ROUTLEDGE HANDBOOK OF CONTEMPORARY INDONESIA

Few countries as culturally rich, politically pivotal, and naturally beautiful as Indonesia are as often misrepresented in global media and conversation. Stretching 3,400 miles east to west along the equator, Indonesia is the fourth most populous country in the world and home to more than four hundred ethnic groups and several major world religions. This sprawling Southeast Asian nation is also the world's most populous Muslim-majority country and the third largest democracy. Although in recent years the country has experienced serious challenges with regard to religious harmony, its trillion-dollar economy is booming and its press and public sphere are among the most vibrant in Asia. A land of cultural contrasts, contests, and contradictions, this ever-evolving country is today rising to even greater global prominence, even as it redefines the terms of its national, religious, and civic identity.

The *Routledge Handbook of Contemporary Indonesia* offers an overview of the modern making and contemporary dynamics of culture, society, and politics in this powerful Asian nation. It provides a comprehensive survey of key issues in Indonesian politics, economics, religion, and society. It is divided into six sections, organized as follows:

- Cultural Legacies and Political Junctures
- Contemporary Politics and Plurality
- Markets and Economic Cultures
- Muslims and Religious Plurality
- Gender and Sexuality
- Indonesia in an Age of Multiple Globalizations

Bringing together original contributions by leading scholars of Indonesia in law, political science, history, anthropology, sociology, religious studies, and gender studies this *Handbook* provides an up-to-date, interdisciplinary, and academically rigorous exploration of Indonesia. It will be of interest to students, academics, policymakers, and others in search of reliable information on Indonesian politics, economics, religion, and society in an accessible format.

Robert W. Hefner is a professor of anthropology and global affairs at the Pardee School of Global Affairs at Boston University. He is also a senior research associate and the former director of the Institute on Culture, Religion, and World Affairs. He has conducted research on politics, ethics, and culture in the Muslim world since the early 1980s. He is the author or editor of some twenty books, including *Shari'a Law and Modern Muslim Ethics* (2016), and is currently completing a book on Islam and citizenship in democratic Indonesia.

ROUTLEDGE HANDBOOK OF CONTEMPORARY INDONESIA

Edited by Robert W. Hefner

Routledge
Taylor & Francis Group

LONDON AND NEW YORK

First published 2018
by Routledge
2 Park Square, Milton Park, Abingdon, Oxon OX14 4RN

and by Routledge
52 Vanderbilt Avenue, New York, NY 10017

First issued in paperback 2020

Routledge is an imprint of the Taylor & Francis Group, an informa business.

British Library Cataloguing-in-Publication Data
A catalogue record for this book is available from the British Library

Library of Congress Cataloging-in-Publication Data
Names: Hefner, Robert W., 1952– editor. | Container of (work): Andaya,
Barbara Watson. Gender legacies and modern transitions.
Title: Routledge handbook of contemporary Indonesia / edited by
Robert W. Hefner.
Description: New York : Routledge, 2018. | Includes bibliographical
references and index.
Identifiers: LCCN 2017037163 | ISBN 9781138644427 (hardback) |
ISBN 9781315628837 (ebook)
Subjects: LCSH: Indonesia—Politics and government—21st century. |
Indonesia—Social conditions—21st century. | Indonesia—Economic
conditions—21st century.
Classification: LCC DS644.5 .R685 2018 | DDC 959.804—dc23
LC record available at https://lccn.loc.gov/2017037163

ISBN 13: 978–0–367–58091–9 (pbk)
ISBN 13: 978–1–138–64442–7 (hbk)

Typeset in Bembo
by Apex CoVantage LLC

CONTENTS

Contents

ACKNOWLEDGMENTS

A book as multi-topical and multi-disciplinary as this one inevitably depended upon the counsel, care, and intervention of more people than I can acknowledge. However, I feel an obligation to express my thanks to a few especially helpful friends and advisors who worked to usher this Handbook forward to production reality. First and foremost are my Routledge Editors, Dorothea Schaefter and Lily Brown. Dorothea helped me to overcome my initial reservations about taking the project on and provided informed suggestions for the list of contributors. Lily made all of our chapters' prose more readable. In addition to all of the contributors to the volume, I want to extend my special thanks for advice and guidance to Amin Abdullah, Muhamad Ali, Azyumardi Azra, Chaider S. Bamualim, Martin van Bruinessen, Greg Fealy, Michael Feener, Jajang Jahroni, Webb Keane, Michel Picard, Zuly Qodir, Sumanto Al Qurtuby, Richard Robison, John Sidel, Rita Smith Kipp, Siti Syamsiyatun, Din Wahid, and Barbara Watson Andaya.

Robert W. Hefner
Boston
October 8, 2017

ILLUSTRATIONS

Tables

Figures

CONTRIBUTORS

Kathleen M. Adams is professor of anthropology at Loyola University Chicago, US.

Dina Afrianty is a senior lecturer and former chair of the Department of International Relations in the Faculty of Social and Political Science at the Syarif Hidayatullah State Islamic University, Jakarta, and research associate at the Institute for Religion, Politics, and Society at the Australian Catholic University.

Barbara Watson Andaya is professor and chair of the Asian Studies program at the University of Hawai'i-Manoa, US, and former director of the Center for Southeast Asian Studies.

Jan S. Aritonang is professor of church history at the Jakarta Theological Institute, Indonesia.

Edward Aspinall is professor in the Department of Political and Social Change, Coral Bell School of Asia Pacific Affairs, Australian National University.

Zainal Abidin Bagir is professor of religious studies and professor of philosophy, Indonesian Associate for UNESCO Chair in Interrreligious and Intercultural Relations, and former director of the Center for Religious and Cross-Cultural Studies, Gadjah Mada University, Yogyakarta, Indonesia.

Ward Berenschot is a political scientist and postdoctoral researcher at the Royal Netherlands Institute for Southeast Asian and Caribbean Studies (KITLV) in Amsterdam, the Netherlands.

Christopher Bjork is Dexter M. Ferry professor of education and coordinator of teacher education in the School of Education at Vassar College, Poughkeepsie, New York, US.

Michael Buehler is senior lecturer in comparative politics in the Department of Politics and International Studies, School of Oriental and African Studies, University of London, UK.

Simon Butt is associate director of the Centre for Asian and Pacific Law at the University of Sydney Law School, Australia.

Sharyn Graham Davies is associate professor of anthropology in the School of Languages and Social Sciences at the Auckland University of Technology, New Zealand.

Zane Goebel is associate professor, Department of Languages and Linguistics, College of Arts, Social Sciences, and Humanities, University of Queensland, Australia.

Vedi R. Hadiz is professor of Asian studies at the Asia Institute, the University of Melbourne, Australia.

Noorhaidi Hasan is professor of Islam and politics and dean of the Sharia and Law faculty at the Sunan Kalijaga State Islamic University, Yogyakarta, Indonesia.

Robert W. Hefner is professor of anthropology and former director of the Institute on Culture, Religion, and World Affairs at the Pardee School of Global Studies, Boston University.

Ariel Heryanto is Herb Feith Professor for the Study of Indonesia, School of Social Sciences, and deputy director of the Monash Asia Institute, Monash University, Australia.

James Bourk Hoesterey is assistant professor of religious studies at Emory University.

Carla Jones is associate professor of anthropology and director of the Center for Asian Studies at the University of Colorado-Boulder, US.

Gerry van Klinken is senior researcher at the Royal Netherlands Institute for Southeast Asian and Caribbean Studies (KITLV) and professor of Southeast Asian history at the University of Amsterdam, the Netherlands.

Juliette Koning is an anthropologist and reader in organization studies and Asian business, Department of Business and Management at the Oxford Brookes University, Oxford, UK.

Tim Lindsey is Malcolm Smith professor of Asian Law, Redmond Barry Distinguished Professor, and Director of the Centre of Indonesian Law, Islam, and Society at the Melbourne Law School, Australia.

Katharine McGregor is associate professor in Southeast Asian history in the School of Historical and Philosophical Studies at the University of Melbourne, Australia.

Jeremy Menchik is associate professor of international relations at the Pardee School of Global Affairs, Boston University, US.

Marcus Mietzner is professor in the Department of Political and Social Change, School of International, Political, and Strategic Studies, Australian National University, Canberra.

Gwenaël Njoto-Feillard is a French political scientist and visiting research fellow at the Institute of Southeast Asian Studies, Singapore.

Raihani is vice dean for Academic Affairs, Faculty of Psychology, Sultan Syarif Kasim State Islamic University, Riau, Indonesia, and a research fellow in the School of Education at the University of Western Australia.

Martin Ramstedt is an associate researcher in the Law and Anthropology Department at the Max Planck Institute for Social Anthropology in Halle, Germany.

Kathryn Robinson is emeritus professor in the School of Culture, History, and Language, College of Asia and the Pacific, the Australian National University.

Arskal Salim is professor of Islamic law and politics and director of the Center for Research and Community Engagement at the Syarif Hidyatullah State Islamic University, Jakarta, Indonesia.

Nancy J. Smith–Hefner is associate professor of anthropology at Boston University, US.

Leo Suryadinata is a visiting senior fellow at the Yusof Ishak Institute at the Institute for Southeast Asian Studies and adjunct professor at the S. Rajaratnam School of International Studies, Nanyang Technological University, Singapore.

Dirk Tomsa is an associate lecturer in the School of Asian Languages and Studies and the School of Government at the University of Tasmania, Australia.

Katrina Trost is a researcher at the Scowcroft Group, Washington, DC, US.

Andrew N. Weintraub is professor of music at the University of Pittsburgh, US.

Chris Wilson is senior lecturer in politics and international relations at the University of Auckland, New Zealand.

PART I

Legacies and junctures

1

INTRODUCTION

Indonesia at the crossroads: imbroglios of religion, state, and society in an Asian Muslim nation

Robert W. Hefner

Few nations as culturally rich, politically pivotal, or environmentally beautiful as Indonesia are so consistently mischaracterized in global media and conversation. No doubt much of this misrecognition has to do with the sheer scale and complexity of this country and with the fact that Indonesia does not conform to received stereotypes of an "Asian" or "Muslim" country. Indonesia is a Southeast Asian nation made up of some 4,000 islands stretching 3,400 miles east to west along the equator and separating mainland Southeast Asia from Australasia. This archipelagic country is home to more than four hundred ethnic groups, 145 of which are recognized in the national census; the two largest ethnic groups (Javanese, 40%, and Sundanese, 15.5%) make up more than half of the population (see Suryadinata chapter, this volume). Some 87.2% of this nation's 260 million residents profess Islam, but there are significant religious minorities as well. A full 9.90% of citizens are Protestant or Catholic, 1.69% are Hindu, 0.72% are Buddhist, and 0.05% self-identify as Confucian. The size of its Muslim population makes Indonesia the largest Muslim-majority and fourth most populous country in the world. No less impressive, Indonesia is also the third largest democracy, having undertaken a return to electoral democracy in 1998–1999 in the aftermath of thirty-two years of authoritarian rule at the hands of President Soeharto's "New Order" regime (see Aspinall, Buehler, Mietzner, and Tomsa chapters, and Aspinall 2005b; Aspinall and Mietzner 2010; Bunte and Ufen 2009; Mietzner 2008).

The restoration of electoral democracy after 1998–1999 was related to other important changes, cultural as well as political, the broader understanding of which lies at the heart of this *Handbook of Contemporary Indonesia*. During the first three years of the post-Soeharto "Reform" (Reformasi) era, eight of the country's (today) thirty-four provinces witnessed outbreaks of ethno-religious violence (Aspinall 2011; Bertrand 2004; Davidson 2008; Duncan 2011; Sidel 2006; Wilson 2008). The violence did much to damage Indonesia's longstanding but too-simple reputation as a tolerant society (see Menchik and Trost chapter and Fealy 2016). However, in its early phases, the conflict had as much to do with the political vacuum created by the sudden collapse of the authoritarian state and the launching of a hastily crafted program of political decentralization in 1999–2000 as it did ethno-religious tensions (see Aspinall, Buehler, and Wilson chapters and Aspinall and Fealy 2003a, 2003b; Schulte Nordholt and van Klinken 2007). Some of the worst violence took place in the provinces of Maluku (the Moluccas) and North Maluku in eastern Indonesia. In several districts where Christians and Muslims live side by side in near-equal numbers, long-simmering resentments between native residents (mostly Christian) and hard-working immigrants (mostly Muslim) made the competition for state spoils and societal advantage especially combustible. Eventually, the violence took the lives of some 15,000 people and displaced more than one million (Duncan 2011; Sumanto 2016; Wilson 2008).

These "small town wars" (van Klinken 2007) also caught the attention of radical Islamist militias from across the nation and the broader Muslim world. One of the larger and the most violent of these organizations, the Jemaah Islamiyah (JI, "Islamic community"), made no secret of its support for al-Qaeda's global campaign against the United States and the West (ICG 2002, Solahudin 2013). On Christmas Eve 2000, JI militants set off bombs outside churches in several major Indonesian cities, killing nineteen people and injuring another 100. On October 12, 2002, JI terrorists set off a truck bomb near a nightclub popular among Western tourists in a resort town in south Bali, killing 202 people and injuring another 290. In the face of these tragic events, some international analysts began to liken Indonesia to Yugoslavia and the former Soviet Union, predicting that the country was on the verge of collapse. Others warned that it was just a matter of time before al-Qaeda succeeded in its goal of turning Indonesia into a "second front" against the West (Abuza 2003; Bond and Simons 2009).

Indonesia does face serious challenges with regard to inter-religious harmony (see Aritonang, Butt, Lindsey, Menchik and Trost, and Ramstedt chapters; and Crouch 2014; Lindsey and Pausacker 2016; Human Rights Watch 2013). Its political and legal systems are tainted by money politics and corruption (see Aspinall, Buehler, and Berenschot and van Klinken chapters; and Aspinall 2014; Butt and Lindsey 2010; Mietzner 2014a). Notwithstanding these problems, however, Indonesia has survived. Today, the country ranks among the most politically consequential nations in the world. It has one of the freest presses in all of Asia. Freedom House – the U.S.-based non-governmental research foundation that evaluates the state of human liberties around the world – has for the past decade ranked Indonesia as the freest country in Southeast Asia, although the country's global ranking has slipped in recent years (see Freedom House 2017). After thirty-two years of Jakarta-biased administration, since 2000, a large share of state power has been decentralized to provinces and districts across the country. An impoverished country in the early 1960s with per-capita incomes on par with Ethiopia, Indonesia today sits squarely in the ranks of the World Bank's "lower-middle income" countries (Hill 1996). It has a trillion-dollar economy and a per-capita income just shy of $4,000; its prospects for future economic growth look strong (Basri and Hill 2010). Taking its pop-cultural cues as much from East Asia as the West or the Middle East, Indonesia's eighty-million strong middle class has an appetite for consumer fashions fully on par with its well-heeled counterparts elsewhere in the world (see Jones chapter, and Dick 1985; Jones 2010; Rakhmani 2016: 99–128; Parker and Nilan 2013). The country is the fourth largest in the world for Facebook subscriptions, with some 111 million users (Yang Hui 2010). High-school girls in *hijabs* gleefully follow trends in Korean pop music (see Heryanto, Robinson, and Smith-Hefner chapters). One of the most celebrated varieties of Indonesian popular music, *dangdut* (Weintraub 2010, and this volume), combines Indian pop cadences with Elvis-Presley vampishness, as well as, however implausibly, appeals for Islamic piety. Management courses popular in Muslim business circles blend sober stories from the life of the Prophet Muhammad with insights from New Age philosophy, Western popular psychology, and Christian prosperity-theology (see Njoto-Feillard and Koning chapters; and Hoesterey 2015; Rudnyckyj 2007; Njoto-Feillard 2012).

All this is to say that, by any and all standards, Indonesia is a richly complex country with not one but a multiplicity of popular cultures, political ethics, and social imaginaries. Not all of the latter soar to their aspirational heights in redolent harmony; this is a land of cultural contrasts, contests, and contradictions. But a vibrant and agonistic plurality of cultures has defined this crossroads of civilizations for more than a millennium (see Watson Andaya chapter, and Cribb 2013; Lombard 1990; Reid 1988, 1993; Watson Andaya 2006; Vickers 1987). As the chapters in this volume suggest, the same trait will likely characterize Indonesia's cultural and political development in years to come, as this nation rises to even greater global prominence (see Hoesterey chapter) and as it refines the terms of its national and civic identity.

From crossroads to critical junctures

All modern societies are ever-evolving and variably cohesive assemblies of diverse social groupings, political projects, and social imaginaries (Barth 1993; Hannerz 1992; Schielke 2015). Although some contemporary academic fashions suggest otherwise, no single discourse ever shapes more than a portion of a society's varied fields and ethico-political orientations. As scholars of law and ethics have long recognized, every society is ethically and legally plural, with a variety of social styles and ethical registers on offer to provide actors with hope, ambition, and moral clarity (see Engle Merry 1988; Laidlaw 2014). At certain "critical junctures" in their development, however, most societies put in place a more-or-less dominant "ideological and institutional legacy" that, however widely contested, attempts to establish ground rules and sensibilities for public co-existence and civic recognition. If it is to endure, and if its terms are not to be pushed aside by rival powers promoting alternate public ethics, this normative work must be scaled up and maintained over time by the "establishment of institutions that generate self-reinforcing path-dependent processes" (Kuru 2009:278; cf. Stepan 2011, 2014). No less important, if it is to remain socially consequential, the charter's discourses and practices must influence sociabilities beyond the confines of state-citizen interaction and give rise to less formal but more pervasive social mores that encourage citizens to experience otherwise abstract categories (citizenship and national identity) as lived realities resonant with a broadly shared and deeply cherished way of life.

The transitions during which civic charters are established may initially be characterized by fierce debates and even violence. Invariably, too, the thorniest disputes center on the terms by which different ethnic, religious, and other identity-based groupings are to recognize and engage each other (see chapters by Bagir, Van Klinken and Berenschott, and Tomsa; Modood 2007; Joppke 2017). Whether on the basis of equality or hierarchy, dominance or marginalization, such social engagements inevitably revive "previous grievances and tensions" (Bertrand 2004: 23). In so doing, the social charters and styles of engagement that emerge from critical junctures put in striking relief what a society once was, is now, and aspires to become.

By all measures, Indonesia today is in the throes of just such a critical juncture, and true to such moments' dynamics, the terms of how a diverse people should live together and flourish figure prominently in public discussion. A great reassessment of self-identities and sociabilities is taking place in this country. In its most public forms, the process concerns state-related matters of constitutionalism, citizenship, party policies, and national education (see chapters by Aspinall, Bagir, Bjork and Raihani, Buehler, Butt, Lindsey, Mietzner, Salim, and Tomsa). But the processes are also unfolding at the grassroots of society, in everyday realities as diverse as gender relations, practical religion, consumer habits, language interaction, and even representations of ethnic cultures in tourism advertising (see Adams, Afrianty, Goebel, Heryanto, Jones, Robinson, and Smith-Hefner chapters). The first and most general aim of this *Handbook* is to highlight the varied forms and meanings of these changes, and to explore just what they imply for culture, politics, and society in contemporary Indonesia.

As hinted above, one set of events illustrates the range of influences at work in this great transition and demonstrates that more is in play than state-shaped policies alone. Whereas in some "Arab Spring" countries after 2011, national elections rewarded Islamist political parties with large electoral pluralities, the national elections held in Indonesia every five years since June 1999 (with direct presidential and gubernatorial elections held since 2004) have consistently shown that only one-sixth of the electorate cares to cast its vote for parties advocating state-enforced implementation of Islamic law (see Aspinall, Butt, Hefner, and Tomsa chapters; and Aspinall 2005a, 2010; Mietzner 2014b, Tomsa 2008, Ufen 2008). Although most Indonesians disapprove of what some describe as a "secular liberal" sequestering of religious ethics from public life, most also subscribe to Indonesia's founding Pancasila ("five principles") philosophy. The Pancasila's first principle affirms that the state is based on and should promote belief in a singular and almighty God (*Tuhan yang Maha Esa*), but should do so while recognizing several faiths, not just the religion of the majority, Islam (see Aritonang, Bagir, Butt, Hefner, Lindsey, and Ramstedt chapters, this volume; and Cribb 2010; Lindsey 2012: 35–65; Lindsey and Butt 2016).

What makes this country's centrist electoral tack since 1999 all the more intriguing is that it has coincided with an ongoing transformation taking place outside the realm of formal state politics – a growing "Islamization" of public culture, gender roles, and consumer fashions in society. "Islamization" is actually not one but many family-related processes, the details of which vary by time and place (Hassan 2007). In today's Indonesia, this multivalent process takes many forms, not all mutually consistent. But Islamization is broadly apparent in everything from the proliferation of Arabic greetings, women's headscarves, and Islam-themed television programming to "shariah-compliant" banks, Islamic study groups (*majlis taklim, pengajian*), and "no-dating" nuptial services (see chapters by Graham-Davies, Hefner, Heryanto, Jones, Robinson, and Smith-Hefner; see also Fealy and White 2008; Howell 2008).

Certainly, the fact that Muslim Indonesia has recently experienced an uptick in popular devotion is less a deviation from the Muslim-world norm than one more striking illustration (Moaddel and Gelfand 2017; Hassan 2002; Pew 2013). In one important respect, however, Indonesia seems different, as if people in this society are especially keen to balance a plural palette of aspirations and "grand schemes" (Schielke 2015; cf. Ewing 1990) rather than bringing all into lock-step alignment. For example, in many Muslim-majority countries, the aftermath of the Islamic awakening (Ar., *sahwa*) has seen growing numbers of believers channel their religious enthusiasm into support for Islamist parties demanding a codified and state-enforced "Islamic law" (*shariah*). This was the pattern in Egypt, Tunisia, and Morocco in the early years of the so-called Arab Spring (Volpi and Stein 2015), and in northern Nigeria after the return to electoral democracy in the early 2000s (Kendhammer 2016). However, although Islam looms larger than ever in Indonesian society, thus far, an Islamist electoral tack does not. Understanding how and why this is so is just one among this Handbook's many concerns. However, because it draws one's gaze toward the varied shapes of self and society in this sprawling country, the topic is a useful point of entry into this Handbook's broader concerns: the imbroglios of politics, law, education, religion, gender, and popular culture in contemporary Indonesia.

Islamization through cultural imbrication

An observer unfamiliar with Indonesian history might speculate that the main reason this country's resurgence has not resulted in an Islamist electoral surge is that its religious awakening has been less pronounced than that of other Muslim-majority countries. However, by all conventional sociological measures, this claim is flatly wrong: Indonesia's Islamic resurgence has in fact been among the more far-reaching and culturally consequential in today's Muslim-majority world (Hassan 2002; Mujani 2003; Pew 2013). The wearing of the Islamic headscarf by women has increased from a small minority in the 1970s to the great majority today (Brenner 2011;

Smith-Hefner 2007; Parker and Nilan 2013). Participation in Islamic study groups has soared, especially among the Muslim middle class (Gade 2004; Howell 2008; Rasmussen 2010). "Islamic arts" once deemed unfashionably provincial are today at the forefront of upper-class cultural consumption (George 2010). Film and television broadcasts once dominated by Western and East Asian programming today have a wealth of Islamically-themed shows (see Heryanto chapter, and Heryanto 2011; Hoesterey and Clark 2012; Rakhmani 2016:33–67). Notwithstanding the lack of electoral support for parties promoting some variety of "Islamic state," the percentage of Muslim citizens endorsing the idea that the state should enforce Islamic law stands at 71%, an above-average figure relative to other Muslim countries (Pew 2013:10). Most tellingly, the syncretic Islamic traditions for which Indonesia was once renowned, and which two generations ago enjoyed the support of the majority of Muslims in Java (Geertz 1960), have today dwindled to the point of near extinction (see Hefner and Ramstedt chapters, and Beatty 1999, 2009; Cederroth 1996; Hefner 2011a; Ricklefs 2007, 2012).

The *longue durée* of Indonesian history provides another perspective on the scale of recent changes – and the way in which "Islamization" itself has meant different things in different periods. Arab Muslim traders first sailed into the Indonesian archipelago in the late seventh century. Widespread conversion to Islam began only six hundred years later, with the adoption of Islam by rulers in several kingdoms in and around northern Sumatra (see Salim chapter). Prior to Islam's arrival, and in fact for most of the period from the ninth to the fifteenth centuries, the larger states in the central and western archipelago subscribed to Hinduism, Buddhism, or some syncretic combination of both (see Pigeaud 1960–63). These religions were one part of a larger "Indic" civilizational package that included Sanskrit-derived alphabets, Indian legal texts, Indian-inspired theater and dance, and state rituals identifying the court as a microcosm of the universe and a meeting point between heaven and earth (Lombard 1990; Schulte Nordholt 1996).

Not all archipelagic societies were swept by the Indic wave. The new civilization had far less impact on the tribal and chiefdom-based peoples of eastern Indonesia, as well as those living in the thickly forested interiors of Sumatra and Kalimantan. Although linked to the people of the coasts by trading alliances, these hinterland societies were less culturally complex and more socially egalitarian than their state-based neighbors, organized around big-men orators and husband-wife households rather than strict class- and status-hierarchies (Atkinson 1987; George 1996; King 1993; Schiller 1997; Tsing 1993). These non-state peoples did not stand apart from the region's trans-territorial flows for reasons of remoteness alone; they guarded their distance out of a desire for autonomy and a fear of slave-raiding by lowland and coastal peoples (Reid and Brewster 1983). In the nineteenth and early twentieth centuries, some among these interior peoples were targeted by Europeans for Christian missionization. The Dutch launched the programs in part so as to prevent the expansion of Islam into their territories (Kruithof 2014; Laffan 2011; Steenbrink 1993:106–11). No longer isolated from national currents, today these populations comprise the demographic core of the country's Christian minority (see Aritonang chapter, and Aragon 2000; Aritonang and Steenbrink 2008; Kipp 1993; Steedly 1993).

Although they still flourish on the island of Bali and in smaller pockets elsewhere in Indonesia (see Ramstedt chapter, and Ramstedt 2004; Hefner 1985, 2004; Vickers 1987), Hindu-Buddhist traditions declined across most of the core state regions with the rise of a new civilizational ecumene, a Muslim one. Islam came to the archipelago not in the company of armies of slave-warriors on horses, as with the early Muslim expansion in the Middle East (Crone 2003), but in association with Indian Ocean traders. From the tenth century onward, much of that trade lay in the hands of Muslim merchants of diverse regional and ethnic provenance. The commerce moved spices, precious metals, luxury cloth, and foodstuffs from southeastern China and the Indonesian archipelago to India, southern Arabia, East Africa, and the Middle East. The great flow brought scholars and Sufi mystics as well as commercial goods. The trade reached its apogee during what the historian Anthony Reid has aptly called the "age of commerce," from the fifteenth to seventeenth centuries. Not coincidentally, it was during this same period that Islam spread to most of the kingdoms in the central and western archipelago (Gibson 2007; Pelras 1996; Reid 1993; Lombard 1990; Ricklefs 2012: 3–12; Vickers 1987).

The social driver for Islamization was not foreign invasion, then, but the desire of local rulers and merchants to join a bustling new world of culture and commerce in which the dominant actors and social mores were, in varied ways, Muslim. The fact that local elites rather than foreigners led the way in the adoption of the new faith gave a distinctive form to the Islamization process. In particular, because most newly converted rulers shared habits of language and culture with their subjects, there was not rupture but considerable continuity from the old culture to the new, not least in matters of governance, the arts, kinship organization, and, most remarkably, gender. The imbrication of Islam with local cultures ensured that social mores and ritual expression in premodern Southeast Asia differed from their counterpart in the Muslim Middle East. The difference would only seriously diminish with the rise of movements of modern Islamic reform from the mid-nineteenth century onward.

Other social factors allowed Muslim societies in Indonesia to develop a regionalized if authentic variant of Islamic civilization, one that long retained social characteristics different from those of the Muslim Middle East and South Asia. During its first centuries, Islam in the archipelago had a "raja-centric" and mystical rather than a legal-minded or jurisprudential (*fiqh*) emphasis (Milner 1995: 146, 271; Burhanudin 2006; cf. Hooker 1984). Rather than madrasa-based legal study, the primary pathway for encountering and enacting Islamic mores was through participation in the pomp and ceremony of Sufi-inflected rituals at the royal court or in villages. The carriers of the tradition included not just erudite scholars (*ulama*) and sacred rulers but village-based healers, mystics, and shrine guardians; all laid claim to different understandings and practices of Islam (see also Gibson 2007; Headley 2004; Pelras 1996; Woodward 1989:164). Court arts of broadly Indic nature, including shadow puppet theater (*wayang*) with its "Hindu" protagonists and Ramayana-influenced dance traditions in which bare shoulders and tight bodices were the female norm, remained popular across the central kingdoms until well into the twentieth century. The latter flourish in south-central Java's Islamic courts to this day (Hughes-Freeland 2008). In most other areas of the archipelago, however, these Indic aesthetic legacies have been displaced in modern times as a result of the growing influence of Islamic reformism (George 2010; Laderman 1991; Peacock 1978).

God's law, plurality, and gender

Another reason Islamic civilization in the archipelago had a less legalistic or *fiqh*-oriented emphasis in its early centuries had to do with the striking absence of an institution at the heart of the transmission of Islamic learning in the Middle East and South Asia: the madrasa. A madrasa is a college or boarding school for intermediate and advanced study in the Islamic sciences in general, and Islamic jurisprudence (*fiqh*) in particular (Hefner 2007). By the twelfth century in the Muslim Middle East, the madrasa had become "perhaps the most characteristic religious institution of the medieval Near Eastern urban landscape" (Berkey 2003: 187; see also Makdisi 1981). Once implanted in a region, madrasas facilitated a great "recentering and homogenization" of elite Islamic knowledge and authority (Berkey 2003: 189). Specialists of the law (*fuqaha*) became pre-eminent among scholars of the Islamic sciences. Jurisprudence (*fiqh*) came to be regarded as the queen of the Islamic sciences. The commanding presence of madrasa scholars ensured that even everyday social mores (*adab*) acquired a significant degree of *fiqh*-mindedness (Sanders 1994; Shoshan 1993).

The fact that, during the first wave of Islamization in the archipelago, the madrasa was notably absent meant that classical Islamic jurisprudence played a limited role in the early Muslim community. Historical studies show that during the first two centuries of Islamization, almost no classical legal texts made their way from the Middle East to the archipelago. By the sixteenth century, Muslim scholars in a few court centers, particularly in northern Sumatra and the Malay Peninsula (in what is today Malaysia), had acquired legal digests that summarized basic judgments of the Shafi'i school of law, the school (*madhhab*) of Islamic jurisprudence still today dominant across Muslim Southeast Asia. Elsewhere, however, the digests were either unknown or drawn little into state legal administration (Hooker 1983: 166). In other words, until well into the modern period, "Legal reality . . . lay outside the [legal] texts" (Hooker 1983: 166; 2008:2; cf. Ricci 2011). So too did the experiential soul of Islam.

There were several small exceptions to Indonesian Islam's less legalistic embedding. In the seventeenth century, rulers in Banten (west Java), Malaya, Makassar, and, most notably, Aceh invoked some aspects of Islamic criminal law to impose severe corporal punishments on those found guilty of gambling, drinking, or theft (Reid 1988: 142). To a degree that departed significantly from the general Indonesian pattern, the sultan's court in Aceh on the northern tip of Sumatra invited and patronized Islamic scholars and Sufi masters. A doctrinal controversy that raged at the court in the seventeenth century shows that some resident scholars (including one especially prominent figure born in Gujarat, India) were both familiar with and committed to an entirely orthodox Islamic theology and at least some features of Islamic law (Riddell 2001: 101–25; Feener 2016:3).

Despite momentary bursts of legal-mindedness, the non-hegemonic nature of Islamic legal traditions in the Muslim archipelago had three important consequences for the practice of Islam in the region. First, and as the historian Merle Ricklefs has observed with regard to central Java (which had one of the least *fiqh*-oriented Islamic traditions of all states in the archipelago; see Hooker 2008), the lesser emphasis on law allowed for a "mystic synthesis" that combined a commitment to a Muslim identity and Sufi illuminationism with "acceptance of the reality of local Javanese spiritual forces such as . . . the Goddess of the Southern Ocean . . . and a host of lesser supernatural beings" (Ricklefs 2012: 7; cf. Beatty 1999; Headley 2004; Ricklefs 2006). In Indonesian territories beyond central Java, the synthesis may not have always been as theologically unconventional as in Java, but cosmological eclecticism – and a colorful parade of ritual specialists laying claim to Islamic authority – remained widespread well into the twentieth century (see, e.g. Cederroth 1981; Gibson 2007; Sakai 1999; and Hefner chapter).

A second consequence of the less legal-minded nature of Islam in the Indonesian archipelago had to do with gender and sexuality. In particular, although some *fiqh*-influenced concerns made their way into popular culture, there was no wholesale reconstruction of gender in line with classical Islamic law. Although a few Indonesian societies (Minangkabau, Balinese) have unilineal descent groups, the most common kinship system in Indonesia is still today a bilateral or "cognatic" arrangement that eschews lineality so as to accord equal weight to maternal and paternal relatives (Karim 1995; Robinson 2009; Schröter 2013). Even where operative (as in Aceh; Siegel 1969; Bowen 1993), patrilineal descent in the archipelago did *not* give rise to the powerful tribes that still today shape politics and society in the Middle East and Central Asia. Nor did this social organization generate strict masculinist cultures of tribal honor and patriarchal control over women, like those associated with what is known as the *hasham* tradition in the Arab Middle East (Abu-Lughod 1986: 105). Although some women wore loose-fitting headscarves (Ind., *kerudung*; Malay, *tudung*), the *hijab* was rare. With the exception of a few aristocrats, female seclusion was unknown (Afrianty, Watson Andaya, and Robinson chapters, and Watson Andaya 2006: 172–78). Contrary to the stipulations of classical Islamic jurisprudence, daughters were usually given inheritance shares equal to those of their brothers; the arrangement provides women with a greater measure of economic autonomy than is the case where women depend for sustenance on fathers, husbands, or sons (Robinson 2009; Schröter 2013). Across the Muslim archipelago, women were also the dominant actors in local markets; men predominated only in long-distance trade (Alexander 1987; Brenner 1998; Reid 1993: 162–64). In matters of sexuality too, the Muslim archipelago was distinctive. Women's active interest in sexuality within the confines of marriage was not regarded as aberrant (see Watson Andaya chapter; and Watson Andaya 2006:153–63). In some parts of the Muslim archipelago, local cultures acknowledged (and still today acknowledge) the reality of a third sex and transgenderism (see Graham Davies chapter, and Graham Davies 2010; Peletz 2009).

A third and final consequence of the less legalistic nature of Islam in premodern and early-modern Southeast Asia is that, when madrasas and a *fiqh*-learning did finally begin to take hold, the scale of the change, and the fact that it coincided with the onslaught of Dutch colonialism, caused a crisis of knowledge, identity, and authority in Muslim society. From the middle decades of the nineteenth century onward, the Indonesian and Malaysian equivalent of the Middle Eastern madrasa, the *pondok* or *pesantren* (see Azra et al. 2007; Dhofier 1999), became a landmark on the cultural landscape and a growing influence on Muslim ethical imaginaries (see Bruinessen 1995; Laffan 2011:27; Ricklefs 2007: 52–72). The spread of *pesantren* ensured that a well organized if at first minority wing of the Muslim community developed a lettered familiarity with Islamic jurisprudence's rules and regulations. During the first years of the twentieth century, the graduates of *fiqh*-oriented boarding schools, commonly referred to as *santri* (i.e., a student of a *pesantren*), used the new social technologies of print, modern social organization, and mass education to promote bold programs of Islamic reform (see Feener 2007; Laffan 2011; Ricklefs 2012). The effects of *this* critical juncture continue to reverberate in Indonesia to this day (see Bagir, Hefner, Lindsey chapters).

Islamic reform and the crisis of tradition

In keeping with the heritage of Indonesian plurality, the *fiqh*-oriented *santri* community was itself divided on religious matters. The most critical divide was that between "old group" (*kaum tua*) traditionalists committed to the study of the Islamic sciences and jurisprudence by way of classical commentaries (known in Indonesia as the "yellow scriptures" or *kitab kuning*; see Bruinessen 1989, 1994) and "new group" (*kaum muda*) reformists or "modernists," who downplayed classical commentaries in favor of a scripturalist return to the Quran and traditions of the Prophet (*Sunna*). The traditionalists tended to be more accommodating of local customs (*adat*) and ritual festivity than were the modernists, tolerating the burning of incense, pilgrimage to saints' tombs, and traditional arts like shadow puppetry and classical dance (see Abdullah 1971; Bowen 1993; Geertz 1960; Peacock 1978). At first, too, the two groups differed on matters of education. Faced with the challenge of European colonialism, modernists in groups like the Muhammadiyah (established in 1912; see Nakamura 2012; Peacock 1978) concluded that the most effective instrument for the improvement of Muslim well-being was not the *pesantren* with its *fiqh*-centered curriculum but the "Islamic day school" (Ind., *sekolah Islam*; see Azra et al. 2007; Hefner 2009). The latter was modeled on a Catholic mission prototype, combining general instruction with religious learning. Although the modernists affirmed the importance of Islamic legal traditions (*shariah*), they also insisted that their proper understanding required that believers make the scriptural message contemporary and consequential by linking the sciences of God to the sciences of nature and the world. In striking contrast to traditionalist educators in some Muslim-majority societies (see Zaman 2002:15), this commitment to modern forms of science and learning was soon adopted by traditionalist Muslims as well. Indeed, by the 1970s and 1980s, Indonesia had established what has come to be regarded as one of the most forward-looking systems of Islamic higher education in the world (see Bjork and Raihani, and Hefner chapters; Abdullah 2006; Azyumardi et al. 2007; Bjork 2005).

Another feature of the new Muslim tradition that emerged over the course of the twentieth century had to do with social organization and civic participation. Seen from a comparative perspective, Indonesia has the most "associationalized" variety of Islam in the world – which is to say, an Islamic community organized around, not living saints or tribal sheikhs, but modern associations with membership lists, social welfare programs, and leaders chosen according to agreed-upon institutional procedures. Indonesia's largest Muslim modernist organization, the Muhammadiyah, today has some twenty-five million members. It manages 12,000 schools, 167 institutions of higher learning, 421 orphanages, 345 polyclinics and hospitals, and a nationwide bank (see Njoto-Feillard chapter, and Njoto-Feillard 2012). Established in 1926 by *pesantren*-based *ulama*, Indonesia's largest traditionalist association (also the largest Muslim social welfare organization in the world), the Nahdlatul Ulama (NU) has some 35 to 40 million followers organized in a loosely coordinated federation. However, NU's role in the management of some 10,000 *pesantren* and many of Indonesia's 30,000 Islamic days schools (see Bush 2009; Feillard 1995; Hefner 2009) shows that it too links Islamic ethical traditions to modern notions of social and educational betterment (see also Feener 2013).

For much of the twentieth century, however, the most politically charged divide within Indonesian society was not that pitting Muslim traditionalists against modernists but that separating Muslims aspiring to a comprehensive realization of Islamic legal traditions from Indonesians favoring a more "secular-nationalist" framework for state and society. The single largest constituency in the latter community was, in fact, Indonesians of Muslim background; many, like Indonesia's first vice president, Mohammad Hatta, were religiously pious. But the secular nationalist community also included syncretic Muslims, Christians, Hindus, Buddhists, Confucians, and the followers of local or traditional religions. In the face of late-nineteenth- and early-twentieth-century calls for radical reform in line with *fiqh*-based Islamic ethics, a small minority from the syncretic wing of the Muslim community began to wonder whether they were really Muslim at all. In the first decades of the twentieth century, and particularly on the densely populated island of Java, new currents of religious "spirituality" (*aliran kepercayaan*) or religious "esotericism" (*aliran kebatinan*) arose among a small portion of this disaffected population, promoting what was in effect conversion away from Islam (see Hefner and Ramstedt this volume; Akkeren 1970; Bruinessen 1994; Stange 1986).

Citizenship as universal or religiously differentiated

Although the Dutch had had a small colonial presence in the Indonesian archipelago for almost three hundred years, it was only in the late nineteenth century that they extended their rule across the breadth of what they called the Netherlands East Indies. The colonial expansion created the need for what Benedict Anderson (1983a) has described as armies of "creole functionaries" (native peoples educated in European-style schools) to meet the administrative needs of the colonial state. The demand for such an educated workforce was especially great because of the scale of Dutch enterprise (one of the most far-reaching in the European-colonized world; see Fasseur 1992) and because of the relatively small size of the European population. However, the Enlightenment values of freedom, equality, and progress that Europeans cited to justify their rule were soon also invoked by educated indigenes demanding a new deal for the native population.

Indonesia's first mass-based movements for national awakening came on the scene in the 1910s (Adam 1995). By the end of the decade, the new movements had mobilized hundreds of thousands of followers across the central territories in the archipelago (Shiraishi 1990). True to Indonesia's legacy of competitive or "agonistic" plurality, the largest movement quickly split along ideological lines, with those committed to a democratic socialist or Marxist variety of anti-colonialism separating from Muslim nationalists intent on ensuring that Islamic law was given pride of place in the new nation. Although its ideological detail and political forms have changed, the contest between Muslim and (broadly defined) secular nationalists has remained one of the critical divides in Indonesian politics and religious governance to this day (Mujani 2003; Salim 2008).

These same processes of modern education, colonial subjectivation, and emancipatory struggle gave rise to the "consciousness of the political category of 'woman'" (Robinson 2009: 34) and a widespread sense that sweeping measures were needed to improve women's situation. The shared concern soon led, however, to the creation of two rival women's movements, one secular nationalist in inspiration and the other modern Islamic (Blackburn 2008; Wieringa 2002). Both wings of the fledgling women's movement agreed on the importance of implementing programs for women's education and welfare. But they parted ways on the question of whether the state should be used to reform family life, especially with regard to matters subject in principle to regulation by Islamic jurisprudence, including divorce, polygamy, and inheritance. These same issues lie at the heart of gender contestations in Indonesia today (see Afrianty, Robinson, Smith-Hefner, and Watson Andaya chapters; and Blackburn 2008; Brenner 2011; Doorn-Harder 2006; Hefner 2016; Robinson 2009).

At the core of this and other contentions lay an even more pervasive normative dispute, which also continues today, over religion and citizenship in the new nation-state. Indonesians committed to a more or less secular nationalist vision of citizenship made their case by bringing Enlightenment ideals of citizen sovereignty together with nineteenth century Romanticism's notion of a "people" united by common culture, as well as, in the case of native Indonesians, shared suffering under European rule. The frame resonated with the Indonesian public, including observant Muslims. To a significant degree, ideas of civic nationhood and sovereignty remain widely supported still today, a fact that stands in striking contrast with national and citizen discourses in neighboring Malaysia (Liow 2009).

> Despite the crisis of official Pancasila ideology during the early years of the democratic transition, the tradition of an inclusive, civic Indonesian national identity that is blind to ethnic difference has proven resilient, including . . . in the everyday political consciousness of many Indonesian citizens.
>
> *(Aspinall 2011: 312)*

By contrast, the discourses associated with liberal citizenship traditions in the modern West (Kymlicka 1995; Turner 1997; cf. for India, Hansen 1999), emphasizing the rights of autonomous individuals, figured much less prominently in early nationalist appeals and have relatively weak purchase in elite and popular political circles to this day. The precedent laid in the early years of the nationalist movement was compounded by two later political developments: New Order and military diatribes against liberalism as antithetical to Indonesian and "Asian" values (Asplund 2009; Honna 2003:113–16; Vickers 1999) and Islamist denunciations of liberalism as un-Islamic (Abdillah 1997). Not surprisingly in light of this legacy, discussions of religious freedom in Indonesia have rarely approached the issue from a perspective that presumes that individual autonomy is a paramount value. They instead highlight a bundle of concerns, revolving around the question of how to balance individual freedom with social order, not least when individuals or religious minorities engage in religious acts majority groupings find heterodox (see Afrianty, Aritonang, Bagir, Butt, Hefner, and Lindsey chapters; and Crouch 2014; Fenwick 2017; Lindsey and Pausacker 2016; Menchik 2016).

Those in the Muslim wing of the nationalist movement have long had a different sense of how to balance the concerns of religion, citizenship, and social order. Most Muslim nationalists and (all the more) today's Islamists (those who see Islam not just as a faith tradition but as a comprehensive and religiously obligatory program for a totalizing reconstruction of state and society; see Bayat 2005) feel that the state has the right and obligation to promote Islamic values and observances among Muslim citizens. Many, but not all, also argue that the enforcement of Islamic law (*shariah*) is necessary to effectively fulfill this prime imperative (see chapters by Afrianty, Bagir, Butt, Hefner, Lindsey, and Salim; and Feener 2007, 2016; Salim 2008). It is important to point out that the "shariah" referenced in such proposals is not the shariah of classical jurisprudence (*fiqh*); nor are its terms laid out by an informal, society-wide network of learned Muslim scholars. This shariah is instead imagined on the model of European, and especially Napoleonic, law as a modernized legal code (which the historical shariah was not; see Layish 2004; cf. Lindsey and Kingsley 2008), crafted by state legislators and enforced by the disciplinary machinery of the high-modern bureaucratic state (see Scott 1998). For Muslims of modernist or Islamist persuasion, the law is additionally imagined as a social blueprint for a far-reaching reconstruction of society, on analogy with high-modernist visions of totalizing reform implemented in other parts of the modern world (see Afrianty and Salim chapters, and Feener 2016: 4; Siegel 1969:98–133). As Sami Zubaida (2003: 135; see also Layish 2004) has remarked with regard to the Muslim Middle East, this emphasis on the étatization and codification of Islamic legal traditions represents nothing less than the "triumph of European models" over classical Islamic conceptions.

On the terms of citizen co-existence, too, Muslim nationalists stand in self-conscious opposition to secular nationalists and liberals. The proponents of a Muslim nation-state conceive citizenship not as a universal status defined by each individual's ownership of an identical array of rights and obligations (van Klinken and Berenschot chapter; see also Turner 1997) but as a *differentiated and asymmetrical* citizenship entailing some shared but also many different rights and duties. Citizenship in this view is *religiously* differentiated (see Kloos and Berenschot 2017: 179; Hansen 1999; Smith 2012) because some of its most urgent rights and duties vary according to one's membership in a religious community. In this sense, too, for Muslim nationalists and Islamists, there can be no silo-like segregation of civic and ethico-religious discourses; specification of the former must include accommodation of mandatory features of the latter (see Hefner 2011b; cf., for India, Hansen 1999:4).

Citizenship for Islamists and Muslim nationalists is *asymmetrical* because, although not enforcing the rules for "protected minorities" (*dhimmi*) that in the classical Middle East accorded second-class status to Christians and Jews (Emon 2012), it nonetheless gives pride of place to Muslim community interests and insists that these too must be accommodated in any proper practice of citizenship. As this stipulation makes clear, Muslim nationalists and Islamists do not see the state as a neutral arbiter among religious communities. Instead, the state is an institution that, while granting rights of representation to non-Muslim minorities, holds the creation of a Muslim moral order among its paramount aims. A key premise of that moral order is that the state has a right and obligation to negatively sanction citizens seen as abusing religious freedoms by promoting deviant understandings of Islam (see Butt and Lindsey chapters; and Crouch 2014; Fenwick 2017; Lindsey and Pausacker 2016).

All this implies a very different understanding of citizenship and religious freedom from that favored by secular nationalists or liberals. The difference has been a point of contention in religious politics since the dawn of the republic. It was to explode with a new intensity after the return to electoral democracy in 1998–1999 (see Afrianty, Aritonang, Hefner, Lindsey, Menchik and Trost, and Ramstedt, this volume).

Democracy and mobilization

Disagreements over religion and citizenship intensified in the aftermath of the Second World War and Indonesia's war for independence (1945–1949). The contests laid the groundwork for culture wars that have continued, albeit with permutations, to this day.

The single most dramatic illustration of the scale of the contention was that, notwithstanding the country's Muslim majority, in the late 1950s, the Indonesian Communist Party leapt forward to become the largest of Indonesia's political parties and the largest communist party in the non-communist world (Mortimer 1974). The party's mass base lay primarily among ethnic Javanese, along with several non-Muslim minorities, like the Balinese (Robinson 1995). Although the communists made use of class appeals, their popularity was also based on their unwavering opposition to proposals for the establishment of an Islamic state. The Indonesian Nationalist Party (PNI) positioned itself similarly, declaring that the state should be neutral on religious matters, rather than an instrument for the creation of an Islamic moral order. The PNI had a significant institutional base in the Ministry of Education, which was regularly locked in struggle with the Muslim-dominated Ministry of Religion (see Boland 1982; Ropi 2012).

In Indonesian studies, the early republican era's pattern of ideologically based political mobilization came to be known as the *aliran* ("current" or "stream") phenomenon (see Aspinall and Tomsa chapters, and Aspinall 2013:32; Feith 2006; Geertz 1960; Ufen 2008). Each vertically integrated current had its own political party, religious preferences, and class dynamics, all of which were put to the task of party mobilization. In the early 1960s, a declining economy, worsening party rivalries, and growing military involvement in national politics overwhelmed the already faltering parliamentary system (see Aspinall and Mietzner chapters, and Mietzner 2009). In the aftermath of a failed left-wing officers coup the night of September 30, 1965, conservative army generals took advantage of *aliran* tensions to mobilize religious organizations to carry out a purge of communists; over the next six months, a half-million alleged communists perished (Cribb 1990; Roosa 2006). Survivors identified as having once been Communist Party members have suffered severe legal and social stigmatization to this day (see McGregor chapter, and McGregor 2009).

At first, many political observers were convinced that President Soeharto's military-dominated "New Order" government (1966–1998) was intent on eliminating ideologically based streams (*aliran*) once and for all, and doing so in a manner designed to especially disadvantage Muslim parties. New Order officials placed strict limits on all political activity except that carried out under the aegis of the government party, Golkar. The number of official political parties was reduced to three. Elections were reduced to state-managed affairs.

The range and ambition of these programs left many observers of Indonesia with the impression that the New Order State was not just a strong state, but one enjoying an unprecedented monopoly of sovereignty, violence, and ideological control (Anderson 1983b; Budiman 1990). In retrospect, and especially in light of the speed with which the regime collapsed in 1998 and new ideological currents emerged, many in Indonesian studies during the New Order period seem to have misjudged the state's cohesiveness and societal penetration. In the post-Soeharto period, the combination of the return of electoral democracy, the decentralization of (certain) state powers, the rise of money politics, and the ascendance of regional alliances and oligarchs has led to a far-reaching decentering of sovereignties and political life in general. Researchers' efforts to come to terms with these developments helped to create one of the most remarkable intellectual events in Indonesian studies in recent years: a profound re-assessment of the nature of the Indonesian state and its varied articulations with society. One of the most pervasive and welcome themes of this new literature has been its insistence on viewing the state not as a "single, homogeneous, and coherent entity with a will of its own" but as "a site of struggle among many competing groups" (van Klinken and Barker 2009:2), each articulating with various class-, ethnic-, and religious groupings in complex ways (see Aspinall, Buehler, Mietzner, Tomsa, Van Klinken and Berenschot, and Wilson chapters; see also Ford and Pepinsky 2014; Hadiz 2010, 2016; Herriman 2012; van Klinken and Barker 2009; Aspinall and van Klinken 2010).

Notwithstanding the New Order's extensive clamp-down on formal party politics, Muslim cultural influence in society grew steadily. In the years following the 1965–1966 campaign, the government cooperated with the Muhammadiyah and Nahdlatul Ulama "to build up" (*membina*) religion in regions where the Communist Party had been influential or where the local population had not yet adopted one of the five religions then recognized by the state (Islam, Catholicism, Protestantism, Hinduism, or Buddhism; since 2000, Confucianism is also recognized). In the late 1960s, the state introduced mandatory religious education in public schools. In Java, Lombok, and south Sulawesi, these initiatives spurred the decline of syncretic variants of Islam, as well as the new religions that had flourished in the 1950s (see Hefner and Ramstedt chapters). The change had lasting implications for national politics, because these latter groupings had earlier formed the base for secular nationalist and left-leaning political parties (see Aspinall and Tomsa chapters, and Aspinall 2013; Geertz 1960; Mortimer 1974; Ricklefs 2012; Ufen 2008).

The New Order also promoted a more circumscribed understanding of Indonesia's state ideology, the Pancasila, in a manner that has influenced debates over citizen rights and freedoms to this day. The Pancasila's first principle provided Muslim leaders in government with a "normative basis for steering the state toward a more Islamised form" (Ropi 2012: 97). The "God's Oneness" principle was incorporated as Article 29 into Indonesia's 1945 constitution, an amended version of which continues to regulate religious affairs today. Although its meaning is subject to diverse interpretations (see Bagir, Butt, Hefner, and Lindsey chapters; and Butt and Lindsey 2012: 223–49, Cribb 2010), Islamists have interpreted Section 2 of Article 29 to mean the state has the right to limit full rights of religious expression to citizens who profess a "religion" (Ind., *agama*, see Atkinson 1987; Picard 2011; Picard and Madinier 2011) recognized by the Ministry of Religion.

In the years since the collapse of the New Order in May 1998, conservative Islamists have invoked this same restrictive interpretation of Article 29 to justify curbs on the freedoms of religious minorities, including Ahmadis, Evangelical Christians, non-conventional Sufis, and Shi'as (see Bagir, Butt, and Lindsey chapters; and Crouch 2014: 69–168; Bagir and Hefner 2016; Human Rights Watch 2013; Lindsey 2012: 401–44). Conservatives have also made use of Indonesia's 1965 presidential edict on religious defamation or "blasphemy," as it is commonly known, which was elevated to the status of national law in 1969 (see Aritonang, Bagir, Butt, Hefner, and Lindsey chapters, and Fenwick 2017; Lindsey and Pausacker 2016; Menchik 2016). Ironically, the defamation law had been only sparingly applied during the authoritarian New Order, which was broadly tolerant of mystical groups and syncretists, even if not according them equal legal standing with state-recognized religions (see Bagir chapter, and Bagir 2013; Crouch 2014; Ropi 2012). By contrast, since the return to electoral democracy in 1998–1999, Muslim conservatives in state and society have used the defamation law to justify programs for policing the boundaries of allowable religious practice and belief, in a manner that has generally disadvantaged religious minorities, including Muslim minorities, like Indonesia's Shi'a (see Crouch 2014; Fenwick 2017; Lindsey and Pausacker 2016; Makin 2017).

The New Order regime also succeeded at implementing programs of mass education, and these laid the groundwork for broader and often unintended social changes, including those impacting women. Between 1965 and 1990, the percentage of literate Indonesians jumped from 40% to 90% of the total population (Jones and Manning 1992; see Bjork 2005, and Bjork and Rahaini chapter). The percentage of youth graduating from high school rose from 4% in 1970 to more than 30% in the same period. There was also a steady growth in private and public Islamic education, which today educates about 15% of the student population (Hefner 2009). No less remarkable, by the late 1990s, the proportion of young women in the *madrasa* student body had grown to over one-half of the total enrollment (Jabali and Jamhari 2002: 68–9). Although officially the New Order state promoted a gender ideology that identified women's "nature" (*kodrat*) with domesticity (Brenner 2011; Robinson 2009), regime programs had the unintended effect of undermining this very ideology. Unlike the pattern seen in some Arab Middle Eastern countries (where higher educational achievement has not led to dramatic increases in female labor force participation; see Adely 2012: 11), advances in women's education have resulted in significantly heightened rates of female labor force participation – two to three times greater than rates seen in the Arab Middle East. These developments have also resulted in changes in courtship habits and a significant increase in age at marriage (see Robinson and Smith-Hefner chapters, and Robinson 2009; Smith-Hefner 2005).

In combination with Indonesia's continuing economic expansion, these developments in the educational field brought a new Muslim middle class into existence and fuelled a popular resurgence in Islamic piety (see Heryanto, Jones, Smith-Hefner, and Weintraub chapters; Parker and Nilan 2013; cf. Tanter and Young 1990). The resurgence was anything but ideologically uniform. Many religious study groups were politically quietist; others were pro-regime; and still others were generally supportive of democratic reform (Abdillah 1997). Whatever their orientation, these varied processes of Islamization had a profound impact on everything from clothing habits and *halal* food items to sociability. Keenly aware of the growing Islamic revitalization, the government made concessions to Muslim interests in the late 1980s and early 1990s. Islamic programming was given a larger presence on state television (Rakhmani 2016). The state moved to expand the jurisdiction of Religious Courts (Cammack 1997). It also worked to create a compilation of Islamic law (Mawardi 2003); to lift the ban on headscarves in schools; to abolish the sports lottery; and to sponsor the organization of a national association of Islamic intellectuals, which quickly became a powerful in-government lobby (see Effendy 2003; Hefner 2000: 128–66).

Faced with a still-growing pro-democracy opposition, the Soeharto regime in the late 1990s took even more desperate defensive measures. It turned away from the country's mainline Muslim associations (which by then were broadly supportive of the pro-democracy opposition), courting conservative Islamists in the Indonesian Council for Islamic Predication (known by its Indonesian acronym, DDII, est. 1967). Under the leadership of Mohammad Natsir (d. 1993; see Kahin 2012), the DDII had positioned itself from the 1970s onward as a leading conduit for Saudi Arabian aid to Islamic schools, mosques, and associations. Some among the graduates of the DDII's scholarship programs in Saudi Arabia returned to Indonesia to lay the foundation for what was to become, in the 1990s and 2000s, the country's small but influential Salafist movement, which was broadly opposed to democracy, liberal citizenship, and women's rights (see Hasan chapter, and Wahid 2013; Hasan 2006). Others attracted to transnational varieties of Islamism looked to the Muslim-Brotherhood more than they did Saudi-style Salafism (see

Hefner chapter, and Bubalo and Fealy 2005; Machmudi 2006). In the final months of the New Order, some in the more radical wing of the Islamist and Salafi communities joined with Soeharto supporters to denounce Christians and Chinese as traitors to the nation. The regime's final days were marked by violent attacks on both minorities (Bertrand 2004; Purdey 2006; Sidel 2006).

Muslim society in New Order Indonesia developed strong pluralist currents as well, some of which went on to play a central role in the culture and politics of the Reformasi era. Whatever its political motives, the New Order regime invested heavily in a reformed and pluralistic variety of Islamic education. The system of State Islamic Universities (IAIN, *Institut Agama Islam Negeri*) expanded to 28 campuses and developed a curriculum that came to include not just Islamic studies but comparative religion, social and political sciences, and training in non-religious professions (Abdullah 2006; Jabali and Jamhari 2002). Today, this country's state-Islamic and Muhammadiyah universities are regarded as among the finest centers of Islamic higher education in the world. Graduates of these Islamic institutions figured prominently among those who engaged in the normative work required to reassure the Muslim electorate that democracy and plural citizenship are compatible with Islam (Abdillah 1997; Barton 1995). In the post-Soeharto Reformasi period, educators in the State Islamic University and Muhammadiyah university system have led the way in the development of a new and boldly democratic curriculum of civic education, one that affirms the public importance of religion while nonetheless rejecting efforts to differentiate citizenship along religious lines (Hefner 2011a; Jackson 2007). No less remarkable, graduates from the highest echelons of the State Islamic University system have consistently supplied the core leadership for the country's fledgling feminist movement, which has both a secular and a significantly larger Muslim-feminist wing (see Afrianty, Hefner, and Robinson chapters, and Doorn-Harder 2006; Rinaldo 2013; Syamsiyatun 2008). In the post-Soeharto Reformasi era, both wings were to encounter growing headwinds. The restoration of electoral democracy created new mobilizational opportunities for Muslim conservatives and Islamists opposed to gender equality and pluralist democracy and favoring a religiously differentiated and hierarchical practice of citizenship (see Afrianty, Robinson, and Smith-Hefner chapters, and Blackburn 2008; Brenner 2011; Robinson 2009).

Democracy renewed and citizenship contested

As the preceding discussion makes clear, the changes Indonesia has undergone since the fall of the New Order in May 1998 have not followed a single ethico-political course, not least with regards to questions of gender, pluralism, and civic tolerance (see Aspinall, Hadiz, and Menchik and Trost chapters; and Aspinall 2010, 2013; Hadiz 2016; Hamayotsu 2011; Menchik 2016). The movement that forced Soeharto from power was a somewhat happenstance coalition and ideologically disunited. Its membership included human-rights activists, left-wing students, mainstream Muslims, disgruntled members of the middle class, and, during Soeharto's final weeks, segments of the military and the then-ruling party, Golkar (see Aspinall, Mietzner, and Tomsa chapters, and Aspinall 2005b; Hefner 2000; Tomsa 2008). For this reason too, many observers were at first skeptical that the successor to Soeharto's "New Order" government would implement the reforms demanded by the democratic opposition. This skepticism was reinforced by the fact that the man who succeeded Soeharto in the presidency was his most loyal of lieutenants and hand-picked vice-president, B. J. Habibie (Fortuna Anwar 2010).

Notwithstanding a significant measure of regime continuity, in the first months of Indonesia's democratic renewal, the government passed laws expanding press freedoms, legalizing independent political parties, and authorizing a referendum on independence in East Timor (which had been forcefully integrated into Indonesia in 1976; Aspinall 2005a). No less significant, the reform government put in place policies designed to separate the police from the military, remove military commanders from civilian government posts, and sever ties between the military and the once-ruling Golkar party (Aspinall and Mietzner chapters, and Mietzner 2009; Honna 2003; Tomsa 2008). In mid-1999, the government also passed two laws that set in motion one of the modern era's most far-reaching programs of administrative decentralization, devolving powers from the nation's capital to provinces, districts, and municipalities (see Aspinall, Buehler, and van Klinken and Berenschot chapters, and Aspinall and Fealy 2003a: 3–4; Schulte Nordholdt and van Klinken 2007). Between 1999 and 2002, Indonesian legislators seemed to crown this list of democratic accomplishments by crafting constitutional amendments designed to strengthen and expand religious freedoms (see Butt and Lindsey chapters, this volume).

From the beginning, however, the country's progress in democratic reform has been accompanied by a generally worsening pattern of religious intolerance (see Aritonang, Aspinall, Bagir, and Wilson chapters; Aspinall 2013; Crouch 2014; ICG 2010; Lindsey and Pausacker 2016). The state and its security forces have made impressive progress toward containing the terrorist fringe of this current, in fact to a degree much greater than most Muslim-majority countries (Jones 2013). Although ISIS has established a few small cells in Indonesia, its efforts have been met with a "strong, unequivocal government and community reaction in rejecting it" (IPAC 2014:23). However, both state and society in Indonesia have shown less ability to deal with the un-civil by-products of the "conservative turn" (Bruinessen 2013a; Burhani 2013; Hefner 2012) seen in Indonesian Islam since the early 2000s. A key feature of the turn has been a striking uptick in inter-religious tensions and the harassment of religious minorities by Islamist vigilantes (Bagir 2013; Crouch 2014; Feillard and Madinier 2006; Human Rights Watch 2013; Menchik 2016; Pausacker 2013; Wilson 2006, 2008).

These and other developments suggest that the more open and competitive environment of the Reformasi era has in several ways played to the advantage of conservative Islamists. Although the latter have never won more than a small portion of the vote in national elections (see Aspinall and Tomsa chapters), in the post-Soeharto period, they achieved new influence in the country's powerful Council of Indonesian Ulama (*Majelis Ulama Indonesia*; MUI). The MUI is a semi-governmental organization created in 1975 to provide a bridge between the government and Islamic scholars (Hasyim 2011, 2014; Ichwan 2013; Olle 2009). Regarded during the New Order period as acquiescent toward the government, in the Reformasi era, the MUI resolved to demonstrate a new spirit of independence. A key tactic in the MUI strategy was to expand its influence by recruiting radical Islamists from groups like the Hizbut Tahrir (Anhaf 2011) and the Majelis Mujahidin Indonesia and by rebranding itself as the national guardian of conservative Islamic morality. From their non-elected but strategic perch, conservative Muslim groupings have been able to compensate for setbacks in the electoral arena and exercise an influence in public life greater than their actual numbers in society (Bruinessen 2013b; Ichwan 2013).

The growing influence of anti-liberal and anti-pluralist ideas in MUI Muslim circles was vividly demonstrated in July 2005, when the Council issued fatwas condemning "secularism, liberalism, and pluralism" as contrary to Islam (Gillespie 2007; Ichwan 2013; see Hefner chapter). Islamists in militant groups cited the declaration to justify verbal and physical attacks on religious minorities (Hilmy 2010: 99–134). The anti-pluralist initiatives have targeted not only prominent national figures and organized religions but minor religious eccentrics in small towns and villages (Telle 2013, 2017). The incidents have raised serious questions about the multicentered nature of sovereignty in contemporary Indonesia, and its implications for religious expression and pluralist co-existence (Human Rights Watch 2013; Lindsey and Pausacker 2016; Bagir and Lindsey chapters).

As the chapters in this Handbook make clear, efforts are underway in contemporary Indonesia to reimagine and remake this huge country; the nation brings disparate resources to the task. This is a country that, notwithstanding its ethno-linguistic diversity, has succeeded at developing a strong sense of national identity and a widely used national language (see Bjork and Raihani, and Goebel chapters; see also Aspinall 2011; Collins 1996; Kuipers 1998). While in some parts of the world Muslim educators have resisted appeals for the reformation of their curricula, their counterparts in Indonesia embraced early on far-reaching programs of educational reform; today the country's State Islamic and Muhammadiyah-based system of Islamic higher education ranks among the finest in the Muslim-majority world. Although not yet winning the international recognition it so richly deserves (but see Kersten 2015), this country's Muslim intelligentsia is innovative, plural-minded, and far-ranging. At a more basic level, Indonesia achieved near-universal literacy in the 1990s. Girls and young women figure prominently in both public and Islamic higher education. At 51%, the country's rate of female labor force participation is two to three times that of many Muslim-majority countries in the Middle East, and roughly on par with figures in Western countries. Although religious minorities today face serious political challenges, they continue to occupy prominent perches in business, the media, and public life. Their public intellectuals figure prominently in public debates (Aritonang and Steenbrink 2008; Bakker 1993; and Aritonang and Ramstedt chapters). In these and many other respects, Indonesia today commands a wealth of social resources for a vibrant national culture and an effective and pluralist democracy (see Stepan 2014).

But Indonesia has legacies of a less plurality-accommodating nature as well. Established in the late 1940s, Indonesia's *Darul Islam* movement is one of the longest-lasting armed Islamist insurgencies in the Muslim-majority world (Dijk 1981; Formichi 2012). Since the early 2000s, the DI's legacy has been radicalized and "trans-nationalized" with the appearance of smaller but more violent groupings professing allegiance to al-Qa'eda and, since 2014, the Islamic State in Syria and the Levant (ISIL, ISIS; see Jones 2013; IPAC 2014). Institutionally speaking, too, the country's political and legal systems remain acutely vulnerable to money politics and corruption (see Buehler, Hadiz, and van Klinken and Berenschot chapters; and Aspinall and van Klinken 2010; Aspinall and Mietzner 2010; Aspinall 2014).

Perhaps even more seriously, the New Order state's habit of mobilizing civilian vigilantes to strike at enemies (Ryter 1998) has given way in the Reformasi era to a less state-monopolized but more socially pervasive pattern of civilian vigilantism; some of its best-organized and most assertive elements operate at the Islamist fringe of the Muslim community (Bakker 2016; Bamualim 2011; Pausacker 2013; Telle 2017; Wilson 2008). No less alarming, in recent years, some among the latter groups have devised a strategy for finally achieving electoral influence by making common cause with anti-democratic populists (see Hadiz chapter). In its final months, the New Order regime had attempted to forge just such a coalition of ethno-religious exclusion (Hefner 2000; Purdey 2006); it failed in large part because of the refusal of Muslim leaders in the Muhammadiyah and Nahdlatul Ulama to accept its terms. As Marcus Mietzner (2014b) and Vedi Hadiz (2016) have both observed, a similarly rightist populist alliance with Islamist militias re-emerged in the 2014 presidential campaign. The tactic had a powerful impact but ultimately fell short of its primary electoral aim (Mietzner 2014b:124). In an important study of secular-nationalist collaborations with hard-line Islamists for the implementation of Islamic legal regulations in several Indonesian regions, Michael Buehler has identified a related populist tack (Buehler 2016). The 2016–2017 "blasphemy" campaign against the Christian governor of Jakarta, Basuki Tjahaja Purnama (popularly known as "Ahok"), marked a new watershed in this long series of uncivil evolutions, and it may well have long-term implications for minorities and citizenship (see Aritonang, Bagir, and Lindsey chapters).

In short, although Indonesia has made great progress toward the goal of creating a national culture and functioning electoral democracy, its efforts to establish an operating consensus on religion and citizenship remain a work in progress. In particular, Indonesia's leaders and its public have yet to resolve the question of whether citizenship – both in formal principle and in lived practice – is to be *universal*, which is to say, a legal and political status extending equal rights and duties to all regardless of religious conviction, or *religiously differentiated*, that is, a civic status extending some rights and obligations to all, but reserving certain rights, duties, and privileges for members of a particular religious community. Since the early 2000s, hard-line Islamists have exploited this uncertainty and taken enforcement of laws on religious defamation into their own hands, effectively circumscribing the rights of religious minorities and non-mainstream Muslims (see Telle 2017).

The fact that Indonesia has long been a crossroads of cultures has always figured among the country's strengths; it has also been its most enduring source of contention. Even as Indonesia achieves greater global prominence over the next generation, this crossroads legacy will likely continue to present challenges to the many Indonesians who aspire to provide their nation with a prosperous, democratic, and plural future. It goes without saying that they are not alone in this regard: ours is an age of new pluralist trial, including in the democratic West (Joppke 2017). This makes the opportunity to come to terms with the cultural richness and political complexity of contemporary Indonesia all the more timely and beneficial.

A renewed Indonesian studies

One challenge of crafting a state-of-the-field *Handbook* like this one is that, not only has Indonesia over the past generation been in the throes of a great transition, but the academic disciplines that seek to make sense of it have undergone seismic shifts of their own. When, in the 1950s and 1960s, Indonesian studies first emerged as an international focus of area studies, the entire undertaking was dominated by a handful of anthropologists, historians, and political scientists from (mostly) the United States and Australia, intent on understanding culture and politics in an emerging but deeply divided nation. The dominant theoretical paradigm of the period, embraced even by figures as intellectually free-ranging as Clifford Geertz, was a modified variant of modernization theory.

Today Indonesian studies is securely established in a broader array of countries and a wider number of disciplines. It is also informed by a richer assortment of theoretical paradigms, from gender, media, and cultural studies to political economy and political ethics. No less significant, today major centers for Indonesian studies operate in Western Europe, North America, Japan, Korea, Hong Kong, Singapore, Malaysia, and, of course, Indonesia itself. One of the most welcome developments in Indonesian studies over the past generation has been the emergence of a new generation of native-born Indonesianists of international standing, based in the country's State Islamic and Muhammadiyah Universities as well as its general (non-religious) universities.

Several Routledge Handbooks on various aspects of politics and economics in Asia have been published over the past ten years, and most have included one or several chapters on Indonesia. In putting together this *Handbook of Contemporary Indonesia*, our aim was to avoid overlap with existing collections by focusing on areas in Indonesian studies of unusually intensive as well as broad research interest. We were also interested in highlighting sub-disciplines and topics where, rather than a handful of researchers in one discipline speaking among themselves, research over the past ten to fifteen years has generated a significant measure of synergy within and across academic disciplines.

With this aim in mind, this volume highlights six fields of inquiry at the heart of Indonesian studies today: political and cultural legacies; democratic politics and societal plurality; markets, ethics, and economic cultures; Islam, minority religions, and pluralist co-existence; the dynamics of gender and sexuality; and Indonesia in an age of political and cultural globalization. Each chapter provides a short, state-of-the-field summary of the topic under consideration in the Indonesian context, and in turn situates the Indonesian sub-field in relation to broader theoretical discussions relevant for other world areas. In so doing, the Handbook is designed to bear witness to both the breadth and richness of Indonesian studies, and its critical relevance for global studies and the contemporary humanities and social sciences as a whole.

References cited

Abdillah, Masykuri. 1997. *Responses of Indonesian Muslim Intellectuals to the Concept of Democracy (1966–1993)* (Hamburg: Abera Verlag Meyer & Co.).

Abdullah, M. Amin. 2006. *Islamic Studies di Perguruan Tinggi: Pendekatan Integratif-Interkonektif* (Islamic Studies in Higher Education: An Integrated-Interconnected Approach) (Yogyakarta: Pustaka Pelajar).

Abdullah, Taufik. 1971. *Schools and Politics: The Kaum Muda Movement in West Sumatra (1927–1933)* (Ithaca: Modern Indonesia Project, SEAP, Cornell University).

Abu-Lughod, Lila. 1986. *Veiled Sentiments: Honor and Poetry in a Bedouin Society* (Berkeley and Los Angeles: University of California Press).

Abuza, Zachary. 2003. *Militant Islam in Southeast Asia: Crucible of Terror* (Boulder and London: Lynne Rienner).

Adam, Ahmat B. 1995. *The Vernacular Press and the Emergence of Modern Indonesian Consciousness (1855–1913)* (Ithaca: Studies on Southeast Asia No. 17, Southeast Asia Program, Cornell University).

Adely, Fida J. 2012. *Gendered Paradoxes: Educating Jordanian Women in Nation, Faith, and Progress* (Chicago and London: University of Chicago Press).

Akkeren, Philip van. 1970. *Sri and Christ: A Study of the Indigenous Church in East Java* (London: Lutterworth Press).

Alexander, Jennifer. 1987. *Trade, Traders and Trading in Rural Java* (Singapore: Oxford University Press).

Anderson, Benedict. 1983a. *Imagined Communities: Reflections on the Origins and Spread of Nationalism* (London: Verso).

———. 1983b. "Old State, New Society: Indonesia's New Order in Historical Perspective," *Journal of Asian Studies* 42: 477–96.

Anhaf, Mohammad Iqbal. 2011. "From Revolution to 'Refolution': A Study of Hizb al-Tahrir, Its Changes and Trajectories in the Democratic Context of Indonesia (2000–2009)" (Ph.D. Thesis. Wellington, NZ: School of Government, University of Wellington).

Aragon, Lorraine V. 2000. *Fields of the Lord: Animism, Christian Minorities, and State Development in Indonesia* (Honolulu: University of Hawaii Press).

Aritonang, Jan S. and Steenbrink, Karel A. eds., 2008. *A History of Christianity in Indonesia* (Leiden: Brill).

Aspinall, Edward. 2005a. "Elections and the Normalization of Politics in Indonesia," *South East Asia Research* 13(2): 117–56.

———. 2005b. *Opposing Suharto: Compromise, Resistance, and Regime Change in Indonesia* (Stanford, CA: Stanford University Press).

———. 2010. "The Irony of Success," *Journal of Democracy* 21(2): 20–34.

———. 2011. "Democratization and Ethnic Politics in Indonesia: Nine Theses," *Journal of East Asian Studies* 11(2): 289–319.

———. 2013. "A Nation in Fragments: Patronage and Neoliberalism in Contemporary Indonesia," *Critical Asian Studies* 45(1): 27–54.

———. 2014. "Parliament and Patronage," *Journal of Democracy* 25(4): 96–110.

Aspinall, Edward and Greg Fealy, eds. 2003a. "Introduction: Decentralisation, Democratisation, and the Rise of the Local," in Edward Aspinall and Greg Fealy, eds., *Local Power and Politics in Indonesia: Decentralizations* (Singapore: Institute of Southeast Asian Studies), pp. 1–11.

———. 2003b. *Local Power and Politics in Indonesia: Decentralisation and Democratisation* (Singapore: Institute of Southeast Asian Studies).

Aspinall, Edward and Gerry van Klinken, eds. 2010. *The State and Illegality in Indonesia* (Leiden: KITLV Press).

Aspinall, Edward and Marcus Mietzner. 2010. *Problems of Democratisation in Indonesia: Elections, Institutions and Society* (Singapore: Institute of Southeast Asian Studies).

Asplund, Knut D. 2009. "Resistance to Human Rights in Indonesia: Asian Values and Beyond," *Asia Pacific Journal on Human Rights and Law* 10(1): 27–47.

Atkinson, Jane Monnig. 1987. "Religions in Dialogue: The Construction of an Indonesian Minority Religion," in Rita Smith Kipp and Susan Rodgers, eds., *Indonesian Religions in Transition* (Tucson: University of Arizona Press), pp. 171–86.

Azra, Azyumardi, Dina Afrianty, and Robert W. Hefner. 2007. "Pesantren and Madrasa: Muslim Schools and National Ideals in Indonesia," in Robert W. Hefner and Muhammad Qasim Zaman, eds., *Schooling Islam: The Culture and Politics of Modern Muslim Education* (Princeton: Princeton University Press), pp. 172–98.

Bagir, Zainal Abidin. 2013. "Defamation of Religion in Post-Reformasi Indonesia: Is Revision Possible?" *Australian Journal of Asian Law* 13(2): 1–16.

Bagir, Zainal Abidin and Robert W. Hefner. 2016. "Christianity and Religious Freedom in Indonesia Since 1998," in Allen Hertzke and Timothy Samuel Shah, eds., *Christianity and Freedom: Contemporary Perspectives*, Vol. II (Cambridge: Cambridge Studies in Law and Christianity, Cambridge University Press), pp. 191–221.

Bakker, F.L. 1993. *The Struggle of the Hindu Balinese Intellectuals* (Amsterdam: Vrij University Press).

Bakker, Laurens. 2016. "Organized Violence and the State: Evolving Vigilantism in Indonesia," *Bijdragen tot de Taal-, Land-, en Volkenkunde* 172(2): 249–77.

Bamualim, Chaider S. 2011. "Islamic Militancy and Resentment Against Hadhramis in Post-Suharto Indonesia: A Case Study of Habib Rizieq Syihab and His Islamic Defenders Front," *Comparative Studies of South Asia, Africa and the Middle East* 31(2): 267–81.

Barth, Fredrik. 1993. *Balinese Worlds* (Princeton: Princeton University Press).

Barton, Greg. 1995. "Neo-Modernism: A Vital Synthesis of Traditionalist and Modernist Islamic Thought in Indonesia," *Studia Islamika: Indonesian Journal for Islamic Studies* 2(3): 1–71.

Basri, M. Chatib and Hall Hill. 2010. "Indonesian Growth Dynamics." Working Papers in Trade and Development No. 2010/10, School of Economics, Australian National University, Canberra.

Bayat, Asef. 2005. "Islamism and Social Movement Theory," *Third World Quarterly* 26(6): 891–908.

Beatty, Andrew. 1999. *Varieties of Javanese Religion: An Anthropological Account.* Cambridge Studies in Social and Cultural Anthropology (Cambridge: Cambridge University Press).

———. 2009. *A Shadow Falls in the Heart of Java* (London: Faber and Faber).

Berkey, Jonathan. 2003. *The Formation of Islam* (Cambridge: Cambridge University Press).

Bertrand, Jacques. 2004. *Nationalism and Ethnic Conflict in Indonesia* (Cambridge: Cambridge University Press).

Bjork, Christopher. 2005. *Indonesian Education: Teachers, Schools, and Central Bureaucracy* (New York and London: Routledge).

Blackburn, Susan. 2008. "Indonesian Women and Political Islam," *Journal of Southeast Asian Studies* 39(1): 83–105.

Boland, B.J. 1982. *The Struggle of Islam in Modern Indonesia* (Netherlands: Koninklijk Instituut voor Taal-Land en Volkenkunde).

Bond, Christopher S. and Lewis M. Simons. 2009. *The Next Front: Southeast Asia and the Road to Global Peace with Islam* (Hoboken, NJ: John Wiley and Sons).

Bowen, John R. 1993. *Muslims Through Discourse: Religion and Ritual in Gayo Society* (Princeton: Princeton University Press).

Brenner, Suzanne. 1998. *The Domestication of Desire: Women, Wealth, and Modernity in Java* (Princeton: Princeton University Press).

———. 2011. "Private Moralities in the Public Sphere: Democratization, Islam, and Gender in Indonesiam," *American Anthropologist* 113(3): 478–90.

Bruinessen, Martin van. 1989. "Kitab Kuning: Books in Arabic Script Used in the Pesantren Milieu," *Bijdragen tot de Taal-, Land-, en Volkenkunde* 146(2–3): 225–69.

———. 1994. "Pesantren and Kitab Kuning: Maintenance and Continuation of a Tradition of Religious Learning," in Wolfgang Marschall, ed., *Texts From the Islands: Oral and Written Traditions of Indonesia and the Malaya World* (Berne: University of Berne Press), pp. 121–45.

———. 1995. "Shari'a Court, Tarekat and Pesantren: Religious Institutions in the Banten Sultanate," *Archipel* 50: 165–200.

————. ed. 2013a. *Contemporary Developments in Indonesian Islam: Explaining the "Conservative Turn"* (Singapore: Institute for Southeast Asian Studies).

————. 2013b. "Introduction: Contemporary Developments in Indonesian Islam and the 'Conservative Turn' of the Early Twenty-First Century," in van Bruinessen, ed., pp. 1–20.

Bubalo, Anthony and Greg Fealy. 2005. *Joining the Caravan: The Middle East, Islamism and Indonesia* (Double Bay [Australia]: Lowy Institute for International Policy).

Budiman, Arief, ed. 1990. *State and Civil Society in Indonesia* Monash Papers on Southeast Asia No. 22 (Clayton [Australia]: Centre of Southeast Asian Studies, Monash University).

Buehler, Michael. 2016. *The Politics of Shari'a Law: Islamist Activists and the State in Democratizing Indonesia* (Cambridge: Cambridge University Press).

Bunte, Marco and Andreas Ufen, eds. 2009. *Democratization in Post-Suharto Indonesia* (London and New York: Routledge).

Burhani, Ahmad Najib. 2013. "Liberal and Conservative Discourses in the Muhammadiyah: The Struggle for the Face of Reformist Islam in Indonesia," in van Bruinessen, ed., pp. 105–44.

Burhanudin, Jajat. 2006. "Kerajaan-Oriented Islam: The Experience of Pre-Colonial Indonesia," *Studia Islamika* 13(1): 33–66.

Bush, Robin. 2009. *Nahdlatul Ulama and the Struggle for Power Within Islam and Politics in Indonesia* (Singapore: Institute of Southeast Asian Studies).

Butt, Simon and Tim Lindsey. 2010. "Judicial Mafia: The Courts and State Illegality in Indonesia," in Edward Aspinall and Gerry van Klinken, eds., pp. 189–213.

————. 2012. *The Constitution of Indonesia: A Contextual Analysis* (Oxford and Portland: Hart Publishing).

Cammack, Mark. 1997. "Indonesia's 1989 Religious Judicature Act: Islamization of Indonesia or Indonesianization of Islam?" *Indonesia* 63: 143–68.

Cederroth, Sven. 1981. *The Spell of the Ancestors and the Power of Mekkah: A Sasak Community on Lombok* (Goteborg: Universitatis Gothoburgensis).

————. 1996. "From Ancestor Worship to Monotheism: Politics of Religion in Lombok," *Temenos* 32: 7–36.

Collins, James T. 1996. *Malay, World Language: A Short History* (Kuala Lumpur: Dewan Bahasa dan Pustaka).

Cribb, Robert. 1990. *The Indonesia Killings, 1965–1966: Studies from Java and Bali*, Monash Papers on Southeast Asia, No. 21 (Clayton, Victoria [Australia]: Centre of Southeast Asian Studies, Monash University).

————. 2010. "The Incredible Shrinking Pancasila: Nationalist Propaganda and the Missing Ideological Legacy of Suharto," in Thomas Reuter, ed., *The Return to Constitutional Democracy in Indonesia* (Canberra, Victoria, Australia: Monash University Press), pp. 65–76.

————. 2013. *Historical Atlas of Indonesia* (London and New York: Routledge).

Crone, Patricia. 2003. *Slaves on Horses: The Evolution of the Islamic Polity* (Cambridge: Cambridge University Press).

Crouch, Melissa. 2014. *Law and Religion in Indonesia: Conflict and the Courts in West Java* (London and New York: Routledge).

Davidson, Jamies S. 2008. *From Rebellion to Riots: Collective Violence on Indonesian Borneo* (Madison: University of Wisconsin Press).

Davies, Sharyn Graham. 2010. *Gender Diversity in Indonesia: Sexuality, Islam and Queer Selves* (London and New York: Routledge).

Dick, Howard W. 1985. "The Rise of a Middle Class and the Changing Concept of Equity in Indonesia – An Interpretation," *Indonesia* 39: 71–92.

Dijk, C. van. 1981. *Rebellion Under the Banner of Islam: The Darul Islam in Indonesia*, Verhandelingen van Het KITLV No. 94 (The Hague: Martinus Nijhoff).

Dhofier, Zamakhsyari. 1999. *The Pesantren Tradition: The Role of the Kyai in the Maintenance of Traditional Islam in Java* (Tempe: Monograph Series, Program for Southeast Asian Studies, Arizona State University).

Doorn-Harder, Nelly van. 2006. *Women Shaping Islam: Indonesian Muslim Women Reading the Qur'an* (Urbana-Champaign: University of Illinois Press).

Duncan, Christopher R. 2011. *Violence and Vengeance: Religious Conflict and Its Aftermath in Eastern Indonesia* (Ithaca: Cornell University Press).

Effendy, Bahtiar. 2003. *Islam and the State in Indonesia* (Singapore: Institute of Southeast Asian Studies).

Emon, Anver. 2012. *Religious Pluralism and Islamic Law: Dhimmis and Others in the Empire of Law.* Oxford Islamic Legal Studies Volume 1 (Oxford: Oxford University Press).

Engle Merry, Sally. 1988. "Legal Pluralism," *Law and Society Review* 22(5): 869–96.

Ewing, Katherine P. 1990. "The Illusion of Wholeness: Culture, Self, and the Experience of Inconsistency," *Ethos* 18(3): 251–78.

Fasseur, Cornelis. 1992. *The Politics of Colonial Exploitation: Java, the Dutch, and the Cultivation System* (Ithaca: Cornell University, SEAP Publications).

Fealy, Greg. 2016. "The Politics of Religious Intolerance in Indonesia: Mainstream-ism Trumps Extremism?" in Tim Lindsey and Helen Pausacker, eds., pp. 115–31.

Fealy, Greg and Sally White, eds. 2008. *Expressing Islam: Religious Life and Politics in* Indonesia (Singapore: ISSEAS Press).

Feener, R. Michael. 2007. *Muslim Legal Thought in Modern Indonesia* (Cambridge: Cambridge University Press).

———. 2013. *Shari'a and Social Engineering: The Implementation of Islamic Law in Contemporary Aceh, Indonesia* (Oxford: Oxford University Press).

———. 2016. "State Shari'a and Its Limits," in R. Michael Feener, David Kloos, and Annemarie Samuels, eds., *Islam and the Limits of the State: Reconfigurations of Practice, Community and Authority in Contemporary Aceh* (Leiden and Boston: Brill), pp. 1–23.

Feillard, Andrée. 1995. *Islam et Armée dans l'Indonésie Contemporaine* (Paris: L'Harmattan).

Feillard, Andrée and Rémy Madinier. 2006. *La Fin de l'Innocence? L'Islam Indonésien Face à la Tentation Radicale de 1967 à Nos Jours* (Paris: Les Indes Savantes).

Feith, Herbert. 2006 (orig. 1962). *The Decline of Constitutional Democracy in Indonesia* (Singapore: Equinox Publishing, 2006).

Fenwick, Stewart. 2017. *Blasphemy, Islam and the State: Pluralism and Liberalism in Indonesia* (London and New York: Routledge).

Ford, Michele and Thomas B. Pepinsky, eds. 2014. *Beyond Oligarchy: Wealth, Power, and Contemporary Indonesian Politics* (Ithaca: Cornell Southeast Asia Program).

Formichi, Chiara. 2012. *Islam and the Making of the Nation: Kartosuwiryo and Political Islam in 20th Century Indonesia* (Leiden: KITLV Press).

Fortuna Anwar, Dewi. 2010. "The Habibie Presidency: Catapulting Towards Reform," in Edward Aspinall and Greg Fealy, eds., *Soeharto's New Order and Its Legacy: Essays in Honour of Harold Crouch* (Canberra, Victoria, Australia: ANU E Press), pp. 99–118.

Freedom House. 2017. "Freedom in the World: 2017 Report." https://freedomhouse.org/report/freedom-world/freedom-world-2017 (Accessed 15 May 2017).

Gade, Anna M. 2004. *Perfection Makes Practice: Learning, Emotion, and the Recited Qur'an in Indonesia* (Honolulu: University of Hawai'i Press).

Geertz, Clifford. 1960. *The Religion of Java* (New York: The Free Press).

George, Kenneth M. 1996. *Showing Signs of Violence: The Cultural Politics of a Twentieth-Century Headhunting Ritual* (Berkeley: University of California Press).

———. 2010. *Picturing Islam: Art and Ethics in a Muslim Lifeworld* (Malden, MA and Oxford: Wiley-Blackwell).

Gibson, Thomas. 2007. *Islamic Narrative and Authority in Southeast Asia: From the 16th to the 21st Century* (New York: Palgrave Macmillan).

Gillespie, Piers. 2007. "Current Issues in Indonesian Islam: Analysing the 2005 Council of Indonesian Ulama Fatwa No. 7 Opposing Pluralism, Liberalism, and Secularism," *Journal of Islamic Studies* 18(2): 202–40.

Hadiz, Vedi R. 2010. *Localising Power in Post-Authoritarian Indonesia: A Southeast Asian Perspective* (Stanford: Stanford University Press).

———. 2016. *Islamic Populism in Indonesia and the Middle East* (Cambridge: Cambridge University Press).

Hamayotsu, Kikue. 2011. "The End of Political Islam? A Comparative Analysis of Religious Parties in the Muslim Democracy of Indonesia," *Journal of Current Southeast Asian Affairs* 30(3): 133–59.

Hannerz, Ulf. 1992. *Cultural Complexity: Studies in the Social Organization of Meaning* (New York: Columbia University Press).

Hansen, Thomas Blom. 1999. *The Saffron Wave: Democracy and Hindu Nationalism in Modern India* (Princeton: Princeton University Press 1999).

Hasan, Noorhaidi. 2006. *Laskar Jihad: Islam, Militancy, and the Quest for Identity in Post-New Order Indonesia* (Ithaca: Southeast Asia Program, Cornell University).

Hassan, Riaz. 2002. *Faithlines: Muslim Conceptions of Islam and Society* (Oxford: Oxford University Press).

———. 2007. "On Being Religious: Patterns of Religious Commitment in Muslim Societies," *The Muslim World* 97(3): 437–78.

Hasyim, Syafiq. 2011. *The Council of Indonesian Ulama (Majelis Ulama Indonesia, MUI) and Religious Freedom* (Bangkok: IRASEC).

————. 2014. "Council of Indonesian Ulama (Majelis Ulama Indonesia, MUI) and Its Role in the Shari-atisation of Indonesia" (Ph.D. Thesis. Berlin: The Free University).

Headley, Stephen C. 2004. *Durga's Mosque: Cosmology, Conversion and Community in Central Javanese Islam* (Singapore: Institute of Southeast Asian Studies).

Hefner, Robert W. 1985. *Hindu Javanese: Tengger Tradition and Islam* (Princeton: Princeton University Press).

————. 2000. *Civil Islam: Muslims and Democratization in Indonesia* (Princeton: Princeton University Press).

————. 2004. "Hindu Reform in an Islamizing Java: Pluralism and Peril," in Martin Ramstedt, ed., pp. 93–108.

————. 2007. "Introduction: The Culture, Politics, and Future of Muslim Education," in Robert W. Hefner and Muhammad Qasim Zaman, eds., *Schooling Islam: The Culture and Politics of Modern Muslim Education* (Princeton: Princeton University Press), pp. 1–39.

————. 2009. "The Politics and Cultures of Islamic Education in Southeast Asia," in Robert W. Hefner, ed., *Making Modern Muslims: The Politics of Islamic Education in Southeast Asia* (Honolulu: University of Hawaii Press), pp. 1–54.

————. 2011a. "Where Have All the *Abangan* Gone? Religionization and the Decline of Non-Standard Islam in Contemporary Indonesia," in Picard and Madinier, eds., pp. 71–91.

————. 2011b. "Human Rights and Democracy in Islam: The Indonesian Case in Comparative Perspective," in Thomas Banchoff and Robert Wuthnow, eds., *Religion and the Global Politics of Human Rights* (Oxford: Oxford University Press), pp. 39–69.

————. 2012. "Islamic Radicalism in a Democratizing Indonesia," in Shahram Akbarzadeh, ed., *The Routledge Handbook of Political Islam* (New York and London: Routledge), pp. 105–118.

————. 2016. "Islamic Ethics and Muslim Feminism in Indonesia," in Robert W. Hefner, ed., *Shari'a Law and Modern Muslim Ethics* (Bloomington and Indianapolis: Indiana University Press), pp. 260–90.

Herriman, Nicholas. 2012. *The Entangled State: Sorcer, State Control, and Violence in Indonesia* (New Haven: Yale University Council on Southeast Asian Studies).

Heryanto, Ariel. 2011. "Upgraded Piety and Pleasure: The New Middle Class and Islam in Indonesian Popular Culture," in Andrew N. Weintraub, ed., *Islam and Popular Culture in Indonesia and Malaysia* (London and New York: Routledge), pp. 60–82.

Hill, Hal. 1996. *The Indonesian Economy Since 1966: Southeast Asia's Emerging Giant* (Cambridge: Cambridge University Press).

Hilmy, Masdar. 2010. *Islamism and Democracy in Indonesia: Piety and Pragmatism* (Singapore: ISEAS Press).

Hoesterey, James B. 2015. *Rebranding Islam: Piety, Prosperity, and a Self-Help Guru* (Stanford: Stanford University Press).

Hoesterey, James B. and Marshall Clark. 2012. "*Film Islami*: Gender, Piety and Popular Culture in Post-Authoritarian Indonesia," *Asian Studies Review* 36(2): 207–26.

Honna, Jun. 2003. *Military Politics and Democratization in Indonesia* (London and New York: LondonCurzon).

Hooker, M.B. 1983. "Muhammadan Law and Islamic Law," in *Islam in South-East Asia* (Leiden: Brill), pp. 160–82.

————. 1984. *Islamic Law in South-East Asia* (Singapore: Oxford University Press).

————. 2008. *Indonesian Syariah: Defining a National School of Islamic Law* (Singapore: Institute of Southeast Asian Studies).

Howell, Julia Day. 2005. "Muslims, the New Age and Marginal Religions in Indonesia: Changing Meanings of Religious Pluralism," *Social Compass* 52(4): 473–93.

————. 2008. "Modulations of Active Piety: Professors and Televangelists as Promoters of Indonesian 'Sufism,'" in Greg Fealy and Sally White, eds., *Expressing Islam: Religious Life and Politics in Indonesia* (Singapore: Institute for Southeast Asian Studies), pp. 40–62.

Human Rights Watch. 2013. *In Religion's Name: Abuses Against Religious Minorities in Indonesia* (New York: Human Rights Watch).

Hughes-Freeland, Felicia. 2008. *Embodied Communities: Dance Traditions and Change in Java* (New York and Oxford: Berghahn).

ICG. 2002. *Al-Qaeda in Southeast Asia: The Case of the 'Ngruki Network' in Indonesia* (Jakarta and Brussels: Asia Briefing No. 20).

————. 2010. *Indonesia: 'Christianisation' and Intolerance.* Asia Briefing N°114 (Jakarta/Brussels: International Crisis Group).

Ichwan, Moch Nur. 2013. "Towards a Puritanical Moderate Islam: The Majelis Ulama Indonesia and the Politics of Religious Orthodoxy," in Bruinessen ed., *Contemporary Developments in Indonesian Islam: Explaining the "Conservative Turn"* (Singapore: Institute for Southeast Asian Studies), pp. 60–104.

IPAC. 2014. *The Evolution of ISIS in Indonesia.* Institute for Policy Analysis of Conflict Report No. 13 (Jakarta: IPAC).

Jabali, Fuad and Jamhari, eds. 2002. *IAIN & Modernisasi Islam di Indonesia* [The State Islamic Institutes and the Modernization of Islam in Indonesia] (Jakarta: Logos Wacana Ilmu).

Jackson, Elizabeth. 2007. "Crafting a New Democracy: Civic Education in Indonesian Islamic Universities," *Asia Pacific Journal of Education* 27(1): 41–54.

Jones, Carla. 2010. "Materializing Piety: Gendered Anxieties About Faithful Consumption in Contemporary Urban Indonesia," *American Ethnologist* 37(4): 617–37.

Jones, Gavin W. and Chris Manning. 1992. "Labour Force and Employment During the 1980s," in Anne Booth, ed., *The Oil Boom and After: Indonesian Economic Policy and Performance in the Soeharto Era* (Kuala Lumpur: Oxford University Press, 1992), pp. 363–410.

Jones, Sidney. 2013. "Indonesian Government Approaches to Radical Islam Since 1998," in Mirjam Künkler and Alfred Stepan, eds., *Democracy and Islam in Indonesia* (New York: Columbia University Press), pp. 109–25.

Joppke, Christian. 2017. *Is Multiculturalism Dead? Crisis and Persistence in the Constitutional State* (Cambridge, UK: Polity Press).

Kahin, Audrey R. 2012. *Islam, Nationalism and Democracy: A Political Biography of Mohammad Natsir* (Singapaore: NUS Press).

Karim, Wazir Jahan. 1995. "Bilateralism and Gender in Southeast Asia," in Wazir Jahan Karim, ed., *"Male" and "Female" in Developing Southeast Asia* (Oxford: Berg), pp. 35–74.

Kendhammer, Brandon. 2016. *Muslims Talking Politics: Framing Islam, Democracy, and Law in Northern Nigeria* (Chicago: University of Chicago Press).

Kersten, Carool. 2015. *Islam in Indonesia: The Contest for Society, Ideas and Values* (London: Hurst and Company).

King, Victor T. 1993. *The Peoples of Borneo* (Oxford: Blackwell).

Kipp, Rita Smith. 1993. *Dissociated Identities: Ethnicity, Religion, and Class in an Indonesian Society* (Ann Arbor: University of Michigan Press).

Kloos, David and Ward Berenschot. 2017. "Citizenship and Islam in Malaysia and Indonesia," in Ward Berenschot, Henk Schulte Nordholt, and Laurens Bakker, eds., *Citizenship and Democratization in Southeast Asia* (Leiden and Boston: Brill), pp. 178–207.

Kruithof, Maryse. 2014. "'Shouting in a Desert': Dutch Missionary Encounters With Javanese Islam, 1850–1910" (Ph.D. Thesis. Rotterdam: Department of History, Erasmus University).

Kuipers, Joel C. 1998. *Language, Identity, and Marginality in Indonesia: The Changing Nature of Ritual Speech on the Island of Sumba* (Cambridge: Cambridge University Press).

Kuru, Ahmet T. 2009. *Secularism and State Policies Toward Religion: The United States, France, and Turkey* (Cambridge: Cambridge University Press).

Kymlicka, Will. 1995. *Multicultural Citizenship: A Liberal Theory of Minority Rights* (Oxford: Oxford University Press.

Laderman, Carol. 1991. *Taming the Wind of Desire: Psychology, Medicine, and Aesthetics in Malay Shamanistic Performance* (Berkeley: University of California Press).

Laffan, Michael. 2011. *The Makings of Indonesian Islam: Orientalism and the Narration of a Sufi Past* (Princeton, NJ and Oxford, UK: Princeton University Press).

Laidlaw, James. 2014. *The Subject of Virtue: An Anthropology of Ethics and Freedom* (Cambridge: Cambridge University Press).

Layish, Aharon. 2004. "The Transformation of the Sharîʿa From Jurists' Law to Statutory Law in the Contemporary Muslim World," *Die Welt des Islams* 44(1): 85–113.

Lindsey, Tim. 2012. *Islam, Law and the State in Southeast Asia.* Vol. I: Indonesia (London and New York: Tauris).

Lindsey, Tim and Simon Butt. 2016. "State Power to Restrict Religious Freedom: An Overview of the Legal Framework," in Tim Lindsey and Helen Pausacker, eds., pp. 19–41.

Lindsey, Tim and Jeremy Kingsley. 2008. "Talking in Code: Legal Islamisation in Indonesia and the MMI Shari'a Criminal Code," in Peri Bearman, Wolfhart Heirichs, and Bernard G. Weiss, eds., *The Law Applied: Contextualizing the Islamic Shari'a* (London and New York: Tauris), pp. 295–319.

Lindsey, Tim and Helen Pausacker, eds. 2016. *Religion, Law and Intolerance in Indonesia* (New York and London: Routledge).

Liow, Joseph C. 2009. *Piety and Politics: Islamism in Contemporary Malaysia* (New York: Oxford University Press).

Lombard, Denys. 1990. *Le Carrefour Javanais: Essai d'histoire globale, Vol 2, Les Réseaux Asiatique* (Paris: Editions de l'École des Hautes Études en Sciences Sociales).

Machmudi, Yon. 2006. "Islamizing Indonesia: The Rise of Jemaah Tarbiyah and the Prosperous Justice Party (PKS)" (Canberra: Ph.d. Dissertation, Faculty of Asian Studies, Australian National University).

Makdisi, George. 1981. *The Rise of Colleges: Institutions of Learning in Islam and the West* (Edinburgh: University of Edinburgh Press).

Makin, Ali. 2017. "Homogenizing Indonesian Islam: Persecution of the Shia Group in Yogyakarta," *Studia Islamika* 24(1): 1–32.

Mawardi, Ahmad Imam. 2003. "The Political Backdrop of the Enactment of the Compilation of Islamic Laws in Indonesia," in Arskal Salim and Azyumardi Azra, eds., *Shari'a and Politics in Modern Indonesia* (Singapore: Institute for Southeast Asian Studies), pp. 125–47.

McGregor, Katharine E. 2009. "A Bridge and a Barrier: Islam, Reconciliation, and the 1965 Killings in Indonesia," in Birgit Brauchler, ed., *Reconciling Indonesia: Grassroots Agency for Peace* (London and New York: Routledge), pp. 214–32.

Menchik, Jeremy. 2016. *Islam and Democracy in Indonesia: Tolerance Without Liberalism* (Cambridge: Cambridge University Press).

Mietzner, Marcus. 2008. "Comparing Indonesia's Party Systems of the 1950s and the Post-Soeharto Era: From Centrifugal to Centripetal Inter-Party Competition," *Journal of Southeast Asian Studies* 39(3): 431–53.

———. 2009. *Military Politics, Islam, and the State in Indonesia: From Turbulent Transition to Democratic Consolidation* (Singapore: Institute of Southeast Asian Studies).

———. 2014a. "Oligarchs, Politicians, and Activists: Contesting Party Politics in Post-Suharto Indonesia," in Michele Ford and Tom Pepinsky, eds., pp. 99–116.

———. 2014b. "How Jokowi Won and Democracy Survived," *Journal of Democracy* 25(4): 111–25.

Milner, Anthony. 1995. *The Invention of Politics in Colonial Malaya: Contesting Nationalism and the Expansion of the Public Sphere* (Cambridge: Cambridge University Press).

Moaddel, Mansoor and Michele J. Gelfand, eds. 2017. *Values, Political Action, and Change in the Middle East the Arab Spring* (Oxford: Oxford University Press).

Modood, Tariq. 2007. *Multiculturalism: A Civic Idea* (Cambridge: Polity Press).

Mortimer, Rex. 1974. *Indonesian Communism Under Sukarno: Ideology and Politics, 1959–1965* (Ithaca: Cornell University Press).

Mujani, Saiful. 2003. "Religious Democrats: Democratic Culture and Muslim Political Participation in Post-Suharto Indonesia." (Ph.D. Thesis. Columbus, OH: Department of Political Science, Ohio State University).

Nakamura, Mitsuo. 2012. *The Crescent Arises over the Banyan Tree: A Study of the Muhammadiyah Movement in a Central Javanese Town, c. 1910s–2010*, 2nd Enlarged Edition (Singapore: ISEAS Press).

Njoto-Feillard, Gwenaël. 2012. *L'Islam et la réinvention du capitalisme en Indonésie* (Paris: Karthala).

Olle, John. 2009. "The Majelis Ulama Indonesia Versus 'Heresy': The Resurgence of Authoritarian Islam," in Gerry van Klinken and Joshua Barker, eds., *State of Authority: The State in Society in Indonesia* (Ithaca: Cornell Southeast Program Publications), pp. 95–116.

Parker, Lyn and Pam Nilan. 2013. *Adolescents in Contemporary Indonesia* (London and New York: Routledge).

Pausacker, Helen. 2013. "Morality and the Nation: Pornography and Indonesia's Islamic Defenders Front." (Melbourne: Ph.D. Dissertation, Law School, University of Melbourne).

Peacock, James L. 1978. *Muslim Puritans: Reformist Psychology in Southeast Asian Islam* (Berkeley and Los Angeles: University of California Press).

Peletz, Michael G. 2009. *Gender Pluralism: Southeast Asia Since Early Modern Times* (London and New York: Routledge).

Pelras, Christian. 1996. *The Bugis* (Oxford: Blackwell).

Pew Forum on Religion and Public Life. 2013. *The World's Muslims: Religion, Politics, and Society* (Washington, DC: Pew Research Center).

Picard, Michel. 2011. "From *Agama Hindu Bali* to *Agama Hindu* and Back: Toward a Relocalization of Balinese Religion?" in Picard and Madinier, eds., pp. 117–41.

Picard, Michel and Remy Madinier, eds. 2011. *The Politics of Religion in Indonesia: Syncretism, Orthodoxy, and Religious Contention in Java and Bali* (London and New York: Routledge).

Pigeaud, Th. G. Th. 1960–1963. *Java in the 14th Century*, 5 Vols (The Hague: Martinus Nijhoff).

Purdey, Jemma. 2006. *Anti-Chinese Violence in Indonesia: 1996–1999* (Singapore: National University of Singapore Press).

Rakhmani, Inaya. 2016. *Mainstreaming Islam in Indonesia: Television, Identity and the Middle Class* (New York: Palgrave Macmillan).

Ramstedt, Martin, ed. 2004. *Hinduism in Modern Indonesia* (London and New York: Routledge).

Rasmussen, Anne K. 2010. *Women, the Recited Qur'an, and Islamic Music in Indonesia* (Berkeley and Los Angeles: University of California Press).

Reid, Anthony. 1988. *Southeast Asia in the Age of Commerce, 1450–1680: Volume One: The Lands Below the Winds* (New Haven: Yale University Press).

———. 1993. *Southeast Asia in the Age of Commerce, 1450–1680: Volume Two: Expansion and Crisis* (New Haven: Yale University Press).

Reid, Anthony and Jennifer Brewster, eds. 1983. *Slavery, Bondage, and Dependency in Southeast Asia* (New York: Palgrave Macmillan).

Ricci, Ronit. 2011. *Islam Translated: Literature, Conversion, and the Arabic Cosmopolis of South and Southeast Asia* (Chicago: University of Chicago Press).

Ricklefs, M.C. 2006. *Mystic Synthesis in Java: A History of Islamization from the Fourteenth to the Early Nineteenth Centuries* (Norwalk, CT: East Bridge).

———. 2007. *Polarising Javanese Society: Islamic and Other Visions (c. 1830–1930)* (Honolulu: University of Hawaii Press).

———. 2012. *Islamisation and Its Opponents in Java: c. 1930 to the Present* (Singapore: NUS Press).

Riddell, Peter. 2001. *Islam and the Malay-Indonesian World: Transmission and Responses* (London: Hurst).

Rinaldo, R. 2013. *Mobilizing piety: Islam and Feminism in Indonesia* (New York: Oxford University Press).

Robinson, Geoffrey. 1995. *The Dark Side of Paradise: Political Violence in Bali* (Ithaca: Cornell University Press).

Robinson, Kathryn. 2009. *Gender, Islam and Democracy in Indonesia* (London and New York: Routledge).

Roosa, John. 2006. *Pretext for Mass Murder: The September 30th Movement and Suharto's coup d'état in Indonesia* (Madison: University of Wisconsin Press).

Ropi, Ismatu. 2012. "The Politics of Regulating Religion: State, Civil Society and the Quest for Religious Freedom in Modern Indonesia." (Ph.D. Dissertation, Canberra, Australia: Australian National University).

Rudnyckyj, Daromir. 2010. *Spiritual Economies: Islam, Globalization, and the Afterlife of Development* (Ithaca and London: Cornell University Press, 2010).

Ryter, Loren. 1998. "Pemuda Pancasila: The Last Loyalist Free Men of Suharto's New Order," *Indonesia* 66 (October): 45–73.

Sakai, Minako. 1999. "The Nut Cannot Forget Its Shell: Origin Rituals Among the Gumai of South Sumatra" (Ph.D. Thesis. Canberra, Australia: Department of Anthropology, Australian National University).

Salim, Arskal. 2008. *Challenging the Secular State: The Islamization of Law in Modern Indonesia* (Honolulu: University of Hawaii Press).

Sanders, Paula. 1994. *Ritual, Politics, and the City in Fatimid Cairo* (Albany: State University of New York Press).

Schielke, Samuli. 2015. *Egypt in the Future Tense: Hope, Frustration, and Ambivalence Before and After 2011* (Bloomington: Indiana University Press).

Schiller, Anne. 1997. *Small Sacrifices: Religious Change and Cultural Identity Among the Ngaju of Indonesia* (Oxford: Oxford University Press).

Schröter, Susanne. 2013. "Gender and Islam in Southeast Asia: An Overview," in Susanne Schröter, ed., *Gender and Islam in Southeast Asia: Women's Rights Movements, Religious Resurgence and Local Traditions* (Leiden: Brill), pp. 7–52.

Schulte Nordholt, Henk. 1996. *The Spell of Power: A History of Balinese Politics, 1650–1940* (Leiden: KITLV Press).

Schulte Nordholt, Henk and Gerry van Klinken, eds. 2007. *Renegotiating Boundaries: Local Politics in Post-Suharto Indonesia* (Leiden: KITLV Press).

Scott, James C., 1998. *Seeing Like a State: How Certain Schemes to Improve the Human Condition Have Failed* (New Haven: Yale University Press).

Shiraishi, Takashi. 1990. *An Age in Motion: Popular Radicalism in Java, 1912–1926* (Ithaca and London: Cornell University Press).

Shoshan, Boaz. 1993. *Popular Culture in Medieval Cairo* (Cambridge: Cambridge University Press).

Sidel, John. 2006. *Riots, Pogroms, Jihad: Religious Violence in Indonesia* (Ithaca: Cornell University Press).

Siegel, James T. 1969. *The Rope of God* (Berkeley: University of California Press).

Smith, Rogers M. 2012. "Equality and Differentiated Citizenship: A Modern Democratic Dilemma in Tocquevillian Perspective," in Partha Chatterjee and Ira Katznelson, eds., *Anxieties of Democracy: Tocquevillean Reflections on India and the United States* (Oxford: Oxford University Press), pp. 117–42.

Smith-Hefner, Nancy J. 2005. "The New Muslim Romance: Changing Patterns of Courtship and Marriage Among Educated Javanese Youth," *Journal of Southeast Asian Studies* 36(3), 441–59.

———. 2007. "Javanese Women and the Veil in Post-Soeharto Indonesia," *The Journal of Asian Studies* 66(2): 389–420.

Solahudin. 2013. *The Roots of Terrorism in Indonesia: From Darul Islam to Jema'ah Islamiyah*. Translated by Dave McRae (Ithaca and London: Cornell University Press).

Stange, Paul. 1986. "'Legitimate' Mysticism in Indonesia," *Review of Indonesian and Malaysian Affairs* 20(2): 76–117.

Steedly, Mary Margaret. 1993. *Hanging Without a Rope: Narrative Experience in Colonial and Postcolonial Karoland* (Princeton: Princeton University Press).

Steenbrink, Karel. 1993. *Dutch Colonialism and Indonesian Islam: Contacts and Conflicts, 1596–1950*. Translated by Jan Steenbrink and Henry Jansen (Amsterdam: Rodopi).

Stepan, Alfred. 2011. "The Multiple Secularisms of Modern Democratic and Non-Democratic Regimes," in Craig Calhoun, Mark Juergensmeyer, and Jonathan VanAntwerpen eds., *Rethinking Secularism* (Oxford: Oxford University Press), pp. 114–44.

———. 2014. "Muslims and Toleration: Unexamined Contributions to the Multiple Secularisms of Modern Democracies," in Alfred Stepan and Charles Taylor, eds., *Boundaries of Toleration* (New York: Columbia University Press), pp. 267–96.

Sumanto, Al Qurtuby. 2016. *Religious Violence and Conciliation in Indonesia: Christians and Muslims in the Moluccas* (London and New York: Routledge).

Syamsiyatun, Siti. 2008. "Women Negotiating Feminism and Islamism: The Experience of Nasyiatul Aisyiyah, 1985–2005," in Susan Blackburn, Bianca J. Smith, and Siti Syamsiyatun, eds., *Indonesian Islam in a New Era: How Women Negotiate Their Muslim Identities* (Clayton: Monash University Press), pp. 139–65.

Tanter, Richard and Kenneth Young. 1990. *The Politics of Middle Class Indonesia*. Monash Papers on Southeast Asia No. 19 (Clayton [Australia]: Centre of Southeast Asian Studies, Monash University).

Telle, Kari. 2013. "Vigilante Citizenship: Sovereign Practices and the Politics of Insult in Indonesia," *Bijdragen tot de Taal-, Land- en Volkenkunde* 169(2013): 183–212.

——— 2017. "Faith on Trial: Blasphemy and 'Lawfare' in Indonesia," *Ethnos*. https://doi.org/10.1080/00141844.2017.1282973 (Accessed 15 May 2017).

Tomsa, Dirk. 2008. *Party Politics and Democratization in Indonesia: Golkar in the Post-Suharto Era* (London and New York: Routledge).

Tsing, Anna Lowenhaupt. 1993. *In the Realm of the Diamond Queen: Marginality in an Out-of-the-Way Place* (Princeton: Princeton University Press).

Turner, Bryan S. 1997. "Citizenship Studies: A General Theory," *Citizenship Studies* 1(1): 15–18.

Ufen, Andreas. 2008. "From *aliran* to Dealignment: Political Parties in Post-Suharto Indonesia," *South East Asia Research* 16(1): 5–41.

Van Klinken, Gerry. 2007. *Communal Violence and Democratization in Indonesia: Small Town Wars* (London and New York: Routledge).

Van Klinken, Gerry and Joshua Barker. 2009. *State of Authority: The State in Society in Indonesia* (Ithaca: Cornell Southeast Asia Program).

Vickers, Adrian. 1987. "Hinduism and Islam in Indonesia: Bali and the Pasisir World," *Indonesia* 44(October): 31–58.

———. 1999. "Asian Values in Indonesia? National and Regional Identities," *Sojourn: Journal of Social Issues in Southeast Asia* 14(2): 382–401.

Volpi, Frédéric and Ewan Stein. 2015. "Islamism and the State After the Arab Uprisings: Between People Power and State Power," *Democratization* 22(2): 276–93.

Wahid, Din. 2013. "Nurturing the Salafi Minhaj: A Study of Salafi Pesantren in Contemporary Indonesia" (Ph.D. Thesis. Utrecht: Department of Religious Studies, Utrecht University).

Watson Andaya, Barbara. 2006. *The Flaming Womb: Repositioning Women in Early Modern Southeast Asia* (Honolulu: University of Hawaii Press).

Weintraub, Andrew N. 2010. *Dangdut Stories: A Social History of Indonesia's Most Popular Music* (Oxford: Oxford University Press).

Wieringa, Saskia. 2002. *Sexual Politics in Indonesia* (New York: Palgrave Macmillan).

Wilson, Chris. 2008. *Ethno-Religious Violence in Indonesia: From Soil to God* (London and New York: Routledge).

Wilson, Ian Douglas. 2006. "Continuity and Change: The Changing Contours of Organized Violence in Post–New Order Indonesia," *Critical Asian Studies* 38(2): 265–97.

———. 2008. "'As Long as It's Halal': Islamic *Preman* in Jakarta," in Greg Fealy and Sally White, eds. pp. 192–210.

Woodward, Mark R. 1989. *Islam in Java: Normative Piety and Mysticism in the Sultanate of Yogyakarta* (Tucson: University of Arizona Press).

Yang Hui, Jennifer. 2010. "The Internet in Indonesia: Development and Impact of Radical Websites," *Studies in Conflict & Terrorism* 33(2): 171–91.

Zaman, Muhammad Qasim. 2002. *The Ulama in Contemporary Islam: Custodians of Change* (Princeton: Princeton University Press).

Zubaida, Sami. 2003. *Law and Power in the Muslim World* (London: I.B. Tauris).

2

GENDER LEGACIES AND MODERN TRANSITIONS

Barbara Watson Andaya

Stretching back deep into the past, the gender legacies of modern Indonesia find their most enduring expression in the innumerable legends through which communities recall their ancestral origins. The outsized figures who populate these stories circulate around a mythological world where the norms of ordinary life have no purchase and where sexual unions between humans and nonhumans can coexist with androgyny, incest, and even adultery. At the same time, the gendered relationships that infuse communal memories also convey potent messages regarding male-female complementarity and the wholeness their conjoining represents. The most significant aspect of this heritage was a tolerance of gender diversity and (as in Southeast Asia more broadly) an environment where women were generally better positioned than in the neighboring world regions of East and South Asia. Yet threading through the historical narrative is a persisting counter theme that presents men's control over women as a visible register of authority and of a virility that harnesses female reproductive power to male advantage.

The pre-nineteenth-century environment

As this volume repeatedly reminds us, generalizations about a country as culturally and ethnically diverse as Indonesia should always be advanced with caution. Nonetheless, from the sixteenth century, the expansion of source material, both indigenous and European, makes it possible to explain why gender relations in pre-nineteenth century Indonesian societies were relatively favorable toward women.

In the first place, women were actively involved in the economy, especially in agriculture and food production. Because the earth was conceptualized as female and the young rice plant as a small child, the nurturing hands of women were needed to transplant seedlings from nurseries into flooded rice fields. In areas that depended on "dry" or unirrigated rice, women dropped the seeds into holes that men had made with dibble sticks, a symbolic representation of the male penetration of the earth (Andaya 2006: 107). A related aspect was female dominance of the marketplace, where women sold surplus food from their gardens or cloth that they themselves had woven. In terms of household expenses, these earnings were a reliable source of income because men were likely to be involved in long-distance trade, caught up in warfare, or summoned for corvée and could therefore be absent from home for long periods of time. Relative economic independence translated into greater female autonomy in relations with men, for although

31

adultery was condemned, at the village level, unsuccessful marriages were easily dissolved and women readily remarried.

In the second place, the nature of kinship and marital customs meant that the birth of a daughter could represent a valuable asset because of the widespread custom of obtaining a wife through bridewealth (*jujur*). Though certainly not universal in Indonesia, these traditions were most frequently referenced in Sumatra, Maluku, and Nusa Tenggara but were also found in other areas as well. Bridewealth typically comprised a combination of gifts and monetary payment from the groom and his family, although the young man might also provide labor for the bride's parents. An eighteenth-century report from Timor thus remarked that even a common man was considered rich if he fathered many daughters, because he received "gold and buffaloes" when they married. In many communities, residence was matrilocal, which meant the husband lived with or near his wife's family. Indeed, it was the "femaleness" of Indonesian households that impressed visitors, who frequently commented that household finances were managed by women and that daughters were valued because they brought men into the family, whereas sons went to live elsewhere.

In societies where mortality was high, a third reason for female status was the fact that women often acted as healers because of their familiarity with the botanical products used in indigenous pharmacology. Numerous reports by Europeans refer to the medicines provided by some local "doctress" that were effective in dealing with diseases ranging from simple fevers and ulcers to gout and gangrene. Further, because supernatural forces were believed to be a primary cause of illness or unexpected death, women as healers and midwives were familiar with the rituals that would ensure benevolent influences, especially in childbirth. This was especially true of older women who had themselves survived the dangers of labor and delivery and through their longevity had acquired the knowledge and experience that enabled them to become conduits to the spirit world. Yet this very power was itself ambiguous, because in certain contexts, such a woman could be accused of marshaling the malevolent forces that caused illness, misfortune, impotency, and even death.

The perceived powers of older women were directly connected to the various ways in which individuals could be located along the gender spectrum. Beyond the age of fertility, senior women had moved into a liminal zone where they occupied a female body but lacked the reproductive capacities that lay at the core of femaleness. In this respect, they resembled the ritually transgendered groups whose clothing and appurtenances combined male and female elements. While symbolizing the wholeness of the sexual union on which life depended, this blurring of gender boundaries also imparted a unique facility to mediate with the spirit world. Scholarly literature has focused on the sacred *bissu* of South Sulawesi (Graham, this volume), who are commonly seen as transgendered males, although in indigenous sources, they are also identified as older women. However, their prominence in Sulawesi's royal courts is not unique. For instance, Banten in West Java was known as a center of Islamic piety, but in 1661, when the ruler's infant son set foot on the earth for the first time, the ritual dance to call up the powers of protection was performed by transgendered men. The *warok* of east Java, whose origins reportedly date from the fifteenth century, may have filled a somewhat similar role. Prohibited from sexual intercourse with women because this would sap their spiritual vitality, *warok* were assisted by young boys known as *gemblak* who were chosen for their beauty (Andaya 2006: 89; Wilson 1999). In this context, Aceh presents a puzzling case. The courtiers termed *sida-sida* (eunuchs) in Acehnese texts and *capados* or "castrated ones" in European documents were extremely influential, especially under the four queens who reigned in the seventeenth century. It is not clear, however, whether they were castrated men (as in Ottoman Turkey, much admired in Aceh), or whether they were transgender *bissu*-like figures thought to possess powers far beyond those of ordinary mortals (Khan 2017).

While transgender priests were said to live with men as if they were married, the sources provide only glimpses of the nature of same-sex relationships. Boys dressed as alluring maidens were a feature of Javanese court dances and might be taken by high-ranking men as lovers, but the provocative singer-dancers who performed in public streets could also be men in women's clothing. From the indigenous perspective, the greatest sexual crimes were adultery and incest, and, for the most part, homosexuality was not a matter of concern as long as a man fathered children and maintained his family obligations. At the court level, however, lack of interest in women could cause a diplomatic crisis because of the high stakes associated with succession and legitimacy. The Muslim contention that homosexuality was a sin against God also carried a heavy weight, and the Kartasura ruler Pakubawana II (1726–42), anxious to rid his court of "immoral" elements, punished offending lords with exile or death (Ricklefs 1998: 222). The nineteenth-century text, the *Serat Centhini*, is often cited for its extensive and apparently tolerant descriptions of same-sex eroticism, but it also displays tensions between *warok* and pious Muslims (*santri*). For their part, Europeans regarded sodomy as an "unnatural" crime that merited death, and there was no toleration for the "situational homosexuality" that occurred, for instance, on board ship or among Batavia's male-dominated Chinese community.

A parallel situation can be found in the women's quarters of Indonesian palaces, which could house hundreds of women as concubines, entertainers, and serving girls. Women took the part of men in court performances, and one of the favorite stories in the Panji cycle tells of a princess, disguised as a man, who enters the women's section of the ruler's palace, and of the flirtation, kissing, and embracing that followed. Gender inversion was also associated with the "lady soldiers" (*prajurit estri*), the female guards of the central Javanese courts, who were praised for their martial skills and whose official costume was that of a male warrior. While it is not difficult to imagine that sexual relationships occurred among royal concubines, a rare mention of their fate comes from a Makassar chronicle, which notes that two palace women found guilty of lesbianism were drowned (Cummings 2010: 283).

Change and continuity

Changing patterns of cultural interaction during what has been termed the "early modern" period of global history (roughly 1500–1800) had far-reaching implications for Indonesia's gender legacy. The most significant development was the advance of Islam across the archipelago and its contested relationship with Christianity. It is generally agreed that Sufi mysticism was a major factor in Islam's appeal, but it also seems that female audiences were taken seriously. Religious texts produced in the late sixteenth and early seventeenth centuries often employed images that women could appreciate, comparing, for instance, the acquisition of mystical knowledge to steps in the weaving process and likening devotees to a batik cloth that Allah waxes and paints in colors chosen according to the divine plan. Rich women could sponsor Islamic teachers, become learned in their own right, and gain a reputation for piety and religious commitment.

Nonetheless, there were also contradictions. Islamic treatises stressed male authority in the household and insisted on premarital chastity, wifely obedience, and complete fidelity. In the Islamic heartlands, seclusion had already become a signifier of respectability and high breeding, since it distinguished elite women from their social inferiors. While lower-class women performed outside work and sold goods in the markets, their well-born sisters demonstrated their Muslim piety by remaining essentially house bound. In royal palaces, religious sanction for four official wives (in addition to numerous concubines) could heighten tensions as women competed for their lord's favor. Although the possession of many women was a public statement of a ruler's wealth, virility, and power, scattered references point to the distaste with which royal consorts were forced to accept the reality of sharing a husband. Behind the scenes, such women might still exercise considerable influence in court politics, but their public space was extremely restricted. Emblematic of this retreat was a 1699 fatwa from Mecca that forbade governance by women and ended a long period of female rule in Aceh. Independent queens did not completely disappear, but it was always assumed that they were acting under the guidance of some male. Upper-class women may also have been expected to demonstrate their adherence to Islam in other ways. Although little is known about female circumcision, the procedure (which involved only a small cut to the clitoris) was evidently practiced among elite families to affirm a daughter's virtue and readiness for marriage.

Our knowledge of the ways in which the adoption of Islam changed village life is similarly limited. Women would certainly have been affected by the prohibition forbidding the eating of pork, a ritual food in much of eastern Indonesia, especially since oversight for domestic animals, including pigs, was a female responsibility. We can assume that healers and midwives incorporated Islamic prayers and invocations into their rituals and channeled advice drawn from Islamic treatises on how to sustain a husband's affection and ward off the possibility of a second wife. In pre-Islamic societies, the powerful dangers of female fertility meant women were excluded from men's houses and forbidden from touching male weapons and tools. In a similar vein, women were excluded from mosques, implicitly reinforcing ideas of women's spiritual inferiority. In many other respects, however, the practicalities of life would have been unchanged, and the economic independence of village women helped sustain the perception of marriage as a partnership by which a wife's family would be dishonored if she were not treated with respect. In some instances, a misunderstanding of Islamic teaching led some men to think that they were required to take another wife, an idea that they roundly rejected as tantamount to adultery (Andaya 2006: 91).

From the early sixteenth century, Islam also faced opposition from the Catholic Portuguese. Intent on dominating the spice trade, they saw the missionizing project as a means of recruiting support and countering the economic and religious influence of Muslims. The greatest success was in eastern Indonesia, where Frances Xavier specifically targeted women and where a number of high-ranking individuals, including Ternate's queen mother, converted to Catholicism. Encouragement to intermarriage and the creation of local Catholic populations gave rise to large numbers of "black Christians" who remained loyal to the Portuguese. For high-ranking men, however, the insistence on monogamy remained a stumbling block to conversion, while women who acted as ritual specialists suffered the deliberate destruction of "heathen" sites and the desecration of ancestral objects. During the seventeenth century, the Dutch East India Company (VOC), which supplanted the Portuguese, adopted similar methods to eradicate "witchcraft," but their Calvinist antipathy toward "papism" meant that evangelism was primarily directed toward the Portuguese-descended Catholic community, with only modest success.

A second feature of the early modern period was the expansion of maritime trade and the rise of new port cities. In the Indonesian archipelago, the most important of these was Dutch-controlled Batavia (modern Jakarta), which from 1619 became the nerve center of VOC operations. Its expanding population included thousands of slaves brought annually from Bali, Lombok, Buton, Timor, and other non-Muslim areas to the east. There was always a good market for healthy young women capable of maintaining a household, helping in business, and satisfying sexual needs, with Chinese traders among the most eager buyers. Legally the property of their owners, the lot of most was not happy, even if they were able to negotiate a degree of independence. A Chinese or Indonesian householder commonly expected that his female slaves would augment the household income through prostitution, and court records are filled with cases of "runaways" fleeing from cruel or abusive treatment (Jones 2010). Slave women bought by Europeans may have been marginally better off, since they usually became nominal Christians and were manumitted if they had born their master children. Those without resources could be eligible for poor relief from the church, but older women also slipped into penury or became procurers for prostitution. The feminization of urban poverty in this period is one of the darker sides of Indonesian history.

Expanding Dutch control in the nineteenth century

Though full-fledged colonialism was not a reality until around 1900, the nineteenth century witnessed the gradual expansion of Dutch territorial control through the archipelago. This exacerbates rather than alleviates the difficulties of generalization, for Java and the main Dutch centers are far better documented than remote areas where many communities never saw a white face. A full study of gender relations during this period has yet to be written, but we can safely assume that for women, many aspects of life were unchanged. They continued to dominate local markets and to play a central role in agriculture; they were involved in income-generating activities, such as pottery, weaving, or spinning cotton thread; they were responsible for time-consuming domestic chores – washing, gathering firewood and water, and preparing food. Above all, they bore and reared children.

Among elite households and in royal palaces, attitudes toward gender relations also showed little change. In deference to Western ideas about monogamy, Muslim rulers were typically photographed with their chief wife, but the belief that plural wives and concubines were a necessary demonstration of superiority persisted. Well into the nineteenth century, Javanese and Balinese texts continued to depict the conjugal bed as a battleground where a man forcefully conquers his reluctant bride. Vanquished, she becomes an exemplar of wifely obedience, completely accepting of her "sisters" who share the same husband (Florida 1996; Creese 2004).

Notwithstanding such continuities, Indonesian societies could not fail to be touched by the increasing pace of global communication, most notably a shift in Islam's doctrinal mood. In 1803, the Wahhabi, determined to eliminate all "non-Islamic" accretions, took control of Mecca. Indonesians had heard the voices of reformist Muslims before, but they could not compare with the strident Wahhabi condemnation of localized Islam. In the Indonesian archipelago, the repercussions were soon apparent. Attention has focused on Minangkabau in Sumatra, where the conflict between local and reformist Islam resulted in prolonged warfare, but moves to impose shariah law by veiling women and restricting male-female interaction were also found in neighboring areas. Women themselves embraced the new reformism, and on the island of Riau, they became active agents in its promotion, producing texts that provided advice on matters such as the duties of a good wife and the application of Islamic law to male-female relations. Ripples spread as far as Ternate, where the sultan issued a proclamation banning un-Islamic funeral customs. Women mourning for a husband or male relative were no longer allowed to wear traditional skirts of sago leaves, perform the customary *lego-lego* (circle) dance, or accompany the body to the graveyard.

Christian missionizing was also reenergized, especially with the arrival of female evangelists from Europe, and in outlying mission stations, the availability of schools and teachers opened up new opportunities for women. The Rhenish mission working among the Batak prioritized female education, and by the 1880s, local women were being trained as teachers. In other areas, nuns in charge of convent schools acted as marriage brokers, cooperating with priests to help find husbands for their pupils and thus lay the basis for a good Catholic family. But mission schooling was also intended to inculcate Christian values, and pressure to limit the expense of bridewealth often resulted in reduced payments that lessened a wife's economic independence.

Unlike missionaries, the colonial government was reluctant to tackle the sensitive issue of polygamy or to oppose pre-Christian spirit veneration. The Dutch Jesuits in Larantuka (eastern Flores) were therefore delighted when the Catholic ruler took a strong stand against "heathen" observations, fining those who missed mass and punishing individuals accused of practicing non-Christian rituals (many of whom would have been women).

The Dutch administration was, however, concerned with public health, especially the spread of venereal diseases in the colonial army and navy. This inevitably led to campaigns for controlling prostitution, and from 1852, prostitutes in Java's major cities were required to register with the police, carry an identity card, and submit to regular medical inspections. Such oversight proved impossible, given that registering hundreds of prostitutes in a port like Surabaya made no allowance for clandestine operations. Homosexual prostitutes were largely ignored, although European sources make occasional references to effeminate men known as *banci* in coastal trading centers. "Banci Batavia" dances and *ludruk* performances that featured young men dressed as women (often in Western clothing) were a popular form of entertainment. But whereas female prostitutes were able to parade openly, the Dutch Indies government so abhorred the possibility of European soldiers engaging in the "unnatural vice" that even in the 1880s, lower ranks were allowed to maintain barrack concubines. Nor was this uncommon, for at the end of the century, half the European men in the Netherlands Indies were still living with Indonesian concubines (Ingleson 1986).

Much has been written about the role of the *nyai* or "housekeeper" as a cultural broker. On the one hand, they could be seen as assisting European men to understand the dynamics of local cultures; on the other, their low status, lack of education, and the racist and sexist manner with which they were treated means it would have been difficult for them to transmit specific knowledge about cultural values in a meaningful way (van Bemmelen et al. 1992). Along the east coast of Sumatra, about 12% of the contracted coolie laborers were young Javanese women. Although some became *nyai* to a European man, many were forced into prostitution by inadequate wages. Because of the demographic imbalance, women were made available to service the sexual and domestic requirements of male workers and to keep them on the plantation (Stoler 1985).

Female victims of the expanding capitalist system have been accorded sympathetic attention by Western scholars, but for Indonesian nationalists, the true patriots were women who took up arms against the Dutch. The most well-known of these "female warriors" is Cut Nyak Dien (1850–1908), who led Acehnese forces against the Dutch following her husband's death. In 1964, President Sukarno installed Cut Nyak Dien (together with her compatriot Cut Meutia, 1870–1910) as a "national heroine," and her story inspired many of the women who in later years joined the separatist Free Aceh Movement (1976–2005). Fighting colonialism is an almost certain guarantee of admittance to Indonesia's heroic pantheon, and today virtually every province can supply stories of female resistance, like the defiant Besse Kajuara, queen of the Sulawesi kingdom of Bone, or Ambon's teenage heroine Martha Christina Tiahahu, who took up arms against the Dutch but died a captive in their hands.

Gender issues in pre-war Dutch East Indies

The ethical policy adopted by the Dutch government in 1901 had significant consequences for women in the Netherlands Indies. Its stated goal was social improvement, and considerable emphasis was therefore given to the expansion of education and health facilities. While government efforts are best documented in Java, Roman Catholic and Protestant missionaries working in the outer islands established schools and medical clinics, becoming in effect an arm of the colonial administration. Because they lived for many years among villagers, missionaries' reports often supply valuable ethnographies; it is thanks to Calvinist pastors, for example, that modern scholars have access to the details of indigenous birth practices in Sulawesi and to information regarding the rituals of transgendered priests and priestesses in Borneo.

Such contexts were a world away from the elite houses of Java, an environment that produced Raden Kartini (1879–1904), a fervent advocate for female education and the most prominent of all Indonesia's national heroines. Nonetheless, there were lesser-known individuals (such as Kartini's elder sister), who also supported the burgeoning nationalist movement in hopes that it would lead to a reshaping of gender relations and a more equal relationship between husbands and wives. Founded in 1912, the first women's organization, Puteri Merdeka (Free Women), and the 1928 Women's Congress were evidence of a new energy directed toward uplifting female status. Women established journals that promoted education for girls, and they contributed to "housewife pages" in local newspapers with discussions of domestic hygiene and house management (Hadler 2008: 83; Parker 2001). While women's organizations were primarily concerned with equipping females for their traditional roles as housewife and mother, they provided a forum for expressing opposition to polygamy, child marriages, forced unions, and prostitution, which they said resulted from the degradation of women in colonial society.

Islam was also responding to new pressures for change that were emanating from Egypt. For Muslim women in Indonesia, the most important organization was Aisyiyah, the women's arm of the modernist movement Muhammadiyah, which was founded in Yogyakarta in 1917. Aisyiyah's leaders were always concerned with female education, but polygamy and marital relations were sensitive topics because any debate would raise questions about conflicts with Islamic law.

During the 1920s, women's organizations became more political, and the major nationalist groups all formed women's branches. Women also joined the Indonesian Communist Party (PKI), and following the abortive 1926–27 communist uprising, a significant number were exiled or followed their husbands to the malaria-infested prison camp of Boven Digul in West New Guinea. For all activist women, a basic question concerned the degree to which political concerns should dominate social ones. Overall, since the primary concern of all anti-colonial groups was political independence, "women's issues" were given only passing attention. Nationalist leaders felt that although women could contribute something to this effort, their more important role was to be supportive wives and mothers. The future president, Sukarno, stressed the notion of *kodrat*, or code of behavior, which comprised both biological traits and a religiously inspired paradigm of harmony. Men and women should have equality but each according to their *kodrat*. Above all, women were told that their organizations should give priority to the nationalist struggle. This argument was persuasive, and while debates about feminist issues often caused divisions within women's groups, they were generally united in endorsing the nationalist cause (Brown 1981).

The 1930s were turbulent years on many levels. The Indies were hard hit by the Depression of 1929, but village women struggling to feed their families and maintain household income would have been especially aware of the impact of high debt, ill health, and poor nutrition. Though wage labor (for instance, as plantation or factory workers) had become an economic necessity for many, women were laid off at a higher rate than men or found their already lower wages cut even further. If anything, the breakdown of the economy strengthened the left wing and nationalist movements, which affirmed colonial fears that extending any political rights to Indonesian women would undermine Dutch control. In 1932, the Minangkabau Rasuna Said became the first Indonesian woman to be arrested because of her radical calls for independence, but other politically active women were also jailed or exiled.

By 1941, suffrage for Indonesian women was introduced for municipal councils, but any progress toward increasing political participation was prevented by the outbreak of World War

II. Pressured on all sides, it may have been the Dutch desire to assert their moral superiority that led to an unprecedented campaign in 1938 and 1939 against the sex industry, targeting and jailing men, regardless of race, who were accused of relations with underage boys (Boellstorff 2005: 64–5). Medical surveys that revealed the prevalence of venereal disease injected greater urgency into efforts to control prostitution by closing brothels and enforcing fines. Women's organizations continued to support such measures, but they remained divided about the issue of polygamy, and divisions between Muslims on the one side and secular or Christian groups on the other were painfully obvious. In 1937, a draft ordinance that would allow for monogamous marriage and divorce on equal grounds for both sexes was withdrawn after vehement protest from Muslim groups with women in the vanguard (Blackburn 2004:120–7).

In 1942, the Japanese invaded Indonesia, which was occupied until 1945. All pre-war women's groups were dissolved, to be replaced by the official women's associations, Fujikini in Java and Bali, and Hahanokai in Sumatra. Following a model established in Japan, these associations urged women to be supporting wives and mothers for their menfolk, and local branches were required to produce and distribute food to the occupying Japanese army. Although the Japanese also promoted the Barisan Srikandi (Srikandi Brigade), which provided military training for young women, as many as 10,000 *jugun ianfu*, or comfort women, may have been forced to provide sexual services to Japanese military. As the economy spiraled downward and the black market flourished, even textiles were in short supply because of the lack of imported yarn; women wore jute sacks and sheets of processed rubber in order to go to the market, and there were reports of farmers working naked in their rice fields. In this situation, it was not difficult for the Japanese to recruit *romusha* (laborers) in projects that cost the lives of untold numbers of men, often in horrific circumstances.

Independence

Following the Japanese surrender in 1945, the Dutch sought to re-impose their colonial regime, despite Indonesia's declaration of independence. During the revolution that followed, women's units cared for wounded soldiers, organized kitchens, served as couriers, and conducted literacy classes. However, the need for guerrillas to be physically able and unencumbered tended to privilege unattached youth, and the revolutionary experience of women was thus often determined by age and marital status. Some young Javanese women joined the "bamboo spears," a revolutionary unit in the Solo area, but there was a general feeling that women should remain at home. This was particularly the case if they were married, but even single women were used reluctantly. Male leaders often regarded women soldiers as a disruptive element, claiming they refused to recognize authority or that they were a distraction to the serious business of fighting the Dutch. Yet regardless of male attitudes, the young women who willingly volunteered as teachers, nurses, and cooks and at times underwent military training were infused with exhilaration at the prospect of an imminent *zaman merdeka* ("independence time"). Involvement in the national revolution was an experience they remembered all their lives (Steedly 2013).

The 1945 Constitution, which had been drawn up as Indonesia declared independence from colonial rule, was a significant document, establishing the basis for the independent government formed after the Dutch withdrew in 1948. The constitution guaranteed that all citizens should have the right to work and be protected by labor laws and that women should be accorded political equality and access to education. PKI women took up the challenge, and their mass movement Gerwani successfully pressured for the inclusion of maternity and menstruation leave in the 1951 Labor Law (Robinson 2009: 58). During the euphoria of independence, a number of other women's organizations were formed, most notably the Kongress Wanita Indonesia, or

Kowani, which has endured to the present day. In the elections of 1955, eighteen women were elected to the 257-member parliament. Nonetheless, resistance to marriage reform from Islamic leaders meant that it was impossible to reach agreement on measures that would give a wife greater protection in relations with her husband. During the 1950s, several different proposals were drafted, but the government was reluctant to introduce laws that would challenge male privileges. When President Sukarno married a second wife in 1954, many women felt betrayed, and his relations with the women's movement deteriorated. Adding to this estrangement was the lack of improvement in women's economic position, since there was still wide discrimination against female workers and the 1957 stipulation of equal pay was regularly flouted (Blackburn 2004: 167–78).

Without the bonding aspect of the nationalist struggle, fissures began to appear in the women's movement, accentuated by the economic and political chaos of the early 1960s and the lack of any one organization to act as head. Muslim women largely retreated from political matters, and even Gerwani accepted the PKI view that feminist issues were not a priority. However, in a time of rising prices, its call for a more equitable economy was a powerful magnet for mothers and wives struggling to maintain a household and feed children. As the economic situation deteriorated, army leaders became increasingly disturbed at the growing communist strength. In 1965, following allegations of a planned coup, they took control of Indonesia's government. The PKI was banned, with Gerwani coming under particular attack. Many of its members were arrested, and the movement itself accused of fostering moral debauchery (later read as lesbianism) (Wieringa 2002). Beyond Java, hostility toward non-normative gender roles was also a feature of Sulawesi's fundamentalist Kahar Muzakkar rebellion (1950–65) and its "Operation Repent" (*Operasi Tobat*). Violently opposed to any practice deemed un-Islamic, the rebels killed numerous *bissu*, whom they accused of communist sympathies. Despite some attempts to revive *bissu* traditions, opposition from reformist Islam has remained strong, and it is unlikely that this legacy of a ritual past will survive.

Gender issues under the New Order, 1966–1998

The "New Order" led by President Soeharto had clear priorities for Indonesia, first among which was economic development, seen as the primary means of combating left-wing activism. There were mixed results for women. For a generation of young people, the rise of a relatively prosperous middle class opened a range of new opportunities, such as overseas study and travel. In rural areas, the benefits were less evident. The adoption of high-yielding rice varieties and technical innovation was lauded as a "Green Revolution," but the introduction of rotary weeders and mechanized rice hullers deprived women of earnings on which households had come to depend. Between 1971 and 1985, the number of Javanese women working in the non-farm sector almost doubled, and the low-wage female factory labor that attracted investors helped spearhead Indonesia's manufacturing expansion (Robinson 2009: 93).

A second element in New Order ideology was the conviction that Indonesian society should rest on the "family principle" (*asas keluarga*) and on normative sex/gender roles, where the household head was male. Although the older term *kodrat* was frequently used, commentators on Indonesia began to refer to an ideology of "state ibuism," that cultivated the image of women as mothers (*ibu*), educators of children, and guardians of the family. Two influential instruments in spreading this message were the government-sponsored wives organizations, *Dharma Wanita* (Women's Service) and the Family Welfare Association (PKK), which encouraged women to devote their energies to husband and children but simultaneously urged them to develop home-based enterprises to augment the family income. Feminist critics have been vocal in condemning policies they regard as tools for the assertion of male authority and endorsement of female dependence (Suryakusuma 1996).

Certainly some advances were made. A 1974 law restricted polygamous marriage so that Muslim men could only take a second wife under stringent conditions, and domestic abuse was grounds for female-initiated divorce. From 1976, which inaugurated the United Nations "Decade for Women," the Soeharto government paid more attention to women's concerns, and a Minister for Women's Affairs was appointed in 1983. Among school pupils, the gender gap that had previously disadvantaged girls was essentially closed by 1990. The focus on women also served the goal of development, which called for a reduction in Indonesia's high birth rate, especially on Java and Bali. Using the extensive PKK network and with the support of Muslim leaders, the National Family Planning program was remarkably successful, and by 1990, the fertility rate had been almost halved, although women were often under extreme pressure to become acceptors of contraception (Blackburn 2004: 152–4).

Yet after twenty years of New Order government, it was impossible to ignore continuing gender disparities, despite Indonesia's economic growth and the overall improvement in the lives of its citizens. In the mid-1980s, two-thirds of all illiterates were adult women, and marriages were still arranged, often at a young age. Divorcées or widows were often left to maintain children without adequate financial support. In the factories developed with foreign investment, women's wages remained significantly lower than those of men, the opportunities for advancement were negligible, and there was little protection from exploitative employers. Political activism among women was low, and they comprised less than 6% of the highest echelon of civil servants. The ways in which women would be affected by a deepening Islamization in society more generally, symbolized by increased adoption of the female headscarf (*jilbab*), were as yet unclear. For most women, the exercise of practical authority and influence was confined to their own families and informal village structures, but as a group, they exerted minimal influence on the nation's political, religious, literary, and artistic life.

Nevertheless, in many respects, the last decade of Soeharto's New Order represented a time of exploration as Indonesians themselves questioned the gender regime that the government had put in place. In 1988, for example, the film *Istana kecantikan* was the first cinematic attempt to present a sympathetic portrayal of individuals in a homosexual relationship. Other films followed, as Indonesians became more familiar with terms such as *gay*, *lesbi*, and *tomboy* that appeared in the print media and on television (Murtagh 2013: 50–76; Blackwood 2010). Frustrated by government indifference, campaigners for gay rights worked to promote more public awareness of HIV/AIDS and discussions of sexual diversity. From 1988, Indonesia's Broad State Guidelines (GBHN) included sections on women's issues and in 1993 envisioned them contributing to development as "equal partners" with men. Women began to publicize sensitive topics, such as sexual harassment, mistreatment of overseas contract workers, violence, and marital rape. Challenges to the government were also evident in Aceh, where the separatist movement attracted a significant number of women combatants. The torture and murder of Marsinah, a young factory worker and union activist, allegedly by the military, generated widespread protests and demonstrations. A growing relaxation of gender boundaries in religious praxis also enlarged female space, and even in the remote highlands of western New Guinea, Christian women were assuming leadership roles. During the 1990s, female ulama in Java initiated training projects so that more women would be able to reach the standards for preaching demanded by Muslim organizations (Nor Ismah 2016). In 1997, the major Muslim organization, Nahdlatul Ulama, endorsed the view that a woman could be vice president.

Frustration with government disinterest in the problems women faced as domestic managers came to a head when the rupiah plummeted during the financial crisis of 1997. It is worth remembering that the Women's Coalition for Democracy and Justice was the first group to demand Soeharto's resignation and that a demonstration led by the Suara Ibu Peduli (Voice of Concerned Mothers) to protest the soaring price of milk became a catalyst for an explosion of support throughout Indonesia. In the face of this challenge, the GBHN of March 1998 formally recognized women as equal partners in development. Yet the fact that these guidelines also referred to women's *kodrat* and their special obligations as mothers points to the continuing ambivalences of Indonesia's gender legacy, tragically demonstrated by the apparent indifference to the gang rapes of Chinese women during the riots of May 1998. A week later, Soeharto resigned, and the New Order came to an end.

Conclusion

Despite commonalities and many shared experiences, independent Indonesia emerged as a nation with hundreds of distinct groups, all with their own histories and sense of identity. In pre-colonial times, societies across this diverse archipelago displayed a remarkable ability to adapt outside influences to the local environment. Although overviews are always problematic, women were generally able to achieve status within communities that respected the complementary of men and women and recognized gender ambivalence as an expression of male-female wholeness. Much of this heritage was retained through the colonial period, in part because the reach of the Dutch Indies Government beyond major centers was constrained by geography and physical distance. Older attitudes still persisted, although the patriarchy of both the colonial government and religious reformists and missionaries did affect gender dynamics in ways that reinforced male status. In the 1950s, women therefore saw Indonesia's independence in terms of new opportunities for partnership with men, but under the Soeharto regime, expectations for wives as citizens were quite different from those of husbands, and there was no place for individuals who did not fit a dimorphic gender division. The collapse of the New Order in 1998 again raised hopes of a more tolerant and inclusive society that would hold true to the gender legacy of earlier times. Despite some progress, the rise of religious fundamentalism and the unwillingness of political leaders to address unresolved gender issues mean that these hopes are as yet unfulfilled.

References cited

Andaya, Barbara Watson. 2006. *The Flaming Womb: Repositioning Women in Early Modern Southeast Asia* (Honolulu: University of Hawai'i Press).

Bemmelen, Sita van, Madelon Djajadiningrat-Niewenhuis, Elsbeth Locher-Scholten and Elly Towen-Bouwsma. 1992. *Women and Mediation in Indonesia* (Leiden: KITLV Press).

Blackburn, Susan. 2004. *Women and the State in Modern Indonesia* (Cambridge: Cambridge University Press).

Blackwood, Evelyn, 2010. *Falling into the Lesbi World. Desire and Difference in Indonesia* (Honolulu: University of Hawai'i Press).

Boellstorff, Tom. 2005. *The Gay Archipelago: Sexuality and Nation in Indonesia* (Princeton: Princeton University Press).

Brown, Colin. 1981. "Sukarno on the Role of Women in the Nationalist Movement," *Review of Indonesian and Malavan Affairs* 15: 68–92.

Creese, Helen. 2004. *Women of the Kakawin World: Marriage and Sexuality in the Indic Courts of Java and Bali* (Armonk and London: M.E. Sharp).

Cummings, William, trans. and ed. 2010. *The Makassar Annals* (Leiden: KITLV Press).

Florida, Nancy K. 1996. "Sex Wars: Writing Gender Relations in Nineteenth-Century Java," in Laurie J. Sears, ed., *Fantasizing the Feminine in Indonesia* (Durham and London: Duke University Press), pp. 207–25.

Hadler, Jeffrey. 2008. *Muslims and Matriarchs: Cultural Resilience in Indonesia Through Jihad and Colonialism* (Ithaca: Cornell University Press).

Ingleson, John. 1986. "Prostitution in Colonial Java," in David P. Chandler and M. C. Ricklefs eds., *Nineteenth and Twentieth Century Indonesia: Essays in Honour of Professor J.D. Legge* (Clayton, Victoria: Centre of Southeast Asian Studies, Monash University), pp. 123–40.

Jones, Eric. 2010. *Wives, Slaves and Concubines: A History of the Female Underclass in Dutch Asia* (DeKalb: Northern Illinois University Press).

Khan, Sher Banu A.L. 2017. *Sovereign Women in a Muslim Kingdom: The Sultanahs of Aceh, 1641–1699* (Singapore: NUS Press).

Murtagh, Ben. 2013. *Genders and Sexualities in Indonesian Cinema: Constructing Gay, Lesbi and Waria Identities on Screen* (London and New York: Routledge).

Nor Ismah. 2016. "Destabilising Male Domination: Building Community-Based Authority Among Indonesian Female Ulama," *Asian Studies Review* 40(4): 491–509.

Parker, Lyn. 2001. "Domestic Science and the Modern Balinese Women," in Susan Blackburn, ed., *Love, Sex and Power: Women in Southeast Asia* (Clayton, Victoria: Monash Asia Institute), pp. 57–74.

Ricklefs, Merle C. 1998. *The Seen and Unseen Worlds of Java 1726–1749: History, Literature, and Islam in the Court of Pakubuwana II* (Honolulu: University of Hawai'i Press).

Robinson, Kathryn. 2009. *Gender, Islam and Democracy in Indonesia* (London and New York: Routledge).

Steedly, Mary Margaret. 2013. *Rifle Reports: A Story of Indonesian Independence* (Berkeley and Los Angeles: University of California Press).

Stoler, Ann Laura. 1985. *Capitalism and Confrontation in Sumatra's Plantation Belt 1870–1979* (New Haven: Yale University Press).

Suryakusuma, Julia L. 1996. "The State and Sexuality in New Order Indonesia," in Laurie J. Sears, ed., *Fantasizing the Feminine in Indonesia* (Durham and London: Duke University Press), pp. 92–119.

Wieringa, S. 2002. *Sexual Politics in Indonesia* (Houndmills: Palgrave Macmillan).

Wilson, Ian Douglas. 1999. "Reog Ponorogo: Spirituality, Sexuality, and Power in Javanese Performance Tradition," *Intersections: Gender and Sexuality in Asia and the Pacific 2*, May. http://intersections.anu.edu.au/issue2/Warok.html.

3

ETHNIC GROUPS AND THE INDONESIAN NATION-STATE

With special reference to ethnic Chinese

Leo Suryadinata

Indonesia is a multiethnic and multi-religious society. According to the 2010 Population Census, there are more than 145 ethnic groups in Indonesia, of which the largest is still the Javanese (40.05%), followed by the Sundanese (15.50%), Malay (3.70%), Batak (3.58%), Madurese (3.03%), Betawi (2.87%), Minangkabau (2.73%), Buginese (2.71%), Bantenese (1.96%), Banjarese (1.74%), Balinese (1.66%), Acehnese (1.44%), Dayak (1.36%), Sasak (1.34%), and Chinese (1.20%) (Ananta et al. 2015: 78). In terms of religion, the population can be divided into Muslims (87.51%), Christians (Catholics/Protestants, 9.90%), Hindus (1.69%), Buddhists (0.72%), and Confucians (0.05%) (Ananta et al. 2015: 257). Why did these multiethnic and multi-religious groups come together to form a country called the Republic of Indonesia?

Dutch colonialism and the birth of modern Indonesia

Indonesian nationalists have argued that Indonesia today is the continuation of the great Buddhist Srivijaya empire (7th to 13th centuries) and the Hindu-Buddhist Majapahit empire (13th to 16th centuries). This is misleading. In fact, Indonesia is a modern construct. The emergence of modern Indonesia is closely linked with Dutch colonialism. It was Dutch colonial rule that united various ethnic groups in the Indonesian archipelago under one colonial administration and one economic and legal system. It was also under Dutch rule that the Dutch East Indies underwent major social change, including the emergence of modern Indonesian elite, which produced a nationalist movement. This nationalist movement emerged in the twentieth century and was led by the Western-educated indigenous Indonesian leaders whose aim was to eliminate Dutch rule and establish a modern Indonesian nation-state along the colonial boundaries, not the earlier empire boundaries.[1]

Indonesian leaders, represented by Sukarno and Mohammad Hatta, declared the country's independence on August 17, 1945, but the actual transfer of power from the Dutch to the Indonesians took place only in December 1949. The inclusion of West Irian (now Papua) into the Indonesian territory took place only in May 1963. Nevertheless, the nationalist movement, which can be seen as part of the nation-building process, had started prior to World War II.

All the Indonesian nationalist symbols were created during the nationalist movement: national language, national anthem, and national flag. Nevertheless, one needs to note that there were at least two types of nationalist movements: secular and Islamic. In the Indonesian youth movement before World War II, the Islamic Youth attended the Youth Congress of 1928 but did not endorse the well-known Youth Pledge (*Sumpah Pemuda*), which advocated Indonesian unity based on a secular nation, unifying language, and unitary state (Suryadinata 1998: 59). During the 1945 Constitution debates, the Islamic groups wanted to insert a clause requiring the Muslims to prac- tice Syariah Law, but it was eventually dropped in order to secure unity (Suryadinata 1990: 26).

The secular nationalist movement appeared to have the upper hand, and therefore, the con- cept of the Indonesian nation was more secular than Islamic even though Indonesia is approxi- mately 88% Muslim. Nevertheless, the cleavages have never been fully bridged. The issue of "Islamic State" continues to surface off and on after Indonesia attained independence.

The nation-building process in Indonesia has not been smooth. Ethnic and Islamic feelings have been strong, and in the earlier period of the republic, there were a number of rebellions, with some having strong ethnic characters and others not. This chapter attempts to examine the policy regarding Indonesian nation-building over the last sixty-five years or so and the chal- lenges faced by the national government. However, as the ethnic Chinese have been seen as a "foreign minority group" without a homeland within Indonesia, their positions in the Indone- sian nation-state and in the nation-building process are different from those of the indigenous Indonesians. This will be examined separately later.

Early ethnic conflicts: challenge to the Indonesian nation-state

Indonesian nationalists proclaimed Indonesia's independence in 1945. The event was followed by the Indonesia-Dutch armed conflict up to 1949 when the Dutch eventually agreed to trans- fer political power to the Indonesians. The form of the Indonesian state was at first federal, which would cater to different regional and ethnic interests. However, a few ethnic groups rebelled against the central government and sought to establish an independent state. The most serious incident was in South Maluku (the Moluccas), the homeland of the Christian Ambonese (Feith 1962: 55–71). In April 1950, Soumokil, the former justice minister of the Dutch-created "East Indonesia" state, with the support of the regional executive council of the area, proclaimed the Republic of the South Moluccas (Republik Maluku Selatan or RMS).

The rebellion enjoyed a great measure of local support, but it was eventually quelled by the central government under the leadership of Sukarno (an ethnic Javanese) and Mohammad Hatta (Minangkabau). The military solution was definitely instrumental in crushing the rebel- lion. However, there were other factors that contributed to the failure of the RMS. Many South Moluccans had family members in other parts of Indonesia, and the rebellion was identified with the Dutch. In the eyes of the Indonesian nationalists, this was a Dutch plot rather than the genuine desire of local people. After the rebellion, Indonesia became a unitary state, which gave more power to the central government in Jakarta.

The second rebellion took place in Aceh, a strongly Islamic area (Sjamsuddin 1985). The Acehnese saw the Indonesian republic as a Javanese- and Minangkabau-dominated state. Aceh was not politically integrated into Indonesia. Communications with the nationalists in Java were weak. Aceh in fact had stronger lines of communication with the Middle East. Initially, Aceh was made a province, but in 1951, the provincial status was abolished, accompanied by the downgrading of the Acehnese leaders, disbanding of Military Division X (the predominantly Acehnese unit of the Indonesian army), and suspension of the right of direct trade with Singa- pore and Penang, which impacted Acehnese revenues.

The local leader, Daud Beureueh, initiated a movement for autonomy, but in 1953, it devel- oped into a separatist movement. He proclaimed Aceh an Islamic state. His troops held many urban centers until 1954. However, the rebellion eventually failed. The government employed soft and hard strategies: it restored the provincial status of Aceh and appointed an Acehnese as the governor. Using strong military operations and the divide-and-rule policy among the Acehnese, the rebellion was eventually crushed.

There was another rebellion in West Java launched in August 1949. This rebellion was initiated by Kartosuwirjo, who attempted to establish an Indonesian Islamic State or Daarul Islam Indonesia (DII). The insurgency reached its peak in 1957 but was largely confined to West Java. It was eventually crushed by the central government in 1962. This rebellion was quite similar to the *Pemerintah Revolusi Republik Indonesia* (PRRI)/Piagam Perjuangan Republik Indonesia (Permesta) rebellion of 1956–1958, which was within the context of Indonesia, not as a separate state based on ethnicity.

The third rebellion involved the Irian Jaya Independence Movement and was known as the Free Papua Movement (Osborne 1985). Unlike the two earlier separatist movements, the Free Papua Movement is recent and smaller in scale. Therefore, it has not yet developed into a major threat. It is clear that the central government did not hesitate to resort to military means to maintain territorial integrity. However, the fact that there were so few separatist movements since the formation of the Republic of Indonesia cannot be solely explained in terms of the government's control and suppression.

Moderate government policy and a certain degree of national integration are two contributing factors that should not be overlooked. In order to hold various ethnic groups together and integrate them into a new form of political unit called Indonesia, Indonesian nationalists have introduced a broad-based policy of national integration. The motto of "unity in diversity" (Bhinneka Tunggal Ika) allows ethnic minorities to retain a large degree of cultural autonomy. However, there is also an integrating force that compels the minorities to join the major stream through the national schools and national institutions. The popularization of national symbols and the national ideology, Pancasila, is also aimed at integrating the multi-ethnic Indonesian society. At one time, during the Sukarno era, the government had also used the creation of an external *konfrontasi* threat to unite the people.

National integration and the Pancasila ideology

The measures of national integration adopted by the Indonesian government since independence include the promotion of a national language, national education, national symbols, national institutions, internal transmigration, and the national ideology or Pancasila.

The most obvious measure was the promotion of an Indonesian national language and education, and this was among the most successful. As Indonesian national schools are required to use Bahasa Indonesia as the medium of instruction, Indonesians of different ethnic groups are "nationalized" by learning the Indonesian language. The 2010 population census shows that 92.08% of Indonesians are able to speak Bahasa Indonesia (Ananta et.al. 2015: 276). However, those who use Indonesian as a daily home language only constitute 19.95%. The majority of Indonesians continue to speak their ethnic language at home, with the exception of three ethnic groups: Betawi, Chinese, and Batak (Ananta et al. 2015: 282).

Indonesian national symbols, such as the national flag, national anthem (Indonesia Raya), and national emblem (the Garuda with its motto: *Bhinneka Tunggal Ika*) are generally accepted by the Indonesian population of various ethnic groups. The presence of national institutions, such as the national armed forces instead of the ethnic armed forces, and national political parties instead of ethnic parties (with the exception of Aceh) indicates the sense of national belonging in the country. Internal transmigration has not been very successful as it often created ethnic enclaves and ethnic conflicts.

Last but not least is the national ideology Pancasila – the "five principles" – which was first formulated by Sukarno during the preparation of Indonesia's independence in 1945. The first principle, "Belief in One Almighty God," was aimed at embracing all religious Indonesians. However, it also denies a special position for Islam, reflecting a secular vision of an Indonesian state and culture. The last four principles – Humanism, Indonesian Unity, Democracy, and Social Justice – are ideas that are supposed to be shared by all ethnic groups.

The state ideology was already a required school subject during the Guided Democracy period (1959–65), but during Soeharto's New Order (1966–1998), the teaching of Pancasila in school was intensified. Between 1978 and 1990, the government established an institute to instill the Pancasila ideology, making it a requirement for all civil servants to take the course and pass the examination. In the view of the Soeharto government, Pancasila meant religious pluralism. Under the umbrella of Pancasila, religious freedom was guaranteed. However, it required Muslim organizations to accept Pancasila as their ideological foundation as well. This was opposed by many Islamists who felt that Pancasila should be subordinate to Islam. The Pancasila ideology attempts to separate Islam as a religion from Islam as a political force. While the government tolerated and even encouraged Islam as a religion (as evidenced in its sponsorship in building mosques and assisting Islamic boarding schools), it suppressed political Islam before 1990.

It is worth noting that Islamists' disagreement with "religious pluralism" is evidence of their opposition to the proposal of Pancasila as the Indonesian ideology during both the Sukarno and Soeharto eras. When Sukarno was in power, Islamic parties (both Nahdatul Ulama and Masyumi) opposed Pancasila; this resulted in the dissolution of the Constituent Assembly in 1959.

During the New Order period, when Pancasila became the sole ideology, there was both peaceful and violent opposition. The Tanjung Priok affair in 1984 and the subsequent bombings were closely related to the Pancasila issue. However, unlike the Sukarno era, Indonesia under Soeharto succeeded in making Pancasila the predominant ideology. Even the official Islamic party, the Partai Persatuan Pembangunan (PPP), was required to drop Islam as its party ideological foundation and profess Pancasila.

The strong defendant of the Pancasila ideology has been the Indonesian military, which is dominated by moderate Muslims and non-Muslims. The military as an institution also serves as a means to integrate Indonesian society.

Soeharto ruled the country for 32 years but was eventually forced to step down in May 1998, following the economic crisis and massive student demonstrations. His vice president B. J. Habibie succeeded him and was forced to introduce reform. The post-Soeharto era is therefore known as the "Reform Era" (Era Reformasi). After the fall of Soeharto, Pancasila no longer had a monopoly of the state ideology. Political parties based on Islam, not Pancasila, emerged. In the 1999 elections, for instance, more than 20 out of 48 parties that participated in the general elections were Islamic Parties; in the 2004 general election, five out of 24 parties were Islamic Parties. In the 2009 general election, five out of 38 parties were Islamic parties, and in 2014, also five out of 12 political parties were Islamic parties (Suryadinata 2014).

Political Islam became respectable and its development is often at the expense of the Pancasila ideology (Suryadinata 1986: 48–9). Nevertheless, Pancasila-based parties are still the largest winners in every general election. Golkar and PDI-P (Partai Demokrasi-Perjuangan) are still based on Pancasila; even some Muslim organization-linked parties have also used Pancasila as the ideology of their parties: the PKB (Partai Kebangkitan Bangsa, linked to NU) and PAN (Partai Amanat Nasional, linked to Muhammadiyah) are two examples. Many have realized that if Pancasila is replaced by Islam, the young Indonesian nation is likely to break up.

If Pancasila was the only ideology used to unite the country in Indonesia before the fall of Soeharto, since his departure, the Majelis Permusyawaratan Rakyat (Supreme Consultative

Council, MPR) has been eager to promote three other ideological pillars: the UUD 1945 (1945 Constitution), the concept of the Indonesian Unitary State (NKRI or Negara Kesatuan Republik Indonesia), and the principle Unity in Diversity (Bhineka Tunggal Ika). The PDI-P, the political party led by Sukarno's daughter Megawati Sukarnoputri, would like to socialize these ideological pillars, but some Islamic parties have disagreed (*Sinar Harapan* 2013).

Nation-building or nation-destroying?

Indonesian national unity encountered a crisis when East Timor left Indonesia to become an independent country. In 1975, Indonesia invaded East Timor and annexed it the following year. This created a major problem for Indonesia later, as Jakarta was determined to integrate East Timor by force. East Timorese rebels were temporarily defeated but opposition to Indonesia never disappeared. The harsh rule of the Indonesian military eventually gave rise to even more fierce resistance. Demonstrations and riots in 1992 and 1996 received international attention and the Soeharto regime was severely criticized for the human rights violations. In 1996, two East Timorese, Bishop Carlos Filipe Belo and Jose Ramos-Horta, received the Nobel Peace Prize, again highlighting the international importance of the East Timor issue. After the fall of Soeharto, clashes and demonstrations continued and UN peacekeeping forces, led by Australian troops moved in. Habibie finally agreed to have a referendum on the independence of East Timor. The referendum (September 1999) confirmed the desire of the East Timorese to leave the Republic of Indonesia. Many maintained that this marked the beginning of the disintegration of the Republic of Indonesia. But this proved not to be the case.

East Timor was unique. It had been a Portuguese colony and was never part of the territories of the Dutch East Indies; its annexation by Jakarta was never recognized by the UN. Therefore, the situation was different from Irian Jaya (Papua) and Aceh. But with the independence of East Timor, many argued that Papua and Aceh might follow suit.

The problems in Aceh and Irian Jaya are not new, however. At one time, they were under control, but harsh military rule during the New Order era resulted in worsening situations. In 1996, the Free Papua Organization (FPO) kidnapped 26 hostages; many of them were Western tourists. They were later rescued by the Indonesian Special Forces. Ethno-nationalism dies hard; the Papuans made use of the Reform Era and the weakened position of Jakarta to demonstrate their resistance against Indonesian rule. In early July, protesters hoisted the separatist West Papuan flag. One person was killed by the police. In the next few days, more flag-hoisting events took place, resulting in violence between Papuans and the police. Up to seven Papuans were killed. At the moment, the separatist movement is still under control.

Toward the end of his presidency, Habibie initiated a major reform in regional administration as reflected in the two laws that he issued in May 1999 regarding the regulations and laws of regional autonomy (Bell 2001). However, these two laws have many ambiguities that have required further refinement. Some considered that these laws were meant to pacify regional ethnic nationalist sentiment, but others argued that in reality they gave rise to minority ethnic nationalism. Regional ethnic identity became stronger, threatening the national unity of Indonesia.

Some regional ethnic groups demanded the state structure be changed from the unitary system to a federal state system, but the central government refused to budge (Nasution et al. 1999). Developments in Aceh after the fall of Soeharto were more promising (Suryadinata 2012b). The post-Soeharto government was eager to resolve the problem, and peace agreements were signed between the government and the rebel group. On December 9, 2002, the Indonesian government and representatives of the Free Aceh Movement (Gerakan Aceh Merdeka, GAM) signed a peace agreement, known as the Cessation of Hostilities Agreement, in Geneva.

The situation after the Bali Bombings on October 12, 2002, no longer favored GAM. In fact, since September 11, 2001, GAM has been regularly threatened with being labeled as a terrorist group. In the general atmosphere of anti-terrorism, GAM had no choice but to return to the negotiating table. The international community, especially the United States, was also willing to play a more active role in mediating the conflict in Aceh. The Acehnese in general felt tired of bloody clashes and longed for peace. By 2002, both sides had come to realize that they would not be able to win by using force. But it took three more years for both sides to come together. The peace agreement was signed on August 15, 2005, after Susilo Bambang Yudhoyono (SBY) became president and Jusuf Kalla vice president (Husain 2007: 3–4; BBC 2005). According to the treaty, Aceh would be given a special broad autonomy. The government troops would be withdrawn in exchange for GAM's disarmament. Local political parties to represent Acehnese interests were allowed. In December 2006, an election was held and the ex-GAM leader Irwandi Jusuf was elected provincial governor.

It should be mentioned that the Indonesian nation during the Soeharto era was defined in terms of an "indigenous" (*pribumi*) nation. The ethnic Chinese did not have a place in this nation unless they completely gave up their ethnic Chinese identity. However, the fall of Soeharto has seen a change in the concept of an Indonesian nation. Multiculturalism is accepted, and the ethnic Chinese are recognized as an integral part of the nation, at least in theory. Under these circumstances, some Chinese Indonesians feel that there is a future for their community in this young secular republic. Let us look at the journey of the ethnic Chinese in the making of the Indonesian nation-state.

Ethnic Chinese and the Indonesian nation

When Sukarno and Hatta declared Indonesia's independence in 1945, Sukarno used the definition of Ernst Renan's concept of nation, which is the politico-cultural definition of nation (*Risalah* 1992: 62–3). Those who regarded Indonesia as their country and were born and lived in the territories of the Republic of Indonesia were recognized as members of the Indonesian nation.

However, Sukarno did not at first explain the terms of membership in the Indonesian nation in any detail. It was only in 1963, when nation-building became a political movement, that Sukarno presented a rather concrete argument. According to Sukarno, the Indonesian nation (*bangsa Indonesia*) comprises various *suku* (ethnic groups).

> Suku [also] means leg, Indonesian nation has many legs, just like a centipede, which possesses Javanese leg, Sundanese leg, Sumatran leg, Irian leg, Dayak leg, Bali leg, Sumba leg, Peranakan Chinese leg, Peranakan Chinese leg is one of the Indonesian national legs.
>
> *(Siauw 1963: 14)*

This was the first time that the president of the Republic of Indonesia clearly stated that the "peranakan Chinese" group is a member (*suku*) of the Indonesian nation. In other words, peranakan Chinese are already members of the Indonesian nation and therefore do not need to be assimilated into the "indigenous Indonesian nation." Nevertheless, Sukarno did not clarify who these peranakan Chinese are. Are they Indonesian-born Chinese who use *Bahasa Indonesia* as their home language or all Indonesian Chinese who have Indonesian citizenship?

Heterogeneous Chinese Indonesians and the nation

In reality, Indonesian Chinese do not constitute a group. They are divided by generation, economic status, citizenship, political ideology, religion, and culture. The majority have become Indonesian citizens and politically oriented toward Indonesia, especially the younger generation. Economically, a large number are in trade and business. In terms of religion, they are Buddhist (53.82%), Christian (35.09%), Muslim (5.41%), and Hindu (1.77%) (Ananta et al. 2008: 30). Culturally, they are quite plural as well. Prior to the Second World War, Indonesian Chinese were divided into "*peranakan* Chinese" and "*totok* Chinese" (or migrant Chinese). The former refers to those Chinese born in Indonesia and influenced by the local (Malay/Indonesian) culture. Peranakan Chinese usually lost their command of the Chinese language and used a local dialect or Malay (Indonesian) as a home language and language of communication. Those Chinese who came to Indonesia during the twentieth century usually still retained the Chinese language and culture. They used a Chinese dialect or Mandarin as their home language and the language of everyday communication. Therefore, they were not classified as "peranakan Chinese." Their children, who were born in Indonesia before or soon after the Second World War, are still closer linguistically and culturally to the "totok Chinese," as they attended Chinese-medium schools and lived in a Chinese community environment.

However, after Soeharto assumed power, he prohibited three cultural pillars of the Chinese overseas (Chinese schools, Chinese organizations, and Chinese mass media), and the descendants of the totok Chinese were transformed into a new type of peranakan Chinese: they used Bahasa Indonesia as the daily language and quickly joined the existing peranakan community. In fact, if the concept of "peranakan Chinese" group as a member of the Indonesian nation had actually been developed, Chinese Indonesian national identity could have been resolved. However, when Soeharto came to power in 1966, he not only refused to acknowledge "peranakan Chinese" as an Indonesian *suku* (ethnic group), but also advocated their total assimilation. He promulgated a "name changing" regulation, "appealing" to Chinese Indonesians to change their names to "Indonesian names."[2] He also restricted the development of the Confucian Religion (Agama Khonghucu), by withdrawing state recognition of Confucianism in 1979 and forbidding the Confucian organization from holding national congresses.

Soeharto's assimilationist policy had a profound impact on the Indonesian Chinese community; Indonesian Chinese in the 32 years of Soeharto rule became "more Indonesianized." But this does not mean that the Chinese Indonesians have been homogenized. The division between "peranakan" and "totok" remains, but the number of totok Chinese has rapidly declined as new Chinese migration has largely stopped and the three Chinese cultural pillars were abolished. However, the totoks are more dynamic in the economic field, and their presence has been strongly felt. It is also worth noting that during the Soeharto rule, almost all totok Chinese obtained Indonesian citizenship and became the new members of the country.

In the era of globalization and democratization, Soeharto was eventually forced to step down, the military power had been undermined, reform was introduced, and political participation had also increased. During the new Reform Era, the government policy also underwent changes. The three pillars of the Chinese culture have largely been restored. Chinese Indonesians have begun to regard themselves as a *suku Tionghoa* ("Chinese ethnicity") within Indonesia. Some Indonesian intellectuals have also begun to accept this concept. During the Reformasi era, the government appears to have accepted multi-culturalism rather than mono-culturalism as the basis of the Indonesian nation. But the 32-year rule of the New Order, during which "indigenism" (pribumi-isme) was the basis of the state policy, remains deeply rooted in many Indonesians' minds. The social distance between Indonesian ethnic groups remains wide. According to a *Tempo* survey (Tempo 2001:12–13), 52% of respondents indicated that they did not approve of their relatives marrying ethnic Chinese; 78% did not approve of Indonesian citizens of Chinese descent speaking a Chinese dialect or Mandarin. These and other indicators show that, for many Indonesians, the expectation is that Chinese Indonesians will integrate themselves into the mainstream of Indonesian society.[3]

It should be noted that the 1945 Indonesian Constitution (before its amendment in 2002) divided Indonesian citizens into *Indonesia asli* (indigenous Indonesian) and *bukan asli* (non-indigenous); it also stipulated that the Indonesian president should be *Indonesia asli*. After the fall of Soeharto, B. J. Habibie issued a Presidential Instruction stating that the division between *pribumi* (indigenous Indonesian) and *non-pribumi* (non-indigenous Indonesian) should be abolished. However, in the amended 1945 Indonesian Constitution, the term *Indonesia asli* continues to be used in the citizenship clause, but the requirement for both Indonesian president and vice president candidacy has been changed to "Indonesian citizen who was born in Indonesia" (*Undang-Undang* 2007:5).

In July 2006, a new Indonesian citizenship law was promulgated. This law abandons not only the division between indigenous and non-indigenous Indonesians but also the male-centered principle (Suryadinata 2016, Vol. I: lii). It defines *Indonesia asli* as an "Indonesian citizen who was born in Indonesia" (Sadeli 2007: 31). Frans H. Winarta, a human rights lawyer, noted that this is "a revolutionary law," which "eliminate(s) all forms of discrimination against ethnic Chinese" (Winarta 2008: 67).

Ethnic Chinese and political participation

Only Indonesian citizens have the right to participate in Indonesian politics. But Chinese Indonesians were not active during the Soeharto era. As soon as Soeharto stepped down, however, there was a rush to establish new political parties. Chinese Indonesians established three political parties: Partai Reformasi Tionghoa Indonesia (Parti), Partai Pembauran, and Partai Bhinneka Tunggal Ika Indonesia (PBI). The Partai Pembauran was transformed into a social organization soon after its formation; Parti did not develop. Only the PBI contested the 1999 election, but it performed poorly, gaining only one seat in the national parliament (from West Kalimantan). It failed to run in subsequent general elections. Based on this and other indicators, efforts to create Chinese political parties in Indonesia now appear finished.

In the four general elections after the fall of Soeharto (1999, 2004, 2009, and 2014), however, many Chinese Indonesians were elected to national and provincial parliaments as members of mainstream party tickets (Suryadinata 2014). In 1999, there were eight Chinese Indonesians in the parliament: five from the PDI-P, one from Golkar, one from PAN, and one from PBI. In 2014, there were 14 Chinese Indonesian MPs: one from PD, one from PKB, one from PAN, and 11 from the PDI-P (Suryadinata 2014).

Since the 1999 general elections, Chinese Indonesians have also been elected to the posts of mayor or deputy regent. These include Basuki Tjahaja Purnama (Zhong Wanxue 钟万学alias Ahok), who was Bupati of East Belitung and later, deputy governor of Jakarta; Hasan Karman (Huang Shaofan 黄少凡), mayor of Singkawang (West Kalimantan); and Tjhai Chui Mei (蔡翠媚), also mayor of Singkawang (Suryadinata 2012a:13; *Harian Yin Hua* 2017).

Outside the field of party politics, many Chinese Indonesians since the fall of Soeharto have established socio-cultural organizations. The Paguyuban Sosial Marga Tionghoa Indonesia (PSMTI) and Perhimpunan Indonesia Tionghoa (INTI) are two prominent ethnic Chinese NGOs. Seen from the mainstream society, the participation in the ethnic Chinese NGOs is less significant compared to that of indigenous Indonesian-dominated NGOs.

While political participation is a way to integrate into Indonesian mainstream society, the process has not always been smooth. Racial and ethnic sentiments have not gone away easily, and racist attacks have been used in order to defeat political opponents. This has happened during many national, provincial, and municipal elections. The most recent examples are the Jakarta gubernatorial elections on July 11, 2012, and February 15, 2017.

Joko (Jokowi) Widodo-Basuki Tjahaya Purnama (alias Ahok) contested the 2012 gubernatorial election as a pair, but Basuki was attacked by their opponents for his ethnic and religious background (Chinese and Christian). Surprisingly, Jakarta voters eventually elected the Jokowi-Basuki pair. Halfway into his gubernatorial term, Jokowi was nominated by the PDI-P to contest the 2014 presidential election; he eventually won. Basuki succeeded him to the governorship. Both Jokowi and Basuki and later, Basuki and Djarot, did a good job in improving the living environment and combating corruption. When Basuki-Djarot announced their intention to run in the 2017 gubernatorial election, their opponents again used ethnic and religious appeals to discredit the pair. Their opponents focused their attacks on Basuki, who was accused of blaspheming Islam, which resulted in two major anti-Basuki demonstrations in Jakarta. In February 2017, Basuki, who had been the most popular candidate before being accused of blasphemy, won less than 50% of the votes and was therefore required to contest a second round. On April 19, 2017, Basuki lost the runoff election to Anies Baswedan. Shortly thereafter he was convicted of blaspheming against Islam and sentenced by a North Jakarta district court to two years imprisonment.

Chinese Indonesian identity and the rise of China

The democratization of Indonesia caused many ethnic minorities, including the Chinese, to be ethnically conscious once again and to aspire to retain their ethnic identity. This is particularly the case with the totok Chinese who have adopted Indonesian citizenship. The rise of China as a major economic, political, and military power is another factor that contributed to the revival of ethnic Chinese identity in Southeast Asia in general and in Indonesia particularly.

Although in law, Beijing today continues to divide Chinese citizens from non-Chinese citizens among the Chinese overseas, in practice, it tends to blur the distinction between Chinese citizens and foreign citizens of Chinese descent; this makes the national status of the ethnic Chinese in Southeast Asia problematic (Yang 2008: 84–5). Policy today tends to regard foreign citizens of Chinese descent as "Chinese citizens"; this makes the national status of the ethnic Chinese in Southeast Asia problematic (Yang 2008: 84–5). Many peranakan Chinese elites in Indonesia have complained that the Chinese embassy has been too close to the Chinese Indonesian associations. During the celebration of the Indonesian Independence Day, for instance, Chinese Indonesian associations only invited Indonesian embassy officials but not Indonesian officials. This could jeopardize the interests of the Chinese Indonesians in the long run (Setiono 2008: 77). The peranakan Chinese elite appealed to the Chinese embassy to implement the Zhou Enlai "Overseas Chinese Policy": to educate Chinese Indonesians to be "loyal to their adopted country" (Setiono 2008:77).

Still today, some Chinese Indonesians have a weak sense of themselves as Indonesian. Under this circumstance, those Chinese who have not integrated themselves into Indonesia's mainstream society will find identifying with Indonesian nation "less attractive," as they have not been part of the Indonesian culture to begin with. In the long run, the rise of China and its ambiguous citizenship policy may have an impact on Chinese integration into the Indonesian nation.

Conclusion

Modern Indonesia was a product of the Indonesian nationalist movement, which emerged in the twentieth century under Dutch colonial rule. The movement eventually united the country's diverse ethnic groups and created the Indonesian nation-state. There were a few ethnic separatist movements, which were quelled by the central government with the exception of that in East Timor, which became an independent state in 2002, but this was a special case. The only remaining ethnic separatist movement of some scale is that in Papua, but it remains weak.

Although the secular ideology as reflected in Pancasila remains dominant, various Islamist ideologies have at times challenged the national ideology. This can be seen in various political events before and after the fall of Soeharto. This may affect the continuing process of nation-building in Indonesia.

The position of ethnic Chinese in the Indonesian nation has greatly improved. Before the fall of Soeharto, they were considered as a non-homeland minority and were expected to assimilate themselves into indigenous society. Since the dawn of Reformasi, however, the government has abandoned the concept of nationhood premised on indigenousness, and ethnic Chinese have been welcome to join the Indonesian nation. However, prejudice against the ethnic Chinese, although diminished, continues.

Notes

1 With regard to the nationalist movement and the emergence of an Indonesian nation, see my discussion in Suryadinata 2015:20–2.
2 Name-changing regulations were promulgated in 1966. It is interesting to note that the so-called Indonesian name is difficult to define; many argued that as long as it is not a "Chinese name," it can be accepted as an Indonesian name.
3 In the late colonial period, the Chinese constituted about 2.8–3% of the total Indonesian population. This was an estimate based on the 1930 population census, which shows that the Chinese constituted 2.03% (Suryadinata 2004). Since 1930, information on the size of the Chinese community in Indonesia has been unavailable. However, since the 2000 population census, the information on the size of the Chinese population has been included again. The census has been based on self-identification reporting. There were about 0.86% Chinese in 2000 and 1.2% Chinese in 2010. The actual number may be higher but not more than 2%, as population growth among Chinese is low, few new Chinese migrants have arrived, and many Chinese emigrated (Suryadinata 2004).

References cited

Ananta, Aris, Evi Nurvidya Arifin, and Bakhtiar. 2008. "Chinese Indonesians in Indonesia and the Province of Riau Archipelago: A Demographic Analysis," in Suryadinata, ed., 30.

Ananta, Aris, Evi Nurvidya Arifin, M. Sairi Hasbullah, Nur Budi Handayani, and Agus Pramono. 2015. *Demography of Indonesia's Ethnicity* (Singapore: ISEAS).

BBC News. 2005. "Aceh Rebels Sign Peace Agreement," 15 August. http://news.bbc.co.uk/2/hi/asia-pacific/4151980.stm (Accessed 9 January 2013).

Bell, Gary. 2001. "The New Indonesian Laws Relating to Regional Autonomy: Good Intentions, Confusing Laws," *Asian Pacific Law and Policy Journal*, 2. www.hawaii.edu/aplpj/2/1.html (Accessed 8 January 2013).

Feith, Herbert. 1962. *Decline of the Constitutional Democracy in Indonesia* (Ithaca: Cornell University Press).

Harian Yin Hua. 2017. "Yinni diyige huayi nu shizhang dansheng" [The First Indonesian Woman Mayor Who Is of Chinese Descent], 23 February.

Husain, Farid. 2007. *To See the Unseen: Kisah di Balik Damai Aceh* (Jakarta: Health Hospital).

Nasution, Adnan Buyung, T. Jakob Koekerits, and St. Sularto. 1999. *Federalisme untuk Indonesia* (Jakarta: Penerbit Kompas).

Osborne, Robin. 1985. *Indonesia's Secret War: The Guerrilla Struggle in Irian Jaya* (Sydney: Allen and Unwin).

Risalah Sidang Badan Penyelidik Usaha-Usaha Persiapan Kemerdekaan Indonesia (BPUPKI) Panitia Persiapan Kemerdekaan Indonesia (PPKI), 29 Mei 1945–19 Agustus 1945. 1992 (Jakarta: Sekretariat Negara Republik Indonesia).

Sadcli, Eddy. ed. 2007. *Undang-Undang Republik Indonesia no. 12 Tahun 2006 tentang Kewarganegaraan Republik Indonesia* (Jakarta: LPPM-TI).

Setiono, Benny G. 2008. "Beberapa catatan mengenai perkembangan Organisasi-Organisasi Tionghoa di Indonesia," *Yinni Jiaodian* (Indonesia Focus) 22: 74–7.

Siauw Giok Tjhan. 1963. "Amanat P.J.M. Presiden Soekarno Pada Kongres Nasional ke-VIII Baperki," in Siauw Giok Tjhan, ed. *Gotong Rojong Nasakom untuk Melaksanakan Ampera* (Djakarta: Baperki).

Sinar Harapan. 2013. "Negara Kesatuan ataukah Negara Persatuan?" 12 June.

Sjamsuddin, Nazaruddin. 1985. *The Republican Revolt: A Study of Acehnese Rebellion* (Singapore: ISEAS).

Suryadinata, Leo. 1986. "Politics in Indonesian Parliament 1966–1985," *Southeast Asian Journal of Social Science* 15(1): 35–52.

———. 1990. "National Ideology and Nation-Building in Multi-Ethnic States: Lessons from Other Countries," in Jon S.T. Quah, ed., *In Search of Singapore's National Values* (Singapore: Times Academic Press), pp. 24–44.

———. 1998. "Indonesian Nationalism and the Pre-War Youth Movement," in Leo Suryadinata, ed., *Interpreting Indonesian Politics* (Singapore: Times Academic Press), pp. 49–68.

———. 2004. "How Many Ethnic Chinese Are in Indonesia?" *Asian Culture*, 28.

———. 2012a. "Integration of Indonesian Chinese to Mainstream Society," *Asian Culture* 36: 9–17.

———. 2012b. "Will There Be Peace in Aceh?" *Straits Times*, 12 December.

———. 2014. "Ethnic Chinese Politics and Indonesian Elections." Paper presented at the Workshop on the 2014 Indonesian Election, ISEAS, 31 October.

———. 2015. *The Making of Southeast Asian Nations: State, Ethnicity, Indigenism and Citizenship* (Singapore: World Scientific).

———, ed. 2016. *Tionghoa dalam Keindonesiaan: Peran dan Kontribusi Bagi Pembangunan Bangsa*, Vol. I (Jakarta: Yayasan Nabil).

Tempo. 2001. "Tionghoa belum diterima apa adanya," 4 February, pp. 12–13.

Undang-Undang Dasar Negara Republik Indonesia Tahun 1945 (Dalam Persandingan Disertai Catatan). 2007 (Jakarta: Forum Konstitusi).

Winarta, Frans H., 2008. "No More Discrimination Against the Chinese," *Suryadinata*: 57–74.

Yang Ping. 2008. "Yan'ge qufen huaqiao huaren de jiexian" [Strictly Differentiate China's Citizens and Foreign Citizens of Chinese Descent], *Yinni Jiaodian (Indonesia Focus)* 22: 84–5.

4

CONSTITUTIONS AND CONSTITUTIONALISM

Simon Butt

Since declaring its independence on August 17, 1945, Indonesia has had four constitutions. The first was the "1945 Constitution," which Indonesia's first president, Sukarno, proclaimed on August 18. The second was the Constitution of the Federal Republic of Indonesia, which lasted from December 27, 1949, until August 17, 1950, when Indonesia's third constitution – the Interim Constitution of 1950 – was brought into force. On July 5, 1959, Sukarno reinstated the 1945 Constitution, which remained in force unamended throughout Soeharto's New Order (1966–1998). After Soeharto's fall, the 1945 Constitution was amended once each year in 1999–2002. Although still entitled the "1945 Constitution," the document is now very different from its original version. The old structural core of the document remains – including Indonesia's national ideology, Pancasila, in the Preamble – but features of liberal democracy have replaced provisions that underlay the authoritarian regimes of Sukarno (from 1959) and Soeharto.

Before 2003, Indonesia had almost no tradition of constitutionalism, in the sense that the government considered itself bound by the Constitution. Indeed, Indonesia's constitutional transitions were, arguably, themselves unconstitutional because they did not take place in accordance with constitutional rules. Importantly, citizens could not hold the government to the Constitution by challenging the constitutionality of government actions. Constitutional review, rightly considered a prerequisite to constitutionalism, was not available in Indonesia until 2003, when a new Constitutional Court (*Mahkamah Konstitusi*) heard its first case.

This chapter will briefly cover Indonesia's constitutional history, outlining the characteristics of each constitution mentioned, the circumstances of the transition from one constitution to the next, and broad indicators of the level of constitutionalism – that is, adherence to the constitution, whether judicially enforced or not – during each period. As we shall see, the primary significance of Indonesia's various constitutions has been largely political rather than legal, except in the post-Soeharto period, when the Constitutional Court was established. This chapter concludes with a brief assessment of the Constitutional Court's contribution to constitutionalism. Has the court effectively kept the government to the constitution? If so, has it done so consistently, and is it likely to perform this function into the future?

The 1945 Constitution

Indonesia's first independent constitution was the result of opportunities occupying Japanese forces gave to Indonesian nationalist leaders to meet to discuss the ideological bases Indonesia might adopt if given limited independence within the Japanese Greater East Asia Co-Prosperity Sphere (Ricklefs 2008). The Japanese established the 62-member *Dokuritzu Zunbi Tjoosakai* (*Badan Penyelidik Usaha-usaha Persiapan Kemerdekaan Indonesia* [BPUPKI] or Investigating Committee for the Preparation of Independence) on April 29, 1945, which, over the course of a few months, hosted debates between prominent Indonesians about whether Indonesia should aspire to liberal democracy, an Islamic state, or totalitarianism. After BPUPKI's final meeting, its chairperson, Radjiman Wedyodiningrat, established the "Committee of 9," chaired by Sukarno (who later became Indonesia's first president), to draft the preamble to the Constitution. Another committee was established to draft the constitution itself (Ranadireksa 2007: 17). The committee was chaired by renowned jurist, Supomo, who earlier had advocated integralist totalitarianism as the best model for Indonesia to adopt and was ultimately primarily responsible for the content of the 1945 Constitution (Lev 1999: 232).

In early August, key Indonesian figures were called to Saigon to meet senior Japanese army figures to discuss Indonesia's transition toward semi-autonomy. These figures included Sukarno, Wedyodiningrat, and Hatta (who later became Indonesia's first vice president and a prime minister). There, the *Dokuritzu Zunbi Iinkai* (*Panitia Persiapan Kemerdekaan Indonesia* [PPKI] or Committee for the Preparation of Indonesian) was established, with Sukarno and Hatta as chair and deputy chair. These figures returned to Indonesia on August 14 – the day before the Japanese surrender. With the Japanese leadership in disarray, they declared independence on August 17, 1945. On the following day, the PPKI proclaimed the 1945 Constitution and decided that it would begin operating on August 19 (Ranadireksa 2007: 20).[1]

The 1945 Constitution was hastily conceived and very short. As discussed in the following,[2] it established the framework under which a strong presidential system flourished, with very few constraints. (As we shall see, from 1959 to 1998, the 1945 Constitution was used to support the successive authoritarian regimes of Sukarno and Soeharto.) While it mentioned a handful of human rights – such as to freedom of speech and association – it did not *grant* them to citizens; rather, it merely ordered the legislature to regulate those rights (Lubis 1993; Manan 2012: 16).

Sukarno and the other drafters clearly saw the 1945 Constitution as an imperfect and temporary measure that would help bring Indonesia together as a nation. In a speech about the 1945 Constitution made before the PPKI on August 18, Sukarno said,

> All you gentlemen certainly understand that the Constitution we have now made is a temporary Constitution. If I may use these words: "this is a lightning (*kilat*) Constitution." Later, when we have come together as a nation, and the situation is calm, we will certainly . . . create a more complete and perfect Constitution.[3]

It was indeed not long before the document was amended, albeit indirectly. Within two months of the 1945 Constitution's introduction, influential figures became concerned that Sukarno and his cabinet were becoming "far too authoritarian" and began agitating for a parliamentary system (Kahin 1952: 152). The Central Indonesian National Committee (Komite Nasional Pusat Indonesia, or KNPI), which had been established soon after Independence to advise the president, was given "real legislative powers," at least until a parliament could be elected and a prime ministership, with its own cabinet, was established (Kahin 1952: 152). These changes were effected by Mahlumat (Decree) No X of October 16, 1945 ("Maklumat X"), brought into law by then–Vice President Hatta.

Many Indonesian constitutional law scholars conclude that Maklumat X amended Article 17 of the constitution, even though no formal changes were made to the text. (Article 17 referred to the president being assisted by ministers, whom he or she could appoint and dismiss. No mention was made of prime ministers and their cabinets.) Some scholars find no fault with this, arguing that Maklumat X simply expressed state convention (Suny 1977; Supomo 1950) or emphasizing that both the president and the Central Indonesian National Committee freely endorsed it (Assaat 1951; Saragih 2006: 39).

Others rightly question whether Maklumat X was a valid exercise of vice-presidential power. Maklumat were not mentioned in the constitution as valid types of legal instruments, and so whether they sit "above" or "below" the constitution in terms of authority is not spelled out (Huda 2008: 160–61). Presumably, however, the constitution – traditionally understood in Indonesia as elsewhere as the *grundnorm* – trumps a Maklumat and cannot, therefore, be amended by one. Other scholars argue that adopting the parliamentary system required following the amendment process contained in Article 37 of the constitution (Manan 2012: 108). This requires two-thirds of the People's Consultative Assembly (*Majelis Permusyawaratan Rakyat* or MPR) members to agree to amendments at a meeting where two-thirds of MPR members are present. (To be fair, the MPR had not yet been established, so this would have been impossible to achieve quickly, but there seems little point in entrenching the constitution if its provisions can be so easily circumvented.) To these criticisms, I would add that convention cannot be established without ever being practiced.

The constitution of the Federal Republic of Indonesia (1949)

The 1949 Constitution was always intended to be temporary. However, it was abandoned perhaps more quickly than most expected, making it Indonesia's shortest-lived constitution. Soon after independence, Dutch forces had returned to Indonesia, seeking to re-establish control. This had met significant resistance from Indonesian fighters and in international fora, and in 1949, the Dutch formally agreed to withdraw their claim of sovereignty. The Dutch then supported efforts for the establishment of a federal system in Indonesia. The Panitia Urusan Ketatanegaraan dan Hukum Tatanegara (Committee for State Affairs and Constitutional Law), which had both Indonesian and Dutch delegates, was established in Holland and met to draft the 1949 Constitution as the legal basis for this system.

This constitution established the Federal Republic of Indonesia, comprising 16 states. It also provided for democratic government, human rights, and judicial review.[4] However, the federal system proved to be deeply unpopular from the very beginning, with many Indonesian politicians suspecting that the Dutch insisted on it to "divide" Indonesia, making it easier for them to resume their rule (Huda 2008: 165). By August 17, 1950, the Federal Constitution had been replaced with the Interim Constitution of 1950.

Like the de facto amendment to the 1945 Constitution by Maklumat X, discussed earlier, the 1949 Constitution was enacted by simple executive instrument: Presidential Decision No. 48 of 1950.[5] Because the legal basis for the adoption of the Federal Constitution was a presidential decision, its legal validity has been questioned on similar grounds to those put forward by critics of Maklumat X. There was, for example, no attempt to use the procedures set out in Article 37 of the 1945 Constitution to bring the Federal Constitution into force. The only legal justification for the 1949 Constitution's introduction, mentioned in the preamble to Presidential Decision No. 48, appears to be the agreement between national and state delegates reached when the constitution was drafted in Holland, which was endorsed by the national and state governments, the Central Indonesian National Committee, and the parliaments of each state.

The Interim Constitution of 1950

As mentioned, the Federal Constitution of 1949 was always intended to be temporary. Article 186 of the 1949 Constitution entrusted its replacement to a Constituent Assembly (*Konstituante*) – a joint sitting of the national parliament and the senate (Article 188). Like Article 37 of the 1945 Constitution, Article 189 of the 1949 Constitution required that replacement or amendment of its provisions be endorsed by a two-thirds majority of the Konstituante at a meeting of the Konstituante attended by at least two-thirds of its members. Yet these provisions were ignored when the 1950 Constitution was introduced – this time by national statute: Law No. 7 of 1950. This left the legal basis for the adoption of the 1950 Constitution highly suspect, just as had been the case for the adoption of the 1949 Constitution.

The 1950 Constitution had been drafted by yet another committee, whose draft was approved on August 14, 1950 (Ranadireksa 2007: 59). The 1950 Constitution retained many aspects of the 1949 Constitution, including a largely democratic system, human rights, and the separation of powers, leading some commentators to suggest that it was, at its heart, really only an amendment to the 1949 Constitution, with the federal system stripped out (Saragih 2006: 40). Under the Interim Constitution of 1950, Indonesia's first democratic elections were held in 1955, as were elections to fill a new *Konstituante* whose job was, again, to draft a permanent constitution. Once more, the 1950 Interim Constitution required at least two-thirds of those present at a meeting of at least two-thirds of *Konstituante* members to approve any new constitution (Article 137). Yet even though the People's Representative Assembly (Dewan Perwakilan Rakyat, or DPR) was democratically elected and had broad legislative powers and the government, run by a cabinet chaired by the prime minister, was formally answerable to it, President Sukarno retained relatively strong authority (Ranadireksa 2007: 64–5). For example, the president was unimpeachable and could, in fact, disband the DPR (Manan 2012: 49).

Within a few years, however, Indonesia's relatively modest democratic experiment met its end. The *Konstituante* had established an 18-member constitution drafting committee in late 1957 but had made very little progress, partly because the committee could not agree on the basis of the Indonesian state (Nasution 1992). Other problems emerged: the 1955 parliament was highly fragmented and became deadlocked, unable to pass legislation; the Indonesian Community Party was garnering widespread grassroots support, which the military perceived as a threat; and numerous regional rebellions threatened the nation's integrity. In response, the army urged Sukarno to return to the 1945 Constitution, and the *Konstituante* was also asked three times to formally revert to it (Huda 2008: 173). Initially both refused, with Sukarno fearing that it would hand the army excessive political power.

However, Sukarno eventually succumbed. As in previous transitions, the applicable constitutional provisions regulating constitutional change were ignored. Here, Sukarno disbanded the *Konstituante* and returned to the 1945 Constitution by issuing a decree on July 5, 1959. The decree criticized the *Konstituante* for failing to return to the 1945 Constitution, despite the urgings of the president and the government "that had been conveyed by the Indonesian people," and for refusing to hold further sessions. According to the decree, this "led to a constitutional situation that endangered the unity and safety of the nation and impeded the development needed to achieve a just and prosperous society." It continued, "With the support of the majority of the Indonesian people, and pushed by my own convictions, I am forced to take the only course to save the Proclaimed Nation." The decree invalidated the 1950 Constitution and reinstated the 1945 Constitution from the date of the decree.

The legality of this constitutional transition is a matter of significant debate (Harahap 2009; Hukumonline 2016), particularly given the subsequent longevity of the 1945 Constitution. Some argue that the decree was justifiable as an exercise of emergency powers (Kusnardi and Ibrahim 1988). These justifications were adopted by the "New Order" (*Orde Baru*) government, under General Soeharto, who had wrestled control of the presidency from Sukarno by 1966. A government dominated by the military, the New Order had a clear interest in maintaining the 1945 Constitution. Implicitly recognizing the legal weakness of the decree, in 1966, the Interim MPR (Majelis Permusyawaratan Rakyat Sementara [MPRS]), constituted after Soeharto took power, issued its own decree to shore up the legitimacy of the transition.[6] This decree repeatedly emphasizes the importance of Soeharto being given the authority to "take all action considered necessary to guarantee the security, calmness, and the stability of the government and the progress of the Revolution . . ." given that, under the previous regime, the 1945 Constitution had been implemented with numerous "deviations" (*penyimpangan*).[7] As for Sukarno's 1959 Decree reintroducing the 1945 Constitution, the MPR Decree justified it on several grounds: as an emergency measure, as being supported by all people, and as being approved soon after by a democratically elected parliament.

These arguments are not particularly convincing. The 1950 Constitution did, in fact, contain provisions dealing with "emergency legislation," which empowered the government to legislate on issues that "because of pressing circumstances needed to be regulated immediately" (Article 96(1)). However, such emergency legislation has the legal status of a statute (Article 96(2)) and cannot, therefore, trump the constitution. As an even weaker form of law, the Presidential Decree of 1959 clearly lacked the legal authority to remove the democratically elected *Konstituante* and to perform the constitutionally mandated function of that body: to devise a new constitution. As mentioned, the 1950 Constitution was, like the 1949 Constitution before it, specific in its threshold requirements for constitutional change, and the *Konstituante* itself had expressly rejected the reversion. It is difficult to reach any conclusion other than that Sukarno's 1959 Decree was unconstitutional.

Nevertheless, the New Order government adopted the 1945 Constitution as its ideological centerpiece, asserting that, under Sukarno, the 1945 Constitution had been neither properly nor consistently implemented. By contrast, the New Order declared that it would act in accordance with the constitution. While this may have served to justify Sukarno's removal, there was very little, if any, legal substance to these assertions. The constitution itself was so threadbare that it was arguably difficult to breach, or at least to prove a breach. In any event, as discussed in the following, constitutional review was not available, so the state could unilaterally interpret the constitution as it saw fit, without being held to account. The result was that the state used the ideological lure of the 1945 Constitution to legitimize its authoritarian rule and policies and even referred to provisions of the constitution to justify legislation but was not, in fact, constrained by those provisions.

One example is the DPR's enactment of Law 5 of 1985, which sought to prohibit amendment to the constitution except by referendum.[8] Under Law 5, if the MPR wanted to amend the constitution, it was required to put the proposal to public vote. An amendment could only be passed if 90% of registered voters participated in the vote and 90% of them agreed to it. Of course, this made it very difficult, if not impossible, to amend the constitution.[9] More important, though, is that this legislation sought to override the Article 37 process, which, as mentioned, requires at least two-thirds of the MPR to vote on any amendment proposal and two-thirds of those voting to agree to it.

The process for presidential "election" that emerged during the New Order provides another example of apparent constitutional non-compliance by the state. Article 6(2) of the original

1945 Constitution provided that the president and vice president were to be elected by majority vote of the MPR. The need for election seems to leave open the possibility that more than one candidate pair could compete for these positions. However, in practice, the process was not competitive, with only one pair in the running and the MPR appointing it by consensus rather than by majority (Huda 2008: 181).[10]

1999 to present

Although the Asian Economic Crisis of 1997–98 was the primary driver of Soeharto's removal from office in May 1998, widespread dissatisfaction about the authoritarian nature of his rule had been steadily building for decades. Fears of continuing unrest, and the prospect of Indonesia "Balkanizing," propelled Indonesia's first post-Soeharto democratically elected parliament toward genuine constitutional change (Horowitz 2013). The four annual amendment rounds that took place in 1999–2002 recalibrated the Indonesian polity toward democracy and effected the redistribution of power from the presidency to various national and subnational institutions (Indrayana 2008).

The First Amendment

The First Amendment was passed on October 19, 1999, and was primarily directed at reducing the presidential power that many thought Soeharto had abused for over 30 years. Originally, the 1945 Constitution referred to power being distributed by the MPR – formally the "highest" institution of state – through to the president and the national parliament. While this meant that the president was accountable to the MPR, his control over that body meant he was never held accountable by it. In practice, the president held significant power, being both head of state and head of government and having an unlimited number of five-year terms. Importantly, the president had both regulatory and legislative powers, including broad emergency powers.

Article 7 now limits any future president from holding office for more than two five-year terms. Amendments also restricted the president's legislative powers in favor of the legislature. The old 1945 Constitution gave the president power to "make legislation with the agreement of the DPR." The president now has power only to "introduce Bills into the DPR" (Article 5(1)) – a power that the president now shares with all DPR members.

The Second Amendment

Perhaps the most significant of the four amendments was the second, enacted on August 18, 2000. This amendment adopted an array of internationally recognized human rights, contained in the Universal Declaration of Human Rights, the International Covenant on Civil and Political Rights, and the International Covenant on Economic, Social and Cultural Rights (Lindsey 2002). Article 28 has been radically expanded to include citizens' rights to

- life, to maintain their lives, and to a livelihood (Article 28A);
- form a family and continue their lineage through a valid marriage (Article 28B(1));
- develop themselves by fulfilling their basic needs; obtain an education; and obtain benefits from science and technology, art, and culture so as to increase their quality of life and further the well-being of humankind (Article 28C(1));
- advance themselves by collectively upholding their rights to develop the community, nation, and state (Article 28C(2));

- just legal recognition, guarantees, protection and certainty, and equal treatment before the law (Article 28D(1));
- employment and to receive just and appropriate reward and treatment, if in an employment relationship (Article 28D(2));
- nationality status (Article 28D(4));
- embrace their respective religions and worship in accordance with their religion; to choose their education, teaching, employment, and citizenship; to choose a residence within the territory of the state, to leave and return to the state (Article 28E(1));
- be convinced of their beliefs and express an opinion and attitude, in accordance with their conscience (Article 28E(2));
- associate, assemble, and express an opinion (Article 28E(3));
- communicate and obtain information to develop themselves and their social environment and to seek, obtain, possess, store, manage, and convey information using all available means (Article 28F);
- protection for themselves and their families, honor, dignity, property rights, and a feeling of security and protection from threats to do or to refrain from something that is a human right (Article 28G(1));
- be free from inhumane torture or treatment and seek asylum to obtain political protection from another country (Article 28G(2));
- physical and mental well-being, a place of residence, a good and healthy environment, and health care (Article 28H(1));
- special treatment to obtain the same opportunities and benefits to achieve equality and justice (Article 28H(2));
- social security that permits holistic self-development as befits human dignity (Article 28H(3));
- personal property rights that cannot be arbitrarily appropriated (Article 28H(4)); and
- protection against discriminatory treatment (Article 28I(2)) (Butt and Lindsey 2012).

Importantly, most of these human rights are subject to Article 28J(2), which permits these rights to be limited by legislation directed at "protecting the rights and freedoms of others and which accords with moral considerations, religious values, security, and public order in a democratic society."

The Constitutional Court has regularly refused to invalidate statutes that breach constitutional rights on Article 28J(2) grounds (Butt 2015).

It seems that the Second Amendment drafters intended that some rights be non-derogable. Article 28I(1) states,

> The right to life, the right to not be tortured, the right to freedom of thought and conscience, the right to religion, the right to not be enslaved, the right to be recognized as an individual before the law, and the right to not be prosecuted under a law of retrospective application are human rights that cannot be limited under any circumstances.

Even though these rights appear intended to be absolute – that is, that Article 28J(2) cannot apply to justify legislation that limits them – the Constitutional Court has in many cases held that Article 28I(1) rights *are* subject to Article 28J(2) (Butt 2015; Butt and Lindsey 2012). In other words, the court has allowed statutes to remain in force even though they breach the human rights of citizens, including these "absolute" Article 28I(1) rights, if the statute upholds the rights of others, and one of the purposes of Article 28J(2), such as religious values or public order (Butt 2016).

The Second Amendment was also particularly significant because it recognized regional autonomy, introduced by national legislation enacted in 1999. The constitution provides subnational governments – that is, provincial, city, and county administrations – with both legislative and regulatory power (Article 18). This power is to be "as broad as possible" but excludes specified issues that fall within the exclusive jurisdiction of the national government (Butt 2010).

Finally, the president's so-called "legislative powers" were further curtailed. Originally, legislation was subject to presidential assent. Article 20(5) now provides that bills come into force automatically 30 days after being passed by the DPR, even if the president does not endorse them.

The Third and Fourth Amendments

The main foci of these amendments, passed in 2001 and 2002 respectively, were reducing the MPR's powers and establishing important new institutions, including the Constitutional Court, a Judicial Commission, and the Regional Representative Council (Dewan Perwakilan Daerah [DPD]). While the MPR still meets to amend the constitution, it no longer has power to pass decrees and set state policy. It also no longer appoints the president. The president and vice president are now directly elected by the people from pairs of candidates proposed by political parties (Article 6A(1)).

The Third Amendment also established that the MPR can impeach the president, on the DPR's recommendation, if the Constitutional Court confirms that the president has committed a serious wrongdoing, such as treason, corruption, or another serious offense, or otherwise no longer meets the requirements to hold office (Articles 7A and 7B).

The constitutional constant: Pancasila

All independent Indonesian constitutions have been similar in one respect: their preambles have contained the principles of Indonesia's national ideology, Pancasila ("the five principles"). Put at their most concise, these principles are

1   *Ketuhanan Yang Maha Esa* (Belief in Almighty God);
2   *Kemanusiaan Yang Adil dan Beradab* (A Just and Civilized Humanity);
3   *Persatuan Indonesia* (The Unity of Indonesia);
4   *Demokrasi*; and
5   *Keadilan Sosial* (Social Justice).

Sukarno introduced Pancasila before the BPUPKI in early June 1945. Largely because these five principles are contained in the preamble, many Indonesian legal scholars and successive governments have claimed that the philosophy has more authority than the constitution itself and is the "source of all sources of law." Most Indonesian jurists consider Pancasila unalterable by way of contemporary legal process (though this is undoubtedly false, as a matter of law. There seems nothing to prevent the DPR, following Article 37 of the constitution, from changing or even removing the preamble). A majority of the Constitutional Court recently confirmed Pancasila's legal pre-eminence as Indonesia's basis of state.[11]

However, Pancasila is a particularly vague ideology that has been very politically malleable. After all, it has appeared as the preamble to very different constitutions, including the more liberal-democratic 1949 and 1950 constitutions and the 1945 Constitution, under which authoritarianism thrived. This vagueness and flexibility arguably makes Pancasila an unsuitable basis for the legal system, at least if legal certainty and consistency are aspired to. Much will depend on the way the Constitutional Court interprets it (Butt 2007). The court appears to have only just begun considering Pancasila in its decision making[12] and has not yet developed sophisticated jurisprudence to explain precisely what its principles mean or require in practical terms.

The Constitutional Court

For the purposes of this chapter, perhaps the most important of the post-Soeharto constitutional reforms was the establishment of the Constitutional Court, the primary task of which is to ensure that the government complies with the constitution, including the human rights adopted in the Second Amendment.[13] This court is the first institution with power to perform constitutional review, and its establishment is the culmination of many long debates and much advocacy.[14]

Whether Indonesia should adopt constitutional review was discussed in the BPUPKI in the lead-up to the declaration of Indonesia's independence on August 17, 1945 (Yamin 1971: 410) and again in the mid- to late 1950s in the Konstituante (Nasution 1992). The ideas had also been discussed during parliamentary debates for a new judiciary law, which was enacted in 1970 (Lev 1978: 57). Each time, proponents of constitutional review were unsuccessful. (It should be noted, however, that some scholars have argued that whether Indonesia should adopt constitutional review was never decided, because supervening events ended these debates before they were fully concluded (Asshiddiqqie 2008: 3)).

Even though constitutional review failed to gain sufficient traction in these debates during the Soeharto regime, the ideal lived on among prominent lawyers, who occasionally publicly proclaimed the virtues of such a system (Lev 1987). This was often met with threats and physical violence from the military, which, reflecting the views of the New Order regime, considered these ideas, at best, as impediments to the main purposes of the state (economic development, which required political stability) and, at worst, as subversion, punishable by imprisonment or death.

The nine-member Constitutional Court struggled through humble beginnings. According to founding chief justice Jimly Asshiddiqqie (2008: 10), the court *mulai dari nol* ("started from scratch"), with little more than the constitution and a copy of the 2003 Constitutional Court Law in hand to support it and almost no budget (Purwadi 2006: 168–69). Indeed, it initially had no permanent offices, locating itself first in the Supreme Court building, before shifting to a Jakarta hotel (Asshiddiqqie 2004: 14). The court was even forced to hold some of its earlier court sessions in the national parliamentary building and even for a time in national police headquarters (Asshiddiqqie 2008: 109). In mid-2005, work began on a grand new Constitutional Court complex in central Jakarta, close to the Presidential Palace, the Supreme Court, and government ministries. Two years later, the court moved into this building and has occupied it since.

The Constitutional Court and constitutionalism

The extent to which the Constitutional Court has contributed to constitutionalism in Indonesia is debated among scholars and practitioners. On the one hand, the court is constrained by its formal jurisdiction, which is outlined in the constitution. It can review only national statutes for compliance with the constitution. This is far from "complete" jurisdiction, because the bulk of Indonesian law is contained in lower-level instruments, such regulations issued by the government, president, and ministers and subnational bylaws. These are simply beyond the purview of the court, which has rejected applications seeking review of them. The court also cannot review the constitutionality of government action and policy, as can constitutional courts in some other countries. The institutional design of the court is weak in another important sense: the court has no formal power to compel the government, or anyone else, to comply with its decisions. There is no concept of contempt of court to punish non-compliance. The court can do very little except issue press releases if, for example, government agencies or even courts continue to apply a statutory provision that the court has formally invalidated, or if they circumvent the court's decision by issuing a type of law that the court cannot formally review, such as a government regulation (Butt and Lindsey 2008).

Partly in anticipation of non-compliance, the court has, almost since its establishment, issued decisions in which it declares statutory provisions to be "conditionally" constitutional or unconstitutional (Butt 2012). In such decisions, the court finds some constitutional defect in the statute under review, but instead of simply invalidating the problematic provisions, the court requires them to be interpreted in a particular way that is constitutional. As I have argued elsewhere, this seems to be tantamount to judicial lawmaking, because the court is often very specific about how the statutory provision should be read in order to maintain constitutionality (Butt 2013).

Perhaps the best example of this is a decision, issued in 2010, in which the court was asked to review Article 43(1) of Indonesia's Marriage Law,[15] which provided that children born out of a valid marriage *only* have a civil relationship with their mothers.[16] One implication of this was that these children could claim neither maintenance nor an inheritance from their biological fathers unless their fathers voluntarily recognized them as part of a formal legal process. The court decided, however, that Article 43(1) was unconstitutional unless interpreted to *add* that such children had a civil relationship with their biological fathers. The effect of the decision was really to change the text of Article 43(1) from "A child born out of marriage has a civil legal relationship with its mother and her family." As the court itself put it,

> A child born out of marriage has a civil legal relationship with its mother and her family, and its father and his family [provided that paternity] can be proven by science and technology and/or another form of legally-recognized evidence that the father has a blood relationship with the child.[17]

Putting aside the obvious desirability of this decision, the court has made a rather radical change to the rights of children born out of wedlock and the obligations of their biological fathers. This is, in my view, a clear exercise of legislative power, because the court has really amended a statute, by purporting to control its interpretation. Yet, the court maintains that it is a "negative" legislator, rather than a "positive" one.[18] The court has sought to justify these decisions by pointing out that Indonesia's national legislature is unresponsive and slow and so simply invalidating statutory provisions is likely to leave long-lasting legal lacunae. While this is undoubtedly a valid concern, "conditional" decisions are highly problematic from a constitutionalism perspective, because the constitution (and the court's founding statute) only permit the court to invalidate legislation it considers to be unconstitutional. The document provides no clear scope for "conditional" decisions. It is, therefore, arguable that these decisions are, themselves, unconstitutional.

Nevertheless, the court attracted mostly positive assessments for its performance during its first decade or so, having invalidated many statutory provisions and even entire statutes for violating constitutional principles. Under the leadership of its founding chief justice, Professor Jimly Asshiddiqqie (2003–2008), the court built a reputation for issuing relatively well-reasoned decisions and for high levels of independence – both as between the presiding judges, as evidenced by the relatively high rates of dissenting judgments and "outside" political interests. The second chief justice, Professor Mahfud, MD (2008–2013), was able to maintain the integrity of

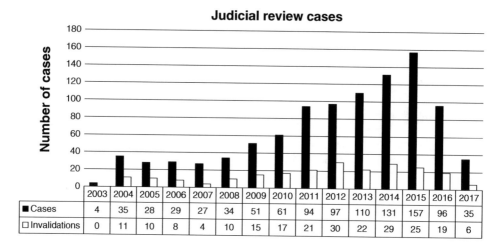

Judicial review cases

	2003	2004	2005	2006	2007	2008	2009	2010	2011	2012	2013	2014	2015	2016	2017
■ Cases	4	35	28	29	27	34	51	61	94	97	110	131	157	96	35
□ Invalidations	0	11	10	8	4	10	15	17	21	30	22	29	25	19	6

Figure 4.1 Judicial Review Cases, 2003–2017

Source: Constitutional Court website: www.mahkamahkonstitusi.go.id/index.php?page=web.RekapPUU

the court, while increasing the impact of the court's decisions, particularly through the issuance of more norm-creating "conditional" decisions.

However, the integrity of the court and the quality of its decision making appears to have declined in more recent years. In 2013, the court's third chief justice, Akil Mochtar, was caught red-handed taking a bribe to fix electoral disputes, for which he was convicted and imprisoned for life in 2014. In 2017, another Constitutional Court judge, Patrialis Akbar, was being pros-ecuted, this time for receiving money to influence a constitutional review case. One also gets the impression that the reasoning of the court has, in some cases at least, become less convincing since the Mahfud era. Nevertheless, this does not appear to have discouraged litigants from using the court, the case load of which remains high, as appears in Figure 4.1.

In total, as of March 1, 2017, the court has decided 938 constitutional review cases and invali-dated legislation in 212 of them.

Conclusions: the future

Many have called for further amendments to the 1945 Constitution, and the idea has enjoyed some political support. However, there does not seem to be a consensus about what needs changing, and most politicians seem wary about the idea. In particular, concern exists that any amendment processes might open a Pandora's box of possibilities, including a greater role for Islam and Islamic law, the removal of institutions established by the constitution, or the under-mining of democratic practices. More prominent have been calls for a return to the "original" 1945 Constitution – that is, the version of the constitution declared on August 18, 1945, and employed from 1966 to 1999. This was, for example, one of the planks of the presidential elec-tion campaign of former Special Forces Commander Prabowo Subianto (Mietzner and Aspinall 2014). However, this, too, is unlikely and would require the DPR and DPD – who, together, constitute the MPR – to agree to reinstate the original version, which would involve them los-ing significant political power to the president. Indeed, the DPD, which was established during the post-Soeharto era, might even cease to exist as a constitutional entity altogether.

The Constitutional Court seems likely to remain the key to Indonesian constitutionalism for the foreseeable future. However, the court's lack of effective enforcement powers makes it vulnerable. If the court's judges and judgments are not seen to be credible, then the government will find it easy to ignore unfavorable court decisions. Much depends on whether, in the aftermath of corruption scandals and widespread critiques of its decision making, it can restore public trust. To do so, the court will need to avoid further impropriety and to establish very strong traditions of judicial reasoning and quality. This will strengthen it as an institution, reducing its reliance on the personalities of its chief justices, which helped build its initial success. Failure to reach these achievements will put Indonesian constitutionalism in jeopardy.

Notes

1 Before submitting the final version of the constitution, the PPKI decided to remove the obligation placed on Muslims – to follow Islamic law – that had been included in an earlier draft. On this, and its implications, see (Lindsey 2012).
2 See the following discussion on the key provisions of the 1945 Constitution and their amendment in 1999–2002.
3 My translation. Original text obtained from (Ranadireksa 2007: iv).
4 See, for example, Articles 7–32, 156–7 of the 1949 Constitution of the Federal Republic of Indonesia.
5 The decree, which was enacted on January 31, 1950, purported to operate retrospectively – that is, it declared that the constitution had been in force since the restoration of Indonesian sovereignty on December 27, 1949 (Saragih 2006: 27). This was confirmed in Article 197 of the constitution itself, which declared itself to have come into force on the same date.
6 MPR Decree No. XX/MPRS/1966 concerning a memorandum to the DPR-GR on the Sources of Law of the Republic of Indonesia and the Hierarchy of Laws in Indonesia.
7 Part 2, MPR Decree.
8 This law was enacted by the national parliament pursuant to MPR Decree No. V/MPR/1983. Of course, Soeharto largely controlled the composition of the DPR, which generally ensured he could control its decision making.
9 This MPR decree was invalidated by MPR No. VIII/MPR/1998, thereby clearing any legal impediments to constitutional amendments in 1999–2002.
10 As is well known, Soeharto controlled the MPR and could, therefore, guarantee his reappointment every five years.
11 Constitutional Court Decision 100/PUU-XI/2013.
12 See, for example, Constitutional Court Decisions 85/PUU-XI/2013 and 3/PUU-XII/2014.
13 According to Articles 24C(1) and 24C(2) of the 1945 Constitution and Article 10 of Law 24 of 2003 on the Constitutional Court, it also has jurisdiction to resolve disputes about the relative jurisdiction of state institutions, the dissolution of political parties, and general election results. It must also "provide a decision" if the DPR suspects that the president or vice president has committed treason or corruption, another serious crime or form of misconduct, or otherwise no longer fulfills the constitutional requirements to hold office.
14 It is not Indonesia's first institution with any powers of judicial review, however. The Supreme Court has, for several decades, been able to review executive regulations and local laws to ensure that they comply with statutes but is unable to review these "lower-level" laws, or statutes, against the Constitution (Hoesein 2009; Lev 1978). However, until relatively recently, the Supreme Court has not actively performed this role with much enthusiasm (Butt and Parsons 2014).
15 Law No. 1 of 1974 on Marriage.
16 Constitutional Court Decision 46/PUU-VIII/2010.
17 Constitutional Court Decision 46/PUU-VIII/2010 para [3.13].
18 For discussion of this concept, see Brewer-Carias 2013.

References cited

Assaat. 1951. *Hukum Tatanegara Republik Indonesia Dalam Masa Peralihan* (Djakarta: Bulan–Bintang).
Asshiddiqqie, Jimly. 2004. "Setahun Mahkamah Konstitusi: Refleksi Gagasan Dan Penyelenggaraan, Serta Setangkup Harapan," in Refly Harun, Zainal A. M. Husein, and Bisariyadi, eds., *Menjaga Denyut Konstitusi: Reflexi satu tahun Mahkamah Konstitusi* (Jakarta: Konstitusi Press).

———. 2008. *Menuju Negara Hukum Yang Demokratis* (Jakarta: Sekretariat Jenderal dan Kepaniteraan Mahkamah Konsititusi).

Brewer-Carias, Allan R. 2013. *Constitutional Courts as Positive Legislators: A Comparative Law Study* (Cambridge, UK: Cambridge University Press).

Butt, Simon. 2007. "Judicial Review in Indonesia: Between Civil Law and Accountability? A Study of Constitutional Court Decisions 2003–2005" (Ph.D. Thesis. Melbourne: Law Faculty, Melbourne University).

———. 2010. "Regional Autonomy and the Proliferation of Perda in Indonesia: An Assessment of Bureaucratic and Judicial Review Mechanisms," *Sydney Law Review* 32(2): 177–91.

———. 2012. "Indonesia's Constitutional Court – The Conservative Activist or Pragmatic Strategist?" in Bjorn Dressel, ed., *The Judicialization of Politics in Asia* (London: Routledge).

———. 2013. "Jurisdictional Expansion, Self-Limitation and Legal Reasoning in the Indonesian Constitutional Court," in D.U.C. Rachmawati and I. Hasan, eds., *Masa Depan Mahkamah Konstitusi* (Jakarta: Setara Institute).

———. 2015. *The Constitutional Court and Democracy in Indonesia* (Holland: Brill).

———. 2016. "Between Control and Appeasement: Religion in Five Constitutional Court Decisions," in Tim Lindsey and Helen Pausacker, eds., *Religion, Law and Intolerance in Indonesia* (London: Routledge), pp. 42–67.

Butt, Simon and Tim Lindsey. 2008. "Economic Reform When the Constitution Matters: Indonesia's Constitutional Court and Article 33," *Bulletin of Indonesian Economic Studies* 44(2): 239–62.

———. 2012. *The Indonesian Constitution: A Contextual Analysis* (Oxford: Hart).

Butt, Simon and Nicholas Parsons. 2014. "Judicial Review and the Supreme Court in Indonesia: A New Space for Law?" *Indonesia* 97(1): 55–85.

Harahap, Krisna. 2009. *Konstitusi Republik Indonesia Menuju Perubahan Ke-5* (Jakarta: Grafitri Budi Utami).

Hoesein, Zainal. 2009. *Judicial Review Di Mahkamah Agung RI: Tiga Dekade Pengujian Peraturan Perundang-Undangan* (Jakarta: RajaGrafindo Persada).

Horowitz, Donald L. 2013. *Constitutional Change and Democracy in Indonesia* (New York: Cambridge University Press).

Huda, Ni'matul. 2008. *UUD 1945 Dan Gagasan Amandemen Ulang* (Jakarta: Rajawali Pers).

Hukumonline. 2016. "Memori Tentang Dekrit Presiden 5 Juli 1959." 4 July. www.hukumonline.com/berita/baca/lt5779f4ef1baf4/memori-tentang-dekrit-presiden-5-juli-1959 (Accessed 21 March 2017).

Indrayana, Denny. 2008. *Indonesian Constitutional Reform 1999–2002: An Evaluation of Constitution-Making in Transition* (Penerbit Buku Kompas).

Kahin, George. 1952. *Nationalism and Revolution in Indonesia* (Ithaca: Cornell University Press).

Kusnardi, Moh and Harmaily Ibrahim. 1988. *Pengantar hukum tata negara Indonesia* (Jakarta: Budi Chaniago).

Lev, Daniel S. 1978. "Judicial Authority and the Struggle for an Indonesian Rechtsstaat," *Law and Society Review* 13: 37–71.

———. 1987. *Legal Aid in Indonesia* (Clayton, Victoria: Centre of Southeast Asian Studies, Monash University).

———. 1999. "Between State and Society: Professional Lawyers and Reform in Indonesia," in Tim Lindsey, ed., *Indonesia: Law and Society* (NSW: Annandale: Federation Press), pp. 227–46.

Lindsey, Tim. 2002. "Indonesian Constitutional Reform: Muddling Towards Democracy," *Singapore Journal of International and Comparative Law* 6(1): 244–301.

———. 2012. *Islam, Law and the State in Indonesia* (London: IB Taurus).

Lubis, T. 1993. *In Search of Human Rights: Legal-Political Dilemmas of Indonesia's New Order, 1966–1990* (Jakarta: Gramedia Pustaka Utama).

Manan, Bagir and Mohammad Fadli (eds.). 2012. *Membedah UUD 1945* (Malang: UB Press).

Mietzner, Marcus and Edward Aspinall. 2014. "Prabowo Subianto Wants Indonesians to Vote for Him, but Just the Once," *Sydney Morning Herald*, 8 July. www.smh.com.au/comment/prabowo-subianto-wants-indonesians-to-vote-for-him-but-just-the-once-20140707-zsymh.html (Accessed 21 March 2017).

Nasution, Adnan Buyung. 1992. *The Aspiration for Constitutional Government in Indonesia: A Socio-Legal Study of the Indonesian Konstituante, 1956–1959* (1st. ed. Jakarta: Pustaka Sinar Harapan).

Purwadi. 2006. *Pendekar Konstitusi Jimly Asshiddiqie: Satria Bijak Bestari dari Bumi Sriwijaya* (Jakarta: Hanan Pustaka).

Ranadireksa, Hendarmin. 2007. *Dinamika Konstitusi Indonesia: Ada Apa Dengan UUD 1945 (Original), Maklumat No. X, UUDs RIS, UUDs 1950, UUD 1945 Pasca Dekrit 5 Juli 1959, UUD 1945 Di Era Orde Baru, UUD 1945 Amandemen I S/D IV?* (Bandung: Fokusmedia).

Ricklefs, M. C. 2008. *A History of Modern Indonesia Since c. 1200* (Stanford: Stanford University Press).

Saragih, Bintan R. (Bintan Regen). 2006. *Perubahan, Penggantian dan Penetapan Undang-Undang Dasar di Indonesia* (Bandung: Utomo).

Suny, Ismail. 1977. *Pergeseran Kekuasaan Eksekutif: Suatu Penyelidikan dalam Hukum Tatanegara* (Jakarta: Aksara Baru).

Supomo. 1950. *Undang-undang Dasar Sementara Republik Indonesia* (Djakarta: Noordhoff-Kolff).

Yamin, H.Muhammad. 1971. *Naskah Persiapan UndangUndang Dasar 1945, Vol 1* (Jakarta: Jajasan Prapantja).

5

MOVING TOWARD STABILITY

Development of the Indonesian education system

Christopher Bjork and Raihani

Education systems are shaped to fit the contours of a nation's political system, culture, and history. This is true of any location. But in Indonesia, these connections are particularly complex and revealing. The goals of the contemporary system, function of schools within society, roles ascribed to teachers, and the government's approach to education development are all rooted in the past. At each stage of the evolution of the Indonesian education system, government leaders treated the schools as an essential tool for uniting the nation in support of national integration and development. Indonesia's long history of colonial rule complicated that process. As the national leadership changed, schools were required to adjust to shifting expectations about what type of citizens would best serve the country. At many points, it was difficult to judge whether the schools were organized to serve politicians or students (Bjork 2003).

Indonesia's remarkable diversity added another layer of complexity to the process of educating the nation's youth. Supporting the motto of *Bhinneka Tunggal Ika* (Unity in Diversity) has created great opportunities – as well as challenges – for education planners. Indonesia is composed of 257 million citizens spread across more than 17,000 islands. Although most citizens speak Bahasa Indonesia, approximately 700 regional languages have been documented (Riza 2008). Indonesian schools, public as well as private, are also responsible for teaching religion. And children, of course, come to school with a wide range of social and cognitive needs.

All of these factors have complicated the work of the educators, administrators, civil servants, and politicians charged with overseeing Indonesian schools. The education system has advanced in a series of fits and starts. The first national education system was not established until 1945 but has already experienced a number of major shifts impelled by leaders with competing visions about how schools should be organized. As the succeeding sections of this chapter will illustrate, the Indonesian education system has demonstrated great resilience in the face of some formidable assaults and is moving closer toward stability and quality.

Early foundations

As was the case in many Asian nations, religious teaching represented the first educational options offered to children living in the islands that eventually became Indonesia. Beginning in the fifth century, Buddhist and Hindu scholars regularly visited the archipelago en route to India, a popular site for pilgrimages. Although no formal schools existed at that time, the visiting scholars provided local citizens with instruction in theology, literature, language, and science (Ricklefs 1981). As a result, the islands developed a reputation as centers of religious study (Djojonegoro 1997). This notion of education grounded in religion continued after the decline of the Hindu-Buddhist period.

Islam first established a foothold in the area in the thirteenth century, when an influx of foreign merchants disseminated their religious beliefs as they traded their wares throughout the region. By the end of the sixteenth century, Islam had become the dominant religion in the archipelago. Indonesia's first system of mass education, the *pesantren*, centered on teaching the language, texts, and doctrine of Islam (Peacock 1973). Life in the pesantren, which were located primarily in rural areas, was an all-encompassing experience: pupils boarded at the institutions and spent a portion of each day laboring in the fields, in addition to studying sacred texts. Students in these institutions included future religious leaders, court poets, and members of the ruling class (Lukens-Bull 2001). The madrasah (Islamic day schools) were also established to cater to the educational needs of Muslim children (Steenbrink 1994).

Another form of religious education was imported to the islands when Portuguese spice traders gained control of the Maluku Islands during the sixteenth century. Roman Catholic priests often followed those traders and established seminaries to serve their children. Hoping to create strong support for their religion in Southeast Asia, the priests inculcated local residents in Catholicism, as well as reading, writing, and mathematics. Although the influence of the Catholic missionaries was limited to a small section of the archipelago, it had an impact that continues to be felt in those areas today.

The educational landscape in Indonesia changed markedly when the Dutch first appeared on the scene at the end of the sixteenth century. Initially, the Dutch made no provisions for the education of Indonesian children. Although small numbers of youth continued to study in pesantren and in schools run by religious missionaries, most Indonesians lacked access to education. Under the Dutch, two social classes developed: peasants, laborers, and servants constituted the lower class; the upper class, or priyayi, was composed of white-collar workers and Indonesian civil servants working in support of the colonial administration (Koentjaraningrat 1975). Ethnic Chinese people living in Indonesia were considered aliens and were not included in either group. Separate school systems served the three different groups (Europeans, Indonesians, and ethnic Chinese). A small number of children of the priyayi were permitted to attend primary schools that served Dutch families, beginning in 1816 (Peacock 1973). In 1848, a second type of elementary school was founded to train the children of pribumi (native Indonesians) to work as clerks in the colonial administration. In addition, in 1851, a group of institutions that aimed to prepare native Indonesians to perform undersupplied technical jobs (such as vaccinator or agricultural development agent) opened their doors. For most families, though, education was regarded as an unattainable luxury.

King's Decree Number 44, enacted in 1893, generated hope that the quantity and quality of education offered to native citizens would improve. This regulation specified two types of schools that would henceforth serve Indonesian children: first-class primary schools (Eerste Klasse) for the children of aristocrats and second-class schools (Tweede Klasse) for the general population (Djojonegoro 1997). In 1907, a third type of school was founded: the Volksschool, or village school, was created as an inexpensive Western-style elementary school for the general population. Unfortunately, all three types of school created in response to King's Decree No. 44 suffered from a lack of funds and qualified teachers. The quality of instruction was of low caliber and dependent on additional financial support from the local communities (van der Veur 1969). The combination of inferior instruction and financial demands placed on parents kept most families from sending their children to school.

The number of schools serving pribumi children did increase under Dutch colonial rule, but investments in education for native children paled in comparison with the resources the Dutch allocated to their own children's schooling. In general, Dutch education for non-Europeans was considered *uitzondering* (the exception) and was organized to train Dutch-speaking workers. Applicants were classified according to parental income, and only the most elite were offered slots. In 1900, for example, the number of Indonesian students enrolled in Dutch elementary schools totaled 1,870, compared with approximately 100,000 in the vernacular schools (van der Veur 1969). At the end of the nineteenth century, school for European children was virtually universal, whereas less than 10% of Pribumi children completed a three-year primary education.

During World War II, the form and focus of education in Indonesia was dictated by yet another foreign power. When the Japanese replaced the Dutch as Indonesia's rulers in 1942, they orchestrated a complete overhaul of the education system. The various systems that had operated under the Dutch were consolidated into a single operation modeled after the Japanese education system. Schools were organized to support the Japanese war effort and the goal of creating a "Greater East Asia Co-Prosperity Sphere." During that period, lessons consisted primarily of physical drills, military training, and indoctrination into Japanese culture. Under Japanese rule, the quality and quantity of instruction declined significantly. Between 1940 and 1945, the primary school population shrank by 30%, and the number of secondary students plummeted by almost 90% (Djojonegoro 1997).

During both the Dutch and Japanese administrations, schooling was organized to support the needs of the occupying powers, not to promote the intellectual development of local children. Religious institutions provided an exception to that pattern, but most schools focused on religious lessons and moral education. Furthermore, the religious schools operated largely in isolation; they did not represent a unified alternative to colonial education. As a result of these factors, when Indonesia gained independence in 1945, the education system that survived was fragmented and unfocused. It also lacked a stable force of experienced teachers.

Creating a national education system

At the conclusion of World War II, Indonesians finally gained the power to form a school system that embodied their own values and aspirations. This presented leaders of the new government with unprecedented opportunities to reshape the education system and increase access to the schools. The first president, Sukarno, and his cadre of assistants regarded education as a key mechanism for breaking down social class barriers and reducing disparities between the rich and poor. In December of 1945, a committee of government officials drafted a plan that outlined the direction of Indonesia's first national education system. The central tenets of that document signaled a rejection of the European system it replaced. Architects of the public school system sought to create institutions that were anti-elitist, anti-discriminatory, and anti-capitalist. Eager to redress the neglect of education of indigenous children under the Dutch and Japanese, Indonesia's first national government made a concerted effort to eliminate the obstacles that previously prevented Indonesian children from enrolling in school. Determined to compensate for the lack of opportunities offered by their former rulers, officials declared that all citizens motivated to study would have access to schooling.

Plans for the new education system did not refer to pesantran or madrasah. In response to protests held by Muslims in 1946, Sukarno's government established a Ministry of Religion (MOR) to manage Islamic affairs, such as marriage, court cases, mosques, and pilgrimages. The MOR was also given responsibility for overseeing all pesantren and madrasah (Mujiburrahman 2006). Although the establishment of the MOR was seen as an accommodation of Muslim interests, the government did not formally consider Islamic education a part of the national education. This dichotomy remained a contentious issue in the country's educational policies and debates.

The freedom to create a new education system virtually from scratch proved to be both liberating and overwhelming. Education planners tried to provide direction to the swarms of newly appointed bureaucrats while they too were navigating unfamiliar pathways. After decades of schooling only for the elite, education was provided to many children whose parents did not enjoy special connections or status. Under Sukarno's leadership, the government made great strides in its goal of providing primary schooling to all Indonesian children. The first public school system was composed of primary schools, lower and upper secondary schools, technical schools, and a number of tertiary institutions. Technical schools, open to primary school graduates, included crafts schools, three types of general technical education institutes, and teacher training schools. Between 1945 and 1950, the number of students attending primary and secondary schools more than doubled, with primary schools experiencing the most dramatic increases.

This influx of new bodies into the schools created strains on a system operating on a shaky foundation. After years of educational neglect, the government was forced to play a serious game of "catch up." Although the government acquired many of the buildings that formerly housed schools operated by the Dutch, the instructional materials left behind by the Europeans were virtually useless to Indonesian educators. Few individuals had any experience managing schools, and only a small number of qualified teachers were available to staff the new institutions. In 1951, it was estimated that 140,000 people would have to be trained as teachers to meet the demand for schooling that was unleashed following independence. In addition, 50,000 active teachers would need to undergo extensive retraining to prepare them to fit into the new system. To overcome this shortage, 500 emergency teacher-training programs were established throughout the country (Djojonegoro 1997).

As he attempted to steer the nation toward stability, President Sukarno was forced to contend with a series of conflicts that divided the population and threatened his own authority. Given their first taste of freedom, Indonesians at all levels of society jockeyed for power and influence. The Sukarno years were plagued by ethnic conflict and outbreaks of regionalism. Political instability and increasingly bleak economic conditions bred criticism of the parliament and the president. Disputes between political parties posed an additional challenge to the nascent government. This instability had important implications for the national education system that was being formed. The effects were most directly felt in two areas: the authority structure used to manage the system and the curriculum. Like all branches of government, the Ministry of Education and Culture (MOEC) was organized vertically, with ultimate authority ensconced at the top of the hierarchy. Education officials in Jakarta were entrusted to make the key decisions that guided the development of schools from Aceh to Kalimantan. They established the objectives that all schools in the country would follow, designed a national curriculum, and oversaw the training of educators. The input of classroom teachers was not solicited. In almost all matters of importance, education decisions were made in Jakarta and transmitted to local levels.

Another manifestation of the political turmoil plaguing Indonesia was the strong connections drawn between education and nation building. Treating the school system as an important vehicle for integrating a nation noted for its ethnic, cultural, linguistic, and economic diversity, government leaders mandated that Bahasa Indonesia be used as the language of instruction in all public schools. Schools were charged with not only inculcating academic skills but also with molding upright citizens.

The massive, unwieldy growth of the education system under President Sukarno paralleled conditions in most sectors of government. Sukarno was more adept at delivering inspiring speeches than at managing government employees. During his tenure, inflation rose at a dangerous rate and unemployment skyrocketed. The president's strategy for reducing unemployment and widening his base of support was to expand the bureaucracy. By 1965, there was a "widespread feeling in Indonesia that the political system could not last as it was for very much longer" (Crouch 1978: 21). When Sukarno was forced out of power in September of that year, the nation was in a state of economic, political, and social chaos.

Charting a new course

The New Order government that replaced Sukarno's Guided Democracy in 1966 was intent on creating stability and uniting a fragmented populace. Soeharto, the new president, quickly mounted a campaign to bolster the authority of the state. Public employees were required to pledge "monoloyalty" to the state and to abstain from joining political organizations. Individuals who refused to acquiesce to such pressure were penalized heavily (Mackie and MacIntyre 1994). One consequence of that overhaul of the government was that civil servants – including teachers – became "transmitters" of directives from their superiors, rather than representatives of communities (Emmerson 1978).

The Soeharto administration set out to create a modern national culture with which all Indonesians could identify. The schools played an essential role in achieving that goal. Kipp observes that during the New Order, the schools became a "powerful means to forge nationalistic loyalties and identities over ethnic, religious, and class divisions" (Kipp 1993: 73). Regarding schools as critical links to national integration, government officials went to great lengths to ensure that members of school communities recognized their identities as Indonesians and respected their obligations to the central government. Behavioral guidelines for teachers and other civil servants became increasingly prescriptive and penalties for non-compliance more severe. Under Soeharto, the government gradually tightened the leash that connected schools to the center. Lacking confidence in the abilities of new teachers, the MOEC attempted to make the schools as "teacher proof" as possible (Shaeffer 1990). New Order leaders framed education as a means of developing a body of citizens who would support the nation, rather than as an opportunity for individuals to acquire skills and knowledge that would reap them rewards.

Convincing citizens with tenuous connections to the central government to conform to New Order plans for change presented a formidable challenge to national leaders. One tool utilized to secure the allegiance of the polity was legislation that aimed to bolster national unity. For example, an Anti-Subversion Law, which carried a maximum penalty of death, made it illegal to commit any acts that "distort, undermine, or deviate from" the principles outlined in Pancasila, the national ideology. The adoption of such policies succeeded in stifling critical voices and encouraging citizens to self-censor their behavior. The government also steadily narrowed the limits of politically acceptable cultural expression in attempt to foster support for the "national culture" it was attempting to develop (Bowen 1994).

Pressure placed on government employees to demonstrate allegiance to the national government further increased in 1971, when Presidential Decision No. 2 established the Corps of Civil Servants of the Indonesian Republic (Korpri) at every level of government (Emmerson 1978). Korpri's guiding objectives stressed discipline, loyalty, and devotion to one's official duties. Even the teachers' union, *Persatuan Guru Republik Indonesia* (PGRI), was utilized to monitor the actions of educators. Formed in 1945, the union was originally created as an umbrella organization to foster teacher unity and professionalism. However, in 1994, the government specified that PGRI was required to "defend and apply Pancasila and the Constitution of 1945 according to the essence of the New Order . . . [and] act as a means of attaining national goals for raising the standard of living" (GOI 1994, chapter IV, section 4). As this language illustrates, under the New Order administration, the PGRI became a mechanism for monitoring teachers rather than a forum through which they could express their opinions and concerns. Teachers may have been expected to act as leaders in the schools, but their autonomy was undercut by rules and regulations designed to minimize the chances that any government employee would undercut national unity.

The heavy emphasis on nation building signaled to teachers that their primary role was to support national goals for the country articulated by leaders in Jakarta. Educators were valued for their ability to loyally follow directives, not their capacity for independent thought. The state stressed teachers' loyalty to the nation above that to their profession. One effect of that emphasis is that teachers did not establish an identity for themselves separate from that applied to all civil servants or a distinct set of professional standards. Following a pattern that Ghazali et al. describe in their study of civil servants, teachers tended to conduct tasks explicitly assigned to them but were careful not to exceed established standards or behave in any way that set them apart from their peers (Ghazali et al. 1986).

The New Order government went to great lengths to ensure that educators supported its plans for social and economic development. The instructor's role as civil servant was emphasized over that of educator, and her opportunities to shape school policy and practice were limited. In co-opting the civil service corps, the government reduced threats to its authority but also undermined the influence of educators. Aware of the potential costs to be paid for displaying resistance to ideas passed down from Jakarta, teachers learned that their wisest course of action was to unquestioningly follow directives from their superiors. Educators came to define their professional responsibilities quite narrowly: to faithfully disseminate a set of ideas formulated in the capital (Bjork 2005, 2013).

Understandably, school employees tended to focus their energies on activities separate from their obligations as government employees. Many had part-time jobs that they took quite seriously. That was partially due to market pressures operating beyond the borders of schools. The income that teachers generated from their extra jobs often depended on the time and effort they invested in that work; government salaries, on the other hand, were primarily based on years of service and levels of education. Family, church, and neighborhood-based activities were also highly valued by government employees. In their neighborhoods and mosques, instructors enjoyed levels of influence that were rarely equaled in the workplace, where they were located toward the bottom of the authority hierarchy. This has had important, though often unrecognized, implications for education reform in Indonesia.

Recent efforts to reform schools

The expansion of the school system that took place during the New Order years was remarkable. As Table 5.1 indicates, the number of students, teachers, and schools all grew dramatically. In addition, education attainment levels and literacy rates steadily increased. Between 1980 and 1990, the literacy rate for citizens aged 15 and older climbed from 67% to 82% and exceeded 90% by 2004 (Unesco Institute for Statistics 2016). However, although the MOEC succeeded in its mission to improve access to the nation's schools, the quality of instruction continued to worry education officials and international consultants. According to a World Bank report, the need to improve the quality of basic education became "a preoccupation for the Government and a central objective of its education policy" (World Bank 1989: i). Recognizing that "teacher quality appears to be the most strategic path to improving primary educational quality" (Suryadi 1992: 81), the MOEC declared its commitment to enhancing the quality of pre-service teacher

Table 5.1 Growth of Total Students and Teachers

	Primary Students	Primary Schools	Primary Teachers
1945	2,523,410	15,069	336,287
1960	8,955,098	37,673	230,838
1975	12,132,667	62,373	1,054,983
1990			
	Lower Secondary Students	Lower Secondary Schools	Lower Secondary Teachers
1945	98,365	322	4,577
1960	670,481	6,312	42,541
1975	1,900,154	7,843	117,584
1990	5,686,118	20,605	409,739

Source: Djojonegoro 1997

education and facilitated a massive re-training of mid-career instructors. The goal of these efforts was to provide teachers with a firmer foundation of subject-based knowledge and to encourage them to shift from transmission-oriented approaches to more student-centered instructional approaches.

Political instability complicated this project. In the late 1990s, after decades of domination by the executive branch, non-governmental organizations, college students, and reformist religious groups pressed for political reform and an end to corruption, collusion, and nepotism (Hefner 2001; Usman 2001). The Asian economic crisis of 1998 heightened that pressure. Widespread civil unrest culminated in the resignation of President Soeharto in May of 1998. This change in leadership sparked hope among Indonesians that an era of increased popular participation, pluralism, and individual freedom was on the way.

In the field of education, the end of the New Order created upheaval but also generated hope that significant changes would be enacted in the schools. After the change in leadership, it appeared that educators would enjoy greater freedom and influence than was true under Soeharto. In 1999, the legislature enacted two laws (Laws 22 and 25 of 1999) that broadened the scope of the government's commitment to decentralization. MOEC officials capitalized on these policies and endorsed a number of initiatives designed to augment the authority of teachers and local education stakeholders. This push for more local control of schools was supported by revisions of the curriculum (such as the addition of local content to the national curriculum), the creation of school committees (which included parent and community representatives), and a general push for more engaging learning activities (Bjork 2013). All of these strategies were employed with the goal of raising standards and levels of achievement in the schools.

Through Law No. 14/2005, the government attempted to improve teachers' qualifications, welfare, and effectiveness (Raihani and Sumintono 2010). This law expanded the prerequisites for teacher certification. It required candidates for certification to provide concrete evidence of their commitment to the profession and to improving their instructional practice. Research that analyzes the effects of the law offers an ambiguous picture. One positive consequence is that teaching has become a more attractive career choice for many citizens, due primarily to substantial increases in the salaries earned by individuals who meet the certification requirements. The impact of Law 14 on teaching quality, on the other hand, has been mixed. Researchers who have studied educators' responses to the legislation indicate that entrenched attitudes and practices are difficult to alter. Abdullah, for instance, documented great variation in the recruitment, pre-service training, and supervision provided to teachers as they worked toward certification (Abdullah 2015).

Another strategy utilized in attempts to raise educational standards was School-Based Management (SBM). After the collapse of the New Order, the government introduced several initiatives that sought to give local citizens greater input into school decision making and, by extension, to raise learning standards (Parker and Raihani 2011). In 2004, a new competency-based curriculum (known as KBK) was piloted in several schools. KBK encouraged teachers to focus on student capacities and to use more active pedagogical approaches as they introduced concepts. Government leaders believed that these changes would augment student achievement and make Indonesia more competitive globally. KBK, later known as KTSP (Kurikulum Tingkat Satuan Pendidikan), became a tool to raise learning standards. The new curriculum also cast teachers as facilitators of student learning, encouraging them to tailor the curriculum to fit the unique interests and capacities of their students (Yamin 2007).

This push for more local autonomy over curriculum and instruction was significant. After decades of tightly controlling all major decisions related to education, the MOEC was delegating unprecedented authority to school employees. Following the new curriculum, however, required educators to change their receptive cultural mind-sets and develop the skills and competencies required to respond to such constructivist teaching requirements. To facilitate this shift in the role of the instructor, two teacher support programs were initiated: KKG (Kerukunan Keluarga Guru), at the primary level, and MGMP (Musyawarah Guru Mata Pelajaran), at the secondary level. Both KKG and MGMP encouraged educators to share their experiences and expertise with one another. These forums provided an ongoing form of professional development for teachers that allowed them to focus on their most immediate concerns.

The government also revised the national examination (*Ujian Nasional*, or UN) in an attempt to ensure that all Indonesian students would meet national competency standards. In the past, the national examination had created extreme anxiety among parents. This sometimes led them to resort to activities such as asking teachers to hold special preparation sessions for the UN, holding communal prayers for entire school communities before test sessions, and, most seriously, attempting to manipulate examination results. Responding to such criticism, the government eliminated the UN as a determinant of high school graduation; instead, UN scores were used only as a source of information for educational improvement.

In 2013, the government introduced yet another new national curriculum, which it labeled Kurikulum 2013 (K13). The MOEC proclaimed its ongoing commitment to producing school graduates who were globally competitive – but also grounded in strong Indonesian values. To support this objective, K13 emphasized students' core competencies, spiritual growth, knowledge, and skills (Machali 2014). Some observers asserted that K13 represented a form of character education, although it was not clear exactly what those values were or how they would be taught. Guidelines for the new curriculum merely stated that teachers should explicitly refer to values or character in their syllabi and lesson plans. Educators were expected to faithfully adhere to the new curricular guidelines, which reduced their autonomy in the classroom. Widespread resistance to K13, however, led the former minister of education, Anies Baswedan, to suspend implementation of K13 until all schools, teachers, and other education stakeholders were fully prepared to enact the curriculum according to plan. In the meantime, he instructed them to revert to the KTSP curriculum.

Response to K13 highlights the challenges that have confronted the MOEC as it attempted to raise learning standards in Indonesian schools. Almost every major education reform policy adopted in the post–New Order years fell short of expectations. Some of the setbacks that occurred were linked to administrative missteps: reform plans were sometimes introduced hastily, before the people and institutions responsible for implementing them fully understood what they were being asked to do. Another obstacle that undermined reform was local resistance (both overt and concealed) to change. The disjointed process of redesigning the curriculum underlined the complexity of altering the attitudes and behaviors of a cadre of teachers who had been socialized to conform to behavioral expectations established over decades. Facilitating changes in classroom interactions proved much more difficult than expanding access to schooling.

One positive outcome of curriculum reform initiatives introduced in the new millennium involved the curricular unification between public schools and madrasah. The Education Law of 2003 facilitated this integration of Islamic and general education. This legislation specified that religious and public institutions should follow the same core curriculum (although madrasah would offer several additional religious subjects). Through this integration, the government aspired to symbolically unite all school graduates as citizens of Indonesia, equally prepared to contribute to national development and unity. Although some managerial and communication problems accompanied this process, unification of the MOEC and MOR promoted equality between the two institutions.

Salient issues and challenges

The shadow of colonialism cast a pall across the Indonesian archipelago for centuries. Dominated by foreign powers with scant interest in enlightening native citizens, Indonesians were forced to make do with limited educational options. Some citizens learned to read and write in local neighborhood schools or pesantren. The most fortunate gained acceptance to Dutch schools and, upon graduation, obtained employment supporting the colonial administration. Under colonial rule, however, the majority of Indonesians did not have access to any formal education. Lacking the skills necessary to improve their income or social status, their futures were often inextricably tied to agriculture.

In the years after independence, the government facilitated a considerable expansion of the school system. A fragmented collection of institutions was consolidated into a unified entity, and new schools were established across the archipelago. The percentage of citizens who attended school and acquired basic numeracy and literacy skills soared. Schools focused on equipping pupils with basic literacy and numeracy skills and on teaching them to act as good citizens.

Once those goals were achieved, the MOEC shifted its focus to more complex challenges. The Indonesian government sought to keep children in school longer and to provide them with a broader, more stimulating form of education. Efforts to alter curriculum and instruction, however, proved more difficult than expanding access to schools. Education officials discovered that modifying behavior was more challenging than constructing new buildings. Though a multitude of circumstances presented challenges to the MOEC as it attempted to raise learning standards, three factors have presented particularly formidable barriers to change.

1) Geography

One factor that has posed ongoing challenges to educational reform in Indonesia is the geographical diversity and the great distances that separate the nation's islands. The MOEC is responsible for overseeing approximately 140,000 primary, 40,000 junior secondary, and 26,000 high schools. Disseminating policy guidelines to schools spread out across more than 17,000 islands (approximately 6,000 of which are inhabited) requires exceptional organization and focus; monitoring the implementation of those initiatives is even more arduous. Traveling from

Jakarta to outer islands can take several days. The distances that separate the MOEC from its sub-national units are more than physical. Ideas are often revised, distorted, or ignored as they are passed from one level or office to the next. As a result, officials stationed in Jakarta often lack a concrete sense of how school employees are responding to policy directives. This loose coupling reduces the stress experienced by education officials – responding to a crisis is not necessary if one is not aware the crisis exists – but can also undermine the process of school reform.

2) *Social diversity*

Although statistics compiled by the MOEC highlight significant reductions in illiteracy and dropout rates over the past 50 years, those figures frequently mask disparities in educational quality between urban, rural, and remote areas. Designing a curriculum that citizens in all corners of the country will find relevant and beneficial to their own needs is no facile task. Indonesia's linguistic, religious, ethnic, and economic diversity complicates this process. Local conceptions about the primary responsibilities of schools may vary significantly from village to village and island to island. Throughout the nation's history, this reality has complicated the challenge of obtaining local buy-in for education policies designed in Jakarta. Critics have highlighted the uneven distribution of resources to schools located in different parts of the country and raised questions about the appropriateness of using a single national examination to measure the performance of all Indonesian students. How was it that children living in remote areas of Papua were assessed using the same standards relied on to evaluate pupils attending schools in Jakarta?

Another factor that has complicated the process of educational reform in Indonesia has been its (in)ability to produce citizens who value and support the nation's multicultural society. The thickening politics of identity – be it religion, ethnicity, or gender – have been overwhelming, partly due to the constellation of global politics and the thrust of transnational ideologies. One example of the charged nature of this topic involved the former governor of Jakarta, Basuki Tjahaya Purnama, who is Christian and ethnically Chinese, was accused of blasphemy after a widely circulated video captured him making a joke about a passage in the Quran that concerns non-Muslims serving as leaders. In the field of education, making the headscarf compulsory for female Muslim students in many schools across the archipelago – and the growing prohibition of this same clothing in Bali – illustrate how education has been vulnerable to these politics. The current education system and its reforms have not shown appropriate responses to this challenge (Raihani 2014).

3) *Culture of teaching*

Indonesian teachers organize their professional lives according to a unique set of assumptions about what an instructor can and should accomplish. When the first national system of education was being established in Indonesia, political leaders focused on creating national cohesion and stability. As a result, teachers came to define their responsibilities quite narrowly: to faithfully disseminate a set of ideas formulated in the capital. Now that the MOEC has shifted its focus to improving the quality of curriculum and instruction, new demands are being placed on educators. After decades of rewarding teachers for dutifully following the orders of their superiors, the ministry is asking them to act autonomously – to shape policy and practice in the schools. This requires a conspicuous shift in the role of the instructor.

As McLaughlin has observed, the effects of any education reform effort will depend on the "incentives, beliefs, and capacity" (McLaughlin 1987: 175) of the individuals entrusted to enact an initiative in the schools. MOEC plans to improve the quality of instruction tend to delegate extensive responsibilities to teachers, who are expected to assume leadership for implementing plans developed in Jakarta. Teachers, however, often lack the capacities to realize those plans. For example, creating a competency-based curriculum that fits the unique needs of students in a particular learning community sounds laudable. But it is also an immense undertaking, likely to prove taxing even to instructors with extensive experience in curriculum design. Few Indonesian instructors have such a background. Historically, they have been rewarded for displaying loyalty rather than initiative or creativity. This mismatch between the objectives of recent education reforms and teacher conceptions of their professional responsibilities frequently impedes efforts to reform the schools.

If teachers are to assume responsibility for improving the quality of curricula and instruction in the schools, they will need to develop the motivation, skills, and sense of collective responsibility required to realize education officials' plans for change. Developing an infrastructure that treats teachers as professionals and gives them the support necessary to act autonomously is an essential antecedent to fundamental reform of the Indonesian education system.

References cited

Abdullah, Umar, 2015. "Learning Through Teacher Professional Training: English Teacher Certification Program in Indonesia" (Ph.D. Thesis. Columbus: The Ohio State University: Graduate Program in Education Teaching and Learning).

Bjork, Christopher. 2003. "Local Responses to Decentralization Policy in Indonesia," *Comparative Education Review* 47(2): 184–216.

———. 2005. *Indonesian Education: Teachers, Schools, and Central Bureaucracy* (New York: Routledge).

———. 2013. "Teacher Training, School Norms and Teacher Effectiveness in Indonesia," in Daniel Suryadarma and Gavin Jones, eds., *Education in Indonesia* (Singapore: Institute of Southeast Asian Studies), pp. 53–67.

Bowen, John. 1994. *Sumatran Politics and Poetics* (New Haven: Yale University Press).

Crouch, Harold. 1978. *The Army and Politics in Indonesia* (Ithaca: Cornell University Press.

Djojonegoro, Wardiman. 1997. *Fifty Years Development of Indonesian Education* (Jakarta: Ministry of Education and Culture).

Emmerson, Donald. 1978. "The Bureaucracy in Political Context: Weakness in Strength," in Karl D. Jackson and Lucian W. Pye, eds.), *Political Power and Communications in Indonesia* (Berkeley: University of California Press), pp. 82–136.

Ghazali, H.A. Syukur, W. Jafidz, and B. Saliwangi. 1986. *Etos Kerja Pegawai Negeri* (Jakarta: Lembaga Ilmu Pengetahuan Indonsia).

Government of Indonesia. 1994. Unduh Keputusan Presiden Nomor 78 Tahun 1994. Jakarta: GOI.

Hefner, Robert W. 2001. "Public Islam and the Problem of Democratization," *Sociology of Religion* 62(4): 491–514.

Kipp, Rita Smith. 1993. *Dissociated Identities: Ethnicity, Religion, and Class in an Indonesian Society* (Ann Arbor: University of Michigan Press).

Koentjaraningrat. 1975. *Introduction to the Peoples and Cultures of Indonesia and Malaysia* (San Francisco: Cummings Publishing Company).

Lukens-Bull, Ronald A. 2001. "Two Sides of the Same Coin: Modernity and Tradition in Islamic Education in Indonesia," *Anthropology and Education Quarterly* 32(3): 350–72.

Machali, Imam. 2014. "Kebijakan Perubahan Kurikulum 2013 Dalam Menyongsong Indonesia Emas Tahun 2045," *Jurnal Pendidikan Islam* 3(1): 71–94.

Mackie, Jamie and Andrew MacIntyre. 1994. "Politics," in Hall Hill, ed., *Indonesia's New Order* (Honolulu: University of Hawaii Press), pp. 1–53.

McLaughlin, Milbrey. 1987. "Learning From Experience: Lessons From Policy Implementation," *Education Evaluation and Policy Analysis* 2: 171–8.

Mujiburrahman. 2006. *Feeling Threatened: Muslim-Christian Relations in Indonesia's New Order* (Amsterdam: Amsterdam University Press/ISIM).

Parker, Lynn and Raihani. 2011. "Democratizing Indonesia Through Education? Community Participation in Islamic School," *Educational Management Administration & Leadership* 39(6): 712–32.

Peacock, James L. 1973. *Indonesia: An Anthropological Perspective* (Pacific Palisades, CA: Goodyear Publishing).

Raihani. 2014. *Creating Multicultural Citizens: A Portrayal of Contemporary Indonesian Education* (New York: Routledge).

Raihani, and Bambang Sumintono, 2010. "Teacher Education in Indonesia: Development and Challenges," in G. Karras and C. C. Wolhuter, eds., *International Handbook of Teacher Education World-Wide: Issues and Challenges* (Athens: Athens–Atrapos Editions), pp. 181–98.

Ricklefs, Merle C. 1981. *A History of Modern Indonesia Since 1300* (Stanford, CA: Stanford University Press).

Riza, Hammam. 2008. "Indigenous Languages of Indonesia: Creating Language Resources for Language Preservation," in *Proceedings of the IJCNLP-08 Workshop on NLP for Less Privileged Languages* (Hyderabad, India), pp. 113–16.

Shaeffer, Sheldon. 1990. *Educational Change in Indonesia: A Case Study of Three Innovations* (Ottowa, Canada: International Development Research Center).

Steenbrink, Karel, 1994. *Pesantren, Madrasah, Sekolah* (Jakarta: Lembaga Penelitian, Pendidikan dan Pengembangan Ekonomi dan Sosial).

Suryadi, Ace, 1992. *Improving the Educational Quality of Primary Schools* (Jakarta: Office of Education and Culture Research and Development).

Unesco, 2016. "Country Study: Indonesia." 6 December 2016. http://en.unesco.org/countries/indonesia.

Usman, Syaikhu, 2001. *Indonesia's Decentralization Policy: Initial Experiences and Emerging Problems* (Jakarta: The SMERU Research Institute).

World Bank. 1989. *Indonesia Basic Education Study* (Jakarta: The World Bank).

van der Veur, Paul W. 1969. *Education and Social Change in Colonial Indonesia* (Athens: Ohio University Center for International Studies).

Yamin, Martinis. 2007. *Profesionalisasi Guru dan Implementasi KTSP* (Jakarta: Gaung Persada Press).

PART II

Democratic politics and plurality

6

DEMOCRATIZATION
Travails and achievements

Edward Aspinall

Indonesia is rightly considered to be one of the great democratization success stories of the last two decades. It is the most populous country to successfully build a new democratic system since the so-called "third wave" of democratization began in Southern Europe in the mid-1970s and now ranks as the world's third largest democracy, after India and the United States. Its democratic progress surpasses that of most of its Asian peers (Aspinall 2015), and within Southeast Asia, it is now the region's democratic giant. Indonesia's democratization is all the more remarkable given that it has occurred as the third wave began to peter out during the early years of the new millennium, giving way to a period of worldwide democratic stagnation, even recession (Diamond 2015).

This success does not mean, however, that Indonesia's democratic achievement has been unqualified. On the contrary, much of the political science literature on Indonesia produced since the collapse of the Soeharto regime in 1998 has focused on identifying shortcomings in the country's nascent democracy. Many such analyses, especially early on, were pessimistic about Indonesia's long-term democratic prospects. As time passed, and immediate threats to the new democratic order receded, some scholars then began to wonder whether Indonesian democracy had become "the only game in town" and could therefore be considered to have become consolidated (Liddle and Mujani 2013). In fact, it has become increasingly obvious that many of Indonesia's democratic deficits were not merely passing phenomena or slowly fading remnants of the old authoritarian past but were instead stable features of the new system (Robison and Hadiz 2004). Accordingly, Indonesia's democratic progress as measured by various global democracy indices, has stagnated (between 2007 and 2017, Indonesia's score in Freedom House's Freedom in the World index, for example, declined slightly from 2.5 to 3.0 (the scores are on a one to seven scale where one is most free). The country is increasingly conforming to, rather than bucking, the international trend of democratic stagnation and even regression.

This chapter reviews Indonesia's democratic progress, two decades after the collapse of the Soeharto regime. It begins by briefly surveying the course of Indonesia's democratization, paying particular attention to two core ingredients of its democratic success: the wide public legitimacy accorded to elections and the strength of its civil society. Attention then focuses on three significant democratic defects: limits on civil liberties, the deep penetration of corruption in state institutions, and the persistence of enclaves of authoritarianism, both in particular state agencies where democratic reform has had limited impact and in various regions of the country where violations of democratic norms are commonplace. The chapter argues that while some of these shortcomings reflect changes in Indonesian society and broad global trends of democratic stagnation, most can be traced to the negotiated, gradual process of regime transition that occurred after the fall of Soeharto in 1998. This process maintained the institutional power and informal influence of key actors and agencies that had been bulwarks of the old Soeharto regime. In conclusion, it is suggested that Indonesia's democratic system has achieved a stable equilibrium, such that dramatic democratic progress is unlikely, although incremental decline or even sudden reversal cannot be ruled out.

Indonesia's democratic achievement

Indonesia's democratic progress was all the more remarkable given that it was so unexpected. The crisis that enveloped the authoritarian Soeharto regime in 1997–98 came suddenly. To be sure, the preceding decade had seen the stirrings of both internal dissent within the regime and political opposition outside it. However, by 1997, Soeharto had reconsolidated his control, sidelining potential critics inside state institutions and forcefully applying repression against opponents outside them. His regime seemed strong, despite its leader's advancing age. Unlike many military-based regimes, there was no long-term plan to "normalize" political conditions and return to democratic rule.

The Asian financial crisis of 1997, which led to a collapse of the rupiah and of virtually the entire Indonesian economy soon thereafter, fundamentally changed the political landscape. During the first months of 1998, public confidence in the government evaporated, and a wave of large student protests spread around the country, testing the resolve of the military. There was also sporadic rioting by urban mobs, culminating in major unrest on the streets of Jakarta (May 12–14, 1998) after troops fired on student protestors at the Trisakti University. Soeharto's position became untenable as students occupied the national parliament, the upper echelons of the political elite began to desert him, and the military wavered, leading to Soeharto's resignation on May 21, 1998.

The crisis had come so quickly that few political forces outside the regime were ready or willing to take over. This oppositional weakness gave Soeharto's successor, B. J. Habibie, breathing space to try to maintain power by conceding to public demands for political change, although he continued to face protests by students and others, as well as growing communal unrest in parts of the country. The seventeen months of his presidency were a dizzying period of reform during which the foundations of the subsequent democratic system were laid. Habibie dismantled major restrictions on freedom of expression, organization, and the media. He allowed free formation of political parties and released most of Indonesia's political prisoners. Habibie also initiated political and fiscal decentralization to Indonesia's districts and allowed an independence referendum to take place in East Timor, leading to the independence of that territory in 2002. Under his presidency, the military also began to withdraw from day-to-day political affairs, realizing its public image had been badly tarred by its support for Soeharto and his regime.

Especially important was Habibie's promise of free elections, which were eventually held in June 1999 and contested by 48 parties. These elections paved the way for the first of several peaceful turnovers in national government, when Habibie was replaced as president by Abdurrahman Wahid, a liberal-minded leader of the Islamic organization, Nahdlatul Ulama, in October 1999, as a result of a vote in the People's Consultative Assembly. Wahid was brought down by in-fighting within his government and was replaced by his deputy, Megawati Sukarnoputri, in July 2001. In turn, in 2004, Susilo Bambang Yudhoyono, a former general and minister, defeated Megawati in the country's first direct presidential election. He held the maximum of two terms and handed power to his directly elected successor, Joko Widodo (Jokowi) in October 2014. In the space of a little over three years, Indonesia had four presidents in quick succession; over the next decade and a half, it had only two, pointing to the stabilization of the new democratic system.

Despite these changes at the top, from the beginning, a degree of continuity in Indonesian national governments was assured by a pattern of broad cross-party power-sharing pursued by all post-Soeharto presidents. All, to varying degrees, formed cabinets based on broad "rainbow coalitions" involving most of the important parties represented in national parliament. From Abdurrahman Wahid's time onward, presidents have also included in their cabinets political actors with roots in the old regime, such as former military generals and leaders of the New Order political party, Golkar, or its successors. On the one hand, this system of broad participation in national government has contributed to the stability of Indonesian democracy, by giving a wide range of important political elites and the constituencies they represent a stake in national government. On the other hand, it has produced a pattern of "cartel" government (Slater 2004) based on the sharing of access to patronage resources among the major players, thus contributing to the pervasive corruption, which we will see continues to be a major feature of the post-Soeharto political order.

Among Indonesia's various democratic achievements, one stands out above all others: the institutionalization of competitive elections as the means to select occupants of political office. The population has embraced electoral politics enthusiastically, and there has also been broad elite buy-in to elections, in part due to the normalization of elections (under highly constrained and undemocratic conditions) during the New Order. From the start, former Golkar politicians, Islamic leaders, and nationalists, as well as former critics of the regime, all believed that they had significant social constituencies that they would be able to mobilize in order to win parliamentary seats. Meanwhile, Indonesia's adoption of a proportional representation rather than winner-takes-all electoral system ensured that parties representing diverse social groups would all be able to gain representation, laying the groundwork for the system of rainbow-coalition governments mentioned earlier.

Indonesian elections are massive affairs. On a five-year cycle, elections are held for legislators at district, provincial, and national assemblies and for district heads, provincial governors, presidents, and their deputies. There are also regular elections for village heads, as well as for neighborhood-level officials who perform important representational and administrative tasks. This means a tremendous number of offices are subject to direct popular choice: in the most recent 2014 legislative election, for example, over 20,000 seats in legislatures around the country were contested by around 200,000 candidates. On the whole, the administration of these elections has been competent, especially at the ballot-booth level, where voting is administered by members of local communities, though vote buying and other forms of clientelism are widespread and malfeasance in counting at higher levels also occurs (Butt 2013). Unlike in some countries, however, electoral violence is relatively rare (Tadjoeddin 2014). Overall, the elective principle is both widely accepted and implemented as a foundation of Indonesian democracy.

Further underpinning Indonesia's democratic success has been the strength of its civil society. It has been observed that Indonesians are unusually likely to join community organizations (Lussier and Fish 2012). Many citizens are active in neighborhood-level government, religious bodies, communal saving groups, and similar bodies, while there is a multiplicity of religious, business, labor, student, professional, cultural, and other social organizations, as well as non-governmental organizations that campaign on issues such as community development, corruption control, and human rights.

The richness of Indonesia's associational life has not been an unalloyed benefit for democratic development. These networks, especially those at the neighborhood level, are prone to capture by elite politicians who use them to distribute patronage at election times. Moreover, Indonesia's civil society involves a fair share of illiberal organizations, such as intolerant Islamist groups or bodies of preman (thugs) who prosper through intimidation and the black economy. Overall, however, Indonesia's civil society provides an important source of Indonesia's democratic resilience, with a rich web of intermediary organizations that represent popular voices in policy making and in decisions on public resource allocation. At various points in Indonesia's recent history, civil society organizations – as well as online networking through social media – have helped to push back against attempts to roll back democratic reforms – such as successful resistance to a law that proposed to end direct elections of local government leaders in 2014. Public protests and other forms of pressure have also helped to shape major policy outcomes in areas ranging from labor law to health-care policy (Aspinall 2013).

Political freedom and civil liberties

It should be obvious from the preceding summary that Indonesia has experienced dramatically expanded political space over the last two decades. Habibie's lifting of restrictions on the media led to a flourishing commercial electronic, online, and print media landscape (Haryanto 2010). The ending of restrictions on organization likewise stimulated dramatic expansion of social organization in areas that had previously been tightly controlled by the government. For example, there was an explosion of labor union organizing in Indonesian factories and other workplaces. Cultural expression has flourished among formerly suppressed or marginal groups – for example, restrictions on ethnic Chinese language and culture were ended, and Confucianism was recognized as an official religion, leading to a cultural and political renaissance in Indonesia's ethnic Chinese communities (Hoon 2008). At the opposite extreme, restrictions on Islamist groups were also loosened, allowing groups that condemned other religions or advocated the adoption of an Islamic state or a universal caliphate to operate more openly.

This opening of space has been accompanied, however, by continuing restrictions on political expression and personal freedom in some areas. Some such restrictions are formal and are legacies of the authoritarian past. Among the most important examples is continuing proscription on advocacy of separatism in peripheral areas of Indonesia like Maluku and Papua. In both places, the authorities have prosecuted, tried, and imprisoned large numbers of non-violent advocates of independence on charges of makar (rebellion; Human Rights Watch 2015). In late 2017, the same charges were brought against several critics of the Joko Widodo government in Jakarta. A proscription on Marxism–Leninism also remains in place from the authoritarian period, and though it is used relatively sparingly by state authorities, it remains symbolically important and is sometimes invoked by Islamist or thug organizations when they burn left-wing books or try to break up meetings of activist groups. This proscription also remains an important obstacle to attempts to investigate the mass killings of leftists that accompanied Soeharto's rise to power in the mid-1960s (see McGregor, this volume).

A new area of restriction on expression in the post-Soeharto era is the online arena. Indonesians, especially those living in big cities, have enthusiastically embraced the Internet and social media, especially since the advent of smartphones. This online participation has dramatically increased the opportunity of ordinary Indonesians to express their political views and cultural identities and to criticize public and private authorities. However, the Indonesian government has responded to this expansion with new limitations, notably passage of the 2008 Law on Information and Electronic Transaction, proscribing online defamation, which has been used to prosecute a range of journalists and ordinary citizens for such acts as criticizing private

businesses on social media or providing evidence of corruption by police or other public officials (Berger 2015: 234).

Other obstacles to civil liberties have, paradoxically, come from the lifting of political restrictions. As noted earlier, a range of illiberal groups populate Indonesia's civil society, some of
which target rival communities. Early in Indonesia's democratization, there was a dramatic spike
in ethnic and inter-religious violence in some parts of the country (Bertrand 2004). Though
mass violence of this sort peaked around 2000–01 and rapidly receded thereafter, pressure against
minority religious groups continues, at least in parts of the country. In particular, there are sporadic public protests and violent attacks against religious minorities, usually members of Islamic
sects, notably Shiites and members of the Ahmadiyah group. Such groups, as well as Christians
and some others, also sometimes face difficulties in erecting houses of worship. In the midst of
what observers have called a post-Soeharto "conservative turn" (van Bruinessen 2013) in Indonesian Islam, local authorities frequently tacitly support such attacks, or at least fail to prevent
them, either fearing the electoral or public order consequences or sympathizing with the views
of the attackers. Various national human rights and pluralism groups try to track the occurrence
of such violations of religious freedom and sometimes release data suggesting an increase (Setara
Institute 2016); in fact, it is difficult to identify long-term trends, though it is certainly clear that
pressures on religious minorities remain a persistent feature of contemporary Indonesian life
(see Bagir chapter, this volume).

Moreover, restrictions on religious expression do not just take the form of pressures by Islamists and vigilantes but are sometimes pursued by state authorities. Indonesia practices a form of
"Godly nationalism" (Menchik 2016) predicated on official recognition and support for the
major monotheistic religions. As a result, authorities, from time to time, prosecute persons on
charges of insulting religion or blasphemy and proscribe so-called "deviant sects" that violate the
religious precepts of the major groups, especially Islam. This form of religious persecution has
been integrated seamlessly into the new Indonesian democracy, as major conservative Islamic
organizations, such as the Indonesian Ulama Council (MUI, Majelis Ulama Indonesia) have
become important pressure groups and as mainstream politicians have striven to accommodate
the interests and attitudes of pious voters. The political benefits of such adaptions to some elite
actors were illustrated by the most controversial, and by far the most politically consequential,
blasphemy trial in recent times: that of the ethnic Chinese and Christian governor of Jakarta,
Basuki Tjahaja Purnama (Ahok). Ahok was charged with insulting Islam in late 2016, in the run
up to his reelection bid, after he criticized those who were invoking the Quran to enjoin Muslims not to support a nonbeliever. The campaign against him dramatically undercut his support
among Muslim voters, advantaging his rivals.

These problems represent real limitations to Indonesian democracy, but they should also
be set against the dramatic overall advancement Indonesia has made in freedom of expression,
association, and assembly since the downfall of Soeharto. The loosening of controls has allowed
often noisy expression of contrary political and social views and interests, such that many in
Indonesia's social and political elite, including some of its presidents, have expressed the view
that democracy has "gone too far" (demokrasi kebablasan; Detiknews 2017).

The quality of democratic institutions

Overt restrictions on political and religious expression are serious problems, but they affect only
aspects of Indonesia's post-Soeharto social and political life and have a direct impact on only a
minority of the country's citizens. A more pervasive, and arguably more fundamental, problem

concerns the quality of democratic institutions, specifically the centrality of informal relationships of power and material exchange in determining how such institutions function in practice, if not in theory.

There are several ways of looking at this problem. Structuralist scholars, such as Robison and Hadiz (2004) and Winters (2011) emphasize the continuing grip on political and economic power exercised by oligarchs – materially endowed actors whose wealth was derived from the fusion of political office and private business during the Soeharto years. During that period, Soeharto and other officials directed contracts, licenses, and other benefits toward favored business actors – often their own relatives. The class of politically connected businesspeople that arose as a result of this process was in most cases able to survive the transition to democracy with their riches intact. Today, many of Indonesia's most prominent politicians are tycoons whose wealth derives from the access they enjoyed to state power under Soeharto. In the regions, leading contestants for elective office are often wealthy state-dependent businesspeople and bureaucrats. Such patterns are not simply a Soeharto-era legacy but point to the continuing centrality of informal relations between political and economic powerholders in the new democratic order: at all levels, public officeholders are enmeshed in symbiotic relationships with private economic actors, trading political favors for material benefits.

Another way of focusing on the same problem is to emphasize the continuing pervasiveness of corruption – the abuse of public office for personal gain – in post-Soeharto state institutions. Civil servants at all levels enrich themselves through multiple techniques, including the levying of informal fees for government services, and straightforward skimming of state budgets, as well as by exchanging contracts, permits and other favors for informal payments from private business actors. According to McLeod (2011), corruption became entrenched when Soeharto converted the bureaucracy into a "franchise system," in which subordinate players were free to use the power of office to extract funds illegally from businesses and the general population, so long as they kept the flow of informal payments moving up through the system. Corruption remains endemic in the state bureaucracy, with numerous analyses detailing phenomenon, such as the manipulation of tendering in the construction sector (Tidey 2013) and the sale of bureaucratic posts and promotions (Kristiansen and Ramli 2006). Indeed, such corrupt behaviors are so widespread that they arguably constitute a central component of the post-Soeharto political order, prompting some observers to point to the interpenetration and interdependence of state and illegality in Indonesia (Aspinall and van Klinken 2011).

Space limitations prevent us from attempting a comprehensive survey of this aspect of post-Soeharto democracy, but let us focus on two institutions that are critical to the functioning of most democratic systems: the legislative and judicial branches of government.

From early in the democratic era, it became obvious that members of Indonesia's legislatures were using their newfound political authority to enrich themselves. They can do so in several ways. For example, they can extract fees – very often straight cash payments – from executive government departments or private business interests in exchange for passing desired laws or even exercising basic legislative tasks. In the regions, for example, legislators often expect payments from the governor or district head in exchange for approving the regional budget. In the national parliament, legislators compete to enter "wet" commissions and legislative bodies, such as those dealing with mining, energy, banking, and budgeting, where they can extract the largest such payments in exchange for passing laws, approving budgets, or cooperating with the executive. Legislators can also intervene directly in the budgeting process in order to direct projects to favored business partners or to insert expenditure items in exchange for fees.

In most, if not all, of Indonesia's legislatures, complex systems of brokerage have grown up around such practices, in which skilled intermediaries negotiate and facilitate payments, often ensuring that all relevant parliamentarians and other actors get a cut and contributing to the broadly inclusive nature of patronage-sharing in Indonesia's system of "promiscuous power sharing" (Slater and Simmons 2013). Such "project brokers" (makelaar proyek) or "budget brokers" (makelaar anggaran) can themselves rise to positions of considerable prominence in Indonesian democracy – for example, the treasurer of President Susilo Bambang Yudhoyono's Democrat Party, Muhammad Nazaruddin, was one such project broker and became a major political player until he was brought down in 2011 by a corruption scandal centering on the construction of an athletes' complex, which ended up claiming the political scalps of several other senior Democrat officials. However, the investigation also revealed that project "fees" had been widely distributed among parliamentarians from several parties. In 2017, the country was rocked by a similar scandal in which it emerged that only 51% of 5.9 trillion rupiah ($440 million) of state funds budgeted for a new electronic ID card program had actually been spent on the project, with the remainder being divided among officials in the Ministry of Interior and national parliamentarians. Little wonder that opinion polls routinely describe the parliament and parties as Indonesia's least trusted institutions.

A similar system of collusion underpins Indonesia's judicial system, which is regularly described as being dominated by a "judicial mafia" (mafia peradilan). Butt and Lindsey (2011) have explained how "case brokers" (makelaar kasus, or makus) facilitate corrupt payments by litigants seeking the resolution of court cases in their favor, with such payments often being shared between judges, prosecutors, police, court officials, lawyers, and other relevant actors. Attempts at promoting judicial reform and integrity have had little impact on this system. For some time, it was believed that Indonesia's new apex judicial body, the Constitutional Court (established in August 2003) was an island of integrity in a generally corrupt system, but this court, too, suffered a major blow to its credibility in 2013 when its chief justice, Akil Mochtar, was arrested and convicted for taking bribes when ruling on disputed local elections. Another constitutional court judge was arrested in 2017 when it was alleged he had accepted bribes from beef importers in relation to a case on the constitutionality of a livestock law.

Leading the key investigations into such corruption scandals has been the country's popular Corruption Eradication Commission (KPK, Komisi Pemberantasan Korupsi). When it began to operate in late 2003, KPK had various institutional features designed to insulate it from corruption and influence-peddling (Schütte 2012), so as to avoid the case brokerage that permeates the rest of law enforcement, and it sent its cases to a specialist corruption court in Jakarta rather than the general court system. Over its first decade, the KPK held a series of highly effective investigations into corruption at senior levels of Indonesian government, arresting and successfully prosecuting a string of officials, including governors, ministers, and senior judges. However, its successes prompted significant resistance from actors within government, the national legislature, and law enforcement agencies, especially the police. A series of high-profile conflicts between the KPK and the police and other elite actors regularly prompted outbursts of public support in favor of the commission but ultimately prompted apparent diminution of the KPK's authority, especially when the commission failed in a high-profile attempt to investigate a senior police officer, Budi Gunawan, in 2015.

It would be easy to make a gloomy account of corruption in all the major state institutions in Indonesia, including the police, civilian bureaucracy, and army. Rather than doing so, let us briefly consider the implications for Indonesian democracy. The preceding analysis suggests that many of the most significant curtailments of Indonesian democracy are informal: rights that citizens are theoretically able to access through the formal operation of the rules and procedures that constitute the state and legal system are often violated in practice. State office holders frequently act as laws unto themselves, evading the chains of accountability that in a democratic system should make state functionaries ultimately subject to citizens. For example, when elected political leaders depend for their campaign financing on donations from business allies, they face strong pressures to reward such supporters with licenses, permits, or other favors rather than to prioritize the public interest when designing or implementing development policy. When court decisions are sold to the highest bidder, ordinary citizens have little chance of enforcing their legal rights even in regular criminal cases, let alone in disputes pitting weak actors, such as poor landholders, against powerful ones, such as plantations or mining companies. To the extent that a functioning rule of law is a prerequisite to a functioning democracy system, that element is all but absent in Indonesia (in 2016, Indonesia ranked 61 out of 113 countries in the World Justice Project's rule of law index [World Justice Project 2016: 21]).

Overall, such phenomena indicate that democratic Indonesia is afflicted by multiple problems of elite capture: state institutions of all sorts typically sacrifice the interests of ordinary citizens, especially poor ones, for the sake of wealthy actors who either directly exercise political and bureaucratic power or who can mobilize the informal networks and material resources to bribe, threaten, or persuade state officials. Such problems not only directly challenge the integrity of Indonesia's democratic order; they also threaten its sustainability by undermining public trust in democratic institutions, a topic we return to in the following.

Authoritarian enclaves

It follows from the preceding analysis that democratization in Indonesia has been experienced unevenly, both in institutional and geographic terms. A few state institutions, such as the KPK or the National Commission of Human Rights, are islands of relative integrity that capture the democratic spirit of the post-Soeharto period. But in large parts of the state bureaucracy, political reform has been layered thinly onto deep structures in which norms, practices, and patterns of thought have changed little since the authoritarian period. Across Indonesia's regions, too, there are great variations in the degree to which citizens can make use of the opportunities afforded by democratization to express themselves politically, demand rights, and hold leaders to account. Indonesia's democratic system is, in short, peppered with authoritarian enclaves, both institutionally and geographically.

In terms of institutional structures, for example, the military is largely unreformed. To be sure, the military no longer plays a central role in government leadership as it did under Soeharto. After the collapse of the Soeharto government, senior officers negotiated their withdrawal from day-to-day political affairs, ending military representation in parliament, ceasing to appoint active officers to most civilian administrative posts, and formally (though in practice only partially) handing responsibility for internal security to the police. But this withdrawal was largely carried out on the military's own terms, with it maintaining considerable autonomy to determine its own doctrine, force deployment, administration, and so on. The Defense Ministry remains essentially a military-controlled agency, and most troops are distributed through the country as part of a "territorial structure" that shadows the civilian administration at every level. This structure provides officers with multiple opportunities for informal political intervention and engagement in economic activities. Anti-corruption investigations in the military have been extremely limited, though corruption in military procurements and management, as well as involvement by officers in the black economy, is endemic. Accordingly, the military and its allies in the bureaucracy have been able to frustrate so-called "second-generation" security sector reforms, which would institutionalize civilian control over the military (Mietzner 2009). Occasional statements by senior generals, most recently Armed Forces Commander (from July 2015) Gatot Nurmantyo, indicate that authoritarian thinking still runs deep in the institution (Forum

Keadilan 2016), and there have been various attempts to reinsert the military into mundane civilian functions, such as fertilizer distribution (see Mietzner chapter in this volume). The military is not poised for a coup, but it has also been only superficially affected by democratic change.

There have been more attempts to reform the police, encouraged in part by the fact that the police have been important beneficiaries of democratization, becoming independent from the military soon after the fall of Soeharto and assuming major responsibility for internal security. Even so, police corruption, involvement in the black economy, extortion of criminal suspects, and brutality all run deep (Baker 2012), and the institution has been able to push back against corruption investigations by the KPK and resist wider attempts at external scrutiny. Similar comments could be made about other components of Indonesia's "deep state," including the intelligence agencies and the Ministry of Internal Affairs.

More broadly still, despite sporadic attempts to promote bureaucratic reform, the entire state bureaucracy in post-Soeharto Indonesia retains significant autonomous political and social weight, rather than being merely a malleable instrument in the hands of elected officials. Ministries can often stonewall or sabotage policies they see as contravening the interest of the bureaucrats, and lobbying and obstruction by civil servants has blunted most attempts to pursue systematic bureaucratic reform. The continuing political influence of the bureaucracy is reflected in the fact that a large proportion of governors, mayors, and district heads in regional Indonesia have backgrounds in the civilian bureaucracy, indicating that the bureaucracy remains a significant source of material wealth and political capital in post-Soeharto Indonesia. Overall, despite the transition to democracy, the state institutions that have long been central to the exercise of political rule (McVey 1982) in Indonesia are not yet fully subordinated to elected politicians.

Regionally, there is also great variation in the depth of democracy across the country. In some locations, notably in urban centers in Java and other densely populated parts of the archipelago, relatively large middle classes, developed and varied economies, dense patterns of associational life, and modern communications facilitate active citizenries. It is noteworthy that many of Indonesia's best known reforming populist political leaders – most famously former Solo mayor and later Indonesian president Joko Widodo – have been products of urban politics, proving themselves as adept media performers, programmatic politicians, and competent administrators in the face of the most politically demanding populations in the country. But in rural and more remote parts of the country, especially where local economies are heavily dependent on state expenditure or on natural resource industries, society is much less assertive. In such places, such as many districts in the interior of Kalimantan, or in large parts of Eastern Indonesia, media are hobbled by their dependence on local governments for advertising revenue, Internet penetration is limited, middle classes are weak or dependent on government employment and resources, local populations have little access to independent sources of information, and civil society organizations are absent or rent-seeking in character. In such locations, powerholders tend to face weak opposition and local governments are often captured by powerful families or other cliques of predatory politicians. In many parts of Indonesia, therefore, the formal rules of democracy are in place, but citizens' capacity to exercise a free choice at elections is in practice severely constrained.

Similar comments could be made about the role of coercion in political life. In some of the more remote provinces, especially where oil palm plantations, mining operations, or other natural resource industries lead to land or labor conflicts with local populations, companies and politicians can mobilize local police, military, and organizations of thugs (preman) to push aside opposition. In such places, preman can also play a role in electoral politics, mixing threats with the usual inducements that are used to mobilize support for incumbent politicians or wealthy challengers (however, it should be stressed that local politics in Indonesia is significantly less violent than in neighboring countries such as Thailand and the Philippines [Buehler 2009]). Special note should be made of Papua and West Papua provinces, where ongoing support for independence has made repression by the security forces a persistent feature of local political life. At the same time, weak state functioning, corruption, and electoral corruption are also especially deeply entrenched in these parts of the country (Anderson 2015; Nolan 2016).

Likewise, citizens' ability to exercise religious freedom varies greatly across the country. There is considerable pressure on members of minority religious groups in regions such as Aceh province and parts of Banten and West Java, where conservative Islamic groups are powerful and where local governments have drafted local regulations that draw inspiration from Islamic legal traditions, or shariah (Buehler 2016). In the anonymity of the big cities, meanwhile, or even in many religiously syncretic rural zones of provinces such as Central Java and Central Kalimantan, there is much greater space for religiously heterodox or irreligious practices.

Conclusion and prospects

Some of these defects of Indonesian democratization reflect slow-moving changes in Indonesian society or echo broad global trends of democratic recession. Instances of violent intolerance of minority religious groups, for example, have a long history in Indonesia, but their prominence in recent times is also linked to the emergence of an increasingly assertive strain of conservative political Islam, a process with roots going back decades. Declining faith in political parties and legislatures, meanwhile, is a trend that has been observed across the democratic world, including in long-established democracies (Foa and Mounk 2016). Likewise, the entrenchment of corruption – and its imperviousness to attempts to root it out through governance reform – is a feature of many recently democratic or semi-democratic regimes (Mungiu-Pippidi 2015).

In terms of recent political history, however, most of Indonesia's democratic weaknesses can be traced to the negotiated form of democratic transition that occurred after 1998, a process that maintained the institutional power of key agencies and actors that had been bulwarks of the old authoritarian regime. As argued elsewhere (Aspinall 2010), conciliating the military and bringing former New Order politicians and oligarchs into post-Soeharto governments helped maintain the stability during the transition, but it also ensured that democratization would be less thorough-going than might otherwise have been the case. The patchiness of Indonesia's democracy is fundamentally a product of this combination: by bringing powerful elite actors into the new democratic order, Indonesia ensured those actors would not destroy that order from the outside; by failing to fundamentally challenge their interests, it ensured they could impede or undermine democracy from within.

Worldwide, it is increasingly obvious that the old teleology of a discrete period or moment of democratization followed by a period of democratic consolidation after which democracy is "out of the danger zone" is no longer tenable, if it ever was. Though Indonesia's democratic achievements have been considerable, their patchiness and the stability and even consolidation of its democratic defects mean that dramatic democratic advancement in the short- to medium- term is unlikely. The current hybrid system represents an equilibrium, even if it is not entirely stable. An optimistic scenario would see elections, free media, and Indonesia's critical citizens continuing to express demands for improved governance, expanding space for political expression, and electing reformist leaders in at least parts of the country, who make incremental improvements in government systems. There is some evidence for this proposition, and most hopeful scenarios for Indonesia focus on reform impulses expressed by local leaders, such as Joko Widodo (though the pressures on such leaders to compromise with oligarchs and conform to dominant political modes, especially as they make the transition to national politics, are also great; see Warburton 2016). It is equally possible, however, to imagine incremental deterioration in aspects of Indonesian democracy, such as freedom of religion or the fight against corruption. In mid-2017, President Joko Widodo himself issued a regulation giving the government much greater powers to ban social organizations, pointing to brewing authoritarian impulses within his own administration. Moreover, underlying popular frustration with corruption, alienation from parties and parliament, and other signs of political anomie also have the potential to provide, as in many countries, space for a successful authoritarian-populist challenge to Indonesian democracy – such as that embodied in the presidential candidacy of former Soeharto son-in-law and disgraced general, Prabowo Subianto, in 2014. Though Indonesia's democratic progress has indeed been substantial, Indonesian democracy is decidedly *not* out of the danger zone.

References cited

Anderson, Bobby. 2015. *Papua's Insecurity: State Failure in the Indonesian Periphery* (Honolulu: East-West Center).

Aspinall, Edward. 2010. "The Irony of Success," *Journal of Democracy* 21(2): 20–34.

———. 2013. "Popular Agency and Interests in Indonesia's Democratic Transition and Consolidation," *Indonesia* 96: 101–21.

———. 2015. "The Surprising Democratic Behemoth: Indonesia in Comparative Asian Perspective," *Journal of Asian Studies* 74(4): 889–902.

Aspinall, Edward and Gerry van Klinken. 2011. "The State and Illegality in Indonesia," in Edward Aspinall and Gerry van Klinken, eds., *The State and Illegality in Indonesia* (Leiden: KITLV Press), pp. 1–28.

Baker, Jacqueline. 2012. "The Rise of Polri: Democratisation and the Political Economy of Security in Indonesia" (Ph.D. Thesis. London: London School of Economics and Political Science).

Berger, Dominic. 2015. "Human Rights and Yudhoyono's Test of History," in Edward Aspinall, Marcus Mietzner, and Dirk Tomsa, eds., *The Yudhoyono Presidency: Indonesia's Decade of Stability and Stagnation* (Singapore: Institute of Southeast Asian Studies), pp. 217–38.

Bertrand, Jacques. 2004. *Nationalism and Ethnic Conflict in Indonesia* (Cambridge: Cambridge University Press).

Buehler, Michael. 2009. "Suicide and Progress in Modern Nusantara," *Inside Indonesia Edition 97*, July–September. www.insideindonesia.org/suicide-and-progress-in-modern-nusantara (Accessed 15 March 2017).

———. 2016. *The Politics of Shari'a Law: Islamist Activists and the State in Democratizing Indonesia* (Cambridge: Cambridge University Press).

Butt, Simon. 2013. "Indonesian Constitutional Court Decisions in Regional Head Election Disputes," CDI Papers on Political Governance. http://archives.cap.anu.edu.au/cdi_anu_edu_au/.IND/2012-13/2013_03_21_RES_IND_PPS_2013.01_cnst_crt_Butt_CBR/2013_PPS01_Butt.pdf (Accessed 15 March 2017).

Butt, Simon and Tim Lindsey. 2011. "Judicial Mafia: The Courts and State Illegality in Indonesia," in Edward Aspinall and Gerry van Klinken, eds., *The State and Illegality in Indonesia* (Leiden: KITLV Press), pp. 189–213.

Detiknews. 2017. "Jokowi: Demokrasi kita sudah kebablasan," *Detiknews*, 22 February. https://news.detik.com/berita/d-3428904/jokowi-demokrasi-kita-sudah-kebablasan (Accessed 20 March 2017).

Diamond, Larry. 2015. "Facing Up to the Democratic Recession," *Journal of Democracy* 26(1): 141–55.

Foa, Roberto Stefan and Yascha Mounk. 2016. "The Signs of Deconsolidation," *Journal of Democracy* 28(1): 5–16.

Forum Keadilan. 2016. "Panglima TNI, Jendral TNI Gatot Nurmantyo," 10 February. http://forumkeadilan.co/wawancara/panglima-tni-jenderal-tni-gatot-nurmantyo/ (Accessed 15 March 2017).

Haryanto, Ignatius. 2010. "Media Ownership and Its Implications for Journalists and Journalism in Indonesia," in Krishna Sen and David Hill, eds., *Politics and the Media in Twenty-First Century Indonesia* (New York: Routledge), pp. 104–18.

Hoon, Chang-Yau. 2008. *Chinese Identity in Post-Suharto Indonesia: Culture, Politics and Media* (Brighton: Sussex Academic Press).

Human Rights Watch. 2015. "Indonesia: Free all Political Prisoners." 9 May. www.hrw.org/news/2015/05/09/indonesia-free-all-political-prisoners (Accessed 15 March 2017).

Kristiansen, Stein and Muhid Ramli. 2006. "Buying an Income: The Market for Civil Service Positions in Indonesia," *Contemporary Southeast Asia*, 28(2): 207–33

Liddle, William and Saiful Mujani. 2013. "Indonesian Democracy: From Transition to Consolidation," in Mirjam Künkler and Alfred Stepan, eds., *Democracy and Islam in Indonesia* (New York: Columbia University Press), pp. 24–52.

Lussier, Dannielle N. and Steven Fish. 2012. "Indonesia: The Benefits of Civil Engagement," *The Journal of Democracy* 23(1): 70–84.

McLeod, Ross H. 2011. "Institutionalized Public Sector Corruption: A Legacy of the Suharto Franchise," in Edward Aspinall and Gerry van Klinken, eds., *The State and Illegality in Indonesia* (Leiden: KITLV Press), pp. 45–63.

McVey, Ruth. 1982. "The Beamtenstaat in Indonesia," in Benedict Anderson and Audrey Kahin, eds., *Interpreting Indonesian Politics: Thirteen Contributions to the Debate* (Ithaca: Cornell University Press), pp. 84–91.

Menchik, Jeremy. 2016. *Islam and Democracy in Indonesia: Tolerance Without Liberalism* (New York: Cambridge University Press).

Mietzner, Marcus. 2009. *Military Politics, Islam, and the State in Indonesia: From Turbulent Transition to Democratic Consolidation* (Singapore: National University of Singapore Press).

Mungiu-Pippidi, Alina. 2015. *The Quest for Good Governance: How Societies Develop Control of Corruption* (Cambridge: Cambridge University Press).

Nolan, Cillian. 2016. "Papua's Central Highlands: The *Noken* System, Brokers and Fraud," in Edward Aspinall and Mada Sukmajati, eds., *Electoral Dynamics in Indonesia: Money Politics, Patronage and Clientelism at the Grassroots* (Singapore: National University of Singapore Press), pp. 398–415.

Robison, Richard and Vedi R. Hadiz. 2004. *Reorganising Power in Indonesia: The Politics of Oligarchy in an Age of Markets* (London: RoutledgeCurzon).

Schütte, Sofie A. 2012. "Against the Odds: Anti-Corruption Reform in Indonesia," *Public Administration and Development* 32(1): 38–48.

Setara Institute. 2016. "Supremasi Intoleransi: Laporan Kondisi Kebebasan Beragama/Beryakinan dan Minoritas Keagamaan di Indonesia Tahun 2016, Pustaka Masyarakat Setara," January 2016. http://setara-institute.org/book-review/supremasi-intoleransi/ (Accessed 15 March 2017).

Slater, Dan. 2004. "Indonesia's Accountability Trap: Party Cartels and Presidential Power After Democratic Transition," *Indonesia* 78: 61–92.

Slater, Dan and Erica Simmons. 2013. "Coping by Colluding: Political Uncertainty and Promiscuous Powersharing in Indonesia and Bolivia," *Comparative Political Studies* 46(11): 1366–93.

Tadjoeddin, Zulfan. 2014. *Explaining Collective Violence in Contemporary Indonesia: From Conflict to Cooperation* (New York: Palgrave Macmillan).

Tidey, Sylvia. 2013. "Corruption and Adherence to Rules in the Construction Sector: Reading the 'Bidding Books'," *American Anthropologist* 115(2): 188–202.

van Bruinessen, Martin. 2013. "Introduction: Contemporary Developments in Indonesian Islam and the 'Conservative Turn' of the Early Twenty-First Century," in Martin van Bruinessen, eds., *Contemporary Developments in Indonesian Islam: Explaining the Conservative Turn* (Singapore: ISEAS), pp. 1–20.

Warburton, Eve. 2016. "Jokowi and the New Developmentalism," *Bulletin of Indonesian Economic Studies*. 52(3): 297–320.

Winters, Jeffrey. 2011. *Oligarchy* (Cambridge: Cambridge University Press).

World Justice Project. 2016. *World Justice Project Rule of Law Index 2016* (Washington, DC: World Justice Project).

7

PARTIES AND PARTY POLITICS IN THE POST-REFORMASI ERA

Dirk Tomsa

Political parties are an essential building block in Indonesia's political system. Though not particularly well institutionalized, most Indonesian parties today have professionally run headquarters and extensive networks of branch offices across the archipelago. Compared to their counterparts in neighboring countries, such as Thailand or the Philippines, they are also more effective in fulfilling at least some important systemic functions, such as the representation of societal interests or the mobilization of citizens for political participation (Mietzner 2013: 192–214). Yet, at the same time, Indonesian parties also still suffer from many weaknesses, including, among others, programmatic shallowness, pervasive corruption, elitism, and lack of meaningful engagement with ordinary citizens. Many of them are highly leader-centric at the top but largely clientelistic at the grassroots, making it difficult to fit them into existing party typologies (Tomsa 2013). Patronage and collusive rent-seeking play a central role in Indonesian party politics; however, parties are more than just "expressions of shifting alliances of predatory interests" (Hadiz 2004: 619).

To illustrate this point, this chapter will provide an overview of some of the key features of contemporary party politics in Indonesia. It argues that despite the parties' poor reputation among both political observers and the Indonesian electorate, the party system is actually showing signs of stabilization, with a clearly discernible core of six parties forming at the heart of the party system. These parties differ significantly from a new crop of presidentialist parties, not only in their organizational structures and in levels of rootedness in society, but also in their ability to fulfill important systemic functions in the broader political system. These differences notwithstanding, Indonesian parties also share some noteworthy commonalities, especially a propensity toward patronage as the driving force behind most, if not all, modes of interaction. This centrality of patronage to party politics has not only damaged the parties' public standing, but it has also affected the broader trajectory of Indonesia's stalled democratization process. Accountability remains poor, political agendas are mainly set by non-partisan actors, and the political soil is becoming increasingly fertile for radical populists keen to undermine the democratic foundations of the post-Reformasi regime.

Structurally, this chapter is divided into four main sections. Following this brief introduction, it will first outline some crucial attributes of Indonesia's contemporary party system and introduce the main parties. The chapter will then proceed to examine how parties engage with each other on a regular basis, highlighting that patterns of interaction are not purely collusive, but

characterized by an often confusing mix of collusion, competition, and quasi-anarchic dynamics. The third section examines to what extent Indonesian parties play constructive roles in the
broader political system, while the fourth and final section before the conclusion identifies some
of the most noteworthy implications of the nature of Indonesian party politics for the country's
democracy.

Indonesia's multi-party system: fragmented, but increasingly stable

Indonesia's current party system has its institutional roots in the path-defining political reforms
that followed the fall of Soeharto in 1998 (Crouch 2010; Horowitz 2013). Although the legislative framework that governs electoral and party politics in Indonesia has undergone substantial
revisions since these initial reforms, the quintessential institutional foundation that underpins
the structure of the party system – a proportional representation (PR) electoral system with
low threshold requirements – has remained in place. As a consequence, the four parliamentary
elections that have been held between 1999 and 2014 have produced a highly fragmented party
system with an average absolute number of legislative parties of 14.0 and an average effective
number of legislative parties of 6.55. In the most recent election in 2014, no less than 10 parties
won seats in the House of Representatives (Dewan Perwakilan Rakyat, DPR).

Highly fragmented party systems are often associated with a lack of continuity and stability
in electoral competition (Mainwaring and Scully 1995). In Indonesia, however, there are some
indications that despite the continued fragmentation the party system is actually stabilizing. First,
while electoral volatility is relatively high, it has remained fairly constant over the years, ranging
from 23.0 in 2004 to 26.3 at the most recent election in 2014 (Higashikata and Kawamura 2015:
8). Second, in the last two elections new parties have found it increasingly difficult to win seats
in parliament. In 2014, only one new party entered parliament, while none of those who had
won seats in 2009 dropped out; accordingly, the national party systems of 2009 and 2014 look
remarkably similar. Third, changed threshold regulations for the local level in the 2014 election
finally ended years of excessive and continuously growing fragmentation in local party systems
(Tomsa 2014), resulting in a convergence between national and local party systems. And fourth,
despite the relatively high volatility, the party system has a clearly discernible core of six parties that have now been consistently represented in parliament since 1999. Importantly, all but
one of these six parties were able to increase their vote share in 2014 after they had suffered
consecutive losses in 2004 and 2009. The combined vote share of these six core parties reached

Table 7.1 Parliamentary election results, major parties only, 1999–2014 (in percent)

Party	1999	2004	2009	2014
Partai Demokrasi Indonesia-Perjuangan (PDIP)	33.74	18.53	14.03	18.95
Partai Golkar	22.44	21.58	14.45	14.75
Partai Kebangkitan Bangsa (PKB)	12.61	10.57	4.94	9.04
Partai Persatuan Pembangunan (PPP)	10.71	8.15	5.32	6.53
Partai Amanat Nasional (PAN)	7.12	6.44	6.01	7.59
Partai Keadilan Sejahtera (PKS)	1.36	7.34	7.88	6.79
Partai Demokrat (PD)	–	7.45	20.85	10.19
Gerindra	–	–	4.46	11.81
Hanura	–	–	3.77	5.26
Nasdem	–	–	–	6.72

63.65% in 2014, after it had previously declined from 87.98% in 1999 to 72.61% in 2004, and 52.63% in 2009.

The resurgence of the core parties is particularly remarkable because party identification among Indonesian voters is relatively low, and scholars have noted clear signs of dealignment over the years as voters became more and more detached from their earlier partisan choices (Ufen 2008). Among the main reasons for this dealignment were a growing lack of trust in political parties and permissive party and election laws that fostered the formation of splinter parties and an individualization of electoral politics. In particular, the introduction of direct elections for presidents and local leaders in 2004 and 2005 respectively and the adoption of an open list PR system for legislative elections in 2009 diminished the role of political parties during electoral campaigns.[1] By 2014, some analysts argued, parties had all but disappeared as influential actors during parliamentary election campaigns as the battle for votes was shaped more by the personal appeal of individual candidates on the party lists and, especially at the local level, the distribution of patronage, club goods, and cash handouts through clientelistic networks (Aspinall and Sukmajati 2016).

And yet, despite the apparent marginalization of *all* parties during the campaign, detailed district-level analyses of voting patterns across the four post-Soeharto elections also show that at least most of the core parties continue to have remarkably distinct constituencies that are deeply embedded in the country's most salient socio-cultural cleavage structures, known in Indonesia as aliran (Fossati 2016). Although dealignment has clearly taken its toll on aliran-based linkages, contemporary Islamic parties, such as PKB, PAN, PPP, and PKS, still have their most loyal support bases in areas where their spiritual predecessors (Masyumi and NU) performed well in 1955 when Indonesia held its first democratic election. Meanwhile, at the secular end of the party spectrum, PDIP also continues to thrive in areas where in 1955 the PNI, PKI, and PSI excelled. Thus, some contemporary parties remain firmly rooted in relatively clearly defined social milieus, thereby adding to the institutionalization of the party system.

By contrast, the new crop of personalistic parties that rose to prominence during the dealignment process in recent years has no such roots in society. Parties like the Democratic Party (Partai Demokrat, PD), the Greater Indonesia Movement Party (Gerakan Indonesia Raya, Gerindra), the People's Conscience Party (Partai Hati Nurani Rakyat, Hanura), and the National Democratic Party (Nasional Demokrat, Nasdem) are often labelled "presidentialist parties" because their main purpose is to serve as electoral vehicles for the presidential ambitions of their leaders. Significantly, all of these parties were founded by or for ex-generals or tycoons formerly linked to Golkar (Aspinall and Sukmajati 2016: 17). Their programmatic outlook is only vaguely defined but ranges from staunchly nationalist (Gerindra) to "religious-nationalist" (PD).

Patterns of interaction: collusive, competitive, or anarchic?

What unites all Indonesian parties regardless of organizational life span, leadership structures, or roots in society is their seemingly insatiable appetite for patronage. The centrality of patronage is often regarded as one of the main pathologies of Indonesia's post-authoritarian regime, but its roots can be traced deep into the preceding New Order regime (and arguably earlier than that), when political and economic power became inextricably intertwined (Robison and Hadiz 2004). Today, its significance for party politics is further amplified by the fact that parties only derive negligible income from regular sources, such as state subsidies or membership dues (Mietzner 2013). Faced with exploding costs for campaigning and the maintenance of increasingly professional headquarters, parties are in constant need to shore up new funds. While some of these funds are coming from wealthy donors and the parties' own members of parliament, more and more parties are now controlled by super-rich oligarchs who are not only bankrolling the party apparatus but, in some cases, have also taken direct charge of leadership boards. Come election time, practically all parties auction off candidatures and party list positions to the highest bidders and then ask the candidates to fund their own campaign activities. But arguably the most lucrative source of funds for Indonesia's political parties is still patronage milked from state institutions, such as the presidency, government ministries, parliament, and state-owned enterprises.

In order to gain access to these state funds, parties exhibit a peculiar pattern of interaction, which mixes competitive, collusive, and quasi-anarchic features. Competition between parties tends to be at its fiercest in the run-up to elections, when parties and candidates will go to great lengths to weaken their opponents. The floating of corruption allegations has been a particularly effective tool in this regard (Tomsa 2015), but as the escalation of sectarian sentiment ahead of the 2017 Jakarta governor election showed, there are few limits to the repertoire of "black campaign" strategies. Another indication of the competitive dimension of electoral politics is that losing parties or candidates often refuse to concede defeat and rather challenge the results in the courts. In 2014, the polarization between the two opposing camps in the presidential election was so intense that losing candidate Prabowo Subianto and the parties that supported him did not shy away from using false exit poll data to claim victory for Prabowo. Only when the Constitutional Court confirmed victory for Joko Widodo (Jokowi), did Prabowo eventually accept the result.

Electoral competition is so fierce because winning means control over the distribution of patronage. Losing, however, does not necessarily mean exclusion from patronage. In some cases, it does, but more often than not, losing parties will still get a share of the pie as they are accommodated in broad coalition governments dubbed "rainbow cabinets." Slater and Simmons (2013: 1370) have described this particular form of collusion as "promiscuous powersharing . . . an especially flexible coalition-building practice, in which parties express or reveal a willingness to share executive power with any and all other significant parties after an election takes place, even across a country's most important political cleavages." Presidents from Wahid and Megawati to Yudhoyono engaged in such promiscuous powersharing, forming oversized coalition cabinets in the hope they would enhance political stability and prevent parliament from moving against the president. Current president Jokowi initially pledged to discontinue the practice of rainbow cabinets and to emancipate the highest political office from the patronage demands of the parties, but he quickly reneged on that pledge. And while Jokowi used rather different methods than his predecessors to persuade former opposition parties like Golkar and PPP to join his coalition (Mietzner 2016), the outcome was the same: a broad rainbow coalition, comprising more than two-thirds of parliamentary seats. Thus, Jokowi had effectively re-established the familiar collusive pattern of executive-legislature relations, further entrenching Indonesia's well-documented "accountability trap" (Slater 2004).

Promiscuous powersharing and rainbow cabinets have earned the Indonesian party system the reputation of a cartel (Ambardi 2008; Slater 2004). Though mostly a post-election phenomenon, in some extreme cases, at the local level, powersharing deals are already sealed before an election, leading to the bizarre situation that a candidate for district head or mayor will contest the election unopposed, as the overwhelming majority of parties represented in the local parliament agreed to nominate the same candidate.[2] Here, cartelization tendencies are undeniable, but it is noteworthy that even in such extreme cases, some parties are always being left out. The same is true for the national level, where, for example, PDIP consistently refused to join Susilo Bambang Yudhoyono's rainbow cabinets between 2004 and 2014. When Jokowi became president in 2014, a whole coalition bloc of opposition parties emerged temporarily, and while several parties have since switched to the government camp, two major parties, Gerindra and PKS, have remained adamantly opposed to Jokowi.

More important, perhaps, large rainbow cabinets have guaranteed neither stability nor efficiency in governance. In fact, behind the veneer of collusive cabinet structures, there is often intense infighting between and even within individual parties over access to the top power brokers and the patronage resources they control. At times, these internal struggles pitch members of parliament directly against cabinet members of the same party, as MPs are trying to use their institutional powers to extract patronage from the government, irrespective of their party affiliations. According to Sherlock (2015: 99), "the concept of cabinet solidarity, under which ministers and affiliated DPR members would defend the administration's policies, never developed." In the House of Representatives, this lack of coalitional coherence is often evident in committee hearings, where ministers are summoned to defend government policies, even though the logic of the rainbow coalition should prevent precisely such critical questioning. In view of such poor cabinet discipline, as well as the usually competitive nature of electoral politics in general, Mietzner (2013: 25) has argued that "if we can speak of a 'cartel' at all, it has quasi-anarchic features."

Functions of parties: what they do and what they don't do

The peculiarities of inter-party competition in Indonesia have produced a party system in which parliamentary opposition is weak but not exactly non-existent. Parties can and do end up as opposition parties, but opposition status rarely translates into the formulation of programmatic policy alternatives that could challenge the government. At the same time, the patronage-driven nature of cabinet formation in Indonesia also makes it difficult for those parties that are joining a ruling coalition to leave clearly identifiable footprints on government policy. As Indonesian cabinets not only feature representatives of large numbers of parties but also many professionals with no party affiliations at all, government policies often lack coherence and a distinct direction that could be associated with one particular party in the coalition. All in all, therefore, Indonesian parties largely fail to fulfill one crucial function of parties in more mature democracies, namely to form a system of government and opposition in which ruling parties dictate and implement policies while opposition parties hold the government accountable and challenge it on the basis of competing policy proposals.

Apart from the supremacy of patronage and power sharing, another reason for the parties' relatively low impact on governance is the fact that political recruitment usually aims at short-term material and electoral interests rather than the development of a strong party apparatus. Unable to fund expensive campaigns for thousands of candidates in the various elections across the archipelago, parties tend to sell nominations for parliament or local executive office to candidates whose main qualifications are cash and charisma rather than political competence or a history of dedicated party activism. Members of political dynasties are also popular as candidates (Aspinall and Uhaib As'ad 2016), and in regions like Banten or South Sulawesi, it is common for powerful families to provide candidates not just for one but for a broad range of parties. As a result, many elected officials, especially at the local level, carry a certain party badge, but they rarely act on behalf of their parties as they represent primarily their own personal interests and those of their families and clientelistic networks.

The parties' recruitment patterns have implications for other indicators of the parties' "systemic functionality" (Webb and White 2007), such as the aggregation and articulation of societal interests and the promotion of political participation. It is noteworthy though that there are significant differences between the national and the local level as well as between individual parties. At the national level, for example, at least most of the core parties do articulate certain societal interests fairly well. As mentioned before, all core parties except Golkar are rooted in specific socio-cultural constituencies, and voters can be reasonably sure that the parties will seek to represent the interests of their core constituencies.

PDIP, for instance, is widely known to defend the interests of religious minorities, while PKS and PPP have built their political identities around issues that are of concern to conservative Muslims. PKB and PAN, meanwhile, are effectively mouthpieces of two moderate Islamic mass organizations (Nahdlatul Ulama and Muhammadiyah), and their political mission is primarily to safeguard the interests of these organizations. The new breed of personalistic parties, by contrast, has no such core constituencies and is therefore far less well-positioned to represent the interests of specific segments of society. Yet they also do not aggregate societal interests very well. While these parties accommodate an extensive range of members with often contrasting views on key issues, this openness to everyone has resulted in incoherent policy positions and a lack of identity that could transcend the appeal of the parties' dominant leaders (Mietzner 2013: 201).

Compared to the national level, local party politics is essentially clientelistic, and the dividing lines between individual parties are often far blurrier. While some parties, like PDIP or PKS, do have a solid grassroots network, whose interests they seek to represent in local governments and parliaments, many local politicians, regardless of their official party affiliation, do not aspire to represent societal interests tied to parties but prefer to focus on distributing club goods to small clientelistic networks. Accordingly, defections and party switching are much more common at the local level, and up until the institutional reforms of 2014, which disqualified most small parties from competing in elections, local parliaments featured even more fragmented party systems than the national legislature (Tomsa 2014). The 2014 reforms may have wiped out the small parties, but the centrality of clientelistic networks at the expense of loyal party affiliations has not diminished; if anything, it has become more severe because of the retention of the open-list electoral system, which has gravely undermined the role of parties in electoral politics (Aspinall and Sukmajati 2016).

At the same time, local executive leaders also often act in contradiction to national party positions as could be seen, for example, in the support for shariah-inspired bylaws by local politicians formally affiliated with the ostensibly secular Golkar Party (Buehler 2013). Moreover, coalition patterns between parties at the local level can differ immensely from national patterns, depending on local power constellations. Even in high stakes elections like the 2017 Jakarta governor election, some parties allied with President Jokowi did not shy away from forging a coalition with Partai Demokrat, one of the few parties remaining outside of Jokowi's rainbow cabinet.

The blatant disregard for party labels by many local politicians also raises questions about the role of parties in mobilizing citizens for political participation. To be sure, the sheer numbers from Indonesian elections are impressive. In 2014, around 200,000 candidates secured party nominations to run for nearly 20,000 seats in the national, provincial, municipal, and district parliaments (detik 2014). Thousands more have contested elections for governor, mayor, or district head over the years, and with the exception of a few independent candidates, the overwhelming majority of these pilkada candidates were also nominated by political parties. It seems therefore fair to say that parties do foster political participation.

However, a significant proportion of these thousands of candidates mobilize their supporters through other means than party machines. While party branches are routinely encouraged to get involved during campaigns, many candidates build their linkages with voters primarily through personal success teams, family networks, religious and ethnic organizations, and numerous other outlets of Indonesia's vivid associational life. Significantly, this increasing marginalization of parties in electoral campaigns could even be observed in the last presidential election, when Jokowi relied more on his relawan (volunteers) than on the parties who had formally nominated him.

Meanwhile, outside the electoral arena, opportunities for ordinary citizens to participate in actual party activities are also limited because the parties' highly elitist organizational structures offer few, if any, opportunities for the rank and file to influence decision-making processes at the top. This is particularly pronounced in the new personalistic parties that are controlled by dominant leaders who do not tolerate party-internal democracy.

Implications for Indonesia's young democracy

That Indonesian parties are struggling to fulfill many of the functions ascribed to them in the academic literature should not be surprising. Parties in many other young democracies and even in some established democracies have similar problems. In Indonesia though, the "standard lament" (Carothers 2006: 175) about elitism, patronage politics, and disregard for constituency service is further compounded by high absenteeism in parliament, low legislative productivity, and frequent corruption scandals. The latter in particular is widely seen as the main reason why many Indonesian citizens hold their parties in very low esteem (see Figure 7.1). And while corruption in Indonesia is by no means confined to parties and parliament, the regularity and sheer scale of corruption scandals involving high-profile party members have caused seemingly irreversible damage to the reputation of Indonesia's parties, as is evident in consistently low trust figures in public opinion polls.[3]

The combination of limited functionality and low appreciation by ordinary citizens makes Indonesian parties the "weakest link" (Carothers 2006) in the country's ongoing democratization process. Significantly though, trust in other key institutions, such as the presidency or the Corruption Eradication Commission (Komisi Pemberantasan Korupsi, KPK), as well as the

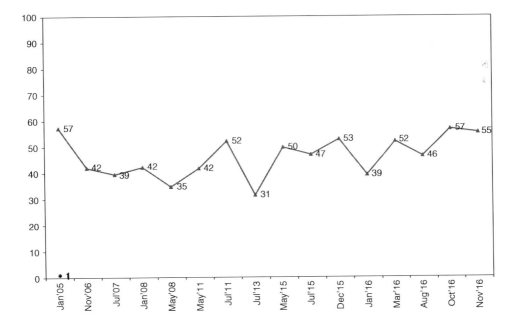

Figure 7.1 Trust toward political parties

Source: Saiful Mujani Research and Consulting (2016), slide reproduced and adjusted with permission of the author.

armed forces, is very high, so that it would be an exaggeration to say that the future of democracy in Indonesia is at imminent risk because of the parties' poor track record. In fact, public support for democracy as the best form of government has been fairly consistent over the last few years, despite a lack of new reform initiatives and an overall sense of democratic stagnation during the Yudhoyono years (Aspinall, Mietzner, and Tomsa 2015).

The broader impact of the parties' underwhelming record of accomplishment on the quality of Indonesia's young democracy should therefore not be overstated. And yet, there are at least three noticeable political trends in Indonesian politics that have the potential to erode the achievements of the democratization process and that can be linked directly or indirectly to the performance of the country's parties. First of all, the supremacy of patronage undermines the notions of both vertical and horizontal accountability (O'Donnell 1994). On the one hand, vertical accountability is "snuffed out" (Slater 2004: 69) by the collusive post-election power-sharing arrangements that make it near impossible for voters to hold individual parties accountable. On the other hand, horizontal accountability is also low because parliament only exercises its oversight function when it wants to extort patronage from the executive, not for the sake of good governance (Case 2011: 29).

Second, parties have largely ceded the initiative to mold political narratives to other non-partisan actors, such as civil society organizations, volunteers, and, of course, presidential and pilkada candidates. Even though Indonesian parties possess much more comprehensive organizational apparatuses than their counterparts in neighboring countries, such as the Philippines, they struggle to use these human resources for setting political agendas and mobilizing people for their cause. As parties seldom formulate comprehensive long-term visions for specific policy issues, they tend merely to respond to emerging policy debates rather than proactively shape public discourse. The retreat from agenda setting is particularly noticeable at the Islamic end of the party spectrum. Here, the Prosperous Justice Party had once set out to champion the Islamist cause not only at the ballot box but also outside election times when most Indonesian parties are essentially inactive (Tomsa 2012). In the early years of the post-Soeharto period, the party often made headlines for its pro-Palestine rallies or its support for the controversial anti-pornography bill. Today, however, non-party actors, such as the notorious Islamic Defenders Front (Front Pembela Islam, FPI), have largely replaced PKS as the public face of Islamist mobilization, as was evident, for example, in the huge mass prayers and protest rallies against Jakarta's former governor Basuki Tjahaja Purnama in late 2016 (Fealy 2016).

Third, the parties must share some of the blame for the growing prominence of populism in Indonesia. As in many other countries, populist candidates have recently emerged as strong contenders in Indonesian elections, both at the national as well as the local level. The most recent presidential election in 2014, for example, was effectively a contest between two populist candidates, although it is important to note that there were significant differences in style and substance between Joko Widodo and Prabowo Subianto (Aspinall 2015; Mietzner 2015). As elsewhere, the rise of populism in Indonesia is driven by widespread disillusionment with elite politics, ineffective institutions, and the centrality of patronage. Of course, parties are not solely responsible for this disillusionment, but as key players in Jakarta's dense web of transactional politics, they are hugely unpopular and a frequent target for public criticism and ridicule.

That the collusive nature of party politics in Indonesia would ultimately trigger a populist backlash was already predicted by Slater and Simmons (2013: 1390), who wrote that "the biggest danger for democratic stability is that oligarchic exclusion will lead them [Indonesian voters] to pursue populist inclusion, unintentionally empowering a strongman with little tolerance for democratic constraints." In 2014, former general Prabowo Subianto came close to making this scenario a reality, but his "challenge to Indonesian democracy" (Aspinall 2015) eventually failed, partly because sizeable sections of the electorate did not regard the political system as sufficiently dysfunctional to hand a mandate to a would-be autocrat. Nevertheless, populist politics is unlikely to go away anytime soon. With Jokowi reneging on his promise to abandon large rainbow coalitions soon after his election and the parties still keen to continue with promiscuous power-sharing arrangements, the soil for another populist challenge in 2019 remains fertile.

Concluding remarks

In conclusion, contemporary Indonesian party politics is characterized by two somewhat contradictory trends. On the one hand, the party system is on its way to become more and more institutionalized. The system now has a clearly discernible core of six parties and the overall number of parties has stabilized. Given the tightened regulations for the formation of new parties, this is unlikely to change drastically in the next legislative election in 2019. Indonesia's party system may be highly fragmented, but this fragmentation is yet to produce the kind of institutionally induced instability or frequent impeachments seen in other multiparty presidential systems (Perez-Linan 2007).

On the other hand, however, parties are struggling to remain relevant as actors both during and outside election times. Parties seldom set the agenda for political discourse and often remain strangely detached from emerging public debates that are not directly linked to electoral competition. Of course, they come to life in the run-up to elections but mainly because they retain the exclusive right to nominate candidates for parliamentary and presidential elections and because electoral laws for local executive elections make it unattractive for candidates to consider running as independents. Once the squabbling over the best candidates is over though and the nominations finalized, parties tend to take a backseat again, leaving most of the electoral campaigning to an eclectic mix of non-party actors, ranging from professional consultants to volunteers, clientelistic networks, and brokers.

There are some signs, however, that the parties are pushing back and trying to reclaim their space at the heart of electoral politics. In the run-up to the hugely important 2017 election for Jakarta governor, for example, parties applied intense pressure on incumbent governor Basuki Tjahaja Purnama (Ahok) after he had publicly toyed with the idea of staging his re-election bid as an independent candidate. Following a string of corruption and fraud allegations against a number of Ahok's advisors and volunteers, the governor eventually relented and announced that he would run with the support of four political parties. His opponents also received high-profile backing from top national party leaders, indicating that parties regarded this election as a proxy battle for the upcoming presidential election in 2019.

The flipside of these renewed efforts by the parties to tighten their grip on electoral politics is that they are likely to resort to familiar political tactics, especially the kind of transactional politics so despised by large sections of the electorate. Unless the incentives and opportunities for patronage politics are systematically reduced – for example through reforms to the party finance system or new electoral rules – there is indeed little prospect for behavioral change among the parties. Accordingly, accountability will remain low while the potential for old and new populists to attack the parties for their self-interest and elitism remains high. Prabowo Subianto, for his part, has already declared his intention to mount another challenge for the presidency in 2019. Thus, even if the formal contours of the party system will stabilize further in the near future, conditions remain ripe for non-party actors to continue raising their profile in Indonesian politics.

Notes

1 Indonesia used an open list PR system in the 1999 legislative election, then a partially open list PR system in 2004, and eventually a fully open list PR system in 2009 and 2014.
2 In December 2015, three local elections had only one candidate. In February 2017, there were nine regions where voters did not have a choice between different candidates (Heryanto 2017).
3 Some of the most prominent corruption convicts in recent years were leaders of political parties, including Anas Urbaningrum (PD), Luthfi Hasan Ishaaq (PKS), and Suryadharma Ali (PPP).

References cited

Ambardi, Kuskridho. 2008. "The Making of the Indonesian Multiparty System: A Cartelized Party System and Its Origins" (Ph.D. Thesis. Columbus: The Ohio State University).

Aspinall, Edward. 2015. "Oligarchic Populism: Prabowo Subianto's Challenge to Indonesian Democracy," *Indonesia* 99: 1–28.

Aspinall, Edward, Marcus Mietzner, and Dirk Tomsa, eds. 2015. *The Yudhoyono Presidency: Indonesia's Decade of Stability and Stagnation* (Singapore: Institute of Southeast Asian Studies).

Aspinall, Edward and Mada Sukmajati. 2016. "Patronage and Clientelism in Indonesian Electoral Politics," in Edward Aspinall and Mada Sukmajati, eds., *Electoral Dynamics in Indonesia: Money Politics, Patronage and Clientelism at the Grassroots* (Singapore: NUS Press), pp. 1–38.

Aspinall, Edward and Muhammad Uhaib As'ad. 2016. "Understanding Family Politics: Successes and Failures of Political Dynasties in Regional Indonesia," *South East Asia Research* 24(3): 420–35.

Buehler, Michael. 2013. "Subnational Islamization Through Secular Parties: Comparing Shari'a Politics in Two Indonesian Provinces," *Comparative Politics* 46(1): 63–82.

Carothers, Thomas. 2006. *Confronting the Weakest Link: Aiding Political Parties in New Democracies* (Washington DC: Carnegie Endowment for International Peace).

Case, William. 2011. *Executive Accountability in Southeast Asia: The Role of Legislatures in New Democracies and Under Electoral Authoritarianism*, Policy Studies 57 (Honolulu: East-West Center).

Crouch, Harold. 2010. *Political Reform in Indonesia After Soeharto* (Singapore: Institute of Southeast Asian Studies).

Detik.com. 2014. "200 Ribu Caleg yang Berebut 19 Ribu Kursi di 2014." *detik.com*, 9 January 2014.

Fealy, Greg. 2016. "Bigger Than Ahok: Explaining the 2 December Mass Rally." *Indonesia at Melbourne*, 7 December. http://indonesiaatmelbourne.unimelb.edu.au/bigger-than-ahok-explaining-jakartas-2-december-mass-rally/ (Accessed 6 March 2017).

Fossati, Diego. 2016. *The Resilience of Partisan Affiliations in Indonesia*. ISEAS Perspective 52 (Singapore: Institute of Southeast Asian Studies).

Hadiz, Vedi R. 2004. "Indonesian Local Party Politics: A Site of Resistance to Neoliberal Reform," *Critical Asian Studies* 36(4): 615–36.

Heryanto, Gun Gun. 2017. "Sole Candidates Harm Political Parties," *The Jakarta Post*, 8 February 2017.

Higashikata, Takayuki and Koichi Kawamura. 2015. *Voting Behavior in Indonesia From 1999 to 2014: Religious Cleavage or Economic Performance?* IDE Discussion Paper No. 512 (Chiba: Institute of Developing Economies).

Horowitz, Donald L. 2013. *Constitutional Change and Democracy in Indonesia* (Cambridge: Cambridge University Press).

Mainwaring, Scott P. and Timothy R. Scully. 1995. "Introduction: Party Systems in Latin America," in Scott P. Mainwaring and Timothy R. Scully, eds., *Building Democratic Institutions: Party Systems in Latin America* (Stanford: Stanford University Press), pp. 1–34.

Mietzner, Marcus. 2013. *Money, Power and Ideology: Political Parties in Post-Authoritarian Indonesia* (Singapore: NUS Press).

———. 2015. *Reinventing Asian Populism: Jokowi's Rise, Democracy and Political Contestation*. Policy Studies No. 72 (Honolulu: East West Center).

———. 2016. "Coercing Loyalty: Coalitional Presidentialism and Party Politics in Jokowi's Indonesia," *Contemporary Southeast Asia* 38(2): 209–32.

O'Donnell, Guillermo. 1994. "Delegative Democracy," *Journal of Democracy* 5(1): 55–69.

Perez-Linan, Aníbal. 2007. *Presidential Impeachment and the New Political Instability in Latin America* (Cambridge: Cambridge University Press).

Robison, Richard and Vedi R. Hadiz. 2004. *Reorganising Power in Indonesia: The Politics of Oligarchy in an Age of Markets* (London and New York: RoutledgeCurzon).

Saiful Mujani Research and Consulting. 2016. *Survei Nasional November 2016* (Jakarta: SMRC).

Sherlock, Stephen. 2015. "A Balancing Act: Relations Between State Institutions Under Yudhoyono," in Edward Aspinall, Marcus Mietzner and Dirk Tomsa, eds., *The Yudhoyono Presidency: Indonesia's Decade of Stability and Stagnation* (Singapore: Institute of Southeast Asian Studies), pp. 93–113.

Slater, Dan. 2004. "Indonesia's Accountability Trap: Party Cartels and Presidential Power After Democratic Transition," *Indonesia* 78: 61–92.

Slater, Dan and Erica Simmons. 2013. "Coping by Colluding: Political Uncertainty and Promiscuous Power-sharing in Bolivia and Indonesia," *Comparative Political Studies*, 46(11): 1366–93.

Tomsa, Dirk. 2012. "Moderating Islamism in Indonesia: Tracing Patterns of Party Change in the Prosperous Justice Party," *Political Research Quarterly* 65(3): 486–98.

———. 2013. "What Type of Party? Southeast Asian Parties Between Clientelism and Electoralism," in Dirk Tomsa and Andreas Ufen, eds., *Party Politics in Southeast Asia: Clientelism and Electoral Competition in Indonesia, Thailand and the Philippines* (London and New York: Routledge), pp. 20–39.

———. 2014. "Party System Fragmentation in Indonesia: The Sub-National Dimension," *Journal of East Asian Studies* 14(2): 249–78.

———. 2015. "Local Politics and Corruption in Indonesia's Outer Islands," *Bijdragen tot de Taal-, Land- en Volkenkunde* 171: 196–219.

Ufen, Andreas. 2008. "From *aliran* to Dealignment: Political Parties in Post-Suharto Indonesia," *South East Asia Research* 16(1), pp. 5–41.

Webb, Paul D. and Stephen White. 2007. "Conceptualizing the Institutionalization and Performance of Political Parties in New Democracies," in Paul D. Webb and Stephen White, eds., *Party Politics in New Democracies* (New York: Oxford University Press), pp. 1–19.

8

THE EPHEMERAL NATURE OF LOCAL POLITICAL MONOPOLIES

Michael Buehler

The decentralization of political and fiscal authority in Indonesia in 1999 triggered a series of studies that predicted the rise of strongmen who would subjugate the local state to their personal interests (see Hadiz 2010). Almost 20 years later, such gloomy assessments no longer dominate scholarship on Indonesian local politics. While many scholars believe that decentralization has failed to improve service delivery and local economic conditions (see Ostwald 2016 et al.), local politics in Indonesia seems to be a lot more dynamic than earlier studies had predicted. While there are undoubtedly oligarchic and dynastic tendencies in Indonesian local politics (Buehler 2013), recent contributions to the debate have emphasized the ephemeral nature of such power constellations (Aspinall and As'ad 2016; Savirani 2016).[1]

Only four election cycles have passed since 1999. It may therefore be too early to reach firm conclusions about the relative dynamism of local politics in Indonesia. However, recent claims that Indonesian dynasties struggle to survive multiple election cycles are suggestive enough to examine the potential reasons for this dynamism more in depth. As most existing studies on Indonesian local dynasties are merely descriptive in nature, it is useful to look at the broader theoretical literature on local political monopolies first.[2]

Literature review

The literature on the durability of local political monopolies falls into two broad groups: the first body of works emphasizes the importance of *local economic conditions*, while the second body of works argues that *institutional conditions* determine the longevity of local political monopolies.

Economic conditions and enduring local political monopolies

In *The Sources of Social Power*, Michael Mann argued that chieftains only managed to establish enduring authority in parts of the world where the local topography allowed them to encage the population. The agricultural surplus that could be expropriated under such conditions then became the nucleus of enduring political systems (Mann 1986: 80). Similarly, McMann (2006) argued that local socio-economic conditions determine to what degree citizens can oppose the monopolization of power in Russian local politics. Montero (2011) stated that demographic conditions, poverty levels, and linkages to urban centers determine whether local incumbents can concentrate power in Brazil. Lankina and Getachew (2012) claimed that education levels resulting from Christian missionary activities increased the level of human capital in some but not other Indian provinces and therefore explain the variance of subnational authoritarianism across the country.

The aforementioned literature finds its counterparts in several works on Southeast Asia. Ockey (1998: 40) and McVey (2000: 12), for instance, both argued that "local godfathers" and "rural big men" came to power in Thai provinces in the 1970s after economic changes acquired political relevance in the context of the (re-)introduction of parliamentary democracy. For the Philippines, Anderson (1988) argued that the concentration of local landholdings gave birth to durable local political monopolies. Similarly, McCoy showed that "a single national highway" in Ilocos Sur province gave rise to a local strongman while "the highway grid that crisscrosses the [Central Luzon] plain lacked comparable choke points," which subsequently prevented the monopolization of local politics in that part of the Philippines (2009: 15). The case that local economic conditions determine the durability of local political monopolies has been made most forcefully by Sidel (2014), who argued that

> [v]ariance in subnational authoritarianism corresponds to local constellations of eco-nomic power, with subnational authoritarian rulers' success in entrenching and per-petuating themselves in power contingent on their ability to constrain the economic autonomy of citizens, voters, local state agents, vote-brokers, and would-be challengers. *By this logic, local economic conditions are determinant of local political outcomes.*
>
> *(2014: 165)[3]*

In other words, wherever local economic conditions create "locked-in electorates" (Scott 1969: 1146, ftn 16) and "pliable populations" (Hale 2003: 229), namely voters who depend eco-nomically on local elites, chances are high that local elites leverage these dependencies into local political monopolies.

However, elites do not simply *encounter* local economic conditions but often actively *construct* them when trying to establish stable local political monopolies. Often, local elites do so with the help of outsiders. Hale (2003), Erie (1988), and Schneider and Schneider (2003) showed the importance of intergovernmental alliances for the establishment of durable local political monopolies in Russia, the United States, and Italy.

> [T]his scholarship suggests that accumulation, concentration, and monopolisation of economic control over a given locality are determined not only by the factor endow-ments and inherited economic structures of a given locality, *but also through interactions between local powerbrokers and supra-local state authorities.* (Emphasis added.)
>
> *(Sidel 2014: 169)*

Furthermore, the durability of local political monopolies is shaped by

> the form of economic control achieved and maintained by subnational authoritarian rulers . . . [S]ubnational authoritarianism is only viable in the long term insofar as pro-prietary wealth and predominance in a local economy of a subnational authoritarian ruler are solidly rooted in property rights in the private economy.
>
> *(Sidel 2014: 179)*

In short, if local politicians can establish local economic monopolies that are based on secure property rights, proprietary wealth, and the private legal realm of the market *and* if these local economic monopolies create sizeable locked-in electorates, local politicians are well-positioned to establish enduring local political monopolies. In contrast, if local politicians depend on privileged access to state resources, rely on the discretionary enforcement of state regulatory powers, and are predominantly involved in illegal economic enterprises, they will struggle to establish enduring economic monopolies (Sidel 2014: 179). The lack of complete control over their economic monopoly makes their local political monopoly more vulnerable to adversarial outside attacks.

The literature emphasizing the importance of economic local conditions for the presence and persistence of local political monopolies can be criticized on several grounds. Since Sidel has most emphatically argued that economic conditions explain the durability of local political monopolies, the following paragraph focuses mainly on his theory. While Sidel differentiates clearly between natural private sector monopolies (1) and private sector monopolies that are created (2), he does not differentiate clearly enough between private sector resources that are created and economic resources that are based on *state-patronage* (3), that is economic resources that flow directly from the state including the "allocation of state budgets and awarding of state loans" (Sidel 2014: 168). He also conflates economic resources and resources that seem to have only *institutional* origins (4), such as "preferential treatment by ... law-enforcement agencies [and] tolerance of electoral fraud and violence, and punitive treatment of rival candidates" (Sidel 2014: 169). Sidel also does not consider explicitly that many economic conditions deemed important for the creation of durable political monopolies are often a function of a country's institutional context. For instance, secure property rights, which are mentioned by Sidel as an important prerequisite for establishing enduring local economic monopolies, are, arguably, determined by a state's overall regulatory framework and how strictly and impartially it is enforced.

In short, the fact that many economic resources flow directly from *the state*, the fact that many resources have *institutional* roots, and the fact that even economic assets in the private sector may be a function of *administrative* powers suggests that enduring political monopolies may be established entirely through the monopolization of resources that have their origins in a country's institutional framework.

Institutional conditions and enduring local political monopolies

A growing literature has emphasized the importance of *institutional* conditions for the emergence of durable local political monopolies. This research strand has been initiated by Gibson, who argued that local political monopolists in nationally democratic countries are challenged by "regime juxtaposition" (Gibson 2012: 5). Since the local political monopoly is undemocratic but national-level politics are democratic, local political monopolists have to find ways to fend off attacks to their local dominance by national-level democratizers or by adversarial alliances between national and local democratizers. In both scenarios, the fate of local political monopolies is determined by how effectively incumbents control the boundaries to their jurisdiction.

The defense capacities of local monopolists are determined by institutional conditions, namely whether a political system is centralized or decentralized, whether provinces are represented in national politics relatively symmetrically or asymmetrically, and how much power a country's institutional framework assigns to government players situated at administrative layers below a local political monopoly (Gibson 2012: 149).

Expanding on Gibson's work, Giraudy (2015) argued that a combination of fiscal and political powers determines the durability of local political monopolies in nationally democratic countries. For example, the size of local fiscal deficits, levels of indebtedness, and the possibility to raise taxes at the subnational level define the fiscal autonomy of local autocrats. If local fiscal deficits and indebtedness are high while possibilities to collect local revenues are scarce, local autocrats have only weak fiscal powers to resist outside attacks. Furthermore, if the party the national executive government head belongs to is highly institutionalized and enjoys high party discipline, outside attacks are more likely to be successful than if these conditions are absent.

To summarize, this literature emphasizes that local political monopolies do not simply "emerge" from local economic conditions but are *actively* constructed through manipulating and bypassing *institutions*. In other words, there is nothing preordained about local political monopolies and they are decisively non-local in origin.

Several critiques can be levelled against this second body of works. First, the potential role local economic conditions play for the rise and survival of local political monopolies is either ignored outright (Gibson 2012) or insufficiently ruled out (Giraudy 2015). Second, these authors also do not address that many of the institutional conditions said to determine the emergence and durability of local political monopolies, such as party institutionalization and party discipline, may themselves be economically conditioned.[4] Third, and most important, aforementioned research on the institutional determinants of local political monopolies is dominated by Latin American experts (Gibson 2012; Giraudy 2015; Gervasoni 2010; Weitz-Shapiro 2015 and various chapters on South America in Behrend and Whitehead 2016). It therefore focuses almost exclusively on *federal democracies*, which are the dominating political system in the Americas.

Most countries in the world are unitary states, however. While unitary states show varying degrees of decentralization, they all have in common that the possibilities for institutional rigging by subnational political players are much more limited compared to federal democracies. Yet, local political monopolies flourish in such countries too. In fact, there is considerable variance *within* these decentralized unitary states with regard to the emergence and durability of local political monopolies despite the fact that such territorial regimes are much more homogenous and national-level control over subnational entities is usually considerable.

In short, there may be a selection bias in findings that local political monopolies are exclusively based on institutional manipulation because most of this research focuses on a region of the world where political systems that are conducive to institutional rigging are prevalent. The great leeway local incumbents in federal democracies have with regard to shaping institutions in their favor allowed scholars working on federal democracies in the Americas to dismiss local economic conditions too quickly.

In the remaining paragraphs, I want to show that combining these two literatures will result in an approach with increased explanatory power. Concretely, I argue that whether a country is a decentralized unitary state or a federal democracy determines whether economic conditions endogenous to localities or institutional conditions exogenous to localities acquire causal primacy in the rise and durability of local political monopolies. In federal democracies, local political monopolies may emerge irrespective of whether local economic conditions lend themselves to elite dominance and the creation of locked-in electorates, because the federal regulatory framework facilitates institutional rigging of the kind described above. This allows local incumbents to establish monopolies based entirely on political resources. Despite the fact that such monopolies may be somewhat detached from local conditions and therefore "built in the air,"[5] they may nevertheless be durable. Said differently, one does not need to "lock-in" the electorate if one can manipulate the election law or the boundaries of electoral districts.

In decentralized unitary states, however, opportunities for institutional rigging are much less available to local incumbents compared to federal democracies. This shifts the focus to local economic conditions as determinants of local political monopolies. In jurisdictions where local economic conditions have created locked-in electorates and where elites have monopolized the private sector economy, there is a high chance that local political monopolies may emerge even though institutions cannot be easily manipulated. If locked-in electorates are created through intra-state alliances and if economic monopolies depend on elites' access to the state, local monopolies are more fragile. These two different economic contexts explain the emergence of enduring local monopolies and single-generation local monopolies within decentralized unitary states, as Sidel has pointed out (2014). Finally, in countries where elites struggle to dominate local economies, where the economic autonomy of local voters is relatively high, *and* where the regulatory framework makes institutional rigging difficult, local political monopolies are less likely to emerge and survive multiple election cycles. Arguably, this is the case in Indonesia, to which I turn now.

Indonesia

Political monopolies are either absent or ephemeral in Indonesian local politics because of two inter-related reasons. First, local economic conditions do not lend themselves to monopolization. Hence, local elites struggle to dominate local economies and the economic autonomy of Indonesian voters is comparatively high. Second, the institutional framework of Indonesia's decentralized unitary state creates formidable obstacles for local incumbents to rig institutions in their favor.

While space constraints make it impossible to provide an exhaustive list of economic and institutional conditions said to facilitate the rise and survival of local political monopolies, the following paragraphs will elaborate briefly on some of the points mentioned in the literature review to illuminate why local politics in Indonesia remain relatively dynamic.

Indonesian elites struggle to monopolize private sector resources

Many democratizing countries are in the Global South, where a large proportion of the electorate works in the agricultural sector. The concentration of land in the hands of a small elite has created tenant farmers whose livelihood depends on landed elites. This has often given rise to political monopolies. In addition to taking advantage of monopolies *inherent* to the private sector economy in a given locality, successful local political monopolists have also used the powers of their office to actively *create* economic monopolies in the private sector as mentioned before. Such strategies included "control over commodity processing centers, markets [and] transportation chokepoints" (Sidel 2014: 169), as well as the use of insider knowledge and political connections to rig the privatization of state-owned enterprises in the manufacturing and heavy industry (Hale 2003: 249). The allocation of concessions for the exploitation of natural resources to allies, friends, and family members, as well as licenses and permits for infrastructure projects on which local economies depend, including bridges, toll roads, ports, and railway tracks, have been used to structure *private sector economic assets* in favor of the incumbent.

In addition to economic power concentration in the hands of an individual politician or a small group of politicians, the rise and endurance of local political monopolies is also determined by the economic autonomy of the electorate. In other words, the lack of an "exit" option for local voters in a jurisdiction where an individual or a small group of individuals have managed to monopolize key economic assets is another important determinant of local political monopolies. One may think that the economic autonomy of local electorates is simply a function of the presence of local economic monopolies. However, local economic monopolies may exist while the livelihoods of the majority of the electorate remain unaffected by such monopolists. Under such conditions, citizens are therefore able to cast freely their ballot on Election Day. In short, it is both the *presence and prevalence* of elite control over the local economy that determines the economic autonomy of voters.[6] Neither inherited private sector economic monopolies nor created economic monopolies are sufficient to establish local political monopolies if the economic autonomy of voters remains high (Sidel 2014: 167).

In Indonesia, it is difficult for local elites to take advantage of natural monopolies or to monopolize local economies in the way described above. In addition, the economic autonomy of voters is relatively high. Concretely, while the quality of data on landownership in Indonesia is notoriously poor, land concentration overall seems to be less prevalent than in other Southeast Asian countries. While there is great variation in land concentration *within* Indonesia (Hefner 1993: 55), the largest concentration of land exists in those parts of Indonesia where the plantation economy looms large (Safitri 2012). However, many of these plantations are under the ownership of *national* elites (Tans 2012: 17) and therefore do not provide *local* elites with leverage over the electorate. About 30% of the plantation sector also consists of small holdings, which explains the fragmented nature of the plantation industry in many parts of the archipelago (Rist et al. 2010: 1112). Finally, provinces and districts receive only a small amount of revenues and export taxes these estates generate (Tans 2012: 58). In areas where there *is* an above average concentration of land in the hands of local players, these pockets of land concentration are often too small to serve as a basis to control significant parts of the electorate. In West Java province, for instance, the higher than usual concentration of landownership (Pincus 1996) is, arguably, neutralized by the population density of the province, which is among the world's highest. Most important, however, the diversification of the rural economy in much of Indonesia since the 1970s (Hart 1986: 192–212) and the accompanying "seasonal or circulatory migration to urban centers or periurban industrial zones" (White 1991: 63) has dramatically reduced the importance of landholdings as a source of political power in past decades.

In short, in areas where land concentration is pronounced, the land is often owned by political players with no interest in establishing local political monopolies. If local economic monopolies in the agricultural and plantation sector exist, they are not capturing enough of the local economy to lock-in sizeable numbers of voters. Finally, the proliferation of new employment opportunities in the country's rural areas has contributed to the relative economic autonomy of Indonesian voters.

With regard to state patronage, corruption and collusion are certainly prevalent in the allocation of licenses and business permits in the natural resource sector. This has not only generated enormous profits for local political elites but also often allowed them to become important economic players or at least interlocutors between local business interests. However, natural resource exploitation does not lend itself to the creation of local economic monopolies that could be turned into local political monopolies. While Law No. 22/1999 initially provided local government with the authority to issue licenses for the logging and plantation industry, this was partially revoked three years later when government regulation PP No. 34/2002 shifted authority over timber permits back to the national Ministry of Forestry (McCarthy 2007). The national government has also used its legal powers to redraw forest boundaries in order to bring more forests under its direct control, thereby depriving local governments of logging opportunities (Tans 2012: 59).

Likewise, large-scale industrialization is absent in Indonesia. Most of the few sizeable industrial assets are in the extractive industry and are either state-owned enterprises under *national* leadership, joint ventures with foreign companies, or under the control of Chinese-Indonesians, who, for historical reasons, constitute a class of pariah capitalists who rarely directly engage in politics. Local mining operations are either too fragmented or too small (Aspinall 2001) to allow local elites involved in such operations to leverage this into political might. With regard to the manufacturing industry, foreign investment in Indonesia's manufacturing industry was always low compared to other Southeast Asian countries (Thomsen 1999). At the time of writing, the sector only employs around 21% of Indonesia's workforce. The largest manufacturing clusters are in Bandung, Jakarta, Medan, and Surabaya, but there are almost no single-company towns (Rothenberg et al. 2016) of the kind that have given rise to local political monopolies in countries such as Russia. In fact, most monopolies in the "good producing industries . . . were eliminated" after the fall of Soeharto, while links between the manufacturing industry and the political establishment largely disappeared after 1998, resulting in "reduced capture" (Kochanova et al. n.y.: 7).

Finally, other state patronage resources with the potential to create locked-in electorates are welfare contributions. While a rudimentary welfare state has developed over the past years in Indonesia, the level of welfare services on offer is not anywhere near the welfare resources available for potential politicization in former post-communist countries. Most Indonesians continue to rely on private savings and family networks when it comes to health and welfare concerns.

In short, the lack of natural private sector monopolies, the absence of large-scale industrialization, the fragmentation of the manufacturing industry, and the insignificance of social services for the livelihoods of Indonesians have resulted in an electorate that remains poor but is also relatively free from economic dependencies.

However, as shown, scholars have argued that even if local elites are unable to make use of natural or created private sector economic monopolies, as well as state patronage, politicians may still be able to establish political monopolies through the concentration of institutional resources. Yet, the institutional framework of Indonesia's unitary state provides limited opportunities for politicians in that respect too.

Institutional constraints on local political monopolies

Research emphasizing the monopolization of political resources through the manipulation of institutions has pointed out that in highly decentralized federal democracies local incumbents have rigged constitutions and electoral rules to their advantage and also manipulated fiscal and regulatory frameworks to either fill their own campaign coffers or to starve off adversarial jurisdictions situated at lower rungs of the institutional hierarchy. In addition, the power to collect and allocate local revenues and to manipulate local indebtedness have all been mentioned as institutional conditions that have shaped the rise and fall of local political monopolies (Gibson 2012; Giraudy 2015).

In Indonesia, however, the decentralized unitary state framework places serious restrictions on the monopolization of institutional resources. For instance, certain amendments to the electoral rules can be made by local governments, but the overall framework regulating local elections is standardized across the country and under the authority of the national election commission (Buehler 2010). Furthermore, unlike in federal democracies, Indonesian local incumbents cannot write their own local constitutions. Consequently, while local incumbents in federal democracies, such as Argentina or Mexico, have written their own constitution to, among other issues, bring the security apparatus stationed in their jurisdiction under their control, the police and the army are under national authority in Indonesia (Kristiansen and Trijono 2005: 237). Likewise, the public prosecutor's office reports to the national level, not the local government (Tans 2012: 14). In short, while there is certainly a fair level of collusion between local governments, the local security apparatus, and the judiciary in many localities, Indonesian local incumbents cannot bring these political resources under their *formal* control. Local political monopolies dependent on such institutional resources are therefore unlikely to be enduring, as they are at constant risk of national government intervention.

Local incumbents face similar obstacles with regard to the manipulation of fiscal resources and budget allocations. After 1998, local governments adopted hundreds of predatory taxes and levies. At the same time, local governments have systematically syphoned off tax revenues that were supposed to go to the national level (Buehler 2009a). However, as part of a re-centralization campaign under the Megawati and Yudhoyono administrations, Law No. 32/ 2004 and Law No. 28/ 2009 confined the number of levies local governments can adopt to 11 taxes (Buehler 2009b). Hence, at the time of writing, local taxation generated only around 10% of the income of local jurisdictions (Ostwald et al 2016: 140).[7] Furthermore, the capacity of the Indonesian government to collect taxes is so weak that the country has one of the lowest tax compliance ratios in the world (Rahman 2017: 2). All this makes predatory levies and the diversion of tax proceeds a blunt tool for the creation of economic monopolies that could be turned into political monopolies.

With regard to the manipulation of budget allocations, Indonesian localities receive on average 90% of their revenues from the national level through block grants (DAU – Dana Alokasi Umum) and special allocation grants (DAK – Dana Alokasi Khusus). While there is a lot of corruption and collusion in intra-governmental budget transfers, the formal allocation mechanism is determined by a standardized regulatory framework under the control of the national level (Brodjonegoro and Martinez-Vazquez 2005). This confines the possibilities of Indonesian local elites to manipulate budget allocations to the degree possible in federal democracies.

Hiring friends and supporters into the local bureaucracy has been mentioned as another tactic to establish local political monopolies. The democratization after 1998 has definitely politicized the local state apparatus. Because there are no local economic monopolies that could serve as a stepping-stone for establishing local political monopolies, the state has become the most integrated tool available for campaigns in most Indonesian localities. Consequently, the majority of candidates running for governor, district head, or mayor hail from within the bureaucracy, turning local executive government head elections essentially into intra-state competition in many districts.

In this context, bureaucrats running in local elections have resorted to using state administrations under their control to campaign on their behalf during election season (Kompas 2005). Local incumbents have also tried to streamline local bureaucracies by promoting, demoting, and transferring local bureaucrats either before or after elections (Ngusmanto 2016) and to expand their electoral vehicle by spending excessive amounts of the local budget on administrative upkeep rather than service delivery (Sjahrir et al. 2013). Finally, bureaucrats have tried to generate resources by selling posts in the local administration (Kristiansen and Ramli 2006).

However, the politicization of the local state apparatus does not automatically translate into political power. While the Indonesian bureaucracy is bloated, the number of people working in the apparatus is small compared to other Southeast Asian countries because of Indonesia's high population density (Buehler 2011: 66). The percentage of the population that directly or indirectly depends on the local state is therefore insufficient to establish political monopolies. In other words, too many people are independent from the state for control over the local state apparatus to yield political leverage sufficiently strong to establish a local political monopoly. The authority of the national government to impose hiring freezes on local administrations and to request five-year placement plans, powers that Jakarta has used in the past, confines the possibilities to co-opt local bureaucracies further (Kompas 2011). Finally, nationwide term limits for local executive government heads add another obstacle to monopolization of bureaucratic power in Indonesia. In short, the rigid structures of Indonesia's decentralized unitary state constrain the development of durable local political monopolies based on the concentration of institutional resources.

In addition to these economic and institutional obstacles to establishing local political monopolies, the broader political context makes it difficult for local politicians to influence national politics in their favor. The major links between national and subnational politics in federal democracies, such as Argentina and Mexico, where incumbents rely on manipulating national institutions to establish local political monopolies are political parties. However, in Indonesia, political parties are poorly institutionalized. Furthermore, party internal hierarchies are top heavy. Therefore, parties do not provide local elites with access to national politics to the same degree as in Argentina or Mexico.

Conclusion

This chapter argued that existing works on local political monopolies may suffer from selection bias, as they either focus on decentralized unitary states or federal democracies. In the former, economic conditions may indeed explain the variance in subnational authoritarianism. In the latter, the possibilities for institutional rigging may explain better the rise and durability of local political monopolies than economic conditions intrinsic to jurisdictions. I have argued that both economic and institutional conditions need to be taken into account to explain the presence or absence of local political monopolies. In Indonesia, the economic autonomy of voters is relatively high, while the possibilities for institutional manipulation are relatively low. Arguably, this combination explains the ephemeral nature of Indonesia's local political monopolies.

There are four main power bases on which local political monopolies can be established, as mentioned. Since private sector economic monopolies, inherited (1) or created (2), are not widespread and because institutional resources (4) are also not as easily captured by local elites compared to federal democracies, the selective distribution of state-patronage (3) is where Indonesian local elites seem to have the most freedom to manipulate the system in their interest. *If* local political monopolies emerge in Indonesia, they will therefore likely be based on the concentration and subsequent dispersion of state patronage.

However, collusive practices with regard to logging licenses, the diversion of plantation revenues and other tax proceeds, the adoption of predatory taxes, and the particularistic delivery of services to select constituencies are all against the law, therefore necessarily *informal* and subject to constant re-negotiations and potential outside intervention. Term limits for local executive government heads add to these obstacles, as regular transition periods allow national elites to renege on informal arrangements. In short, local political monopolies may emerge in Indonesian politics, but they are unlikely to be very durable because risks of outside intervention are high.

Against this backdrop, the *dynastic* nature of existing local political monopolies and the prevalence of *money politics* in local elections are not to be seen as indicators for the growing entrenchment of particularistic interests but as indicators for the rather unstable basis of local political monopolies across the archipelago state. Since locked-in electorates are largely absent in Indonesia, politicians trying to establish local political monopolies are always confronted with the risk that voters, vote-canvassers, and power brokers will take their money and run. Local elites therefore rely on family and clan networks to minimize the risk of defection. Similarly, the prevalence of money politics in Indonesian local politics should be seen as an indicator for the relative dynamism of local politics. Indonesian politicians need to engage in money politics because they cannot coerce voters to support them at the ballot box. Locked-in electorates, in other words, would not have to be paid for electoral support, as they have no other option than to vote for the candidate on whom they depend economically.

While it may look like the ephemeral nature of Indonesian local monopolies bodes well for the democratization of Indonesian politics, the absence of local authoritarianism does not automatically translate into progressive and democratic politics. While predatory elites struggle to entrench themselves in local politics, so do progressive politicians. As Trounstine (2008) has shown, successful reformers rely on monopolistic government arrangements as much as local bosses. More likely then, the scenario for future local politics in Indonesia is one where different predatory networks and local mafias will jostle for power and the support of the electorate without providing much in terms of policy agendas that would address the country's many problems.

Notes

1 There is no doubt that only a sliver of Indonesian society has the means to compete in local executive and legislative elections. Indonesian politics remain elite-dominated. However, the point made here is that power dynamics *within* this elite are more competitive than scholars had expected when Indonesia decentralized its political and fiscal structures.

2 The burgeoning literature on local strongmen, dynasties, oligarchies, and subnational autocratic regimes all have in common that they focus on power constellations in which competition is confined. I therefore call such power constellations "local political monopolies."

3 Emphasis added.

4 Panebianco (1988) showed how economic structures may shape party discipline in the long run. Buehler (2012) applied this argument to the Indonesian context.

5 In contrast to Democratic machines, Republican machines in the United States were built "in the air" Lincoln Steffens pointed out in his classic study of American political machines, "The Shame of the Cities," published in 1904.

6 Of course, local economies may be completely monopolized, but voters remain relatively autonomous because their livelihoods do not depend on the private sector but state resources, such as welfare programs that are under the control of the national government.

7 In April 2017, the Indonesian Supreme Court struck down Article 251 in Law No. 23/ 2014 on Regional Governance. Article 251 allowed governors and ministers to revoke district regulations that were violating provincial and national law. This means that the notoriously slow and corrupt Supreme Court is now the only institution that can revoke local regulations. *De facto*, this has empowered district government heads.

References cited

Anderson, Benedict. 1988. "Cacique Democracy and the Philippines: Origins and Dreams," *New Left Review* 169: 3–31.

Aspinall, Clive. 2001. "Small-Scale Mining in Indonesia," *Mining, Minerals and Sustainable Development* 79 (September) (London: International Institute for Environment and Development and World Business Council for Sustainable Development).

Aspinall, Edward and Muhammad Uhaib As'ad. 2016. "Understanding Family Politics: Successes and Failures of Political Dynasties in Regional Indonesia," *South East Asia Research* 24(3): 420–35.

Behrend, Jacqueline and Laurence Whitehead. 2016. *Illiberal Practices: Territorial Variance Within Large Federal Democracies* (Baltimore MD: Johns Hopkins University Press).

Buehler, Michael. 2009a. *Predatory Tax Practices Are Entrenched.* (Oxford: Oxford Analytica). http://michael buehler.asia/wp-content/uploads/2017/03/PredatoryTaxSystem.pdf (Accessed 16 March 2017).

———. 2009b. "The New Regional Taxation Law: An End to Predatory Taxation?" *Van Zorge Report* XI(8). http://michaelbuehler.asia/wp-content/uploads/2012/06/BuehlerVanZorge2009.pdf (Accessed 16 March 2017).

———. 2010. "Decentralisation and Local Democracy in Indonesia: The Marginalisation of the Public Sphere," in Edward Aspinall and Marcus Mietzner, eds., *Problems of Democratisation in Indonesia: Elections, Institutions and Society* (Singapore: ISEAS), pp. 267–85.

———. 2011. "Indonesia's Law on Public Services No. 25/ 2009: Changing State-Society Relations or Continuing Politics as Usual?" *Bulletin of Indonesian Economic Studies* 47(1): 65–86.

————. 2012. "Revisiting the Inclusion-Moderation Thesis in the Context of Decentralized Institutions: The Behavior of Indonesia's Prosperous Justice Party in National and Local Politics," *Party Politics* 19(2): 210–29.

————. 2013. "Married With Children: The Second Round of Direct Elections for Governors and District Heads Shows That Democratisation Is Allowing Powerful Families to Entrench Themselves in Local Politics," *Inside Indonesia* 112 (July–September). www.insideindonesia.org/married-with-children (Accessed 23 December 2016).

Brodjonegoro, Bambang and Jorge Martinez-Vazquez. 2005. "An Analysis of Indonesia's Transfer System: Recent Performance and Future Prospects," in Jorge Martinez-Vazquez, Sri Mulyani Indrawati, and James Alm, eds., *Reforming Intergovernmental Fiscal Relations and the Rebuilding of Indonesia: The "Big Bang" Program and Its Economic Consequences* (Cheltenham: Edward Elgar Publishing), pp. 159–98.

Erie, Steven P. 1988. *Rainbow's End: Irish-Americans and the Dilemmas of Urban Machine Politics* (Berkeley and Los Angeles: University of California Press).

Gervasoni, Carlos. 2010. "A Rentier Theory of Subnational Regimes: Fiscal Federalism, Democracy, and Authoritarianism in the Argentine Provinces," *World Politics* 62(2): 302–40.

Gibson, Edward. 2012. *Boundary Control: Subnational Authoritarianism in Federal Democracies* (New York: Cambridge University Press).

Giraudy, Augustina. 2015. *Democrats and Autocrats: Pathways of Subnational Undemocratic Regime Continuity Within Democratic Countries* (New York: Oxford University Press).

Hadiz, Vedi. 2010. *Localising Power in Post-Authoritarian Indonesia: A Southeast Asian Perspective* (Stanford: Stanford University Press).

Hale, Henry E. 2003. "Explaining Machine Politics in Russia's Regions: Economy, Ethnicity, and Legacy," *Post-Soviet Affairs* 19(3): 228–63.

Hart, Gillian. 1986. *Power, Labor, and Livelihood: Processes of Change in Rural Java* (Berkeley: University of California Press).

Hefner, Robert. 1993. *The Political Economy of Mountain Java: An Interpretive History* (Berkeley: University of California Press).

Kochanova, Anna, Bob Rijkers and Mary Hallward-Driemeier. n.y. "Cronyism and Competition in Indonesian Manufacturing Pre and Post Suharto," Society for Institutional and Organizational Economics. http://papers.sioe.org/paper/1373.html (Accessed 16 March 2017).

Kompas. 2005. "Kilasan Peristiwa: Pilkada Datang, Pejabat Hilang," *Kompas*, 31 July: 14.

————. 2011. "Pegawai Negeri Sipil: Moratorium Peluang Jual–Beli Formasi," *Kompas*, 16 September: 2.

Kristiansen, Stein and Muhid Ramli. 2006. "Buying an Income: The Market for Civil Service Positions in Indonesia," *Contemporary Southeast Asia* 28(2): 207–33.

Kristiansen, Stein and Lambang Trijono. 2005. "Authority and Law Enforcement: Local Government Reforms and Security Systems in Indonesia," *Contemporary Southeast Asia* 27(2): 236–54.

Lankina, Tomila and Lullit Getachew. 2012. "Mission or Empire, Word or Sword? The Human Capital Legacy in Postcolonial Democratic Development," *American Journal of Political Science* 56(2): 465–83.

Mann, Michael. 1986. *The Sources of Social Power Volume 1: A History of Power From the Beginning to AD 1760* (Cambridge: Cambridge University Press).

McCarthy, John. 2007. "Sold Down the River: Renegotiating Public Power Over Nature in Central Kalimantan," in Henk Schulte Nordholt and Gerry van Klinken, eds., *Renegotiating Boundaries: Local Politics in Post-Suharto Indonesia* (Leiden: KITLV Press), pp. 151–76.

McCoy, Alfred. 2009. *An Anarchy of Families: State and Family in the Philippines* (Madison: University of Wisconsin Press).

McMann, Kelly M. 2006. *Economic Autonomy and Democracy: Hybrid Regimes in Russia and Kyrgyzstan* (New York City: Cambridge University Press).

McVey, Ruth. 2000. "Of Greed and Violence and Other Signs of Progress," in Ruth McVey, ed., *Money and Power in Provincial Thailand* (Copenhagen, NIAS Press), pp. 1–29.

Montero, Alfred. 2011. "The New Boss Same as the Old Boss? Incumbency and the Decline of Conservative Rule in the Brazilian Northeast." *American Political Science Association Meeting*. Seattle. http://people.carleton.edu/~amontero/The%20New%20Boss%20Same%20As%20the%20Old%20Boss.pdf (Accessed 15 March 2017).

Ngusmanto, Ngusmanto. 2016. "*Pilkada 2015* and Patronage Practice Among Bureaucrat in West Kalimantan, Indonesia," *Asian Social Science* 12(9). http://dx.doi.org/10.5539/ass.v12n9p236 (Accessed 24 December 2016).

Ockey, James. 1998. "Crime, Society, and Politics in Thailand," in Carl A. Trocki, ed., *Gangsters, Democracy, and the State in Southeast Asia.* Vol. 17 (Ithaca: SEAP Publications), pp. 39–54.

Ostwald, Kai, Yuhki Tajima and Krislert Samphantharak. 2016. "Indonesia's Decentralization Experiment: Motivations, Successes, and Unintended Consequences," *Journal of Southeast Asian Economies* 33(2): 139–56.

Panebianco Angelo. 1988. *Political Parties: Organization and Power* (London and New York: Cambridge University Press).

Pincus, Jonathan. 1996. *Class Power and Agrarian Change: Land and Labour in Rural West Java* (London: St. Martin's Press).

Rahman, Abdul. 2017. "Tax Compliance in Indonesia: The Role of Public Officials as Taxpayers." (Unpublished Ph.D. Thesis. Enschede, The Netherlands: University of Twente). http://doc.utwente.nl/102666/ (Accessed 16 March 2017).

Rist, Lucy, Laurene Feintrenie, and Patrice Levang. 2010. "The Livelihood Impacts of Oil Palm: Smallholders in Indonesia," *Biodiversity and Conservation* 19(4): 1009–24.

Rothenberg, Alexander D., Samuel Bazzi, Shanthi Nataraj and Amalavoyal Chari. 2016. "Assessing the Spatial Concentration of Indonesia's Manufacturing Sector: Evidence From Three Decades." Rand Working Paper Series WR-1180. https://papers.ssrn.com/sol3/papers.cfm?abstract_id=2897162 (Accessed 16 March 2017).

Safitri, Hilmayati. 2012. "Economic Corridor Policy, Land Concentration and 'Social Exclusion.'" (unpublished MA Thesis. The Hague, The Netherlands: Institute of Social Studies). https://thesis.eur.nl/pub/13083/

Savirani, Amalinda. 2016. "Survival Against the Odds: The Djunaid Family of Pekalongan, Central Java," *South East Asia Research* 24(3): 407–19.

Schneider, Jane C. and Peter T. Schneider. 2003. *Reversible Destiny: Mafia, Antimafia, and the Struggle for Palermo* (Berkeley and Los Angeles: University of California Press).

Scott, James C. 1969. "Corruption, Machine Politics, and Political Change," *American Political Science Review* 63(4): 1148–58.

Sidel, John T. 2014. "Economic Foundations of Subnational Authoritarianism: Insights and Evidence From Qualitative and Quantitative Research," *Democratization* 21(1): 161–84.

Sjahrir, Suharnoko Bambang, Kristina Kis-Katos and Günther G. Schulze. 2013. "Administrative Overspending in Indonesian Districts: The Role of Local Politics," University of Freiburg: Department of International Economic Policy Discussion Paper Series No. 24.

Steffens, Lincoln. 1904. *The Shame of the Cities* (New York: Hill and Wang).

Tans, Ryan. 2012. *Mobilizing Resources, Building Coalitions: Local Power in Indonesia* (Honolulu: East–West Center).

Thomsen, Stephen. 1999. "Southeast Asia: The Role of Foreign Direct Investment Policies in Development," OECD Working Papers on International Investment, 1999/01 (OECD Publishing). http://dx.doi.org/10.1787/431857742281

Trounstine, Jessica. 2008. *Political Monopolies in American Cities: The Rise and Fall of Bosses and Reformers* (Chicago: The University of Chicago Press).

Weitz-Shapiro, Rebecca. 2015. *Curbing Clientelism in Argentina: Politics, Poverty, and Social Policy* (New York: Cambridge University Press).

White, Ben. 1991. "Economic Diversification and Agrarian Change in Rural Java, 1900–1990," in Paul Alexander, Peter Boomgaard, and Ben White, eds., *In the Shadow of Agriculture: Non-Farm Activities in the Javanese Economy, Past and Present* (Amsterdam: Royal Tropical Institute), pp. 41–70.

9

ETHNIC, RELIGIOUS, AND REGIONAL CONFLICT

Chris Wilson

In early 1998, Indonesia was a highly authoritarian and corrupt state, ruled since 1966 by President Soeharto. It is now the most democratic state in Southeast Asia. The transition was rapid and remarkable, but it was also violent in some areas. Over four tumultuous years, Indonesia saw its worst violence since the extermination of the Left in 1965 and 1966. Eight provinces of the country saw extensive violent conflict, either renewed insurgency against the state or communal violence between ethnic and religious communities. Between 10,000 and 20,000 people died in this turmoil, and hundreds of thousands fled their homes by land or sea. But almost as quickly as it exploded, this conflict disappeared. By 2005, Indonesia was once again stable and mostly peaceful and now has a democratically elected government.

This series of conflicts between 1998 and 2005 was clearly connected to the dramatic political transition triggered by the resignation of President Soeharto in May 1998. Soeharto's repressive New Order had mostly kept the peace, but it was at a cost. Politics had become collusive, corrupt, and nepotistic and state institutions had been hollowed out. As minor violent events set off simultaneous crises in multiple areas, transitional governments in Jakarta grappling with their own survival proved unable to prevent their escalation. That violent conflict should occur during rapid democratization after a long period of authoritarian rule was not, in retrospect at least, surprising. Scholars of conflict elsewhere have demonstrated how elites threatened by political liberalization often use nationalist rhetoric to gain or retain power, facing little resistance from and exploiting weak state institutions (Mansfield and Snyder 2005: 54). Indonesia appears to have followed this pattern during the transition period beginning in 1998. Known as Reformasi in Indonesia, the sudden onset of political participation brought a rush of new political parties, intensified competition for office among national and local elites, and evoked fervor on the streets.

Yet this political transformation affected all provinces and districts of Indonesia, but only a very small proportion suffered ethnic or secessionist war. Further, none of the eight main conflicts should be understood as simply provoked by national elites afraid of losing power. In some areas, histories of state abuse or intercommunal rivalry interacted with the national transition in particularly volatile ways. This chapter will not present case studies of each conflict but will instead identify important similarities and differences between them.

Secessionist conflict

The conflict literature would categorize Indonesia as an archetypal insurgency-prone state. With many ethnic groups concentrated in remote, inaccessible, and resource-rich sub-state regions and with a long, sometimes brutal authoritarian history, the country had many conditions conducive to separatist conflict. Three such regions – East Timor (now Timor Leste), Aceh, and Papua – waged rebellions of varying intensity for much of the period since they were incorporated into the country. With the resignation of President Soeharto in May 1998 and the onset of democratization, many in each region again demanded greater self-determination or independence.

Both East Timor and Papua were incorporated into modern Indonesia against their will and well after the country's independence. As a Portuguese colony, East Timor had never been part of the Dutch East Indies. Ostensibly in response to a communist takeover, the Indonesian military invaded East Timor in December 1975, and six months later, the territory became the country's twenty-seventh province. A combined political and military resistance against Indonesia emerged and continued until eventual independence in 1999. Papua had been part of the former colonial unit but had been retained by the Netherlands until the early 1960s. In keeping with the anti-colonial *zeitgeist* or the era, the United States sponsored an agreement by which the territory would be transferred to the United Nations, then to Indonesia, and then offered self-determination. In 1969, carefully selected Papuan elders instead voted to become part of Indonesia through the highly coercive "Act of Free Choice." Soon after, the Free Papua Organization (Organisasi Papua Merdeka, OPM) began a low-level armed resistance. Aceh had, by contrast, been part of Indonesia since the country's inception, but an early dispute over the role of Islamic law in the constitution led many Acehnese to join the Darul Islam rebellion. While that uprising was quelled, a new insurgent organization, the Free Aceh Movement (Gerakan Aceh Merdeka, GAM), was formed in 1976. GAM waged two periods of insurgency against the Soeharto regime. In each case, but particularly in Papua and Timor, a strong sense of national distinctiveness and belief that the region had been incorporated illegally provided separatist movements with a powerful rationale of resistance.

Yet there was nothing inevitable about rebellion in any of the regions, despite their forceful inclusion into the republic. Had Jakarta offered greater autonomy and a more inclusive, less abusive approach, this would likely have engendered a greater willingness to integrate into Indonesia (as can be seen in contemporary Aceh, discussed in the following). New Order repression simply strengthened distinct Acehnese, Papuan, and Timorese identities in opposition to Indonesia. While revived by democratization, all three insurgencies had their roots in the predemocratic era.

Human rights abuses were central to all three insurgencies. While rebel groups sometimes brutalized civilians, particularly migrants from elsewhere in the country, the security forces did so with much greater regularity and impunity. Military operations involved extra-judicial killings, shootings on civilian crowds, rapes, forced displacement, routine assaults, and the disappearance of activists. The first years of Indonesia's occupation of East Timor were particularly brutal: several hundred thousand people were forced into resettlement camps, and perhaps 100,000 people died from mistreatment, disease, or starvation (Cotton 2000: 3). The killing of 250 peaceful protesters at the Santa Cruz cemetery in Dili in 2001 was just the most internationally known of these events. Similar events occurred elsewhere with enough regularity to create widespread support for secession. GAM's independence struggle prompted a repressive military occupation, which lasted from the late 1980s until the fall of the New Order in 1998. Approximately 1,000 people were killed and many more disappeared during this operation, abuses which played a major role in renewed rebellion during the democratization period. The Achenese, Papuans, and Timorese had little choice but to accept these abuses during the New Order period, but the instability accompanying the fall of Soeharto's New Order regime provided a striking opportunity for self-determination.

Other developments increased tension in the three provinces. Migration of people from elsewhere in Indonesia increased anxiety and anger among indigenous communities, particularly in Papua. The impact of in-migration in Papua has been extensive: from being 96% of the local population in 1971, Papuans now comprise less than half. Often described as an intentional government program of "transmigration," the majority of those moving to Papua have done so independently in search of economic opportunity. This transformation has been most visible in major cities, such as Jayapura, where non-Papuans make up approximately 65% of the population (Chauvel 2008: 151). Periodic riots driven by migration-related tension have occurred since the 1980s. In East Timor, animosity toward migrants led to riots between Timorese and Bugis migrants in the mid-1990s.

Chronic poverty and poor governance also played a role in driving support for independence. Although Aceh and Papua were home to the nation's most valuable natural resources in the form of the Arun gas field and Grasberg gold and copper mine (the world's largest gold mine and Indonesia's biggest taxpayer), local communities continued to live with some of the lowest human development indicators in the country, particularly in Papua and East Timor. The extraction of local resources enriched New Order officials and resource companies but left little benefit for the provinces. Indeed, in causing the degradation of rivers, soil, and forests and through the extraction of land and exclusion of marine areas, large-scale resource projects have often undermined local development.

While support for secession from Indonesia was strong in each province, the armed movements varied in their capacity to challenge the state. The low-level insurgency in Papua by the OPM has been too fragmented to mount a serious challenge to Indonesian sovereignty in the way GAM and Falintil did in Aceh and East Timor. The latter organizations were more structured and hierarchical and had better access to weapons and a greater international profile and support. This varied capacity influenced the events in each province in the democratization era. Also important was the material and ideological value Indonesia placed on each region. Aceh and Papua were not only rich in natural resources and tax income but were seen as integral parts of the Indonesian nation in a way that East Timor was not.

The surprising decision in early 1999 by the Habibie administration to offer the Timorese a referendum on independence set off a demonstration effect in the other regions. By 1998, Indonesia was facing substantial international criticism over its continued occupation of East Timor. In January 1999, interim president B. J. Habibie requested that the United Nations hold a referendum in the province, giving the Timorese a choice: remain as part of the country and enjoy special autonomy or secede. When it became clear that the vast majority of Timorese supported withdrawal from Indonesia, pro-integration militias carried out a campaign of violence against civilians. These killings were tolerated, if not orchestrated, by the Indonesian security forces. Approximately 1,500 people had lost their lives by the time the Australian-led intervention force established security. By 2002, the Democratic Republic of Timor Leste became the first newly sovereign state of the twenty-first century.

Partly in response to this offer to the Timorese, Acehnese, and Papuans also rallied and demanded a similar vote. However the result of the referendum in Timor had raised nationalist concerns among the political and military elite, and there was resistance to any further risk to

Indonesian sovereignty. As the reformist, if erratic, government of Abdurrahman Wahid attempted to assuage anger in Aceh by freeing political prisoners and offering to punish abusive military personnel, GAM used this new space to mobilize support and establish a form of parallel state in controlled areas. A renewed military offensive saw abuses by both sides and numerous civilian casualties. The two sides were at a stalemate by the end of 2004 when the Indian Ocean tsunami devastated coastal areas of the province. Within months, both sides had seized the opportunity for peace.

Protest and mobilization also increased in Papua at the eastern end of the country as the political landscape opened in 1998. After the Timorese voted to secede in 1998, the Indonesian Government was reluctant to offer Papuans a similar choice. But with the Papuans choosing non-violent mobilization, the government was willing to make other concessions to anti-integration sentiment in the province. The Wahid government offered a package of special autonomy to the region, but this has been much less successful than that in Aceh, as discussed in the following section. Papua continues to see sporadic attacks against security forces, human rights abuses, and the detention of those supporting separatist sentiment.

Communal war

Even more violent than the secessionist struggles were a series of local wars between ethnic and religious communities, or at least their most militant members. Serious communal violence was confined to five provinces – Maluku, North Maluku, Central Sulawesi, West Kalimantan, and Central Kalimantan, sometimes concentrated in particular districts within them. Communal clashes had started before Soeharto's resignation, suggesting intergroup tension was already becoming endemic to the authoritarian era. Mobs attacked Chinese churches in the cities of Situbondo and Tasikmalaya in 1996. In 1997, in the dying days of the Soeharto regime, violence between local Dayaks and migrants from the island of Madura caused over 500 deaths in the province of West Kalimantan. Yet the ethnic and religious violence that broke out after the democratic transition began was on an unprecedented scale. Approximately fifteen thousand people died, more than one million were displaced, and large areas of affected provinces were destroyed.

There are important differences between the five large communal wars. Most notably, the foremost cleavage differed from place to place. Religion was central in the conflicts in the east of the country (in Maluku, North Maluku, and Sulawesi), where large Christian communities make up a sizeable proportion of the local population. In West and Central Kalimantan, however, ethnic animosity was paramount. Some conflicts burned themselves out quickly, such as those in Kalimantan, where the Madurese were quickly expelled from the province. Others, such as that in Maluku, remained at a high intensity for several years.

Yet the five ethnic and religious conflicts share some important similarities, which present lessons for understanding collective violence both in Indonesia and elsewhere. Most clearly, all took place against a backdrop of dramatic political change emanating from Jakarta. Between 1998 and 1999, the Asian Financial Crisis first devastated many local economies, driving people from formal employment into the informal sector and sending prices skyrocketing. The resignation of Soeharto compounded this turmoil, bringing both excitement over a new democratic future but also concerns over what that reality would look like. Most important, democratization raised questions over who would now assume power in each province, city, and district. Where two religious or ethnic communities laid claim to local dominance, those concerns led to tension and ultimately violence. In most cases, the triggering incidents of these large conflicts were minor, most often public fights between youths. These normally routine individual disputes were enflamed by two larger surrounding phenomena: a contest for status between communities and a general social breakdown from rapid political and economic change.

Contrary to many claims at the time, the violence in remote areas of the archipelago was not incited from Jakarta, either by the armed forces or former members of the New Order regime attempting to retain power. Violence in one location often had a "spillover" effect on another province, heightening tension and introducing new repertoires of ethnic contention. But while the conflicts were not provoked from the center, instability in Jakarta and the crises in legitimacy faced by the Habibie and Wahid administrations meant that violence in remote areas like Maluku or Kalimantan could rapidly escalate and spread.

The end of decades of military rule in Indonesia brought a swift decline in the capacity and morale of state security institutions. As they were blamed for the worst depredations of the New Order, morale among personnel plummeted. The fear of prosecution sometimes deterred the security forces from using the force necessary to stop escalating violence. In some locations, the army and police lacked the capacity to respond effectively. In rural areas, like Kao Malifut in North Maluku or Sampit in Central Kalimantan, only a handful of personnel faced large mobs. With so many conflicts occurring simultaneously, many troops were diverted elsewhere, including approximately 18,000 troops diverted to East Timor in the lead up to the August 1999 referendum (Crouch 2010: 249). In Ambon, military units departed to quell minor disturbances on surrounding islands just before Christian and Muslim rioting broke out in the capital. Yet the security forces were far from blameless in the turmoil. In most areas, sufficient personnel were present to prevent attacks yet chose to withdraw. In North Maluku, soldiers allowed a jihadist attack on the village of Duma, which claimed the lives of 250 people. In some areas, an overzealous response from security forces aggravated the killing. The military and police came into often violent confrontation over resources in many areas. Personnel also often exploited the fear and instability of conflict to extract rents from victims (Davidson 2008: 142; Wilson 2008: 174) or became involved in the fighting out of communal solidarity.

All five communal conflicts were preceded by tensions over changing demographic conditions through the movement of people within and between provinces over the past decades. Connections to place have long been important in Indonesia: when the country democratized, claims of indigeneity became increasingly politically salient. This was most clearly seen in Kalimantan, where Dayaks and Malays both sought to dominate "homeland" districts, using violence against the Madurese to underline their political claims. Migration was also a crucial source of tension before the religious conflicts. In Ambon, large numbers of migrants from South Sulawesi had altered the demographic and economic and political balance over previous decades, and Muslims were increasingly occupying high-status roles in the civil service and politics. In Poso, migration from South Sulawesi as well as government-sponsored transmigration swung the demographic balance in favor of Muslims (Aragon 2001: 56–7; McRae 2013: 26–7). In the front line of all the conflicts, in places like Ambon, Poso, Malifut, and Sampit, tensions over employment, land use, and crime grew over time. Both indigenous and migrant communities became anxious over a loss of political and economic control. Many saw in the national transition either the opportunity to rectify this decline or feared that their position might become dramatically worse. Ethnic affiliation became a key determinant of political support.

The communal conflicts were not just a matter of intergroup animosities, however, nor of the political opportunity afforded by the nationwide political transition. The national changes also created powerful incentives for elites to mobilize people along identity lines and to manipulate ethno-religious tensions. Three nationwide changes had major consequences for life in the regions: democratization, the decentralization of political and financial authority to the local level, and the process of redistricting of new administrative units known as pemekaran. While violence did not always emerge as electoral contests were in full swing, the question of who was to hold local power was never far from the minds of the main protagonists.

Far more than for national-level elections, winning and losing local office held immense consequences for local elites and their followers. The public service is a crucial source of employment and access to state resources in Indonesia, particularly in areas with little private sector and high rates of urbanization (Van Klinken 2007: 42). Employment in local government departments and the large offices of the governor and district heads is often the only stable career available. These positions also provide officials with the possibility of extracting further wealth through bribes and other forms of corruption, particularly in so-called "wet" departments with large and difficult-to-monitor budgets. From late 1998, parties and politicians now needed to compete for popular support to win seats in local legislatures. Contests over who would become the local executive became heated affairs, both in parliaments and among followers on the streets.

The significance of winning local political office increased further with a dramatic process of decentralization initiated early in the transition. With two laws passed in 1999, Indonesia moved from being highly centralized to devolving substantial political and financial authority to provincial, city, and district governments. Local governments were now to receive a far greater proportion of revenue from natural resources and government transfers. Whole government departments were to be transferred from Jakarta or created anew in the regions, generating new lucrative bureaucratic employment opportunities and construction contracts. Although there were substantial benefits from this change, the process itself was fraught with risks so soon in the democratization process. Dominating local office became increasingly valuable at the very time elites needed to compete for office but before democratic institutions and norms had been established.

Accompanying the process of decentralization of authority was the proliferation of dozens of new districts and provinces known as pemekaran (literally "blossoming," but more aptly "redistricting"). The number of districts (kabupaten) in Indonesia increased from 341 in 1999 to 497 by 2010. While certainly "bringing government closer to the people," as was its stated goal, pemekaran also emphasized the importance of local ethnic and religious identities. Claims to indigeneity and a special right to political dominance in one's homeland became a crucial path to power. While some administrative units had indeed been too large and unmanageable, the motive of local leaders in demanding a new district was often primarily to exploit new opportunities for patronage, government contracts, and bureaucratic employment. Demands for and the creation of new administrations frequently created tensions. In North Maluku, for example, the creation of a new province and its impending division into numerous new districts was central to the initiation and escalation of ethnic and religious fighting in the area.

The intensified political competition from 1999 cannot by itself explain the communal violence in five Indonesian provinces of course. Electoral contests, decentralization, and the division of districts took place elsewhere with no violence. And some of the worst clashes, such as those in Ambon in January 1999, occurred many months before elections were to be held. Ethnic and religious violence is rarely purely instrumental: emotion, status rivalries, and contingency all also play their part. Political campaigning from late 1998 was sharpened not only by the rewards of political office but by the fears some groups had of being dominated by an ethnic or religious other, a sense of injustice at loss of control in one's homeland, distrust of the security forces, and inter-group animosities.

Ending violence and building peace

In the worst affected areas, the consequences of conflict were extensive and took years to dissipate. By 2001, there were 1.4 million internally displaced persons in Indonesia (Hedman 2008: 4). Approximately half that number remained displaced by 2004, many IDPs remaining in camps with security concerns hindering their return or because resettlement funds provided by the central government and international agencies had been corrupted by local government. In addition to the extensive loss of life and displacement, much of the infrastructure of affected provinces or districts was destroyed, compounding the effects of the Asian Financial Crisis. As protagonists took control of enemy territory, they destroyed schools, health clinics, markets, and gardens. Poverty increased in conflict-affected areas more than other Indonesian provinces that had suffered the impact of the financial crisis but not experienced extensive collective violence. In Aceh, for example, the poverty rate increased from 14.8% of the population in 1998 to 28.4% in 2004 (Barron 2008: 2). The violence undermined trust in neighboring communities and in state security institutions suspected of provocation and failing to defend victims from attacks.

While at their height, these conflicts appeared as if they might lead to state failure or even Indonesia's disintegration; in fact, they were a temporary and violent recalibration of the country after centuries of indigenous and colonial authoritarian rule. By 2005, the country's state institutions and economy had stabilized and major violent conflict had disappeared. The consolidation of democracy facilitated peace in many areas, allowing a political compromise between the government and GAM in Aceh for example. However, the eight conflicts discussed in this chapter ended in very different ways. The most dramatic finale was that in East Timor, where a referendum on independence saw the vast majority of voters elect to secede from Indonesia.

In the other secessionist insurgencies, the government used a combination of ongoing repression and concessions. Aceh is now recognized as a remarkably successful case of negotiated settlement to civil war. Following the Indian Ocean tsunami, the government and GAM seized the opportunity for peace. A central step in bringing the rebellion in Aceh to an end was a new willingness on the part of GAM for Aceh to remain part of Indonesia. From that concession, the path to the Memorandum of Understanding (MoU) between GAM and the government of Indonesia was clear. The government also made important concessions toward GAM and Aceh, in particular allowing local political parties to contest elections in the province, something disallowed elsewhere in the country. In permitting GAM to form one of these parties and go on to win office, the government gave the former rebels the incentive to lay down their arms. The agreed package of special autonomy also stipulated that Aceh would receive 70% of local oil and gas revenue and increased revenue from the central government. President Yudhoyono's past as a former general gave him an almost unique position to convince the military to accept the outcome of negotiation. Former GAM rebels have dominated politics and important economic sectors in Aceh (Aspinall 2009), meaning the most likely "spoilers" of the peace have been neutralized.

While the Wahid government made similar concessions to Papua, violence has continued. Local leaders and the government agreed on a special autonomy package, granted by Law No. 21, 2001, which devolved authority of many elements of governance similar to that in Aceh. A new Papuan People's Assembly (MRP) was established to represent indigenous Papuans, while the central government transferred large fiscal resources to the region. Yet special autonomy has been far less successful in Papua than in Aceh. As subsequent administrations failed to implement the agreement fully, and many Papuans believed the law had been imposed on them rather than negotiated in good faith, secessionist activity and violence continued (Bertrand 2014: 176). The division of the region into two provinces, Papua and West Papua (with a third not yet formalized), by presidential instruction, divided the independence movement and created competition within the Papuan elite over new government positions and contracts. Predations by the security forces have also continued, exemplified by the killing of independence leader Theys Eluay. Most areas of Papua continue to have limited state services with few clinics or education facilities and inadequate staff to maintain them. The failed promise of special autonomy likely increased secessionist sentiment and explains a period of renewed instability beginning in 2009.

The religious conflicts ended through a messy combination of government and grassroots initiatives. A great deal of the impetus for peace in these areas came from local communities themselves. Motivated by the devastation wrought by conflict and now wary of provocateurs seeking to create tensions, many local communities took the initiative in building peace. In Maluku and North Maluku, Christian and Muslim leaders used security personnel to facilitate small meetings, gradually preparing the way for the return of IDPs and larger processes of reconciliation. While religion had been used to provoke violence, leaders now used it to facilitate peace, creating interfaith fora in Maluku, North Maluku, and Poso (Al Qurtuby 2016: 127). In some areas, communities have turned to local cultural traditions (adat) to build peace and prevent the escalation of small incidents. In Maluku, Christians and Muslims have revived old village alliances of mutual assistance known as pela gandong. While these traditions may create greater bonds between indigenous communities, there is some risk they may enhance cleavages between locals and migrants however.

In West and Central Kalimantan, successful campaigns of ethnic cleansing brought the killings to a halt. Most Madurese were expelled from the provinces or forced into restricted areas, the government prioritizing stability over the IDPs' rights to reside anywhere in the country. Little in the way of reconciliation has been attempted, and many districts now operate under a form of Dayak and Malay ethnic nationalism.

Central and local governments played a crucial role in building peace in the communal conflicts. Once the turmoil of the Habibie and Wahid administrations had subsided, the central government provided the necessary political space and security for the above grassroots initiatives. It also convened much larger meetings, including those leading to the Malino I and II agreements, which helped end the Poso and Maluku conflicts. While the central government has led many peace initiatives, it has fallen to provincial and district governments to implement their terms and deal with the volatile nature of post-conflict contexts (Al Qurtuby 2016: 159). Local initiatives have been varied and tailored to specific contexts. In several cases, local governments have co-opted militia members into local political and economic life as a way of preventing a return to violence. The governments in Maluku and North Maluku provided important roles to the leaders of both Christian and Muslim militias.

Political leaders and parties have also developed peacebuilding mechanisms designed to depoliticize ethno-religious identity. In many post-conflict elections, candidates have chosen to run for office with a member of the opposing community, an agreement that both increases the pair's potential number of supporters but also motivates the candidates to moderate their rhetoric so as to win support from both communities. In elections for the governor of Maluku, held in 2003 and 2008, all pairs of candidates had both a Christian and Muslim on the ticket (Crouch 2010: 268). The same arrangement was used in Poso in 2008 (Aspinall 2011: 303). In West Kalimantan, Dayaks and Malays also shared the ballot in 2005.

The role played by security forces varied from place to place and over time. The implementation of civil emergency in Maluku and North Maluku led to a gradual decline in violence from mid-2000. Personnel were given greater authority to use force and external troops acted more professionally and impartially than local units, which had often become heavily involved in the fighting. In Maluku, for example, thousands of security personnel had joined the fighting on both sides, escalating and prolonging the fighting (Crouch 2010: 250, 256). In some areas, while not joining the violence, military and police personnel exploited the fear of and breakdown in law and order to extract money or belongings from those at risk of attack or fleeing their homes. In others, they attempted to derail a return to normalcy by provoking further conflict so they could continue to benefit from instability, either through receiving greater allowances for service in designated conflicts zones or from the security payments from local businesses. Military abuses also exacerbated the situation in Papua, Aceh, and East Timor.

Ongoing challenges and continuing violence

While the decline of violent conflict in Indonesia has been remarkable and a similar recurrence of the violence of 1999 to 2002 is highly unlikely, several risks remain. There have been few prosecutions of those involved in the worst human rights abuses, either from ethnonationalist militias or the security forces, thereby maintaining a culture of impunity. Important issues remain unresolved, including rivalries between the military and police and disagreements over their relative responsibilities and the military's "territorial command structure" through which locally based units remain involved in off-budget economic activities. The military and police continue to be involved in resource extraction, such as logging, leading to the intimidation of local communities protesting over land expropriation and environmental degradation. The most serious risks of large-scale conflict are in Papua, where the government continues to enjoy a large power advantage but weak legitimacy. Partly because of the lucrative nature of resource extraction in the region, the security forces have little interest in total reconciliation with the OPM or other Papuan groups. While the independence movement remains severely fragmented and poses no threat to Indonesian sovereignty, members of the security forces continue to periodically fire on unarmed protesters while militant Papuan factions sometimes attack guard posts. Of concern, some militants see their best chance of self-determination in provoking a military crackdown (IPAC 2015: 22), a strategy almost certain to lead to large loss of life and little positive change in Papua. There is unlikely to be a military end to the conflict in Papua. If the region is to be fully integrated into Indonesia, the government should focus on further removing the security forces from extra-curricular economic activities, curbing abuses, reintegrating militants, and reducing resource- and land-related grievance in the region.

Despite the dramatic decline in ethnic and religious violence in Indonesia, large-scale conflict has not disappeared altogether. Since 2011, large communal riots have occurred in Ambon, Tarakan in East Kalimantan, and Lampung in Sumatra. Each case demonstrated that many of the same causes of intergroup conflict remain in Indonesia, including the role of patronage in local government and volatile land- and identity-based tensions (Wilson 2015). In each case, however, the response of the central government and national security forces has been rapid and more vigorous than during the transition. Jakarta quickly sent reinforcements to halt the violence, and such clashes have rarely lasted more than a few days. There are several reasons for this improved response, including a far more stable political situation in the capital, widespread memory of the escalation that occurred from 1999, and the fact that recent incidents have been isolated rather than occurring simultaneously in many areas.

Of additional concern, Indonesia has witnessed ongoing repression of religious minorities by Islamist extremists. Mobs have attacked followers of the Ahmadiyah religion in Cikeusik in Banten; Christians in Bekasi, Central Java, and elsewhere; and Shi'a in Madura (Wilson 2015). Neither the central government nor the justice system has done a great deal to prevent these attacks while local politicians have increasingly seen the utility of aligning themselves with extremist groups, such as the Islamic Defenders Front (FPI). Groups such as FPI have been allowed to proliferate and grow and been used at opportune times by local and even national politicians, most notably during the 2017 Jakarta elections.

Conclusion

The communal and separatist violence that erupted between 1998 and 2002 never threatened the Indonesian state. With the secession of Timor Leste, only seven of Indonesia's twenty-six provinces were beset by large-scale violent conflict. Yet for the approximately fifteen million people living in those provinces, the conflicts were devastating. In addition to the thousands who died, many more were injured or traumatized by witnessing the violence firsthand. More than one million people were displaced to IDP camps, often remaining in poor conditions for several years. The conflicts destroyed local economies and infrastructure and left opposing communities lacking the trust and cohesion to rebuild them. Until around 2003, several district and provincial governments ceased to function.

As tragic as the explosion of violence in so many parts of the country was, it quickly dissipated. Elections were held, many incumbents were ousted peacefully, the economy grew again, and the country stabilized. Organized violence has not disappeared altogether, nor have many of the causes of the earlier conflicts. But major outbreaks are now rare, and the government's response is quicker and more effective than before. In most areas of the country, there is little elite or societal support for collective violence. Papua remains the region most at risk of mass violence. Security force involvement in resource extraction and a repressive response to any displays of Papuan nationalism, along with factionalism among the Papua separatist movement, all create a volatile situation that requires far greater attention by Jakarta. Violence against minorities remains a serious, if sporadic, problem. Indonesia's progress has been remarkable, from an authoritarian state with disdain for human rights to a vibrant democracy. As the country has democratized, most localized conflicts have been resolved, but risks of organized violence remain. Further progress will require further steps toward a rights-based liberal democracy.

References cited

Al Qurtuby, Sumanto. 2016. *Religious Violence and Conciliation in Indonesia: Christians and Muslims in the Moluccas* (London and New York: Routledge).

Aragon, Lorraine V. 2001. "Communal Violence in Poso, Central Sulawesi: Where People Eat Fish and Fish Eat People," *Indonesia* 72: 45–79.

Aspinall, Edward. 2009. "Combatants to Contractors: The Political Economy of Peace in Aceh," *Indonesia* 87: 1–34.

———. 2011. "Democratization and Ethnic Politics in Indonesia: Nine Theses," *Journal of East Asian Studies* 11: 289–319.

Barron, Patrick. 2008. "Managing the Resources for Peace: Reconstruction and Peacebuilding in Aceh." World Bank online publication. www.c-r.org/accord-article/managing-resources-peace-reconstruction-and-peacebuilding-aceh (Accessed 2 February 2017).

Bertrand, Jacques. 2014. "Autonomy and Stability: The Perils of Implementation and 'Divide and Rule' Tactics in Papua, Indonesia," *Nationalism and Ethnic Politics* 20(2): 174–99.

Chauvel, Richard. 2008. "Refuge, Displacement, and Dispossession: Responses to Indonesian Rule and Conflict in Papua," in Eva-Lotta Hedman, ed., *Conflict, Violence, and Displacement in Indonesia* (Ithaca: Cornell Southeast Asia Program Publications), pp. 147–72.

Cotton, James. 2000. "The Emergence of an Independent East Timor: National and Regional Challenges," *Contemporary Southeast Asia* 22(1): 1–22.

Crouch, Harold. 2010. *Political Reform in Indonesia After Soeharto* (Singapore: Institute of Southeast Asian Studies).

Davidson, Jamie. 2008. *From Rebellion to Riots: Collective Violence on Indonesian Borneo* (Madison: The University of Wisconsin Press).

Hedman, Eva-Lotta. 2008. "Introduction: Dynamics of Displacement in Indonesia," in Eva-Lotta Hedman, ed., *Conflict, Violence, and Displacement in Indonesia* (Ithaca: Cornell Southeast Asia Program Publications), pp. 3–27.

Institute for Policy Analysis of Conflict (IPAC). 2015. "The Current Status of the Papuan Pro-Independ
ence Movement." IPAC Report no 21 (Accessed 20 May 2016).

Mansfield, Edward D. and Jack Snyder. 2005. *Electing to Fight: Why Emerging Democracies Go to War* (Cambridge, MA: MIT Press).

McRae, Dave. 2013. *A Few Poorly Organized Men: Interreligious Violence in Poso, Indonesia* (Leiden and Boston:
Brill).

Van Klinken, Gerry. 2007. *Communal Violence and Democratization in Indonesia: Small Town Wars* (London and
New York: Routledge).

Wilson, Chris. 2008. *Ethno-Religious Violence in Indonesia: From Soil to God* (London and New York:
Routledge).

Wilson, Chris. 2015. "Illiberal Democracy and Violent Conflict in Contemporary Indonesia," *Democratization* 22(7): 1317–37.

10

HISTORICAL JUSTICE AND THE CASE OF THE 1965 KILLINGS

Katharine McGregor

In transitions from authoritarian to democratic societies, efforts to deal with human rights claims relating to past cases of state violence and associated justice measures are generally at the forefront of societal and governmental agendas. This is because such initiatives can serve to mark out a clear break with the past. They can work to end discrimination against persecuted groups. In the early post-Soeharto era, there were signs that Indonesia too would make a break from past traditions of violence, impunity, and discrimination and pay greater attention to human rights abuses. Yet in the case of the most violent episode in Indonesian history, the 1965 killings and imprisonments, there has been mounting resistance, largely from the military and Islamic organizations implicated in the violence, to any forms of historical justice.

In this chapter, I survey a range of efforts to address this case since 1998. I use the broad term *historical justice* – by which I mean all forms of possible redress for past violence, including trials, apology, reparation, reconciliation, memorialization, and truth seeking – to assess multiple approaches to dealing with this past. I examine how the government responded to demands for reform through new human rights laws and mechanisms that could have enabled the government to achieve historical justice for this case. I trace the bases of ongoing resistance to any forms of historical justice that emanate from an alliance of Islamic groups backed by the military. I argue that this alliance is based both on a historical partnership and new trends in Indonesian politics, including increasing emphasis on Islamic values. It is furthermore underpinned by a broader pact of impunity for the military.

Alongside this trend, however, I argue that activists, including those from within communities implicated in the violence, have tried to achieve historical justice particularly by emphasizing alternative truth telling and attempting to re-humanize survivors. Using the fiftieth anniversary of the violence as a point of reflection, I analyze the increasing emphasis in activism on demanding an end to impunity for past human rights crimes and the increasingly defiant positions of government, military, and religious officials toward this case. But first, let us review current understandings of the 1965 violence.

Background to the violence

From its beginnings in 1920, the Indonesian Communist Party (Partai Komunis Indonesia, PKI) targeted workers promoting an anti-imperialist critique of Dutch colonialism. The PKI experienced the first attack in 1948, during the independence struggle against the Dutch (1945–1949), when following the seizure by leftist troops of the local government in Madiun, the republican army took revenge and executed party leaders without trial. By the mid-1950s, however, the party had recovered by building a mass base among workers and peasants. It achieved 16.4% of the vote in the 1955 elections.

In 1959, President Sukarno introduced a new system of government known as Guided Democracy, during which there were no national elections and only "functional groups" that vied for influence through ministerial posts, mass mobilizations, and presidential favor. The army supported this system primarily to block the PKI's potential electoral success because the army leadership held its own ambitions of an increased political role.

By 1965, the PKI had a membership of 3.5 million, with 20 million more members of affiliated or closely aligned organizations (Mortimer 1974: 366). The party continued to follow a strategy of working within the existing political system, yet the party leadership was also concerned about a repeat of the Madiun incident. To balance the armed power of the military, the PKI began to call for the formation of a fifth force comprised of armed civilians. This was an idea that Sukarno began to back early in 1965 as a way of checking the army's influence (Mortimer 1974: 381–2). The army, however, blocked the proposal.

Sukarno was successful in his campaign for the return of West Irian (now West Papua) from the Dutch. Nevertheless, his more controversial "Confrontation" campaign, designed to prevent the formation of the British-backed new nation of Malaysia, on the grounds that it was an imperialist project, raised alarm in Western countries and led them to increasingly support anti-communists in the army (Simpson 2008: 122–44). These countries especially feared that resource-rich Indonesia might become communist, which could jeopardize foreign investment.

Several factors contributed to increased tensions in Indonesian society in the 1960s. First, President Sukarno promoted the concept of "three pillars" of Indonesian society, Nasakom (Nationalisme, Agama, Komunisme), or nationalism, religion, and communism. This led to competing accusations from the PKI of the army being communist-phobic or from religious organizations of the PKI being anti-religion. Second, the passage of legislation in 1959 and 1960 enabling land reform led to increasing frustration when bureaucrats stalled in implementing these reforms. In parts of Indonesia, peasants began to seize land, leading to violent clashes with those with large land holdings, such as the Nahdlatul Ulama (NU) in East Java. In response, NU created a defense force called Banser (Barisan Ansor Serbaguna, Multipurpose Ansor Troops) to defend land interests, especially in East Java, and in preparation for future armed clashes with the PKI (Fealy and McGregor 2010: 40–1). Third, the failing economy resulted in spiraling inflation and widespread poverty.

Looking back on this period, historians have increasingly emphasized the army's preparation for some form of clash with the PKI. Roosa (2006: 31) argues that that the army was waiting for a "pretext" to crush the party. Melvin (2017) points more specifically to the army's use of the Confrontation campaign to arm and train anti-communist civilians in Sumatra in preparation for such a clash.

In the early hours of October 1, 1965, a group calling itself the September 30th Movement kidnapped and killed six leading generals and one military aide. The corpses of the generals were discarded in a disused well on the outskirts of Jakarta in an area known as Lubang Buaya (Crocodile Hole). The army, under the leadership of Major-General Soeharto, as head of KOSTRAD (Komando Stratégis Angkatan Darat, Army Strategic Command) moved quickly to crush the movement and to label it a PKI plot. PKI members were falsely accused of torturing and mutilating the generals before their deaths (Wieringa 2002: 291). The army then orchestrated mass demonstrations by student and religious organizations, which led to attacks, first on the properties associated with the PKI and then on those labeled "communist." During the course of late 1965 through to 1968, between 500,000 or one million Indonesians were killed by the army, police, and civilian vigilantes (Cribb 1990: 1). More than one million people were imprisoned, mostly without trial (Amnesty International 1977: 41–4). They targeted all persons who were suspected of being "communist," including not only PKI members but also members of all PKI-aligned or affiliated organizations and persons with any ties to the party or these organizations.

Due to limited access to sources and conflicting accounts from participants, it has been difficult for historians to pinpoint precise responsibility for the violence (Roosa 2016: 286–91). There is now increasing consensus, however, that the violence was orchestrated by the anti-communist leadership of the army. In her pathbreaking work, Melvin (2017) has uncovered evidence of extensive planning by Soeharto as commander of KOSTRAD and the regional army commander in Aceh to crush the PKI by deploying trained civilians. It is likely that similar efforts were made to co-ordinate attacks with other regional army commanders. In some provinces, such as East Java, this was more difficult because of loyalties within the army to Sukarno. Here, Soeharto relied more heavily on co-operation with NU's Banser forces (Fealy and McGregor 2010: 43–4). The violence was particularly fierce in Bali, East Java, and Central Java, where the PKI had strong support. In Bali, RPKAD (Resimen Pasukan Komando Angkatan Darat, Army Commando Regiment) forces relied on tameng (guards) associated with the right wing of the Indonesian National Party (Robinson 1995: 299–301). In Eastern Indonesia, the army co-opted Christian and Catholic anti-communists (Webb 1986: 98–9). In Sumatra, the army used Pemuda Pancasila (Pancasila Youth) (Ryter 1998: 55–6). Despite army complicity, the army promoted the fiction that it was "spontaneous violence" (Roosa 2016: 283–5). Western governments also supported a thorough purge of communists (Simpson 2008: 184–94).

Most people were killed after being held for short periods of time in police and military facilities. Quotas of prisoners were taken by civilian militias at night and shot, beheaded, or bludgeoned to death in remote locations, such as forests (Kammen and McGregor 2012: 17–20). Prisoners suffered from inadequate food, torture, sexual violence, and lack of medicines. The army subjected prisoners detained in remote prison camps, such as Buru or Moncongloe in Sulawesi, to forced labor (Ahmad 2012: 174–80).

The 1965–1968 violence cleared the way for a new military-dominated government. The army was regularly used to crush dissent, and anti-communism became a cornerstone of the regime. The families of those imprisoned and killed and former political prisoners suffered through intense stigmatization due to official versions of history, including textbooks, the annual screening of the docudrama *Pengkhianatan G30S/PKI* (The Betrayal of the 30 September Movements/PKI), the Sacred Pancasila Monument, and annual commemoration of October 1, which demonized those branded PKI as national traitors (McGregor 2007: 61–111). Further to this, a series of laws barred them from working in occupations such as teachers, journalists, or civil servants (Bedner 2015). The long duration of the regime (32 years) meant that anti-communist propaganda became entrenched and advocacy for survivors was limited. The label "communist" was also used to discredit any critics of the regime. This elaborate web of anti-communism contributed to fears of expressing sympathy for those persecuted.

Democratization and advocacy for historical justice

The Indonesian government took critical steps toward democratization following Soeharto's resignation, including paying new attention to human rights and winding back the political influence of the Indonesian military. In 1999, the government passed Law No. 39 on human rights, which committed the state to respecting, upholding, and advancing human rights consistent with the international human rights agreements to which Indonesia is a signatory. Then with Law No. 26 of 2000, the government set up a new mechanism for the prosecution of past cases of human rights abuses via either Ad Hoc Human Rights Courts or a Truth and Reconciliation Commission (TRC), following investigations by the National Commission of Human Rights (Komisi Nasional Hak-Hak Asasi Manusia, KOMNAS HAM). Work began on drafting a law for the formation of a TRC. The military technically rescinded its political role and gave up previously reserved seats in the parliament, and the police force separated from the armed forces.

The interim president, Habibie, signaled some loosening of the intense anti-communism of the past, first by releasing all remaining political prisoners from the 1965 case. These prisoners had been detained for so long on the grounds that they, as die-hard communists, remained a threat to society. Furthermore, Habibie cancelled the annual compulsory screening on state television of the docudrama about the September 30th Movement and promised revisions to school history textbooks that had previously promoted vigilant anti-communism. By shutting down the Ministry of Information and ending press censorship, he created a public space for survivors and activists to air new versions of history, focusing no longer on the terror of communists, but on the intense and enduring suffering of persons accused of being communist.

Seizing on this new space, some high-profile former political prisoners formed the organization YPKP (Yayasan Penelitian Korban Pembunuhan 1965/66, Foundation for Research into the 1965/66 Killings).[1] YPKP's membership comprised mostly former political prisoners, for whom there was a sense of urgency about gaining recognition and redress for their suffering. They placed a strong emphasis on rebutting versions of history in which they were dehumanized, by publishing memoirs about experiences of detention. Further to this, and building on global trends, they sought to document the locations and details of mass graves from 1965, so as to present society with undeniable evidence of the atrocities committed against alleged communists (McGregor 2012: 242).

In this immediate transition period, other human rights activists and lawmakers looked to examples of recent transitions for inspiration. The 1990s seemed to offer many examples. South Africa's then recent TRC guided the formulation of Indonesia's draft TRC legislation. The wave of apologies from state leaders for past crimes or neglect of human of rights violations that characterized the 1990s (Barkan 2000: xvii) may also have in part inspired the newly elected president Abdurrahman Wahid. In 2000, he offered a personal apology for the role of NU in the 1965 violence and proposed lifting the long-standing 1966 ban on communism. Coming from the man who had headed NU in the 1980s, this was very significant, for it suggested that he was speaking on behalf of the largest Muslim community in Indonesia.

Although this was an important and rare form of recognition from a senior government official for the suffering of those targeted in 1965, it remained a personal apology. Furthermore, the apology and the proposal to lift the ban on communism generated mass public protests. Scores of protestors in Jakarta and Medan took to the streets, using the names of new and sometimes established Islamic organizations, such as NU and Forum Ukhuwah Islamiyah (Islamic Fraternity Forum), a puritanical organization created in 1989 and loosely aligned with the conservative Majelis Ulama Indonesia (MUI, Indonesian Ulama Council), to present an "Islamic" protest against the revival of communism in Indonesia ("New Wave of Protests Target Plan on Communism," 2000). A year later, when the YPKP sought to rebury the remains of unidentified persons from the exhumed grave in Wonosobo, a coalition of "Islamic groups" violently disrupted the reburial on the grounds that the town of Kaloran was no place for communists (McGregor 2012: 246–7). This protest was based on the rejection of any effort to rehumanize and potentially memorialize victims.

As indicated previously, some Islamic organizations participated in the killings, and thus they are invested in the narrative that the violence was justified. However, in the post-Soeharto era, the military has also, behind the scenes, encouraged protests in the name of Islam as a way of blocking developments that would also implicate the military, given that it can no longer itself use violence to crush such actions (Mietzner 2008: 366–7). This tactic has been effective because of an increasing emphasis on so-called "Islamic values" in society and politics such that framing any debate in terms of Islam can draw support from Islamic groups.

The story is, however, more complex than this, because alongside the military's use of political Islam, activism for historical justice has also come from within so-called "implicated communities" (Morris-Suzuki 2005: 26–7). One of the most remarkable examples is Syarikat (Masyarakat Santri untuk Advokasi Rakyat, Santri Society for People's Advocacy) which was formed by young people in NU in 2000, in an effort to address the stigma attached to NU youth as a result of Banser's actions in the 1960s, and to promote reconciliation between survivors and NU members. Inspired by a new emphasis on human rights and tolerance from within NU after the 1980s and with the support of Abdurrahman Wahid, they conducted research into NU's role in the violence by interviewing survivors and published some of these accounts in internal NU publications as a way of rehumanizing those branded "communist." They promoted joint community projects and discussions involving survivors and NU members in East Java, as a way of bringing together these long opposing communities. In an effort to challenge entrenched anti-communism in the broader populace, they ran a film-making competition among students and hosted an exhibition in Yogyakarta on the women's prison Plantungan (McGregor 2009: 206–15). They also assisted with securing community approval and providing security during the YPKP's exhumation of the mass grave at Wonosobo. Syarikat activists, however, faced intense pressure from more conservative members of NU, and they enjoyed less and less protection following Wahid's impeachment as president and the backlash against both him and so-called liberal Islam more generally (McGregor 2009: 215–21).

There were many additional setbacks during the presidencies of Megawati Sukarnoputri (2001–2004) and Susilo Bambang Yudhoyono (2004–2014). It was during their terms that the new human rights laws and mechanisms were really tested. A series of cases of past human rights abuses were investigated by KOMNAS HAM, but senior military men continued to obstruct investigations by refusing summons to appear at hearings (Setiawan 2016: 25). Only two cases advanced from an investigation to an Ad Hoc Human Rights Court: the violence following the independence ballot in East Timor (1999) and the shooting of Muslim protestors in Tanjung Priok (1984). In each case, however, only low-ranking officers were convicted, and all their sentences were eventually overturned. This suggests that senior military figures remained above the law. By 2004, the legislation for establishing a TRC was ready for the parliament, but in response to objections to amnesty provisions, the Constitutional Court rejected the entire bill rather than addressing those particular provisions (Pohlman 2016: 70). Lawmakers seemed unwilling to risk confrontation with the military, the organization most likely to be investigated by a TRC.

The government did, however, give KOMNAS HAM a new mandate in 2008 to undertake a nationwide investigation into the 1965 violence. In 2012, the commission announced its findings of gross human rights violations, including killings, exterminations, slavery, forced removal from an area, restrictions on physical freedom, torture, rape and other forms of sexual violence, and forced disappearances.[2] Further to this, the commission attributed responsibility for the violence to Soeharto and to regional and local military commanders. The findings were quite remarkable because they directly pointed the finger at the military and at the former general who had led Indonesia. Commissioners recommended further investigations by the attorney general. This could have led to the formation of an Ad Hoc Human Rights Court or a non-judicial settlement if agreed to by survivors.

The announcement of the findings put some pressure on President Bambang Yudhoyono to respond. There were rumors of a potential apology for all cases of past human rights abuses, yet following an intense public backlash from both Islamic organizations and retired military men, this did not eventuate (Revianur 2012). Further complicating matters was Yudhoyono's position as a son-in-law of the former RPKAD Commander Sarwo Edhie, who was celebrated in New Order historiography for crushing the communists. By apologizing for the violence, he would have undermined both his family and the Indonesian military, an institution to which he, as a former general, also remained loyal. His links to the repression remind us of some of the reasons politicians will not address this case. Meanwhile, successive attorney generals repeatedly declared the evidence in the KOMNAS HAM report to be inadequate and refused to proceed with further investigations. To date, the full report is under embargo and has not been released to the public. As a result, the report cannot serve the function of an alternative state-authorized history of the violence.

Despite these challenges, activism for the survivors of 1965 continued and took many forms reflecting grassroots-based recognition of the need for historical justice for survivors. In Bali, for example, in 2005, young people created a community space called Taman 65 (1965 Park) within a family complex for the purposes of hosting discussions and exhibitions related to the 1965 violence, which had deeply impacted the local community. The collective behind the park also conducted oral history interviews to record testimonies of survivors. In 2015, they recorded some of the songs of former Balinese political prisoners to connect new audiences with these experiences for the purposes of challenging long-held stigmas against this community (*Bali Tribun News* 2015). Among the Taman 65 collective are those whose families had been killed and those who had participated in the killings, thereby creating difficult fractures in understanding this past (Dwyer 2015: 22–5). These activists have also faced military, police, and community surveillance.

In the city of Solo, activists and survivors formed the organization SEKBER 65 (Sékretariat Bersama 65, Joint Secretariat 65) in 2005. SEKBER 65 is run by two activists who co-ordinate a support and advocacy network for hundreds of survivors in the Solo area and surrounding districts. Emphasizing reconciliation, they have focused on hosting discussions and events with survivors and other community groups, including students and fiercely anti-communist groups, as a way of building greater understanding and lobbying the local government to support survivors' health care (Wardaya 2015).

In other cases, advocacy work for 1965 survivors has arisen out of the work of local organizations with wider ambits than this case alone. From 2004, for example, a broader victims' advocacy group in Sulawesi, SKP HAM (Solidaritas Sulawesi Korban Pelanggaran Hak Asasi Manusia, Sulawesi Solidarity for the Victims of Human Rights Violations), took up advocacy for victims of the 1965 violence. This organization focused on truth seeking by conducting oral history research with survivors and reparation. After socializing their ideas in community discussions in 2012, the mayor of Palu offered an official apology to the victims of the violence (Lamasitudju 2014: 380–3).

Similarly in Eastern Indonesia, the Network of Women of Eastern Indonesia for the Study of Women in Religion and Culture (Jaringan Perempuan Indonesia Timur, JPIT) decided in 2010 to research the case of the 1965 violence in the region of East Nusa Tenggara. Researchers documented the experiences of women survivors of the violence in this region, and applying ideas from liberation theology, they sought to understand how the Protestant church and its members contributed to the suffering and how they could work to remedy this suffering (Kolimon 2015:

4–7). JPIT emphasizes "truth telling" and ongoing support for survivors. JPIT members have also faced some societal resistance.

Some advocacy groups have focused on evidence gathering and working toward legal forms of justice. Most groups, however, have decided that an important part of their work is to first confront stereotypes about those branded PKI, by engaging in alternative truth telling, by sharing the stories of suffering of survivors. One survivor of the violence, the former political prisoner Ibu Kadmiyati puts it this way:

> I also demand and hope for justice for the violence against the victims of 1965. For the sadistic torture and killing of millions of people and those detained up to 14 years. When will the law be upheld? . . . Who is sadistic and cruel? The communists? Or the perpetrators of the killings? Find out the truth.
> *(Ibu Kadmiyati, cited in Yuniar and Easton 2015)*

She and many activists continue to push for recognition at a government level of the suffering of survivors of state violence for the purposes of endorsing a new social consensus about the effects of the 1965 violence and creating a genuine break from the past and associated anti-communism.

Based on the failure of all legal avenues for redress and the failure to pass new legislation for a TRC, activists from a broad coalition of the activists groups, including some mentioned above, calling itself KKPK (Koalisi Keadilan dan Penungkapan Kebenaraan, Coalition for Justice and Truth Telling), joined together from 2008 onward to perform the work of a TRC outside of a formal state process. From 2012–2013, which they dubbed "The Year of Truth Telling," they hosted independent public hearings across different cities of Indonesia for multiple cases of past human rights abuses (Pohlman 2016: 64–5). By bringing in respected members of society, they used the hearings to assist in validating the experiences of survivors and to try to build a stronger consensus on the need for action.

The year 2014 was highly significant for human rights activists, because of the presidential election contested by the populist civilian governor of Jakarta, Joko Widodo (Jokowi), who had no links to the New Order regime, and the retired general Prabowo, who was accused of complicity in past human rights crimes. Sparked in part by fear of a Prabowo presidency and his apparent popularity among young people, activists launched a campaign during the election to "oppose the forgetting" of all cases of human rights abuses that remained unaddressed (Hutabarat 2012).

With the electoral win of Jokowi over Prabowo, activists were optimistic of greater attention to the 1965 case because one of Jokowi's electoral promises was to address past human rights abuses, including this case. To conclude this chapter, I will reflect on the fiftieth anniversary of the violence in 2015, to consider the latest developments in activism for this case and signs of intensified resistance to these initiatives during Jokowi's presidency.

The fiftieth anniversary of the 1965 violence

Anniversaries of major historical events can serve as triggers for significant reflection and sometimes action on cases of past violence. For this reason, there was some anticipation that in 2015, his first full year as president, Jokowi might finally seek to deal with the 1965 case. In May 2015, he announced the formation of a Reconciliation Committee that would investigate past human rights cases. The membership of this committee was, however, troubling because it included the attorney general's department, which had repeatedly refused to proceed with investigations, and members of the military and police who were for the most part the accused parties (Aritonang 2015). Already it seemed that Jokowi was making major compromises on addressing human rights cases.

Perhaps more disheartening for survivors was Jokowi's attendance on October 1 at the ceremony at the Sacred Pancasila Monument at Lubang Buaya, where he categorically rejected offering an apology to survivors (Suwanti 2015). It is not clear what prompted this statement, but due to his party's minority position in the parliament, he faced pressure to build a broader coalition of support. As a concession, he appointed the highly conservative General Gatot Nurmantyo head of the Indonesian military earlier in the year (Fikri 2015). Jokowi may well thus have made this statement to shore up support from military men and from Islamic constituencies.

In a show of force designed to consolidate the support of Islamic groups for anti-communism, the military commander for the district of Jakarta held a mass prayer at the monument on the night before the ceremony, which was attended by the army chief of staff and the families of the military victims of 30 September Movement (Pratiwi 2015). An official from MUI used the anniversary to call for the return of compulsory screening of the docudrama *The Betrayal of the 30th September Movement/PKI* (*MUI Minta Film G 30 S-PKI Kembali Diputar*).

In recent years, former executioners have also been more vocal in rejecting historical justice for 1965 survivors. In a 2015 press interview, a self-confessed former executioner Burham, who goes by the name "the Butcher" and is now part of the Front Anti-Komunis Indonesia (Indonesian Anti-Communist Front) in Yogyakarta, stated that if the president made the apology, "this would be a betrayal" (Affan 2015). His reaction conveys the strength of conviction felt by some who participated in the killings that what they did was righteous.

In 2015, anti-communist actions seemed to intensify. Members of local society, for example, forcibly cancelled a planned YPKP meeting in West Sumatra in February, on the basis that they were "afraid of a revival of PKI ideology" (Agustino 2015). The military and police also became more heavy-handed. In the small city of Salatiga, Central Java, the police forced students from Satya Wacana University to withdraw from circulation an edition of their magazine devoted to local experiences of the violence and reports on mass graves and killings (Suherdjoko 2015). In Bali, police threatened to cancel the permit for the Ubud Writers and Readers' Festival scheduled for late October, if the organizers did not cancel three sessions, a film screening, a book launch, and a photo exhibition related to the 1965 violence (Erviani and Anindita 2015).

Meanwhile, activists tried to use the new global spotlight on the 1965 violence, generated largely through the acclaim of the 2012 film *The Act of Killing*, to their benefit. A group of activists headed by Indonesian human rights lawyer Nursyahbani Katjasungkana began to prepare an International People's Tribunal (IPT) for the 1965 case to be heard by a panel of international judges in The Hague in November 2015. The IPT, built on the precedent of multiple people's trials, aimed to perform the work that no trial in Indonesia seemed capable of doing: hearing witness testimony, processing case submissions, and forming a judgment.

A host of government and military officials tried to dismiss it on the basis that the Indonesian government would handle the case. Representatives from NU and Pemuda Pancasila respectively went so far as to call for the prosecution of those involved in the IPT on the basis that they were betraying the nation by holding this tribunal abroad (Pemuda Pancasila 2015). Indicative of the general tone of former military men serving in the government, former KOSTRAD commander retired General Luhut Panjaitan, who was then coordinating minister for politics, law, and security and in charge of resolving past human rights cases, deflected attention from the tribunal. He suggested that it was just not clear who would be put on trial, given generals were killed and communists were killed (Henschke 2015).

The purpose of the IPT was to increase pressure on the Indonesian government to address this past. Yet the only feeble step that the government took was to host the first national symposium on the events of 1965 in April 2016. The most senior military representative in attendance, retired Lieutenant-General Sintong Panjaitan, used the opportunity to cast doubt on the number of people killed, claiming that only one person died during the time he and his troops were in Central Java (Affan 2016). Minister Luhut took this denial further by asking the press where all the mass graves were from 1965, if indeed so many people had been killed. This outraged activists and survivors who had for years documented such graves ("Djokowi Perintahkan" 2016). The minister reiterated that the government would never apologize for this case. These increasingly assertive statements by retired military men seemed a far cry from the steps taken by Presidents Habibie and Wahid over fifteen years earlier, to begin to recognize the suffering of 1965 survivors and to put an end to vengeful anti-communism.

In June 2016, two months after this symposium and as an anti-PKI symposium was being held in Jakarta, the judges of the ITP 1965 announced their findings that the Indonesian state was responsible for multiple crimes against humanity, describing the violence as "a genocide" (IPT 1965, 2016). They recommended that the government should quickly address these crimes.

At the time of writing (March 2017), no further progress has been made on this case. Meanwhile, survivors of the violence are rapidly aging and passing away. Neither they, nor all activists, agree on what forms of historical justice should be applied. Yet they hope at the very least, as does Ibu Kadmiyati (quoted earlier in this chapter), for a significant break from the past and for new histories of 1965 in which those targeted in the violence are no longer portrayed as sadistic and evil and in which their suffering and the scale of violence against them are finally recognized.

Acknowledgment

This chapter has been completed with the support of the Australian Research Council Future Fellowship (FT130100957) for the project *Confronting Historical Injustice in Indonesia: Memory and Transnational Human Rights Activism*.

Notes

1 YPKP was founded by the high-profile former political prisoner and novelist Pramoedya Anata Toer, the prominent former Gerwani activist and political prisoner Sulami, and the political exile Umar Said, who campaigned for years abroad in France for justice for this case. YPKP had strong representation around Indonesia and adopted several strategies to gain redress.
2 Komnasham, *Pernyataan Komnasham tentang Hasil Penyelidikian Pelanggaran HAM yang Berat Persitiwa 1965–1966*, at http://stopimpunity.org/content/stopimpunity/eksekutif_summary_peristiwa_1965_4.pdf, accessed July 20, 2012.

References cited

Affan, Heyder. 2015. "Jumat Pagi Bersama Algojo Pemburu PKI," *BBC Indonesia*, 1 October, at www.bbc.com/indonesia/berita_indonesia/2015/10/150922_indonesia_lapsus_penolakanmasyarakat (Accessed 25 February 2017).
———. 2016. "Penyangkalan Pembunuhan Massal di Simposium 1965," *BBC Indonesia*, 19 April. www.bbc.com/indonesia/berita_indonesia/2016/04/160418_indonesia_simposium1965 (Accessed 25 February 2017).
Agustino, Yudi Prama. 2015. "Diusir Warga, Pertemuan YPKP 65 Pusat dengan YPKP SUMBAR Batal Terlaksana." Radio Republik Indonesia, 22 February. www.rri.co.id/post/berita/142178/nasional/

diusir_warga_pertemuan_ypkp_65_pusat_dengan_ypkp_sumbar_batal_terlaksana.html (Accessed 8 November 2015).

Ahmad, Taufik. 2012. "South Sulawesi, The Military, Prison Camps and Forced Labour," in Douglas Kammen and Katharine McGregor, eds., *The Contours of Mass Violence in Indonesia, 1965–68* (Singapore: NUS Press), pp. 156–81.

Amnesty International. 1977. *Indonesia: An Amnesty International Report* (London: Amnesty International).

Aritonang, Margareth. 2015. "Luhut Expected to Accelerate Reconciliation," *The Jakarta Post*, 20 August. www.thejakartapost.com/news/2015/08/20/luhut-expected-accelerate-reconciliation.html (Accessed 30 August 2015).

Bali Tribun News. 2015. "Prison Songs: Nyanyian yang Dibungkam," 22 August. http://bali.tribunnews.com/2015/08/22/prison-songs-nyanyian-yang-dibungkam-lagu-lagu-eks-tahanan-politik-1965 (Accessed 17 February 2017).

Barkan, Elazar. 2000. *The Guilt of Nations: Restitution and Negotiating Historical Injustices* (London and New York: W. W. Norton and Company).

BBC Indonesia. 2016. "Djokowi Perintahkan Pencariaan Kuburan Massal Korban Peristiwa 1965," 25 April. www.bbc.com/indonesia/berita_indonesia/2016/04/160425_indonesia_luhut_pki (Accessed 26 April 2016).

Bedner, Adriaan. 2015. "Citizenship Restored," *Inside Indonesia*, 30 September. www.insideindonesia.org/citizenship-restored (Accessed 13 October 2015).

Cribb, Robert. 1990. "Introduction: Problems in the Historiography of the Killings in Indonesia," in Robert Cribb, ed., *The Indonesian Killings 1965–1966: Studies From Java and Bali* (Clayton, Vic: Centre of Southeast Asian Studies, Monash University), pp. 1–44.

"Djokowi Perintahkan Pencariaan Kuburan Massal Korban Peristiwa 1965," 2016. *BBC Indonesia*, 25 April, at www.bbc.com/indonesia/berita_indonesia/2016/04/160425_indonesia_luhut_pki (Accessed 26 April 2016).

Dwyer, Leslie. 2015. "Beyond Youth Inclusion: Intergenerational Politics in Post-Conflict Bali," *Journal of Peacebuilding and Development* 10(3): 16–29.

Erviani, Ni Komang and Erkia Anindita. 2015. "Ubud Festival Banned Drom Discussing 1965 Massacre," *The Jakarta Post*, 23 October. www.thejakartapost.com/news/2015/10/23/ubud-festival-banned-discussing-1965-massacre.html (Accessed 23 October 2015).

Fikri, Ahmad. 2015. "Pengamat: Pilih Gatot Nurmantyo: Djokowi Butuh Sokongan TNI," *Tempo*, 10 June. https://m.tempo.co/read/news/2015/06/10/078673921/pengamat-pilih-gatot-nurmantyo-jokowi-butuh-sokongan-tni (Accessed 10 March 2017).

Fealy, Greg and Katharine McGregor. 2010. "Nahdlatul Ulama and the Killings of 1965–66: Religion, Politics, and Remembrance," *Indonesia* 89: 37–60.

Henschke, Rebecca. 2015. "Luhut: PKI Ada Dibunuh, Jenderal Ada Dibunuh, Siapa Mau Diadili?" *BBC Indonesia*, 11 November. www.bbc.com/indonesia/berita_indonesia/2015/11/151111_indonesia_lunch_with_luhut (Accessed 12 November 2015).

Hutabarat, Restraia F. 2012. *Melawan Lupa: Narasi-Narasi Komunitas Taman 65 Bali* (Denpasar: Taman 65 Press).

IPT 1965. 2016. *Final Report of the IPT 1965: Findings and Documents of the International People's Tribunal on Crimes Against Humanity Indonesia 1965* (The Hague, Jakarta: IPT 1965 Foundation).

Kammen, Douglas and Katharine McGregor. 2012. "Introduction: The Contours of Mass Violence in Indonesia, 1965–68," in Douglas Kammen and Katharine McGregor, eds., *The Contours of Mass Violence in Indonesia, 1965–1968* (Singapore: NUS Press), pp. 1–21.

Kolimon, Mery. 2015. "Forbidden Memories: Women Victims and Survivors of the 1965 Tragedy in Eastern Indonesia," in Mery Kolimon, Liliya Wetangterah and Karen Campbell-Nelson, eds., *Forbidden Memories: Women's Experiences of 1965 in Eastern Indonesia* (Victoria: Herb Feith Foundation and Monash University Publishing), pp. 1–20.

Lamasitudju, Nurlaela, A. K. 2014. "Rekonsiliasi dan Pernyataan Maaf Pak Wali Kota Palu," in Baskara Wardaya, ed., *Luka Bangs Luka Kita: Pelanggaran Ham Masa Lalu dan Tawaran Rekonsiliasi* (Yogyakarta: Galang Pustaka), pp. 371–84.

McGregor, Katharine. 2007. *History in Uniform: Military Ideology and the Construction of Indonesia's Past* (Singapore: NUS Press).

———. 2009. "Confronting the Past in Contemporary Indonesia: The Anti-communist Killings of 1965–66 and the Role of the Nahdlatul Ulama," *Critical Asian Studies* 41(2): 195–224.

———. 2012. "Mass Graves and Memory of the 1965–66 Killings," in Douglas Kammen and Katharine McGregor, eds., *The Contours of Mass Violence in Indonesia, 1965–1968* (Singapore: NUS Press), pp. 234–62.

Melvin, Jessica. 2017. *The Indonesian Genocide Files: How the Indonesian Military Initiated and Implemented the Indonesian Genocide, the Case of Aceh* (forthcoming).

Mietzner, Marcus. 2008. "Controlling the Military: Conflict and Governance in Indonesia's Consolidating Democracy," in Marcus Mietzner, ed., *Military Politics, Islam and the State in Indonesia: From Turbulent Transition to Democratic Consolidation* (Singapore: Institute of Southeast Asian Studies).

Morris-Suzuki, Tessa. 2005. *The Past Within Us: Media, Memory and History* (London: Verso).

Mortimer, Rex. 1974. *Indonesian Communism Under Sukarno: Ideology and Politics* (Ithaca: Cornell University Press).

"MUI Minta Film G 30 S-PKI Kembali Diputar," 2015. *Republika*, 1 October, at www.republika.co.id/berita/nasional/umum/15/10/01/nvjid6330-mui-minta-film-g-30spki-kembali-diputar (Accessed 5 October 2015).

"New Wave of Protests Target Plan on Communism," 2000. *The Jakarta Post*, 8 April. http:www.thejakarta post.com/Archives/ArchivesDet.asp?FileID=20000408.@02 (Accessed 17 November 2000).

Pemuda Pancasila. 2015. "Pemuda Pancasila mengutuk keras sidang International People Tribunal, Todung Mulya Lubis PENGECUT !" Pemuda Pancasila website, posted 12 December. www.pemuda-pancasila.or.id/index.php/app/berita/112 (Accessed 15 December 2015).

Pohlman, Annie. 2016. "A Year of Truth and the Possibilities for Reconciliation in Indonesia," *Genocide Studies and Prevention* 10(1): 60–78.

Pratiwi, Priska Sari. 2015. "Renungan Peringatan G30S Digelar di Lubang Buaya," *Berita Satu*, 1 October, at www.beritasatu.com/politik/311045-renungan-peringatan-g30s-digelar-di-lubang-buaya.html (Accessed 5 October 2015).

Revianur, Aditya. 2012. "PBNU Tolak Permintaan Maaf Kepada Korban Tragedi 65," *Kompas*, 15 August. http:wwwi.kompas.com/printenews/xml/2012/08/15/20243252/PBNU. Tolak.Permintaan.Maaf.Kepada.Korban (Accessed 12 September 2012).

Robinson, Geoffrey. 1995. *The Dark Side of Paradise: Political Violence in Bali* (Ithaca: Cornell University Press).

Roosa, John. 2006. *Pretext for Mass Murder: The September 30th Movement and Suharto's Coup d'etat in Indonesia* (Madison: University of Wisconsin Press).

———. 2016. "The State of Knowledge About an Open Secret: Indonesia's Mass Disappearances of 1965–66," *Journal of Asian Studies* 75(2): 281–97.

Ryter, Loren. 1998. "Pemuda Pancasila: The Last Loyalist Free Men of Suharto's New Order," *Indonesia* 66: 45–73.

Setiawan, Ken. 2016. "From Hope to Disillusion: The Paradox of Komnas Ham, the Indonesian National Human Rights Commission," *Bidragen tot de Taal, Land-en Volkenkunde* 172(1): 15–26.

Simpson, Bradley R. 2008. *Economists With Guns: Authoritarian Development and US-Indonesian Relations, 1960–1968* (Stanford: Stanford University Press).

Suherdjoko. 2015. "Student Magazine Withdrawn for Publishing About 1965 Massacre," *The Jakarta Post*, 20 October. www.thejakartapost.com/news/2015/10/20/student-magazine-withdrawn-publishing-about-1965-massacre.html#sthash.mjsS9Kvc.dpuf (Accessed 25 October 2015).

Suwanti, Nina Cucu. 2015. "Jokowi Tidak Akan Minta Maaf kepada Korban 65/66," *Sinar Harapan*, 1 October. www.sinarharapan.co/news/read/151001059/jokowi-tidak-akan-minta-maaf-kepada-korban-65-66 (Accessed 5 October 2015).

Wardaya, Baskara T. 2015. "Reconciliation Without Politics," *Inside Indonesia*, October-December. www.insideindonesia.org/reconciliation-without-politics-2 (Accessed 1 March 2017).

Webb, Paul R. A. F. 1986. "The Sickle and the Cross: Christians and Communists in Bali, Flores, Sumba and Timor, 1965–1967," *Journal of Southeast Asian Studies* 17: 94–112.

Wieringa, Saskia E. 2002. *Sexual Politics in Indonesia* (New York: Palgrave Macmillan.)

Yuniar, Dodi and Matt Easton, eds. 2015. *Enduring Impunity: Women Surviving Atrocities in the Absence of Justice* (Jakarta: AJAR). http://asia-ajar.org/2015/11/enduring-impunity-women-surviving-atrocities-in-the-absence-of-justice/ (Accessed 10 November 2015).

11

THE INDONESIAN ARMED FORCES, COALITIONAL PRESIDENTIALISM, AND DEMOCRATIZATION

From praetorian guard to imagined balance of power

Marcus Mietzner

In November 2016, President Joko Widodo (or "Jokowi") toured a number of military units. In his speeches, he reminded the assembled troops of their obligations to be loyal to him and the state. "As commander-in-chief," he said on November 11 to the marines corps, "I want to make sure that everyone is loyal to the state, Pancasila [its ideology], the constitution, and the principle of diversity" (Detik 2016). He then paused for a moment before repeating, "I just want to make sure." Obviously, Jokowi's rather awkward address did not occur in a vacuum. In early November, hundreds of thousands of Islamist demonstrators had staged a protest in Jakarta, demanding the prosecution for blasphemy of the Christian-Chinese governor of Jakarta, Basuki Tjahaja Purnama (or "Ahok"), who was a Jokowi ally and running for re-election. Some of the protesters had threatened to storm the presidential palace, and violent clashes erupted. As the protest unfolded, Jokowi sat in a lounge at Jakarta airport, discussing with his aides what to do. Primarily, they concluded, he had to ensure that the military was on his side (Interview with a Jokowi confidant, Jakarta, November 15, 2016). Clearly shaken by the sudden outburst of populist Islamist power, the president believed that without the military's backing, his rule could be under threat.

This episode highlights an apparent paradox in Indonesia's civil-military relations almost two decades after Soeharto's fall. On the one hand, the armed forces – the "praetorian guard" of Soeharto's authoritarian regime – have been nominally depoliticized, with active officers withdrawn from cabinet and the legislature. The military's notorious dual function, which allowed it to play a role in both defense and politics, was shelved, and official military businesses were shut down. But as Jokowi's actions show, the military's political weight – whether real or perceived – has remained an important factor in Indonesian politics. Authors focusing on Indonesian military affairs have given different answers to explain this phenomenon: they have pointed out that the military's territorial command structure is still in place, providing the military with a formidable resource of continued power (Ate 2010); that civilian elites have retained the military's power to deal with internal security threats (Honna 2013); that the military's remaining business interests make it both powerful and accepting of the democratic status quo (Beeson 2008); that excess numbers of military officers push the armed forces back into the civilian realm (Laksmana 2016); or that civilians are either incapable of or politically unwilling to take charge of the security sector, leaving the military with significant influence (Sebastian and Iisgindarsah 2013).

While all of these approaches capture key patterns of post-Soeharto civil-military relations, this chapter advances an alternative explanation for the continued power of the military during critical political junctures – and, by implication, the chances for further military reform. Drawing from new studies on coalitional presidentialism, it argues that the level of the military's political influence rises and falls with the threat perception of incumbent presidents vis-à-vis the security of their rule. If presidents feel secure from such threats, windows of opportunity for military reform open – as they did in the early phases of the B. J. Habibie, Megawati Sukarnoputri, and Susilo Bambang Yudhoyono presidencies. If, on the other hand, presidents sense that their civilian coalition partners are unreliable or popular mobilization could destabilize their government, they are likely to turn to the military to consolidate their power. Importantly, presidents do not only react to actual threats. Rather, they *anticipate* the possibility of them occurring (whether on strong grounds or not), thus making the military a near-permanent fixture in the architecture of presidential coalitions. Eventually, the armed forces acquire the same status as an important political party in the presidential alliance, giving it an extent of influence that arguably exceeds its security and political capacities. In order to develop these arguments, the chapter proceeds in four steps. It first outlines the concept of coalitional presidentialism. It then discusses the presidencies regulated by pre-2002, pre-amendment constitutional arrangements – the presidencies of B. J. Habibie, Abdurrahman Wahid, and Megawati. The third section focuses on the post-amendment presidencies of Yudhoyono and Jokowi, followed by the conclusion.

Coalitional presidentialism and the military

The concept of coalitional presidentialism developed in the context of a long and intensive debate about the stability of presidential systems operating in a multi-party landscape. Traditionally, leading political scientists have postulated that presidential systems with multi-party legislatures are less stable than presidential systems with only two parties, or pure parliamentary systems (Mainwaring 1993; Linz 1994). However, this skepticism has recently been challenged by authors who maintain that presidents in multi-party systems can maintain stability by building carefully balanced parliamentary coalitions. For instance, Chaisty, Cheeseman, and Power (2015: 1) found that "the ability of presidents to form coalitions has meant that the anticipated 'difficult combination' of multiparty politics and presidential systems has not proved detrimental to political stability." In order to achieve this stability, presidents use five main tools: cabinet authority, budgetary power, partisan power (i.e., the influence that presidents can wield over their own party), legislative power, and the exchange of favors (Chaisty, Cheeseman and Power 2015: 1). Among these, cabinet powers are often seen as the most effective instrument.

In Indonesia, post-Soeharto presidents have picked extensively from the coalitional presidentialism menu. Using their constitutional powers over appointments and budgets, presidents have tried to maintain cabinet loyalty through a mixture of "persuasion" and pressure (Mietzner 2016). Indeed, some authors have asserted that such inclusivist coalition-building has already taken the form of "promiscuous powersharing" (Slater and Simmons 2013). But neither coalitional presidentialism theorists nor Indonesia-focused scholars have paid much attention to the military as an integral part of Indonesian presidential coalitions after 1998. Instead, the almost exclusive emphasis of both has been on parties and parliament as targets of presidential accommodation. The military has been mostly treated as an entity presidents avoid alienating because of its control over the state's defense and security arsenal (Sebastian 2006). Arguably, however, the military needs to be analyzed in the same framework of coalitional presidentialism that parties and legislators are conceptualized in. Like parties and parliamentarians, the military trades its support to presidents against concessions and rewards, and like the former, it can increase its demands in situations where presidents face difficulties in sustaining the loyalty of other coalition partners. Within this framework, the fluctuations in the political weight of the military and the progress or stagnation of military reform become functions of the president's ability to control the overall stability of his or her coalition.

To be sure, some scholars of civil–military relations have described a menu of options presidents typically use in democratic transitions to secure the support of the armed forces for democratization (Croissant, Kuehn, Lorenz, and Chambers 2013). This menu includes accommodation of the military's interests in exchange for concessions as well. But the main purpose of this strategy is to prevent the military from becoming an anti-democratic spoiler, and – in the worst-case scenario – from launching a coup (Croissant et al. 2013). It is, therefore, mostly applicable for states in vulnerable phases of post-authoritarian transition, or political systems in a deep crisis of legitimacy. This chapter, by contrast, proposes to interpret the military as a "normal" coalition partner of presidents in states that have passed the democratic transition stage. As such, the strategies applied are not (only) coup-proofing strategies but options for presidents to consolidate their rule should other coalition partners, or external popular mobilizations, appear as threats to the president's position or ability to govern effectively.

Pre-amendment presidents and the military: Habibie, Wahid, and Megawati

The level of threat that presidents sense from their coalition partners depends to no small extent on the existing constitutional arrangements. Presidents may feel less pressure on their positions – and the need to accommodate – in executive-heavy systems than in regimes with significant legislative authority. Indonesia's early post-Soeharto system belonged to the latter category. While Soeharto had manipulated the 1945 constitution to build his strongly presidentialist regime, the charter's original form – which now serves as the foundation of the democratic state – was of a hybrid character. It gave robust powers to the president, but he or she was elected by the People's Consultative Assembly (Majelis Permusyawaratan Rakyat, MPR), the country's highest legislative body. And although impeachment proceedings were not spelled out in the constitution, the logic of its institutional hierarchies indicated that the MPR could dismiss the president. Thus, a democratic interpretation of the 1945 Constitution suggested that the president needed to maintain a solid majority in the MPR – which consisted of elected members of parliament and non-elected delegates – in order to stay in power. It was this constitutional hybrid between presidentialism and parliamentarism that Soeharto's successors had to work with, and it had significant repercussions for their approach to both civilian and military allies.

But while Habibie, Wahid, and Megawati worked within the same constitutional system, they did so under very different circumstances. To begin with, Habibie's parliament had been elected in the last pre-democratic ballot in 1997, giving him some assurance that the MPR would not move against him until new elections were held. Moreover, the opposition – consisting of newly founded parties without parliamentary representation – had agreed to tolerate Habibie as a transitional president, securing his position unless he violated the consensus of fresh elections and political reforms (Mietzner 2013: 93). Consequently, as long as Habibie interpreted his role as transitional and saw himself primarily as the organizer of post-authoritarian elections, he was under little pressure to build a presidential coalition inside or outside of parliament. This also gave him room to maneuver vis-à-vis the military. On his first day in office, Habibie demonstrated his constitutional powers by proposing to replace Wiranto, the military commander (Wiranto 2003: 93–4). Wiranto asked Habibie to reconsider and promised in return to fully support the president. Habibie agreed to this deal. Unsurprisingly, then, it was in this early period of Habibie's presidency (from late May 1998 to around January 1999) that the most important military and political reforms were decided and passed. The dual function was abolished, multi-party democracy was launched, and East Timor was granted a referendum for independence.

The key to the partial success in depoliticizing the armed forces in the early post-authoritarian period, therefore, was the low necessity for Habibie to uphold the principles of coalitional presidentialism. With a transitional president and a parliament constituted under authoritarianism, coalitional presidentialism in Indonesia was still in an embryonic phase. But all of this changed in the beginning of 1999, when it became clear that Habibie would no longer limit himself to the role of transitional ruler but was keen to enter the presidential race himself. Importantly, with that decision came the need to form coalitions ahead of the MPR session scheduled for October 1999. However, as Habibie's support by his own party, Golkar, was shaky, he turned to Wiranto for assistance – indeed, he offered him the vice presidency if he threw the support of the armed forces behind him (Mietzner 2009: 204). In the period of Habibie's courtship of the armed forces – from around March to October 1999 – military reform not only stagnated but regressed. In September 1999, the military committed severe abuses in East Timor after its population had profoundly endorsed independence. Still hoping for Wiranto's support in the upcoming presidential ballot, Habibie did nothing to rein in the military. Worse still for the president, important factions in Golkar deserted him, and Wiranto also withdrew his support. Ultimately, after the MPR rejected his accountability speech, Habibie decided not to stand for re-election.

As Habibie's successor, the MPR elected Wahid, the erratic leader of the traditionalist Muslim organization Nahdlatul Ulama (NU). But while his election marked the formal beginning of coalitional presidentialism in Indonesia, Wahid fundamentally misunderstood the concept. For him, presidential coalitions were only necessary to *win* power, not to *maintain* it. Thus, he assembled a coalition of parties and MPR delegates – including from the military – to support his candidacy. And despite his NU-affiliated party having collected only 12.6% of the votes in the preceding parliamentary elections, he won the MPR ballot decisively. However, Wahid thought that the necessity of coalition-building had ended with his election and that Indonesia's constitution gave him unlimited executive powers (interview with Wahid confidant, Jakarta, November 10, 1999). In the first half year of his presidency, he indeed acted like a president without partners, and this had repercussions for the political position of the armed forces. Like Habibie in his early period in power, Wahid used the president's (in his case, imagined) political independence to push for a further reduction in the military's political role: he fired Wiranto from cabinet in February 2000 (he had appointed him as a price for the military's support of his candidacy); he promoted known reformers to key positions in the armed forces; he signaled willingness to negotiate with separatist rebels in Aceh and Papua; and he supported initiatives to reform, and eventually abolish, the military's territorial command structure.

But Wahid's ignoring of the logic of coalitional presidentialism proved unsustainable. After he dismissed several party-linked ministers in the first half of 2000, most parties in parliament turned against him. A cabinet reshuffle in August 2000 achieved a temporary reconciliation, but this unraveled too, and parliament began impeachment proceedings in February 2001. Under threat from a powerful party alliance, Wahid felt forced to court the military (Honna 2003: 184). As part of this approach, Wahid gradually gave up on all military reform efforts he had launched earlier; he removed reformers from the military leadership, rescinded offers of negotiations with separatists, and abandoned all further structural military reform (Mietzner 2009: 217). Apparently, Wahid believed that by aligning with the military, he could save himself from impeachment. But there is little evidence to suggest that the military could have protected Wahid even if it wanted to – the civilian anti-Wahid alliance was simply too strong. Nonetheless, as the impeachment process shifted to the MPR in May 2001, Wahid continued to plead with the military to discipline his opponents. The military refused and voted with the other MPR parties for his impeachment in July 2001. Hence, Wahid's over-estimation of his presidential autonomy, his under-estimation of the need to work with civilian coalition partners, and his false emphasis on the armed forces as a potential savior not only premeditated his downfall but also rolled back military reforms – fortunately, however, not far enough to undo the changes of the early Habibie period.

Wahid's vice president Megawati succeeded him, and while she inherited an unchanged institutional framework, she assumed power under profoundly different conditions. First, she did not have to build a coalition to get elected – she automatically became president after Wahid's impeachment. Second, she only agreed to endorse Wahid's removal after senior party leaders swore that she would not suffer the same fate during the remainder of her term, which expired in 2004. Third, as part of the deal with Wahid's opponents, she consented to the election of a conservative Islamic party chairman as her vice president, reducing the risk of attacks on her from Muslim groups (Crouch 2010: 32). Thus, Megawati held a number of insurance policies against her impeachment, and she accepted that she had to hand cabinet posts to most parties in return. In other words, she built her government on principles of coalitional presidentialism, but she knew that the probability of her getting prematurely dismissed was low. Importantly, the circumstances of her ascension to power also meant that she was not dependent on the military to maintain it. To be sure, she wanted the military to be on her side, and she personally did not see military reform as a priority. As president, therefore, she did not take the lead on initiating further reform in and of the armed forces. But when the military in August 2002 proposed to her to abort the ongoing process of constitutional amendments and return to the original 1945 document, she refused (Crouch 2010: 60). Instead, she joined the other party leaders in passing a constitutional reform package that would see the introduction of direct presidential elections and the complete removal of the armed forces from all legislatures, both national and local, by 2004.

In hindsight, the 2002 constitutional amendments were the most important watershed in Indonesian civil-military relations since the early Habibie reforms. They marked the military's worst political defeat since Soeharto's fall, with a united civilian coalition ignoring its calls for the abandonment of much of the democratic experiment. This feat was only possible because the incumbent president perceived the threat of being removed by her coalition partners to be low, and the military hence was not required as a stabilizer of the presidential alliance. It was this constellation that allowed Megawati to act without having to ponder a backlash from the armed forces. Indeed, Megawati's situation was not dissimilar to Habibie's in the second half of 1998, when his relative autonomy as a transitional president allowed him to make decisions on political reform that heavily impacted on the military's standing. But like Habibie, Megawati also saw her position changing as she faced the challenge of re-election. The pre-election lobbying dissolved the foundations upon which Megawati's coalition had been based, with parties now viewing the 2001 agreement as obsolete. For the president, the perspective had changed too: she had to stitch together an electoral coalition, without the insurance policies that she enjoyed while in office. And it was this increased uncertainty over shifting patterns of coalitional presidentialism that further weakened her (already not very strong) inclination to take on the armed forces.

Nowhere was Megawati's changing relationship with the military more visible than in the Aceh conflict. In early 2002, almost parallel to the process of constitutional reforms, Megawati agreed to peace negotiations with the Acehnese rebels. Although the military opposed this move, a cessation of hostilities agreement was signed in December 2002. But key military figures sabotaged the cease fire, and while Megawati had rebuffed the military in mid- and late 2002, she no longer showed such courage in mid-2003. As she considered which parties and groups to include in her electoral coalition, she gave in to the military's request in May 2003 to cancel the agreement and launch an all-out war (Aspinall and Crouch 2003). To be sure, Megawati was not predisposed against tough military action, but her rapid approval of the military's agenda – after having invested in a peace process – was a clear sign of the military's rising political weight ahead of the elections. And Megawati's proclivity to keep the military on board only increased as it became clear that her main challengers in the election would be Wiranto and Yudhoyono, both retired generals. Thus, the years 2003 and 2004 saw standstill and even regression in military reform efforts, as the military was once again viewed as a significant factor in the balance of coalitional presidentialism. Her courting of the military notwithstanding, Megawati lost the elections against Yudhoyono, who became the first president of the post-amendment regime.

Post-amendment presidents and the military: Yudhoyono and Jokowi

The 2002 constitutional amendments addressed the problems inherent in both the original 1945 constitution and in its experimental post-1998 implementation within a democratic polity. The reforms gave the president a popular mandate through direct elections, eliminating his or her dependence on the MPR; established presidential impeachment procedures, making it much harder to remove an incumbent head of state; and handed the parliament additional powers too but clearly defined the demarcation lines between presidential and legislative powers. The new impeachment procedures in particular were significant in – theoretically, at least – reducing the president's need to permanently maintain a majority coalition in the legislature. Under the post-2002 constitutional rules, a president can only be impeached if a) two-thirds of parliamentarians decide to ask the Constitutional Court (also newly established by the amendments) to rule on whether the president has violated the constitution or the law; b) the court then decides that that was the case; c) a follow-up session of the MPR after the court's verdict is attended by three-fourths of MPR members; and d) two-thirds of attending MPR members vote to impeach the president. In practice, then, a president can fend off impeachment threats if he or she maintains a 25 percent blocking minority in the MPR – which not only includes parliamentarians but also members of the mostly ceremonial Regional Representative Council (Dewan Perwakilan Daerah, DPD). For the parliament, this presidential blocking minority is one-third of the members.

But despite these vastly changed circumstances, post-amendment presidents have not acted much differently from their predecessors. After initially experimenting with notions of increased presidential autonomy, Yudhoyono and Jokowi too eventually came to view themselves as unremittingly under threat of impeachment, requiring control over large legislative majorities to neutralize it (Aspinall, Mietzner and Tomsa 2015; Mietzner 2017). Evidently, this approach impacted on their relationship with the military as well. Following some bold posturing at the beginning, both presidents either dropped military reform initiatives or decided not to start new ones. Partly, Yudhoyono and Jokowi's continuously high threat perceptions were due to the strong role that the post-amendment constitution had left for parties and parliament: presidents could only be nominated by parties or coalitions of parties, and that was later defined by law as those having obtained 20% of the seats in parliament or 25% of the votes in the last legislative election; parliament had the right to approve both the state budget in its entirety and its various line items; and the legislature could block key appointments. Whether these constitutional arrangements pose real threats to a president's position is debatable, but it is clear that both Yudhoyono and Jokowi believed that they did.

Unsurprisingly, then, the only major case of Yudhoyono seriously confronting the armed forces fell into his first year in office, when he still drew from early post-amendment ideas of enlarged presidential autonomy. Yudhoyono had won a decisive victory over Megawati, and his vice president Jusuf Kalla had broadened the base of the government coalition by taking over the chairmanship of the large Golkar party in December 2004. Feeling secure in his position, he quickly approved the beginning of fresh negotiations with the Aceh rebels, which he knew would irritate the military. Ignoring the military's misgivings, Yudhoyono's government signed a wide-ranging peace accord in August 2005. This was an important military reform step, but it turned out to be Yudhoyono's first and last. Two developments led Yudhoyono to believe that it was unwise to challenge the armed forces any further after Aceh: first, his coalition partners became increasingly unruly, with party leaders sharply criticizing government policy. Indeed, in 2006, a Golkar meeting deliberated whether to withdraw from the cabinet (Mietzner 2013: 155). The president's increased sense of coalitional insecurity culminated in 2009, when he asked his coalition parties to sign a contract of loyalty for his second term. This contract, however, proved toothless when the government suffered a series of defeats in parliamentary votes between 2009 and 2011. For Yudhoyono, the disloyalty of his coalition partners and the need to accommodate them nevertheless confirmed a view that he had formed in his time as minister to Wahid: that the Indonesian polity was, in effect, "semi-parliamentary, semi-presidential" (interview, Cikeas, December 2, 2014). This, he was now convinced, had not changed with the constitutional amendments of 2002.

The second reason for Yudhoyono's reluctance to initiate more military reform steps was his own experience with the armed forces during the Aceh negotiations. While the military eventually relented, it only did so after intensive internal rifts. The then commander of the armed forces, Endriartono Sutarto, reported to Yudhoyono that several senior officers had raised the possibility of rejecting the president's orders on Aceh and that it took much effort to persuade them otherwise (interview, Jakarta, June 11, 2007). Accordingly, parallel to Yudhoyono's increasing suspicion of his coalition parties' loyalty, his sense was firming that the military was turning impatient too. Convinced that he needed the military to counter-balance the weakening support of his civilian partners, Yudhoyono eventually decided to appease it. As a result, the president dragged his feet on the legally mandated disbandment of military businesses, before signing a decree in 2010 that was acceptable to the armed forces; he ignored a 2009 call by parliament to launch human rights trials on the kidnappings and killings of 1998, which involved senior army leaders; he refused to issue a government apology to the victims of the army's anti-communist purges of 1965/66, despite having declared in 2012 that he considered doing so; and he stonewalled any discussion on the reform of the territorial command structure. Given that he had started his presidency with a daring breakthrough in civil-military relations, this obstructionism may appear odd, but it perfectly aligns with the shifting power constellations in Yudhoyono's presidential coalition and the president's consolidating views on the limitations of his authority.

Similar to Yudhoyono, Jokowi began his presidency in the belief that the post-amendment constitution might give him extensive powers. But unlike Yudhoyono, who already had acquired a pragmatic skepticism toward the influence of the presidency while serving in Wahid's cabinet, Jokowi learned his lessons about the intricacies of Indonesia's coalitional presidentialism in an abrupt and traumatic manner. Jokowi had run his campaign on a platform of being different from Yudhoyono, who he thought had been held hostage by his coalition partners. If elected, he pledged, he would not make compromises with the parties willing to support him. He won on that pledge, and in an interview in September 2014, one month before his inauguration, Jokowi was bursting with presidential self-confidence. Although only enjoying the support of 37% of parliament members, he predicted that his executive powers would trump all other forces (interview, Jakarta, September 15, 2014). Claiming that parliament only had very limited functions, he threatened that if it didn't approve his budget, he'd just govern based on the budget outlines of the previous year. Similarly, if parties rejected his policies, he'd turn to the people to force the elite to reconsider. "Watch me," he proclaimed when asked whether it would really be that easy. But the bitter awakening came only a week after his swearing-in ceremony. Pressured by his coalition parties, Jokowi had to abort one planned announcement of his cabinet, and shortly before the second, he was informed by Megawati – whose party had nominated him – that it would withdraw its support for his presidency if he insisted on appointing a party cadre she did not support. Visibly shaken, Jokowi gave in and had brutally landed in reality.

Under pressure from his own party and other coalition partners, Jokowi felt he had no political capital to spend on military reform, even in his early presidency. On Megawati's insistence, he appointed Ryamizard Ryacudu, a conservative military officer dismissed by Yudhoyono, as minister of defense. Ryamizard moved swiftly to implement his agenda, which reflected traditional army notions of the military's "fusion" with the people. He conceptualized a "state defense" program for civilians – essentially a paramilitary training exercise to spread military values to the population. After a long preparation phase, the project was launched in October 2015, with Jokowi's support. Meanwhile, Jokowi's standing vis-à-vis his presidential coalition had deteriorated further in the first half of 2015. In January, he nominated a Megawati protégée as chief of police but cancelled that nomination after the latter was declared a suspect in a corruption investigation. As a consequence, both Megawati and the police turned against Jokowi, with members of her party even raising the possibility of impeachment. Despite its practical unlikelihood, Jokowi was deeply anxious about the threat of impeachment and concluded that he needed to strengthen his ties to the military. He began visiting military units more often, and in June 2015, he wore full military fatigues in a meeting with Islamic leaders at the palace. Jokowi allowed the armed forces to re-engage with civilian policy areas, such as agricultural and village development (IPAC 2015), and in August, he appointed Gatot Nurmantyo, a known army conservative, as new military commander. Unlike many of his predecessors, then, Jokowi did not even have early successes in military reform.

Jokowi's position only improved after he chose to strengthen his presidential coalition with rather unconventional methods. Instead of exclusively focusing on the accommodation of partners with concessions (which had shown little effect), he prioritized a more coercive approach (Mietzner 2016). Using his powers to fuel internal splits in opposition parties, he managed to install loyalists at the helm of two of them by early 2016. A third party had already replaced its anti-Jokowi leadership in the previous year. As a result, his support in the legislature grew from 37 to 69%. And it was in this period, not coincidentally, that he took initial steps toward a progressive agenda critical of the military. First, in April 2016, Jokowi approved a seminar sponsored by his security minister, Luhut Pandjaitan, on the 1965 events, at which victims demanded a government apology. Second, he supported an initiative – by Luhut as well – to investigate past human rights abuses in Papua. But even as Jokowi tightened his grip, he soon got second thoughts about his newfound courage vis-à-vis the armed forces. After the military conveyed its objections about the 1965 and Papua initiatives to him, he felt it necessary to give a speech at military headquarters in June 2016 in which he assured the officers that a) he had no intention of apologizing to former members of the Communist Party, and b) he was determined to maintain the territorial command system. Two months later, he replaced Luhut with

Wiranto – another military conservative. With Wiranto's appointment, the two projects that Luhut had driven were effectively halted.

It is unclear why Jokowi concluded that it was impossible for him to see the 1965 and Papua initiatives through. He commanded a super-majority in parliament, his approval ratings were at record heights, and the threat by the police had subsided. Thus, he could have taken on the military without endangering his own position. Arguably, Jokowi was unwilling to risk alienating the armed forces for something he did not deem a strategic priority. However, if his enthusiasm for military reform was low while at the peak of his political strength, his interest diminished further when the Ahok demonstrations started in November 2016. It was not only the extent of Islamist mass mobilization that shocked him, but also the fact that members of three parties from his coalition were among the crowds. In addition, Yudhoyono supported the rallies, as did two other opposition parties (Prabowo Subianto's Gerindra later disengaged after Jokowi invited him for several meetings). For Jokowi, the protests revived the ghosts of impeachment and even non-constitutional removal, leading him to once more cultivate the military as an ally against the unreliability of his coalition parties and the unpredictability of the Islamist masses. In a speech at military headquarters in January 2017, the president lobbied the armed forces as an important partner on both the domestic and international stages (Sekretariat Kabinet 2017). Whether justified or not, Jokowi had returned to the conventional wisdom of many of his predecessors that aligning with the military was the best protection against unstable civilian politics.

Conclusion: how coalitional presidentialism shapes military reform patterns

This chapter has shown how the dynamics of coalitional presidentialism can explain fluctuations in the political influence of Indonesia's armed forces. Four major points need to be emphasized in this regard. First, within the concept of coalitional presidentialism, it is the *threat perception* of presidents vis-à-vis the safety of their position that has been the most decisive factor in creating political space for the military. Low threat perceptions have led them to impose limitations on the political role of the armed forces, while the military managed to defend its interests when presidents felt high levels of threat from their civilian coalition partners. Second, and following from this, the paradigm of coalitional presidentialism allows us to identify the *timing* of low and high levels of military influence on politics, or, in other words, the precise *periods* when successful military reform efforts occurred. Indonesia's most far-reaching military reforms fell into periods when presidents sensed no threat toward their position because they had either a) been given guarantees by key civilian forces that they could serve out their terms (Habibie in 1998 and Megawati in 2001/2002) or b) built a stable early coalition and still believed in their extensive executive powers (Yudhoyono in 2004/2005). Conversely, the political weight of the armed forces increased when a) nearing elections meant that coalition partners cut their ties to the president (Habibie in 1999 and Megawati in 2003/2004); b) continuously disloyal cabinet parties made presidents aware of the limitations of their power (Yudhoyono 2006–2014); c) presidents grossly overstepped their powers and lost all civilian support as a result (Wahid 2000/2001); or d) incumbents faced mass mobilizations supported by parts of the political establishment (Jokowi 2016).

It is obvious, then, that military reform efforts in Indonesia have had a higher chance of succeeding in the early phases of presidencies, when upcoming elections didn't unsettle coalitions and presidents sensed a higher level of independence from the armed forces. It is also clear that not a single military reform initiative was launched in later periods of any presidency, suggesting that the incumbent's increasing disillusionment about his or her presidential powers, frustration over the lack of loyalty within government coalitions, and heightened pre-election conflict ultimately serve as disincentives against risky attempts to reform the armed forces. This, however, brings us to the third main point emerging from this chapter's discussion: that is, the question of whether the threat perceptions of Indonesian presidents and their evaluation of the strength of the armed forces have been based on rational calculations of power constellations or – alternatively – on overestimations of both former factors. As indicated earlier, there are strong indications that both Yudhoyono and Jokowi did not fully grasp the fact that only a three-fourths majority in the MPR could impeach them after a verdict by the Constitutional Court. And indeed, neither has met a single incident in which impeachment proceedings were seriously considered, much less initiated against them. As far as the armed forces are concerned, it is difficult to ascertain what exactly they could do to either unseat a president who alienated them or protect one they supported from impeachment proceedings. In both scenarios, the president's ability to maintain a solid presidential coalition is much more crucial in determining the eventual outcome than the military's maneuvering. Wahid, for instance, did not fall because of the violence the military allegedly stirred up in several regions – he fell because his antics had driven away all civilian allies.

Fourth and finally, it is important to restate that coalitional presidentialism is a useful but not the only lens through which to assess the extent of the military's political influence. As indicated in the introduction, there have been other approaches to exploring this issue, and they remain valid. In the same vein, my discussion of coalitional presidentialism in this chapter further develops, rather than supersedes, some of the propositions I advanced in earlier works – for example, that the Indonesian military's weight in the transition was determined by intra-civilian conflict (Mietzner 2009) as well as by the quality of presidential leadership (2011). This chapter has adopted these points and framed them more specifically in relation to the way presidents build coalitions, allowing for a more precise identification of how, when, and why presidents caused an expansion or contraction of the military's political space. However, the slight change in perspective can alter some judgments: if assessed by the stability of civilian democracy, for example, it remains true that Yudhoyono maintained solid subjective civilian control over the military (Mietzner 2011), but the approach chosen here directs our attention to the lack of any military reform project in his second term and the reasons for that lack. In essence, the concept of coalitional presidentialism applied here explains why Indonesian presidents at critical junctures still perceive the military as a veto player with the same weight as influential political parties – while there is little evidence that the armed forces actually deserve such a perception.

References cited

Aspinall, Edward and Harold Crouch. 2003. *The Aceh Peace Process: Why It Failed* (Washington, DC: East West Center).

Aspinall, Edward, Marcus Mietzner, and Dirk Tomsa. 2015. "The Moderating President: Yudhoyono's Decade in Power," in Edward Aspinall, Marcus Mietzner, and Dirk Tomsa, eds., *The Yudhoyono Presidency: Indonesia's Decade of Stability and Stagnation* (Singapore: ISEAS), pp. 1–21.

Ate, Jan Pieter. 2010. "The Reform of the Indonesian Armed Forces in the Context of Indonesia's Democratisation." Shedden Papers, Centre for Defence and Strategic Studies, Australian Defence College.

Beeson, Mark. 2008. "Civil – Military Relations in Indonesia and the Philippines: Will the Thai Coup Prove Contagious?" *Armed Forces & Society* 34(3): 474–90.

Crouch, Harold. 2010. *Political Reform in Indonesia After Soeharto* (Singapore: ISEAS).

Chaisty, Paul, Nic Cheeseman, and Timothy Power. 2015. "The Coalitional Presidentialism Project: How MPs Understand Coalitional Politics in Presidential Systems." Research Report, Oxford University, January.

Croissant, Aurel, David Kuehn, Philip Lorenz, and Paul Chambers. 2013. *Democratization and Civilian Control in Asia* (Basingstoke: Palgrave).

Detik. 2016. "Jokowi ke Marinir: Sebagai Panglima Tertinggi Saya Ingin Pastikan Semua Loyal," 11 November. https://news.detik.com/berita/d-3342914/jokowi-ke-marinir-sebagai-panglima-tertinggi-saya-ingin-pastikan-semua-loyal.

Honna, Jun. 2003. *Military Politics and Democratization in Indonesia* (London: Routledge).

———. 2013. "Security Challenges and Military Reform in Post-Authoritarian Indonesia: The Impact of Separatism, Terrorism and Communal Violence," in Jurgen Rueland, Maria-Gabriela Manea, and Hans Born, eds., *The Politics of Military Reform: Experiences from Indonesia and Nigeria* (New York: Springer), pp. 185–200.

IPAC. 2015. "The Expanding Role of the Indonesian Military," *IPAC Report* No. 19, 25 May.

Laksmana, Evan A. 2016. "Reshuffling the Deck? Explaining the Rotational and Promotional Patterns of Indonesian Military Officers, 2005–2016," Paper Presented at the Conference *Two Decades of Reformasi*, University of Melbourne, 3–4 November.

Linz, Juan J. 1994. "Presidential or Parliamentary Democracy: Does It Make a Difference?" in Juan J. Linz and Arturo Valenzuela, eds., *The Failure of Presidential Democracy: The Case of Latin America* (Baltimore: Johns Hopkins University Press), pp. 3–87.

Mainwaring, Scott. 1993. "Presidentialism, Multipartism, and Democracy: The Difficult Combination," *Comparative Political Studies* 26: 198–228.

Mietzner, Marcus. 2009. *Military Politics, Islam, and the State in Indonesia: From Turbulent Transition to Democratic Consolidation* (Leiden: KITLV Press).

———. 2011. "Conflict and Leadership: The Resurgent Political Role of the Military in Southeast Asia," in M. Mietzner, ed., *The Political Resurgence of the Military in Southeast Asia: Conflict and Leadership* (London and New York Routledge), pp. 1–23.

———. 2013. *Money, Power, and Ideology: Political Parties in Post-Authoritarian Indonesia* (Honolulu: Hawaii University Press).

———. 2016. "Coercing Loyalty: Coalitional Presidentialism and Party Politics in Jokowi's Indonesia," *Contemporary Southeast Asia* 38(2): 209–32.

———. 2017. "Indonesia in 2016: Jokowi's Presidency Between Elite Consolidation and Extra-Parliamentary Opposition," *Asian Survey* 57(1): 165–72.

Sebastian, Leonard C. 2006. *Realpolitik Ideology: Indonesia's Use of Military Force* (Singapore: ISEAS).

Sebastian, Leonard C. and Iisgindarsah. 2013. "Taking Stock of Military Reform in Indonesia," in Jurgen Rueland, Maria-Gabriela Manea, and Hans Born, eds., *The Politics of Military Reform: Experiences From Indonesia and Nigeria* (New York: Springer), pp. 29–56.

Sekretariat Kabinet. 2017. "Hadiri Rapim TNI 2017, Presiden Jokowi Minta TNI Antisipasi Cepatnya Perubahan Dunia," 16 January. http://setkab.go.id/hadiri-rapim-tni-2017-presiden-jokowi-minta-tni-antisipasi-cepatnya-perubahan-dunia/.

Slater, Dan and Erica Simmons. 2013. "Coping by Colluding: Political Uncertainty and Promiscuous Powersharing in Indonesia and Bolivia," *Comparative Political Studies* 46(11): 1366–93.

Wiranto. 2003. *Bersaksi di Tengah Badai: Dari Catatan Wiranto, Jenderal Purnwirawan* (Jakarta: Ide Indonesia).

12

EVERYDAY CITIZENSHIP IN DEMOCRATIZING INDONESIA

Gerry van Klinken and Ward Berenschot[1]

Citizenship is arguably the biggest elephant in the room of Indonesian public debate. Take a newspaper on a given day, and you might read about sanctions against LGBT people or a proposal to prohibit alcohol. Land conflicts between villagers and palm oil and mining companies feature often, as does provincial shariah law, proscribing indecent behavior by, particularly, women. Expansion of the government's subsidized health care might be there, and education and social security and street protests about these things. Each one of these stories illustrates the evolving, highly political, nature of citizenship in Indonesia. Each concerns the state's responsibilities to its citizens and how it enables or restricts those rights. Each also conveys an interpretation of how "proper" citizens should behave. Yet paradoxically, the media seldom discuss these issues in terms of citizenship. Normative discussion on the extent to which the state can interfere in the private lives of citizens, for example, is rare. The Indonesian term for citizenship, *kewarganegaraan*, has an alien, technical ring to it. Today, it is used almost exclusively to describe the legal status of Indonesia's ethnic Chinese minority. And it is the term used in rather arid high school civics textbooks.

This reluctance to discuss public issues in terms of citizenship harks back to the New Order (1966–1998). Propaganda of the period gave it a particularly paternalistic interpretation. Kewarganegaraan signified obedience and an inclination to prioritize harmony over protest. Child-father images described the ideal citizen–state relation (Shiraishi 1997). Deference toward bearers of state authority was essential. Citizen rights hardly figured, as did the idea that the state also had obligations. The New Order mutilated the concept of citizenship so that it became virtually impossible to connect it meaningfully to the democratic politics that followed. But there are signs that Indonesians are rediscovering the riches of a citizenship perspective, and this chapter will explore some of them.

Indonesia's Reformasi reflected broader transformations affecting states, markets, and the political integration of citizens around the world. In the English-speaking world at least, these global shifts *have* greatly intensified public debate about citizenship since the early 1980s.[2] The decline of the welfare state and the Soviet collapse in the Global North, the Third Wave of democracy in the South, state decentralization, and market globalization everywhere – all conspired to undermine old certainties about citizen rights.

In Indonesia, after 1998, "Asian values" talk justifying the authoritarian bargain disappeared. In its place have come new ideas of welfare rights, protests against "corrupt" politicians, and, out in the provinces, alternative political communities based around religious or local identities. Underlying these discussions is an awareness that democratization has not been an all-out success. The public sphere is free and open, and civil society lively. Legislative reforms are expanding citizen rights. Yet free and fair elections seem to have done little to curtail the dominance of oligarchic elites. Some have called Indonesia a "patronage democracy" (Klinken 2009). "Predatory elites" (Hadiz 2010) win elections by using their "money power" to buy voters or, if that fails, the "muscle power" of allied criminal elements to coerce them (see Aspinall chapter, this volume). In our view, however, "stagnating" democratization (Mietzner 2012) cannot be attributed solely to institutional shortcomings or selfish elites. Citizens would seem to have the casting vote to break this strange impasse of blatant manipulation amid discursive openness. Yet we do not know much about their thinking.

Observing how ordinary citizens relate to power holders and state institutions is a way of studying democratization "from below." Citizenship studies can offer insights that other approaches miss. Neo-statist analyses emphasizing the autonomy and capacities of state institutions, for example, rang true during the authoritarian New Order. But they are elitist and did not foresee the extent of democratization that would follow. Democratization theory *is* sensitive to popular movements and casts light on the institutionalization of democracy since 1998. But it has trouble with the high degree of informality that runs through actual democratic practices. By bringing the everyday lives of large numbers of ordinary citizens back into the picture, citizenship studies offer a more panoramic view than elite-centered and formal-institutional approaches have done.

This chapter has three aims. First, we wish to develop the argument that a citizenship perspective on political change is fruitful. Second, we want to understand the everyday citizenship regime emerging in democratizing Indonesia today. Why do citizens have so many rights on paper they cannot enjoy in reality? The answer, we argue, should be sought in the highly informal, personalized, and mediated character of that citizenship. Thirdly, we seek to explain this pattern of citizenship historically. The decentralization that paralleled democratization is of particular interest to us.

Why "post-colonial" citizenship?

Citizenship is the basis of all politics. It is the "organizing principle of state-society relations in modern states" (Butenschøn, et al. 2000: 8). If a polity consists of the state and its people, then citizenship is about who those people are and how they relate to each other and to the state. Put more operationally, citizenship denotes the relationship between citizens and agents of the state, referring to both the rights citizens enjoy as well as obligations to contribute to public life (Tilly 1996: 8). Citizenship studies traditionally follow one of three approaches. All three consider citizenship vital to democratic consolidation. A liberal tradition examines the legal status of the individual and is thus primarily concerned with membership conditions in the political community. It inspires arguments about the importance of actually realizing civil and political rights. A communitarian one focuses on the management of societal diversity. How can peace be maintained while respecting minority rights? This is of clear relevance to Indonesia (Hefner 2001). A republican tradition, meanwhile, emphasizes the role of an active and informed citizenry. De Tocqueville's study of the lively public sphere underpinning democracy in 19th-century America is a famous republican example. Democratic accountability depends on citizens collectively demanding that state agents actualize rights. The civic culture that makes democracy work rests on trust, tolerance, participation, associational activity, and a sense of affiliation with national or even global polities (Pattie et al. 2004). Republican citizenship speaks strongly to Indonesia's democratization. We broadly adopt this third perspective here but at the same time find it is due for renewal.

The field of citizenship studies emerged out of Western experiences with democratization, and still displays Western biases. Yet today democratization is most intense in the non-Western, post-colonial world. There, conventional approaches to the study of citizenship face considerable conceptual and methodological challenges. At first sight, "real" citizenship seems largely absent. The rights-claiming, autonomous, and individualistic citizens celebrated in the mainstream literature exist in post-colonial countries only in small numbers. Just as problematic is the post-colonial institutional setting. Conventional citizenship studies assume the context of a liberal, high-capacity welfare state. Those who, by contrast, examine the patterns of state-citizen interactions in a weakly institutionalized state and a predominantly clientelistic political system make intriguing discoveries (Cornwall, et al. 2011; Lazar 2012; Robins, et al. 2008). Citizens relate to each other and to power holders in more communitarian, clientelist, and hierarchical ways than Western scholars are used to. Post-colonial citizens apparently cannot assume the law will protect them while they protest. Instead, they negotiate, improvise, and above all relate personally to those in power around them.

Idealized images of citizenship as reflected in the standard literature have proven seductive throughout the world. But it is not productive to study actual post-colonial state-citizen interactions primarily in terms of their deviation from those ideals. Rather, we observe particular conceptions and practices of rights, reciprocity, and representation. And we want to know how these relate to the political economy and post-colonial history of state formation. Researchers before us have fruitfully posed these questions particularly in Africa and India (Chabal and Daloz 1999; Chatterjee 2004; Kaviraj 2001; Mamdani 1996). They have generally shed the expectation that citizenship in post-colonial states is "on its way" to evolving into something more akin to Western patterns. They argue that the socio-cultural embeddedness of the market and the state historically conspired to prevent autonomous citizens from emerging in large numbers. In short, what Engin Isin (2005) called "citizenship after orientalism" requires an open conceptualization and a reflexive interaction with the normative baggage that comes with the concept of citizenship.

Part of that reconceptualization of citizenship involves a fresh appreciation for passion, for antagonism, in short, for "the political." Post-colonial citizenship relations frequently play out beyond the legal framework, which is weak. This is true at the scale of everyday personal negotiation but also at that of the convulsive upheaval involving riots, church burnings, or land occupations, as the newspaper stories opening this chapter illustrated. A tendency to transgress the formal rules stretches the conventional "civic" celebration of the active citizen. As it happens, the recognition among scholars of post-colonial societies that citizenship is fundamentally volatile is paralleled in the Global North. There, too, resurgent interest in elemental citizenship questions since the 1980s has fed distrust of prevailing prescriptions for a politics of "good governance" and for "post-partisan" and "post-political" "consensus democracy" (Mouffe 2005).

Engin Isin (2002), for reasons such as this, proposed to distinguish "critical" citizenship studies from conventional ones by the former's heightened attention precisely to the political. He urged that the study of citizenship should be a historical and empirical science, rather than primarily normative. Moreover, besides studying the practices of those who already belong to the political community – "history's victors" – he wanted to observe those moments in which outsiders and strangers challenge the rules while demanding entry to that community for themselves. We argue here that in Indonesia this dynamic largely plays out informally. Decisive to the question of who is "in" or "out" is not simply the content of laws or policies but rather how these boundaries are negotiated on the ground.

To begin our "post-colonial" study of citizenship in Indonesia, we will focus in the following section on the everyday practices that express what it means to be an ordinary, non-elite citizen in "normal" times. Rather than looking for "participating" or "rights-claiming" citizens, as normative theory would urge us to do, the aim here is to detect the strategies, values, and attitudes that people express through everyday interactions. This means doing ethnographic fieldwork on how, for example, they access subsidized health care or defend land rights. Every day, citizens relate to each other and to the state in ways that tend to conform to a habitual pattern. From these concrete interactions, we try to grasp some key characteristics of the social pact among citizens and between citizens and the state. This complex agreement comprises the complete range of prevailing rights and duties (written and unwritten), and ideologies and laws, as well as the daily practices in which those things are supported, evaded, or (rarely) contested. Such a pact has been called a "citizenship regime" (Isin and Nyers 2014: 151).

In the subsequent section, we ask a historical question: how does such a regime come about? We argue that its emergence is not "natural," but the outcome of a complex and frequently antagonistic set of socio-economic processes. Particularly the question of who is "in" and who is "out" of the body politic and what rights the "ins" have, normally not salient, can become pressing at contentious moments. Which historical forces conspired to create a citizenship regime in which citizens have so many more rights on paper than in their everyday lives?

Informality and rights

Nearly two decades after the fall of Soeharto, citizenship is characterized by a particular paradox. On the one hand, new laws and regulations have considerably expanded citizen rights. Yet, on the other hand, the capacity of citizens to actually realize these rights has not increased and, in some areas, has even decreased.

If we restrict our view to laws and regulations, it would appear that citizenship in Indonesia has deepened considerably. New laws on the press (1999), labor (2003), citizenship (2006), freedom of information (2009), and legal aid (2011) substantially strengthened the power of citizens vis-à-vis state authorities. Moreover, the social security law (2011) and expanded subsidized health care dramatically increased citizen welfare rights – and that while Western welfare states are shrinking. Not less important, after decades of forced evictions under Soeharto, citizens now have greater security of land tenure, at least on paper. A spatial planning law was adopted in 2007 and a land acquisition law in 2012, while Indonesia's Constitutional Court recognized communal land rights in 2012.

Yet, citizens often cannot realize those rights. In the face of expanding palm oil and mining concessions, village communities still find it difficult to protect their land (Cramb and McCarthy 2016). Thuggish organizations, often with good political connections, disrupt demonstrations by progressive organizations. Expanding welfare programs suffer from mistargeting as the poorest struggle to gain access (Mulyadi 2013). Despite constitutional guarantees, minority groups have trouble building houses of worship or protecting themselves from violence. Papua remains a dark place. Critical journalists and even official investigators face intimidation when they dare to look into the dealings of Indonesia's rent-seeking elites. When NGOs take labor disputes, environmental conflicts, or land disputes to court, judges rule remarkably often in favor of their corporate or state adversaries (Nicholson 2010).

Such gaps between law-on-paper and law-in-practice are, we argue, largely due to the highly informalized character of the Indonesian state. As we will explore in the next section, this informalization is not just a legacy of the New Order but also a product of Indonesia's democratization process. A long history of political interference in bureaucratic processes has inhibited bureaucratic autonomy, limited the regulatory capacity of state institutions, and thus generally weakened the rule of law. As a consequence, ordinary citizens experience state laws and policies as a random and unpredictable force. They see that personal influence, politics, and money shape bureaucratic outcomes just as much as do formal rules. So they resort to personal connections with influential go-betweens to work around them. This reliance on informal connections constitutes an important element of state-citizen interaction in Indonesia, as it does in many other post-colonial states (Lazar 2012). The weakly institutionalized nature of many post-colonial states is forcing citizens to take recourse to informal connections.

The importance of personal connections in the everyday functioning of the state helps explain the implementation gaps mentioned earlier. Whether one considers access to welfare, land rights, human rights, social security, or minority rights, the actual capacity of citizens to realize such rights depends on the character of their informal, personal networks. Take, for example, the access to Indonesia's expanding welfare programs. In theory, the selection of beneficiaries for such programs is based on formal criteria. In practice, however, village heads have considerable influence over this selection (Mulyadi 2013; Sambodho forthcoming). They face strong incentives to direct the benefits to family members and supporters. A similar example concerns access to subsidized health care. Poorer patients are regularly turned away at hospitals and clinics and feel intimidated by complex paperwork. Various kinds of brokers have emerged to help people work around these obstacles, using their skills and knowledge of procedures to solve bureaucratic hurdles and to pressure hospital staff into providing beds and subsidized medicines (Hanani forthcoming).

Informal contacts also play a large role in the many land conflicts plaguing Indonesia. The difficulties rural communities have with incoming palm oil or mining companies are not only caused by Indonesia's vague and contradictory legal framework. They are exacerbated by the informal connections between these companies and regional political and bureaucratic elites (Lucas and Warren 2013). In exchange for secretive forms of profit-sharing, such as election campaign contributions, companies obtain support from local elites to evade regulations and suppress protests (Aspinall and Berenschot forthcoming). Even the courts are not above such exchanges (Pompe 2006). Conversely, rural communities that chose to cultivate strong connections with power holders stand a better chance of protecting their land than those that resist (Afrizal 2013; Muur forthcoming).

Similar informal mechanisms can be observed to lie behind clashes with minority groups, such as the mob attacks on an Ahmadiyah community in Cikeusik (West Java) in 2011 and on a Shia community in Sampang (Madura) in 2012. Growing intolerance and religious fanaticism do not exhaust all possible explanations for these outbursts of violence. Perpetrators such as the Islamic Defenders Front (FPI), a hard-line Islamist organization, enjoy impunity because they are clandestinely connected to the police. They extort "un-Islamic" businesses like nightclubs or liquor stores and share the profits with security personnel (Baker and Milne 2015). Such organizations can also deliver votes, and this cements their connection with politicians. Minority groups, by contrast, lack such informal connections, with serious consequences for their own security (Soedirgo 2016).

The recurring theme in these examples is that the character of informal personal networks shapes the actual capacity of citizens to realize their rights. Shaping these interactions between state institutions and citizens is a particular layer of intermediaries. These range from political actors and local fixers to quasi-state representatives like village heads and RT/RW heads. Indonesia is not unique in this respect. Poorer citizens in many states, particularly in the Global South, rely on this kind of "political mediation" to deal with state institutions (Berenschot 2011). Faced with under-resourced and un-responsive state institutions, a range of brokers have emerged who use their social contacts and knowledge of state procedures to pressure institutions on behalf of their clients. Partha Chatterjee (2004) coined the term "political society" to refer to this sphere of informal mediation between citizens and the state. He noted that in many post-colonial democracies claims to public services are not justifiable rights. They are more likely to be settled through informal, politicized negotiations. For this reason, the struggle for fuller forms of citizenship does not only take place in parliament or on the streets in big demonstrations. It repeats itself every day in government offices throughout Indonesia, wherever citizens need to muster both *savoir-faire* and connections to pressure authorities. These are the everyday politics of citizenship that a weakly institutionalized state generates.

How does this reliance on informal connections affect citizenship in Indonesia? Scholars of conventional citizenship studies may not even agree that these interactions should qualify as citizenship. The impersonal, legal, contractual element is missing. Yet the view that there is "something missing" with citizenship in Indonesia is too restrictive. It makes no sense to conclude that citizens are only those upper-class persons who can afford to negotiate with state institutions purely on the basis of their rights. The analytical challenge is rather to discover the *particular form* of citizenship that is generated by this informal and mediated interaction with state institutions. As a preliminary answer to that question, we propose three key observable characteristics of everyday citizenship in democratizing Indonesia.

A first key aspect is that *citizenship is socialized*. The quality of one's personal networks and the sense of obligation embedded in these networks shapes the quality of one's citizenship. Individuals enjoying more wide-ranging contacts with influential and responsive people have a stronger capacity to realize their rights. This makes membership of a religious or ethnic community a valuable asset – it comes with useful contacts as well as a sense of solidarity and mutual obligation. One gains access to important resources (land, education, health care, and so on) not only by virtue of one's national citizenship, but also by virtue of one's age, gender, ethnicity, membership in a community, and other forms of "local citizenship" (Lund 2016).

A citizenship of informal connections is highly differentiated. Those with strong connections enjoy a fuller form of citizenship, while citizens lacking them might not even try to go to a government office by themselves, and they are likely to fail if they do (Sambodho forthcoming). Whole communities who lack influential connections – such as the minority Ahmadiyah community – are at a disadvantage. To a much larger extent than by laws and policies, the distinction between "in" and "out" groups is determined by the quality of the social connections an individual or community enjoys. Class speaks loudly here. Those with the lowest incomes and social status possess the least effective connections. Mediated citizenship reflects and reproduces social inequalities.

A second key aspect is that *citizen rights are personalized*. The experience of citizen rights is not only practically but also normatively mediated. Alongside the formal rules, the expectations and attitudes of citizens vis-à-vis state institutions are shaped by informal institutions, such as patron-client relations and norms of reciprocity. Citizen expectations about the kinds of services the state should deliver – and hence the type of pressure they are prepared to exert on the state to get them – are shaped by obligations embedded in personal relationships. Rights such as access to subsidized health care are experienced as a personal privilege rather than as an impersonal right. In this sense, mediated citizenship is self-reproducing: the experience that connections matter more than formal rights in itself discourages citizens from engaging in claim-making and adopting a discourse of rights. Habituation to informal mediation limits the pressure on state institutions to reduce the implementation gap and strengthen rights guarantees.

A third aspect is *the socialization of political agency*. Nurturing personal relationships constitutes an important form of agency. Such an observation might seem to go against conventional ideas about political participation, which focus on demonstrations, petitions, and other rights-claiming behavior. But autonomous political agency – participating in a rally, speaking out critically – risks alienating the important contacts poorer citizens depend on. Mediated citizenship in this sense constrains agency. Furthermore, the clientelistic and mediated access to state benefits creates a sense of indebtedness that discourages open critique of power holders. Citizens feel "tied in" (*terikat*).

Yet an exclusive focus on claim-making overly restricts the view of political agency. In the context of informal, mediated state institutions, political agency also takes the form of cultivating personal bonds with influential power holders. Clientelism is a two-way street: citizens make active, conscious use of the obligations embedded in the exchange. Invoking a family relation, presenting oneself as somebody's "underling" (*anak buah*), unquestioningly supporting a patron, obsessively socializing with bureaucrats – all are useful means for the marginalized to strengthen social bonds that also serve to defend their interests. This might not constitute "civic" behavior in the narrow, Western meaning of the term. But this behavior does constitute an important form of political agency that citizens possess in the context of highly informalized state institutions. The cultivation of personal connections plays an important role in the everyday struggles of citizens to realize their rights.

That does not imply, however, that all citizens are necessarily content with their dependency on such clientelistic relationships to get things done. As we explore in the next section, there are good reasons to attribute the periodic outbursts of popular demands to alter Indonesia's citizenship regime, at least in part, to boiling resentment over precisely these everyday interactions.

Critical junctures

Reformasi was such a moment in which citizens challenged the citizenship regime created by the New Order. Often forgotten is that it was a double movement – one for democracy, another for decentralization. Organizationally distinct, they sprang sequentially from different social formations. In this section, we link citizenship movements to a specific history of state formation and of political economy. We will argue that the mediated citizenship regime we described was, at least in part, the result of Reformasi contestation. Where the democracy movement aimed to enhance impersonal citizen rights, decentralization effectively emasculated them once more.

The passionate protests in Indonesia's biggest cities that brought down President Soeharto in May 1998 had democracy as their theme. Students demanded political freedoms and elections, the army out of politics, an end to corruption and violence, and lowered prices (the latter demand triggered by the economic crisis). They continued to press Soeharto's successor Habibie. Through most of 1998, the media were full of "democracy" talk, while the word *decentralization* was hardly heard. Unfortunately, the democratizing demands did not enjoy strong political party support. Unlike in Spain after Franco, no socialist party emerged to fill the gap on the left of the spectrum left by the destruction of the PKI in 1965. A few years later, one experienced observer concluded that democratic reform had been "half-hearted" (King 2003).

By the end of 1998, however, a new demand was heard from a different source. Demonstrations in provincial towns beyond the central island of Java began to demand "autonomy." The troubled regions of East Timor, Papua, and Aceh started it. Soon other regions chimed in too with veiled threats to secede if not granted more autonomy. The most prominent spokespersons were not necessarily democrats. They were members of local governments, often deploying a language of ethnic chauvinism. For them, decentralization was as much a way of resisting Jakarta elites as of advancing a broad citizenship agenda in their own region. They represented a rapidly growing *lower* middle class in hundreds of small and medium provincial towns. Their prosperity

depended on state patronage, and their politics ran through the bureaucracy (Klinken and Berenschot 2014). Multilateral agencies like the World Bank, already deeply engaged with the Indonesian government because of the Asian Financial Crisis, urged decentralization for reasons that
may have had more to do with their distrust of strong state apparatuses. Jakarta listened, and from
this point on, much of the country's political energy went in that direction. The decentralization
reforms were carried through with an intensity the World Bank described as "Big Bang," making Indonesia "one of the most decentralized countries in the world" (World Bank 2003: 28).

By conflating it with democracy, proponents of decentralization in 1998 obscured a history
in which the two have at times been opposed to each other. Democracy and decentralization
are conceptually distinct. The first is about the mobilization of citizens to participate, directly
or indirectly, in ruling through the state. The second concerns the institutional structure of that
state, the object of politics. A centralized, high-capacity state is in direct contact with most citizens. A decentralized state may be decentralized by fate (poverty and conflict) or by design (a
desire to limit central powers). Its central apparatus tends to have only indirect contact with most
citizens, leaving much of the work to locally embedded elites. Decentralization can, of course, be
democratic as well – that was the hope during Reformasi – but it was a mistake to expect that
decentralization would foster democratization.

The biggest clash between decentralization and democracy occurred during the iconic anti-
colonial Revolution of 1945–1949. This was a complex episode. Groups with many ideological orientations – some secular, others religious – took part in the struggle. But nearly everyone
agreed broadly on some version of state socialism. The main goal was the creation of a *centralized*
democratic state, one capable of providing welfare for everyone. Of course, leading republicans had
pragmatic reasons for wanting centralized control in the midst of Indonesia's regional diversity. But
their argument that the republic should be "unitary" also carried great, modernizing legitimacy. It
represented the future-oriented alternative to what they called colonial "feudalism." The popular
cry of "Merdeka!" – freedom! – in 1945 supported that dream. It expressed as much a personal
yearning for emancipation from oppressive patrons as one for national independence (Reid 1998).

Opposed to the passionate vision of a centralized republic was one the colonial Dutch had
invented in the first decades of twentieth century. Seeking both to preserve indigenous forms
of rule and to save money on the construction of an ambitious modern state, the Dutch built
indirect rule into many parts of their territorial system. They trusted local aristocrats to mediate to their indigenous subjects the little governing the state did commit to. By enhancing the
prestige of local old men and their conservative rural norms (*adat*), they hoped to restrain those
dynamic elements most threatening to social stability: youth, women, transients, labor, and dis-
sident intellectuals. Rather than relying on law impersonally administered by a central state, the
colonials trusted the "culturally authentic" personal authority these men had built up within
the informal and hierarchical world of local social exchange. Local elites liked indirect rule and
continued to push for it under the name of federalism or decentralization even after 1945. In
areas of the archipelago where the Dutch regained control following the Japanese defeat, they
established a federal state structure in which the pre-war families were once more preeminent.

Post-Reformasi decentralization shares some characteristics with colonial indirect rule.
National elites justified both on the basis that the legitimacy of the locally rooted, communitarian (hierarchical) political community is more robust than that generated by modern, national
legality. Behind the public justification in both cases lay an elite preference for striking personal
deals with loyal provincial elites – "betting on the strong" (Wertheim 1964) – over an impersonal principle of rule. And in both cases, those elite beliefs more or less consciously ran counter
to a conception of democratic rule from a national center. These convictions helped create the
"mediated" citizenship regime we observe in Indonesia today.

In part, this conservative colonial vision was sustained by the overwhelmingly rural political economy of the archipelago. As late as 1945, only 10% of the population lived in urban areas. Traditional deference and clientelistic dependency flourished under rural circumstances. But already by the mid-1930s a good observer of the Dutch indirect rule system was skeptical that a system so bound to the assumption of rurality could be sustained without violence. Rupert Emerson wrote of "this extraordinarily difficult task of bringing back to life communities which shall still have the semblance of growing from the soil." He thought of a "violent and bloody trial of strength [as] ... inevitable ... [I]t is difficult to see how the new society can break through the artificially petrified crust of the old traditions without violent conflict" (Emerson 1979 [1937]: 436, 493, 518–9).

The Revolution of 1945–1949 was the first of three critical junctures when the everyday citizenship regime was called into question. Each was at once a struggle over democracy and one over the structure of the state. The second was the bloody birth of the New Order in 1965–1966. By the mid-1960s, the central state had grown significantly in its capacities. But military and other central state elites felt that excessive citizen mobilization – largely leftist – made the country ungovernable. Ironically, they found themselves forming alliances with non-communist parties that, by virtue of their local ethnic, religious, or elitist values, were less committed to the republican ideal than the PKI. The 1965 upheaval can be seen as a counter-revolutionary push to build a modern authoritarian state by depoliticizing citizenship while retaining central state capacities. It was growing popular dissatisfaction with this centralized "authoritarian bargain" that made the argument for democratic decentralization so compelling in late 1998. But the republican image of a state that could be both centralized and democratic had been dealt a serious blow. This was another way in which the New Order mutilated citizenship aspirations.

By the end of the third contentious moment, Reformasi, it was decentralization that had shaped state-citizen relations more than democratization. Numerous studies on local politics since 1998 confirm that today's decentralized state appears to be less capable of autonomous action and more socially embedded in local hierarchies than seemed to be the case even a couple of decades ago. Particularly inhibiting to the institutionalization of the state since 1998 have been predatory *local* politics. Decentralization has permitted local elites to maintain and sometimes expand their capacity to bend the implementation of state policies and laws to their needs (Aspinall and Klinken 2011; Klinken and Barker 2009). Struggles about "ins" and "outs" in the provinces effectively redefined "outs" as those who lacked influential personal connections. In defiance of constitutional law, members of ethnic, religious, sexual, and other minorities were left to fend for themselves as best they could. For the "ins," the net consequence of Reformasi has been that the mobilization of citizens for competitive politics, amid insecurities caused by weak rule of law, has reclientelized state-citizen relations. Vote-buying is routine and omnipresent. Clientelistic exchanges such as those we examined in the previous section are the essence of most of these politics (Aspinall and Berenschot forthcoming).

Arguably the citizenship regime in Indonesia today would have been different – less clientelist, more rule-based, more effective – if democratization had not been immediately followed by decentralization.

Conclusion

We have argued in this chapter for a post-colonial approach to studying citizenship in Indonesia. It is a research endeavor that calls for some critical distance from the conventional interpretations of citizenship. It is open to the idea that post-colonial state-citizen relations have a reality not fully captured by the ideal image of the autonomous, individualistic, rights-claiming citizen. And it pays attention to political economy, to the history of state formation, and to informality.

In the first substantive part of this chapter, we highlighted our observation that the nature of citizenship in Indonesia today is not only a product of formal laws and legislation but also of the quality of personal relationships and informal networks. As a result of the weakly institutionalized, socially embedded nature of state institutions, citizens regularly depend on personal connections to realize rights and to bend rules in their favor. Their reliance on personal connections mutes the experience of "rights." Instead, citizens continually negotiate their relations with those in power. Rather than being primarily legal in nature, relations are interpersonal, at times antagonistic, in short, political. Mediated citizenship is highly differentiated. There are strong class differences between citizens who can and others who cannot easily access the benefits of state services on a daily basis.

In the second substantive part, we argued that the citizenship regime described in the first arises from a particular political economy and history of state formation in Indonesia. Economically, it grew out of the predominantly rural and small-town demographics of the colonial period. Politically, it is the outcome of political struggles that peaked at certain critical junctures. The latest of these, in 1998–1999, was to a great extent won by predatory provincial elites, who saw Reformasi as an opportunity to capture key resources of the state and control the flow of them to their local clients. Decentralization has come at a great cost to the quality of citizenship, particularly for the poor majority of the population.

How might change come to this "mediated" citizenship regime? The mediated character of citizenship in Indonesia dissuades citizens from concerted efforts to push the state toward a fuller realization of rights. The irony of Indonesia's democratization is that many newly emerging citizenship struggles are not formulated in terms of a universal "right" but in terms of particular (community-based) claims. This might gradually change. The slow social transformation wrought by urbanization and a growing middle class might eventually create more demanding, autonomous citizens. Protests against "corrupt" politics have been effective in the bigger cities of Indonesia, and this could be a harbinger of the "post-clientelist" politics of the future (Manor 2013). It does seem unlikely that a single political party will emerge that can aggregate such impulses in the direction of a centralized, democratic republic. But conscious, cross-class bridge-building between political communities in cities and provincial areas could work wonders. Some of this is happening already, and it is likely to grow stronger as urbanization and globalization continue to transform the social landscape. It could be the beginning of Indonesian citizens reclaiming the centralized, republican state.

Notes

1 This chapter builds on the results of an international research program on citizenship and democratization in Indonesia we helped to run between 2012 and 2017. "Clients to citizens? Emerging citizenship in democratizing Indonesia" (www.kitlv.nl) was funded jointly by the Royal Netherlands Academy of Arts and Sciences (KNAW), the Indonesian Ministry of Research and Technology, and the Indonesian Ministry of Education and Culture, under the Third Scientific Program Indonesia-Netherlands (SPIN-3). We gratefully acknowledge insights gained from discussions particularly with the other core researchers: Retna Hanani, Prio Sambodho, Zamzam Fauzanafi, Willem van der Muur, Vita Febriany, and Chris Chaplin.
2 Try typing "citizenship" into https://books.google.com/ngrams.

References cited

Afrizal. 2013. "Oil Palm Plantations, Customary Rights and Local Protests: A West Sumatran Case Study," in Anton Lucas and Carol Warren, eds., *Land for the People: The State and Agrarian Conflict in Indonesia* (Athens: Ohio University Press), pp. 149–83.

Aspinall, Edward and Ward Berenschot. Forthcoming 2018. *Democracy for Sale: Elections, Clientelism and the State in Indonesia* (Ithaca: Cornell University Press).

Aspinall, Edward and Gerry van Klinken, eds. 2011. *The State and Illegality in Indonesia* (Leiden: KITLV Press).

Baker, Jacqui and Sarah Milne. 2015. "Dirty Money States: Illicit Economies and the State in Southeast Asia," *Critical Asian Studies* 47(2): 151–76.

Berenschot, Ward. 2011. *Riot Politics: Hindu-Muslim Violence and the Indian State* (London: Hurst & Co).

Butenschøn, Nils, Uri A. Davis, and Manuel Hassassian, eds. 2000. *Citizenship and the State in the Middle East: Approaches and Applications* (New York: Syracuse University Press).

Chabal, Patrick and Jean-Pascal Daloz. 1999. *Africa Works: Disorder as Political Instrument* (Oxford: James Currey).

Chatterjee, Partha. 2004. *The Politics of the Governed: Reflections on Popular Politics in Most of the World* (New York: Columbia University Press).

Cornwall, Andrea, Steven Robbins, and Bettina Von Lieres. 2011. "States of Citizenship: Context and Cultures of Public Engagement and Citizen Action," IDS Working Paper Series No. 363 (Brighton, UK: Institute of Development Studies at the University of Sussex).

Cramb, Rob, and John F. McCarthy, eds. 2016. *The Oil Palm Complex: Smallholders, Agribusiness and the State in Indonesia and Malaysia* (Singapore: NUS Press).

Emerson, Rupert. 1979 (1937). *Malaysia: A Study in Direct and Indirect Rule* (Kuala Lumpur: University of Malaya Press).

Hadiz, Vedi. 2010. *Localising Power in Post-Authoritarian Indonesia: A Southeast Asia Perspective* (Stanford, CA: Stanford University Press).

Hanani, Retna. Forthcoming. "Between Patronage and Empowerment: Citizenship and Health Care in Indonesia." (Ph.D. University of Amsterdam, Amsterdam).

Hefner, Robert W., ed. 2001. *The Politics of Multiculturalism: Pluralism and Citizenship in Malaysia, Singapore, and Indonesia* (Honolulu: University of Hawai'i Press).

Isin, Engin F. 2002. *Being Political: Genealogies of Citizenship* (Minneapolis: University of Minnesota Press).

Isin, Engin F. 2005. "Citizenship After Orientalism: Ottoman Citizenship," in Fuat Keyman and Ahmet Icduygu, eds., *Citizenship in a Global World: European Questions and Turkish Experiences* (New York and London: Routledge), pp. 31–51.

Isin, Engin and Peter Nyers, eds. 2014. *Routledge Handbook of Global Citizenship Studies* (New York and London: Routledge).

Kaviraj, Sudipta. 2001. "In Search of Civil Society," in Sudipta Kaviraj and Silnani Khilnani, eds., *Civil Society: History and Possibilities* (Cambridge: Cambridge University Press), pp. 287–324.

King, Dwight Y. 2003. *Half-Hearted Reform: Electoral Institutions and the Struggle for Democracy in Indonesia* (Westport, CT: Praeger).

Klinken, Gerry van. 2009. "Patronage Democracy in Provincial Indonesia," in Olle Törnquist, Neil Webster, and Kristian Stokke, eds., *Rethinking Popular Representation*, pp. 141–59 (Basingstoke: Palgrave Macmillan).

Klinken, Gerry van and Joshua Barker, eds. 2009. *State of Authority: The State in Society in Indonesia* (Ithaca: Cornell University Southeast Asia Program).

Klinken, Gerry van and Ward Berenschot, eds. 2014. *In Search of Middle Indonesia: Middle Classes in Provincial Towns* (Leiden: Brill).

Lazar, Sian. 2012. "Citizenship Quality: A New Agenda for Development?" *Journal of Civil Society* 8(4): 333–50.

Lucas, Anton and Carol Warren, eds. 2013. *Land for the People: The State and Agrarian Conflict in Indonesia* (Athens: Ohio University Press).

Lund, Christian. 2016. "Rule and Rupture: State Formation Through the Production of Property and Citizenship," *Development and Change* 47: 1199–228.

Mamdani, Mahmood. 1996. *Citizen and Subject: Contemporary Africa and the Legacy of Late Colonialism* (Princeton: Princeton University Press).

Manor, James. 2013. "Post-Clientelist Initiatives," in Kristian Stokke and Olle Törnquist, eds., *Democratization in the Global South: The Importance of Transformative Politics* (Basingstoke: Palgrave Macmillan), pp. 243–53.

Mietzner, Marcus. 2012. "Indonesia's Democratic Stagnation: Anti-Reformist Elites and Resilient Civil Society," *Democratization* 19(2): 209–29.

Mouffe, Chantal. 2005. *On the Political* (London: Routledge).

Mulyadi. 2013. "Welfare Regime, Social Conflict, and Clientelism in Indonesia" (Ph.D. Thesis. Canberra, Victoria, Australia: Australian National University).

Muur, Willem van der. Forthcoming. "State or Adat Lands? Territorial Disputes and the Claim to Indigeneity in Indonesia" (Ph.D. Thesis. Leiden: Leiden University).

Nicholson, David. 2010. *Environmental Dispute Resolution in Indonesia* (Leiden: Brill).

Pattie, Charles, Patrick Seyd, and Paul Whiteley. 2004. *Citizenship in Britain: Values, Participation and Democracy* (Cambridge: Cambridge University Press).

Pompe, Sebastiaan. 2006. *The Indonesian Supreme Court: A Study of Institutional Collapse*, (Ithaca: Cornell University, Southeast Asia Program).

Reid, Anthony. 1998. "Merdeka: The Concept of Freedom in Indonesia," in David Kelly and Anthony Reid, eds., *Asian Freedoms: The Idea of Freedom in East and Southeast Asia* (Cambridge: Cambridge University Press), pp. 141–60.

Robins, Steven, Andrea Cornwall, and Bettina von Lieres. 2008. "Rethinking 'citizenship' in the post-colony," *Third World Quarterly* 29(6):1069–86.

Sambodho, Prio. Forthcoming. "Levelling the Playing Field? Democratic Reform and Citizenship in Rural Indonesia." (Ph.D., University of Amsterdam, Amsterdam).

Shiraishi, Saya S. 1997. *Young Heroes: The Indonesian Family in Politics* (Ithaca: Cornell Southeast Asia Program Publications).

Soedirgo, Jessica. 2016. "Citizenship Gaps and Patronage Structures: Religious Minorities in Indonesia." Paper presented at the Conference *From Clients to Citizens? Citizenship in Democratizing Indonesia*. Universitas Gadjah Mada, Yogyakarta, December 10.

Tilly, Charles, ed. 1996. *Citizenship, Identity and Social History* (Cambridge: Cambridge University Press).

Wertheim, W. F. 1964. "Betting on the strong?," W. F. Wertheim, ed., *East-West Parallels: Sociological Approaches to Modern Asia*, pp. 259–77 (The Hague: Van Hoeve).

World Bank. 2003. "Cities in Transition: Urban Sector Review in an Era of Decentralization in Indonesia," East Asia Urban Working Paper Series, Dissemination Paper No. 7 (World Bank, Urban Sector Development Unit; Infrastructure Department; East Asia).

PART III

Markets and economic cultures

13

NEW MUSLIM CULTURES OF CAPITALIST ENTERPRISE

Gwenaël Njoto-Feillard

Islam and the material sphere have long been connected. The sacred texts of Islam are well known to feature many commercial components, which celebrate the figure of the merchant and encourage trade, albeit on an ethical basis. The Prophet Muhammad and his wife were themselves tradespeople. But what is new today is the over-arching extension of contemporary capitalism into globalized Muslim societies. Modern capitalism is now transnational and highly consumerist, while "public religious culture has become more pluralized and agonistic" (Hefner 2017: 271). The first stage in this evolution was the emergence of "Islamic economics" (i.e. Islamic banking, finance, and insurance) in the 1970s, funded by the Middle Eastern oil boom. Various observers have argued that this was an Islamic adaptation to modern capitalism, reflecting Muslim societies' integration into a globalized world, not an identitarian withdrawal (Beaugé 1990: 27; Tripp 2006: 149; Utvik 2006: 37). Others, however, have been more dubious. Turkish-American scholar Timur Kuran (2004: 39) has argued that Islamic economics can be used as an instrument of legitimization and political manipulation that hampers sound economic reform and fuels poverty and under-development. As Islamic economics originally emerged from cooperation between Islamist movements and Saudi fundamentalism, Kuran claims it can further promote the institutional development of identitarian exclusionism. In some cases, Islamic banking has even been proven to fund radical and violent movements (Kepel 2000: 156–7).

"Market Islam" (Rudnyckyj 2009) or *Islam de marché* (Haenni 2005), which emerged in the 2000s, seemed less open to such criticism. This openly pro-market current in Islam praised non-confrontational "pious materialism" (Wuthnow 1993). As Patrick Haenni (2005: 13–33) has shown, this has partly stemmed from progressive Islamists' quest for new ways to tackle ideological and political deadlock within Islamism. Market Islam's prosperity preachers and pious businessmen are an apparent feature of "post-Islamism" (Roy 2004), promising to help the Ummah reclaim its rightful place among the great world civilizations through peaceful economic development. Market Islam, as a by-product of the recent emergence of the Muslim middle classes, has been presented as a possible force for moderation and Muslim societies' integration into a globalized world (Nasr 2009: 12).

With the possible exception of Indonesia, this idea has come into question since the failure of the 2011 "Arab Spring" and its wide-reaching fallouts. Indonesia has undergone rapid development over the past decade, with an average growth rate of 5%. It has often been cited as an example of how Islam, democracy, and economic development can thrive together. But as Indonesia's successive governments have regularly noted, the country seems to lack businessmen. In May 2016, the current president, Joko Widodo, declared that the country needed up to 5.8 million entrepreneurs to reach 4% of the population, which is the ASEAN average ratio (Antara News 2016). Throughout most of its history as an independent nation, Indonesia's business class has largely been of ethnic Chinese minority origin (officially 1.7% of the population). But post-Soeharto era democratic reforms, deregulation, and decentralization may be bringing change. As Edward Aspinall notes, "private capital is far stronger than it was 25 years ago; the domestic bourgeoisie has grown enormously in wealth and we must therefore assume in political influence" (2013: 9). He adds that there seems to be a "growing layer of middle-sized capitalists who neither need nor benefit from state patronage" (ibid.). Max Lane (2014: 51) has also discussed how decentralization has weakened crony conglomerate capital, shifting the balance of power toward a growing number of local, smaller capitalists. Moreover, Indonesian society is now seeing growing interest in entrepreneurship, especially among the younger generations. Since the presidency of Susilo Bambang Yudhoyono (r. 2004–2014), and even more so the current president Joko Widodo (2014–), the Indonesian government has adopted various institutional and educational measures to encourage a stronger domestic business class.

How do Market Islam and its new Muslim culture of capitalist enterprise come into this equation? Will they encourage a large Muslim business class to emerge with the potential to rival the economic weight of the ethnic Chinese – as some religious and political leaders have been hoping since the 1990s? Are opportunistic agents just using Islam as a sales pitch, or is Islam encouraging a new generation of true entrepreneurs? How might this affect intercommunity and interfaith relations? While these questions are not easily answered because the processes involved are still ongoing, this chapter proposes some elements of reflection. It will describe Market Islam's main stakeholders in Indonesia, both in terms of their economic-religious values and their business practices, with a special focus on previously unexplored cases.

New Islamic prosperity theology and its business practices

In the late 1990s and early 2000s, a new type of Islamic preaching emerged in Indonesia. Its central message was that Muslim piety and wealth were entirely compatible and that Muslims should seek out wealth to develop the Islamic community through religious alms and entrepreneurship. In many Muslim countries, from Malaysia and Pakistan to Egypt, such "pious materialism" became a major paradigm shift in Islamic discourse. During these times, the Muslim world seemed to be developing its own prosperity gospel in the style of North American televangelists. In Indonesia, these preachers' calls for pious materialism criticized what was thought to be a rampant idealization of poverty (as a means of spiritual development, promoted by some brands of ascetic Sufism and Javanese mysticism). It was argued that the only way for the Muslim Umma to regain its rightful place among civilizations and to challenge Western secularist domination was through economic development. Everyone was thus entitled – and indeed had the duty – to be rich. At a time when Indonesia was witnessing the growth of Islamic extremism and economic insecurity, the population widely welcomed such preaching for tolerance and prosperity for all. Young, charismatic Islamic preachers mostly spread this message. They were often inspired by American self-help and psycho-spiritual literature, such as the works of Norman Vincent Peale, Steven Covey, Napoleon Hill, and Robert Kiyosaki.

The first preacher to use this self-help *cum* prosperity theology – and make an apparently lucrative business out of it – was Abdullah Gymnastiar (widely known as Aa Gym or "Brother Gym"). In the early 2000s, he built a "religious tourism" complex in the city of Bandung. His followers could stay overnight and hear him preach, visit his family home, and buy his books and DVDs. The "Daarut Tauhid" complex housed a hotel, a supermarket, a bookstore, an Islamic boarding school, and a personal development institute. At the height of Aa Gym's popularity, tens of thousands of people were visiting his Daarut Tauhid complex, many of whom were women. As James Hoesterey (2015: 215) remarked,

> The figure of Aa Gym consolidated the aura of media technologies and global self-help psychology with aspirations of the middle-class Muslims in search of piety and prosperity and the anxieties of the Indonesian women who try to balance their careers with demands of emotional labor at home. Aa Gym offered hope in uncertain times.

To further develop his business ventures, Aa Gym also created a holding company called Manajemen Qolbu corporation (MQ Corp.), i.e., the "Management of the Heart." It consisted of a dozen businesses, ranging from TV and radio shows to multimedia businesses, travel agencies, and a multilevel marketing firm. Quite naturally, these enterprises were primarily built on Aa Gym's popularity. In 2006, it emerged that the preacher had taken a second younger and "prettier" wife. This, to his female followers, undermined his message of controlling one's "passions," as Hoesterey has noted. Daarut Tauhid fell empty, and MQ Corp's various businesses were severely damaged by this fall from grace.

With the fall of Aa Gym, other preachers quickly filled the gap in this new spirituality marketplace. Each had his own trademark: Jeffry Al-Buchory focused on young people and often appeared on TV shows, preaching in "cool" language (he however died in a motorcycle accident in 2013 at the age of 40). Arifin Ilham is currently one of the major players in the new preaching scene. He does not focus on pious enrichment *per se* in his addresses but has used the thousands of followers his "Majelis Az-Zikra" movement has attracted over the years as the basis for business ventures. Ilham is indeed typical of what Julia Day Howell (2001) has termed "Neo-Sufism." Membership is open to all (unlike the traditional *tarekat* system), as are its communal acts of worship (*zikir*). In the mid-2000s, Ilham set up a travel agency (PT.[1] Andiarta Wisata), offering luxury haj tours (known as "Haji Plus") to his followers. In the light of his flock's rapid expansion, the preacher created an Islamic gated community (Bukit Sentul Azzikra) on the outskirts of Jakarta, together with a local real estate company and the World Islamic Call Society (WICS), a proselytizing institution that received funding from the Libyan state during the Muammar Qaddafi era. In this three-way arrangement, Ilham was given a large house in the complex in exchange for moving his preaching business there. His thousands of followers had been expected to follow him in this "Hijra"[2] and buy houses in the ideal place to practice the Islamic faith. The WICS meanwhile contributed roughly 5.2 million USD to build the complex's main mosque (named the Muammar Qaddafi Mosque). This move showed the extent of the Libyan leader's drive to extend his influence to Indonesia. The project did not, however, achieve the hoped-for results. It became mired in construction and logistical problems, and Ilham only came to the complex to preach at events on weekends. In 2013, only 350 houses had been sold (with about 50 being permanently occupied) as opposed to the original target of 2,000 (Madinier 2016: 118).

The more prosperity-oriented preacher Yusuf Mansur has now clearly replaced Aa Gym in popularity, after starting out as a junior preacher at Aa Gym's Daarut Tauhid. He primarily encourages Muslim entrepreneurship through a spiritual technique involving intensive daily prayer sessions (*sholat*) and invocations (*doa*). While five daily prayer sessions are obligatory in Islam, Mansur tells his followers to do seven, viewing them as having a true performative power (Mansur 2012: 53–61). For him, it is a good thing to ask God to be wealthy and an entrepreneur (and thus to help the Muslim community).

Mansur is typical of a subtle, interesting evolution within Islamic prosperity preaching. Firstly, he adopts the well-known "seed-faith" principle typical of charismatic neo-Protestant mega-churches (if you "give to God," he will give you back a hundred-fold, making you rich in this very life). While Abdullah Gymnastiar focused on professionalism and a religious-ethical attitude for attaining success, Mansur's preaching focuses on the power of *sedekah* (voluntary almsgiving) for the individual to seek wealth through "doing business with God" (Kailani 2015: 57, 79). Secondly, Mansur openly adopts a religious-nationalistic approach to his business ventures. In 2013, he created Veritra Sentosa International (VSI), an online payment service for Indonesian customers to bypass the banking system, which Mansur castigates for its links to "foreign interests." Through a multi-level marketing (MLM) scheme, VSI allows its customers to pay their phone and electricity bills, taxes, travel costs, religious donations, educational fees, and more (for a study of Islamic MLMs in Indonesia, see Njoto-Feillard 2016). The sign-up fee to the system, which is called Veritra Pay, is 350,000 Rp (30 USD). New members receive a welcome package, including a smartphone application. For each new recruit, members receive 30,000 Rp in cash and an additional 20,000 Rp for their VP account. Two types of bonuses can be earned through this scheme: first, on every transaction made by downline members and second, for every new member recruited. VSI's advertising claimed that after 10 months, every person could receive monthly payments of up to 112 million Rp (9,000 USD) for only four transactions, and 840 million Rp (70,000 USD) for 30 transactions. The South Sumatra branch of the Ulama Council (MUI, Majelis Ulama Indonesia) discredited this blatant "pyramid scheme" in March 2014, accusing VSI of taking advantage of people's gullibility (Lestari 2014). The service was later modified and renamed TRENY, with a revised income scheme.

A year before, the Jakarta MUI chapter had criticized another Mansur-run business, where the preacher had been offering 12 million Rp (1,200 USD) shares with an 8% annual interest rate. The funds were destined for the booming real-estate market in the Indonesian capital. In 2012, a year after its creation, the business had attracted over 2,000 people and 18 million USD in total (Sipahutar 2013). But as the company was operating without the required official approval (under Indonesian law for private individual capital), it was forced to close. Mansur then set up another organization called the Indonesian Islamic Community's Cooperative (Koperasi Indonesia Berjamaah, KIB) with the stated goal of "buying back the national economy," here again with religious-nationalistic overtones (Tempo 2013). One of KIB's investments is a "Sharia-compliant" hotel called SITI, close to Jakarta's airport in Tangerang. Other activities have included setting up an online fee-paying "business school" for would-be Islamic entrepreneurs (Wisata Hati).

Not all the newly emerged Market Islam preachers have been hit by such controversy. Ari Ginanjar, the creator of the ESQ (Emotional Spiritual Quotient) program, is another major "brand" in this new spirituality marketplace. This program features the same mix of spirituality, psychology, and management. While it has now lost momentum, it is thought to have had hundreds of thousands of followers in the 2000s. Daromir Rudnyckyj has carried out a case study on the Krakatau Steel Company and the workings of ESQ on the ground. He considers this phenomenon (which he dubs "spiritual economies") as the "extension of economic rationality into domains of life from which it was previously limited." Applied to the managers of Krakatau Steel, the ESQ program as a "sober, austere, rationalized way of life entailed configuring labor as religious calling and the methodical cultivation of Islamic virtues" (Rudnyckyj 2010: 254).

But as Rudnyckyj asks, does the "spiritual reform" the new Islamic preachers call for actually work? Are such entrepreneurial and spiritual ethics creating a new brand of Muslim entrepreneurship? While he suggests a favorable conclusion on the positive effects of such an ethic on honesty and professionalism, he rightly notes that results are difficult to gauge, as it is difficult to produce measurement factors and most of the available data come from self-reporting. This not only goes for Ari Ginanjar's ESQ program, but for the new preachers of Market Islam more generally. The organizational manifestations of this new entrepreneurial paradigm in Indonesian Islam, however, are easier to observe.

The "Islamic sub-economy": negotiating tensions between religion and capitalism

In the mid-1990s, Timur Kuran noted how, in contrast to "Islamic economics," little research had been done on the "Islamic sub-economy." With this latter term, Kuran meant a sector composed of a variety of "nonfinancial enterprises that advertise their operations as Islamic" as they "shun interest, abide by Islamic norms, and make conscious efforts to support and promote Islamic causes" (Kuran 1995: 167). The Islamic sub-economy has since rapidly developed in various directions (including, as discussed above, new Islamic preachers setting up business ventures). While this is still a niche market sector in Indonesia, its share is growing daily, fueled by a conspicuously pious and consumerist emerging Muslim middle class. Halal certification (on what Muslims may consume) is one example of what is financially at stake with these newly developing consumption patterns. The process had been in the hands of the Indonesia Council of Ulamas (MUI) for years (see Lindsey 2012),[3] but there is now rivalry between the MUI and the Ministry of Religious Affairs. The latter wants to end the MUI's monopoly by also issuing certificates (companies applying for a halal certificate must pay a fee and the process is renewable every two years). The parliament is moreover reviewing a law that could make halal-certification compulsory for all products on sale in Indonesia. Up to now, there has been a legal uncertainty as to whether the certification is mandatory or not. Only producers and importers of products claimed to be halal have been concerned (Lindsey 2012: 268).

Compliance with Muslim ethical standards is no longer limited to consumer goods in the new Islamic sub-economy. In Indonesia's major cities, more and more "Sharia-compliant" hotels (such as the Sofyan Hotels) are being built. They of course offer services such as halal menus but also single-sex swimming pools; couples also have to present a marriage certificate to book a room. Alcohol is not sold, and the call for daily prayers is loud enough for all guests to hear. In a similar quest for a more "authentic" Islamic lifestyle, Islamic gated communities have sprung up around the country. As Rémy Madinier (2016: 113) has shown, this venture had already been introduced in the early 1970s, as idealized communal Islamic living based on cooperation and mutual assistance. One example is the "Islamic Village" in Tangerang, which was founded by Yunan Helmi Nasution, a military Islamic chaplain who became a preacher and founded his own group. In the 1990s, however, Nasution's children made the scheme for-profit, founding a real-estate company called PT. Mustika Hadriasi. Other players are now also involved in such marketing, including PT. Orchid Reality and PT. Bumi Darussalam, who claim that buying houses in such gated communities is "economic jihad," or again part of the "creation of paradise on earth" (Hew 2014: 9). Buyers must certainly be Muslim, but there is no obligation to be actively observant (e.g., in mosque attendance). As Madinier (2016: 117) argues, the process is more about self-emulation in religious practice among middle-class Muslim Indonesians, rather than a drive for segregation from the rest of society.

While there has been an abundance of new stakeholders in the Islamic sub-economy, Indonesia's oldest and largest organizations have also been involved. To be sure, both the traditionalist Nahdlatul Ulama ("The Renaissance of Ulama") and modernist Muhammadiyah ("The Path of Muhammad") have commercial roots. Muslim traders (and rural landlords in the case of the NU) founded these organizations in the early twentieth century. Both organizations were religious, social, and educational, but at various stages in their history, they endeavored to develop moneymaking ventures to fund their philanthropy – albeit with limited success (Njoto-Feillard 2014). The 2000s, nevertheless, marked the beginning of a wholly new economic movement, in step with the rise of Market Islam. Both organizations' leaders realized they were being challenged by new players of the likes of Abdullah Gymnastiar, who was delivering an appealing, "simpler" message of piety and prosperity for all with new, effective, and lucrative tools over the Internet and SMS. Indeed, there was also an economic dimension to the "fragmentation of religious authority" (Eickelman and Piscatori 1996: 58) experienced by Indonesian Islam.

But NU and Muhammadiyah also realized that new sources of funding would be profitable to set up and that their millions of members and supporters were essentially a captive market of potential consumers, preferably of products from the organizations' own business lines. Accordingly, they attempted to revive their "entrepreneurial spirit" both through discourse and practice. NU launched the NUQua mineral water brand and the Tali Jagat brand of clove cigarettes in partnership with the Bentoel conglomerate. Both ventures faltered, because members preferred to stick to their familiar old brands. Muhammadiyah was more ambitious (see Njoto-Feillard 2017). In the 2000s, it set up several companies, which it consolidated under the PT. Solar Global International Holding Corporation. Their operations included trading, garages and auto parts, chemicals, agricultural food production, and fisheries. Here too the Libyan proselytizing organization WICS played a key role (as in the case of Arifin Ilham). WICS partly financed Muhammadiyah's economic venture through a company called PT. Solar Sahara Investment. Muhammadiyah's leaders also set up a bank (Bank Persyarikatan), not only to meet its members' and supporters' banking needs but also those of its thousands of branches and institutions (clinics, universities, schools, orphanages, and so on). Interestingly, this was a conventional rather than an Islamic bank. This was quite bold because charged interest (*riba*) is forbidden (*haram*) in classical Islamic jurisprudence, although Muhammadiyah had declared that the bank would become Islamic in its workings in the future. It was also remarkable during this economic conjuncture that Muhammadiyah created a membership card called KATAM, which also served as a debit card and a health insurance scheme and which allowed members to automatically transfer membership fees and donations to the Muhammadiyah. In theory, given Muhammadiyah's millions of supporters, the organization was sitting on an enormous source of income. In practice, however, neither KATAM nor any of the other projects succeeded. This was for various reasons, which include management issues and the involvement of dishonest individuals (an outsider to Muhammadiyah brought financial scandal to Bank Persyarikatan). Clearly, Muhammadiyah's and NU's religious leaders were not the same savvy Muslim merchants as those of the early twentieth century.

Interestingly, it proved difficult for NU and Muhammadiyah, as socio–religious institutions positioned within a philanthropic habitus, to move in a new economic direction and to work effectively in the moneymaking sphere. As Max Weber argued, religion encountering modern capitalism illustrates a "struggle in principle" between "ethical rationalization and the process of rationalization in the economic sphere" (Weber 1978: 584). These tensions were hard to negotiate in the case of Muhammadiyah, as they were exacerbated by specific structural and organizational factors. Its economic venture entailed rationalizing and centralizing a funding system that had always been managed locally on various hierarchal levels. The central leadership's initiatives of the 2000s struck members as a way not only to "commercialize" Muhammadiyah's charitable foundations but also to set up fierce competition for funds. In the words of a cadre, Muhammadiyah had been infected by the "virus of capitalism" (Suara Muhammadiyah 2005: 8). As Robert Wuthnow (1994: 632) has argued, one of the more efficient ways to mediate the tensions of the encounter between religious ethics and capitalist rationalization is "institutional differentiation." This entails bracketing-off a religious organization's moneymaking activities into a separate entity that can be both formally and symbolically dissociated from the main organization's charitable vocation. Muhammadiyah's economic endeavors in the 2000s abolished just this kind of separation.

We would also like to discuss some other ways in which these tensions are mediated, for instance in the case of the mass-based Muslim social movement, Hidayatullah. This is currently one of Indonesia's main neo-fundamentalist organizations and one of the most under-researched of its Islamic organizations. It also perhaps ranks after NU and Muhammadiyah as the third-largest Islamic organization in terms of members and supporters. Abdullah Said set up Hidayatullah in the early 1970s on the outskirts of Balikpapan in East Kalimantan as a self-sufficient religious-educational community for following the early ideals of the Prophet Muhammad. It offered teaching for free, giving disadvantaged children the highest priority. At that stage, its teaching consisted of English and Arabic classes, as well as religious teaching. But to develop its infrastructure, manual work also quickly became an important part of the curriculum. Pupils, who had paid little or no tuition, were directly put to work for their labor to help the institution to develop.

Moreover, outsiders wanting to join the community were told to donate all their belongings and entirely devote themselves to the cause. With the network's economic development, a wage system was introduced, giving all members compensation called *natura*. Endogamy became one of the cornerstones for the growth of the community. Male and female pupils got married at the end of their schooling in marriages that were jointly arranged by their parents and Hidayatullah's leaders. The young couples were then sent to various parts of the archipelago on proselytizing missions.

While the organization at first relied on donations, it managed to diversify its funding sources, notably thanks to a network of 141 cooperatives (Inkophida or Induk Koperasi Hidayatullah) and to a variety of economic ventures: retailing, printing services, telephone communications, a bakery in Jakarta, and a new-technology consulting company (PT. Totalindo Rekayasa Telematika). The organization also sought to control the transformation and distribution of its agricultural products (fish, sheep, and cattle farming) by creating the Sakinah Group.

Meanwhile, Hidayatullah's leadership drove through a rationalization process of its organizational capacity and internal funding mechanisms. In 2000, it indeed underwent a relatively unnoticed transformation process. Owing to its expansion ambitions, it had decided to abandon its "closed system" in favor of an "open system," adopting the legal status of "social organization" (ormas, organisasi kemasyarakatan). This might have been a seemingly minor development had it not been symptomatic of a deeper change. With the constant enrollment of new members, the old internal-wage system no longer came to be thought of as economically viable. The assembly therefore decreed that members should invest in their own profitable ventures, rather than being automatically and inefficiently incorporated into Hidayatullah's educational and economic organizations. The organization also stopped trying to manage every aspect of its members' lives, announcing that it no longer wanted to get involved in local conflict management, geographical transfers, changes of residency, or even its management's career choices. While its activists had formerly been strictly forbidden from working outside of the community, from 2000, they were given no choice but to look for gainful employment, creating acute tensions between members and their leadership. The Hidayatullah case illustrates perfectly Paul Seabright's remarks: "[W]here competition between religious organizations to attract members is reasonably vigorous, the strategic considerations underlying the management of religious organizations has much in common with that of other businesses" (2016: 215).

For Abdullah Said's organization, this "openness" policy also stemmed from its growing interest in the charitable donations sector. Indeed, the change in legal status in 2000 was also intended to allow Hidayatullah, as a newly-acknowledged social organization (*ormas*), to officially apply to become a national religious-donations-collection organization (LAZNAS, Lembaga Amil Zakat Nasional), that is, primarily for the collection of legal charity (*zakat*), free donations (*infaq*), and religious endowments (*waqf*). The financial stakes were clearly exceptionally high. Since the launch of the system by the Ministry of Religious Affairs in 1999, only around ten institutions had received the accreditation, giving them access to a huge "salvation goods" market (the number of LAZNAS had reached 16 in 2016). Given its network of Islamic schools and highly committed preachers, Hidayatullah doubtless recognized its strong potential to take on other large organizations in the industry, such as Muhammadiyah and Nahdlatul Ulama.

In 2001, the Ministry of Religious Affairs officially recognized Hidayatullah as an institution authorized to collect religious donations on a national level. Its preachers, who were spread out across the archipelago, would henceforth be expected to directly turn over all their religious donations to the Baitul Maal Hidayatullah network (BMH, its central institution for donations), rather than these going from person to person, as had been the case. Crucially, BMH's management announced its aim to put part of these donations toward capital for Islamic micro-finance institutions (BMT, Baitul maal wa tamwil). These, it must be remembered, are profit-making enterprises. Issuing micro-loans became integral to the organization's preaching and growth strategies. Marketplaces are some of the most fertile places for Hidayatullah's traveling sales representatives, as small traders are often in need of a quick, one-time loan. BMT's activists approach these traders and offer them a loan, on the condition that they join in the organization's acts of worship. Such participation is expected to lead them eventually to genuine commitment and becoming fully fledged members. As the case of Hidayatullah shows, the charitable and lucrative spheres can also merge successfully in the new Islamic sub-economy in Indonesia, as is the case in other parts of the Muslim world (Atia 2013).

Conclusion: Islam as spiritual capital?

We have observed that the new Muslim cultures of capitalism take a variety of forms, from prosperity preaching and halal consumption, to Islamic gated communities and the turning of religious organizations to the "material sphere." This prosperity theology and its associated practices are products of the current anxieties and aspirations of the emerging Muslim middle classes in a rapidly urbanizing Indonesia. Here, as in other parts of the Muslim world, "entrepreneurship – combining material success with moral connectedness – is coming to be seen as the exemplary contemporary way of being a modern, moral Muslim" (Osella and Osella 2009: s204).

The effects of this new economic ethic still need further research, notably as to whether it can promote the creation of extended and durable entrepreneurial networks. In the case of Java, which contains half of the Indonesian population, studies have suggested that entrepreneurship is chronically confronted by the problem of trust and institutionalization. As Clifford Geertz noted in the 1960s in his study of Muslim entrepreneurs in Modjokuto (Pare in East Java), businesses had difficulties developing beyond the immediate family circle. They lacked "the capacity to form efficient economic institutions"; in other words, they were "entrepreneurs without enterprises" (Geertz 1963: 28). This problem of "scaling up" seems to be still present to this day.[4] Eldar Bråten (2013: 264) shows that there is strong concern for individual autonomy in intra-family relations; entrepreneurs at the "micro-level are involved in socio-ritual cycles of reciprocity that affect their dispositions with regards to business" and are confronted by a "reluctance about mutual entrusting of individual resources" in business ventures (*ibid.*).[5]

Research on religion and trust seems key to better understanding the possible effects of these new Muslim cultures on the longer term development of capitalist enterprise. There are good reasons to think that trust facilitates growth (Arrow 1972), as high levels of it minimize transaction costs in societies. Trust therefore is an essential aspect of social capital and, in this scheme, religion is considered as one of the main binders of individuals (Boettke 2011). One can thus wonder whether Market Islam's developing "moral economy" has the potential to produce such "social capital."[6] Since the early twentieth century, both NU and Muhammadiyah have attempted to revive domestic enterprise through their own membership networks. They have managed to do so, albeit on a limited scale, at the local branch level. Hidayatullah has also been attempting to do so by building a database of its entrepreneurs and creating an internal market, where members coordinate supply and demand. Yusuf Mansur's economic theology is producing its own various networks, mixing business initiatives and charities, some building upon a new Muslim indigenous entrepreneurial identity in opposition to the "foreign."

As Greg Fealy (2008: 34–5) suggests, changes in Islam in Indonesia have been driven by various factors. These are notably linked to the country's national socio-political situation and relations between Western and Muslim nations. But all things being equal, its current marketization is not much of a threat to its moderate character. When Fealy draws on the work of Peter Berger and Wade Roof, he interestingly posits that the convergence of two trends can promote plurality and tolerance: first, plurality emerges out of wide freedom of choice owing to the individualization of contemporary religious practices; tolerance comes about when individuals and institutions looking to enter the "spiritual marketplace" are compelled to be as inclusive and moderate as possible to maximize their potential "consumer-believer" base.

But if economic performance is contingent on moderation/inclusiveness in this new, dynamic spiritual marketplace, one might also ask whether radicalism/segregation can also be a factor for entrepreneurial success. Looking at the various manifestations of Market Islam in Indonesia, we sometimes find sales pitches to the effect that the Islamic economy is superior and fundamentally opposed to the "unbeliever" (*kafir*) conventional economy. Businesses sometimes loudly claim as much, which would seem to confirm one of Timur Kuran's hypotheses (2004: 5–7): the "cultural difference" of Muslims from the rest of the world counts more here than sharing any common ground with a global civilization.

Kuran (2004: 51) also claims that one factor behind the growing momentum of the "Islamic sub-economy" is how it helps to enhance micro-economic efficiency. Building trusting relations within this moral community can minimize transaction costs. Newcomers looking to integrate within a new urban setting draw on their former regional or ethnic solidarity networks. They thus turn to the Islamic sub-economy where news of dishonesty travels quickly. Christine Dobbin has explored this through her research on the economic efficacy of a religion-based commune in her study of the Padri, a Wahhabi-inspired movement in Sumatra (1784–1847). She notes that where there is "extra-territoriality," with moneymaking activities taking place outside usual places of residence or origin, Islam and its system of law allow the establishment of a "moral community" that facilitates economic exchange (Dobbin 1977: 38).

Like political Islam, Islamic economics and the Islamic sub-economy have the potential to be instrumentalized in the various power plays that Indonesia is experiencing in the age of democracy and ongoing economic development. For the moment, the country has not experienced a state-sponsored Islamization of the economy with ethno-nationalist overtones, as has been the case in Malaysia (Fischer 2008). But some actors might see an opportunity in promoting an exclusivistic, communitarian economy. The new networks of entrepreneurial-charitable spheres certainly often carry an inclusive and moderate character.[7] However, others seem intent on "taking back" the national economy from so-called foreign agents and the ethnic Chinese minority.[8] This issue reflects the long-raging debate as to whether Islam can be considered as producing "spiritual capital," defined by Peter Berger and Gordon Redding (2011: 2) as a "subset of social capital." Robert Hefner (2011: 193) sees spiritual capital as the cultural and ideological content that flows through networks, cooperation, and trust; he further suggests that spiritual capital can be negative or positive in its social effects. In the case of Market Islam in Indonesia, we can indeed observe evidence of just such a dichotomy.

Notes

1 PT is an acronym for *Perseroan Terbatas*, a term that represents a limited liability company in Indonesia.
2 In reference to the Prophet Muhammad's migration from Mecca to Medina in 622 CE.
3 MUI is defined by Lindsey as "nominally independent" but "endorsed and funded by the state that under the New Order often worked with the Ministry of Religion." This relation has changed, however, as MUI has reinforced its independence and at the same time its influence over the state for the administration of Islamic legal traditions, notably the Islamic economy sector (Lindsey 2012: 255).
4 Mario Rutten's study (2012) questions, however, this problem of scaling up, with the case of Central Javanese businesses. He suggests that there are in fact forms of co-operation beyond the nuclear unit, both within the family and outside, particularly through subcontracting processes involving clusters of family businesses.
5 It should be noted that Bråten sees these characteristics as a result of the Javanese micro-enterprises' embeddedness in specific social, cultural, and political contexts.
6 Social capital is defined as "a society's ability to make the process of social and economic exchange run smoothly and fully, by drawing upon norms about cooperation and about the public good" (Berger and Redding 2011: 2).
7 For example, Mansur's inspired Sedekah Rombongan [Voluntary almsgiving group] that caters to both Muslim and non-Muslim people in need (see Kailani 2015: 132).
8 For example, the Majelis Ta'lim Wirausaha ("Entrepreneurial Congregation") that proposes a scheme whereby landowners wanting to sell their property are put in contact with Muslim "native" buyers (www.mtw.or.id/). Interestingly, this initiative is presented as the economic continuation of the "212 Movement" initiated by fundamentalists to prevent the possible election of Basuki Tjahaja Purnama, the acting governor of the Greater Jakarta region in 2017, a Christian and ethnic Chinese, who took over the position in 2014 when Joko Widodo was elected to the presidency of the republic.

References cited

Antara News. 2016, May. "Indonesia Needs Millions of New Entrepreneurs: President Jokowi," *AntaraNews.com*, 23 www.antaranews.com/en/news/104826/indonesia-needs-millions-of-new-entrepreneurs-president-jokowi (Accessed 27 March 2017).

Arrow, Kenneth J. 1972. "Gifts and Exchange," *Philosophy and Public Affairs* 1(4): 343–62.

Aspinall, Edward. 2013. "The Triumph of Capital? Class Politics and Indonesian Democratization," *Journal of Contemporary Asia* 43(2): 226–42.

Atia, Mona. 2013. *Building a House in Heaven: Pious Neoliberalism and Islamic Charity in Egypt* (Minneapolis: University of Minnesota Press).

Beaugé, Gilbert. 1990. *Les capitaux de l'Islam* (Paris: Presses du CNRS).

Berger, Peter L. and Gordon Redding. 2011. "Introduction: Spiritual, Social, Human, and Financial Capital," in Peter L. Berger and Gordon Redding, eds., *The Hidden Form of Capital: Spiritual Influences in Societal Progress* (London and New York: Anthem Press), pp. 1–13.

Boettke, Peter. 2011. "Spiritual Capital and Economic Development: An Overview," in Peter L. Berger and Gordon Redding, eds., *The Hidden Form of Capital: Spiritual Influences in Societal Progress* (London–New York: Anthem Press), pp. 28–39.

Bråten, Eldår. 2013. "Embedded Micro-Businesses: Trust, Incorporation and Scaling in Javanese 'Family Firms'," in Eldår Braten, ed., *Embedded Entrepreneurship: Market, Culture, and Micro-Businesses in Insular Southeast Asia* (Leiden: Brill), pp. 253–74.

Dobbin, Christine. 1977. "Economic Change in Minangkabau as a Factor in the Rise of the Padri Movement, 1784–1830," *Indonesia* 23: 1–38.

Eickelman, Dale F. and James P. Piscatori. 1996. *Muslim Politics* (Princeton: Princeton University Press).

Fealy, Greg. 2008. "Consuming Islam: Commodified and Aspirational Pietism in Contemporary Indonesia," in Greg Fealy and Sally White, eds., *Expressing Islam: Religious Life and Politics in Indonesia* (Singapore: ISEAS), pp. 15–39.

Fischer, Johan. 2008. *Proper Islamic Consumption: Shopping Among the Malays in Modern Malaysia* (Copenhagen: NIAAS Press).

Geertz, Clifford. 1963. *Peddlers and Princes: Social Development and Economic Change in Two Indonesian Towns* (Chicago: University of Chicago Press).

Haenni, Patrick. 2005. *L'islam de marché: L'autre révolution conservatrice* [Market Islam: The Other Conservative Revolution] (Paris: Le Seuil et La République des Idées).

Hefner, Robert W. 2011. "Islam and Spiritual Capital: An Indonesian Case Study," in Peter L. Berger and Gordon Redding, eds., *The Hidden Form of Capital: Spiritual Influences in Societal Progress* (London-New York: Anthem Press), pp. 191–211.

———. 2017. "Epilogue: Capitalist Rationalities and Religious Moralities – An Agonistic Plurality," in Juliette Koning and Gwenaël Njoto-Feillard, eds., *New Religiosities, Modern Capitalism, and Moral Complexities in Southeast Asia* (Singapore: Religion and Society in Asia Pacific Series, IRASEC-Palgrave Macmillan-Springer), pp. 265–85.

Hew, Wai Weng. 2014. "Making 'New' Muslim Places in Urban Malaysia and Indonesia," *IIAS Newsletter* 67(9): 9.

Hoesterey, James Bourk. 2015. *Rebranding Islam: Piety, Prosperity, and a Self-Help Guru* (Stanford: Stanford University Press).

Howell, Julia Day. 2001. "Sufism and the Indonesian Islamic Revival," *The Journal of Asian Studies* 60(3): 701–29.

Kailani, Najib. 2015. *Aspiring to Prosperity: The Economic Theology of Urban Muslims in Contemporary Indonesia* (Ph.D. Thesis. Canberra, Victoria, Australia: School of Humanities and Social Sciences UNSW Canberra).

Kepel, Gilles. 2000. *Jihad: expansion et déclin de l'islamisme* (Paris: Gallimard).

Kuran, Timur. 1995. "Islamic Economics and the Islamic Subeconomy," *Journal of Economic Perspectives* 9(4): 155–73.

———. 2004. *Islam and Mammon: The Economic Predicaments of Islamism* (Princeton: Princeton University Press).

Lane, Max. 2014. *Decentralization & its Discontents: An Essay on Class, Political Agency and National Perspective in Indonesian Politics* (Singapore: ISEAS).

Lestari, Wiji. 2014. "Bisnis Haram Berkedok Syariah [A Proscribed Business Wearing the Mask of Sharia]," *KabarSumatera.com*, 11 March. http://kabarsumatera.com/2014/03/11/bisnis-haram-berkedok-syariah/ (Accessed 22 March 2017).

Lindsey, Tim. 2012. "Monopolizing Islam: The Indonesian Ulama Council and State Regulation of the 'Islamic Economy.'" *Bulletin of Indonesian Economic Studies* 48(2): 253–74.

Madinier, Rémy. 2016. "Du phalanstère au marché de niche: Genèse et évolution de l'immobilier islamique indonésien [From the Phalanstery to the Niche Market: Genesis and Evolution of Islamic Real-estate in Indonesia]," *Archives de Sciences Sociales des Religions* 61(175): 111–34.

Mansur, Yusuf. 2012. *Semua Bisa Jadi Pengusaha* [Everyone can be an Entrepreneur] (Jakarta: YM Books).

Nasr, Seyyed Vali Reza. 2009. *Forces of Fortune: The Rise of the New Muslim Middle Class and What It Will Mean for Our World* (New York: Free Press).

Njoto-Feillard, Gwenaël. 2014. "Financing Muhammadiyah: The Early Economic Endeavors of a Muslim Modernist Mass Organization in Indonesia (1920s–1960s)," *Studia Islamika* 21(1): 1–46.

———. 2016. "Le marketing relationnel de multiniveaux islamique en Indonésie [Islamic Multilevel Marketing in Indonesia]," *Archives de Sciences Sociales des Religions* 175; 135–57.

———. 2017. "Muhammadiyah vs. Mammon: The Economic Trials and Tribulations of an Islamic Modernist Mass Organization in Indonesia (1990s–2000s)," in Juliette Koning and Gwenaël Njoto-Feillard, eds., *New Religiosities, Modern Capitalism, and Moral Complexities in Southeast Asia* (Singapore: IRASEC-Palgrave Macmillan-Springer), pp. 17–38.

Osella, Filippo and Caroline Osella. 2009. "Muslim Entrepreneurs in Public Life Between India and the Gulf: Making Good and Doing Good," *Journal of the Royal Anthropological Institute* 15(S1): S202–S221, Osella Filippo and Benjamin Soares (eds.), Special Issue: Islam, Politics, Anthropology.

Roy, Olivier. 2004. *Globalized Islam: The Search for a New Ummah* (New York: Columbia University Press).

Rudnyckyj, Daromir. 2009. "Market Islam in Indonesia," *The Journal of the Royal Anthropological Institute* 15(S1): S183–201, Osella Filippo and Benjamin Soares (eds.), Special Issue: Islam, Politics, Anthropology.

———. 2010. *Spiritual Economies: Islam, Globalization, and the Afterlife of Development* (Ithaca: Cornell University Press).

175

Rutten, Mario. 2012. "Individualism and Collective Forms of Business Organization: Rural Capitalists in India, Malaysia and Indonesia," in Thomas Menkhoff and Solvay Gerke, eds., *Chinese Entrepreneurship and Asian Business Networks* (London and New York: Routledge), pp. 295–318.

Seabright, Paul. 2016. "Religion and Entrepreneurship: A Match Made in Heaven?" *Archives de Sciences Sociales des Religions* 61(175): 201–19.

Sipahutar, Tassia. 2013. "OJK Grills Cleric Over Investment." *The Jakarta Post Online*, 23 July. www.theja kartapost.com/news/2013/07/23/ojk-grills-cleric-over-investment.html (Accessed 27 March 2017).

Suara Muhammadiyah. 2005. "Bencana Ekonomi Nasional, Bencana Kemanusiaan [National Economic Catastrophy, Humanitarian Catastrophy]," *Suara Muhammadiyah* 90(6).

Tempo. 2013. "Bisnis Baru Yusuf Mansur Membeli Ulang Indonesia [Buying Back Indonesia, Yusuf Mansur's New Business]." *Tempo Online*, 5 September. http://bisnis.tempo.co/read/news/2013/09/05 /092510519/bisnis-baru-yusuf-mansur-membeli-ulang-indonesia (Accessed 27 March 2017).

Tripp, Charles. 2006. *Islam and the Moral Economy: The Challenge of Capitalism* (Cambridge and New York: Cambridge University Press).

Utvik, Bjørn Olav. 2006. *The Pious Road to Development: The Ideology and Practice of Islamist Economics in Egypt* (London: Hurst & Co).

Weber, Max. 1978. *Economy and Society: An Outline of Interpretive Sociology, Vol.2*, Guenther Roth and Claus Wittich, eds. (Berkeley: University of California Press).

Wuthnow, Robert. 1993. "Pious Materialism: How Americans View Faith and Money." *The Christian Century*, 3 March. www.questia.com/PM.qst?a=o&d=5000161726 (Accessed 17 March 2017).

———. 1994. "Religion and Economic Life," in Neil J. Smelser and Richard Swedberg, eds., *The Handbook of Economic Sociology* (Princeton and New York: Princeton University Press, Russel Sage Foundation), pp. 620–46.

14

CHINESE INDONESIANS

Businesses, ethnicity, and religion

Juliette Koning

This chapter is based on my research into the relationship between religion and business among Chinese Indonesians. Fieldwork was conducted in 2004, 2007, and 2011 as well as several shorter visits up until the present day. Over the years, I have collected life-business narratives of middle-class ethnic Chinese business owners from Yogyakarta who have converted to Pentecostal-charismatic Christianity, combined with observations at two Pentecostal-charismatic churches while participating in their Sunday worship meetings and interviews with church leaders and church staff, joining meetings of the Full Gospel Business Men Fellowship International chapters in Yogyakarta, and following Chinese Indonesian business owners in their businesses and other meetings (Koning 2017, 2013, 2011, 2009; Koning and Dahles 2009; Koning and Susanto 2014; Koning and Waistell 2012). These ethnographic encounters sensitized me to some of the core features of Pentecostal-charismatic Christianity as well as to the lives of Chinese Indonesian groups in Indonesia (see Koning and Ooi 2013). The aim of this chapter is to highlight the most important findings on this business–religion relationship. The following sections discuss the ethnic and economic position and positioning of Chinese Indonesians in Indonesia over the last few decades and the upsurge of the charismatic movement in Indonesia since the 1980s. The chapter also analyzes why Pentecostal-charismatic Christianity speaks to the imagination of Chinese Indonesian business owners in particular. The majority of the business owners who participated in my research own small and medium enterprises (mainly retail and services, with some manufacturing), share a common descent from southern China, and are mostly second- or third-generation Chinese born in Indonesia. Before joining the Pentecostal-charismatic movement, the majority was already Christian (traditional Protestant), while others adhered to Buddhism and Confucianism.

Chinese Indonesians: ethnicity and business

Researching Chinese Indonesian economic and religious questions requires taking into consideration the role of the state in "the selective creation and manipulation of ethnic identities" (Tan 2001: 952). Indonesia's process of nation building has been characterized by forging a national identity out of a multi-ethnic populace. As has been argued by Aguilar (2001:505), the "alienness of Chinese can be understood as the ideological product of sociohistorical processes specific to Indonesia, particularly in its construction of nationhood." One of the more important facets from that history lies in the Dutch colonization policy that positioned the Chinese as inter-mediaries for European enterprises. The colonizers also assigned Chinese shares in the lucrative opium trade, at the expense of native entrepreneurs. As a result, the gap between local popula-tions and the Chinese only grew (Hefner 2001: 17–19). This legacy turned out to be crucial in the formative years of independence and thereafter.

The colonial government's division of Indies society into Europeans, foreign Orientals (such as the Chinese), and pribumi ("indigenous," lit., "children of the soil"), each with different rights, continued after the formation of the nation-state. In particular, during the New Order (1966–1998) various restrictive laws for Chinese Indonesians were installed in order that "such citizens shall be assimilated as to avoid any racial exclusiveness and discrimination" (Winarta 2004:72). Examples include the restriction of traditional Chinese religious expressions to the family home, recommendations that Chinese names be changed to Indonesian ones, the ban-ning of Chinese language from the public sphere, and the obligation to always carry a letter to prove Indonesian citizenship. Most of these discriminatory regulations date from the early years of the New Order regime when the assimilation policy was aimed at repudiating Chineseness (Lindsey 2005:54). As Heryanto notes (1998: 104), Chinese identities have been "always under erasure."

The Assimilation Program was an attempt to construct a national identity by "identifying significant others," the most significant other being the non-pribumi Chinese (Hoon 2006: 151). Such systematic "othering" resulted in an anti-Chinese rhetoric and many violent attacks. For Chinese Indonesians, the choice was an either-or proposition; they could either be Indonesian or Chinese, but not both: "to be completely Indonesian, the Chinese had to give up all their 'Chineseness'" (Hoon 2006: 152). The possibility of a hybrid identity, according to Ang (2001), the more logical outcome of a Chinese migrant's daily life in a non-Chinese environment, was never a real option. Coppel (2004: 20) shows that even after generations of settlement in Indo-nesia and speaking the national language (and often not being able to speak any of the Chinese dialects), ethnic Chinese were still not allowed "to call Indonesia 'home.'" In discussions on being Chinese, the state (bureaucracy and instruments of government) has been one of the most important "variables, which has contributed to the 'separateness' of the Chinese in Indonesia, particularly in Java" (Suryadinata 1993: 77).

In the more recent history of Chinese Indonesians, the year 1998 takes on a special signifi-cance. Although it is the year President Soeharto was forced to step down (May 21) and as such marked the end of the New Order regime that had severely restricted Chineseness, one week earlier (May 13–14), many Chinese Indonesians were attacked during violent mass riots. The country was suffering from a prolonged economic crisis during which basic goods, including fuel and energy, became extremely expensive. People took to the streets to protest, and some protests changed into massive attacks on people of Chinese descent. Unfortunately, that 1998 incident was one in a line of historical incidents in which people of Chinese descent were tar-geted as scapegoats. Many Chinese Indonesians fled the country. Those who stayed encountered heightened feelings of insecurity (Purdey 2006; Susanto 2006). This traumatic event and many before have left their mark on any subsequent issue related to their "identity."

The fall of the New Order regime a week later and the subsequent reformation years did, however, open up the country to expressions of Chinese Indonesian culture. For exam-ple, interim president Habibie (May 1998–October 1999) approved the formation of Chinese political parties and issued a decree to stop the official use of the terms *pribumi* and *non-pribumi*. In 2000, Abdurrahman Wahid (president from October 1999 until July 2001) abolished the law on the manifestation of Chinese cultural and religious expression and Megawati Sukarnoputri (in office from July 2001 until October 2004) issued a decree making Im Lek (Chinese New

Year) a national holiday. If we fast-forward to the present, there has indeed been an upsurge in cultural and political expression in the public domain with Chinese New Year being a national holiday, the re-emergence of Chinese organizations, and an increasing demand by non-Chinese Indonesians for courses in Mandarin. There has also been an interesting political turn. Whereas during the New Order, "Chinese Indonesians were noticeably absent from politics, today, Chinese Indonesian politicians are present at various levels of government as administrators and elected members of parliament, most notably in the controversial figure of Jakarta Governor Basuki Tjahaja Purnama (Ahok)" (Setijadi 2016: 3).

With the Chinese Indonesian and Christian Ahok running for re-election as governor of Jakarta (which involved a second round in April 2017), ethnic and religious tensions were on the rise again as the following quote from the *Jakarta Post* (January 27, 2017) shows: "A day before the Nov. 4, 2016 (411) rally, a noodle seller near my apartment advised me to stay home because 'we never know what could happen.' The feeling of trauma from the 1998 riots suddenly arose." At the same time, in Yogyakarta, the 1975 decree according to which Chinese Indonesians cannot "own" land is still active as an interview with a Chinese Indonesian in the *Washington Post* (March 18, 2017) shows:

> When Willie Sebastian bought a tiny piece of land to build a storage space, government officials in the heart of Java island delivered him an unpleasant surprise. He could not register the purchase, since he was of Chinese descent, and therefore the land would belong to the local sultan.

Chinese descent/ethnicity has thus time and again been exploited in times of social, economic, and political upheaval. There is, however, also a rather persistent economic discourse hovering in the country denoting all "ethnic" Chinese as wealthy and rich. Whether there is an economic domination and the extent to which this is related to a particular Chinese way of doing business in which Chineseness matters, it is important to point out that Chinese Indonesians historically were not allowed to occupy civil servant positions or own land. In the New Order period (1965–1998), they "were prohibited from participating fully in political, civic and military affairs" (Freedman 2000: 3) and, as a result, ended up in entrepreneurial and business occupations; the majority, in fact, are small shopkeepers and traders. Politically excluded and in a hostile environment, the Chinese had to establish themselves without the benefit of outside support. The fact that they had an outsider status contributed to the creation of "closely knitted Chinese business networks" in order to secure start-up capital and labor (Ooi 2007:122). Only some Chinese Indonesians, the so-called *cukong* – a Hokkien term to refer to ethnic Chinese businessmen who cooperate with the power elite (Suryadinata 1997: 8) – were chosen as business partners by the Soeharto regime and received favors not accessible to others. This very small group of *cukong* became synonymous with "the ethnic Chinese" in general; their conspicuous wealth further heightened "hatred" against Chinese Indonesians as an ethnic group.

In short, there are lingering sentiments toward Chinese Indonesians such as the idea that Chinese Indonesians have always benefited disproportionately from cronyist economic opportunities and that Chinese Indonesians are foreigners whose national loyalty is unclear (Freedman 2000; Setijadi 2016). This is a tough "message" for many Chinese Indonesians, including my research participants; as one interviewee put it, "We want to correct the wrongs being done to the Chinese, to get rid of the discrimination. We want the same rights as other Indonesians." How does religion and in particular their conversion to Pentecostal-charismatic Christianity in the largest Muslim country in the world fit into this story?

Chinese Indonesians: religion and religious tensions

According to the 2000 Census, approximately 35% of Chinese Indonesians are Christians (both Protestants and Catholics). This proportion is second only to Buddhism, which accounts for some 54% (Ananta, Arifin, and Bakhtiar 2008: 30). The Chinese Christian population, however, increased to almost 43% in the 2010 Census (Ananta et al. 2013: 21) most likely due to conversion in Pentecostal-charismatic churches. The latter are part of one of the fastest growing religious movements in the world today and their growth is mainly taking place outside the West (Anderson 2013; Hefner, 2013a), including Indonesia. Chinese Indonesians play an important part in these movements as church leaders, church members, and church supporters.

The Pentecostal-charismatic movement is a global phenomenon that shares similar practices of a born-again experience across a wide range of cultures, ethnic groups, classes, genders, and ages, facilitated by Internet, smartphones, and social media; these enable the use of similar music, worship styles, and recruitment strategies across the globe. Hunt (2000) dubbed this Christian movement a "global winner" because of its adaptation to local circumstances; Robbins (2011: 63) argues that the intensive involvement of its members is based on the fact that each and every one are qualified to engage in "core ritual performances," such as praying and singing. This, he contends, fosters the kind of trust that connects Pentecostals across ethno-cultural boundaries.

In their recent study on Asian Pentecostalism, Chong and Goh (2014: 403) point to three "Asian" characteristics: the simultaneous movement of indigenization and transnationalization, the trend to build mega-churches in tandem with worship services in small groups, and new ways of social engagement. Other ostensibly Asian features highlighted in the literature include Biblical literalism, personal salvation, moral chastity, evangelical activism (Anderson 2005), and the "more positive, this-worldly message to the prevailing pessimistic or even escapist world of Christian thought" (Ma 2005: 61). Furthermore, the Asian movements are characterized as "young" both in terms of their recent expansion and growth and in the age groups that are drawn to these religious practices. Messages in church include practical tips on how to conduct business, plan a career, and manage personal relationships. Worship and preaching thus not only provide for sin and salvation but for "daily needs, healing, God's favor in business and others" (Ma 2005: 71). The latter is a message that Chinese Indonesian business owners in my research often referred to as their reason for joining these churches.

Pentecostal-charismatic organizations started to gain more prominence in the Indonesian religious landscape in the 1980s and 1990s, particularly in urban Java where mega-churches became the most visible sign of the growing presence of the so-called third wave of Pentecostalism associated with prosperity gospel (Hefner 2013a). However, many of the Pentecostal-charismatic organizations gather in less visible and formal settings, such as private homes, restaurants, and abandoned sales rooms, as they struggle to obtain a government permit to officially act as a house of worship. Pentecostalism in Indonesia is characterized by many schisms due to doctrinal differences and leadership and personality clashes. Burgess (2002) concludes that from its humble beginning in 1921, the Pentecostal movement in Indonesia has produced thousands of new churches. One schism in more recent times led to the creation of the Indonesia Bethel Church (GBI, Gereja Bethel Indonesia) that has seen a "tremendous quantitative growth" (Wiyono 2005: 317). According to Andaya (2009), this is the largest Pentecostal denomination with over 5,000 congregations, many of which qualify as mega-churches (more than 2,000 members). The churches in my research belong to this GBI strand.

The GBI churches generally adopt a congregational system of governance, which "allows the local churches sovereignty and autonomy to draft work programs, doctrine, finance, and mission" (Wuysang and Tahun 2014: 113). The worship style is entertaining with singers, musicians, and dancing groups and pragmatic preaching in which personal stories and testimonies figure centrally. Many of the preachers are former businessmen or professionals, and church marketing (advertisements in newspapers, Christian broadcast, and celebrities who give a testimony) can be aggressive. There is a strong emphasis on the miraculous, as in divine healing (Wiyono 2005) and on multiplication and growth.

Pentecostal-charismatic churches in Indonesia are interesting in several ways: they blend an individual religious experience with a collective dimension of sharing experiences through worship and testimonies, and their constituency is young, educated, and middle class, with a strong Chinese Indonesian presence (Gudorf 2014). There is also a strong leadership cult and a "theology of practice" (Anderson 2003: 8) comprehensible to all with practical lessons on how to address or solve personal, family, career, or business problems. Sermons are explicitly in tune with this - worldly affairs and experiences of churchgoers. There is an ethos of giving, charity, and rewards, expressing specific ideologies of social justice, for example helping the (village) poor, supporting orphanages, and donating money (beyond tithing) but also of individual growth, success, health, and wealth.

The growth of these movements is taking place in a context fraught with religious tensions. Although Christianity is a minority religion in Muslim-dominated Indonesia, some Muslims perceive the Christian presence as a threat. According to Hoon (2013: 467), this is based on misperceptions that Christians are a homogenous group that aims to "Christianize Indonesia." Melissa Crouch (2013) shows that such mutual tensions are driven by fears of proselytization, Christianization (Kristenisasi), and Islamization (Islamisasi). Inter-religious tensions are not limited, however, to Christians and Muslims. According to a recent report, there is an alarming rise of religious intolerance in Indonesia, which includes all religious groupings and denominations; it is seen as one of "the most worrying developments in post-Soeharto Indonesia" (CSW 2014). As Hefner (2013b: 24) aptly argues, obstacles to pluralist freedom in Indonesia "include the continuing inability or unwillingness of Indonesian authorities to enforce existing laws and constitutional provision on religious freedom in a consistent manner."

The Chinese Indonesian business owners in my research all found their way to Pentecostal-charismatic Christianity in severe periods of business and personal crisis, often involving feelings of extreme insecurity in Indonesia. In the next section, I address why, against this backdrop, it made sense for some Chinese Indonesian business owners to convert to Pentecostal-charismatic Christianity.

Religious conversion: networks, prosperity, and morality

Pentecostal-charismatic Christianity is, according to many analysts, frequently found among ethnic minorities, stigmatized as inferior, where it "acts as a revitalization and assertion of moral standing" (Martin 2005: 28). In such instances, converting is an act of empowerment and religion works as an identity marker. One research participant stated,

> If we look at the facts, we can say that in the past the Chinese felt like a group that was held down. They were afraid and fearful. This is exactly why they went looking for justice, love, mercy, spirituality, protection, God.

And "we [Christians and Chinese] cannot join practical politics. We can only follow the politics of the Lord." A history of insecurity, including the 2016 and 2017 protests and court case against candidate Ahok, convinces many Chinese Indonesians that their long felt insecurity is far from over. As a global revitalization movement, Pentecostal-charismatic Christianity holds the promise to offer protection beyond the nation-state: "Christian churches have links to powerful international constituencies that eagerly defend the rights of Christian minorities worldwide" (Brazier 2006). The charismatic movement also aptly uses its international networks "for syncretizing salvationary ideologies with local experiences" (Lee and Ackerman 1997: 143–4).

The May riots and the regime change in 1998 and the more recent unrest around the Jakarta election convince many Chinese Indonesians that there is no safe place for them in their own country. All of a sudden, being seen as "Chinese" instead of "Indonesian" meant, according to Fuyuan (2003), for many Chinese Indonesians a "forced" reorientation on their current lives. Some left the country, while others turned to religion. Pentecostal-charismatic Christianity is a religion that is "change" oriented. It is believed and expressed vehemently that "only the power of the Holy Spirit makes this change possible" and that "from this change, other change will follow, be it personal or social transformational" (Ma 2005: 66). This message fell on fertile ground among Chinese Indonesians at such crucial moments in their lives.

In such insecure circumstances, engagement in the Pentecostal-charismatic churches and in the business clubs that are associated with it, such as local branches of the Full Gospel Business Men Fellowship International (which by nature is interdenominational), offered a trustworthy environment. Religiously active entrepreneurs often have strong personal ties of trust with co-worshippers, "the network reinforces the behavioural norms of the faith, and also provides a primary source of contacts for the individual" (Dodd and Seaman 1998: 73). This blending of religion, ethnicity, and professionalism can be interpreted as a form of sociocultural capital (cf. Bourdieu 2011), as the religious networks offer information, contacts, sharing, and guidance in both practical and spiritual ways.

Because "stereotypes do not disappear so fast, [and] the equation of 'Chinese' and 'rich' is deeply embedded" (Chua 2004: 476), this co-worship network is particularly important. Business experiences are shared in church and religious gatherings, something most other religious groupings do not offer. The sharing of family and business problems offers comfort, safety, and a feeling of belonging. Networks of co-worshippers fuse ethnicity and religion and often also enhance members' economic identities as business owners; as one of the business owners revealed,

> Most of our problems are not discussed in the mainstream churches. But the Full Gospel meetings can be used to discuss business opportunities although this is not among the major intentions. A while ago some property deals were closed via Full Gospel. It is rather natural that business issues arise among this group.

Pentecostal-charismatic Christianity is known for being among the few religions that explicitly endorse wealth creation and the accumulation of capital. As Meyer (2006: 11) has argued, "Born Again Christians have a right to enjoy prosperity by the grace of God." Although Chinese Indonesians share with Christian churches the importance of the family, the more mainstream Christian churches do not speak to the business spirit of Chinese Indonesians (Wijaya 2002). "In contrast to Buddhism or Catholicism, the charismatic churches endorsed the accumulation of wealth – a message that is attractive to a group for whom money has been a major cushion in a boisterous and volatile society" (Brazier 2006). These are not unimportant issues for the business owners in my research. In the words of one of the interviewees, "In business, the Chinese can be very pragmatic. The most important thing is profit. Maybe being a minority has taught the Chinese to be opportunistic and pragmatic at the same time." Whereas Weber suggested that capital accumulation was the unintentional consequence of a "calling" in combination with a Puritan ethic (Weber 1995/1930), little is unintentional in the capital accumulation of converted Chinese Indonesian Christians. In fact, there is a very intentional appeal to spiritual guidance, support by God, and the reception of "gifts of the spirit" – in return for praying, leading an honest life, and paying tithe.

The Full Gospel Business Men Fellowship International meetings are often organized around obtaining a better understanding of the Bible, discussing and sharing everyday (business) problems, and doing charity. In various writings on the Pentecostal-charismatic movement, we find reference to the role and meaning of words, praying, speaking in tongues, and testimonies but also of money (tithing) and giving (charity). Words and giving in these settings act as agency and carry meaning beyond their immediate existential significance in that they enhance charismatic power within but also beyond. Words and charity are not just "pure gifts: as there is an expected return, that of prosperity and . . . continued development as a 'powerful charismatic personality.'" Hence, words and charity can be argued to reinforce "the charismatic persona of both donors and recipients" (Coleman 2000: 201).

This born-again culture brings with that the born-again personhood firmly believes in material success: "God wants the faithful to be rewarded with prosperity" (Bielo 2007: 318). It has to be added, however, that there is more to the so-called prosperity gospel than pure individual gain and the so-called subordination of society to impersonal economic powers (Hefner 1998, 2017). This comes to the fore in processes of moral re-embedding, a process that among my research participants plays out at two levels. The first is a moral re-embedding in the family of co-believers as everything in the Pentecostal-charismatic churches is geared to offer a "sense of therapeutic community and belongingness" (Anderson 2013: 140). The second is a moral re-embedding in wider society with the congregation offering a moral compass and a focus on others. This comes to the fore most clearly in the charity and social mission activities in which all participants are involved. The Indonesian situation in which religious tensions are strongly experienced, however, restricts such activities to fellow Christians.

Lacking political power, to become engaged in the "politics of the Lord," as one participant said, is more than a second-best option. Refuge in the Lord is felt as strengthening both business leadership and ethnic solidarity. Hence, whereas conversion has a clear personal intensity and leads to improved self-esteem, an important characteristic for business leaders is their faith's guiding and protective dimension. In other words, the born-again status can be empowering at an individual and group level and for social life as well as spiritual fulfillment.

Conclusion

The Pentecostal-charismatic movement and Chinese Indonesian business owners have encountered and engaged each other in a dialectical process of empowerment that has profound implications for both business and ethnic life. The Pentecostal-charismatic movement offers a this-worldly, global, and modern "alternative" that provides spiritual guidance and social resources for effective business leadership. The prosperity gospel identifies wealth creation as a reward, an expected return to giving (charity, tithing) and praying. But the gospel also facilitates an inner reward of spiritual growth and self-esteem. In addition, religious gatherings provide a forum where insecurities and business problems can be addressed simultaneously.

There is also empowerment at the level of Chinese converts' specific position of ethnic and social vulnerability. The Pentecostal-charismatic movement is a global phenomenon capable of taking on varied local colors. Because of these linkages between the local and the global, individual members may feel connected to believers all over the world, not only sharing the gospel but also a social position and, in some sense, destiny. The experience may reduce one's sense of political insecurity and offer an escape – imagined or real – from a depressing situation in which wealth and economic success offer no guarantee of political power. An important conclusion must be that, for these new believers, the prosperity gospel offers more than inward purity; it is also about the "building of moral identity," a process that, paradoxically, reconnects Chinese Indonesians with Indonesia (Bielo 2004: 276).

References cited

Aguilar, Filomeno. 2001. "Citizenship, Inheritance, and the Indigenizing of 'Orang Chinese' in Indonesia," *Positions* 9(3): 501–33.

Ananta, Aris, Evi Nurvidya Arifin, and Bakhtiar. 2008. "Chinese Indonesians in Indonesia and the Province of Riau Archipelago: A Demographic Analysis," in Leo Suryadinata, ed., *Ethnic Chinese in Contemporary Indonesia* (Singapore: Institute of Southeast Asian Studies).

Ananta, Aris, Evi Nurvidya Arifin, M. Sairi Hasbullah, Nur Budi Handayani, and Agus Pramono. 2013. "Changing Ethnic Composition: Indonesia, 2000–2010." Paper presented in the XXVII IUSSP International Conference, Busan, 26–31 August.

Andaya, Barbara. 2009. "Contextualizing the Global: Exploring the Roots of Pentecostalism in Malaysia and Indonesia." Paper presented to a Symposium on Management and Marketing of Globalizing Asian Religions, International Convention of Asia Scholars, 11–14 August.

Anderson, Alan. 2003. "The Proliferation and Varieties of Pentecostalism in the Majority World." Lecture at the Symposium Non-Western Pentecostalism (Amsterdam).

———. 2005. "The Charismatic Face of Christianity in Asia," in Alan Anderson and Edmond Tang, eds., *Asian and Pentecostal. The Charismatic Face of Christianity in Asia* (Regnum Books International), pp. 1–12.

———. 2013. *To the Ends of the Earth. Pentecostalism and the Transformation of World Christianity* (Oxford: Oxford University Press).

Ang, Ien. 2001. *On Not Speaking Chinese: Living Between Asia and the West* (London: Routledge).

Bielo, James S. 2004. "Walking in the Spirit of Blood: Moral Identity Among Born-Again Christians," *Ethnology* 43(3): 271–89.

———. 2007. "'The Mind of Christ': Financial Success, Born-again Personhood, and the Anthropology of Christianity," *Ethnos* 72(3): 315–38.

Bourdieu, Pierre. 2011. "The Forms of Capital (1986)," *Cultural Theory: An Anthology* 1: 81–93.

Brazier, Roderick. 2006. "In Indonesia, the Chinese Go to Church," *International Herald Tribune*, 26 April.

Burgess, Stanley M. ed. 2002. *The New International Dictionary of Pentecostal and Charismatic Movements* (Michigan: Zondervan).

Chong, Terence and Daniel Goh. 2014. "Asian Pentecostalism: Revivals, Mega-Churches, and Social Engagement," in Bryan Turner and Oscar Salemink, eds., *Routledge Handbook on Religions in Asia* (London: Routledge), pp. 402–17.

Chua, Christian. 2004. "Defining Indonesian Chineseness Under the New Order," *Journal of Contemporary Asia* 34(4): 465–79.

Coleman, Simon. 2000. *The Globalization of Charismatic Christianity. Spreading the Gospel of Prosperity* (Cambridge: Cambridge University Press).

Coppel, Charles. 2004. "Historical Impediments to the Acceptance of Ethnic Chinese in a Multicultural Indonesia," in Leo Suryadinata, ed., *Chinese Indonesians: State Policies, Monoculture, and Multiculture* (Marshall Cavendish Academic), pp. 17–28.

Crouch, Melissa. 2013. "Proselytization, Religious Diversity and the State in Indonesia: The Offense of Deceiving a Child to Change Religion," in Juliana Finucane and Michael Feener, eds., *Proselytizing and Limits of Religious Pluralism in Contemporary Asia* (Singapore: Springer), pp. 17–40.

CSW Christian Solidarity Worldwide. 2014. "Indonesia: Pluralism in Peril. The Rise of Religious Intolerance Across the Archipelago." www.csw.org.uk/2014/02/14/report/179/article.htm.

Dodd, Sarah and Paul Seaman. 1998. "Religion and Enterprise: An Introductory Exploration," *Entrepreneurship, Theory and Practice* 23(1): 71–86.

Freedman, Amy. 2000. *Political Participation and Ethnic Minorities. Chinese Overseas in Malaysia, Indonesia and the United States* (London and New York: Routledge).

Fuyuan, Zhou. 2003. "Ethnic Voices Where Do We Belong?" *Asian Ethnicity* 4(3): 453–9.

Gudorf, Christine E. 2014. "The Pentecostal/Charismatic Movement in Indonesia," in Christine Gudorf, Zainal Abidin Bagir and Marthen Tahun, eds., *Aspirations for Modernity and Prosperity. Symbols and Sources Behind Pentecostal/Charismatic Growth in Indonesia* (Adelaide: ATF Theology), pp. 1–13.

Hefner, Robert W. 1998. *Market Cultures: Society and Morality in the New Asian Capitalisms* (Boulder, CO: Westview Press).

————. 2001. "Introduction: Multiculturalism and Citizenship in Malaysia, Singapore, and Indonesia," in Robert Hefner, (ed.), *The Politics of Multiculturalism. Pluralism and Citizenship in Malaysia, Singapore, and Indonesia* (Honolulu: University of Hawai'i Press), pp. 1–58.

————. 2013a. "Introduction: The Unexpected Modern – Gender, Piety and Politics in the Global Pentecostal Surge," in Robert Hefner, (ed.), *Global Pentecostalism in the 21st Century* (Bloomington: Indiana University Press), pp. 1–36.

————. 2013b. "The Study of Religious Freedom in Indonesia," *The Review of Faith & International Affairs* 11:(2):, pp. 24.

————. 2017. "Epilogue: Capitalist Rationalities and Religious Moralities – An Agonistic Plurality," in Juliette Koning and Gwenaël Njoto-Feillard, (eds.), *New Religiosities, Modern Capitalism, and Moral Complexities in Southeast Asia* (New York: Palgrave/MacMillan), pp. 265–285.

Heryanto, Ariel. 1998. "Ethnic Identities and Erasure. Chinese Indonesians in Public Culture," in Joel Kahn, ed., *Southeast Asian Identities. Culture and the Politics of Representation in Indonesia, Malaysia, Singapore, and Thailand* (London: I. B. Tauris Publishers), pp. 95–114.

Hoon, Chang-Yau. 2006. "Assimilation, Multiculturalism, Hybridity: The Dilemmas of the Ethnic Chinese in Post-Suharto Indonesia," *Asian Ethnicity* 7(2): 149–66.

————. 2013. "Between Evangelism and Multiculturalism: The Dynamics of Protestant Christianity in Indonesia," *Social Compass* 60(4): 457–70.

Hunt, Stephen. 2000. "'Winning Ways': Globalisation and the Impact of the Health and Wealth Gospel," *Journal of Contemporary Religion* 15(3): 331–47.

The Jakarta Post. 27 January 2017. "Chinese Indians Caught Up in the Storm of Identity Politics." www.thejakartapost.com/academia/2017/01/27/chinese-indonesians-caught-up-in-the-storm-of-identity-politics.html

Koning, Juliette. 2009. "Singing Yourself Into Existence; Chinese Indonesian Entrepreneurs, Pentecostal-Charismatic Christianity, and the Indonesian Nation State," in Julius Bautista and Francis Lim Khek Gee, eds., *Christianity and the State in Asia: Complicity and Conflict* (London: Routledge), pp. 115–31.

————. 2011. "Business, Belief and Belonging: Small Business Owners and Conversion to Charismatic Christianity," in Marleen Dieleman, Juliette Koning and Peter Post, eds., *Chinese Indonesians and Regime Change* (Boston: Brill), pp. 23–46.

————. 2013. "Generational Change in Chinese Indonesian SME's," in Thomas Menkhoff, Chay Yue Wah, Hans-Dieter Evers, and Hoon Chang Yau, eds., *Catalysts of Change: Chinese Business in Asia* (Singapore: World Scientific Publishing), pp. 231–250.

————. 2017. "Beyond Prosperity Gospel: Moral Identity Work and Organizational Cultures in Pentecostal-Charismatic Organizations in Indonesia," in Juliette Koning and Gwenaël Njoto-Feillard, eds., *New Religiosities, Modern Capitalism, and Moral Complexities in Southeast Asia* (New York: Palgrave/MacMillan), pp. 39–64.

Koning, Juliette and Heidi Dahles. 2009. "Spiritual Power: Ethnic Chinese Managers and the Rise of Charismatic Christianity in Southeast Asia," *Copenhagen Journal of Asian Studies* 27(1): 5–37.

Koning, Juliette and Can Seng Ooi. 2013. "Awkward Encounters and Ethnography," *Qualitative Research in Organizations and Management* 8(1): 16–32.

Koning, Juliette and Andreas Susanto. 2014. "Apprehension, Admiration and Ambiguity: Chinese Indonesians Talking About Business Opportunities in China," in Emile Kok-Kheng Yeoh, ed., *China: Developmental Model, State-Civil Societal Interplay and Foreign Relations* (Kuala Lumpur: University of Malaya Press), pp. 707–30.

Koning, Juliette and Jeff Waistell. 2012. "Identity Talk of Aspirational Ethical Leaders," *Journal of Business Ethics* 107(1): 65–77.

Lee, Raymond and Susan Ackerman. 1997. *Sacred Tensions. Modernity and Religious Transformation in Malaysia* (Columbia: University of South Carolina Press).

Lindsey, Tim. 2005. "Reconstituting the Ethnic Chinese in Post-Soeharto Indonesia: Law, Racial Discrimination, and Reform," in Tim Lindsey and Helen Pausacker, eds., *Chinese Indonesians. Remembering, Distorting, Forgetting* (Singapore: Institute of Southeast Asian Studies), pp. 41–76.

Ma, Wonsuk. 2005. "Asian (Classical) Pentecostal Theology in Context," in Alan Anderson and Edmond Tang, eds., *Asian and Pentecostal. The Charismatic Face of Christianity in Asia* (Regnum Books International), pp. 59–92.

Martin, David. 2005. "Issues Affecting the Study of Pentecostalism in Asia," in Alan Anderson and Edmond Tang, eds., *Asian and Pentecostal. The Charismatic Face of Christianity in Asia* (Regnum Books International), pp. 27–36.

Meyer, Birgit. 2006. "The Pentecostal Aesthetic and the Spirit of Modern Consumerism: Faith, Prosperity and Vision in African Pentecostal-Charismatic Churches." Princeton Lecture in Religion and Global Culture, Centre for the Study of Religion (Princeton University, 26 April 2006).

Ooi, Can-Seng. 2007. "Un-Packing Packaged Cultures: Chinese-ness in International Business," *East Asia: An International Quarterly* 24(2): 111–28.

Purdey, Jemma. 2006. *Anti-Chinese Violence in Indonesia, 1996–1999* (Singapore: Singapore University Press).

Robbins, Joel. 2011. "The Obvious Aspects of Pentecostalism: Ritual and Pentecostal Globalization," in Martin Lindhardt, ed., *Practicing the Faith. The Ritual Life of Pentecostal-Charismatic Christians* (New York and Oxford: Berghahn Books), pp. 49–67.

Setijadi, Charlotte. 2016. "Ethnic Chinese in Contemporary Indonesia: Changing Identity Politics and the Paradox of Sinification." ISEAS Perspective, No. 12. https://web5.iseas.edu.sg/images/pdf/ISEAS_Perspective_2016_12.pdf.

Suryadinata, Leo. 1993. "The State and the Chinese Minority in Indonesia," in Leo Suryadinata, ed., *Chinese Adaptation and Diversity. Essays on Society and Literature in Indonesia, Malaysia & Singapore* (Singapore: Singapore University Press), pp. 77–100.

———. 1997. *The Culture of the Chinese Minority in Indonesia* (Singapore: Times Books International).

Susanto, Andreas. 2006. "Safety-First: Strategies of Managing Insecurities Among Chinese Indonesians in Yogyakarta," in Juliette Koning and Frans Hüsken, eds., *Ropewalking and Safety Nets: Local Ways of Managing Insecurity in Indonesia* (Leiden and Boston: Brill), pp. 107–24.

Tan, Eugene. 2001. "From Sojourners to Citizens: Managing the Ethnic Chinese Minority in Indonesia and Malaysia," *Ethnic and Racial Studies* 24(6): 949–78.

The Washington Post. 18 March 2017. "Ethnic Chinese still grapple with discrimination despite generations in Indonesia." www.washingtonpost.com/world/asia_pacific/ethnic-chinese-still-grapple-with-discrimination-despite-generations-in-indonesia/2017/03/17/4abba780-0444-11e7-ad5b-d22680e18d10_story.html?utm_term=.fa023b211113

Weber, Max. 1995 (1930). *The Protestant Ethic and the Spirit of Capitalism* (London and New York: Routledge).

Wijaya, Yahya. 2002. *Business, Family and Religion: Public Theology in the Context of the Chinese-Indonesian Business Community* (Bern: Peter Lang AG).

Winarta, Frans. 2004. "Racial Discrimination in the Indonesian Legal System: Ethnic Chinese and Nation-Building," in Leo Suryadinata, ed., *Ethnic Relations and Nation-Building in Southeast Asia. The Case of the Ethnic Chinese* (Singapore: ISEAS Publications), pp. 66–81.

Wiyono, Gani. 2005. "Pentecostals in Indonesia," in Alan Anderson and Edmond Tang, eds., *Asian and Pentecostal: The Charismatic Face of Christianity in Asia* (Regnum Books International), pp. 307–28.

Wuysang, A.O. and Marthen Tahun. 2014. "Autonomy, Splintering and Growing Ecumenism: Governance and Organisation in Pentecostal and Charismatic Synods in Indonesia," in Christine Gudorf, Zainal Abidin Bagir and Marthen Tahun, eds., *Aspirations for Modernity and Prosperity. Symbols and Sources Behind Pentecostal/Charismatic Growth in Indonesia* (Adelaide: ATF Theology), pp. 111–38.

15

CONSUMPTION AND THE NEW MIDDLE CLASSES

Carla Jones

Descriptions of Indonesia frequently emphasize its exceptional, often large, status. It is the world's largest majority-Muslim country. It is the fourth largest country in the world. To these, one can now add the fact that in 2010 Indonesia established a world record in consumer confidence (121.6) and that that rank has continued into 2017 (150.8) (Roy Morgan 2017). Taken together, the size and enthusiasm of Indonesian consumer sentiment may seem like another piece of the broader story of Indonesia's unique standing in the world. Compared to similar indicators from the growing economies of China (111) or India (136) or the nervous polities of Europe and North America, this may be accurate. These indicators have also been in dialogue with a claim that economic liberalization has allowed Indonesia to officially become a "middle-income" country. Often read as a significant stepping-stone on a global ladder of progress, middle-income status fundamentally derives from a shift in a national economy oriented from production of consumer goods exported for consumers elsewhere to enjoy to a national economy that consumes its own or imported goods. Most measures suggest that approximately 60% of Indonesia's GDP derives from domestic consumption (comparable to the United States and double that of China) and that approximately 43% of the population can be classified as middle class (World Bank 2015). Statistics such as these fuel debates inside and outside of Indonesia about whether the growth of middle-class populations in formerly colonized and impoverished countries necessitates a concomitant decrease in middle-class segments in developed economies.

Rather than question the accuracy of these claims, I instead focus in this chapter on the assumptions that generate them and the details they may miss. In what follows, I ask how an affective indicator, consumer confidence, is in dialogue with a contrasting but equally powerful affective aspect of middle classes, anxiety. I further suggest that the particular roots and form of middle-class anxieties in Indonesia are historically specific. Three features – status, corruption, and shame – illustrate some less celebratory and uniquely Indonesian contours to the role of consumption in middle-class membership and its twin, middle-class exclusion. In particular, concerns about propriety and excess shape debates about respectable, rather than conspicuous, consumption. Each of these suggest that confidence and anxiety are mutually formed conditions of class relations and are, as Christine Walley has recently argued for the United States, "bound up with projections onto others of our own hopes and fears about the future" (2017: 2).

Consumer confidence surveys demand imagining the future. As elsewhere, market research firms, transnational banks, and state agencies in Indonesia cooperate in generating quarterly data on consumer sentiment by querying approximately 2,000 respondents in thirty cities and smaller towns (Guharoy 2006). Respondents are asked if they feel optimistic about their current financial condition and if they anticipate buying a variety of commodities in the next three, six, and twelve months, ranging from inexpensive to expensive "durable" goods (Guharoy 2009). These correspond to questions about whether they anticipate Indonesia will experience financial "good times" or "bad times," thereby linking personal and household consumption to national sentiment. In the process, the acquisition of particular commodities, such as smartphones, motorcycles, or personal-care items, fuse the concept of a consumer good to a good feeling. That personal and collective affect can be measured through possession of key objects is also central to measurements of socioeconomic class in Indonesia, as census surveys ask respondents to declare household monthly income; levels of education; home ownership; refrigerator, motorcycle, or car ownership; and possession of indexical furniture such as sideboards.

To raise cultural components of class formation and membership is to also raise a fundamental tension in social scientific treatments of class. Political economists have emphasized the material features of class formation, specifically the relationship of individuals within a class to the means of production. Put simply, in a capitalist system, people either sell or purchase human labor, making them members of either the proletariat or the bourgeoisie. Alternative or complicating interpretations point out that this Marxian perspective limits analysis of middle classes, treating them as either non-existent or as politically conservative. By contrast, perspectives inspired by Max Weber have emphasized the moral roots of capitalist systems, systems that may ultimately produce high inequality but that can be saturated with ideological affiliation to status, respectability, education, white-collar work, and, frequently, frugality (1947, 1958, 1968). Whether emphasizing a material or a cultural foundation, both perspectives work well with European and North American examples of capitalist class systems, with roots in Protestant Christianity and industrial production. In these settings, working classes were drawn into industrial labor regimes by virtue of their location in centers of empire and a naturalized racial logic of white progress through which middle-class identity came to refer to an unmarked norm earned through hard work and merit.

While much of the symbolic anthropology of Java benefited from a strong Weberian foundation, that approach focused more on interpretation than social class. For example, James Peacock's (1968) analysis of working-class theater employed Weberian and psychological categories, and the influence of Weber, through Talcott Parsons, was an essential component of Clifford Geertz's strain of symbolic analysis of Javanese religion (1976) and agriculture (1963). However, by 1963, Hildred Geertz described a "metropolitan superculture" that included educated, artistic, and economically stable Indonesians for whom the national language, chosen in 1928 as part of the revolution against the Dutch, was a primary tongue. Geertz described this superculture as "still in the process of formation" (35–7) but as mostly focused on cultural and political, rather than economic, characteristics. It emphasized a transnational awareness but a national consciousness, especially through employment in the civil service. Two years after Geertz's observation, President Soeharto, who ruled from 1965–98, began what would ultimately be three decades of authoritarian rule framed as anti-communist. Talk about class suggested a Marxist orientation that was almost instantly banned as part of a broader domination of political discourse. The site of the largest communist party in the world outside of the socialist bloc in the early 1960s, the country was ravaged by anti-communist mass killings by the late 1960s, and the very term *kelas* (class) became imbued with strong leftist overtones. By 1985, Howard Dick argued that while there had been considerable intellectual interest among Indonesianists about the developmentalist and modernizing promise of an urban middle class in the 1950s and 60s, it had dissipated with "a focus on the 'elite' [which] seems to have blinded social scientists to its middle-class nature"

(1985: 71). Significantly, he observed that the central organizing principle of the growing middle classes was the "privatization of the means of consumption" (75) that was "unsoftened by any trace of *noblesse oblige*" (74).

The privatization to which Dick referred was both commercial and domestic, in the sense that these processes were market-based and took place in secured, private spaces, such as homes. Henk Schulte Nordholt (2004) argues that the intellectual silences, both within Indonesia and by foreign scholars, have entrenched a lack of awareness of the demographic reality of changing Indonesian social and economic relations around class. He has called for research on the new Indonesian middle classes as essential to "decolonizing Indonesian historiography," because they are "people without history" for whom the old colonial social categories no longer apply (16). The energetic expression of democratic participation in the past two decades following Soeharto's rule is evidence to scholars, such as Gerry Van Klinken, of the rise of a substantial, though still insecure, Indonesian middle class (2014).

The more recent increase of multinational capital production and urban economic growth suggests that newer social differentiations in Indonesia are indeed amenable to a class analysis. In addition to national political control, Soeharto's authoritarian techniques opened the country to international investment in private industry, which benefited from military suppression of organized labor in offshore, flexible, feminized, multi-national manufacturing. While this combination of rule and recruitment relied on a mobile and rural population, a middle-income demographic segment also grew during that period, through both civil service and private entrepreneurship. Measuring that group and figuring out what to call it have become industries unto themselves in Indonesia since the 1990s, but undergirding both the measurement and the analysis of the middle classes is a tension over whether they are conscious of their privilege or are sympathetic to less secure classes. One way to identify that consciousness is through attitudes about consumption.

Anxiety

The apparently unproblematic celebration of the joys of consumption is therefore complex, suggesting ambivalence and critique about the relationship between consumption and morality. The highly visible consumption in many of the Asian capitals during the 1990s has generated research on the novelty of what was dubbed the "new rich" of Asia (Pinches 1999; Robison and Goodman 1996). Indonesian middle classes do vary from their Western counterparts in key ways. For example, middle-class households benefit from the same rural, flexible, vulnerable populations that multi-national factories do, allowing them to have domestic staff in a way that would be impossible for comparable households in Europe or North America. Yet much of the "new rich" scholarship has conflated the more visible and even flamboyant displays of wealth, reminiscent of European nouveaux riches (or what have been called "Orang Kaya Baru," or OKB, literally New Rich People, in Indonesian), with evidence of a more moderate, self-conscious, and anxious middle class (Barker 2009). Indeed, common descriptions of OKB start and stop with descriptions of either residential aesthetics or women's dress, suggesting that the newer middle classes are recognizable for lifestyle and the charged boundary between public and private spaces.

It is therefore intriguing that for all the rhetorical power of describing Indonesians as enthusiastic consumers, most of the Indonesian families I know, citizens who would certainly qualify as middle-class according to the measures I have described, avoid calling themselves *kelas menengah* (literally "middle class"). Instead, they name neighbors or friends as middle-class but then go on to say they are "lower" middle class or avoid a classed term altogether. This contrasts strongly

189

with the American pattern in which middle-class membership is a mode of majority belonging, a move that has the effect of minimizing class differences in the nation. Instead, the term *kelas menengah* clearly circulates as a term of distinction, referring to wealth. James Siegel has argued that Indonesian nationalism has discouraged citizens from imagining themselves as members of classes in favor of imagining the "nation composed of kin" (2002: 222) in which class affiliations might produce cleavages in the national family.

This reticence to identify as middle class is unique but bears some resemblance to anxieties consistent with middle classes elsewhere. Indeed, anxiety seems to be a central and increasingly common feature of middle-class life. As Heiman et al. (2012) argue, middle classes globally experience a mix of aspiration and anxiety that they express through a desire for security and disciplined consumption. Mark Liechty describes anxiety among middle-class Nepalis in Kathmandu as the enactment of respectability through restrained consumption, with specific expectations for male and female codes of display (2003). Linked to increasingly precarious access to income, middle classes may consume in reference to neighbors or social peers but do so worrying about the future for themselves or their children, what Barbara Ehrenreich describes as "fear of falling" (1989). Anxiety of this sort is both a sentiment and a powerful correlate to facts that are not as frequently cited in the triumphal descriptions of Indonesia's growing middle class. As the World Bank documents, Indonesia's robust growth in GDP since the 1998 Asian financial crisis has not been associated with broad increases in employment and has instead been a "jobless" recovery (2010). Much of this income has been based on repatriated income from exported labor, rather than exported commodities. In addition, the Asian Development Bank's description of a doubling of the middle class in Indonesia in the first decade of the new millennium was achieved in part through lowering the minimum income to classify as "middle class" to US$2 a day. It is therefore not surprising that one economic measure of inequality, the Gini coefficient, worsened from 29 in 1990 to 39 in 2011 (Kanbur, et al. 2014: 9), suggesting that the increased wealth in Indonesia is also increasingly concentrated among the upper strata of the population. Although these alternative indicators may contradict the more optimistic depictions of a large middle class, they also suggest that the idea of the middle class remains a powerful, relevant category for Indonesians imagining either utopian or dystopian futures.

How does one therefore reconcile the apparently contradictory mix of anxiety and consumption in contemporary Indonesia? I suggest that these feelings co-exist in part because of overlapping concerns with three criteria: status, corruption, and shame.

Status

Perhaps nothing denotes the display of new wealth in Indonesian households more than the emulation of high-status taste. Typical in domestic features, such as gold-gilt furniture or elaborately decorated house gates, these aesthetic statements are recognizable to the more modest middle classes as quintessentially OKB. In other words, they are forms of what Thorstein Veblen (1899) described as conspicuous consumption, in that they are aspirational and are guided by the social group situated above them in the social hierarchy. Veblen's analysis focused less on status than class but placed consumption at the center of the analytical frame. These Indonesian examples recall that specific and historically ethnic conceptions of status have been central to social differentiation in regions of Indonesia with traditions of nobility. Status has been an illuminating tool for analysts, as well, interpreting the complex hierarchy of Javanese and Balinese social relations, well outside the formal, feudal settings of kingdoms. From language to ideas about refinement, etiquette, and comportment, status has been considered a more appropriate analytic tool than wealth. Ward Keeler (1990) has described status as the essential social differentiator in Java, resting on the linguistic and aesthetic enforcement of Javanese hierarchy that privileges the nobility (*priyayi*). Indeed, the anthropology of Indonesia, especially in the scholarship of Clifford Geertz, influenced the discipline's turn toward symbolic and interpretive anthropology during the 1970s and 1980s, a turn that arguably reflected the concerns with status in the central Javanese communities he studied.

Although both the national revolution of 1945 and the student activist movements of the 1980s and 1990s framed calls for democratic self-rule through critique of *feodal* (feudal) privilege, much of the middle-class style of the New Order reproduced priyayi conventions. Indeed, although there are a number of terms for poverty in Indonesian parlance, including the direct phrase of *orang miskin* (literally, "poor person"), the more polite appellations obliquely use status terms such as *orang kecil* or "little people." Nowhere is this more apparent than in the Javanese ambivalence around money. Although Javanese nobility often lived in large extended households, decorated with powerful objects that might use gold, or appear gilted or even ostentatious to outsiders, conceptions of power framed that wealth as an effect, rather than the source, of high-born status. A gold object in a family collection might well be a form of fungible precious metal but was foremost a treasure imbued with sacred power. As a result, wealth was not something one should pursue or even desire. Rather, elites in this status-focused system were to value spiritual potency (Anderson 1972) over monetary wealth. Suzanne Brenner (1998) demonstrates how those values can be adopted and reproduced by non-elites in her analysis of the stigma female Javanese batik traders experienced in the 1980s and 1990s. Their comfort with handling and managing money in the marketplace meant they had to offset this shame through endorsing priyayi ideologies that denigrated the pursuit of wealth. Nonetheless, as Brenner describes, these women's income could not directly accrue as capital, but had to be "domesticated" back into familial status through the purchase of goods associated with priyayi style, a process that ultimately bankrupted many of the families she knew. Brenner (1998: 119) articulates the process she analyzed as intersecting with capitalist modes of production but as not directly capitalist; instead, it was a combination of Dutch colonial intervention in sultanate rule and Javanese conceptions of trade. Conspicuous consumption therefore entailed using capital to acquire goods associated with a higher status, rather than a higher class.

A powerful effect of these ideologies has been to delink consumption from production in polite discourse. Because priyayi families never seemed to need to work or worry about where money came from, work become a marker of low status. There is now no faster way to signal one's high status standing than to appear not to know or care how luxury goods come into one's life. This has meant that owning a luxury good can suggest power and even provoke envy, but it is inappropriate to inquire how someone might acquire such a good. One cannot directly inquire about how money circulates or where it settles. This code of propriety generates its own parallel universe of suspicion.

One concept in particular illustrates these intersecting tensions over the visible public style of consumption by the newly wealthy and the older ambivalences around the relationship between production and consumption: *pamrih*. Variously understood as profiteering or, worse, uncontrollable greed, pamrih is a critique of inappropriate pursuit of illicit wealth. Rooted in priyayi privilege, it has now become part of democratic activist rhetoric in Indonesia that identifies excessive consumption with excessive power. To accuse others of pamrih is to implicitly accuse them of immorality, to suggest that they have sought power without fully disclosing an intent to defraud or profit.

Corruption

Although rooted in a system of nobility, concepts like pamrih have acquired a new legitimacy in the last two decades because they provide an explanation for the visible circulation of wealth and the sense of illegitimacy that anxious middle-class citizens feel about it. Besides Indonesia's other unique rankings in the world, many middle-class Indonesians are highly aware of one particular statistic: that Indonesia consistently scores poorly by corruption watchdog organizations, such as Transparency International. In 2016, Indonesia was ranked 90 out of 176 countries for its perception of corruption (Transparency International 2017). Although apparently in the middle of a global index, measures such as this reflect a widespread sense among middle-class Indonesians that while capital is abundant, it is only available to those with connections to elite power or those willing to use those connections.

Deep suspicion about wealth therefore plays in to broader middle-class insecurities, which then fuel fascination with tales of excessive consumption among corrupt fellow citizens. Transforming access to the state into wealth has long been a trait associated with Indonesians seeking entry to and beyond the middle classes. Sociologist Justus M. van der Kroef described, in 1956, "a 'national' social class system . . . in its infancy" (138) but which featured entrepreneurs and intelligentsia engaging in "unprecedented corruption and collusion" (143). While critiques of corruption, such as van der Kroef's, focus on production, through facilitating illicit access to state funding, infrastructure, or authority, the particular discourse around corruption in Indonesia has also centered on consumption. As a result, Indonesians who feel that corruption is rampant feel that they cannot trust what they see. For example, the same indexical commodities about which census or consumer confidence surveys inquire may have been acquired through ill-gotten means, but neither surveys nor neighbors can ask about that. In a sense, an earlier status system that made it impolite, and potentially irrelevant, to ask about the ability to consume now intersects with a contemporary class system that makes those sources of consumption deeply suspect.

Some brief historical context is helpful. As a mode of economic exchange that appears to be out of public view, exchange labeled as "corrupt" is recognizable to Indonesian citizens and to international organizations like Transparency International alike as illegitimate because of its secrecy. The national Corruption Eradication Court, or Komisi Pemberantasan Korupsi, was established in 2002 and has become a unique part of the post-Soeharto political landscape. It was charged with curtailing what feels like a rise in corruption in spite of, or perhaps because of, the atmosphere of reformist freedom following Soeharto's resignation. Although President Soeharto enriched himself and his family through secretive financial deals (estimates range to around US\$35 billion), the decade since his resignation is widely perceived by Indonesians to have fostered even more corruption. As Nils Bubandt has described, power has become murky, intermittently visible as untraceable wealth but still rooted in access to spiritual potency. This murkiness has fed a fascination with rumor and suspicion, which is especially acute around accounts of corruption (2008, 2014).

Preoccupation with secrecy further fuels an industry of documentation and revelation in which the corruption court is the most central site. The KPK system is intentionally separate from the federal court system in hopes of ensuring independence and holds both corrupting private citizens and corrupted civil servants liable for actions that enrich themselves or cost the state. The logic of legal authority in corruption trials borrows from other technologies of justice, emphasizing particular kinds of evidence and measurement that appear to be neutral reflections, rather than productions, of power (Tidey 2013). Convicted citizens are then sentenced to fines, reparations to the state, and terms in a white-collar prison system. A common phrase is that corrupt citizens are not afraid of prison, but they are afraid of poverty. The particularly Indonesian performances of corruption trials suggest that revelation of wrongdoing in trials involves more than just techniques of truth but a particular focus on transparency, which Karen Strassler has described as uniquely concerned with the form and symbolism of money itself (2009). More than a medium of exchange that can be transformed into anything, it is both public and yet unavailable to the majority of the public. In dialogue with the gold goods that preceded it in a feudal past, currency is a curious thing, a simultaneously mass and inalienable good that can telegraph the desires of a middle class.

Corruption trials have therefore emerged in the last decade in Jakarta as an appealing legal and cathartic solution to a national problem in which currency and corruption figure centrally. Originally (but no longer) televised live on a dedicated channel, trials involve thorough recounting of secret details of corrupt transactions, with the accused typically asked to detail the burner cellphones, secret codes, brown paper bags of cash, or ways they spent their wealth. The accused almost always sit on a lone chair in front of a panel of judges, while TV cameras capture every bead of sweat or expression of privileged indifference. In the first few years of these televised cases, many of my friends would find it almost impossible not to watch, the promise of seeing and hearing about how much money was changing hands and how it was happening was just too much to resist. As a long-time fellow enthusiast of Indonesian soap operas, I can attest that the most expressive gasps of shock, amusement, and heartbreak I have witnessed in response to TV viewing have not been to scripted programs but to the detached accounting of otherwise melodramatic details in corruption trials. Tales of wealth wasted in debauched ways, such as drug addiction, were especially satisfying.

Shame

By trafficking in exposure, corruption trials apply a middle-class feeling to elite crimes: embarrassment. Defendants who fail to fully express shame in these accounts fail to grasp that the crime is as much performative as material. Indonesian folk culture is replete with morality tales about the dangers of excess desire, where it is associated with the possibility of being recognized as someone whose individual desire for social mobility threatens family and community. Clifford Geertz called this a kind of "stage fright" (*lek* or *isin*), less about guilt than the fear that "for lack of skill or control an illusion will not be maintained, that the actor will show through her part" (1973: 402).

Shame adds an affective component to political and economic conditions, returning us to our opening question about the intersection of affect and consumption in Indonesia. The context I have outlined suggests that consumer desire is not merely an unmediated expression of net worth. Rather, it is informed by status and political and historical context. In an environment in which money seems to circulate with abundance and ease, it has been wrenching for me to see how that money never seems to settle with many of the families I know. Instead, their efforts to claim and hang on to capital feels, to them, like evidence of the fact that there is also something suspicious about capital, that one can never know the real origins of the neighbors' new addition on their house or new car. It is therefore not surprising that middle-class citizens rarely identify as such.

Shame can motivate both conspicuous and frugal consumption. Veblen's analysis of conspicuous consumption focused in large part on how much shame can motivate consumption beyond one's means. Victorian-era domestic accounts situated in nineteenth-century England exquisitely detailed the suffering of those who might fail to meet status and class demands of a system in which being middle-class could itself be an embarrassment. In what I have detailed here, there are both similar and different foundations for shame. Acquiring the requisite goods for a respectable life can run afoul of a system in which ostentatious expenditure can provoke accusations of pamrih. Yet failing to acquire the appropriate goods can also be paralyzing, as Johan Lindquist describes of the lives of working-class migrants in Indonesia who find they are unable to complete labor sojourns if they are ashamed to return home empty-handed (2008).

In this context, spaces outside of the home, and especially those that involve consumption, have become especially charged, precisely at a time in which much of the flagrant forms of development have generated new public spaces of consumption throughout Indonesian cities. Lizzy Van Leeuwen (2008) argues that the contemporary Indonesian middle class is drawn to the public space of the mall because they imagine it as a space where nothing detrimental to the political and social body might occur. Yet, as she also argues, that ideal exists precisely because malls are the spaces where so much more might occur. Rumors abound about how young women might find the excess consumer desire of the stylish mall environment so powerful that they might engage in commodified sex in order to fund fashionable shopping. The intersection of consumer and sexual desire in these settings has fueled anxiety among middle-class parents, as Nancy Smith-Hefner has demonstrated, encouraging a youth movement toward Islamic piety and earlier marriages (2007). Again, this is in contrast to middle-class demographics elsewhere, where education and professional employment usually lead to later ages for first marriage.

The potent mix of affect and national fortunes are evident in national economic policy over the last two decades. During the Asian economic crisis, the federal government fought capital flight among wealthy and less wealthy Indonesians alike by discouraging converting Indonesian rupiah into foreign currency. A national campaign linked shame for being caught converting rupiah into foreign currency into affection for the currency through a campaign called "Love the Rupiah." In the past decade, in the wake of that period, the campaign was expanded to encourage middle-class Indonesians to use their disposable income to support national industries through "loving" domestically produced goods rather than buying imported goods, again suggesting that negative effects of economic liberalization should be offset through moral middle-class consumption. The growth of credit card use in Indonesia has generated related worries about excess and lack of self-control. A notorious case in 2011 humanized the fact that consumer banking debt had grown by 20% a year between 2005 and 2010. Irzen Octa, a Citibank customer, died in the presence of outsourced debt collectors after he was shocked to learn of the true size of his outstanding loan. In 2016, new laws ostensibly designed to help citizens resist credit-card-based consumption required banks to limit clients to two credit cards per issuer. The same law has also been widely interpreted by middle-class citizens as cracking down on the abuse of credit cards by corrupt elites as a way to avoid taxes and to launder money.

The growing appeal of Islamic alternatives for clean consumption underscores the intimate fusion of morality and money and the widespread worry about unmanaged consumer desire. Daromir Rudnyckyj argues that shame has been a powerful motivator for corporate employees and Islamic banking executives alike, providing an avenue to channel critiques of capitalism into inspiring disciplined labor at work (2010) and promoting pious financial instruments for those same middle-class investors (2017). These religious critiques of capital may celebrate pursuing wealth but cannot, as James Hoesterey has demonstrated for Islamic entrepreneurial efforts in Indonesia, "be reduced . . . to the neoliberal logics of the free market" (2017).

Conclusion

In addition to triumphant praise for Indonesia's march through a global ladder of class progress, experts in and out of the country also express worry about the risk of Indonesia entering a period of stasis, something labeled the "middle-income trap." Broadly defined as a failure to move from dependence on natural resource extraction and on to high-value commodity production, Indonesia's economists are advising the government to take steps that may feel familiar to the citizens I have described here, such as encouraging even higher domestic consumption and decreasing social inequality. Rather than an engine for national development, the "arrival" of national middle-income status now generates a new reason for worry, stalled broad-based growth (Deutsch 2011). A middle-income trap may seem like a remote risk to American or European middle-class segments worried about losing standing, but it now occupies front-page news accounts in much of Southeast Asia. I began this chapter by identifying Indonesia's exceptional status in the world. In closing, we might recall that while Indonesian middle classes are indeed unique, this uniqueness is nonetheless familiar in that it is at once both material and immaterial, global and local. At a historical moment in which middle-class belonging elsewhere is in doubt and exclusion from the middle classes is motivating political movements, we do well to acknowledge that Indonesia's anxieties may be our own.

References cited

Anderson, Benedict. 1972. "The Idea of Power in Javanese Culture," in Claire Holt, Benedict Anderson and James Siegel (eds.), *Culture and Politics in Indonesia* (Ithaca: Cornell University Press), pp. 1–69.

Barker, Joshua, et al. 2009. "Orang Kaya: Figures of Indonesian Modernity," *Indonesia* 87: 35–72.

Brenner, Suzanne. 1998. *The Domestication of Desire: Women, Wealth, and Modernity in Java* (Princeton: Princeton University Press).

Bubandt, Nils. 2008. "Rumors, Pamphlets, and the Politics of Paranoia in Indonesia," *The Journal of Asian Studies* 67(3): 789–817.

———. 2014. *Democracy, Corruption and the Politics of Spirits in Contemporary Indonesia* (London and New York: Routledge).

Deutsch, Anthony. 2011. "Middle Income: Indonesia Promoted," *Financial Times*, 7 February. http://blogs.ft.com/beyond-brics/2011/02/07/promotion-indonesia-becomes-middle-income (Accessed 1 April 2011).

Dick, Howard. 1985. "The Rise of a Middle Class and the Changing Concept of Equity in Indonesia: An Interpretation," *Indonesia* 39: 71–92.

Ehrenreich, Barbara. 1989. *Fear of Falling: The Inner Life of the Middle Class* (New York: Pantheon).

Geertz, Clifford. 1963. *Agricultural Involution: The Process of Ecological Change in Indonesia* (Berkeley: University of California Press).

———. 1973. *The Interpretation of Cultures* (New York: Basic Books).

———. 1976. *The Religion of Java* (Chicago: University of Chicago Press).

Geertz, Hildred. 1963. "Indonesian Cultures and Communities," in Ruth McVey, ed., *Indonesia* (New Haven: HRAF Yale University Press), pp. 78–84.

Guharoy, Debnath. 2006. *Redefining Indonesia's Socio-Economic Strata* (Jakarta, Indonesia: Roy Morgan Research Reports).

———. 2009. "As Poverty Declines, 'Upward Mobility' Is Being Redefined," *Jakarta Post*, 8 September.

Heiman, Rachel, Mark Liechty, and Carla Freeman. 2012. "Introduction: Charting an Anthropology of the Middle Classes," in Rachel Heiman, Carla Freeman, and Mark Liechty, eds., *The Global Middle Classes: Theorizing Through Ethnography* (Santa Fe: School for Advanced Research Press), pp. 3–29.

Hoesterey, James Bourk. 2017. "Marketing Islam: Entrepreneurial Ethics and the Spirit of Capitalism in Indonesia," *Practical Matters Journal* (April 14). http://practicalmattersjournal.org/2017/04/14/marketing-islam/.

Kanbur, Ravi, Changyong Rhee, and Juzhong Zhuang. 2014. "Introduction," in Ravi Kanbur, Changyong Rhee and Juzhong Zhuang, eds., *Inequality in Asia and the Pacific: Trends, Drivers and Policy Implications* (London and New York: Routledge), pp. 1–36.

Keeler, Ward. 1990. "Speaking of Gender," in Jane Atkinson and Shelly Errington, eds., *Power and Difference: Gender is Island Southeast Asia* (Palo Alto, CA: Stanford University Press), pp. 127–52.

Liechty, Mark. 2003. *Suitably Modern: Making Middle-Class Culture in a New Consumer Society* (Princeton: Princeton University Press).

Lindquist, Johan. 2008. *The Anxieties of Mobility: Migration and Tourism in the Indonesian Borderlands* (Honolulu: University of Hawai'i Press).

Peacock, James. 1968. *Rites of Modernization: Symbolic and Social Aspects of Indonesian Proletarian Drama* (Chicago: University of Chicago Press).

Pinches, Michael. 1999. "Cultural Relations, Class and the New Rich," in Michael Pinches, ed., *Culture and Privilege in Capitalist Asia* (London and New York: Routledge), pp. 1–55.

Robison, Richard and David Goodman, eds. 1996. *The New Rich in Asia: Mobile Phones, McDonalds and Middle-Class Revolution* (London and New York: Routledge).

Roy Morgan Research. 2017. "Roy Morgan Indonesian Consumer Confidence Up in March 150.8 (up 4.3pts.); Highest Since September 2016," Finding No. 7228, April 28 (Jakarta: Roy Morgan Research).

Rudnyckjy, Daromir. 2010. *Spiritual Economies: Islam, Globalization and the Afterlife of Development* (Ithaca: Cornell University Press).

———. 2017. "Debating Form, Consuming Substance: Halal Authenticity in Malaysian Islamic Finance," *Practical Matters Journal* (April 17). http://practicalmattersjournal.org/2017/04/17/debating-form/.

Schulte Nordholt, Henk. 2004. *De-Colonising Indonesian Historiography* (Lund, Sweden: Center for East and South-East Asian Studies, Lund University).

Siegel, James. 2002. "The Idea of Indonesia Continues: The Middle Class Ignores Acehnese," *Archipel* 64(1): 199–229.

Smith-Hefner, Nancy. 2007. "Youth Language, *Gaul* Sociability, and the New Indonesian Middle Class," *Journal of Linguist Anthropology* 17(2): 184–203.

Strassler, Karen. 2009. "The Face of Money: Currency, Crisis, and Remediation in Post-Suharto Indonesia," *Cultural Anthropology* 24(1): 68–103.

Tidey, Sylvia. 2013. "Corruption and Adherence to Rules in the Construction Secotre: Reading the 'Bidding Books," *American Anthropologist* 115(2): 188–202.

Transparency International. 2017. "Corruption Perceptions Index 2016." www.transparency.org/news/feature/corruption_perceptions_index_2016, published 25 January 2017 (Accessed 18 May 2017).

Van der Kroef, Justus. 1956. "The Changing Class Structure of Indonesia," *American Sociological Review* 21(2): 138–48.

Van Klinken, Gerry. 2014. "Introduction: Democracy, Markets and the Assertive Middle," in Gerry van Klinken and Ward Berenschot, eds., *In Search of Middle Indonesia: Middle Classes in Provincial Towns* (Leiden and Boston: Brill), pp. 1–34.

Van Leeuwen, Lizzy. 2008. *Lost in Mall: An Ethnography of Middle-Class Jakarta in the 1990s* (Leiden: KITLV Press).

Veblen, Thorstein. 1899. *The Theory of the Leisure Class: An Economic Study of Institutions* (New York: Palgrave Macmillan).

Walley, Christine. 2017. "Trump's Election and the 'white working class': What we missed," *American Ethnologist* 44(2): 1–6.

Weber, Max. 1947. *The Theory of Social and Economic Organization*. A. M. Henderson and Talcott Parsons, trans. (New York: Free Press).

———. 1958. *The Protestant Ethic and the Spirit of Capitalism* (New York: Scribners).

———. 1968. *Economy and Society: An Outline of Interpretive Sociology*. Guenther Roth and Claus Wittich, eds. (New York: Bedminster).

World Bank. 2010. *Indonesia Jobs Report: Towards Better Jobs and Security for All* (Jakarta and New York: The World Bank).

———. 2015. "Household Final Consumption Expenditure, % of GDP." http://data.worldbank.org/indicator/NE.CON.PETC.ZS?locations=ID.

16

REVISITING "WONDERFUL INDONESIA"

Tourism, economy, and society

Kathleen M. Adams

Hailed as an important dimension of the nation's economy, tourism has played a complex role in the culturally-diverse nation of Indonesia. Like Oz's proverbial "yellow brick road," tourism development was initially envisioned as a pathway to empowerment. Beginning in the late 1960s and early 1970s, a growing chorus of Indonesian politicians and tourism consultants extolled tourism as an avenue for generating foreign exchange, fostering sustainable development, and enhancing national identity and pride. Yet, just as Oz's yellow brick road was riddled with unanticipated twists, detours, and challenges, so, too, has been the story of tourism in Indonesia. In broad terms, this chapter examines the interplay between tourism development (both planned and unplanned), local dynamics, and intergroup sensibilities in Indonesia.

More specifically, as I will underscore in the pages that follow, both domestic and international tourism in Indonesia are entwined with nation-building, inter-ethnic, religious, and regional political dynamics. Likewise, the government's relentless pursuit of UNESCO World Heritage sites and its tourism awareness campaigns (such as the current, foreigner-oriented "Wonderful Indonesia" and the "Sapta Pesona" or "Seven Charms" promotion for Indonesians) have had reverberations for many Indonesians' understanding of their places in the world. The expansion of tourism and travel-oriented campaigns in the archipelago has not only transformed the aspirations and leisure-time activities of middle-class Indonesians with disposable incomes; it has also subtly reconfigured the ways in which local groups imagine themselves and their relationship to the nation. This is the case not only for those whose ethnic homelands have become established tourist destinations, but also for some groups residing in remote locales far from the tourist trail. This chapter traces the history of tourism projects and policies in Indonesia and spotlights case studies from various regions of Indonesia to address the interplay between tourism development and local understandings of identity, cultural heritage, and the state. Ultimately, this chapter showcases how tourism is entangled with a variety of sociocultural dynamics in Indonesia, ranging from economic and environmental transformations to shifting sensibilities about lifestyle and "place," to reconfigured understandings of ethnic, regional, religious, or national identities.

Tourism visions: from the colonial era into the New Order

Most scholars of Indonesian tourism trace the birth of international tourism back to the colonial era, when the Dutch colonial tourist bureau published the first Bali guidebook in Batavia in 1914, just six years after their conquest of the island – a conquest which had entailed the slaughter and exile of thousands of Balinese (Picard 1993: 75; Kodhyat 1996; Dahles 2001: 28; Hampton and Clifton 2017: 181). As Adrian Vickers observed in his history of Bali as a "created" paradise, "the scar on the liberal imagination of the Netherlands produced by these massacres had to be healed, and the preservation of Balinese culture, in combination with tourism, were the most effective balms for the healing process" (Vickers 1989: 91). In this period, Dutch-produced tourism pamphlets gradually shifted the older popular image of "savage Bali" to a new vision of an unspoiled Eden, fit for genteel tourism centering on cultural arts. These idyllic images coalesced in the late 1920s, as Bali attracted international artists and writers whose works further enhanced Bali's reputation as the "most romantic" stop on cruises that included various Javanese ports. By 1940, "paradisiacal Bali" was drawing 250 international tourists monthly, a sizable number given the high costs of travel at the time (Vickers 1989: 97–8).

World War II, the Indonesian post-war struggle for independence, and the politically tumultuous violence of the 1960s interrupted international tourism in the archipelago. Likewise, domestic tourism in this era was either a political activity for government officials or a leisure pursuit restricted to only the most economically privileged citizens (Gunawan 1997: 18; Dahles 2001: 28). Nevertheless, Indonesia's first president, Sukarno, imagined a broader, transformative role for tourism in national development, both economically and culturally.[1] Soon after independence, in the early 1950s, Sukarno began promoting Bali abroad as an international tourism destination and eventually drew on Japanese war reparation funds to construct Bali's first international-class hotel and begin airport expansions (Hitchcock and Putra 2007). While formal national tourism policy was scant in this post-independence era, by 1958, Sukarno sensed a need to cultivate local tourism consciousness and minted an Indonesian term for tourism, *pariwisata* (Kodhyat 1996: 66).

Sukarno's seemingly instinctive tourism-as-nation-building efforts were not limited to Bali. From early in his presidency, he envisioned the construction of a national monument in the center of Jakarta that would serve as the symbol of the nation, akin to Paris's Eiffel Tower. In Sukarno's vision, the structure's architecture would incorporate ancient "Indonesian" symbols (conveying the naturalness of the nation) and would both commemorate Indonesia's struggle for independence and showcase the grandeur of the nation. Its museum spaces would display national icons, such as the nation's first flag, and historical dioramas. Monas, as the national monument has come to be known, was ultimately built over the course of two presidencies; as a prime destination for touring school groups and domestic tourists (as well as a symbolically potent site for political demonstrations), the monument continues to promote leisure-time lessons in citizenship.

It was not until after General Soeharto took power in 1966–1967 that large-scale international tourism began to take center stage in government planning initiatives, eventually emerging as the country's most important economic sector, after oil and gas. In this era, international tourist arrivals went from less than 100,000 visitors annually in the 1960s to an all-time peak of 5,185,000, just before the economic turmoil that led to the collapse of Soeharto's regime (World Bank 2017). Beginning in 1969, Soeharto's New Order regime initiated a series of Five-Year Plans (*Repelita*) aimed at generating economic growth over a 25-year period. The first plan (1969–74) identified five key tourist zones for development (Bali, Jakarta, Yogyakarta, Solo, and North Sumatra) and outlined a tourism policy aimed at augmenting foreign exchange earnings, promoting Indonesia's natural and cultural resources, and reinforcing national and global solidarity. While the emphasis was heavily economic, Michel Picard observes that one should not underestimate the government's political objectives; just as Dutch colonialists had lassoed tourism's romantic imagery to expunge memories of their massacre of Balinese, the New Order regime's promotion of tourism helped replace international memories of Soeharto's violent rise to power with images of a peaceful and orderly multi-cultural nation (Picard 1996: 44).

Domestic tourism and nation-building

Indonesia's second Five-Year Plan (1975–1979) mapped a more specific growth plan and high-lighted tourism's contributions to local communities and national unity. This era saw the opening of Jakarta's "Beautiful Indonesia in Miniature Park" (*Taman Mini*), an ethnic theme park that exemplifies tourism's linkages to nation-building in the New Order era. Hailed as recreating Indonesia's cultural diversity in miniature, the park was designed to showcase Indonesia's exemplary cultural heritage to both insiders and outsiders (Pemberton 1994: 255). From the outset, as First Lady Soeharto explained at the park's opening ceremony, Taman Mini would encourage Indonesian visitors to "understand the culture, language and customs of their brothers from the other islands . . . [thereby] consolidat[ing] the cohesion and the unity of the nation" (cited in Freeman 1984: 231). The organization of the park conveys these unity-building aims: park zones for each of the nation's provinces showcase full-sized replicas of indigenous houses, dance performances, and regional material culture drawn from the same set of categories (weapons, baskets, marriage garments, and so on), regardless of the relevance of these categories to the particular ethnic group on display. For instance, the South Sulawesi pavilion displays wedding costumes of local groups, such as the Bugis and the Toraja, even though funeral attire would have been a more relevant category for the Toraja. Adherence to a uniform set of categories communicates that despite superficial differences, there is underlying commonality among the groups that constitute the nation (Adams 1998: 85).

Moreover, the park was designed to be experienced in provincial terms: the primary signs visible from the park's thoroughfares indicate only the names of provinces, not ethnic groups. The take-away point is that the province (not the ethnic group) is the source of regional culture (Hitchcock 1998: 131–2; see also, Picard 1997: 197–8).[2] As depicted in Taman Mini, provinces contribute colorful cultural pinnacles to Indonesia's national culture (Picard 1993: 93). In essence, for domestic tourists, the park aims to naturalize the state.

Yet, as anthropological studies of domestic tourists visiting New Order–era national-consciousness-building destinations in the 1990s and 2000s suggest, tourists bring their own cultural and persona agendas, which may contrast with or conflict with the state's vision of the sites' function. For instance, Edward Bruner's observations of Jakarta migrant Toba Batak families making recreational weekend visits to Taman Mini suggest that provincial and national identity are not salient to their visits. Rather, these Jakarta-based migrant Bataks celebrate and create their own versions of ethnic identity via picnics, concerts, and fashion shows in the park's Batak area, which serves as a homeland surrogate. As Bruner argues, urban Bataks reared far from the ancestral homeland are recreationally toying with ethnic identity in a space where they are "simultaneously the tourists and the toured" (Bruner 2005: 227). The Batak domestic tourists Bruner observed were exploring identity and heritage at a distance, through a sanitized version of their homeland. In this at-a-distance leisure setting, idealized ethnic identities seldom have occasion to clash with the often economically and emotionally charged familial and clan identities given preeminence in the Batak homeland.

In a similar vein, state-sponsored cultural festivals and official museum displays designed to foster shared provincial and national identities by stressing similar cultural themes for each provincial district (e.g., housing, textiles, and livelihoods) sometimes produced ironic outcomes. For instance, Alorese domestic tourists observed visiting Nusa Tenggara Timur's Provincial Museum in Kupang voiced disgruntlement at their island's frozen-in-time depiction in the museum's displays, which featured 1930s-era photographs, images of traditional houses, bronze drums, and what they considered poor-quality textiles. For many Alorese visitors, the displays (which stood adjacent to cases of sumptuous East Timorese textiles) were evidence of the province's disrespect for them as "backwards." Likewise, Chinese residents of Kupang voiced dismay at their absence from the museum's displays, which was, for them, a powerful reminder of their exclusion from the New Order era's vision of the nation (Adams 1999, 2003). In short, for some minority groups, domestic tourist sites sometimes inadvertently produce a sense of disenfranchisement from province or nation.

Blurring culture, tourism, and economics: "touristification," socioeconomic dreams, and schisms

Indonesia's Five-Year Plans of the last three and a half decades not only continue to emphasize tourism's role in strengthening national unity and identity, but (in tandem with rising tourist arrivals) these campaigns have also, directly and indirectly, encouraged even those residing far from the beaten tourist track to reimagine ethnic identities in terms of tourism. For instance, in preparation for a series of international tourism drives (e.g. Visit Indonesia Year 1991, Visit ASEAN Year 1992, and so on), in 1989, the Indonesian government initiated a Tourism Consciousness Campaign, which has continued to the current day (e.g. Departemen Kebudayaan dan Pariwisata 2008). The campaign delineated the "Seven Charms" (sapta pesona) to which all Indonesian groups should aspire. These tourist-pleasing charms included security, orderliness, friendliness, beauty, comfort, cleanliness, and memories. To this day, these "seven (touristic) charms" are featured in regionally-distributed booklets, detailed in Indonesian newspapers and blogs, discussed in local workshops, and posted on plaques in villages throughout Indonesia (e.g. http://pariwisata.ponorogo.go.id/articles/view?detail=gerakan-sadar-wisata-dan-aksi-sapta-pesona-di-telaga-ngebel, April 6, 2017).

For instance, as early as the mid-1990s, Indonesia's ubiquitous Tourism Consciousness Campaign was inspiring villagers on the seldom-visited island of Alor in East Nusatenggara to weigh and tout their own touristic charms and attracting powers vis-à-vis other more touristically famous Indonesian ethnic groups. As Alorese acquaintances were fond of declaring, the Seven Charms were every bit as present on Alor as they were on Bali, if not more so, since Alor lacks the debauchery for which Bali's Kuta Beach has become famous. Although the Tourism Consciousness Campaign has clearly helped craft visions of a new kind of "imagined community" based on shared notions of one's homeland's tourist-drawing charms, the competitive representation of Alor's "greater" (but still unrecognized) touristic charms merits our attention, as some local groups cannot help but recognize and resent that certain groups receive more promotion and tourism revenues than others (Adams 1997: 157–8; 2004:119).

It also pays to note that although local groups are reimagining themselves and their homelands in terms of the Tourism Consciousness Campaign's seven "touristic charms," the state's emphasis on these charms does not necessarily entail prioritizing the needs, comforts, or rights of indigenous groups. This has been a painful lesson for some groups who have found themselves on the wrong side of state tourism development plans. For instance, many Sasak residents of Gili Trawangan (a small island off Lombok's northwest coast in Eastern Indonesia) enjoyed a modest economic boost from small-scale, impromptu backpacker and dive tourism from the mid-1980s through the early 1990s. As the island gained popularity, backpackers began to establish tourism businesses and labor migrants began arriving from nearby islands, prompting population pressures and climbing land prices (Kamsma and Bras 2000; Hampton and Jeyacheya 2015). Elite national and regional investors eventually became aware of the economic potential of the island,

and soon thereafter, a new provincial Tourism Master Plan slated the island for beach and dive resort development. Locals were ordered to clear the zones designated for development, which they initially refused to do. This prompted a series of army-led land clearance operations in 1992, 1993, and 1995 that destroyed local tourism businesses and homes, displacing locals to fringe areas of the island (Kamsma and Bras 2000; Dickerson 2008).

While the New Order government clearly did not shy from using force to achieve its ends when local groups opposed national economic interests, the Reformasi era that began with Soeharto's fall in 1998 has ushered in new policies that ostensibly promise to return decision-making capabilities to local hands. The 2001 Autonomy Act initiated a process of decentralization that devolved financial and administrative decision making to regional and local governments. As part of decentralization, the central government now steers sizable tourism development funds to the local level to enact locally determined tourism development policies (Hampton and Jeyacheya 2015: 489).[3] Under Reformasi, the violent displacements on Gili Trawangan have ceased, yet islanders have yet to receive financial assistance from the regency and still find themselves unable to control tourism decision making on their island (Hampton and Jeyacheya 2015: 489). As Hollin Dickerson observes, "On the one hand, decentralisation could provide opportunities to resolve these conflicts through the local political process. On the other hand, it might give local governments a chance to assert greater authority over local land rights with no national oversight" (Dickerson 2008: n.p.).

The Reformasi era's decentralization policy has also had reverberations for regional campaigns and festivals targeting domestic tourists. (Under Reformasi, domestic tourism has become an increasingly important building block of recent Indonesian tourism policy, which now recognizes not only the nation-building potential but the economic potential of domestic tourists, who far out-number international tourists). Maribeth Erb (2009) studied several cultural festivals organized in two recently-divided Manggerai districts in western Flores. These cultural festivals were part of the Ministry of Tourism and Culture's "Archipelagic Tourism Glitter" (Geybar Wisata) domestic tourism campaign initiated in 2003. As she notes, the two districts' tourism boards conceptualized the "glitter" promised via tourism in very different ways and organized tourism endeavors accordingly. The Tourism Board head in Ruteng envisioned travel as a "new necessity" – part of a modern lifestyle increasingly important for the younger generation – and therefore set about identifying local leisure sites that promised to appeal to local residents (rather than targeting domestic and international tourists via cultural displays). His vision was to develop facilities and activities for the pleasure of local urban and nearby rural dwellers: playgrounds, beachside toilets, and concerts catering to local music tastes. By "civilizing" local behaviors via glittering touristic amenities and by cultivating local leisure tastes, he hoped to integrate tourism into the lives of Manggeraians, thereby engaging in a kind of cultural "ordering" that schooled locals in modernity (Erb 2009:180–1). In contrast, the neighboring Tourism Board in Labuan Bajo (a town planned in the 1980s as the "gateway" to Komodo National Park) opted to pursue the economic glitter embodied in international tourists and organized cultural displays, ethnic wedding song performances, races, and feasts targeting ever-elusive international visitors.[4] As Erb notes, these dreams of attracting foreign revenues took on a life of their own, as tourism board officials sought and received funding from Jakarta for their structural and cultural projects in the name of tourism (Erb 2009: 178, 181). In both these contrasting cases, we see visions of tourism routinizing ways of thinking about and mobilizing culture.

The reformulation of Indonesian cultural identities in terms of tourism is perhaps best exemplified by Michel Picard's long-term research on Bali. In the early years of New Order tourism development, a number of foreign consultants and anthropologists warned of mass tourism's looming threat for the vitality of local Indonesian cultures, and for Balinese culture in particular.

However, as Picard chronicles for Bali, older colonial, anthropological, and touristic representations of Bali in tandem with the New Order's conception of "culture as art" (Acciaioli 1985) so thoroughly homogenized and reified Balinese culture that tourism became inseparable from Balinese ideas about themselves, a phenomenon Picard terms "touristification" (Picard 1996, 2003).[5] In the post-New Order era of Reformasi, Balinese intellectuals, well aware of tourism's entanglement with their cultural notions of identity, have drawn on the idea of "Balineseness" in debates concerning the future course of tourism and the rights of Balinese to craft tourism policies that benefit Balinese, rather than outsiders (Picard 2003: 111).

Here, it is worth underscoring that the top-down mega-tourism development initiated in the Soeharto era has ultimately marginalized many Balinese who are largely unable to compete with outside investors. Although Bali's tourism sector generates US$3–5 billion annually, an estimated 85% of the tourist economy is controlled by non-Balinese (MacRae 2010; Cole 2016: 42). Not only has tourism drawn outside investors to Bali, but it has also attracted impoverished, predominantly Muslim migrant workers from other regions of Indonesia seeking tourism-sector jobs, a phenomenon Balinese perceive as unjust since the government pressed unemployed Balinese to transmigrate off-island (Picard 2003: 112). Bali's touristic image as an island paradise has also inspired an additional 30,000 foreign migrants to move to Bali (Cohen 2008, cited in Cole 2016: 36), creating further inequities in wealth and privilege. Tourism has thus fueled debates about which groups of Indonesians (wealthy Jakarta investors, Balinese, migrants, foreigners, and so on) have the right to shape Bali's future.

As tourism development has resulted in the disappearance of an estimated 1,000 hectares of rice fields annually, growing numbers of Balinese are finding themselves disenfranchised from landownership (Picard 2003: 111). Unrestrained tourism development has also resulted in overuse and contamination of Bali's groundwater, which has had ramifications for the health and well-being of the Balinese. With 65% of the island's water now diverted to tourism and the water table unsustainably low, poorer and lower-caste Balinese women have suffered the heaviest burden, as it is they who are responsible for securing water for washing and meal preparation. These women have little recourse when wells run dry, as they can ill afford to purchase bottled water (Cole 2016: 41). Moreover, poorer, lower-caste women are least able to register concerns in this patriarchal society, where only male household heads may participate in local decision making via territorial socio-cultural units known as *banjars* and where they risk being doubly censured for more public outcry (Cole 2016: 31, 41). In short, the flow of tourism-derived economic benefits and deficits is far from uniform, giving rise to additional caste, class, gender, and even regional tensions on the island.

Tourism in tumultuous times[6]

From the 1970s into the 1990s, the New Order's ability to keep religious and inter-regional tensions at bay benefitted tourism development, which in turn contributed to the nation's economic growth in this era (Dahles 2001: viii). The 1998 collapse of the New Order not only relaxed the government's top-down control of tourism in Indonesia's regions, but it also unleashed an era of more politicized ethnic and religious identities, as well as new shocks to Indonesia's tourism industry (Picard 2003: 109). Beginning around the time of the New Order's demise, Indonesia was struck by a series of crises that plummeted tourism arrivals to all-time lows. The Indonesian economic crisis (*krismon*) in early 1998, anti-Chinese rioting in Jakarta soon thereafter, inter-ethnic/religious violence elsewhere in Indonesia, the 2002 and 2005 bombings of tourist gathering spots in Bali, the 2003 Jakarta Marriott Hotel bombing, the Southeast Asian SARS scare, outbreaks of Avian influenza in Indonesia, earthquakes, and tsunamis, all took their tolls on tourism to the archipelago. For much of the 2000s, the external perception of Indonesia had shifted from tropical paradise to tropical disaster zone.

Yet, even in this context of diminished visitors, tourism has offered a lens for Indonesians to rethink ideas about self and other. For instance, Andrew Causey (2007) documents how Christian Toba Bataks, well aware of Western tourist fears of religious violence, encouraged tourists to spend their vacations in the hinterland Sumatra Batak homeland, since the Batak and their homeland are "safe." Via his study, we catch a glimpse of an emergent new twist on Toba Batak sensibilities concerning their group identity. Whereas in the past Toba Batak remoteness and traditional spiritual practices branded them as "dangerous headhunters," in the post-Bali-bombing and post-9/11 era, their remoteness becomes an asset and their Christianity facilitates bridge-building between themselves and Western tourists.

The tropes of safety and danger were equally relevant to the trickle of Western danger-zone tourists visiting East Timor in the late 1990s at the height of Indonesia-backed paramilitary genocide in the now-independent nation. Although drawn to East Timor for varied reasons (e.g. activism, desires to witness news as it unfolded, pursuit of adrenalin-rush experiences), the activities and blog reports of these tourists subtly shaped outsider understandings of the Indonesian state and had reverberations for nearby islanders' understandings of themselves. In the mid- and late 1990s, I interviewed a number of danger-zone tourists who had stopped on the nearby island of Alor while en route home from witnessing violence in East Timor. Most had not planned to visit Alor but were seduced by the tranquility of Alor's scenic port. On these stopovers, impromptu visitors readily shared with locals their impressions of the contrasts between East Timor's tensions and violence and the peacefulness of Alor. Alorese self-representations had long stressed "ruggedness," the island's profusion of languages, or its abundance of bronze gongs, yet by the late 1990s, the image of ruggedness was receding, and some Alorese were foregrounding these newer, danger-zone-tourist-inspired images of "peacefulness" and "beauty." As the Alor case suggests, even small numbers of tourists visiting Indonesia in tumultuous times can play a potent role in reshaping indigenous self-imagery and sensibilities concerning place (Adams 2001).

Some of the most interesting research on tumult, tourism, and identity dynamics in the current era derives from Bali. The aftermath of the 2002 and 2005 Bali bombings prompted tourism scholarship on the complex (and sometimes deadly) interplay between religious, cultural, ethnic, and regional identities and tourism, all of which are in dialogue with state policies and global religious movements. From Picard (1996, 2009) and Pederson (2009), we know that Bali's touristic packaging as a lone Hindu zone in a Muslim nation obscured the actual religious diversity on the island. Moreover, the ubiquitous travel imagery of Bali as an idyllic Hindu island rendered Bali's historic Muslim communities and immigrant Muslims seemingly out-of-place "outsider" ethno-religious groups. Hitchcock and Putra (2007) have chronicled how, in the aftermath of the bombings, religiously and culturally diverse local and global stakeholders came together to rebuild Bali's devastated tourism-based economy.

Shinji Yamashita (2012) recently offered further evidence of the convergence of tourism, spiritual healing, and multiculturalism in the form of an annual "Echo of Peace Event" (Gema Perdamaian) initiated in 2012 by Bali's tourism business community. Initially a tourism-resuscitation strategy, this annual spiritual festival has blossomed into a movement that fosters a new kind of plural, multi-ethnic, multi-religious conception of a broader peace-oriented community. As Yamashita describes, it draws together tourists and locals from different faiths to dance together to Hare Krishna music in their own styles. Via his study, we can see how sites of tragedy can become creative venues for fostering new spiritual identities and for fueling novel "umbrella group" sensibilities. In sum, spiritual tourism appears to have a diverse array of ramifications for ethnicity in today's era of heightened religious identity consciousness.

Merantau and tourism: back to the future?

When the tumult of the late 1990s and 2000s struck, many Indonesian communities that had come to depend on tourism-derived income faced the challenge of finding new audiences for their cultural "products." While the national government turned to pushing domestic tourism more aggressively (as noted earlier), hotels, restaurants, and travel agencies in many areas still faced sluggish revenues. This was the case in the Sa'dan Toraja highlands in Upland Sulawesi, where I have based much of my research since the mid-1980s. At tourism's mid-1990s apex, 50,000 foreign tourists and 200,000 "domestic tourists" were visiting annually (Adams 2006). A decade later, international tourism had slowed to a trickle, severely damaging the local economy. In 2006, local Toraja officials gravitated to a new source of revenue: Courting Toraja migrants and their families to return to the ancestral homeland for vacation visits. An initial "Lovely December Festival" – subsequently dubbed a "Longing to Return Home to Toraja Festival" – was organized to boost tourism revenues and hotel bookings during the tourist off-season. Entertainment, welcoming parades, food, and dance displays as well as holiday fireworks and hotel discounts were all part of the enticement. Heavily promoted on social media and in the news, the event was a resounding success. Today, the festival is an annual event, drawing thousands of return migrant-tourists each December.

In many ways, the festival can be seen as reconstituting, in novel form, an older Indonesian pattern of mobility known as *merantau* (a form of circular migration wherein one voluntarily departs one's homeland seeking livelihood, fortune, or experience, ultimately returning home with enhanced status). As Noel Salazar (2016) notes, for many Indonesians, merantau has evolved from circular migration to more permanent migration, yet the ubiquity of cell phones, cyber-, and actual travel means that "home" is no longer located in a fixed locale. For a number of the Toraja migrants I interviewed, the allure of a temporary "touristic" return for the Lovely December Festival was the promise of being able to satisfy one's longings for home without the daunting financial burdens and expectations normally tethered to a more permanent return.

Here, a clarification concerning Toraja ritual practices is necessary. For Torajans, ancestral houses and funerals are inseparable from cultural and familial identities. Contributing funds to house consecration rituals and repaying prior generations' mortuary debts by gifting exorbitantly priced water buffalo at funerals for house-based kin are key paths for maintaining and nurturing familial relations. Yet, for many Toraja migrants toiling in low-paying jobs, these costs entailed in returning temporarily for funeral rituals (or more permanently) are prohibitive. Thus, the migrant-oriented Lovely December Festival provides an alternative and far less costly avenue for temporary return visits. As Lina, a first-generation migrant, explained, "I don't want to oblige my kids to get tangled up in Toraja ritual customs [euphemism for debt], but the Lovely December Festival interests me. There's art, Toraja clothing, bamboo music, traditional dances." Lina's comments suggest that part of the festival's appeal is the opportunity to connect to ancestral heritage, but not too deeply. The connections being forged are all aesthetic yet anesthetized, divorced from the realm of house-family duties and funeral debts. In short, Lina and other migrant-tourists returning for the Lovely December Festival are consuming Heritage-Lite. In the creative touristic borderzone space of the festival, they have found a less-burdensome way to periodically re-inhabit their ancestral culture.

Closing thoughts

As these case studies illustrate, tourism in Indonesia is far more than simply a component of the economy that contributes to Indonesia's foreign exchange revenues. Tourism has a long history of being entangled in political projects, beginning with the Dutch and running through the New Order to the present day. New Order–era tourist sites, such as Taman Mini, were designed not only to showcase Indonesia's glorious cultural heritage to the world, underscoring the nation's worthiness on the global political stage, but also to instill a sense of "unity in diversity" and nourish national pride among visiting domestic tourists. Yet domestic tourists digest the state's messages at these sites in their own ways, filtering them through their own ethnic and personal perspectives.

Likewise, the state's use of tourism to cultivate provincially oriented identities and to fuse these identities with the arts has had unexpected reverberations on Bali and elsewhere, where tourism has become an inextricable dimension of ethno-cultural identity. Moreover, state-, provincial-, and regency-based tourism campaigns and festivals, which are often designed to chase revenues, have prompted Indonesian groups to re-imagine themselves and mobilize culture in new ways. In sum, "Wonderful Indonesia's" yellow brick road of tourism may not always lead to riches (particularly in tumultuous times), but it always seems to meander into the terrain of politics, identity, and inter-group sensibilities.

Notes

1 We catch a glimpse of this via a scene in the classic 1955 political satire *Tamu Agung*, which depicts a Javanese village head discussing plans to embrace tourism development to enable the village to join the modern world (Vickers 2011: 460).

2 Writing about New Order–era tourism, Wood suggests that this de-emphasis on ethnicity per se

> presumably serves to mask Javanese political dominance and Chinese economic dominance [in the New Order era] . . . touristically, Indonesia's Chinese minority – the largest in Southeast Asia – is completely erased. . . [from] government tourist promotion and not recognized at Mini Indonesia or its regional institutions.
>
> *(Wood 1997: 26)*

Likewise, Indonesia's museum displays and cultural festivals in this era (destinations frequented by school groups and domestic tourists) reflected similar erasures of the nation's Chinese population and Chinese spiritual practices (Adams 1999, 2003). A Chinese temple pavilion was added to Taman Mini after the fall of the New Order government.

3 As of 2010, these funds amounted to over US$200,000 annually (Furqan and Puad Mat Som 2010, cited in Hampton and Jeyacheya 2015: 489).

4 Most tourists visit the islands that constitute Komodo National Park by boat, thus they rarely set foot in Labuan Bajo, Flores.

5 Various scholars have explored the ways in which tourism has comingled with cultural arts and ethnic identity in different Indonesian locales, highlighting in particular relationships between tourist-inspired arts and individual and group agency (e.g. Forshee 2001, Causey 2003, Adams 2006).

6 Similar versions of paragraphs 2, 4, and 5 of this section were previously published (Adams 2016).

References cited

Acciaioli, Greg. 1985. "Culture as Art: From Practice to Spectacle in Indonesia," *Canberra Anthropology* 8(1–2): 148–72.

Adams, Kathleen M. 1997. "Touting Touristic Primadonas: On Tourism, Ethnic Negotiation, and National Integration in Sulawesi Indonesia," in Michel Picard and Robert Wood, eds., *Tourism, Ethnicity, and the State in Asian and Pacific Societies* (Honolulu: University of Hawaii Press), pp. 264–275.

———. 1998. "Domestic Tourism and Nation-Building in South Sulawesi, Indonesia," *Indonesia and the Malay World* 26(75): 77–96.

———. 1999. "Identités Ethniques, Régionales et Nationales dans les Musées Indonésiens," *Ethnologie Française* 29(3): 355–64.

————. 2001. "Danger-Zone Tourism: Prospects and Problematics for Tourism in Tumultuous Times," in Peggy Teo, T. C. Chang and K. C. Ho, eds., *Interconnected Worlds: Tourism in Southeast Asia* (Oxford: Elsevier Science), pp. 265–81.

————. 2003. "Museum/City/Nation: Negotiating Meaning and Identities in Urban Museums in Indonesia and Singapore," in Robbie Goh and Brenda Yeoh, eds., *Theorizing the Southeast Asian City as Text: Urban Landscapes, Cultural Documents and Interpretative Experiences* (Singapore: World Scientific Press), pp. 135–58.

————. 2004. "The Genesis of Touristic Imagery: Politics and Poetics in the Creation of a Remote Indonesian Destination," *Tourist Studies* 4(2): 115–35.

————. 2006. *Art as Politics: Re-Crafting Identities, Tourism, and Power in Tana Toraja, Indonesia* (Honolulu: University of Hawaii Press).

————. 2016. "Tourism and Ethnicity in Insular Southeast Asia: Eating, Praying, Loving and Beyond," *Asian Journal of Tourism Research* 1(1): 1–28.

Bruner, Edward M. 2005. "Taman Mini: Self Constructions in an Ethnic Theme Park in Indonesia," in Edward Bruner, ed., *Culture on Tour* (Chicago: University of Chicago Press), pp. 211–30.

Causey, Andrew. 2003. *Hard Bargaining in Sumatra: Western Travelers and Toba Bataks in the Marketplace of Souvenirs* (Honolulu: University of Hawaii Press).

————. 2007. "'Go Back to the Batak: It's Safe There': Tourism in North Sumatra During Perilous Times," *Indonesia and the Malay World* 35(103): 257–71.

Cole, Stroma. 2016. "A Gendered Political Economy of Tourism and Water," in Mary Mostafanezhad, Roger Norum et al., eds., *Political Ecology of Tourism: Community, Power and the Environment* (London: Routledge), pp. 31–49.

Dahles, Heidi. 2001. *Tourism, Heritage and National Culture in Java* (Leiden: International Institute for Asian Studies/Curzon).

Departemen Kebudayaan dan Pariwisata. 2008. *Sadar Wisata dan Sapta Pesona: Buku Saku* (Jakarta: Direktorat Jenderal Pengembangan Destinasi Pariwisata, Departemen Kebudayaan dan Pariwisata).

Dickerson, Hollin. 2008. "Trouble in Paradise," *Inside Indonesia* 92, April-June, at www.insideindonesia.org/trouble-in-paradise (Accessed 28 March 2017).

Erb, Maribeth. 2009. "Tourism as Glitter: Re-examining Domestic Tourism in Indonesia," in Tim Winter, Peggy Teo, and T. C. Chang (eds.) *Asia on Tour: Exploring the Rise of Asian Tourism* (London: Routledge), pp. 170–82.

Forshee, Jill. 2001. *Between the Folds: Stories of Cloth, Lives and Travels From Sumba* (Honolulu: University of Hawaii Press).

Freeman, John. 1984. "Taman Mini: A Nation in Miniature," *Kaleidoscope International* 9(1): 230–5.

Furqan, Alhilal and Ahmad Puad Mat Som. 2010. "Effects of Decentralization Policy on Island Destinations in Indonesia," *World Applied Sciences Journal* 10: 63–70.

Gunawan, Myra P. 1997. "National Planning for Indonesia's Tourism," *Pacific Tourism Review* 1(1): 47–56.

Hampton, Mark P. and Julian Clifton. 2017. "Tourism in Indonesia," in C. Michael Hall and Stephen J. Page, eds., *The Routledge Handbook of Tourism in Asia* (London and New York: Routledge), pp. 181–90.

Hampton, Mark P. and Julia Jeyacheya. 2015. "Power, Ownership and Tourism in Small Islands: Evidence from Indonesia," *World Development* 70: 481–95.

Hitchcock, Michael. 1998. "Tourism, *Taman Mini*, and National Identity," *Indonesia and the Malay World* 26(75): 124–35.

Hitchcock, Michael and I. Nyoman Darma Putra. 2007. *Tourism, Development and Terrorism in Bali* (Burlington: Ashgate Publishing Company).

Kamsma, Theo and Karin Bras. 2000. "Gili Trawangan: From Desert Island to 'Marginal' Paradise Local Participation, Small-scale Entrepreneurs and Outside Investors in an Indonesian Tourism Destination," in Greg Richards and Derek Hall (eds.), *Tourism and Sustainable Community Development* (London and New York: Routledge), pp. 170–84.

Kodhyat, H. 1996. *Sejarah Pariwisata dan Perkembangan di Indonesia* (Jakarta: Gramedia Widiasarana Indonesia untuk Lembaga Studi Pariwisata Indonesia).

MacRae, Graeme. 2010. "If Indonesia Is Too Hard to Understand, Let's Start With Bali," *Journal of Indonesian Social Sciences and Humanities* 3: 11–36.

Pederson, Lene. 2009. "Keeping Bali Strong," *Inside Indonesia*, 95. 8 February 2009. www.insideindonesia.org/keeping-bali-strong (Accessed 18 October 2016).

Pemberton, John. 1994. "Recollections from 'Beautiful Indonesia' (Somewhere Beyond the Postmodern)," *Public Culture* 6(2): 241–62.

Picard, Michel. 1993. "'Cultural Tourism' in Bali: National Integration and Regional Differentiation," in Victor T. King and Michael Parnwell, eds., *Tourism in Southeast Asia* (London: Routledge), pp. 71–98.

———. 1996. *Bali: Cultural Tourism and Touristic Culture* (Singapore: Archipelago Press).

———. 1997. "Cultural Tourism, Nation-Building and Regional Culture: The Making of a Balinese Identity," in Michel Picard and Robert Wood, eds., *Tourism, Ethnicity and the State in Asian and Pacific Societies* (Honolulu: University of Hawaii Press), pp. 181–214.

———. 2003. "Touristification and Balinization in a Time of Reformasi," *Indonesia and the Malay World* 31(89): 108–18.

———. 2009. "Tourism and Balinese Identity in the Aftermath of the Kuta Bombing," in Michael Hitchcock, Victor T. King, and Michael Parnwell (eds.), *Tourism in Southeast Asia: Challenges and New Directions* (Copenhagen: NIAS Press), pp. 99–131.

Salazar, Noel B. 2016. "The (Im)mobility of *Merantau* as a Sociocultural Practice in Indonesia," in Nataša Gregorič Bon and Jaka Repič, eds., *Moving Places: Relations, Return and Belonging* (New York and Oxford: Berghahn), pp. 21–42.

Vickers, Adrian. 1989. *Bali: A Paradise Created* (Berkeley: Periplus Editions).

———. 2011. "Bali Rebuilds its Tourist Industry," *Bijdragen tot de Taal-, Land- en Volkenkunde* 167(4): 459–81.

Wood, Robert. 1997. "Tourism and the State: Ethnic Options and Constructions of Otherness," in Michel Picard and Robert Wood, eds., *Tourism, Ethnicity and the State in Asian and Pacific Societies* (Honolulu: University of Hawaii Press), pp. 1–34.

World Bank. 2017. "International Tourism, Number of Arrivals." *Data by Country (Indonesia).* http://data.worldbank.org/indicator/ST.INT.ARVL?locations=ID&view=chart (Accessed 22 February 2017).

Yamashita, Shinji. 2012. "*Gema Perdamaian*: Tourism, Religion and Peace in Multicultural Bali." Paper presented at the Conference Bali in Global Asia Between Modernization and Heritage Formation, Den Pasar, Bali, July 16–18.

PART IV

Muslims and religious plurality

17

THE RELIGIOUS FIELD

Plural legacies and contemporary contestations

Robert W. Hefner

In all modern societies, the public nature and influence of religious traditions depend upon an evolving interplay of societal values, state practices, and competition between rival socio-political groupings intent on promoting their vision of and structures for religious flourishing. A Muslim-majority country characterized by a high degree of religious plurality, Indonesia has long witnessed competition between, on one hand, conservative groupings hoping to restrict the country's religious diversity and, on the other, pluralist actors determined to defend Indonesian traditions of nationalist pluralism and co-existence. In the post-1998 Reformasi era, these contests have been drawn into ongoing discussions as to whether Indonesia can serve as a model with regard to Islam, pluralism, and democracy or whether current trends place the country's pluralist legacies in peril.

This chapter examines the nature of the religious field in Indonesia. It focuses in particular on trends in and interactions between state and religious society since 1998 and the social and political history that gave rise to Reformasi-era dynamics.

Muslim majority, religiously plural

Of Indonesia's almost 260 million people, some 87.2% self-identify in national censuses as Muslim. Although the country has dozens of smaller religious currents, only six are accorded state recognition as "religions" (*agama*). The latter standing brings with it administrative bureaus in and subsidies from the Ministry of Religious Affairs (MORA). In addition to Islam, the state-recognized religions include Catholicism and Protestantism (each counted as a separate religion, with Protestants comprising 7% and Catholics 2.9% of the national population); Hinduism (1.69%); Buddhism (0.72%); and Confucianism (0.05%). Although official data are lacking, there are also some two or three hundred thousand practitioners of local religions, which are not recognized by the state, and a comparable number of people in various new religious movements, commonly referred to as, not religions, but *kepercayaan* (lit., "beliefs," "spiritual beliefs") or *aliran kebatinan* ("spiritual currents").

The question of just how the country's diverse faith traditions are to co-exist within the framework of the Indonesian nation-state has been a matter of dispute since the dawn of the republic in 1945 (see Bagir, Butt, Lindsey, and Ramstedt chapters). The constitution and the associated state philosophy, known as the Pancasila ("Five Principles") affirm principles of religious freedom but do so in a way that balances religious freedom with other interests, including national security and public morals (Butt and Lindsey 2012).

The first of the state philosophy's principles is *Ketuhanan yang Maha Esa*, or "belief in Almighty God." This principle had its origins in a longer formulation approved by secular and Muslim nationalist leaders at a meeting of the Japanese-convened Investigating Body for the Preparation of Independence (BPUPK) on June 22, 1945, in the run-up to the Indonesian declaration of independence on August 17, 1945. In its original and longer form, this principle included seven words that stipulated that the state was obliged "to carry out Islamic shariah for Muslim adherents," a phrasing that in the years since has come to be known as the Jakarta Charter. One day after the declaration of independence, the seven words were abruptly deleted from the Pancasila. The deletion occurred after the second most prominent of the new republic's leaders, Mohammad Hatta, approached Muslim delegates on the independence committee to plead that Christian leaders in eastern Indonesia might withdraw from the republic if the newly formed government mandated state implementation of Islamic law. As a concession to Muslim delegates, the first principle's reference to "belief in God" (Ketuhanan) was expanded to include the words, *yang Maha Esa* ("belief in an all-powerful God"); the phrase is typically interpreted to imply the state is committed to promoting a monotheistic form of religiosity broadly consistent with the core Islamic doctrine of God's unicity (*tauhid*). Muslim party leaders are also said to have agreed to the Ketuhanan switch because they were confident that, once national elections were held, parties committed to the implementation of Islamic law would prevail. As it turned out, Muslim parties were to be disappointed in this latter regard during each of the country's subsequent elections. As a result, revival of the Jakarta Charter has remained a rallying cry among Indonesian Islamists to this day.

Although designed to underscore that Indonesia is not a secularist state but a religious nation founded on belief in God, the first principle of the Pancasila also implies that, although Muslims might comprise the majority of Indonesia's population, neither Islam nor any other religion is accorded the privileged status of sole religion of the state. Article 29 in the original 1945 Constitution reinforces this message, stating that "The state guarantees all persons the freedom to embrace their religion and to worship (*beribadat*) in accordance with their religion (*agama*) and beliefs (*kepercayaan*)." However, in article 28J(2), the 1945 Constitution also makes clear that under certain conditions, religious freedom can be limited, especially when it imperils "the rights and freedoms of others," or is in some way deleterious to the "moral considerations, religious values, security, and public order in a democratic society."

Since the final years of Indonesia's "Guided Democracy" (1959–1965) and over the course of the authoritarian New Order state (1966–1998), Indonesia's rulers have invoked the latter clause to justify significant restrictions on religious freedoms. Against this backdrop, in 2001, reform-minded legislators introduced a constitutional amendment (article 28E) designed to strengthen protections for religious life. The amendment stated that, "Each person is free to embrace their religion and to worship (*beribadat*) in accordance with their religion," and "Each person has the freedom to possess beliefs (*kepercayaan*), and to express their thoughts and attitudes in accordance with their conscience." Another amendment (28I(1)) included among the same package of Reform-era amendments borrowed language from the Universal Declaration of Human Rights to state that that the "right to have a religion" (Ind., *hak beragama*) was one among several human rights "that cannot be limited under any circumstance" (Lindsey and Butt 2016:22; cf. Hosen 2007).

Although the Reform-era amendments seemed to strengthen constitutional protections for religious freedom, the second of the two amendments mentions only the "right to have a religion" and does not explicitly protect public *practices* associated with a religion. It thus leaves the door open to the understanding that, although private beliefs enjoy constitutional protection, religious practices that undermine public order or morality might yet be legitimately circumscribed. As it happened, after the dizzy days of liberal democratic reform from 1999–2002, Indonesia's Constitutional Court (Mahkamah Konstitusi) issued rulings affirming just such a restrictive interpretation of religious freedom. Established in 2003, the court was intended by its designers "to re-establish Indonesia as a liberal constitutional democracy with a separation of powers" (Lindsey and Butt 2016: 20; see also Butt and Lindsey chapters). To a significant degree, the Constitutional Court *has* succeeded in strengthening the separation of state powers, a separation that was regularly compromised in the 1950s and during Soeharto's New Order government (1966–1998; see Feith 2006). On matters of religious freedom, however, the court has also made clear that it views the right as more readily subject to circumscription than most human-rights activists had hoped. In this regard, the court's non-liberal views are consistent with those held by most of the Indonesian public.

Campaigns for state-enforced shariah

It was not just the Constitutional Court that pushed questions about religion and public life into the public square in the early Reformasi period. A new generation of conservative Islamists appeared on the scene during these same years and proclaimed that shariah law is of a higher legal and moral standing than national law and that the state must recognize this fact and make greater accommodations to Islamic legal traditions. This was not just a matter of polite legal argument. Citing the longstanding Islamic ethical principle to "command right and forbid wrong" (Cook 2001), militants in vigilante groups like the Islamic Defenders Front (FPI, see Bamualim 2011; Pausacker 2013; Wilson 2006) took advantage of the relative vacuum of state power in the early Reform era to mount shows-of-force aimed at imposing their ethical views on business and social establishments. The vigilantes also attacked Muslim minorities they regarded as "deviant" (*sesat*) and moved to monitor and restrict the construction of Christian churches in urban areas the activists deemed Muslim (Ali-Fauzi et al. 2011; Crouch 2014:127–28; Human Rights Watch 2013). Some among these Islamist militias, including the leader of the Islamic Defenders Front (Front Pembela Islam), insisted that democracy *is* un-Islamic and that the only form of government consistent with Islam is a state based on shariah law (Feillard and Madinier 2006: 117–20; Jamhari and Jahroni 2004). This view was at variance with majority opinion among the Muslim public at large.

The campaign to bring about a greater accommodation of Islamic norms (conservatively understood) in national law also took place through legislative channels. In 2000–2001, the Islamist leadership of the Moon and Stars Party (Partai Bulan Bintang, PBB) and the United Development Party (Partai Pembangunan dan Persatuan, PPP) introduced a proposal to amend the constitution so as to require the state to enforce Islamic law for Muslim citizens, as the Jakarta Charter had envisioned. Notwithstanding pressure from Islamist conservatives, in 2001, Indonesia's parliament voted down the proposal. One of the reasons the "nay" vote proved so one-sided is that the leadership of Indonesia's two largest Muslim associations, the Muhammadiyah and Nahdlatul Ulama, made clear their opposition to the amendment (Salim 2008). The largest Muslim social welfare association in the world, the Nahdlatul Ulama has some 35–45 million followers; more urban, centralized, and middle class, the Muhammadiyah has 25 million. Although their membership's political views range from puritan-conservative to pluralist progressive (Feillard 1995; Kersten 2015; Nakamura 2012), the leadership of both organizations in the early Reformasi period used their organizational perches to defend electoral democracy and Indonesia's Pancasila heritage of multi-religious nationalism (cf. Burhani 2013).

Having failed in 2001 to secure a constitutional amendment in parliament, some in Indonesia's Islamist community began to explore other avenues in their campaign for state-enforced shariah. The two most important strategies pursued were, first, pressuring provincial, district, and city governments to implement "regional bylaws" (*peraturan daerah*) designed to promote shariah-compliant behaviors in matters of dress, worship, and entertainment, and, second, using the courts to challenge state-imposed limitations on the jurisdiction of Islamic law, on the grounds that such limitations infringe Muslims' constitutionally protected religious freedom.

In the six years that followed the defeat of the constitutional amendment requiring implementation of shariah law at the national level, conservative Muslim activists joined forces with political parties – including some long regarded as "secular nationalist" rather than Islamist (see Buehler 2016) – to pass "shariah-oriented regional regulations" (*peraturan daerah syariah Islam*) in 53 of the country's 470 districts and municipalities. The substance of almost half of these regulations is not directly derived from shariah but seeks simply to outlaw or limit gambling, prostitution, and the consumption of alcohol (Bush 2008:176; Salim 2008). The remaining 55% of the regional regulations *do* reference explicitly Islamic concerns, mandating mastery of basic religious skills or duties, such as reading the Quran or paying religious alms (zakat), and the wearing of dress deemed Islamic in schools and government offices.

With the notable exception of the special province of Aceh (see Afrianty and Salim chapters, and Feener 2013), none of the regional regulations sought to enforce Islamic criminal law; none too applied the harsh *hudud* penalties mandated in classical Islamic jurisprudence. However, the more controversial features of Islamic law were by no means entirely missing from public discussion. Militants involved in the regional campaigns, like the Party of Liberation (Hizbut Tahrir) and the Indonesian Council of Jihadi Fighters (MMI), continued to call for a totalizing implementation of Islamic law, on the grounds that this alone could "save" (*selamatkan*) Indonesia from moral and political decline (cf. Fealy and Hooker 2006: 163–65, 178–80). Although less inclined to call for sweeping changes to the constitution, conservative activists on the Indonesian Council of Ulama (MUI; Hasyim 2014; Ichwan 2013) also sought to extend the scope of shariah-influenced legislation.

The courts have proved another channel through which conservative Islamists have sought to extend the scope of shariah regulations. In 2007, a Muslim plaintiff petitioned the Constitutional Court claiming that Law No. 1 of 1974 on Marriage – which does not forbid but places serious legal restrictions on Muslim men's right to have more than one wife (see Butt and Lindsey chapters, and Cammack, Young, and Heaton 1996; Robinson 2009: 84–7) – violated his religious freedom as a Muslim. In a separate case in 2008, another plaintiff filed a petition with the Constitutional Court, arguing that Law No. 7/1989 on Religious Courts violated his religious freedom by not allowing Islamic courts to operate in all domains of public life, including in matters of criminal law. This plaintiff's legal team argued that God intended Islamic law to apply to the whole of human experience. Legislation that precludes the law's implementation in, for example, matters of criminal law, then, violates Muslims' freedom of religion.

In 2007 and 2008, the Constitutional Court issued rulings flatly rejecting these claims. In the polygamy case, the court argued that the state had not just the authority but the *obligation* to restrict the right of men to have more than one wife, so as to safeguard the rights òf mothers and children. In its 2008 ruling on the Islamic courts and criminal law, the court declared that, "In this Republic of Indonesia, the highest law is the 1945 Constitution, not the Qur'an," and it went on to state that the jurisdiction of the Religious Courts was to be determined solely by the nation's legislature (Lindsey and Butt 2016: 21). In these and other Reformasi-era rulings, the Constitutional Court has consistently ruled against conservative Islamists, upholding the principles of Indonesia as a sovereign and multi-religious nation-state.

Even as it has deflected conservative Islamist appeals, the Constitutional Court has made clear that it regards the state as having a legitimate stake in the promotion of religion and the curbing of heterodoxy. This ruling has been one element in a series of changes that have shaken religion–state relations since the Reformasi era, not least with regard to the policing of religious expression.

Religious freedom and blasphemy controls

One of the most decisive rulings the Constitutional Court made in its first years of operation concerned the state's right to take action against those who "misuse" or "defame" any of the religions officially recognized in Indonesia. The law this ruling upheld is commonly referred to as Indonesia's "Blasphemy Law." However, the law actually touches on matters more far-reaching than religious defamation alone (see Bagir 2013, and this volume). It 1) affirms the state's right to restrict religious activity in the name of public order, 2) distinguishes a higher and more legally authoritative category of "religion" (agama) from a less extensively protected category of "spiritual beliefs" (kepercayaan), 3) authorizes the state to take action against those who show "enmity" toward or otherwise misuse, dishonor, or deviate from state-recognized religions, and 4) encourages the state in conjunction with religious authorities in society to protect orthodox religion from religious deviation.

The court's 2010 ruling built directly on two legal precedents, both products of troubled periods in Indonesian history. The first and most important precedent was an edict issued by President Sukarno on January 27, 1965, and known as Presidential Stipulation No. 1/PNPS/1965 on "Preventing the Misuse and Defamation of Religion" (Penetapan Presiden No. 1/1965 tentang Pencegahan, Penyalagunaan, dan/atau Penodaan Agama). Sukarno issued this edict just eight months prior to the catastrophic violence that led to his ouster and the rise of Soeharto's New Order in late 1965. Four years later, Sukarno's 1965 stipulation was given full legal standing when Soeharto's New Order regime elevated it to the status of national law (Law No. 5/PnPs/1969). A telling indication of the law's high-modernist spirit, New Order legislation described the law as authorizing the new, military-dominated government "to guide (*memberikan bimbingan*), administer (*pengurusan*), and control (*pengawasan*) all religious activities" (Ropi 2012: 154).

The fact that in January 1965, it was the staunchly nationalist President Sukarno who put in place the legal foundation for far-reaching controls on religion and heterodoxy has long struck observers as paradoxical, because the community most harmed by the regulation was the syncretic or non-standard Muslims (see below) who were among Sukarno's most loyal supporters. However, the rationale for the edict lay less in the president's religious preferences than in his desperate effort at the time to hold up a collapsing base of support in the Muslim wing of his ruling coalition. Six years prior to issuing the presidential stipulation, Sukarno had dismissed Indonesia's parliament and introduced a presidentially dominated "Guided Democracy" (Feith 2006; Lev 1966). In an effort to forge a new governing coalition, Sukarno cobbled together what he described as the NASAKOM alliance (an acronym for "Nationalism-Religion-Communism"), which rested on three pillars: Sukarno's nationalist supporters, the even larger Indonesian Communist Party, and the wing of the Muslim community associated with the traditionalist and fiercely anti-communist Nahdlatul Ulama (see Boland 1982: 102). A teetering edifice from the start, by late 1964, the three partners in the NASAKOM alliance had fallen into infighting. This conflict between ostensible coalition allies gave strategic urgency to Sukarno's issuing of the presidential stipulation, widely seen as a palliative to the Muslim wing of his coalition.

What made Sukarno's edict of particular interest to NU and others in the Muslim community was not coalitional politics but a matter of a more specifically religious nature: the fact that the fifteen years prior to the edict had seen the explosive growth of new religious movements known as aliran kebatinan, "spiritual belief currents." Although the earliest aliran kebatinan movements had been established in Central Java in the 1890s, most of the better organized aliran kebatinan had been founded in the last years of Dutch colonial rule (Geels 1997; Mulder 1978; Stange 1980). They experienced their most spectacular growth in the Javanese countryside in the 1950s, as rival Muslim, nationalist, and communist organizations used religious appeals to mobilize followers. Not coincidentally, the larger kebatinan groupings recruited their core membership from among ethnic Javanese of less orthodox Muslim persuasion. They did so at a time when party rivalries and Muslim reformist campaigns were leading some syncretic Muslims to wonder whether they were really Muslim at all. In 1955, kebatinan groups joined forces to form the Congressional Body for Indonesian Kebatinan (Badan Kongres Kebatinan Indonesia). In 1957, the congress issued a declaration stating that the first or Ketuhanan principle of the Pancasila was actually a concept inspired by kebatinan, not by Islam. Congressional officials also declared that their religion was the "original religion" (*agama asli*) of all Indonesians. A small minority in the kebatinan community even spoke disparagingly of Islam as "an imported religion" (Ropi 2012:141). These anti-Islamic declarations confirmed Muslim leaders' belief that the kebatinan movement was an imminent and growing threat.

This, then, was the context in which President Sukarno issued his edict on religious defamation. What made the edict of such lasting political importance was that it affected, not just kebatinan groups, but the entire landscape of state policy on religion. In particular, buried in the edict's four articles were two measures long advocated by officials in the Ministry of Religious Affairs as well as by Muslim social organizations but long opposed by secular nationalists, religious minorities, and the nationalist and communist leadership.

The first of the two measures was that, for the first time in the republic's history, the state listed just which among the nation's many faith traditions it officially recognized as "religions" (agama). The Muslim-dominated Ministry of Religious Affairs (MORA) had long argued for the creation of such a list and had quite specific ideas of what was required to be included on it. When first approached in 1952 by Balinese requesting that their Hindu faith be included among those recognized by the state, MORA officials responded by explaining that a "religion" (agama) had to meet three doctrinal criteria: recognize a unitary God, acknowledge a prophet or founding seer, and preserve and transmit a holy scripture (*kitab*). In addition, the ministry explained, the religion had to enjoy international recognition; it could not merely be a local religion (Ropi 2012:138; see also Bakker 1993; Picard 2011; see also Ramstedt chapter). Based on a Muslim reformist understanding of religion but broadly consistent with Indonesian Christian sentiments (Aragon 1996; Atkinson 1987), this restrictive formula was to have a transformative effect on religious governance in Indonesia.

The second of the two regulatory shifts inaugurated by the 1965 presidential edict had to do with prohibiting state support for spiritual movements deemed to be "deviating from" (*sesat*) or showing "enmity" toward the country's state-recognized religions (Crouch 2014: 22–3, 161–63; Lindsey and Butt 2016: 24). Articles 2 and 3 put in place mechanisms by which the president can warn, ban, or jail those who misuse or defame one of Indonesia's recognized religions. Article 4 put in place provisions in the criminal code to allow authorities to take action against citizens alleged to have violated the regulation, with a threat of imprisonment for up to five years.

In short, the 1965 edict and its 1969 legislative successor laid the legal foundation for heighted state involvement in the policing of religious orthodoxy and the prosecution of heterodoxy. The legislation extended state recognition and support to the category of faith traditions officially recognized as "religion" (agama). In principle, the constitution still extended legal protections to "spiritual beliefs" (kepercayaan), and during the heyday of amendment-making in the early post-Soeharto era, those provisions were strengthened, at least on paper. However, the Defamation Law established a clear and asymmetrical hierarchy between religion and spiritual beliefs. Over time, this made the latter variety of religiosity (kepercayaan) vulnerable to challenge by religious conservatives who alleged that spiritual-belief adherents were defaming or otherwise deviating from state-recognized religions. In the rough-and-tumble atmosphere of the post-Soeharto Reformasi era, this prospect was to become a growing and occasionally violent reality.

Culture shift and religionization

The Constitutional Court's 2010 ruling affirming the state's right to promote and defend religious orthodoxy was made politically intelligible as a result of one other, longer-term development in the religious field: a shift in popular understanding of the concept of religion from the plurality of viewpoints common at the dawn of the republic to the narrower and standardized view long promoted by Muslim parties and the Ministry of Religious Affairs.

In the first years of the independence era, the religion-belief binary (agama-kepercayaan) referenced in the 1945 Constitution and promoted by the Ministry of Religion had not yet been adopted by most of the tribal or chiefdom-based societies that had recently been incorporated into the new Indonesian nation. In the republic's early years, there were still hundreds of thousands of Indonesians in interior stretches of the central and eastern archipelago who practiced indigenous religions (Aragon 1996; Atkinson 1987; George 1996; Hoskins 1987; Kuipers 1998; Tsing 1993: 54–5). These remote island and tropical forest territories had remained largely aloof from the great flow of commerce, people, and religious discourses that from the thirteenth century onward had served to bring the majority of Indonesian peoples to Islam (Lombard 1990; Reid 1993; see also Introduction). After independence, most of these hinterland peoples regarded their own faith traditions as every bit as deserving of state recognition as Christianity or Islam. But Muslim and Christian scholars were unwilling to extend the standing of agama to these localized traditions, regarding them as a lesser species of religiosity, better characterized as "spiritual beliefs" (kepercayaan), if not outright "superstitions" (*takhyul, kurafat*).

For Muslim leaders in independent Indonesia, however, there has always been a larger and more troubling category of religious community than the country's local religions: the millions of Indonesians who self-identified as Muslim but who nonetheless subscribed to syncretic cosmologies and ritual traditions at odds with mainstream Sunnism. Nineteenth-century Dutch missionaries working on the island of Java were the first to draw attention to this category of "non-standard" Muslims (Kruithoff 2014:111–21; Ricklefs 2006: 89–104). When, in the mid-twentieth century, Western anthropologists carried out research in rural Java, they confirmed that the non-standard Muslim community was vast and that its largest concentration was among ethnic Javanese in the provinces of East and Central Java (Hefner 1987; Ricklefs 2006, 2007, 2012).

This was no mere academic matter. In the early years of the republic, ethnic Javanese comprised almost half of Indonesia's population, and at the time, these non-standard Muslims constituted the majority of Javanese. Studies also confirmed that this population formed the backbone of the country's two most important non-Islamic parties, namely, the Indonesian Nationalist Party (PNI) and the Indonesian Communist Party (PKI; see Geertz 1960; Jay 1969). These non-standard Muslims were commonly referred to as *abangan*, lit., "red," or, alternately, *kejawen*, "Javanists" (see Hefner 1987; Kersten 2015: 225–27). The abangan were distinguished from Indonesians of more normative Sunni persuasion, who were referred to as "whites" (*putihan*) or "*santri.*" The latter term refers to Muslims who have spent time in madrasa boarding schools, which in Java and most of Indonesia are known as pesantren or pondok pesantren (Azra et al.

2007; Dhofier 1999). Across the Muslim-majority world, madrasas are boarding schools for intermediate and advanced study in the Islamic sciences, including Islamic jurisprudence (fiqh; see Berkey 1992). One of the most striking differences between the diffusion of Islam to Southeast Asia as compared with the Middle East and South Asia was that institutions of higher Islamic learning like the madrasa arrived, not *with*, but centuries *after* Southeast Asia's first wave of Islamization from the thirteenth to seventeenth centuries (see Introduction). Boarding schools for the study of the Islamic sciences were established in large numbers across the central archipelago only from the mid-nineteenth century onward (Bruinessen 1994, 1995; Hefner 2009, 2016), and they soon played a major role in the promotion of a more shariah-minded Islam.

Although the phrase *abangan* was not used for self-identification among any ethnic grouping other than the Javanese, elsewhere in early republican Indonesia, there were other populations who self-identified as Muslim but preserved traditions as indifferent to fiqh orthodoxy as those of Java's abangan. The most prominent of these non-standard Muslims were the *wetu telu* Sasak of Lombok (Cederroth 1981, 1996), certain sub-ethnic groupings among the otherwise Muslim Bugis and Makassar peoples of southern Sulawesi (Pelras 1996; Rossler 1997; Gibson 2007), and the Gumai of Sumatra's southern highlands (Sakai 1999). A related tradition of non-standard Islam had also once existed among the Malay peoples in what is today Malaysia (see Laderman 1991; Peletz 1996). Although their adherents self-identified as Muslim, most among these non-standard varieties of Islam had hereditary ritual specialists who burned incense, recited formulaic prayers, and presented offerings (*sajen, sesajen*) to various ancestral, guardian, and world spirits. Most of the latter spirits were understood by way of cosmologies and liturgies that drew lightly on Islamic traditions but more substantially on narrative traditions that had long flourished alongside Islam (see Pelras 1996; Gibson 2007; cf. Headley 2000; cf. Smith-Hefner 1992).

As Indonesian and Western anthropologists first reported in the 1980s, with the annihilation of the Communist Party in 1965–1966, the reining in of the Nationalist Party, and the consolidation of the New Order government, the political supports for this non-standard variety of Islam collapsed; as a result, the ranks of non-standard Muslims have fallen precipitously since the early years of the New Order (Hefner 1987, 2011; Kim 1996; Pranowo 1991; Picard and Madinier 2011; Ricklefs 2012). In the years following the 1965–1966 massacres, as many as 1.75 million syncretic Muslims converted to Christianity, in part because Christianity appeared to offer an especially safe shelter against allegations that one might be a communist (Akkeren 1970; Boland 1982: 232–33; Hefner 1993). About one-sixth that number of people converted to Hinduism (Ramstedt 2004). Although in subsequent years, the ranks of Hindu converts in Java have shrunk as a result of significant reversion to Islam (Hefner 2004), the Christian community has flourished. Today Christians are well represented in the ranks of the middle class and university graduates; own several of the country's largest and most respected media conglomerates; figure prominently in the ranks of artists, public intellectuals, and celebrities; and occupy mid-level or senior leadership positions in most of the country's non-Muslim political parties. The single most striking index of the community's relative social health is that in the seven decades since Indonesian independence, Christians have seen their percentage share of the national population triple in size (Hefner 2017).

The single greatest beneficiary of the decline of syncretic Islam, however, has been the mainstream Sunni community. The New Order government and its democratic successor implemented programs of compulsory religious education from grade school through college, and this instruction has driven home the idea that all religions must conform to an officially recognized normative core. Urbanization, rising educational levels, exposure to international media, and the growth of the new Muslim middle class have also undermined the appeal of once-popular varieties of non-standard Islam, particularly those associated with traditional social authorities, making the latter appear "not only suspiciously syncretic … but unappealingly parochial" (Howell 2007: 227; 2008; cf. Bruinessen and Howell 2007).

A new but agonistic plurality

Even as more unconventional varieties of Islam have declined, the Muslim community in the late New Order and Reformasi periods has developed a new religious plurality. Since the 1990s, for example, growing numbers of people in the new Muslim middle class have developed an interest in Islamic spirituality or Sufism (*tasawwuf*). Although Sufi orders have been a prominent feature of Indonesian Islam since at least the sixteenth century, Indonesians in the "neo-Sufi" movement of the 1990s have eschewed the formal hierarchies of the traditional orders in favor of personalized programs of *tasawwuf* study in adult Islamic education programs, or by way of self-study on the Internet (Howell 2007:230–34; cf. Hoesterey 2015).

Islam in New Order and Reformasi Indonesia developed pluralist intellectual currents as well. Under the direction of a series of forward-looking ministers of religion, the New Order regime invested heavily in a reformed variety of Islamic education, which encouraged civic, general, and technical education as well as religious instruction. The achievement has had a direct effect on Indonesian democracy, inasmuch as graduates of these institutions have figured prominently among those who have succeeded in reassuring the Muslim electorate that Islam, democracy, and religious plurality are compatible (see Introduction, and Abdillah 1997; Jackson 2007).

Another area of striking pluralization in the religious field over the past generation has involved Muslim women. Today, the proportion of young women comprising the madrasa student body has grown to over one-half of the total enrollment (Jabali and Jamhari 2002: 68–9). Young women's enrollment in the country's prestigious state Islamic University system has also climbed steadily, from just 3% of the student body in 1988 to about 40% today (Jabali and Jamhari 2002: 47). No less remarkably, the state Islamic educational system has served "as a major source for women's religious empowerment" (Syamsiyatun 2008, 144; cf. Rinaldo 2013), with women graduates of the state Islamic university system figuring prominently in the ranks of the new generation of Muslim feminists that emerged in the 1990s. As in much of the Muslim world (Badran 2007; Mir-Hosseini 1999), this is a second-generation Muslim feminism, a successor to that which emerged during the 1920s and 1930s in the context of the anti-colonial struggle. Most of the leading figures in the first-generation movement had ties to mass-based social organizations, whether secular or Muslim nationalist, and invoked Enlightenment ideals of freedom and equality to frame their appeals. By contrast, the second-generation Muslim feminists are more self-consciously concerned with the reformulation of Islamic thought and jurisprudence than Enlightenment ideals per se. The main pathway to the new Muslim feminism has been by way of small study circles engaged with new international currents of Islamic feminist thought and preoccupied with formulating a scripturally-defensible reform of Islamic law and ethics on matters involving women.

The Reformasi era has provided new opportunities for anti-pluralist currents in the religious field as well. These currents are not new: Muslim conservatives and Islamists in the Indonesian Council for Islamic Predication (known by its Indonesian acronym, DDII, est. 1967) had served since the 1970s and 1980s as the leading intermediary for Saudi Arabian aid to Islamic schools, mosques, and associations. From the 1980s onward, some graduates of the DDII's scholarship programs in Saudi Arabia returned to Indonesia to spearhead what was to become the country's small but influential Salafist movement, which was broadly opposed to democracy, pluralism, and gender equality (see Noorhaidi chapter, and Hasan 2006). Other activists of anti-pluralist persuasion have looked to the Muslim Brotherhood more than Saudi-style Salafism for inspiration (Hasan 2006). Brotherhood ideals were popular among the many Indonesian students returning from study in Egypt, Syria, and Saudi Arabia in the 1980s and 1990s. Known in Indonesia as the *tarbiyah* ("education," "ethical socialization") movement, the Brotherhood-influenced movement went on in the Reformasi era to develop the most successful of the new Islamist parties, known today as the Prosperous Justice Party (PKS; Machmudi 2006). The party has consistently secured 7% of the vote in national elections (see Bubalo, Fealy, and Mason 2008: 49–74).

Although conservative Islamists have been unable to win any more than a small share of the vote in national elections, in the post-Soeharto period, they have succeeded in securing representation on the country's semi-governmental Council of Indonesian Ulama (Majelis Ulama Indonesia; MUI). The latter had been created in 1975 to provide a bridge between the government and Islamic scholars (Ichwan 2013). In the Reformasi era, the MUI resolved to demonstrate its independence by recruiting hard-line Islamists from groups like the Hizbut Tahrir and the Majelis Mujahidin Indonesia, and by rebranding itself as the guardian of Islamic morality (Bruinessen 2013b; Hasyim 2014; Ichwan 2013). The growing influence of anti-liberal and anti-pluralist ideas in Muslim debates reached a polemical crescendo in July 2005, when the MUI issued fatwas condemning "secularism, liberalism, and pluralism" as contrary to Islam (Gillespie 2007; Ichwan 2013; Olle 2009). Muslim democrats responded by insisting that the MUI had twisted the meaning of each of these terms. Hard-line Islamists in Hizbut Tahrir Indonesia, the Majelis Mujahidin Indonesia, and the Islamic Defenders Front cited the declaration to justify harsh criticisms of and regular confrontations with Muslim democrats and religious minorities (Hilmy 2010: 99–134; Human Rights Watch 2013).

Whither the religious field?

Seen against the backdrop of the country's changing religious field, one can better appreciate that the Constitutional Court's 2010 affirmation of restrictions on religious freedom was not judicial overreach out of step with long-term trends in society. In fact, if the court's decision illustrates anything, it is that, rather than standing apart from society, the justices who sat on the Constitutional Court were very much in its sway. The example also provides one more reminder that, contrary to our stereotypes of the putatively all-powerful Indonesian state, the state in the Reformasi era has been highly permeable to society-based cultural trends, not least when it comes to matters of religious governance (see Introduction, and Jones 2013; Bruinessen 2013a, 2013b).

Notwithstanding these developments, Indonesia still has an impressive network of Muslim intellectuals and civic organizations committed to multi-religious citizenship and a pluralist if not liberal interpretation of Islam. It has an equally impressive array of Christian, Hindu, and Buddhist activists equally dedicated to the ideals of Indonesian nationalism. Notwithstanding their setback in efforts to reform the country's marriage laws (Lindsey 2012; Hefner 2016), gender reformers and Muslim feminists figure prominently in public debates. In fact, after having been banished from the leadership of organizations like the Muhammadiyah in 2005 (Brenner 2011; Dewi 2008; Syamsiyatun 2008), women activists have quietly returned to play prominent roles once more. In a few cities, including Ambon and Jakarta, local branches of the Indonesian Council of Ulama (MUI) have even broken with the national leadership and lent their support to programs of inter-faith cooperation.

Notwithstanding civil initiatives like these, one of the most significant developments in Reformasi Indonesia has been the consolidation of a new non-governmental structure of socio-religious control linking the quasi-official Majelis Ulama Indonesia (MUI) to populist Islamic militias in society (see Hadiz and Hefner chapters, this volume). Neither of these two entities is subject to any significant measure of democratic control. It would be a mistake, however, to conclude that all blame for Indonesia's spike in religious violence lies with the country's Islamist militias. Certainly, this network and the MUI are the two most consequential new players on the Reformasi-era religious scene. However, survey data and field research indicate that growing numbers of Muslim Indonesians today hold views similar to those of the MUI leadership (see Menchik and Trost chapter, and Fealy 2016). This is not particularly surprising in light of Indonesia's decades-long culture shift toward popular acceptance of the idea that the state has an interest in promoting orthodoxy and prosecuting religious deviation.

Although national elections continue to indicate that starkly intolerant policies do not sell in the electoral marketplace, the Muslim public in Indonesia appears to be grappling with the question of how to balance the aspiration for personal and public religiosity with pluralist citizenship. This public ethical ambivalence is a quality they share, of course, with national publics in much of the late modern world, including in Western democracies. Here in Indonesia, the outcome of this struggle over religion, citizenship, and nation will likely determine the future of religious pluralism in this richly diverse and robustly democratic, but ethically divided, society.

References cited

Abdillah, Masykuri. 1997. *Responses of Indonesian Muslim Intellectuals to the Concept of Democracy (1966–1993)* (Hamburg: Abera Verlag Meyer & Co).

Akkeren, Philip van. 1970. *Sri and Christ: A Study of the Indigenous Church in East Java* (London: Lutterworth Press).

Ali-Fauzi, Ihsan, Samsu Rizal Panggabean, Nathanael Gratias Sumaktoyo, Anick H. T., Husni Mubarak, Testriono, and Siti Nurhayati. 2011. *Kontroversi Gereja di Jakarta* [The Church Controversy in Jakarta] (Yogyakarta: CRCS Press).

Aragon, Lorraine V. 1996. "Reorganizing the Cosmology: The Reinterpretation of Deities and Religious Practice by Protestants in Central Sulawesi, Indonesia," *Journal of Southeast Asian Studies* 27(2): 350–73.

Atkinson, Jane Monnig. 1987. "Religions in Dialogue: The Construction of an Indonesian Minority Religion," in Rita Smith Kipp and Susan Rodgers, eds., *Indonesian Religions in Transition* (Tucson: University of Arizona Press), pp. 171–86.

Azra, Azumardi, Dina Afrianty, and Robert W. Hefner. 2007. "Pesantren and Madrasa: Muslim Schools and National Ideals in Indonesia," in Robert W. Hefner and Muhammad Qasim Zaman, eds., *Schooling Islam: The Culture and Politics of Modern Muslim Education*, (Princeton: Princeton University Press), pp. 172–98.

Badran, Margot. 2009. *Feminism in Islam: Secular and Religious Convergences* (Oxford: One World).

Bagir, Zainal Abidin. 2013. "Defamation of Religion in Post-Reformasi Indonesia: Is Revision Possible?" *Australian Journal of Asian Law* 13(2): 1–16.

Bakker, F.L. 1993. *The Struggle of the Hindu Balinese Intellectuals: Developments in Modern Hindu Thinking in Independent Indonesia* (Amsterdam: VU University Press).

Bamualim, C.S., 2011. "Islamic Militancy and Resentment Against Hadhramis in Post-Suharto Indonesia: A Case Study of Habib Rizieq Syihab and His Islamic Defenders Front," *Comparative Studies of South Asia, Africa and the Middle East* 31(2): 267–81.

Berkey, Jonathan. 1992. *The Transmission of Knowledge in Medieval Cairo: A Social History* of Islamic Education (Princeton: Princeton University Press).

Boland, B.J. 1982. *The Struggle of Islam in Modern Indonesia* (Leiden: Koninklijk Instituut voor Taal- Land en Volkenkunde).

Brenner, Suzanne. 2011. "Private Moralities in the Public Sphere: Democratization, Islam, and Gender in Indonesia," *American Anthropologist* 113(3): 478–90.

Bruinessen, Martin van. 1994. "Pesantren and Kitab Kuning: Maintenance and Continuation of a Tradition of Religious Learning," in Wolfgang Marschall, ed., *Texts From the Islands: Oral and Written Traditions of Indonesia and the Malaya World* (Berne: University of Berne Press), pp. 121–45.

———. 1995. "Shari'a Court, Tarekat and Pesantren: Religious Institutions in the Banten Sultanate," *Archipel* 50: 165–200.

————, ed. 2013a. *Contemporary Developments in Indonesian Islam: Explaining the "Conservative Turn"* (Singapore: ISEAS).

————. 2013b. "Introduction: Contemporary Developments in Indonesian Islam and the 'Conservative Turn' of the Early Twenty-First Century," in van Bruinessen, ed., pp. 1–20.

Bruinessen, Martin van and Julia Day Howell, eds. 2007. *Sufism and the "Modern" in Islam* (London and New York: I.B. Tauris).

Bubalo, Anthony, Greg Fealy, and Whit Mason. 2008. *Zealous Democrats: Islamism and Democracy in Egypt, Indonesia, and Turkey* (Double Bay, Australia: Lowy Institute for International Policy).

Buehler, Michael. 2016. *The Politics of Shari'a Law: Islamist Activists and the State in Democratizing Indonesia* (Cambridge: Cambridge University Press).

Burhani, Ahmad Najib. 2013. "Liberal and Conservative Discourses in the Muhammadiyah: The Struggle for the Face of Reformist Islam in Indonesia," in van Bruinessen, ed., pp. 105–44.

Bush, R. 2008. "Regional Sharia Regulations in Indonesia: Anomaly or Symptom?" in Greg Fealy and Sally White, eds., *Expressing Islam: Religious Life and Politics in Indonesia* (Singapore: Institute of Southeast Asian Studies), pp. 174–91.

Butt, Simon and Tim Lindsey. 2012. *The Constitution of Indonesia: A Contextual Analysis* (Oxford and Portland: Hart Publishing).

Cammack, Mark, Lawrence A. Young, and Timothy B. Heaton. 1996. "Legislating Social Change in an Islamic Society: Indonesia's Marriage Law," *American Journal of Comparative Law* 44(1).

Cederroth, Sven. 1981. *The Spell of the Ancestors and the Power of Mekkah: A Sasak Community on Lombok* (Goteborg: Universitatis Gothoburgensis).

————. 1996. "From Ancestor Worship to Monotheism: Politics of Religion in Lombok," *Temenos* 32: 7–36.

Cook, Michael. 2001. *Commanding Right and Forbidding Wrong in Islamic Thought* (Cambridge: Cambridge University Press).

Crouch, Melissa. 2014. *Law and Religion in Indonesia: Conflict and the Courts in West Java* (London and New York: Routledge).

Dewi, Kurniawati Hastuti. 2008. "Perspective Versus Practice: Women's Leadership in Muhammadiyah," *Journal of Social Issues in Southeast Asia* 23(2): 161–85.

Dhofier, Zamakhsyari. 1999. *The Pesantren Tradition: The Role of the Kyai in the Maintenance of Traditional Islam in Java* (Tempe: Monograph Series, Program for Southeast Asian Studies, Arizona State University).

Fealy, Greg. 2016. "The Politics of Religious Intolerance in Indonesia: Mainstream-ism Trumps Extremism?" in Tim Lindsey and Helen Pausacker, eds., pp. 115–31.

Fealy, Greg and Virginia Hooker, eds. 2006. *Voices of Islam in Southeast Asia: A Contemporary Sourcebook* (Singapore: Institute of Southeast Asian Studies).

Feener, R. Michael. 2013. *Shari'a and Social Engineering: The Implementation of Islamic Law in Contemporary Aceh, Indonesia* (Oxford: Oxford University Press).

Feillard, Andrée. 1995. *Islam et Armée dans l'Indonésie Contemporaine* (Paris: L'Harmattan).

Feillard, Andrée and Rémy Madinier. 2006. *La Fin de l'Innocence? L'Islam Indonésien Face à la Tentation Radicale de 1967 à Nos Jours* (Paris: Les Indes Savantes).

Feith, Herbert. 2006 (orig. 1962). *The Decline of Constitutional Democracy in Indonesia* (Singapore: Equinox Publishing, 2006).

Geels, Anton. 1997. *Subud and the Javanese Mystical Tradition* (Richmond, UK: Curzon).

Geertz, Clifford. 1960. *The Religion of Java* (New York: The Free Press).

George, Kenneth M. 1996. *Showing Signs of Violence: The Cultural Politics of a Twentieth-Century Headhunting Ritual* (Berkeley: University of California Press).

Gibson, Thomas. 2007. *Islamic Narrative and Authority in Southeast Asia: From the 16th to the 21st Century* (New York: Palgrave Macmillan).

Gillespie, Piers. 2007. "Current Issues in Indonesian Islam: Analysing the 2005 Council of Indonesian Ulama Fatwa No. 7 Opposing Pluralism, Liberalism, and Secularism," *Journal of Islamic Studies* 18(2): 202–40.

Hasan, Noorhaidi. 2006. *Laskar Jihad: Islam, Militancy, and the Quest for Identity in Post-New Order Indonesia* (Ithaca: Southeast Asia Program, Cornell University).

Hasyim, Syafiq. 2014. "Council of Indonesian Ulama (Majelis Ulama Indonesia, MUI) and Its Role in the Shariatisation of Indonesia." (Ph.D. Thesis. Berlin: The Free University).

Headley, Stephen. 2000. *From Cosmogony to Exorcism in a Javanese Genesis* (New York: Oxford University Press).

Hefner, Robert W. 1987. "Islamizing Java? Religion and Politics in Rural East Java," *Journal of Asian Studies* 46(3) (August): 533–54.

———. 1993. "Of Faith and Commitment: Christian Conversion in Muslim Java," in Robert W. Hefner, ed., *Conversion to Christianity* (Los Angeles: University of California Press), pp. 99–125.

———. 2004. "Hindu Reform in an Islamizing Java: Pluralism and Peril," in Martin Ramstedt, ed., *Hinduism in Modern Indonesia: A Minority Religion Between Local, National, and Global Interests* (London: RoutledgeCurzon), pp. 93–108.

———. 2009. "The Politics and Cultures of Islamic Education in Southeast Asia," in Robert W. Hefner, ed., *Making Modern Muslims: The Politics of Islamic Education in Southeast Asia*, (Honolulu: University of Hawaii Press), pp. 1–54.

———. 2011. "Where Have All the *Abangan* Gone? Religionization and the Decline of Non-Standard Islam in Contemporary Indonesia," in Picard and Madinier, eds., pp. 71–91.

———. 2016. "Islamic Ethics and Muslim Feminism in Indonesia," in Robert W. Hefner, ed., *Shari'a Law and Modern Muslim Ethics* (Bloomington and Indianapolis: Indiana University Press), pp. 260–90.

———. 2017. "Christians, Conflict, and Citizenship in Muslim-Majority Indonesia," *Review of Faith and International Affairs* 15(1): 91–101.

Hilmy, Masdar. 2010. *Islamism and Democracy in Indonesia: Piety and Pragmatism* (Singapore: Institute for Southeast Asian Studies Press.

Hoesterey, James. 2015. *Rebranding Islam: Piety, Prosperity, and a Self-Help Guru* (Stanford: Stanford University Press).

Hosen, Nadirsyah. 2007. *Shari'a and Constitutional Reform in Indonesia* (Singapore: ISEAS Press).

Hoskins, Janet. 1987. "Entering the Bitter House: Spirit Worship and Conversion in West Sumba," in Rita Smith Kipp and Susan Rodgers, eds., *Indonesian Religions in Transition* (Tucson: University of Arizona Press), pp. 136–60.

Howell, Julia Day. 2007. "Modernity and Islamic Spirituality in Indonesia's New Sufi Networks," in Martin van Bruinessen and Julia Day Howell, eds., pp. 217–40.

———. 2008. "Modulations of Active Piety: Professors and Televangelists as Promoters of Indonesian 'Sufism,'" in Greg Fealy and Sally White, eds., *Expressing Islam: Religious Life and Politics in Indonesia* (Singapore: Institute for Southeast Asian Studies), pp. 40–62.

Human Rights Watch. 2013. *In Religion's Name: Abuses Against Religious Minorities in Indonesia* (New York: HRW).

Ichwan, Moch Nur. 2013. "Towards a Puritanical Moderate Islam: The Majelis Ulama Indonesia and the Politics of Religious Orthodoxy," in van Bruinessen ed., pp. 60–104.

Jabali, Fuad and Jamhari, eds. 2002. *IAIN & Modernisasi Islam di Indonesia* [The State Islamic Institutes and the Modernization of Islam in Indonesia] (Jakarta: Logos Wacana Ilmu).

Jackson, Elizabeth. 2007. "Crafting a New Democracy: Civic Education in Indonesian Islamic Universities," *Asia Pacific Journal of Education* 27(1): 41–54.

Jamhari, and Jajang Jahroni. 2004. *Gerakan Salafi Radikal di Indonesia* [Radical Salafi Movements in Indonesia] (Jakarta: PT Raja Grafindo).

Jay, Robert R. 1969. *Javanese Villagers: Social Relations in Rural Modjokuto* (Cambridge, MA: MIT Press).

Jones, Sidney. 2013. "Indonesian Government Approaches to Radical Islam Since 1998," in Mirjam Künkler and Alfred Stepan, eds., *Democracy and Islam in Indonesia* (New York: Columbia University Press), pp. 109–25.

Kersten, Carool. 2015. *Islam in Indonesia: The Contest for Society, Ideas, and Values* (London: Hurst and Company).

Kim, Hyung-Jun. 1996. "Reformist Muslims in a Yogyakarta Village: The Islamic Transformation of Contemporary Socio-Religious Life." (Ph.D. Thesis. Canberra, Victoria, Australia: Department of Anthropology, Australian National University).

Kruithof, Maryse. 2014. "'Shouting in a Desert': Dutch Missionary Encounters With Javanese Islam, 1850–1910." (Ph.D. Thesis. Rotterdam: Department of History, Erasmus University).

Kuipers, Joel C. 1998. *Language, Identity, and Marginality in Indonesia: The Changing Nature of Ritual Speech on the Island of Sumba.* Studies in the Social and Cultural Foundations of Language 18 (Cambridge: Cambridge University Press).

Laderman, Carol. 1991. *Taming the Wind of Desire: Psychology, Medicine, and Aesthetics in Malay Shamanistic Performance* (Berkeley: University of California Press).

Lev, Daniel S. 1966. *The Transition to Guided Democracy: Indonesian Politics, 1957–1959* (Ithaca: Modern Indonesia Project, Southeast Asia Program, Department of Asian Studies, Cornell University).

Lindsey, Tim. 2012. *Islam, Law and the State in Southeast Asia.* Vol. I: Indonesia (London and New York: Tauris).

Lindsey, Tim and Simon Butt. 2016. "State Power to Restrict Religious Freedom: An Overview of the Legal Framework," in Tim Lindsey and Helen Pausacker, eds., pp. 19–41.

Lindsey, Tim and Helen Pausacker, eds. 2016. *Religion, Law and Intolerance in Indonesia* (New York and London: Routledge).

Lombard, Denys. 1990. *Le Carrefour Javanais: Éssai d'histoire globale, Vol 2, Les Réseaux Asiatique* (Paris: Editions de l'École des Hautes Études en Sciences Sociales).

Machmudi, Yon. 2006. "Islamizing Indonesia: The Rise of Jemaah Tarbiyah and the Prosperous Justice Party (PKS)" (Ph.D. Dissertation. Canberra: Faculty of Asian Studies, Australian National University).

Mir-Hosseini, Ziba. 1999. *Islam and Gender: The Religious Debate in Contemporary Iran* (Princeton: Princeton University Press).

Mulder, Niels. 1978. *Mysticism and Everyday Life in Contemporary Java: Cultural Persistence and Change* (Athens, OH: Ohio University Press).

Nakamura, Mitsuo. 2012. *The Crescent Arises Over the Banyan Tree: A Study of the Muhammadiyah Movement in a Central Javanese Town,* c. 1910s–2010. 2nd Enlarged Edition (Singapore: ISEAS Press).

Olle, John. 2009. "The Majelis Ulama Indonesia Versus 'Heresy': The Resurgence of Authoritarian Islam," in Gerry van Klinken and Joshua Barker, eds., *State of Authority: The State in Society in Indonesia* (Ithaca: Cornell Southeast Program Publications), pp. 95–116.

Pausacker, Helen. 2013. "Morality and the Nation: Pornography and Indonesia's Islamic Defenders Front" (Ph.D. Dissertation. Melbourne: Law School, University of Melbourne).

Peletz, Michael G. 1996. *Reason and Passion: Representations of Gender in a Malay Society* (Berkeley and Los Angeles: University of California Press).

Pelras, Christian. 1996. *The Bugis* (Oxford: Blackwell).

Picard, Michel. 2011. "From *Agama Hindu Bali* to *Agama Hindu* and Back: Toward a Relocalization of Balinese Religion?" in Picard and Madinier, eds., pp. 117–41.

Picard, Michel and Remy Madinier, eds. 2011. *The Politics of Religion in Indonesia: Syncretism, Orthodoxy, and Religious Contention in Java and Bali* (London and New York: Routledge).

Pranowo, Bambang. 1991. "Creating Islamic Tradition in Rural Java" (Ph.D. Thesis. Melbourne, Australia: Department of Anthropology and Sociology, Monash University).

Ramstedt, Martin. 2004. *Hinduism in Modern Indonesia* (London and New York: Routledge).

Reid, Anthony. 1993. *Southeast Asia in the Age of Commerce, 1450–1680,* vol. 2, *Expansion and Crisis* (New Haven: Yale University Press).

Ricklefs, Merle C. 2006. *Mystic Synthesis in Java: A History of Islamization From the Fourteenth to the Early Nineteenth Centuries* (Norwalk, CT: East Bridge).

———. 2007. *Polarising Javanese Society: Islamic and Other Visions (c. 1830–1930)* (Honolulu: University of Hawaii Press).

———. 2012. *Islamisation and Its Opponents in Java: c. 1930 to the Present* (Singapore: NUS Press).

Rinaldo, R. 2013. *Mobilizing Piety: Islam and Feminism in Indonesia* (New York: Oxford University Press).

Robinson, Kathryn. 2009. *Gender, Islam and Democracy in Indonesia* (London and New York: Routledge).

Ropi, Ismatu. 2012. "The Politics of Regulating Religion: State, Civil Society and the Quest for Religious Freedom in Modern Indonesia." (Ph.D. Dissertation. Canberra, Australia: Australian National University).

Rossler, Martin. 1997. "Islamization and the Reshaping of Identities in Rural South Sulawesi," in Robert W. Hefner and P. Horvatich, eds., *Islam in an Era of Nation-States: Politics and Religious Renewal in Muslim Southeast Asia* (Honolulu: University of Hawaii Press), pp. 275–306.

Sakai, Minako. 1999. "The Nut Cannot Forget Its Shell: Origin Rituals Among the Gumai of South Sumatra" (Ph.D. Thesis. Canberra, Victoria, Australia: Department of Anthropology, Australian National University).

Salim, Arskal. 2008. *Challenging the Secular State: The Islamization of Law in Modern Indonesia* (Honolulu: University of Hawaii Press).

Smith-Hefner, Nancy J. 1992. "Pembaron: An East Javanese Rite of Priestly Rebirth," *Journal of Southeast Asian Studies* 23(2): 237–75.

Stange, Paul. 1980. "The Sumarah Movement in Javanese Mysticism" (Ph.D. Dissertation. Madison, WI: Department of History, University of Wisconsin-Madison).

Syamsiyatun, Siti. 2008. "Women Negotiating Feminism and Islamism: The Experience of Nasyiatul Aisyi-yah, 1985–2005," in Susan Blackburn, Bianca J. Smith, and Siti Syamsiyatun, eds., *Indonesian Islam in a New Era: How Women Negotiate Their Muslim Identities* (Clayton: Monash University Press), pp. 139–65.

Tsing, Anna Lowenhaupt. 1993. *In the Realm of the Diamond Queen: Marginality in an Out-of-the-Way Place* (Princeton: Princeton University Press).

Wilson, Ian Douglas. 2006. "Continuity and Change: The Changing Contours of Organized Violence in Post-New Order Indonesia" *Critical Asian Studies* 38(2): 265–97.

18

ISLAMIZATION, LAW, AND THE INDONESIAN COURTS

The more things change . . .

Tim Lindsey

Like the governments of all Southeast Asian states with significant Muslim populations, the governments of independent Indonesia have been adept at using the bureaucratic and legal mechanisms of state to assert control over the interpretation of Islam, the religion of at least 80% of the population. They have done this by close management of the administration of a restricted selection of Islamic legal traditions, interpreting, and often altering, them to suit their wider political aims. Generally, the result is a distancing of Islamic law from its traditional sources of authority, creating what amounts to a *de facto* state madhhab, or school of law.[1]

This was a strategy modern Indonesia inherited from Dutch colonial rule. It was state policy for much of Soeharto's New Order from 1966 to 1998, a period when Islam was constructed as a potential political threat to the centralized, authoritarian, and nationalist state the military had created, to be crushed, tightly controlled, or co-opted. Overt repression of political Islam diminished significantly after Soeharto's fall in May 1998. Many of the New Order restrictions placed on the public expression of Muslim identity – political and legal – were lifted soon after his resignation.

Since then, much attention has been paid to the so-called Islamic "revival"[2] seen as having taken place in Indonesia. Popular calls for greater recognition of shariah are identified as characteristic of this phenomenon and the challenges they present for post-Soeharto governments have been the subject of much analysis.[3] It is a common theme that the "Islamization of law in modern Indonesia" constitutes a direct "challenge to the secular state" (Salim 2008). There is little doubt that many "hard-line" (*garis keras*) conservative proponents of *Syariahisasi* (shariah-ization or legal Islamization) do seek to bring precisely such a challenge. Certainly, many of those who oppose them see the hard-liners' efforts to win greater formal recognition of Islamic legal traditions as ultimately intended to create an Islamic state. They see this as anathema to Indonesia's essentially secular democracy and its religiously and culturally diverse society (Mujani and Liddle 2009: 577). In fact, the opponents of legal Islamization regard pluralism as fundamental to the political bargain struck in 1945 that led to the creation of a united archipelagic republic and thus essential to the continued coherence of the nation.

To justify their position, the pluralists – who include Muslims as well as non-Muslims – rely heavily on the Pancasila, the Indonesian state ideology embedded in the preamble to the Constitution in 1945. The first *sila* states that "The state is based on . . . Belief in Almighty God (Ketuhanan yang Maha Esa)," and for them, this is a guarantee of religious pluralism that would prevent the privileging of Islam or any other religion by the state. Indeed, the word *Islam* does not even appear in the Constitution. The result of increasing Islamist challenges to the pluralist position (which was dogma under the Soeharto regime) is a growing polarization of the Muslim community since 1998 (Ricklefs 2008). This was made very clear by the inflamed rhetoric and tensions sparked by the recent candidacy of Basuki Tjahaja Purnama (known as "Ahok"), a Chinese Christian, for the governorship of Jakarta. For many, the challenges to the state posed by post-Soeharto Syariahisasi seem to amount to an existential struggle between supporters of the Pancasila state and their Islamizing enemies.

The situation is, however, much less clear-cut than either of the groups at the extremes of this debate would admit. It is, in fact, by no means the case that recent, often successful, efforts at legal Islamization have necessarily diminished the state's influence over the religious lives of Muslim Indonesians or represent a shift toward an alternative model of the state based on Islamist norms – let alone the dismantling of the state madhhab. This is largely because the proponents and opponents of Islamization both look to the state to mediate in their favor. Strategies for and against Syariahisasi in Indonesia are thus most often expressed in terms of state regulation of Islamic legal traditions, that is, firmly within the framework of the state. Syariahisasi may reflect social and cultural changes post-Soeharto, but it does not necessarily point to a weakening of long-standing state strategies for control of Islamic legal traditions.

Expanding Islam, expanding the state

In fact, the state's capacity to intervene in the religious lives of Muslims in Indonesia has, in some respects, expanded rather than contracted since Soeharto fell twenty years ago. A pattern is now evident of the state responding to pressure from Muslim groups to revise and extend the scope of Islamic legal traditions in Indonesia but usually doing so in a way that keeps those traditions captured by the legal and administrative institutions of the state. Attempts to create a formal system of law for Muslims that is derived from conservative Islamic norms, let alone independent of the state, are inevitably stymied.

Islamic legal traditions have certainly grown beyond the narrowly limited private law sphere to which they were largely (and often forcibly) confined in the colonial period and under Sukarno and Soeharto (albeit in different ways and to different extents under these leaders). Post-Soeharto regulation and bureaucracy has, however, expanded with them. The state has usually been able to retain interpretative authority over Islamic law and a wide power of intervention in its application, even if these are not always exercised and are sometimes challenged by conservative Muslim groups. It is therefore highly unlikely that the state will grant autonomy to Islamic legal traditions in the form of an Islamic judicial system that is not under the firm control of the state and less likely still that such a system could be achieved without state sanction. Even in Aceh, where formal legal Islamization has gone further than anywhere else in the republic, the local shariah judges and prosecutors are members of national agencies and remain answerable to their Jakarta superiors, with the Supreme Court retaining ultimate appellate authority (Lindsey 2012: 297–325).

It is not surprising that the Indonesian state remains the arbiter of the content of Islamic law in Indonesia. As An-Na'im (2008) has shown, when a modern state seeks to regulate a religion by passing laws and creating legal and bureaucratic institutions to control that religion's expression and application, it usually finds itself called upon to determine its substance too. In other words, once the state uses law to regulate and administer Islam, as the Indonesian state has always done, it cannot avoid a normative role as well. The state thus finds itself the context in which disputes about the substance and legal status of shariah are fought out (for example, through elections, like the Jakarta gubernatorial elections; in the legislature, by making laws; in the production by government of executive regulation; and so forth). In many cases, it also finds itself the judge of those contests (for example, through the courts, the bureaucracy, law-enforcement agencies, and the policies it develops in response to such contests).

This is why the strategies of most proponents of legal Islamization since 1998 (and even before then) are, as mentioned, marked by the use of the secular structures of the state to strengthen their positions. Muslim groups, particularly conservative ones, have (perhaps ironically) sought to use the legal mechanisms the state has developed to restrict Islam in their efforts to force the state to accept a normative religious role and, of course, adopt the conservative norms they propose. In other words, to return to An-Na'im's model, they now seek to reassert revelation precisely through the bureaucratic agencies of the state they see as having distorted it in the past.

Some marginal, violent extremist Islamist groups – Jemaah Islamiyah and its offshoots, for example – follow a different path, confronting the state and aiming for its violent displacement but without any real prospect of success. However, most mainstream conservative Muslim groups – for example, the most prominent Islamist party, PKS (Partai Keadilan Sejahtera, Justice Welfare Party), and MUI (Majelis Ulama Indonesia, Council of Indonesia Ulama), a highly influential and conservative state-endorsed NGO – do not overtly seek to displace the state, at least not in the near future (Shihab and Nugroho 2008). Instead, they claim to work within the secular framework of the existing polity to transform it, seeking to remake it in their own image.

They have sought to do this through a diverse variety of means, including proposing regional and national legislation, for example: Islamizing *perda* (*peraturan daerah*, regional regulations) at the local government level, including the regressive Aceh "Perda Shariah" or *Qanun*, and the Anti-Pornography Law, No .44 of 2008 (Lindsey 2012: ch.11, 13). They have also provoked litigation against minority religious groups, including so-called "deviant sects" or aliran sesat. This has typically taken the form of complaints to police that lead to state prosecutions under the provisions of the criminal code popularly referred to the "Blasphemy Law" (discussed further later). In addition, conservatives have relied on the *fatwa* (legal opinion of a Muslim religious scholar), the traditional instrument available to ulama. Fatawa[4] issued by MUI denouncing pluralism and liberalism are a good example of this, as are the more specific MUI fatawa that are routinely used as decisive evidence in blasphemy prosecutions.

In the remainder of this chapter, I present two short case studies to show how the state, though the courts, has responded to the challenges presented by conservative Islam as Indonesian political life has transformed, opened up, and created room for Islam in the two decades since Soeharto resigned in 1998: judicial interpretation of the law on freedom of religion and decision-making in Indonesia's Islamic courts. These two examples will focus on how Indonesia's judicial institutions have declined to take opportunities to support Islamization, refusing to roll back state authority over the interpretation and application of Islamic law, instead confirming it and, in some cases, expanding it.

Before turning to these case studies, however, a disclaimer is required. By "state," I mean "government" and the bureaucracies through which it governs. I accept that the state is not a homogenous entity and to treat it as though it is homogenous involves significant generalization and distortion. Differences, even conflicts, frequently exist both between and within the branches of government and, as governments change, so do state policies and institutions. Nonetheless, it is my argument that broad patterns can be identified in the approaches toward Islamic legal traditions of Indonesian governments and their bureaucracies.

Freedom of religion in the courts

Freedom of religion[5] is guaranteed in the Indonesian Constitution of 1945. Article 29 paraphrases the first principle of the Pancasila in paragraph 1 and then states that

> 2   The State guarantees all persons the freedom of religion (*memeluk agamanya*), each according to their own religion and beliefs (*kepercayaan*).

Article 28E, which was added to the constitution during the post-Soeharto amendment process, repeats and elaborates the guarantees in Article 29:

> 1   Each person is free to profess their religion and to worship in accordance with their religion
> 2   Each person has the freedom to possess convictions and beliefs, and to express their thoughts and attitudes in accordance with their conscience.

These two provisions are strengthened by Article 28I(1), which renders them non-derogable, that is, prohibits them from being qualified or diminished in any way:

> The right to life, the right to not be tortured, the right to freedom of thought and conscience, *the right to have a religion (hak beragama)*, the right to not be enslaved, the right to be recognized as an individual before the law, and the right to not be prosecuted under a law of retrospective application *are human rights that cannot be limited under any circumstances*. [emphasis added]

Despite the plain words of this Article, however, the Constitutional Court has repeatedly held that the human rights mentioned in it (including in relation to religion) are, in fact, capable of derogation.

In a series of cases,[6] the Constitutional Court was asked to consider whether the freedom from prosecution under retrospective laws, the freedom from torture, and the right to life (all Article 28(I) rights) are, in fact, absolute. The Court decided that they can be set aside if the interest to be protected by doing so is particularly important. This means Articles 28E and 29 also need to be understood as granting rights to religious freedom that can, in fact, be restricted by the state in certain circumstances. This seems contrary to express terms of Article 28(I) but it is hardly revolutionary. Few states anywhere in the world allow their citizens to exercise unrestricted religious freedom. The more important question it provokes, however, is how far that power to restrict reaches – in precisely what circumstances is the state entitled to limit religious freedom?

The answer to this is found in Article 28J(2) of the constitution, which provides that

> In carrying out his or her rights and freedom, every citizen has the *responsibility to abide by the restrictions set out by legislation* protecting the rights and freedoms of others and *which accords with moral considerations, religious values, security and public order* in a democratic society. [emphasis added]

The Constitutional Court has made it clear that this article allows the government to legislate in ways that limit citizens' rights. In fact, rights may even be set aside if that is necessary to fulfill "just demands in accordance with moral, religious, security and public order considerations."[7] Accordingly, any decision as to whether the limitation of rights by the state in a particular case is valid requires a weighing up of the rights of an individual against the rights of others, where "others" is defined by the state by reference to its obligation to safeguard the morality and religion of those "others" as well as its obligation to ensure "public order" (*ketertiban umum*) – a nebulous term once beloved of the New Order and capable of almost infinite expansion.

How does this work in the day-to-day practice of law making and law enforcement? Again, a series of Constitutional Court decisions offer answers.[8] In the Religious Courts Case in 2008,[9] the Constitutional Court held that the extent of the jurisdiction of the Religious Courts (*Pengadilan Agama*) – Indonesia's shariah courts – was not a matter for Islamic legal tradition but a matter to be determined by the legislature, at its discretion; it alone had the authority to determine what parts of Islamic law applied in Indonesia and to what extent.[10]

In this, the court was simply confirming what it had decided a year earlier in the *Polygamy Case*,[11] when it found that, as might be expected, Indonesian Muslims do not have unlimited rights to apply Islamic family law but are bound by state law in that area, and, more significantly, the state is not bound by Islamic law but rather has not just the power to interpret and restrict the application of Islamic law but also a duty to do so.

In the *Polygamy Case*, the applicant, M. Insa, an Islamist, objected to provisions in Law 1 of 1974 on Marriage that he claimed prevented him from engaging in polygamy[12] (for reasons discussed further later). He argued that Article 28E(1) of the constitution guarantees citizens freedom to embrace a religion and to worship in accordance with that religion. Restricting polygamy, he said was tantamount to breaching Islamic law, thus denying him that freedom. This was an "all or nothing" argument: Insa's position was that the grant of religious freedom meant absolute freedom, with the state having no right to intervene or regulate. The court absolutely rejected this. It held that Article 28J(2) in fact *requires* the state to impose limits on the human rights guaranteed by the constitution, including religious rights:

> The state as the highest organization in a community, created on the basis of agreement, *not only has the authority to regulate but also the obligation to regulate* [and] the authority to determine the requirements which must be fulfilled by citizens who wish to enter into a polygamous marriage in the interests of the public benefit. [emphasis added]

This position was further confirmed in the 2009 *Blasphemy Law Case*,[13] a case brought this time by the pluralists. This resulted in a highly controversial Constitutional Court judgment that became a watershed of the post-Soeharto debate over religious freedom in Indonesia. In it, the court affirmed that the state's Article 28(J)(2) power to restrict public expression of religious freedom to ensure public order is a very broad one and may be exercised more or less as it sees fit.

The issue before the court was the constitutionality of a religious defamation statute known as the "Blasphemy Law": Law No. 1/PNPS/1965 on Preventing the Abuse/Dishonoring of Religion.[14] In its Elucidation (*penjelasan*, explanatory memorandum), this law lists the six religions recognized by the state (Islam, Catholicism, Protestantism, Hinduism, Buddhism, and Confucianism). It also distinguishes between these "religions" (agama) and mere "beliefs" (kepercayaan). These two provisions are fundamental to the state's management of religion in Indonesia. Article 1 of the Blasphemy Law also prohibits public support for "deviant" (sesat) "beliefs." In Article 2, it establishes a system by which the president may issue warnings and then ban such deviant religious groups (Article 2) and jail their members for up to five years (Article 3). Article 4 then inserts Article 156a in the criminal code (Kitab Undang-Undang Hukum

Pidana, KUHP), providing the basis for such prosecutions. This is the provision generally used to prosecute members of unorthodox religious sects – that is, in most cases, "beliefs" seen as outside the six state-sanctioned religions, for so-called blasphemy. It states that

> Any person who intentionally and in public expresses sentiments or carries out acts that (a) are principally of a nature of enmity toward, misuse of or dishonoring (*penodaan*) of a religion adhered to in Indonesia (b) are intended to stop a person believing in any religion [agama] that is based on an Almighty God will be sentenced to imprisonment for up to 5 years.

The applicants in this case were a disparate group of many NGOs, as well as prominent public figures, including former president Abdurrahman Wahid, once head of Indonesia's largest Muslim mass organization, Nahdlatul Ulama. Most were Muslims, with some representatives of other religions, but all were united by their support for pluralist values. They claimed that the Blasphemy Law was inconsistent with the rights to freedom of religion in Articles 29 and 28E of the constitution. They argued that the law undermined rights to freedom of belief, expression, and thought by allowing the government to identify religious interpretations as deviant and prohibit and disband "deviant" religious activities and sects. The law, they said, further infringes freedom of religion because it gives the state power to determine which interpretations of religious beliefs are "correct" and which are "wrong," allows punishment of people holding different beliefs or interpretations, and discriminates against those whose beliefs fall outside the six state-recognized religions. The Constitutional Court rejected these submissions. Instead, it followed its earlier decisions and upheld the Blasphemy Law as a valid exercise of the state's virtually unlimited power to restrict the right to religious freedom.

In doing so, it found that Indonesia is not an Islamic state, nor is it, however, a secular one. Instead, Indonesia is "a religious country," and the meaning of this term is to be understood (and limited) by reference to a wide range of regulatory features of the state, principally the Constitution.[15] In other words, Indonesia's religiosity is defined and confined by the constitution and laws made under it, not by religious laws such as shariah. The court then borrowed from well-established American jurisprudence[16] (although this was not acknowledged) to find that the right to freedom of religion protected by the constitution is nothing more than a private right to hold a religious belief (*forum internum*). The state may place limitations on individuals' rights to publicly express or manifest such private belief (*forum externum*). The rights to public expression of religious freedom (like all rights in Articles 28A–28I) are therefore not absolute. Instead, they may be limited pursuant to Article 28J.[17]

In this way, the decision in the *Blasphemy Law Case* upheld the state's broad right to deal with religious issues, including to enforce its interpretation of religious orthodoxy to ensure public order. In the case of Islam, the court suggested that the government should do this by reference to the opinions of leading ulama organizations.[18] Implicitly, however, decisive power in this process always remains with the state because its ultimate duty is not to enforce the views of the *ulama* (which, after all, are rarely homogenous) but rather to have reference to those views to achieve the higher constitutional duty to prevent "conflict, unrest, disintegration and animosity in the community."

In summary, despite the plain words of Articles 28E, 29, and 28I(1) of the constitution, the right to religious freedom is not a "human right that cannot be limited under any circumstances." Rather, the national government has largely unlimited scope to restrict public expression of religion for reasons of public order. In other words, despite the post-Soeharto insertion into the constitution of expanded guarantees of religious freedom, the state has the same power to override religious norms, more or less at will, that it enjoyed under the New Order. This means that the extent of Syariahisasi and the manner in, and extent to which, Islamic legal traditions are to be interpreted and applied is ultimately its decision alone.

The Religious Courts

The Indonesian courts that exercise this state authority to apply Islamic legal traditions in Indonesia have three tiers: the *Pengadilan Agama* (Religious Court), the *Pengadilan Tinggi Agama* (High Religious Court), and the *Mahkamah Agung* (Supreme Court).[19] The Religious Courts are the exclusive court of first instance[20] for cases where the parties are Muslim[21] and which concern, among other things,[22] marriage (including polygamous marriage,[23] as regulated by the Marriage Law No. 1 of 1974).[24] The Religious Courts' docket is overwhelmingly dominated by such cases, especially those relating to divorce.

The legislation applicable to the Religious Courts does not expressly state the sources of law on which Religious Court judges may rely in coming to their decisions. In practice, however, the panels of three judges who hear cases generally apply the version of Islamic law embodied in national regulation – chiefly the Law on Marriage and its implementing Government Regulation, No. 9 of 1975, as well as a range of ministerial regulations and circular letters (*surat edaran*). The chief source, however, is the state-sanctioned *Kompilasi Hukum Islam* (Compilation of Islamic Law, Presidential Instruction No. 1 of 1991), issued by former President Soeharto as a "guide" for Religious Court judges. The *Kompilasi* is narrow in scope, covering only marriage, inheritance, and *wakaf*,[25] and its provisions allow only a very restricted application of Islamic legal traditions. For nearly two decades, however, the Religious Court judges have relied heavily on the *Kompilasi*, the Marriage law, and Government Regulation No. 9 of 1975 – and not traditional understandings of Islamic law – to deal with divorce and related cases.

To give an example of the approach of these courts, consider the position of M. Insa, the applicant in the Constitutional Court Polygamy Case, referred to above. According to traditional fiqh,[26] a Muslim man has a more or less absolute right to take up to four wives at once. The *Kompilasi* permits this in principle but only if he can prove that he is able to deal equally with all wives (and their children).[27] This is a significant obstacle, especially when read with the conditions of which the Religious Court must satisfy itself before formally allowing the polygamous marriage sought. The husband must, for example, show that his existing wife is unable to "perform her function as a wife," is incurably ill, physically incapacitated, or barren.[28] Even where these can be shown, Art. 58(1) of the *Kompilasi* states that the husband must also fulfill the conditions in Art. 5 of the Marriage Law, namely, he must have his wife's permission and must be able to fulfill the basic needs of his wives and children.[29] These provisions are supported by the 1974 Marriage Law, Government Regulation No. 9 of 1975 on the Implementation of Law No. 1 of 1974 Marriage (Chapter VIII, Arts. 40–4), and by criminal penalties. Under Article of 279 of the Criminal Code, parties to a polygamous marriage that is not judicially approved face five to seven years' imprisonment. More recently, Law No. 23 of 2006 on Civil Registration strengthened these provisions by imposing a penalty for failure to register a registrable marriage of RP 1 million and adding fines of RP 50 million and imprisonment for ten years for bureaucratic fraud associated with marriage registration.[30]

Insa's complaint was that these provisions constitute a formidable barrier to polygamous marriage, making it virtually impossible for him to exercise what he saw as his religious right. He was right in this. That was, in fact, precisely the purpose of these provisions; they were specifically intended to displace the traditional fiqh for the purposes of social engineering, including "the creation of stable families, control of population growth, control of divorce and polygamy, equalisation of rights and status of women... [and] unification of the nation through unification of the Law" (Salim and Azra 2003: 88).

It thus follows that, whatever the issue for decision, traditional Islamic legal sources are seldom cited in Religious Court judgments today – and then usually only to support propositions of law in national regulation. As I have previously explained,[31] only in 30% of 85 Religious Court decisions that I have analyzed was any sort of Islamic legal source referred to at all. None of the Supreme Court decisions studied cited any Islamic sources at all. Across all three levels of the Islamic judicial system, the Quran and ḥadith – the basic scriptural sources of Islam – were relied upon even less frequently than fiqh. Traditional fiqh textbooks were cited in 72.7% of the small number of cases where Islamic sources were used. Next, came the Quran, cited in 54.5% of cases that relied on Islamic sources, while only 27% cited ḥadith. In none of the cases studied were fatawa cited at all, despite being the basic tool by which fiqh is applied in traditional Islamic jurisprudence.

Nurlaelawati (2010) has suggested that the Religious Courts are more ambivalent toward the *Kompilasi* and more ready to rely on fiqh sources than my selection suggests, although her selection of cases is very much smaller. Wahid (2010: 13–14), however, refers to research conducted by the Directorate of Religious Justice in 2001, which concluded that 100% of 1,008 Religious Court decisions surveyed were based on the *Kompilasi*, with 71% explicitly stating this in the judgment itself. This is understandable. From a formalist point of view, it is perhaps surprising that the courts ever cite sources of Islamic law at all. There is no express authority to do so in the legislation that establishes and regulates them. Accordingly, even if the Religious Courts do consider traditional sources of Islamic law, they may not use them to contradict or set aside national (non-Islamic) law, and indeed, they never do.

As might be expected, these entrenched characteristics of formalistic bureaucratic positivism permeate the entire Islamic judicial system in Indonesia. The judgments of these courts, like the procedures they follow, differ little from decisions of Indonesia's secular courts, and both are influenced heavily by European "Civil Law" traditions of judicial decision making and not at all by the Muslim *qadi* (judge) tradition – in fact that word is not used at all in the Indonesian Islamic judicial system. This is to be expected, given the Religious Courts are supervised by the secular Supreme Court, both through administrative oversight, career structure, and the appeal process, and that is a very formalistic and civil law institution. Like the Religious Courts and High Religious Courts, the Supreme Court almost never gives detailed attention to Islamic sources of law in its judgments, instead restricting itself to state regulation.

Even recent efforts to offer the Religious Courts new areas of Islamic legal tradition in which to work have not changed these patterns. Law No. 3 of 2006 amending Law No. 7 of 1989 on the Religious Courts expressly granted them a new and very wide jurisdiction over "syariah economy"[32] in the revised Article 49 of Law No. 7 of 1989 (confirmed by Art. 55 of Law No. 1 of 2008 on syariah banking). As might be expected, a new, specific-purpose guide-book for judges was also developed – the *Kompilasi Hukum Ekonomi Syariah* (KHES, Compilation of Syariah Economic Law) – to enable them to make decisions in this area without the need for recourse to the uncomfortable debates of fiqh. This has all proved fruitless, however, because judges have been slow to explore the technically complex and challenging area of Islamic finance, with few or no decisions issued in this area to date.

In summary, Indonesia's Religious Courts are an intrinsic part of Indonesia's secular judicial system, not the world of the ulama. Islamic jurisprudence, or fiqh, is almost entirely irrelevant to their decisions, while state regulation is the *sine qua non*: a reader of the *Kompilasi*, could predict most decisions; a reader of traditional *fiqh* could not.

As I have argued before, these are certainly courts for Muslims – indeed, in many areas of private law, they have exclusive jurisdiction for Muslims – but they are not Islamic courts. It may seem remarkable that they appear to have been so far almost entirely untouched by the huge shifts toward a more conservative religious identity that have marked the wider Muslim community in post-Soeharto Indonesia, despite the widening of their jurisdiction in that time to enable them to deal with areas in which legal Islamization has taken place, such as Islamic banking. The reason for this is simply that these courts are oriented almost exclusively toward the state – they are creatures of the bureaucracy not the mosque. They look inward and upward, taking their cues on Islam from the Supreme Court and the judicial administrative system, not from MUI or any other Muslim organization.

Conclusion

Despite popular perceptions of an erosion of state authority vis-à-vis Islam in religiously polarized post-Soeharto Indonesia, the state has, in fact, often been able to exploit its continuing central place as the source of laws and law enforcement. It has even been able to use challenges brought by the proponents of legal Islamization as opportunities to reform the formal legal institutions of Islam in Indonesia in ways that have allowed it to consolidate or even expand its control, albeit often subtly. In this, the state has been particularly successful as regards the management of philanthropy (zakat[33] and wakaf), shariah banking, and Islamic education, all of which are the subject of amended regulatory schemes that reconfirm the state's decisive authority to interpret and apply Islamic legal norms.[34]

The state has also been able to avoid fully complying with the demands of conservatives to enforce their interpretations of orthodox shariah, for example in the Constitutional Court. It has, however, sometimes tolerated their efforts to enforce it through other means, so long as this happens within the framework of the state. These efforts include, among others, local and (to a lesser extent) national regulation reflecting Islamic norms, the formation of the Mahkamah Syar'iyah in Aceh – a state agency – and, of course, blasphemy trials in the criminal courts, in which the state is the prosecutor and judge. These efforts, however, have had very little impact on the orientation of most state law agencies, as the example of the Religious Courts shows.

Throughout, the state has sought to maintain its role as arbiter of the argument about Islam and law, although it has sometimes done so by declining to act at all, as in the case of the Religious Courts. As a result, both sides of the legal Islamization debate – pluralists and Islamists – still construct their claims in terms of appeals to the state and its legal framework, rather than in terms of the creation of an Islamic state (except at the militant fringe). In the process, the state, while generally resisting the more challenging demands of the Islamists, has used its position in the debate to expand its legal presence in Muslim religious life. It has used tactics of institutional passivity or co-option and regulatory intervention to do this, even while struggling to manage growing polarization among Muslims about Syariahisasi. I conclude that, even when the state appears to have been swayed by proponents of legal Islamization, the results usually take the form of legal institutional change that is cast firmly within the existing structure of the secular state's legal system. This is true whether the change is regulatory (for example, the Anti-Pornography Law) or judicial (for example, the creation of Aceh's Islamic courts).

In simple terms, the proponents of legal Islamization seek legitimation from the state, and that allows the state to maintain authority, and often control, over the messy business of Syariahisasi. The contest that legal Islamization has provoked in Indonesia, between Muslims and other religionists, between the state and religious groups and, above all, between different groups of Muslims – pluralists and Islamists – is undoubtedly complex and dynamic. Its trajectory is thus hard to predict. Despite this, it does seem possible that the trend may still be toward consolidation of state bureaucratic control of Islamic legal traditions in Indonesia, rather than its diminution.

Notes

1 For a more detailed version of this argument, see Lindsey (2012), on which this chapter draws extensively. It also consolidates material from Lindsey and Butt (2016) and Lindsey (2017).

2 "Revival" implies a renewing, or recovery, of something that already existed. Whether contemporary legal Islamization is reviving the Indonesian past or is the creation of something new (and alien) in Indonesia is hotly disputed there. See Lindsey (2012: 6–9).

3 See, for example, Salim (2008), Hooker (2008), Mietzner (2009), Bush (2008), and Shihab and Nugroho (2008), among a large number of others.

4 *Fatāwā* (Ar.) is the plural of *fatwā*.

5 This section in based on Lindsey and Butt (2016). I am grateful to Simon Butt for his generous permission to do so.

6 See: the Soares Case (Constitutional Court Decision 065/PUU-II/2004); the Death Penalty Case (Constitutional Court Decision 2–3/PUU-V/2007); and Firing Squad Case (Constitutional Court Decision 21/PUU-VI/2008).

7 See the Soares Case (Constitutional Court Decision 065/PUU-II/2004), p. 51.

8 See the Polygamy Case (Constitutional Court Decision No. 16/PUU-VI/2008) and the Blasphemy Case (Constitutional Court Decision No. 140/PUU-VII/2009).

9 Constitutional Court Decision No. 16/PUU-VI/2008.

10 The court here relied on Art. 24A(5) of the constitution: "The structure, position, membership and procedural law of the Supreme Court and the courts below [which under art. 24(2) include the Religious Courts] shall be regulated by statute."

11 Constitutional Court Decision No. 16/PUU-VI/2008.

12 In fact, "polygamy" refers to the taking of multiple spouses by either a man or a woman. "Polygyny" refers to a man taking multiple wives. In Indonesia, however, *poligami* is the term used for polygyny and that usage is followed here.

13 Constitutional Court Decision No. 140/PUU-VII/2009.

14 This was originally Presidential Decision No. 1/PNPS/1965 but was upgraded to become a law (*undang-undang*, statute) by Law No. 5 of 1969.

15 Constitutional Court Decision No. 140/PUU-VII/2009, p. 275.

16 The forum internum/forum externum (idea/action) distinction "explained by the United States Supreme Court has, under different terminology, been broadly accepted in international human rights jurisprudence" (Witte and Greene 2011: 258). See also Uitz (2007: 31), and *Reynolds v. US*, 98 US 145 (1878), para. 166.

17 Constitutional Court Decision No. 140/PUU-VII/2009, p. 293.

18 Constitutional Court Decision No. 140/PUU-VII/2009, p. 291–2.

19 Art. 4(1), Law No. 7 of 1989.

20 Art. 6(1), Law No. 7 of 1989.

21 Arts. 1(1) and 49(1), Law No. 7 of 1989.

22 The other areas that fall within the jurisdiction of the Religious Courts are inheritance (Art. 49(b), Law No. 7 of 1989 on Religious Justice); Muslim wills and testaments (Art. 49(c)); charitable bequests (hibah) (Art. 49(d)); wakaf or Islamic charitable trusts (Art. 49(e)); Islamic philanthropy (Art. 49(f), (g) and (h)), comprising zakat (charitable payments obligatory for Muslims) and *infaq* and *sadaqah* (voluntary charity); and "shariah economy" (*ekonomi syari'ah*) (Art. 49(i)).

23 Art. 49(a), Law No. 7 of 1989 on the Religious Courts, as amended by Art. 37, Law No. 3 of 2006.

24 Elucidation to Art. 49(2), Law No. 7 of 1989, and Elucidation to Art. 49(a), Law No. 3 of 2006, Section 37.

25 *Wakaf* (Ar. *Waqf*): The permanent dedication by a Muslim of property, usually land, for purposes recognized by Islamic law as pious, religious, or charitable.

26 *Fiqh* (Ar.): Islamic jurisprudence, the contested body of scholarly interpretation.

27 Arts. 55–9, *Kompilasi*. See also Arts. 4 and 5(1)(c) of the Marriage Law, which are essentially the same as Arts. 57 and 59 of the *Kompilasi*).

28 Art. 57, *Kompilasi*.

29 Art. 58(3), *Kompilasi*. It is open to the judge to dispense with this requirement if permission is not forthcoming and there has been no word from the wife or wives for at least two years or permission is impossible to obtain.

30 See Arts. 90, 92–8, Law No. 23 of 2006 on Civil Registration.

31 For this and the next paragraph, see Lindsey (2017).
32 The Elucidation to Art. 37 of Law No. 3 of 2006 provides that "shari'a economy" includes Islamic banking, Islamic micro-finance, Islamic insurance, Islamic contracts, Islamic securities, Islamic pawn-broking (*penggadaian*), and "Islamic business." For more description of these areas of jurisdiction, see also the Elucidation to Art. 49(2), Law No. 7 of 1989 on Religious Justice, and the Elucidation to Art. 49(a), Law No. 3 of 2006, Section 37.
33 *Zakat* (Ar.): charitable payments obligatory for Muslims.
34 For Islamic banking, see Law No. 1 of 2008 on syariah banking and Lindsey (2012: ch. 6); for Islamic education, see Law No. 20 of 2003 on National Education, Government Regulation No. 55 of 2007 on Religious Education for the Recognized Religions, and Lindsey (2012: ch.7); for zakat and wakaf, see Law No. 23 of 2011 on Zakat Management, Law No. 41 of 2004 on Wakaf, and Lindsey (2012: ch. 5).

References cited

An-Na'im, Abullahi Ahmed. 2008. "Shari'a in the Secular State: A Paradox of Separation and Conflation," in Peri Bearman, Wolfhart Heinrichs and Bernard G. Wiess, eds., *The Law Applied: Contextualizing the Islamic Shari'a, A Volume in Honor of Frank E Vogel* (London and New York: IB Tauris), pp. 321–41.

Bush, Robin. 2008. "Regional 'Sharia' Regulations in Indonesia: Anomaly or Symptom?" in Greg Fealy and Sally White, eds., *Expressing Islam: Religious Life and Politics in Indonesia* (Singapore: Institute of Southeast Asian Studies), pp. 171–91.

Hooker, M.B. 2008. *Indonesia Syariah: Defining a National School of Islamic Law* (Singapore: ISEAS).

Lindsey, Tim. 2012. *Islam, Law and the State in Southeast Asia, Vol. I: Indonesia* (London: I.B. Tauris).

———. 2017. "Islamic Courts in Three Southeast Asian Countries," in Christoph Antons, ed., *Routledge Handbook of Asian Law* (London: Routledge), pp. 341–61.

Lindsey, Tim and Simon Butt. 2016. "State Power to Restrict Religious Freedom: An Overview of the Legal Framework," in Tim Lindsey and Helen Pausacker, eds., *Religion, Law and Intolerance in Indonesia* (London: Routledge), pp. 19–41.

Mietzner, Marcus. 2009. *Military Politics, Islam and the State in Indonesia* (Singapore: ISEAS).

Mujani, Saiful and William Liddle. 2009. "Muslim Indonesia's Secular Democracy," *Journal of Democracy* 21(2): 35–49.

Nurlaelawati, Euis. 2010. *Modernisation, Tradition and Identity: The Kompilasi Hukum Islam and Legal Practice in the Indonesian Religious Courts* (Amsterdam: Amsterdam University Press).

Ricklefs, Merle C. 2008. "Religion, Politics and Social Dynamics in Java: Historical and Contemporary Rhymes," in Greg Fealy and Sally White, eds., *Expressing Islam: Religious Life and Politics in Indonesia* (Singapore: ISEAS), pp. 115–36.

Salim, Arskal. 2008. *Challenging the Secular State: The Islamization of Law in Modern Indonesia* (Honolulu: University of Hawai'i Press).

Salim, Arskal and Azyumardi Azra (2003), *Shari'a and Politics in Modern Indonesia* (Singapore: ISEAS).

Shihab, Najwa and Januar Nugroho. 2008. "The Ties That Bind: Law, Islamisation and Indonesia's Prosperous Justice Party," *Australian Journal of Asian Law* 10(2): 233–67.

Uitz, Renata. 2007. *Freedom of Religion* (Strasbourg: Council of Europe).

Wahid, Marzuki. 2010. "Reformation of Islamic Family Law in Post-New Order Indonesia: A Legal and Political Study of the Counter Legal Draft of the Islamic Law Compilation," in Ota Atsushi, Otomato Masaaki and Ahmad Suaedy, eds., *Islam in Contention: Rethinking Islam and the State in Indonesia* (Jakarta: The Wahid Institute; Japan: Centre for Southeast Asian Studies, Kyoto University; Taiwan: Centre for Asia-Pacific Area Studies), pp. 77–120.

Witte, John and Christian M. Greene. 2011. *Religion and Human Rights: An Introduction* (Oxford: Oxford University Press).

19

THE SPECIAL STATUS OF ISLAMIC ACEH

Arskal Salim

By the end of 2012, Indonesia had 34 provinces. Earlier, during the New Order period (1966–1998), Indonesia had 27 provinces, including East Timor. After East Timor became an independent state in 1999, Indonesia acquired several new provinces upon splitting up those provinces that had large land areas or big populations. Of these 34 provinces of Indonesia, five have special status in that they are allowed to make special arrangements in particular aspects of government. These provinces include Aceh, Jakarta, Yogyakarta, Papua, and West Papua. However, Aceh is the only province granted special autonomy for the implementation of Islamic law or shariah.

In 1999, following the collapse of the authoritarian Soeharto regime in 1998, Aceh was awarded autonomous status, with special privileges in the social, legal, and cultural domains. This autonomy includes the formal implementation of shariah in Aceh by way of three administrative instruments: recognizing a distinctive court (Mahkamah Syar'iyah) to have wider jurisdictions, legislating locally certain Islamic criminal laws, and founding relevant state institutions to support the implementation of shariah in the region.

This chapter seeks to explain how and why the current special status of Islamic law in Aceh was achieved and has been implemented. The current special status of Islamic Aceh is a result of a (re)assertion of Islamic identity that led to the official enforcement of shariah in the province. Before delving into the discussion of the basis of Islamic identity in Aceh, the next section provides a theoretical overview of how Islamic identity has been constructed. The sections that then follow deal with Aceh's Islamic identity from the historical perspective. The discussion seeks to answer the question of what has made Aceh a distinctive region and why it deserves a special status. Before the conclusion, I review current developments with regard to the special status of Islamic Aceh (see also Afrianty chapter, this volume).

Islamic identity construction

Schwedler (2001: 2–5) mentions that there are at least three elements in the construction of Islamic identity. First, there are historical processes and experiences through which Muslim individuals and groups come to see themselves. Second, the relationship between Muslims and those around them may possibly allow or deny a mutual recognition. And third, the location where Muslims live contributes to the construction of their identity. All this suggests that from the very beginning, Islamic identity not only originated from Islamic doctrines but also emerged as a result of Islam's responses to social and political challenges.

Pratt (1999: 7–11) adds six factors that make up the basic Islamic identity. They are (1) the concept of *umma* as a united community, (2) the creed of either Sunnism or Shi'ism as a tradition and history, (3) the Quran and the Sunna as the ultimate sources and inspiration for personal piety, (4) belief in and practice of the Five Pillars of Islam in daily life, (5) the geographic location where identification of ethnic with religious identity occurs, and (6) the shariah or divine law, which structures relationships within Muslim life.

Of all these six factors, shariah may be regarded as especially critical for Islamic identity. This is not surprising given that the essence of Islam is conveyed in both belief and law, and in fact, the term *shariah* frequently is meant to cover both. Moreover, a sharp distinction between Islam and shariah is hardly ever identified. This helps explain further why the implementation of shariah is central to the agenda of current political Islam in many Muslim regions. In the context of Aceh, Michael Feener (2013) has demonstrated that shariah plays a greater role in a way that it has become an instrument for social engineering for shaping the future definition of Acehnese society.

Historical context of Aceh's Islamic identity

A number of historical facts have made the Acehnese especially proud of their strong Islamic identity. First, Aceh was the first region in Indonesia to embrace Islam. Second, the first Muslim kingdom in Indonesia was established in Aceh. The gravestone of the first Muslim ruler of Samudra, Sultan Malik as-Salih, is dated 1297. According to Merle Ricklefs (2001), this is the earliest clear evidence of the existence of a Muslim dynasty in Indonesia. And third, the history of shariah implementation in Aceh has a long pedigree and was very clear compared to other areas in Indonesia. Based on the journals of European travelers who visited Aceh during the seventeenth century, Reid (1988, 1993) describes how shariah was already applied in Aceh by way of an Islamic court that imposed *hudud* punishments on thieves, drunkards, and others seen as having violated God's law.

Islamic identity also played an important role in providing the Acehnese with a rallying point to resist the colonial power of the Dutch (1873–1903). The idea of *Perang Sabil* or "war in the way [of God]" was clearly invoked by the ulama to justify resistance to Dutch rule. The war in Aceh lasted for more than thirty years and was the toughest and longest war fought by the colonial Dutch in the East Indies. The crucial position of Islamic identity and the role of ulama in the Aceh war have strengthened a sense of intertwined regional and Islamic identity among the Acehnese.

Having said that Islamic identity has long been embedded in the minds of the Muslim Acehnese and that ulama played an important role in implanting such an identity, it is necessary to describe the rise of a new generation of ulama in Aceh in the late 1930s. Under a new organization established in 1939 called PUSA (*Persatuan Ulama Seluruh Aceh*; All-Aceh Ulama Association), the ulama sought to mobilize support for their idea of an Islamic society. By holding rallies throughout Aceh, they invited people to unite under the banner of Islam and to be alert to shariah rules and religious duties. The result was, to use Morris's (1985: 87) words, "a heightened consciousness of their identity as Acehnese Moslems that transcended kinship, village, and territorial identities." Indeed, it was the ulama who became the agents for the translation of Islamic identity into socio-political action in Muslim society.

The first years after the independence of Indonesia in 1945 found the ulama controlling political positions in the Acehnese regional government. The *uleebalang* (traditional aristocratic rulers) were attacked because of their having collaborated with the colonial Dutch. Many leading *uleebalang* were killed in the 1948 Cumbok massacre (Syamsuddin 1985). With power in their hands, the ulama then set out to redefine Acehnese identity in accordance with Islamic doctrines. For the ulama, it was now time to realize "their primary aim [which] was to apply as much Islamic law as possible in Acehnese society. The Indonesia national revolution was, therefore, seen by [the] ulama as an opportunity to restore the validity of Islamic law in the region" (Syamsuddin 1985: 111).

As their first step, the ulama demanded the establishment of a province for the Aceh region. This was intended not only to buttress their authority but also as a means of protection of the Acehnese identity as Muslims (Salim 2004). Aceh's provincial status did not last long, however. The province of Aceh was incorporated in 1950 into the province of North Sumatra, with Medan as the capital. This administrative reorganization resulted in Aceh being absorbed and subsumed into North Sumatra, a region with plural socio-cultural life and a strong Protestant population.

The dissolution caused deep disappointment among the ulama. The ulama wanted to build an Islamic society in Aceh; by contrast, the national leadership in Jakarta sought to create a religiously neutral state with the Pancasila as its principal ideology. The disagreement led to open rebellion, and under the leadership of Teungku Daud Beureueh, Aceh was declared separate from the Republic of Indonesia and part of the Negara Islam Indonesia (Indonesian Islamic State) led by Sekarmadji Maridjan Kartosuwiryo in West Java (Syamsuddin 1985). This revolt was only brought to an end in the early 1960s.

The New Order period

During more than three decades of the New Order (1966–1998), the ulama in Aceh were provided with respectable status and generous incomes by the government. As Ricklefs (2001) has observed, it was in this way that the ulama were co-opted and made dependent on the state. The impact of the co-optation policy of the New Order deeply compromised the autonomy of the ulama and gradually led many to put aside their appeals for the implementation of shariah. During the New Order period, all forms of Islamic identity expression in Aceh were undermined. The regime refused to validate the Regional Regulation 6 of 1968 on the Implementation of Shariah Law in Aceh. The reason put forward was that Indonesian law forbade the decentralization of religious affairs to a provincial government. The regime's actions signaled clearly that any effort to implement an Islamic agenda in Aceh would not be tolerated.

Faced with this impasse, some Acehnese leaders put forth a new and more rebellious alternative. In December 1976, under the leadership of Teungku Hasan M. Tiro, the well-known Free Aceh Movement (GAM, or Gerakan Aceh Merdeka) replaced this Islamic rationale as the motive of struggle. According to Hasan Tiro, the discourse of Islamic identity would only obstruct international support for the struggle for self-determination in Aceh (Syamsuddin 1985). For this reason, Tiro developed a discourse of Javanese colonialism and economic deprivation to justify his demands for the right to self-determination (Kell 1995:64). This discourse was regarded as a much more viable means of gaining national sympathy and international concern.

Post–New Order era (1998 onward)

The post–New Order period saw the continuing marginalization of Islamic identity discourse in Aceh. This was because the rebels (GAM) were mainly driven by aspirations for full independence rather than by an Islamic agenda. Despite the Indonesian government offering two laws on regional autonomy (Law 44 of 1999 on the Administration of Aceh as a Special Province and Law 18 of 2001 on the Extensive Autonomy for the Special Province of Aceh as Nanggroe Aceh Darussalam), the GAM leaders were of the view that all these offers were only attempts at political co-option.

Ironically, at the time when Islamic identity was discounted by Aceh's rebel movement, the Indonesian government provided wholehearted support to the consolidation of Aceh's Islamic identity. For the Indonesian government, the offer of allowing the implementation of shariah in the restive province was seen as an effective way to win the hearts and minds of the Acehnese people. By enacting laws that granted greater regional authority over religious life, customs, and education while also strengthening the role of the ulama, the Indonesian government hoped the widespread resentment in Aceh might be overcome and the province would remain happily within the fold of the unitary state of Indonesia (Salim 2003).

During the years of Aceh's political transition (1998–2001), the voices of the rural ulama began to be articulated. The ulama founded a new organization called Himpunan Ulama Dayah Aceh (HUDA or the Association of the Dayah Ulama of Aceh) in September 1999. In their view, the New Order regime's policies had eroded Aceh's Islamic identity, resulting in widespread social and moral problems. The solution to this crisis, HUDA ulama believed, was the reinstatement of Islamic shariah for the Acehnese. This view was welcomed by the post-New Order governments. In fact, in mid-2001, when the existing ulama council (MUI) was transformed into Majelis Permusyawaratan Ulama (MPU – the Consultative Council of Ulama), many HUDA figures were recruited to take up important positions in the council.

As the central government considered the only group that could counter the legitimacy of opposition groups in Aceh was the ulama, their major role in mediation efforts in the post-Soeharto era was given prominence. Putting the ulama forward as regional leaders was an excellent strategy for the central government to combat its main opponents in Aceh, namely GAM. This government's effort to strengthen the ulama's role, however, was alleged by the GAM leaders to sow the seeds of internal conflict between the Acehnese themselves. As observed by McGibbon (2006: 335), the GAM leaders "were not only deeply critical of what they claimed as HUDA's pro-government stance, but saw them as potential rivals for [local] leadership."

The special status

Inasmuch as one of the most important features of Islamic identity formation is shariah, the special status granted to Aceh is centered on how shariah rules are to be constructed and enforced. This raises further questions: What legal basis is needed to validate shariah implementation? What is the level or scope of its legal instruments? What are the legal institutions required to uphold the Islamic regulation? What aspects of law do those Islamic regulations cover? Would everyone in Aceh, regardless of personal religious affiliation, be subject to shariah regulations?

Legal and political basis

All legal and political platforms invoked or earlier proposed (either during the Sukarno presidency 1959–1965 or during the Soeharto regime 1966–1998) to support the implementation of shariah in Aceh were annulled by later republican governments. It was only after the departure of the Soeharto regime that the implementation of shariah in Aceh was again given official legal standing. As mentioned, the first law implementing the arrangement was Law 44 of 1999, which granted the provincial government the right to initiate and establish policies on particular issues, such as religion, customs (*adat*), education, and the role of ulama. The second was Law

18 of 2001, which allowed for economic concessions and detailed how those particular issues in the previous statute were to be directed and locally managed, including the institutionalization of shariah. Other than these two laws, there was an additional special enactment following the 2005 Peace Agreement between the rebels (GAM) and the Indonesian government. A year after this agreement, Law 11 of 2006 on the Governance of Aceh was promulgated. This Law was considered a "constitution" of Aceh within the unitary state of the Republic of Indonesia.

Legal institutions

When the Indonesian government granted Aceh autonomy in three administrative jurisdictions (religion, local custom, and education), the ulama were inevitably required to become actively involved in managing these three areas. In fact, the idea of the implementation of shariah must implicitly entail handing over some authority to the ulama because they are the only ones with appropriate knowledge of Islamic law. For this reason, a provincial regulation, locally known as Qanun, assigns the Acehnese ulama organization (MPU) responsibility for several critical administrative functions. Based on the Qanun 2 of 2009, the MPU has the following responsibilities and authority:

a   issuing legal opinions on governance, development, the economy, and socio-cultural life;
b   offering directions over conflicting ideas on religious issues either within Muslim communities or among believers of different religions
c   providing feedback and recommendations to the government of Aceh and the provincial legislature in the shariah-based lawmaking process
d   supervising the undertaking of governance and the implementation of regional policy in accordance with Islamic shariah

The other institution responsible for managing the implementation of shariah in Aceh is the religious bureaucracy known as the Dinas Syariat Islam (DSI), or the provincial Office of Islamic Shariah. The head of this institution reports directly to the governor of Aceh. This office has sub-branches at the district level across Aceh. The office has played a more active operational role than the ulama council (MPU) in enforcing the Qanun on shariah rules. The provincial religious bureaucracy has been engaged in, among other things, planning future activities, recruiting staff for the shariah enforcement police (*wilayatul hisbah*), preparing manuals, disseminating information and guidelines, coordinating the meetings of all relevant provincial institutions, and supervising the application of shariah.

With all these mandates, the DSI acquired a greater share of the regional budget than that allocated to the ulama council. All this suggests that in the modern state, the religious bureaucracy appears to have a wider job scope and hence is more functionally significant than the ulama in the implementation of shariah. This confirms Vogel's study (2000) on the competing role between the Wahhabi ulama and the Saudi bureaucracy in the implementation of shariah. Vogel observes that the religious bureaucracy pays attention to procedural matters and has been more imperative in the successful implementation of shariah than the ulama, who mostly focus on the legislative content of sharia.

One important aspect of the special status of Islamic Aceh is the operation and scope of shariah courts (Salim 2010). These have broader jurisdiction than Religious Courts elsewhere in Indonesia. In the post–New Order period, they have also been given a new form as Mahkamah Syar'iyah. The expansion of Mahkamah Syar'iyah's jurisdiction, which previously only dealt with personal or family issues, now extends to certain criminal acts, including gambling, alcohol consumption, and adultery. With this judicial development, proponents of shariah implementation hoped that they could restore the earlier form of shariah courts in Aceh while also reviving Acehnese identity.

As elsewhere in Indonesia, Aceh has two parallel yet equal state courts (Civil Court and Mahkamah Syar'iyah) that co-exist in every district or municipal region. In cases of legal appeal, appellate courts for both systems are present at the provincial level. The same is true for further appeal that must go to the Supreme Court in Jakarta, which exercises the powers of cassation. Under the terms of the 2006 Law on the Governance of Aceh, the Mahkamah Syar'iyah's jurisdiction on some penal cases was extended to allow non-Muslim offenders to be adjudicated by this shariah court. In addition, the shariah court was also granted the authority to examine disputes over property ownership between Muslim parties, a matter previously under the jurisdiction of the Civil Court.

Legal provisions

The 2006 Law on the Governance of Aceh incorporated new provisions while also updating certain points pertaining to the implementation of shariah in Aceh. There are many shariah-related provisions in this law, such as on the application of Islamic shariah (Articles 125–7), the shariah court (Articles 128–37), the MPU or ulama council (Articles 138–40), the police force (Articles 207 (1 and 4)), the public prosecutor (Articles 208 (2) and 210), and human rights (Article 227 (1c)). All these have strengthened the legitimacy of existing shariah Qanun and the jurisdiction of the shariah court. Most of these, however, required further implementing regulations in the form of Qanun or regional regulations of the Aceh legislature.

As far as Islamic legal aspects incorporated into the provincial regulations are concerned, at least 17 (seventeen) Qanun were enacted between the years 2000 and 2006 (Salim 2008). The preparation and enactment of Qanun became less frequent after 2006, especially after Irwandi Yusuf became provincial governor for the first time (2007 to 2012). This coincided with the dominance of Partai Aceh, a non-religious party linked to the Free Aceh Movement, over the Aceh legislature following the 2009 legislative elections. The opposition of both Governor Irwandi and Partai Aceh to the legislation of shariah has to do with a possible implication on the position of Aceh in the world, which would make it economically and politically disadvantaged (Salim 2015: 101). The vision of Partai Aceh and Governor Irwandi (although the two were not always united on other issues) had dominated the provincial legislature from October 2009 through to 2014.

During Governor Irwandi's term in office, only two Qanun of shariah nature were passed (Qanun 2 of 2009 on the Ulama Consultative Council and Qanun 10 of 2007 on Islamic Treasury). In fact, the governor refused to sign legislation on the draft Qanun on criminal law (*jinayah*) because the earlier legislature (2004–2009) included the stoning to death of adulterers (Salim 2009). However, after the departure of Governor Irwandi from the office, the provincial legislature (2009–2014) enacted the Qanun on *jinayah* that included 100 lashes for adulterers but stopped short of requiring their execution by stoning. This Qanun was then signed by Governor Zaini Abdullah (2012–2017), Governor Irwandi's successor.

From late 2014 to mid-2017, Governor Zaini Abdullah signed eight additional Qanuns, which were shariah related. Those Qanuns include the following:

1 Qanun 6 of 2014 on the Islamic criminal rules (jinayah)
2 Qanun 8 of 2014 on the fundamentals of Islamic Shariah
3 Qanun 9 of 2014 on the founding of Shariah Aceh Bank

4 Qanun 7 of 2015 on the division of authorities pertaining to Islamic shariah between pro-vincial and district/municipal governments
5 Qanun 8 of 2015 on the fostering and the protection of Islamic creed
6 Qanun 4 of 2016 on the guidance of maintaining religious harmony and building worship places
7 Qanun 8 of 2016 on the assurance system of halal products
8 Qanun 13 of 2016 on the formation and the structure of Aceh governance auxiliaries

It must be noted that the crafting of these Qanun has had a lot to do with both legislative and governor elections. The 2014 legislative election motivated the incumbent legislature to promise and pass more Qanuns on shariah in 2014 for appeasing their constituents and getting re-elected. Meanwhile, the 2017 governor election led the incumbent governor to approve the Qanun legislation in 2015 and 2016, a move he believed would improve his chances for re-election. He and other politicians in the province were afraid of losing political support should they be portrayed as being "anti-shariah." However, not many people in Aceh were persuaded by this political maneuver. In the 2014 legislative election, the share of the vote for Partai Aceh declined, and the incumbent governor failed to win re-election in 2017.

Legal scope

Until early 2017, numerous Qanun on shariah rules were crafted, covering varied aspects of law. The institutions affected ranged from the ulama to the bureaucracy, the court, the task force unit, and local village, provincial, and district leadership. Meanwhile, the content of these Qanun touched on rituals, family issues, education, public decency, halal food, religious creed, Islamic economy, and criminal law (jinayah). The only aspect of jinayah that has yet to be legislated are its most severe punishments, including execution for murder, amputation for theft, and stoning to death for adultery. Whether these punishments will be legislated in the future depends very much on the extent to which the Aceh provincial legislature would have undisputed consensus formulated in the amended Qanun on jinayah. Although it is not impossible, this is very unlikely to happen in the near future, especially because of the opposition of Irwandi (Aceh's governor-elect 2017–2022) to harsher varieties of jinayah punishment.

The Qanun rules apply to any Muslim resident of Aceh, but non-Muslims who live in Aceh may be subject to the Qanun as well. Non-Muslims are expected to comply with Islamic injunctions implemented in Aceh, including those prohibiting gambling, alcohol consumption, and khalwat (illicit proximity of an unmarried couple). Non-Muslim women are also expected to abide by the Islamic dress code for women. Any violation of these injunctions results in prosecution in the Shariah Court of Aceh regardless of the religious affiliation of the offenders.

There are two circumstances in which non-Muslim residents in Aceh are subject to Qanun laws (Salim 2015). The first is based on the jurisdictional principle. If an offense is committed within the boundaries of the Aceh region, this principle covers perpetrators who are either Muslim or non-Muslim, Acehnese or non-Acehnese, and Indonesian citizens or foreign citizens. The second scenario is based on the principle of voluntary legal subjection. This principle is the exception rather than the rule in the implementation of shariah in Aceh. If non-Muslims, for one reason or another, voluntarily choose to comply with a particular shariah law in the Qanun, their choice is considered valid and acceptable. And, as far as the principle of voluntary legal subjection is concerned, there is no legislation in Indonesia that prohibits non-Muslims from opting to be examined by Aceh's Shariah Courts. Additionally, no valid legal reason exists for judges to prevent this from taking place.

Despite these two legal provisions, the principles for applying the caning penalty on non-Muslim offenders remain unclear. It has been argued that caning is a corporal punishment that is intended not to injure but to humiliate an offender of Qanun. In other words, caning is not to enforce painful punishments but rather to educate society (Feener 2013: 233–7). However, all this becomes ambiguous when it comes to the caning penalty for non-Muslim offenders. As non-Muslims had violated the Qanun and were increasingly willing to opt for a caning penalty instead of secular punishment (imprisonment), many wonder what would be the implications of such corporal punishment on non-Muslim offenders. Would it achieve the ultimate goal of Islamic punishment, that is, to wound the pride more than the flesh? As a matter of fact, some non-Muslim offenders have chosen the caning penalty because they do not want to spend time in prison, as they lack basic facilities. For these non-Muslim offenders, the choice is merely pragmatic. They look for something that minimizes their misery.

Conclusion

The foregoing discussion demonstrates that the special status of Islamic Aceh has been historically constructed by way of a longstanding and evolving process of Islamic identity formation. Its genealogy can be traced back to the region's early Islamic kingdoms. Its current expression is the result of social and political dynamics relative to the unitary state of Indonesia. Its special status has not only presented Aceh as a distinctive province among others, but also has created precedents for law and governance elsewhere in Indonesia. Of these precedents, the legislation of Qanun on shariah rules in Aceh has encouraged other provinces and districts to enact bylaws that incorporate and enforce Islamic injunctions for their Muslim residents. However, these bylaws do not have the solid legal and constitutional status that the Qanun have in Aceh.

Finally, we can ask, does the special autonomy of Islamic Aceh bring something meaningful and for which the Acehnese feel grateful? The answer to this question varies depending on the way actors conceive the role of shariah in Acehnese life. The Acehnese people and the ulama seem broadly satisfied with the current achievement of the special status of Islamic Aceh (Feener et al. 2015). Nevertheless, many feel that the social and moral changes resulting from this status are more nominal and less significant than hoped. Many have been disappointed to discover that the main objectives of shariah (justice, prosperity, safety) they thought would be fulfilled by the official implementation of shariah remain to be achieved.

References cited

Feener, R. Michael. 2013. *Shari'a and Social Engineering: The Implementation of Islamic Law in Contemporary Aceh, Indonesia* (Oxford: Oxford University Press).

Feener, R. Michael, Kloos, David and Samuels, Annemarie, eds., 2015. *Islam and the Limits of the State: Reconfigurations of Practice, Community and Authority in Contemporary Aceh* (Leiden: Brill).

Kell, Tim. 1995. *The Roots of Acehnese Rebellion, 1989–1992* (Ithaca: Cornell Modern Indonesia Project).

McGibbon, Rodd. 2006. "Local Leadership and the Aceh Conflict," in Anthony Reid, ed., *Verandah of Violence: The Background to the Aceh Problem* (Singapore: NUS Press).

Morris, Eric. 1985. "Aceh: Social Revolution and the Islamic Vision" in Audrey R. Kahin, ed., *Regional Dynamics of the Indonesian Revolution: Unity From Diversity* (Honolulu: University of Hawaii Press), pp. 83–110.

Pratt, Douglas. 1999. *Identity and Interaction: Islam and the Challenge of Interreligious Dialogue* (Sydney: Charles Strong Memorial Trust).

Reid, Anthony. 1988. *Southeast Asia in the Age of Commerce 1450–1680: Volume One. The Lands Below the Winds* (New Haven: Yale University Press).

————. 1993. "Islamization and Christianization in Southeast Asia: The Critical Phase, 1550–1650," in Antony Reid, ed., *Southeast Asia in the Early Modern Era: Trade, Power, and Belief* (Ithaca: Cornell University Press), pp. 151–79.

Ricklefs, Merle C. 2001. *History of Modern Indonesia Since c. 1200*. 3rd Edition (Stanford: Stanford University Press).

Salim, Arskal. 2003. "Shariah in Indonesia's Current Transition: An Update," in Arskal Salim and Azyumardi Azra, eds., *Shariah and Politics in Modern Indonesia* (Singapore: ISEAS), pp. 213–34.

Salim, Arskal. 2004. "Shari'a from Below in Aceh (1930s–1960s): Islamic Identity and the Right to Self Determination with Comparative Reference to the Moro Islamic Liberation Front (MILF)," *Indonesia and Malay World* 32 (March): 80–99.

Salim, Arskal. 2008. Challenging the Secular State: The Islamization of Law in Modern Indonesia (Honolulu: Hawai'i University Press).

————. 2009. *Politics, Criminal Justice and Islamization in Aceh* (Melbourne: ARC Federation Fellowship, Centre for Islamic Law and Society, Melbourne Law School, University of Melbourne).

————. 2010. "Dynamic Legal Pluralism in Indonesia: The Shift in Plural Legal Orders of Contemporary Aceh," *Journal of Legal Pluralism and Unofficial Law* 42(61): 1–29.

————. 2015. *Contemporary Islamic Law in Indonesia: Shariah and Legal Pluralism* (Edinburg: Edinburgh University Press).

Salim, Arskal and Azumardi Azra. 2003. "Introduction: The State and Shari'a in the Perspective of Indonesian Legal Politics," in Salim, Arskal and Azyumardi Azra, eds., *Shariah and Politics in Modern Indonesia* (Singapore: ISEAS), pp. 1–16.

Schwedler, Jillian. 2001. "Islamic Identity: Myth, Menace, or Mobilizer?" *SAIS Review* 21(2): 1–17.

Syamsuddin, Nazarudin. 1985. *The Republican Revolt: A Study of the Acehnese Rebellion* (Singapore: Institute of Southeast Asian Studies).

Vogel, Frank E. 2000. *Islamic Law and Legal System: Studies of Saudi Arabia* (Leiden, Boston, and Köln: Brill).

20

SALAFISM IN INDONESIA

Transnational Islam, violent activism, and cultural resistance

Noorhaidi Hasan

The eruption of religious conflicts and sectarian violence that have engulfed the political arena of post-Soeharto Indonesia appears to be more an anomaly than a prevailing feature when located in a broader picture of the country's history. Despite the fact that a large majority of Indonesia's population is Muslim, pockets of multi-religious and multi-ethnic communities that enjoyed ages of peaceful coexistence were established across the archipelago. In fact, Indonesian Muslims have traditionally been known for their accommodative and tolerant stance toward local custom and religious diversity. Nonetheless, migration, industrialization, mass education, and the advancement of media and communication technology have affected traditional values and local wisdoms, which had been keys in the establishment of peaceful coexistence in this plural society. Due to the intensification of globalization, Indonesia has likewise been increasingly susceptible to the influence of transnational Islam, which aggressively promotes rigid purification of faith under the banner of Salafism.

The collapse of Soeharto's New Order regime in May 1998 heralded Reformasi. Along with the dynamics of political transition and democratic reforms after Soeharto, a more complicated political landscape emerged. Not only did this Reformasi lead to the abrupt end of authoritarian government and repressive measures employed by the state in dealing with criticism and opposition; it also created opportunities for suppressed ethnic identities and religious ideologies to come to the surface (Sidel 2006: 9–10). Eventually, a number of militant Islamist groups achieved notoriety by taking to the streets to demand the comprehensive implementation of the shariah and raiding cafés, discotheques, casinos, brothels, and other dens of vice. More important, they called for jihad in a number of Indonesia's trouble spots, such as Ambon. In the provincial capital of Maluku, a bloody communal conflict had erupted between Christians and Muslims in 1999. During the conflict, thousands of Salafis from Java and other islands of Indonesia ventured to the frontlines to fight jihad against Christians and establish their footholds.

The expansion of Salafism in Indonesia

Salafism began to flourish in Indonesia in the second half of the 1980s, evident in the appearance of young men wearing long beards (*lihya*), Arab-style flowing robes (*jalabiyya*), turbans (*imama*), and ankle-length trousers (*isbal*) and women wearing a form of enveloping black veil (*niqab*) in public places. Identifying themselves as Salafis, followers of the pious ancestors (*Salaf al-Salih*), members were inclined to stand distinctly apart from the "anything goes" open society around them. They lived in small, exclusive, tight-knit communities. Under the changing political circumstances during the 1990s, the movement evolved rapidly to the extent that it succeeded in establishing an exclusivist current of Islamic activism organizing study sessions openly in university campuses and mosques located both in city outskirts and villages in the countryside.

Before the collapse of the New Order, Salafism was relatively consistent in developing a stance of apolitical quietism. The movement's main concern emphasized the purity and oneness of God, meaning to accept and believe in the oneness of God and his absolute authority, considered the foundation of Muslim life; other Salafi concerns centered on the call for a return to strict religious practice as well as the moral integrity of individuals. Seemingly trivial, superficial issues, such as jalabiyya, imama, lihya, isbal, and niqab have constituted the main themes in their day-to-day discussions. A commitment to wear the jalabiyya by men and the niqab by women, for instance, has been viewed as much more important than taking part in political activities. Salafis believe that Muslim society must first be Islamized through a gradual evolutionary process that includes education (*tarbiyya*) and purification (*tasfiyya*) before the comprehensive implementation of the shariah can be realized. As a strategy to achieve this end, they have been fervently committed to da´wa activities, participating in the establishment of *halqa*s (study circles) and *daura*s (workshops).

Salafism can be conceptualized as a form of reconstituted Wahhabism, marked by its concern with matters of creed and morality, including strict monotheism, divine attributes, purification of Islam from accretions, anti-Sufism, and development of the moral integrity of the individual. Because of the pejorative connotation of the term *Wahhabi* among Muslims, the term *Salafi* has been used as the banner of the movement (Delong-Bas 2004: 123–4; Hasan 2007: 85; Commins 2009: ix). The genealogy of Salafism can be traced back to the efforts made by classic Salafi articulators, including Ahmad ibn Hanbal (d. 855), Ahmad ibn Taymiyya (d.1328), and Ibn Qayyim al-Jawziyya (d. 1350), to advocate a return to pure Islam; these predecessors inspired Muhammad ibn 'Abd al-Wahhab (d. 1787) to denounce religious practices prevalent in the Arabian society, such as the cult of saints. Known as Wahhabism, the movement was later enshrined as Saudi Arabia's state religion (Nevo 1998; Al-Rasheed 2002; Delong-Bas 2004; Lacroix 2011).

Salafism has developed as a consequence of Saudi Arabia's immensely ambitious global campaign for the Wahhabization of the Muslim umma. This campaign can be seen against the background of the Arab Cold War, especially when Saudi Arabia tried hard to reinforce its position as the center of the Muslim world following the fading influence of Arab socialist nationalism developed by Gamal Abdul Nasser after the Arab-Israeli War of 1967 (Kepel 2002: 46). Thanks to the skyrocketing of world oil prices, which gave considerable economic benefits to Saudi Arabia during the 1970s, this kingdom had the opportunity to sponsor a variety of da´wa activities all over the Muslim world, the purpose of which was to ensure the acquiescence of the Muslim world, boost Saudi legitimacy at home, and fulfill Western political projects (Fraser 1997: 222; Al-Rasheed 2008: 2). In this way, Wahhabism was exported and spread, together with the Muslim Brotherhood ideology as a by-product of the campaign. This campaign was later intensified, particularly in the aftermath of the Iranian Revolution and the takeover of the Masjid al-Haram by Juhayman-led group in 1979 (Abukhalil 2004; Trofimov 2007). In fact, the political developments in Saudi Arabia during the 1980s and 1990s informed much about the changing landscape of Salafism. Rivalries and alliances established as a consequence of the Juhayman's takeover of the Masjid al-Haram urged the establishment of the circle of prominent Salafi authorities serving as the main patrons of the Saudi state around Muslim clerics like 'Abd al-Aziz bin Baz (d. 1999), Nasir al-Din al-Albani (d. 1999), and Muhammad bin Salih al-Uthaimin (d. 2001).

With the world's largest Muslim population and its strategic position in Southeast Asia, Indonesia was of particular interest to Saudi Arabia. The inflows of Salafism came particularly from the Indonesian Council for Islamic Propagation (Dewan Dakwah Islamiyah Indonesia, DDII) and the Jakarta-based College for the Study of Islam and Arabic (Lembaga Ilmu Pengetahuan Islam dan Arab, LIPIA). With generous financial support from Saudi Arabia, DDII was active not only in sponsoring the construction of mosques and Islamic schools but also in the dispatching of Indonesian youths to study in various universities in the Middle East. An international branch of Imam Muhammad Ibn Saud University in Riyadh, LIPIA came to intensify the Saudi campaign by providing free higher education for a younger generation of Indonesian Muslims (International Crisis Group 2004: 7–8). Thousands of madrasa graduates received the opportunity to study at LIPIA; some then had the chance to continue their studies in Saudi Arabian universities, particularly at the Islamic University of Madina. Despite LIPIA's curricula and teaching materials imbued with Saudi anti-pluralistic Wahhabi ideology and political propaganda, the Indonesian government allowed the institution to operate, as it was seen as helping Indonesia to solidify its bilateral relations with Saudi Arabia (Kovacs 2014: 5–6). One of the most remarkable impacts of the Salafi campaign was the emergence of a new type of Muslim intellectual who had the zeal to disseminate Salafism. These actors set up foundations and madrasas financed directly by philanthropic agents in the Middle East, which played a crucial role in the further expansion of Salafism.

The rapid proliferation of Salafism was coupled with the eruption of tension among its protagonists, particularly following the Afghan War in the late 1980s. The Salafis were divided into three factions: purists, politicos, and jihadists. While the purists were primarily concerned with the purity of Islam and thus rejecting political activism, the politicos were politically minded and highly critical of incumbent regimes. Close to the latter, the jihadists believed in the necessity of jihad to fight for Islam (Wiktorowicz 2006: 217–28). These three categories are identical to what Hegghammer and Lacroix (2007: 105–17) refer to as quietists, reformists, and jihadists respectively. Reflecting on what occurred in Saudi Arabia, the increasing number of Salafis returning to Indonesia from the Salafi teaching centers in the Middle East resulted in the competition for the position as the legitimate representative of the movement. The upshot was that fragmentation and conflict became inevitable. All of the rivals claimed to be authentic Salafis committed to the purity of the movement goal and in so doing gained generous financial support from Saudi Arabia and other Persian Gulf countries. They were split into two main currents: the so-called Sururis and non-Sururis. For the latter, the former were followers of Syrian Muhammad Surur al-Nayib Zayn al-'Abidin, one of the main critics of the Saudi regime. Despite their anti-regime criticism, the Sururis remained the most favored group to receive money from Saudi Arabia and Kuwait through funding agencies operating in Indonesia (Hasan 2009). To boost their legitimacy, the non-Sururis strengthened their alliance with Muqbil Ibn Hadi al-Wadi'i of Yemen and were thus also known as the Yemenis.

Political and Jihadi activism

Salafism captured Indonesia's public attention when its activities began to be associated with violent jihadism. The trigger was the involvement of its proponents in responding to Indonesian political developments after Soeharto. Through various mass religious gatherings, *tabligh akbar*, Salafi activists lost no time in attempting to engage in the changing political landscape. Under the leadership of Ja'far Umar Thalib, one current set up the Forum Komunikasi Ahlus Sunnahh wal Jama'ah (the Communication Forum for Followers of the Sunnah and the Community of the Prophet, FKAWJ) in February 1999. Subsequently, they issued a resolution calling on

Indonesian Muslims to perform jihad in Maluku, where skirmishes between local Christians and Muslims had escalated into full-blown communal conflicts (Hasan 2006; van Klinken 2007). This call was legitimized by fatwas, religious legal opinions, given by a number of prominent Salafi 'ulama in the Middle East (Hasan 2005). On April 6, 2000, Ja'far Umar Thalib's supporters gathered in the Senayan Main Stadium in Jakarta to state their determination to fight jihad. Under the auspices of Laskar Jihad (Jihad Force), thousands of them in fact enlisted to venture to the frontlines and fight against Christians. Until its disbanding in October 2002, Laskar Jihad dispatched more than 7,000 fighters to confront Christians in Maluku.

The Laskar Jihad was not the only Salafi group mobilizing fighters to fight jihad in Maluku. Laskar Mujahidin, for instance, also mobilized volunteers, who were believed to have certain historical linkages with the home-grown Darul Islam and al-Qaeda-linked Jamaah Islamiyyah. Given their differing doctrinal interpretations and ideological orientations, Laskar Jihad and Laskar Mujahidin often displayed mutual hostility (Hasan 2006: 196–7). Often portrayed as a quietist Salafi group, the former justified its resort to political activism and violence by emphasizing the necessity for Muslims to protect their Muslim brothers from the attacks of belligerent infidels. Associated with the Salafi jihadi ideology, the latter, on the contrary, highlighted their operation in Ambon as just a preliminary action in a greater jihad against enemies attacking Muslims all over the world.

Laskar Mujahidin's successful operations in Ambon convinced Jamaah Islamiyah to strengthen their foothold in Indonesia. During the first phase leading up to the Reformasi from January 1993 to May 1998, Abdullah Sungkar and Abu Bakar Ba'asyir, founders of Jamaah Islamiyah, operated freely out of Malaysia and developed Jamaah Islamiyah's organizational capacity, focusing on recruitment and building operational bases. By the late 1990s, six *wakalah*, or subdivisions, had been set up in Malaysia, as well as a seventh in Singapore. At the same time, the group maintained its network in Indonesia. During a second phase, from May 1998 to December 2000, following Sungkar's and Ba'asyir's return from Malaysia to Indonesia, the leaders further expanded and consolidated their network, organizing the first coordinated attacks on a dozen churches on Christmas night of 2000 (Solahudin 2013: 6–8).

The rise of Jamaah Islamiyah (JI) is of particular importance because the group constitutes the strongest expression of Salafism in the political landscape of post-Soeharto Indonesia. Despite its historical ties to the Darul Islam, JI remains a new phenomenon that demonstrates how transnational dynamics have transcended established cultural and political boundaries and penetrated different milieus. JI is believed to be the most active group in disseminating the Salafi jihadi ideology in Indonesia. The ideology prospered during the Afghan War via Abdullah Azzam's thoughts. He managed to contextualize Sayyid Qutb's radical view to obliterate the "infidel" regimes in power in the respective countries (the so-called near-enemy) to push for offensive jihad against the infidels wherever they are. The latter is deemed to be an integral part of the jihad against *jahiliyahism* (the state of non-Islamic "ignorance"), in which every Muslim is obliged (as a *fard 'ayn*) to participate in order to fortify the integrity of the Islamic territory. In the mid-1990s, Ayman al-Zawahiri, known to be close to Osama bin Laden, developed an alternative vision of the jihad movement: the war against jahiliyyahism had to attack its source directly, that is, had to attack the "Salabis," whom he identified as the United States, its Western allies, and Zionist Israel (Gerges 2009). His ideas clearly shifted the focus of jihad toward the "distant enemy" that bin Laden adopted, which had been formulated at the end of the 1980s and had become the backbone of the creation of the World Islamic Front for Jihad in 1998, which later transformed into the infamous al-Qaeda.

From 1985 to 1990, some 200 Darul Islam members in the *usroh* network were in fact dispatched to Afghanistan to participate in military training (*i'dad ashkari*) at Harby Pohantum, founded by Shaikh Rasul Sayyaf. The purpose was to acquire military knowledge and skills for jihad against the New Order government. In Afghanistan, the militants became acquainted with the jihadi Salafi teachings. Their adoption of jihadism stirred up conflicts in the internal *usroh* network. They criticized the ideology of the vanguard of the Darul Islam leadership believed to be imbued by traditional Islamic teachings. One important target of their critiques was Ajengan Masduki, the then DI commander deemed to have deviated from the fundamental Islamic teachings by joining a Sufi order (Solahudin 2013: 145–8). Sungkar led the campaign against Masduki. Shortly thereafter, he established Jamaah Islamiyah.

With the support of Abu Bakar Baasyir, Sungkar responded to bin Laden's message to shift from a local jihad to implement the shariah law to an international jihad targeting America by joining the World's Islamic Front for jihad. While many senior members in Regional Command (Mantiqi) I of Jamaah Islamiyah, such as Hambali and Mukhlas, supported Sungkar and Ba'asyir's call, Mantiqi II officials like Ibnu Thoyib, Achmad Roihan, and Thoriqudin rejected it. The debates were set aside after serious communal conflicts exploded in Ambon and Poso. In the eyes of Jamaah Islamiyah's leaders, these communal conflicts had opened the door to jihad. Conflicts of interest among its protagonists have also informed the dynamics of Jamaah Islamiyah after the death of Sungkar in 1999, a situation that eventually gave rise to various factions planning terror operations without any recourse to the leadership's decisions (Solahudin 2013). Baasyir, who came to replace Sungkar, called Muslims to unite and fight for jihad, believed to be the only way to implement the law of Allah (Abuza 2003: 167). He resigned in 2000 and was quickly replaced by Abu Rusdan and, subsequently, by Abu Dujana, who continued the previous confrontational stance of Jamaah Islamiyah (Pavlova 2006: 4). Despite such fragmentation, the Jamaah Islamiyah network and its offspring remain alive and well in Indonesia particularly because they are grounded in the Salafi jihadi ideology. From his cell in Nusakambangan prison, in July 2008, Baasyir established Jamaah Anshorut Tauhid, a splinter faction from JI; in July 2014, the organization pledged its loyalty to the Islamic State in Syria and Iraq (ISIS), calling for jihadists to perpetrate terror attacks.

Salafism in the age of war against terrorism

Following the 9/11 attacks, Jakarta came under increasing international pressure to act swiftly against the radical Islamist groups. Initially, the Indonesian government was hesitant. Traumatized by the New Order's repressive security measures, the Indonesian civil society reminded President Megawati Sukarnoputri's administration of the danger of employing the enemy-centric model of repression. Faced with intricate political problems, Megawati attempted not to "hurt" Islamist groups and remained idle in countering the threats posed by Islamist radicalism. All of this changed dramatically after the 2002 Bali bombing, which demonstrated the grave threat radical Islamist groups posed to Indonesia. In spite of Vice President Hamzah Haz's initial denial of information provided by Singaporean, Malaysian, and US authorities about the cells of the Jamaah Islamiyah masterminding a series of bombing attacks in Indonesia, including those on Bali, the police investigation quickly punctured the idealistic bubble. It appeared that Jamaah Islamiyah had some 2,000 members and a wider support network of about 5,000 people. The police also uncovered the strong ties Jamaah Islamiyah had with al-Qaeda. The message was clear: the War against Terrorism had come to Indonesia. Particularly in response to the Bali bombing, the Indonesian parliament passed two anti-terrorism laws: Law No. 15/2003 provides the legal basis for the police to detain terrorist suspects up to six months before an indictment is drawn up, while it gives to prosecutors and judges the authority to block bank accounts belonging to individuals or organizations believed to be funding terrorist activities, and Law No. 16/2003 aims specifically at retroactively prosecuting the Bali bombers.

Just five days after the first Bali bombing in October 2002, the Laskar Jihad leadership surprisingly announced the organization's dissolution. The disbanding had to do with the dispute between Ja'far Umar Thalib and his main lieutenants about the purity of their jihad activism. Some Salafis on the advisory body of Laskar Jihad began to feel that the political steps taken by Ja'far Umar Thalib had deviated from the Salafi fundamental teachings on avoiding politics, let alone violence. A number of these critics, including Abu Munzir Dzul Akmal and Abu Muhammad Dzulqarnain, requested clarification from Ja'far Umar Thalib. Dissatisfied with his explanation, they mobilized support from other Salafis to work toward the disbanding of Laskar Jihad. As far as they were concerned, Laskar Jihad had strayed from Salafist doctrine because of the personal – politico-economic – interests of its top leadership. They held Ja'far Umar Thalib responsible for making Laskar Jihad part of an embarrassing political game (Hasan 2006: 211–12). Dzul Akmal and Dzulqarnain sent a letter to the Saudi Salafi scholar, Rabi' ibn Hadi al-Madkhali, requesting a fatwa concerning the existence of Laskar Jihad. In response, the *mufti* issued a *fatwa* recommending Laskar Jihad disband.

Laskar Jihad's dissolution confirms the vulnerability of the Salafis to tensions and conflicts imbued by ideological disputes and political-economic rivalries. In fact, after the disbanding of Laskar Jihad, the Salafis who had been united under the influence of Ja'far Umar Thalib became divided into three major groups under the command of three rival leaders: Lukman Ba'abduh, Dzulqarnain, and Abu Turab al-Jawi (Sunarwoto 2016: 206–7). Lukman Baabduh was deputy commander of Laskar Jihad in Maluku, whereas Dzulqarnain was the head of its fatwa section. Abu Turab came late to Maluku and was not part of the Laskar Jihad elite group. However, he was able to exert his influence among certain Salafi circles because of his loyalty to Yahya al-Hujuri, the successor of al-Wadi'i in leading Darul Hadith in Yemen. After the death of al-Wadi'i, rivalry and conflict occurred between al-Hujuri and Abd al-Rahman al-Mar'i al-Adeni. While Baabduh sided with al-Adeni, Abu Turab decided to defend al-Hujuri.

It is of interest to note that all the Salafi authorities associated with Laskar Jihad, including Ja'far Umar Thalib, came to actively engage in countering violent jihadism. Endorsing what Nasir Abbas, former commander of Jamaah Islamiyah, said in his *Uncovering Jamaah Islamiyah: Confession of a Former JI Member*, Ja'far Umar Thalib has strongly criticized the interpretation of bin Laden on jihad and the Jamaah Islamiyah decision to follow the interpretation. He asserted that bin Laden did not qualify as a mufti so that his fatwa should be ignored. According to Ja'far, jihad is legitimate only under certain conditions, including with the approval from the competent political authority and only for defensive purposes. Abu Hamza Yusuf also criticized Imam Samudra (one of the Bali bombers), who also claimed to be Salafi. According to Yusuf, the claim is false because Samudra had idolized problematic personalities, such as Safar al-Hawali, Salman al-Awdah, Osama bin Laden, Abdullah Sungkar, and Abu Bakar Ba'asyir.

Lukman Ba'abduh took more significant steps toward condemning Salafi jihadists by publishing a book entitled *They Are Terrorists*. In this book, he condemns bin Laden as a *Kharijite*, which is to say (in Salafi parlance) one who destroys Islam by spreading the doctrine of "excommunication" (*takfir*) and perpetrating terror. In another book, Ba'abduh reiterates his criticism of Imam Samudra and other like-minded individuals as a deviant group that is too quick to apply the doctrine of takfir to legitimate rulers and Muslims who hold different views. Differences among Salafi jihadists and Salafi quietists in interpreting jihad and other key Salafi doctrines have prevented them from establishing a hegemonic discourse, crucial in the dynamics of Indonesia's Counter Violent Extremism (CVE).

The waning appeal of the Salafis

In response to the growing difficulties confronting Salafism after 9/11, certain groups of Salafis have demonstrated their readiness to accommodate calls for reforms and movement toward the Islamic mainstream. For instance, they did not hesitate to undertake a review of their school curriculum and incorporate both religious and secular worldly knowledge into course syllabi. Accordingly, the curriculum adopted in their madrasas helps somehow to bridge the educational dualism that has characterized Muslim education for almost two centuries. Yet the main character of the madrasas is maintained as Islamic teaching centers aimed to train a new generation of Muslims rooted in and committed to the dissemination of the Salafi faith (Wahid 2014). Interestingly, with this reformed system and relatively modern management requiring students to pay tuition fees and living costs, the madrasas have apparently facilitated the mobility of Salafi teachers and students in Indonesia. At some Salafi madrasas in Indonesia, for instance, it is not difficult to find students from neighboring countries like Malaysia and Singapore. Those madrasas apparently have succeeded at creating a system that enables them to operate independently, without Saudi money. This is particularly the case for the madrasas under the control of Dzulqarnain and his allies. Some of the madrasas have even successfully evolved into established Islamic education institutions attracting middle-class families.

In tandem with the significant changes in Indonesia's political context after Soeharto and the dynamics after 9/11, the space for maneuvering available to the Salafis is no longer sufficient to maintain their footholds at the grassroots. Elsewhere (Hasan 2010), I have argued that the attempt to set up Salafi madrasas as the node for informal social network for the purpose of propagating Salafi ideology in remote areas of abangan villages, which were perceived to be the "red" areas imbued with syncretic, communist influences, was largely ineffective, owing to the Salafis' exclusivist and self-limiting character. Though generally located in areas of urban or semi-urban settlement, these madrasas have emerged as enclaves that draw a firm distinction with the "anything goes" open society around them. Teachers, students, and other members of the madrasa form tight-knit communities restricting contacts with outsiders. Except for certain important reasons, students are not allowed to have contact with people from the surrounding community. Their daily life is routine to the point of being monotonous. The main components of their activities consist of praying, studying, and memorizing the Quran.

The rigid Salafi religious doctrines and exclusivist lifestyle taught in the Salafi madrasa have attracted only a small number of abangan children and thus not brought about significant change in the larger Muslim population as a whole. These young Muslim recruits were disaffected youth eager to feel a sense of empowerment and declare their independence from village elders. The rest remained skeptical regarding the Salafis' claim to promote authentic Islam while criticizing local religious practices. Instead, the proliferation of Salafi madrasas has compelled villagers to practice Islam and traditional rituals as their attempt to de-contextualize the Salafi call for purifying Muslim beliefs and practices.

This was the course of events in Batikan, Muntilan, a village located several kilometers from Borobudur, where the Madrasa Minhaj al-Sunnah was established with the financial support of a local businessman and owner of a network of restaurants in Central Java. No doubt, the presence of this madrasa inspired more villagers to attend Friday congregation and daily collective prayers and more women to wear headscarves. Nonetheless, they have been also very active in attending *selamatan*, *barzanzi*, and *hadrah*, traditional rituals and practices deemed *bid'a* (religiously unacceptable "innovation") by the Salafis. These performative events have been organized as a cultural strategy employed by the villagers to resist Salafism. They believe that there is no need for the Salafis to keep promoting the strict version of Salafi Islam if it only disturbs their village conviviality and harmonious life.

The failure of the Salafis to win followers is likewise evident in the case of Kepakisan, an *abangan* village located in densely populated hill country twenty-five kilometers to the north of the town of Wonosobo on the Dieng Plateau. When I visited the community in the early 2000s, the Salafis had expanded their influence so as to dominate the village. Almost half of the five hundred families in the village transformed themselves into Salafis, and more than thirty of them joined the Laskar Jihad mission in Maluku. Interestingly, they have remained modest farmers or agricultural laborers working every day on ex-plantation farmland owned by affluent business-men, planting potatoes, carrots, cabbages, and other vegetable crops. But one hour before the noon prayer, these believers usually rush home to take a bath, don the jalabiyya, and go to the mosque. The conversion of the Kepakisan people to Salafism appears in many instances to have involved the conversion of whole families, though it was not always the head of each family who led the conversion – the eldest son was more often the catalyst.

Some elites in Kepakisan, including the then-village head Supoyo, supported the develop-ment of Salafism in their village as part of their effort to get closer to the New Order political forces and mainstream religious groups. The village elites were involved in supporting the Salafi propaganda through their sponsoring of the building of Salafi da'wa infrastructure. Mosques and teaching centers of Salafism were established, including three educational institutions for children, men, and women, known as Tarbiyatul Atfal, Tarbiyatul Rijal, and Tarbiyatul Ummahat respectively. To fortify their stronghold in Kepakisan, the proponents of Salafism were keen to establish contacts with fellow Salafi followers in other Indonesian cities. *Daurahs* and other reli-gious gatherings were held regularly at Masjid Baitul Makmur. With the presence of prominent Salafi *ustadh*s, including Lukman Baabduh, Muhammad Umar As-sewed, Qomar Suaidi, Muslim Abu Ishaq, and Afifuddin, the events succeeded in consolidating followers and further promot-ing the Salafi messages. The return of a group of native Salafis from a younger generation of Kepakisan, who had completed their studies in various Salafi madrasas, intensified Salafi da'wa activities in Kepakisan.

Nevertheless, the "golden age" of Salafism in Kepakisan has apparently come to an end. When I returned to the village in 2015, the influence of Salafism was waning. After Pak Poyo passed away in 2002, tensions rose, involving conflicts between Salafi and non-Salafi villagers. The latter, who had from the outset felt threatened by the Salafi da'wa expansion, launched measures against the Salafis. The position of Salafi opponents strengthened too as a result of changes to the political map of Kepakisan. Pak Poyo's close family, including some of his sons, not only withdrew their support, but also appeared to have become the main agents of the anti-Salafi opposition. They felt that the Salafis' presence in their villages had contributed to the deterioration of family relations and village conviviality.

Krismono (2016: 207–8) indicated that the growing influence of Tablighi Jamaat, which was brought by Nur Syam, the eldest son of Khairuddin, a senior *takmir* of Masjid Baitul Makmur, has also helped to accelerate the declining influence of Salafism in Kepakisan. Nur Syam had studied at Pesantren Payaman Magelang, which is one of the centers of Tablighi Jamaat in Cen-tral Java. After returning home to the village, he actively promoted Tablighi Jamaat doctrines with the help of senior *tablighi ustadh*s from Temboro of East Java. Both Nur Syam and Khair-uddin assumed that the da'wa methods of Tablighi Jamaat are more suitable to the Prophet's Sunnah when compared to the Salafi method that was inclined to accuse villagers of *bid'a* and *shirk*. Nur Syam built a center of Tablighi Jamaat in Musalla Al-Hidayah, not far from Masjid Baitul Makmur, and actively preached tablighi teachings from door to door. Conflict becomes inevitable. Proponent of the Salafis and Tablighi Jamaat engaged in heated debates. For the Salafis, Tablighi Jamaat's ideology deviates from the fundamental tenets of Islam. While in the eyes of the proponents of Tablighi Jamaat, the Salafi ideology has not only endangered village cultural practices but also divided the community.

When Salafism flourished in Kepakisan, some people who disagreed with the Salafi ideology chose to send their sons to NU religious schools (pesantren). After returning home, these young ustadhs sought to promote their more moderate version of Islam and were involved in the resistance against Salafism. Ramadan, for example, took a step further by establishing the Irsyadul Mubtadin Quranic Kindergarten. This institute developed rapidly and soon transformed itself into a *diniyah* school that drew growing attention from Kepakisan children. There they studied theology, fiqh, and hadith by using books commonly used in NU pesantrens. More important, Ramadan sought to revive traditional religious rituals, such as *barzanzi*, *salawatan*, and *yasinan* which had been prohibited when Pak Poyo was serving as Kepakisan village head (Krismono 2016: 211). Such traditional rituals and gatherings have gradually evolved and attracted growing numbers of villagers.

Bambang, the eldest son of Pak Poyo, has also been very active in organizing resistance against Salafism. He was eager to challenge the Salafis by recruiting and mobilizing followers. To win the competition between him and the proponents of the Salafis, Bambang made an alliance with NU's Barisan Ansor (Banser) at Batur Sub-District. He encouraged villagers to organize a demonstration in front of the village office to challenge the Salafis' influence (Krismono 2016: 213). Eventually, Bambang and his followers succeeded in taking control of Masjid Baitul Makmur, which had been the main center of Salafi da'wa activities. The local Salafi movement did not give up. They tried to consolidate themselves in the al-Huda musalla (prayer house), which they also began to use for their Friday congregational worship. This marked the first time in the community that congregational worship was held simultaneously in two adjacent mosques.

There is no doubt that, despite their continuing efforts to maintain a foothold in Indonesia, growing social resistance against Salafism has put a halt to their expansion. Recently, Ja'far Umar Thalib sought to extend his network of followers to Papua. His plan to build a pesantren in Arso 14 Jayapura and to establish 20 others across Papua sparked strong opposition from local Papuans. They organized meetings and coordinated with local government agencies to oppose the presence of Ja'far Umar Thalib and his pesantren, which they believe would threaten peaceful life and inter-religious harmony in Papua (Al-Makassary 2017). According to them, tensions had been increasing when the so-called Tolikara incident of clashes occurred on Idul Fitri 2015, between the congregation of the Gereja Injili di Indonesia (GIDI) and Muslims. Comprehending the seriousness of the situation, the provincial branch of the Council of Indonesian Ulama (MUI) eventually issued a call to expel Ja'far Umar Thalib from the islands.

Conclusion

The efflorescence of Salafism in Indonesia cannot be isolated from Saudi Arabia's immensely ambitious global campaign for the Wahhabization of the Muslim umma. Part of the Saudis' politics of expanding their geo-political and geo-strategic influence across the Muslim world, the campaign succeeded in creating networks of loyalty and allegiance, based on real benefits and clothed in the language of Islamic solidarity and brotherhood. Saudi Arabia realized the importance of local partners in running the campaign. In the Indonesian context, we cannot underestimate the role played by DDII and LIPIA in marketing Saudi religious ideology. Da'wa activities linked to the campaign proliferated, followed by the establishment of Salafi foundations and madrasas in many parts of Indonesia's provinces.

For many years, the expansion of Salafism seemed unabated. A group of quietist Salafis, under the leadership of Ja'far Umar Thalib, resorted to political activism by calling for jihad in Maluku. In the midst of the bloody communal conflict in the islands, the home-grown Darul Islam-linked Jamaah Islamiyah rose. They claimed to be the real Salafis who would fight for Islam against belligerent infidels. Debates over authenticity among Salafis were rife. These fragments informed the dynamics of Salafism in Indonesia, which reflects how dimensions of transnational Islam are entangled with local politics. The dynamics of Salafism in Indonesia also adds to debates about current dimensions of identity politics molded by transnational forms of political organization, mobilization, and practice which are coming into being through globalized political and social spaces.

Today, however, the expansion of Salafism in Indonesia appears to have ended in failure. The cases of Muntilan and Kepakisan described in this chapter illustrate two things: (1) that the Salafi campaign to take root in Javanese abangan villages depends much upon a supportive social and economic configuration and the absence of support from local elite and influential personalities makes the campaign vulnerable to resistance and opposition from villagers who felt threatened by the Salafi exclusivist ideology and self-limiting character, and (2) that a Javanese village cultural mechanism is at work to counter the expansion of the rigid ideology promoted by Salafism; the villagers would react against Salafism by de-legitimizing Salafi claims and reviving traditional cultures and rituals.

References cited

Abukhalil, As'ad. 2004. *The Battle for Saudi Arabia, Royalty, Fundamentalism, and Global Power* (New York: Seven Stories Press).

Abuza, Zachary. 2003. *Militant Islam in Southeast Asia: Crucible of Terror* (Boulder, CO: Lynne Rienner Publishers Inc.).

Al-Makassary, Ridwan. 2017. *Insiden Tolikara dan Ja'far Umar Thalib: Kontroversi Mushalla yang Dibakar dan Drama Jihad di Tanah Papua* (Jayapura: Kementerian Agama Provinsi Papua).

Al-Rasheed, Madawi. 2002. *A History of Saudi Arabia* (New York: Cambridge University Press).

———. 2008. "Introduction: As Assessment of Saudi Political, Religious and Media Expansion," in Al-Rasheed, Madawi, ed., *Kingdom Without Borders Saudi Arabia's Political, Religious and Media Frontiers* (London: Hurst), pp. 1–38.

Commins, David. 2009. *The Wahhabi Mission and Saudi Arabia* (London: I.B. Tauris).

Delong-Bas, Natana J. 2004. *Wahhabi Islam, From Revival and Reform to Global Jihad* (London: I.B. Tauris).

Fraser, Cary. 1997. "In Defense of Allah's Realm: Religion and Statecraft in Saudi Foreign Policy Strategy," in Susanne Hoeber Rudolph and James Piscatori, eds., *Transnational Religion and Fading States* (Oxford: Westview Press), pp. 226–34.

Gerges, Fawaz, A. 2009. *The Far Enemy Why Jihad Went Global* (2nd ed., Cambridge: Harvard University Press).

Hasan, Noorhaidi. 2005. "Between Transnational Interest and Domestic Politics: Understanding Middle Eastern *Fatwas* on Jihad in the Moluccas," *Islamic Law and Society* 12(1): 73–92.

———. 2006. *Laskar Jihad: Islam, Militancy and the Quest for Identity in Post-New Order Indonesia* (Ithaca: Southeast Asia Program, Cornell University).

———. 2007. "The Salafi Movement in Indonesia: Transnational Dynamics and Local Development," *Comparative Studies of South Asia, Africa and the Middle East* 27(1): 83–94.

———. 2009. "Ambivalent Doctrine and Conflict in the Salafi Movement in Indonesia," in Roel Meijer, ed., *Global Salafism: Islam's New Religious Movement* (London and New York: Hurst/Columbia University Press), pp. 223–43.

———. 2010. "The Failure of the Wahhabi Campaign: Transnational Islam and the Salafi Madrasa in Post-9/11 Indonesia," *South East Asia Research* 18(4): 705–35.

Hegghammer, Thomas and Stéphane Lacroix. 2007. "Rejectionist Islamism in Saudi Arabia: The Story of Juhayman al-'Utaybi Revisited," *International Journal of Middle East Study* 84(4): 103–22.

International Crisis Group. 2004. "Indonesia Backgrounder: Why Salafism and Terrorism Mostly Don't Mix," *ICG Asia Report* 83: 1–53.

Kepel, Gilles. 2002. *Jihad, the Trail of Political Islam* (London: I.B. Tauris).

Kovacs, Amanda. 2014. "Saudi Exporting Salafi Education and Radicalizing Indonesian Muslims," *German Institute of Global and Area Studies Focus* 7: 1–8.

Krismono, 2016. *Ekonomi-Politik Salafism di Pedesaan Jawa* (Yogyakarta: Pascasarjana UIN Sunan Kalijaga).

Lacroix, Stéphane. 2011. *Awakening Islam: Politics of Religious Dissent in Contemporary Saudi Arabia*, trans. George Holoch (Cambridge, MA: Harvard University Press).

Nevo, Joseph. 1998. "Religion and National Identity in Saudi Arabia," *Middle Eastern Studies* 34(3): 34–53.

Pavlova, Elena. 2006. "From Counter-Society to Counter-State: Jemaah Islamiyah According to PUPJI," Working Paper 117 (Singapore: Institute of Defense and Strategic Studies).

Sidel, John. 2006. *Riots, Pogroms, Jihad: Religious Violence in Indonesia* (Ithaca: Cornell University Press).

Solahudin. 2013. *The Roots of Terrorism in Indonesia: From Darul Islam to Jema'ah Islamiyah*, trans. Dave McRae (Ithaca: Cornell University Press).

Sunarwoto. 2016. "Salafi Dakwah Radio: A Contest for Religious Authority," *Archipel* 91: 203–30.

Trofimov, Yaroslav. 2007. *The Siege of Mecca* (New York: Doubleday).

Van Klinken, Gerry. 2007. *Communal Violence and Democratization in Indonesia, Small Town Wars* (London and New York: Routledge).

Wahid, Din. 2014. "Nurturing the Salafi Manhaj: A Study of Salafi Pesantrens in Contemporary Indonesia" (Ph.D. Thesis. Utrecht, The Netherlands: Faculty of Arts, Utrecht University).

Wiktorowicz, Quintan. 2006. "Anatomy of the Salafi Movement," *Studies in Conflict and Terrorism* 29(3): 207–39.

21

CHRISTIANS IN INDONESIA

Jan S. Aritonang

There are numerous important issues and developments concerning Christianity and Christians in Indonesia during the so-called Reformation Era, from May 1998 to today. This chapter focuses on three issues: denominational and organizational development, inter-faith relations, and political and economic life.

Denominational[1] and organizational[2] development

Indonesia is a country with many Christian church denominations and organizations, although the total number of Christians, according to official statistics, is not more than 10% of the population, i.e., around 25 million out of 257 million in 2016. Until the beginning of the twenty-first century, there were some 15 major denominations: Roman Catholic, Lutheran, Eastern Orthodox, Reformed (Calvinist, Presbyterian), Anglican (Episcopal), Mennonite, Baptist, Methodist, Pentecostal, Charismatic, Evangelical, Adventist, Jehovah's Witness, Mormon, and Christian Scientist. Those denominations are adhered to by some 400 church organizations. The adherence is twofold – denominational and organizational. The Pentecostal denomination, for example, is adhered to by over 100 Pentecostal church organizations, while one church organization, such as Gereja Bethel Indonesia (Indonesian Bethel Church) adheres simultaneously to three different denominations – Pentecostal, Evangelical, and Reformed.[3]

Each denomination and organization has its unique history in this country. The Roman Catholic Church (RCC) started its mission at the beginning of the sixteenth century. After a two-century break (seventeenth to eighteenth century) except in some islands (Flores and the surrounding small islands), RCC returned to this country in the beginning of the nineteenth century and has flourished up to today. It is now the largest church in Indonesia with some seven million members. Its impact and contribution to the life of the nation are also very remarkable, among other things through education (from kindergarten to university), health care, agricultural extension, media (radio, television, newspaper, and so on), and diaconal ministry.

The Eastern Orthodox Church, one of the oldest denominations in the world, entered this country in the nineteenth century but was unable to grow and increase significantly. This church is further divided into several organizations, among others Greek, Syrian, and Coptic Orthodox. The Greek Orthodox in the beginning of the twenty-first century also split into several organizations. The total number of the members of the Orthodox churches in this country is quite small, not more than 100,000.

The Reformed Church (*Gereformeerd*, Calvinist, Presbyterian) started at the beginning of the seventeenth century during the rule of the Vereenigde Oost-Indische Compagnie (VOC, the Dutch East Indies Company). However this church only grew significantly from the beginning of the nineteenth century, as a result of the efforts of several Dutch missionary societies. Recently, among the some 400 church organizations, 50 profess adherence to the Reformed or Calvinist denomination in spite of differences in grade and understanding of what Calvinism is.

Certain churches have combined Reformed doctrine with Evangelical, like the Gereja Reformed Injili Indonesia (GRII; Indonesian Evangelical Reformed Church). The current total numbers of the members of the so-called Reformed churches is some six million. Some larger churches in terms of membership include the Gereja Masehi Injili Minahasa (GMIM; the Minahasa Evangelical Christian Church), Gereja Protestan Maluku (GPM, the Moluccan Protestant Church), and Gereja Masehi Injili Timor (GMIT; the Timor Evangelical Christian Church) with respectively around one million members.

The Lutheran Church began its local operations in the eighteenth century through the officials of the VOC, among others Baron Gustaaf van Imhoff, the governor general in 1743–50 (Aritonang et al. 2008: 123). But significant church growth began only in the second half of the nineteenth century, especially through the work of a German missionary society, Rheinische Missions-Gesellschaft (RMG, the Rhenish Mission Society) in Batakland and the surroundings. RMG was not purely Lutheran, because it came from a church that adopted Uniert (a combination of Lutheran and Reformed) tradition. But most (around 10) of its established churches in Indonesia, with a membership of six million, claim to be Lutheran and affiliate with the Lutheran World Federation (LWF). The largest of such churches is the Huria Kristen Batak Protestan (HKBP; the Protestant Batak Christian Church) with some 3.5 million members (Aritonang 2016: 27).

The Anglican denomination is represented through just one church organization. The church was set up in 1822 in the colonial capital, Batavia (present-day Jakarta), in the post-British colonial rule in 1811–1816 (the British ruled Sumatra through 1825). When it was officially established in 1829, its name was the British Protestant Community at Jakarta; a Congregation of British Protestants of East Java was established in Surabaya almost one century later in 1928. The membership today is quite limited (less than 10,000) and is significant in only four cities (Jakarta, Surabaya, Batam, and Nunukan; Aritonang 2016: 112–5).

The Mennonite denomination is represented through three organizations: Gereja Injili di Tanah Jawa (GITJ, Evangelical Church in Java Land), Gereja Kristen Muria Indonesia (GKMI; Indonesian Muria Christian Church), and Jemaat Kristen Indonesia (Indonesian Christian Congregation). The first of these churches is the fruit of the Mennonite mission from the Netherlands, i.e., Doopsgezinde Zendingsvereeniging (DZV) that started to work in Java in the 1850s. Although DZV also worked in Papua and in North Sumatra, the Christians resulting from mission work joined non-Mennonite churches already established in their respective territories. The membership in the three Mennonite churches today numbers less than 200,000. Unlike their sibling Baptist churches, these churches have joined the Communion of Churches in Indonesia (Persekutuan Gereja-gereja di Indonesia or PGI), the national council of churches (Aritonang 2016: 139–42; BAKI 2017, 308–32).

The Baptist denomination is represented by some eight organizations, including independent Baptists, and is scattered across most of the country. The Baptist Missionary Society started its work in the 1810s but ceased operations from the 1850s until the 1940s; Baptist organizations were re-established in the 1950s. Although total membership of the Baptist churches is less than

500,000, their contribution in health ministry is quite remarkable. These churches are also active in operating theological schools. Until 2010, there were some ten Baptist theological schools, from North Sumatra in western Indonesia to Papua in eastern Indonesia (Direktori 2011: 342–55). The Baptist churches have their own communion, the Union of Indonesian Baptists; consistent with their self-understanding as free churches, they have not joined the Communion of Churches in Indonesia or PGI (Aritonang 2016: 165–70).

Methodism was brought to the Dutch East Indies by way of Singapore and Malaya in the 1880s. Its initial work was among Chinese and Indian-Tamils but then widened to reach indigenous people, mainly the Batak. The main church organization is Gereja Methodist Indonesia (GMI, the Indonesian Methodist Church), but there are also smaller organizations, which together have some 150,000 members. Although the GMI has on occasion been disturbed by internal conflict, mainly between the Chinese and the Batak, this church is well-known for its initiatives in the fields of health and education (from kindergarten to university).

The Pentecostal, Charismatic, Evangelical, Adventist, Jehovah's Witness, Mormon, and Christian Science groups are "made-in-America" denominations that came to Indonesia in several waves from the end of the nineteenth century through the second half of the twentieth century. The fastest growing yet most fissiparous currents are the Pentecostals and their younger sibling, the Charismatics. There are several doctrinal and practical differences between the Pentecostals and the Charismatics. The Charismatic movement started in the United States in the 1960s and entered this country in the 1970s. It does not place as much emphasis as the Pentecostals on baptism of the Spirit and glossolalia (speaking in tongues); at first, too, it was not usually institutionalized as a church organization. Despite their doctrinal differences on matters like baptism, in recent years, the Pentecostals have tended to downplay their differences. Today there are more than 100 Pentecostal-Charismatic churches and a comparable number of theological and Bible schools, many of them family enterprises. The total number of Pentecostal-Charismatics is around eight million. Many of their members are also registered in other churches. These Christians' aggressive efforts to establish churches in Muslim-majority regions have often strained Christian-Muslim relations.

Evangelicals in Indonesia, some of whom also bear the Pentecostal-Charismatic banner, have some 50 church organizations, with approximately two million members. Their ranks include the Salvation Army, the Seventh-Day Adventists, Jehovah's Witnesses, the Church of Jesus Christ of the Latter-Day Saints, and the Church of Christ, Scientist. In total, these churches have some one million members, with the Seventh-Day Adventists being the largest.

The Dewan Gereja-gereja di Indonesia (DGI, the Council of Churches in Indonesia), an ecumenical institution, was established in 1950, a product of the global ecumenical movement. In 1984, its name was changed to Persekutuan Gereja-gereja di Indonesia (PGI, Communion of Churches in Indonesia). Although the PGI aspires to unite all denominations and church organizations in Indonesia, through 2014 only 89 church organizations had joined this institution.[4] Most of the so-called evangelical churches and their evangelism ministries (around 120) came together to established the Persekutuan Gereja-gereja dan Lembaga-lembaga Injili Indonesia (PGLII, Communion of Evangelical Churches and Institutions), while most (around 100) of the Pentecostal-Charismatic churches founded the Persekutuan Gereja-gereja Pentakosta di Indonesia (PGPI, the Communion of Pentecostal Churches in Indonesia). In addition to these three umbrella institutions, there are others, including the Persekutuan Baptis Indonesia (the Union of Baptists in Indonesia), Persekutuan Gereja-gereja Tionghoa di Indonesia (the Union of Chinese Churches in Indonesia), and Persekutuan Gereja-gereja Mandiri di Indonesia (the Union of Self-Reliant Churches in Indonesia). Some churches opt not to affiliate with any of these umbrella organizations.

The complicated nature of denominations and organizations in Indonesia challenges any attempt to provide accurate estimates of the total number of Christians in the country. The multiple memberships across denominations and organizations further complicate such attempts. If all church organizations and memberships were combined, the total number might be as high as 40–50 million, a figure that would no doubt startle and disturb some Muslim officials. Fortunately, this exaggerated number is never used as an official statistic and profile.[5]

Interfaith, especially Christian-Muslim encounters

The beginning of the New Order or Soeharto regime, especially in the period from 1966–1978, was marked by tensions between Muslims and Christians. These were caused by, among other things, the conversion of many Muslims to Christianity. To counteract this so-called "Christianization" current, Muslim parties in cooperation with the government issued laws and regulations to curb Christian missionizing. Since the 1970s interfaith dialogue has also intensified. However, all of these efforts have not diminished tensions between the two communities. As noted by Mujiburrahman (2006), both sides shared the same sense and feeling of "being threatened."

Since the fall of the Soeharto regime in 1998, other incidents have disturbed interfaith and especially Muslim-Christian ties. A series of conflicts in Poso (Central Sulawesi) from 1998 to 2002, in Maluku from 1999 to 2004, in West and Central Kalimantan from 2000 to 2001, the bombings of Christian churches in several cities on Christmas Eve of 2000, and the bomb blast in Bali on October 12, 2002, caused much damage to Muslim-Christian ties (Aritonang 2015: 538–75). Some analysts argue that these were not purely inter-religious conflicts but also involved political-economic interests. Whatever the causes, these events heightened tensions and mistrust.

The allegations directed against the Christian minority include long-heard claims that it seeks to dominate the nation through evangelism, education, health ministry, the founding of new churches, the economy and business, and the control of government positions. With regard to evangelism through education, Muslims have long objected to the regulation in Christian schools that all students, including the Muslims, are required to take the Christian religion as a compulsory course. To address this problem, article 12, verse 1(1) of the 2003 Law on National Education System of 2003 states that "every student in an educational entity is a subject in a process of education and has a right to receive religious education according to her/his religion and taught by a teacher of the same religion." Christians objected to this stipulation, not just on technical and financial grounds (adding classrooms, teachers, and so on) but on the additional grounds that such courses are a vital feature of Christian education. This law, however, has been applied since 2004 (Aritonang 2015: 588–91; Crouch 2014: 71–81).

With regard to church building, since the beginning of the New Order regime, there were accusations that many Christians or church organizations build houses of worship without permission either from the government or the people from other faiths in the surrounding community. During an interreligious meeting on November 30, 1967, initiated by the government, Muslim leaders again raised this objection. On September13, 1969, the government through the Ministers of Religious Affairs and Home Affairs issued a joint decision nr. 1/1969 concerning the responsibility of government officials to ensure the orderliness of worship activities by the adherents, including the building of worship facilities (Aritonang 2015: 397–405).

Muslims and Christians found that this joint decision lacked clarity and specificity. After a long debate, the government issued the Joint Regulation of Ministers of Religious Affairs and Home Affairs number 9/8 (2006). The regulation stipulates that to build a worship building requires the written support of at least 90 congregants and at least 60 people from other faiths who live in the area. The building must also have a building constructing permit (Izin Mendiri-kan Bangunan or IMB) from the local government and be approved by the Interreligious Har-mony Forum (Forum Kerukunan Umat Beragama or FKUB), a state-sponsored group that is made up of representatives from Indonesia's six state-recognized religions (Gultom 2006: 61–75; Direktori 2011: 37–50).

The joint regulation aims at building understanding and goodwill among the frequently conflicting parties. The fact is, however, there are obstacles to its effective implementation. For example, a local congregation that belongs to the Presbyterian Gereja Kristen Indonesia, the GKI Yasmin in Yasmin Garden, Bogor, West Java, had to close its church even though it had a construction permit since July 13, 2006, after earlier waiting for four years. It also secured for-mal approval from the surrounding community after three meetings in 2002, March 2003, and January 2006. With these documents in hand and the support of then Mayor of Bogor Diani Budiarto, this church started the building project. However, just as the project got underway, some Muslim groups, among them the Islamic Defender Front (Front Pembela Islam or FPI), the Prosperous Justice Party (Partai Keadilan Sejahtera or PKS), and Ulama Forum of Bogor launched protests against the project. On February 14, 2008, the mayor and the head of the City of Bogor Administration and Planning suspended the project. They also prohibited the con-gregation from worshipping in the building (Victor Silaen 2012: 33–74; Crouch 2014: 124–5).

GKI appealed the case from the District Court to the Supreme Court. Its efforts were sup-ported by other Christian groupings and many moderate Muslim organizations and figures. This case was even brought to the ombudsman and discussed at the United Nations. The church eventually won the case. Undeterred, the mayor issued another letter on March 11, 2011, cancel-ling the building permit for a second time. On July 8, 2011, the ombudsman issued a recom-mendation instructing the mayor to cancel the second letter. The ombudsman also advised the minister of Home Affairs to monitor the situation to ensure that the church could continue the building project and submitted its report to the national legislature and President Susilo Bambang Yudhoyono. To this day, however, the church remains shuttered, and the congregation performs its Sunday services in front of the presidential palace or in congregants' homes. In spite of the pos-sibility of corruption and bribery behind this case (Silaen 2012: 74–6), the Australian researcher, Melissa Crouch, concludes that this dispute demonstrates the limited capacity for enforcement of legal rulings regarding religious minorities where political will is lacking (Crouch 2014: 125–6).

Another strategy of conservative and hard-line Muslim groups to implement their aspirations to transform Indonesia into an Islamic state has been through the issuance of regional regulation (Peraturan Daerah or Perda). After their failure in the early independence era to implement the seven-word clause "with obligation to apply Islamic Syariah by the adherents" (dengan kewa-jiban menjalankan Syariat Islam bagi pemeluk-pemeluknya) of the Jakarta Charter (adopted on June 22, 1945) and after the failure to win passage of a similar constitutional amendment dur-ing the People's Consultative Assembly (Sidang Majelis Permusyawaratan Rakyat or MPR) of 1999–2002, Islamist activists attempted to set up a number of syariah-based regional regulations, in accordance, they argued, with Indonesia's Law on Decentralization. Under the terms of this law, provincial, district, or city governments may pass regional regulations, known as peraturan daerah or Perda, on all matters except those reserved for the national government, such as for-eign affairs, national defense and security, judicial affairs, economic policy, and religion. Since the failure of the Jakarta Charter enforcement at the national level, some Islamists have sought to implement shariah-influenced laws at the regional level. The regulations deal with nine catego-ries of activity: religious rituals (such as Friday prayer), management of zakat (almsgiving), Mus-lim clothing (wearing jilbab or hijab), prostitution, vice (maksiat), alcohol and drugs, Quranic education, local governance, and non-Islamic regulations (Crouch 2014: 55–6).

Although non-Muslims are generally exempt from complying with the Perda Syariah, the introduction of religious matters, including Quranic education, has been an issue of concern for Christians. One counter-response from a predominantly Christian region was the perda draft issued by the city government of Manokwari in West Papua, the so-called "City of the Gospel," in March 2007. The draft law proposed to prohibit use of religious symbols other than Christian ones in the city. If this regulation had passed, non-Christians would have found it difficult to practice their religion in Papua. The draft legislation was rejected in 2007, however, and although a revised version was drafted in 2008, it too was not approved as law (Crouch 2014: 56). This conservative Christian initiative was rejected by most Christian groups, including the Conference of (Catholic) Bishops (Konferensi Waligereja Indonesia or KWI) and PGI. The draft was also criticized by Muslim leaders and organizations.

For Crouch (2014: 57), the decentralization of power in the post-Soeharto era has led to a greater politicization of religion at the regional level, through the use of religion for political gain. This has heightened tensions between Muslims and Christians, as well as within Muslim and Christian communities. Despite these and other religious conflicts, Indonesia and its religious and political leaders have been recognized internationally for inter-religious harmony and tolerance. For example, President Susilo Bambang Yudhoyono received the World Statesman Award on May 30, 2013, from the Appeal of Conscience Foundation (ACF), an organization in New York, United States. This recognition, however, was criticized by some leading observers, including Father Franz Magnis-Suseno, through his e-mail (May 15, 2013) when this awarding was still planned.[6]

Surveying the broader course of recent religious tensions and conflicts in Indonesia, Susanne Schröter provides the following summary assessment:

> Since that time [Soeharto's resignation in 1998] orthodox and fundamentalist Islamic tendencies have increasingly gained ground in Indonesia. New political parties were founded. . . . New organizations formed as well; some of them, such as the Islamic Defenders Front (*Front Pembela Islam*) and the Holy War Warriors (*Laskar Jihad*) mobilized the fight against both "infidels" and Muslims suspected of living [a] non-Islamic way of life. Since the introduction of democracy, Islamist groups have attacked numerous Western institutions and Christian churches. . . . In 2005 the powerful Council of Indonesian Ulama (*Majelis Ulama Indonesia*; MUI) issued eleven *fatwas* in which they explicitly condemned liberalism, secularism, and pluralism as being un-Islamic. Moreover, Muslims were forbidden to pray jointly with members of other faiths, and to intermarry with Christians. These decrees issued by the MUI resulted in the closing of numerous small churches. According to Indonesian law, religious centers need to be accepted by the respective neighborhoods surrounding them; if they are not, permission to build and maintain such buildings will not be granted. This is why many Christian churches are semi-legal, merely tolerated institutions. After the *fatwas* had been proclaimed, Muslims mobilized against these small houses of worship, and within a short time forced dozens of them to close. Violence against individual Christians is increasing as well, most notably in hot spots. On October 16, 2006, for example, the secretary general of the Protestant Church of Central Sulawesi, the Reverend Irianto Kongkoli, was killed by a shot in the head in broad daylight in the town of Palu. The resurgence of an orthodox and neo-orthodox Islam is highly visible in public life. Islamic clothing is dominating the streetscapes outside Jakarta, and a so-called anti-pornography law issued in 2008 criminalizes everything that does not conform to the moral ideas of Islamic hardliners. . . . As a consequence, students in the city of Padang

(West Sumatra) are now required to furnish proof that they are familiar with the Koran, female students and government employees have to wear the Islamic headscarf (*jilbab*), and the population has to participate in Islamic training courses. Since these measures were introduced there have been repeated assaults on women who were out in the public without a male escort, or whose clothing was not in conformity with Islam.

(2010: 22–3)

Christians' place in political and economic life

Christians have been appointed to high government positions in Indonesia for most of the republic's history. During Abdurrahman Wahid's presidency (1999–2001), Christians such as Purnomo Yusgiantoro, Luhut Binsar Panjaitan, Bungaran Saragih, Alexander Sony Keraf, and Freddy Numberi were appointed as cabinet ministers. Megawati Sukarnoputri (2001–2004) also appointed Christian ministers, including Jacob Nuwa Wea, Purnomo Yusgiantoro, Bungaran Saragih, and Manuel Kaisiepo. Susilo Bambang Yudhoyono (2004–2014) appointed Purnomo Yusgiantoro, Mari Elka Pangestu, Freddy Numberi, Nafsiah Mboi, Balthasar Kambuaya, and E. E. Mangindaan. More recently, President Joko Widodo (Jokowi) (r. 2014–) has appointed Christian ministers as well, including Luhut Binsar Panjaitan, Yasonna Laoly, Ignasius Jonan, Thomas Trikasih Lembong, Enggartiasto Lukita, and Johana Yembise. Besides these names on the central level, we can also mention a number of high-ranking Christian officers and governors of provinces.[7]

Nevertheless, the appointments of the Christians in high-ranked positions has not always gone smoothly, especially after the founding of the All-Indonesia Association of Muslim Intellectuals (Ikatan Cendekiawan Muslim Indonesia or ICMI) on December 7, 1990 (Aritonang and Steenbrink 2008: 217–8). One such example concerned the military commander, Johny Lumintang. According to Richard Daulay (2015: 275–7), during the last years of the New Order/Soeharto regime, there was factionalism within the Indonesian Army (Tentara Nasional Indonesia Angkatan Darat or TNI AD), between "Green" (Islamic) and "Red-White" (nationalist) officers. Baharuddin Jusuf Habibie, then chairperson of ICMI and the newly appointed president after Soeharto's resignation on May 21, 1998, asked General Wiranto, then armed-forces commander, to fire Lieutenant General Prabowo, then commander of the Army Strategic Command (Panglima Kostrad), because Prabowo was suspected of having plotted a coup against the president. Consistent with military protocol, Wiranto was to appoint Major General Johny Lumintang to replace Prabowo. Contrary to this instruction, the office of chief of staff of the army was not handed from Prabowo to Lumintang but to the Muslim officer Subagyo, on May 22, 1998. At 7:00 p.m., Subagyo handed over the office to Lumintang. But shortly after midnight, Wiranto called Subagyo and ordered him to hand over the office of Panglima Kostrad from Lumintang to Major General Djamari Chaniago. The formal reason was that there had been a mistake in the previous Letter of Decision of the Army Commander. According to Wiranto, Lumintang was only appointed as the interim Panglima Kostrad. Although confused by and disagreeing with his commanding officer's decision, Subagyo transferred the office of Panglima Kostrad from Johny Lumintang to Djamari Chaniago at 11.00 a.m. on May 23, 1998. Lumintang had held the office for only seventeen hours. Lumintang was angry and offended. As an army officer, however, he had to accept the order. He soon learned that the real reason for his repositioning had to do with matters of religion. With Jun Honna, a political scientist from Ritsumeikan University, Japan, Daulay concludes

At the time of personnel change in May 1998, Wiranto chose Maj. Gen. Johny Lumintang to succeed Prabowo as Kostrad Commander. But the ICMI camp that formed the core of the Habibie government demanded Wiranto to retract the appointment because Lumintang was a Catholic,[8] not a Muslim. Wiranto had no choice but to comply with this demand.

(Daulay 2015: 279)

After the dramatic appointment and discharge, Lumintang was appointed to several strategic positions, among others, vice head staff of the army, governor of the National Defense Institute, and general secretary of the Department of Defense. Nevertheless, wrote Daulay (2015: 251), he never reached the highest position in the army because of his Christian background. Since that time, few if any Christians have been appointed to top positions in the army or police.

A second example of controversy with regard to Christians in high office concerns Basuki Tjahaja Purnama or Ahok, a Chinese-Indonesian politician. He is a member of the evangelical Church of Christ Jesus (Gereja Kristus Yesus) and a spiritual son of Stephen Tong, the founder and leader of the Indonesian Evangelical Reformed Church (Gereja Reformed Injili Indonesia). He had served earlier as the regent of Belitung Timur (2005–2006), his homeland, and as a member of the People's Representative Assembly from 2009 to 2012. In 2012, he was elected the vice governor of the Jakarta Special Region, with Joko Widodo (Jokowi), the elected governor. When Jokowi was elected president of Indonesia in 2014, Ahok was elevated to the post of governor of Jakarta. His promotion was soon challenged, however, by several militant Muslim organizations.

Ahok introduced a series of bold changes in government policy and practice. He promoted good governance and clean government policy and battled against bureaucratic corruption, including that in the Regional DPR of Jakarta. He also launched programs in transportation, the environment, and low-income housing. These policies and actions stimulated protest and resistance from many groups, including some conservative Muslims. He was supported, however, by many communities and former leaders, both Muslims and Christians. Ahok and Djarot Saiful Hidayat (who is Muslim) ran as the incumbents for a second term as the governor and vice governor respectively of Jakarta on April 19, 2017, but they failed to win the election.

Among many issues, the former governor's speech in Kepulauan Seribu (a sub-region of Jakarta, off the north coast of Java) on September 27, 2016, sparked controversy. In it, he advised his audience not to be fooled by certain religious leaders citing the Quranic verse Sura Al Maidah 51.[9] This statement triggered unrest among many Muslim organizations, including the Council of Indonesian Ulama (MUI). The MUI leadership accused Ahok of blasphemy and insulting the Holy Quran. Although Ahok apologized on several occasions and explained that he never intended to insult the ulama and the Holy Quran, protesters urged the government to dismiss and imprison him.

On November 4, 2016, a huge demonstration was organized in central Jakarta, assembling some 200,000 protesters from some 25 Muslim organizations. The protesters urged the government to expedite the legal process against Ahok. Similar demonstrations took place the same day in Surabaya, Makassar, and several other cities. The Jakarta demonstration went peacefully for most of the day, but around 9:00 p.m. violence broke out and was only brought under control hours later.

President Jokowi declared publicly that he would not interfere in the legal case against Ahok. After an intensive investigation, on November 16, the police announced that Ahok was to be charged with religious blasphemy and brought to trial. Notwithstanding the legal proceedings, further mass demonstrations took place on December 2, 2016, and February 21, 2017, involving hundreds of thousands of Muslim protesters. Fortunately, the government and police kept the situation under control, but suspicions remained that some political figures were behind this

protest. On May 9, 2017, after 22 sessions, the court ruled that Ahok was guilty of religious defamation of Islam and the Quran and sentenced him to two years prison, to begin immediately.
Ahok and his legal team have appealed the ruling.

Besides the installment of a number of Christians to high-ranked political positions, some
Christians, especially of Chinese descent, live lucrative lives and dominate Indonesia's economy.
A number of big corporations were founded and owned by Chinese-Indonesians, many of
whom are Christians. They are widely seen as among Indonesia's most privileged economic
elites. Although they employ large numbers of Muslims in their corporations, socio-economic
resentment of their status is widespread and contributes to anti-Chinese and anti-Christian
unrest.

* * *

This brief description of the Christians in Indonesia shows that Christianity is quite dynamic
in this country. At the same time, continuing internal and external challenges remind Christian
Indonesians that they must reflect on their situation and strive to make improvements. It might
be unfair to compare the situation of Indonesian Christians with those in other Asian countries.
But the Christians in Indonesia deserve to thank God that their life situation and conditions are
generally better than their Christian counterparts in many Middle Eastern countries. Although
the Christians in Indonesia still face serious challenges, they can give thanks that they are able
to practice their faith in relative peace and freedom.

Notes

1 In this chapter, "denomination" refers to some ecclesial stream, like Lutheranism, the Reformed,
  Church, Baptists, Methodists, or Pentecostals.
2 Here "organization" means an institution operative at the synod level, like Gereja Kristen Indonesia
  (Indonesian Christian Church).
3 For detailed information on denominations and church streams in Indonesia, see Jan S. Aritonang,
  Berbagai Aliran di dalam dan di sekitar Gereja (Jakarta: BPK Gunung Mulia, 15th [revised edition] 2016).
4 For the list of the PGI members as well as the number of its respective members, see *Buku Almanak
  Kristen Indonesia (BAKI)* 2017, 308–32.
5 According to Agus Indiyanto (2013: 18), based on the population census of 2010, the total number of
  Christians (incl. the Catholics) is 23,436,386 out of the total population of Indonesia of 237,641,326.
  Whereas according to *Direktori Gereja-gereja* (2011: 301–11, 333) (probably from an older resource), the
  total number of the Christians is 22,036,060 out of 233,184,852.
6 This is Magnis-Suseno's letter (accessed from http://nasional.kompas.com/read/2013/05/17/1100
  0272/ on November 7, 2016):

> *Ladies and Gentlemen of the Appeal of Conscience Foundation (ACF),*
>   *I am a Catholic Priest and professor of philosophy in Jakarta. In Indonesia we learnt that you are going to
> bestow this year's World Statesman Award to our President Susilo Bambang Yudhoyono because of his merits
> regarding religious tolerance. This is a shame, a shame for you. [. . .] How can you take such a decision without
> asking concerned people in Indonesia? [. . .] Do you not know about the growing difficulties of Christians to get
> permits for opening places of prayer, about the growing number of forced closures of churches, about the growth of
> regulations that make worshipping for minorities more difficult, thus about growing intolerance on the grass-root
> level? And particularly, have you never heard about the shameful and quite dangerous attitudes of hard-line
> religious groups towards so called deviant teachings, meaning members of the Achmadiyah and the Shia com-
> munities, and the government of Susilo Bambang Yudhoyono just doing nothing and saying nothing to protect
> them? [. . .] Do you not know that President Susilo Bambang Yudhoyono during his up to now 8 1/2 years
> in office has not a single time said something to the Indonesian people, that they should respect their minori-
> ties? [. . .] What could be your motivation to bestow upon this President a reward for religious tolerance who so
> obviously lacks any courage to do his duty protecting minorities? I have to add that I am not a radical, not even*

a "human right extremist" (if such exist). I am just appalled about so much hypocrisy. You are playing in the hands of those – still few – radicals that want to purify Indonesia of all what they regard as heresies and heathen.

Franz Magnis-Suseno SJ

7 These data were accessed from *Wikipedia* on October 29, 2016.

8 Daulay (2015: 278) inserts a footnote noting that Johny Lumintang is not Catholic but Protestant; he came from GMIM (Minahassan Church) and in Jakarta joined the GPIB, GMIM's sister church.

9 Sura Al Maida 51 in the English version, relates: "O you who believe! Do not take the Jews and the Christians as allies; some of them are allies of one another. Whoever of you allies himself with them is one of them. God does not guide the wrongdoing people" (www.quranwow.com/#/ch/5/t1/ar-allah/t2/en-itania/a1/alafasy-64/a2/itania-64/v/0, accessed on October 29, 2016).

References cited

Agus, Indiyanto. 2013. *Agama di Indonesia dalam Angka – Dinamika Demografis Berdasarkan Sensus Penduduk 2000 dan 2010* (Religion in Indonesia in Number – Demographic Dynamics Based on Population Census of 2000 and 2010) (Yogyakarta: CRCS).

Aritonang, Jan S. 2015. *Sejarah Perjumpaan Kristen dan Islam di Indonesia* (A History of the Encounter of Christian and Islam in Indonesia) (Jakarta: BPK Gunung Mulia).

———. 2016. *Berbagai Aliran di dalam dan di sekitar Gereja* (Various Streams Within and Surrounding the Churches) (Jakarta: BPK Gunung Mulia, [revised edition]).

Aritonang, Jan S. and Karel Steenbrink, eds. 2008. *A History of Christianity in Indonesia* (Leiden: Brill).

Buku Almanak Kristen Indonesia (BAKI) 2017 (Jakarta: PGI).

Crouch, Melissa. 2014. *Law and Religion in Indonesia* (London and New York: Routledge).

Daulay, Richard M. 2015. *Agama dan Politik di Indonesia* (Religion and Politics in Indonesia) (Jakarta: BPK Gunung Mulia).

Direktori Gereja-gereja, Yayasan, Pendidikan Agama dan Pendidikan Keagamaan Kristen di Indonesia (Directory of Churches, Foundation, and Christian Religious Education in Indonesia). 2011 (Jakarta: Kementerian Agama, Direktorat Jenderal Bimbingan Masyarakat Kristen).

Gultom, Gomar, ed. 2006. *Dari SKB ke PBM* (Jakarta: PGI).

Mujiburrahman. 2006. *Feeling threatened: Muslim-Christian Relations in Indonesia's New Order* (Leiden: Amsterdam University Press).

Schröter, Susanne, ed. 2010. *Christianity in Indonesia – Perspective of Power* (Berlin: LIT Verlag).

Silaen, Victor, ed. 2012. *Bertahan di Bumi Pancasila – Belajar dari Kasus GKI Yasmin* (Defense on the Earth of Pancasila – Learning from the Case of GKI Yasmin) (Jakarta: Bina Kasih).

22

HINDUISM AND BUDDHISM

Martin Ramstedt

In order to understand the dynamics that are important for both the Hindu and the Buddhist community in Indonesia today, we have to briefly revisit the history of the difficult beginnings of these two communities. Their beginnings were difficult because of three inter-related factors that have played out quite differently for each community from independence onward: (1) the predicament of "indigenous" ethnic groups and their respective traditions; (2) the predicament of "foreign" ethnic groups and their respective traditions; and (3) the inadvertent tension between national and transnational orientations in the development of both Hinduism and Buddhism in post-colonial Indonesia.

These factors continue to effectively shape the individual trajectories of both communities, including their attitude and standing vis-à-vis the increasing Islamization of Indonesian society, and have thus stayed highly topical to this day.

The predicament of Indigenous ethnic groups

The ethnic identities of most indigenous Indonesians are moored in local customary laws (*adat*). These customary law traditions are in many cases still embedded in sacred cosmologies, which the Indonesian Ministry of Religious Affairs (MORA), the legal successor institution of the colonial Office of Religion dedicated to the supervision of Muslim affairs only (Locher-Scholten 2000: 193), has never recognized as part of religion proper. Rather, MORA's Decree No. 9/1952 classified these sacred cosmologies as "currents of spiritual belief." On the basis of the first foundational principle of the Indonesian state, contained in the Preamble of Indonesia's Basic Law from 1945, "Belief in the One Almighty God" is mandatory for each Indonesian citizen. MORA (then under the leadership of Haji Mohamad Rasjidi, an alumnus of Al-Azhar University in Cairo) further specified that the term "religion" was to solely refer to divine revelation of a universal message, transmitted in a holy book to a holy prophet. Moreover, religious worship was to take place in specific buildings, such as mosques, or churches, that is, spaces intended for worship of a transcendent principle and not for "nature worship."

While the belief dimension of ethnic traditions was challenged by the state definition of "religion," its customary law aspect was threatened by state attempts of legal unification (Holleman 1981, lxiv; Lev 2000, 56–9); this was despite the fact that Article 18 of the Indonesian Basic Law demanded some recognition of the customary laws of those regions that had retained a special cultural character. It was the combination of the increasingly restrictive and prescriptive legal notion of "religion" pushed through by the Indonesian state and the growing restrictions on local customary laws that was a major motor of the formation of a multi-ethnic Hindu community in Indonesia under the leadership of ethnic Balinese between 1958 and 1980. By 1964, the state had recognized Hinduism as one of the religions adhered to by the Indonesian people (Ramstedt 2004a: 11–17; Picard 2004: 58–9, 61–7).

From 1964 onward, members of other ethnic groups latched on to the successful Balinese Hindu movement, most notably Javanese from Central and East Java, as well as Tengger Javanese inhabiting the area in and around today's Bromo-Tengger-Semeru National Park. While orthodox Islam had become more and more influential in urban areas since independence, syncretistic millenarian Javanese mystical groups had mushroomed in rural areas. Many members of these groups had also been leftists, and some in their ranks had been killed by predominantly Muslim militias that aided Soeharto in his purge (see McGregor 2009). In the wake of these events, a Hindu revival movement rapidly spread throughout Java, which invoked the pre-Islamic golden past of Javanese history, the age of the Hindu-Buddhist empires of ancient Java-Mataram, Singhasari, and, foremost, Majapahit (Geertz 1972: 69; Mayor Polak 1973, 1977; Lyon 1977: 64–103; Howell 1977; Hefner 1985: 15–17, 41, 66, 72, 140–1; Suwandi 2000: 52–4).

Conversion to a recognized religion was also imperative for members of Javanese mystical groups because from among them repeatedly arose staunch criticism of the Soeharto regime (Suwandi 2000: 113–24, 162–72). A case in point was the heavily mediatized Sawito affair. In 1978, a court of law finally pronounced guilty the Javanese mystic Sawito Kartowibowo for his criticism of Soeharto, which had found resonance among influential people (Bourchier 2010).

Similar developments were taking place beyond Bali and Java. In South Sulawesi, a non-Muslim Bugis group, called To Wani To Lotang, as well as non-Christianized members from among the Sa'dan and Mamasa Toraja, sought state recognition for their ethnic religions as being a local variant of Hinduism. In response to this request, Government Decree No. 6/1966 permitted the development of Hinduism in South Sulawesi, even though there was scant evidence of historical influence of either ancient India or the Old Javanese Hindu-Buddhist empires in the region (Ramstedt 2004b: 185–206).

In North Sumatra, it was the Karo ethnic group still largely adhering to the indigenous belief and ritual systems that requested official recognition of their local tradition as "Hindu." The vicinity of their homelands to the port town of Medan, a hotbed of communism since colonial times (Loderichs 1997: 39; Benda and McVey 2009: Pos. 2374–2393; Mortimer 2006: 431–3), and the fact that a Trotskyite party had taken root in the area since 1959 (Alexander 1991: 534) made them targets of anti-communist scrutiny. Consequently, after 1965, they sought to affiliate with Hinduism, or, alternatively, with Islam and Protestantism. In 1985, the association of Karo "Hindus" was incorporated into the representative body of Indonesian Hindus, the Parisada Hindu Dharma Indonesia (PHDI).

In Kalimantan, last but not least, Christian proselytizing put an increasing strain on the ethnic groups collectively known as Dayak who still largely practiced slash-and-burn agriculture while adhering to their ethnic religion, called *Kaharingan*. MORA had followed the assessment of Christian missionaries in classifying Dayak as "people still without religion," a policy that added fuel to discontent that in 1957 had led to the so-called Dayak insurrection. The leaders of the insurrection called for the establishment of a separate Dayak territory to achieve a measure of autonomy from the Muslim Banjar inhabiting the southern coastal region around the port town of Banjarmasin. Until 1957, the interior and the coastal region had been joined in one administrative unit. In response to the insurrection, Sukarno accorded what the Dayak saw as their territory the status of a province, the Province of Central Kalimantan (Weinstock 1984: 11–12, 89–97, 134–5; Baier 1998: 50).

While Central Kalimantan developed into a center of timber production, it was predominantly members of the Ngaju and Luangan Dayak who sought to protect their land, customs, and culture by aligning themselves with the Indonesian Hindu movement, which they deemed more tolerant to their spiritual, socio-legal, and material heritage. In 1980, their ethnic tradition was officially recognized as a local variant of Hinduism, on the strength of archaeological evidence indicating Hinduism and Buddhism had been influential in Borneo prior to the advent of Islam. The Great Council of the Hindu Kaharingan Religion was subsequently integrated in the PHDI (Weinstock 1984: 12, 190–4).

The predicament of "foreign" ethnic groups

The traditions of non-autochthonous, non-Muslim ethnic groups in Indonesia, who had been classified as "foreign Orientals" in the colonial Constitutional Regulation of the Netherlands Indies from 1854, that is, primarily the Indians and Chinese (*SvhKdN* 1883: 267; Thung 2011: 199–200), faced different challenges to their religious traditions in the course of their integration into the Indonesian nation state (see also Bachtiar 2006). Neither of these "alien" ethnic groups was homogenous in composition.

As to the Indians, there were first of all the descendants of indentured Tamil laborers on the plantations of North Sumatra, who had arrived en masse after the great famine of 1876–77 in the Madras residency. Members of other ethnic and caste groups from India, like Chettyars, Sindhis, and Sikhs, had subsequently been attracted to Medan because of the flourishing economic conditions the plantation industry had brought to the region. The colonial census of 1930 had counted some 21,000 Indians in North Sumatra, comprising Hindu and Muslim Tamil plantation laborers, some Telugus, former sepoys from Bengal, and Sikhs from Gujerat. A comparatively small group of Indians, comprising altogether 5,500 Muslim and Hindu Tamils, Muslim and Hindu Gujeratis, and Hindu Sindhis and Sikhs had settled in Java; 2,900 in Kalimantan; and about 1,500 on other islands. Most of them had been single males, who had already been born in Indonesia (Vignato 2000: 69–76; Mani 2006a: 49–51, 57, 2006b: 100–4; Bachtiar 2006: 135; Basarsyah 2008: 10–12; Ramstedt 2011: 523–4).

After the partition of India, another wave of Indian migrants reached Indonesia, consisting primarily of some two thousand Sindhis who also eventually became Indonesian nationals. In 1955, at the height of Indian-Indonesian non-bloc cooperation, a branch office of the Indian Council for Cultural Relations (ICCR), the Jawaharlal Nehru Cultural Centre (JNICC), was established in Jakarta in order to cater to the cultural needs of the Indian diaspora in Indonesia (Mani 2006b: 109–10; Ramstedt 2008: 1230).

The Hindus among the Indian migrants had already early on established their own religious institutions, like the Shri Mariamman Temple in Medan, built in the 1880s. The Deli Hindu Sabha was founded in 1913 also in Medan (Basarsyah 2008: 24). Further organizations were the Adi Dravida Hindu Sabha and the Krishna Sabha. All of them survived into the 1950s (Mani 2006a: 63).

While from the start, MORA recognized the Tamil Hindu tradition as "religion," it nevertheless encouraged the Hindu Tamil community, particularly after 1965, to de-emphasize ethnic and cultural differences. Their independent Hindu organizations had to join the PHDI, and in 1973, MORA prohibited the performance of traditional rituals deemed primitive and repellent, like the annual fire walking at the Shri Mariamman Temple on the occasion of the five-day Bekala festival and the so-called self-mutilation or immolation rituals on the occasion of the three-day Thaipusam festival (Vignato 2000: 162–5, 2004: 243–4; Mani 2006a: 72–82; cf. Bachtiar 2006: 135, 143–4). Thereafter some Tamil-Indonesians celebrated these ceremonies with the Tamil-Malaysian community in nearby Penang (Basarsyah 2008: 26).

Tamil Hindu traditions were under attack not only from Indonesian government institutions. Tamils in Sumatra were themselves abandoning the religion of their forebears in response to the dissemination, in Indonesia, of the Tamil Self-Respect movement, founded by E.V. Ramaswamy in Tamil Nadu in 1925, and the Dalit movement, catalyzed by B. R. Ambedkar's call for the conversion of Dalits to Buddhism in 1956 (Vignato 2000:77, 83, 165–9; Mani 2006a: 61–7, 79, 83; Basarsyah 2008: 26; Ramstedt 2011: 524).

The Buddhist movement among the Tamils in Medan had already commenced in 1930, instigated by the Buddhist scholar and Tamil Dalit leader Iyothee Thass, who had come to Sumatra from India for the very purpose of spreading Buddhism among the Adi Dravida diaspora (Mani 2006a: 84; see also Omveldt 2003: 2, 234–42). Moreover, in 1929, a branch of the International Buddhist Mission in Thaton (Burma), the Association for the Propagation of Buddhism in Java, had opened in Batavia. It later became independent from its Burmese mother organization under the name of Java Buddhist Association. Its leadership and members consisted of Dutch colonial officers, along with aristocratic Javanese and Chinese (Juangari 1995: 3–4; Brown 2004: 46–52; Ramstedt 2011: 525).

Both the Tamil Buddhist community and a small community of Javanese Buddhists survived into the post-colonial period. A third group of Buddhists was formed by members of different Chinese communities in the archipelago, adhering to either Chan or Pure Land, the two major schools of contemporary Han Chinese Buddhism (Juangari 1995: 2, 5; Ling 2004: 16; see also Ashiwa and Wank 2005: 223–4, 227–8, 232–3). Finally, there was a group of Chinese adhering to local varieties of what has been called the syncretistic Chinese "folk religion," containing a mixture of Buddhist, Daoist, and Confucian elements, along with the veneration of local guardian deities. Their roots reached back into the colonial period and more precisely to the association called Sam Kauw Hwe (Juangari 1995: 5; Kimura 2003: 55; Brown 2004: 48–9; see also Seiwert 1997: 43).

It was, however, not until 1966 that Buddhism was officially recognized as a "religion." Buddhism did not neatly fit MORA's definition of a religion, particularly not in its overly "Chinese" cultural form. Most Indonesian Muslim intellectuals and politicians had viewed China with a decidedly critical eye, despite, or rather because of the fact that Sukarno had visited the People's Republic in 1956 and had subsequently established his version of Guided Democracy in a manner akin to Mao's style of socio-political mobilization. Sukarno's sympathies for Mao's China were later seen to incriminate Sino-Indonesians as a kind of fifth column (Chen 2005: 39–44; Hong 2011: 9–10, 73–7, 132, 148, 200, 213–22). When Soeharto established himself as president in 1968, China had definitely fallen from grace. What lingered from the previous period was the unresolved issue of the citizenship of the people of Chinese descent in Indonesia, with some Indonesians, among them military leaders, regarding the Chinese as a national security issue. All expressions of Chineseness, including Chinese dialects, personal names, and religious as well as cultural traditions, were henceforth forbidden, as Sino-Indonesians were subjected to a forced Indonesianization process (Purdey 2005: 9, 14–15, 18–29; Hong 2011: 162–70, 180; Thung 2011: 201–4).

Consequently, a large number of Sino-Indonesians officially converted to Islam, Catholicism, or Protestantism. A much smaller number tried to salvage the tradition of their forefathers, by seeking protection under the mantle of Buddhism. The task of bringing Buddhism in line with MORA's definition of religion and of turning the highly heterogeneous Buddhist groups into a unified national organization, was to be carried out by a Dutch-educated Sino-Indonesian, born Tee Boan An.

Having been an active member of the Theosophical Society and the syncretistic Sam Kauw Hwe association already in the Netherlands Indies, in 1954, Tee Boan An began to study Chan Buddhism under the Chinese Chan monk Pen Ching. Unable to go to China for further training, because he did not speak any Chinese, Tee Boan soon turned to the founder of the Vipassana movement, Mahasi Sayadaw, in Burma, where in the same year he received ordination as a full monk of the Burmese Theravada tradition, with the name of Ashin Jinarakkhita (Juangari 1995: 38–55; Kimura 2003: 57; Brown 2004: 47; Racheman 2010: 214). Ashin Jinarakkhita returned to Indonesia in 1955, where he espoused an ecumenical, universal notion of Buddhism, called Buddhayana or Ekayana, which was generally popular among both eastern and western Buddhists at the time, in order to bridge the differences among Indonesia's highly diverse Buddhist schools (Dharmawimala 2012: 9; Racheman 2010: 213, 217–19; Sudhamek 2012: 19–21). With this encompassing approach, he was eventually successful in bringing into the fold members of other ethnic groups, including the Balinese, the Tengger, and the Buda Sasak (Juangari 1995: 61–80; MacDougall 2005).

In order to further the development of monasticism in Indonesia, Ashin Jinarakkhita invited renowned Buddhist monks from Sri Lanka, Burma, Thailand, and Cambodia to Indonesia. In 1959, the first Indonesian monks were ordained. They joined the newly founded national organization for Buddhist monastics, the Sangha Sutji Indonesia, as novices. In 1969, the Indonesian novices became fully ordained monks, on the occasion of which the Sangha Sutji Indonesia changed its name to Maha Sangha Indonesia. A couple of years later, its name changed again to Sangha Agung Indonesia (Juangari 1995: 84–194; Dharmawimala 2012: 10).

In 1966, MORA finally extended formal state recognition to Buddhism. However, Buddhism was placed in close state administration with Hinduism. From 1967 onward, Buddhism was represented in MORA by a joint Secretariat General for the Guidance of the Hindu Balinese and Buddhist Communities (Sekretariat Jenderal Bimbingan Masyarakat Hindu Bali dan Buddha, Bimas Hindu Bali dan Buddha).

State recognition was also predicated upon the formulation of an equivalent to the "Belief in the One Almighty God" required of all national religions. Bhante Ashin proposed the worship of the Adhi Buddha, a concept from an Old Javanese tantric Buddhist text, *Sanghyang Kamahayanikan*. But this was deemed apocryphal by many Buddhists, particularly by the members of the Thailand-educated Theravada-section of the Sangha Agung Indonesia. The controversy did not abate, and by 1978, the Sangha Agung Indonesia had splintered into three monastic subsections: Buddhayana, Theravada, and Mahayana. In addition to these monastic organizations, there were four lay organizations: (1) Kasogatan, representing a group of Javanese Buddhists who embraced the reimagined Old Javanese tantric Buddhist heritage from the times of the Hindu-Buddhist Empires of Singhasari and Majapahit; (2) the Nichiren sect derived from Japan; (3) Chinese Maitreya Buddhism; and (4) Chinese Tridharma.

MORA pressured all these Buddhist organizations into joining one single representative body. In 1979, the Leadership of Indonesian Buddhists (Perwalian Umat Buddha Indonesia, abbreviated WALUBI) was established, marking a further step in the recognition of Buddhism in Indonesia. Vaisak became a national holiday in the same year, and, a year later, the Bimas Hindu dan Buddha was split into two subsections, the Office of Hindu Affairs and the Office of Buddhist Affairs (see also Juangari 1995: 195–207; Kimura 2003: 57–66; Brown 2004: 52–3).

Tension between national and transnational orientations

The integration of Buddhism into Soeharto's nationalist fold for a while succeeded in covering up the "theological" tensions between the three subsections of the Sangha Agung Indonesia, particularly between the Sangha Theravada and the Sangha Buddhayana. The protagonist of the Thai-oriented Theravada faction was the renowned Balinese monk Bhikkhu Girirakkhito, alias Bhante Giri, abbot of the Brahmavihara Arama monastery in North Bali.

Bhante Giri had originally been one of Bhante Ashin Jinarakkhita's first Indonesian students. In 1958, Bhante Ashin had visited Bali together with the Sinhalese monk Narada Mahathera; the visit of the two monks inspired Ida Bagus Giri to set up a simple meditation place in the Village of Banjar, in the vicinity of Singaraja. The following year, Bhante Ashin visited Giri's meditation center, together with a number of monks from Sri Lanka, Burma, Thailand, Malaysia, and Indonesia. During this visit, he ordained Giri as a novice. In 1966, Giri received full ordination as Bhikkhu Girirakkhito in Bangkok. Upon his return to Bali, Bhante Giri's meditation center in North Bali quickly developed into a full-fledged monastery, called Brahmavihara Arama. In 1971, it hosted its first Vaishak celebration, which was honored by the presence of an assembly of Theravada monks from Thailand. In the same year, the incumbent president of the World Association of Buddhism, Princess Poon Pismai Diskul, an aunt of Thailand's King Bhumibol Adulyadej, paid a visit to the Brahmavihara Arama. In 1982, the Dalai Lama also visited Bhante Giri. Visits by such exalted personages naturally added to the monastery's legitimacy and renown.

These visits also underscored the necessity to develop translocal and international ties with co-religionists abroad, in order to be recognized as a true world religion at home. However, the recourse to and cultural translation of foreign Buddhist, and for that matter Hindu, traditions into "Indonesian Buddhism" and "Indonesian Hindu Dharma," often caused tensions with local Hindu and Buddhist traditions or ran afoul of MORA and other state policies on religion.

With the help of the recognized religious institutions, Soeharto's "New Order" regime in fact kept all religious communities under tight surveillance. Actual interference by religious organizations from abroad was strictly forbidden. It is thus not surprising that the activities of transnational, devotional religious movements, which demonstrated a strong zest for proselytizing, like the Hare Krishna movement and the Satya Sai Baba movement in the case of Hinduism or Nichiren in the case of Buddhism were vehemently opposed by the officially recognized representative bodies of the respective religions.

The Sindhi community in Jakarta began in 1973 to develop ties with the transnational Satya Sai Baba movement. In 1977, other Indian-Indonesian Hindus invited Swami Bhaktivedanta Prabhupada, the founder of the International Society of Krishna Consciousness (ISKCON), to Jakarta (Ramstedt 2008: 1242). These two devotional (bhakti) and anti-caste movements were spreading fast throughout Indonesia's Hindu community, attracting a significant number of modernists, intellectuals, and youth to their mission. Fearing the loss of their authority and the decline of their ritual tradition, in 1984, the high-caste Balinese conservatives within the official Hindu institutions succeeded in having IKSCON banned. It was to take another ten years before the Satya Sai Baba movement was banned as well. Although these two movements were allowed to continue to exist in Indonesia, their activities were effectively curtailed (Howe 2001: 163–98).

There were also other Indian Hindu organizations that steadily extended the sphere of their activities in Indonesia. In contrast to the Hare Krishna and the Sai Baba movement, they succeeded in staying below the radar of state supervision. Ananda Marga, for example, had entered Indonesia via Indian-Indonesian networks in 1980. It opened its first center in Bali in 1984. The organization soon became well known for the excellence of its yoga training. Another popular organization is Brahma Kumaris, whose first meditation center was established in Jakarta in 1982. The first Brahma Kumaris meditation center in Bali opened in 1990.

Within the Indonesian Buddhist community, it was the Nichiren School of Japanese Buddhism that met with fierce opposition from WALUBI. Nichiren had first established a branch in Indonesia in 1964. In 1987, Nichiren was declared a deviant sect, consequently losing its representative seat within WALUBI. Like ISKCON and the Satya Sai Baba groups, Nichiren was nevertheless allowed to continue to exist at the margins of official religion (Steenbrink 2013).

Hinduism and Buddhism through the Fall of Soeharto

By the mid-1980s, both Hinduism and Buddhism enjoyed an institutional recognition in Indonesia, which – regardless of their communities' comparatively small size – was officially proportionate to that of the three Abrahamic religions (Islam, Protestantism, and Catholicism). The Directorate of Hindu Affairs initiated the establishment of three Hindu colleges in Denpasar (Bali), Blitar (East Java), and Klaten (Central Java), where schoolteachers could acquire the necessary training that qualified them to teach Hinduism in state schools throughout the country. The Directorate of Buddhist Affairs equally funded the establishment of Buddhist teacher training schools and colleges in Jakarta, Banyumas (Central Java), Ampel Boyolali (Central Java), Medan (North Sumatra), and Bogor (West Java). Hindu temples and Buddhist monasteries, supervised by the respective government institutions, were established on an even larger scale.

In 1989, however, the Indonesian government suddenly abandoned its policy of equal treatment as a result of Soeharto's strategic "turn to Mecca," by which he sought to attenuate the criticism that had arisen not only in the form of the middle-class pro-democracy movement but also within the military leadership, hitherto dominated by Christian and secular nationalist generals. This sudden change of religious policy was marked by the enactment of several laws that reflected an increasing normative and institutional recognition of Islam in Indonesia's state law. Law No. 2/1989 on the National Education System, for instance, stipulated that the government was to provide appropriate funding for the private Islamic schools, hitherto only supervised but not sponsored by MORA (Zuhdi 2006: 416–24). At the same time, state funding for Hindu and Buddhist educational institutions dried up. Of the three aforementioned Hindu colleges, only the one in Denpasar survived. The two in Java soon had to close down for want of public funding (see also Hefner 2004: 94). The Buddhist schools and colleges experienced a similar loss of funding; in Medan, Jakarta, and Bogor, however, the cutbacks were cushioned by private funding on the part of the local Sino-Indonesian community, whose members were usually much more affluent than the Buddhist constituency in rural Central Java.

In 1990, the Association of Indonesian Muslim Intellectuals (Ikatan Cendekiawan Muslim Indonesia, ICMI) was founded. It was chaired by Soeharto's protégé, Minister of Research and Technology B. J. Habibie, who was instrumental in the rapid occupation of the ranks of the Indonesian bureaucracy by ICMI members. By 1992, ICMI members already dominated the cabinet and the ruling party, Golkar. ICMI's rise to power caused further normative and institutional accommodation of Islam on the part of the Indonesian state (see also Ramstedt 2012a: 7).

I do not have the space here to describe the legal accommodation of Islamic norms and institutions in more detail. Pertinent for our topic here, though, is, first of all, that the Indonesian Council for Islamic Predication (Dewan Dakwah Islamiyah Indonesia, DDII) was now allowed to do "internal" missionary work among Javanese Christians, Hindus, and Buddhists, on the grounds that the latter had turned away from Islam and had thereby committed apostasy, a wrong that needed to be righted. Secondly, Soeharto's Presidential Instruction No. 1/1991 strengthened the jurisdiction of the Islamic courts, which eventually led to the state publication of a Compilation of Islamic Law as their officially recognized source of law (see also Ramstedt 2009; 340, 2012a: 8).

The strengthening of Islamic jurisdiction proved particularly burdensome for those members of the Hindu and Buddhist communities whose official religious affiliation had not been registered as such. Even today, mistaken registration of non-Muslim citizens' religious affiliation is not unusual, particularly among Sino-Indonesian Buddhists and non-Balinese Indonesian Hindus. There are a number of reasons why a person may not be registered under the religion to which he or she professes allegiance. One concerns the availability of qualified people to officiate a wedding ceremony. In Indonesia, weddings are lawful only when they are conducted in a religious context, which requires the respective families to invite a qualified Hindu or Buddhist officiant to lead the wedding ceremony. Many communities have long suffered from a lack of resident Hindu priests or Buddhist officials to officiate. Under such circumstances, families have had to choose between the costly option of flying in a qualified officiant from another region or having the wedding couple pose as members of another religious community, with wedding officiants ready at hand. Another reason for mistaken registration has to do with access to modern education. In the predominantly Christian mountainous region of South Sulawesi, for instance, access to schools has been made difficult for children of Hindu Toraja background, which is why parents have often, at least nominally, converted to either Catholicism or a variety of Protestantism to help their children to make their way in the world.

In Java, non-Muslim Javanese have quite frequently not been registered under their professed religions, not the least because of the impact of the rhetoric of the DDII, geared to denounce Javanese Hindus and Buddhists as apostates from Islam. One hears similar complaints from Sino-Indonesians who have found themselves registered as Christians rather than Buddhists. Against the backdrop of such cases of mistaken registration, it is obvious that the legal strengthening of Islamic jurisdiction, in conjunction with the empowerment of the DDII, has increased pressures on the Hindu and Buddhist communities, especially in Java (Ramstedt 2004b: 212, 2009: 340–2, 2012a: 8).

The pressure caused by the growing Islamization of Indonesian society has been exacerbated by the fact that Islam has also become more influential in the armed forces. Formerly, both military and police had tended to protect recognized religious minorities, especially when the leading commander had been of Hindu or Buddhist persuasion. Quite a few Balinese and non-Balinese Hindus as well as Javanese Buddhists had in point of fact pursued a career in the armed forces. Buddhist monasteries and Hindu temples had frequently been built in close proximity to military barracks. With the increasing number of "green generals" from the 1990s onward, however, it is not surprising that more and more incidents have occurred in which mobs have damaged or destroyed Hindu temples and Buddhist monasteries. These developments have contributed to a growing disenchantment among members of the Hindu and Buddhist community with the politics within their representative institutions.

In 1994, simmering tensions between the Sangha Theravada, led by Bhante Giri, and the Sangha Buddhayana, led by Bhante Ashin, finally erupted over the issue of whether Buddhists would be allowed to worship the South Indian guru, Satya Sai Baba, whose alleged magical powers were dazzling growing numbers of people across Southeast Asia, including Indonesia. In 1984, Bhante Ashin, who was renowned for his own alleged power to heal, had visited Satya Sai Baba and claimed that the guru had cured leg pain from which he had long suffered; henceforth, he regarded Satya Sai Baba as his own guru (Kimura 2003: 62). Bhante Ashin's unwillingness to withdraw his open admiration of the Indian saint deepened the rift between the Theravada and the Buddhayana factions within the Indonesian Sangha Agung, leading to the Indonesian Buddhayana Council and the Buddhayana Sangha's departure from WALUBI in 1994 (see also Steenbrink 2013: 7).

Among the non-Balinese members of the Hindu community, a general discontent had become palpable by the early 1990s, because of the unchanged hegemonic position of Balinese priests in official Hindu institutions and representative bodies. The political dominance of the Balinese had furthermore resulted in a one-sided accommodation of Balinese concepts and rituals in modern Indonesian Hinduism. The suppression of local tradition was especially galling because the adoption of Hinduism ended up offering so little in terms of basic protection, let alone access to the benefits of modernity. In the end, many non-Balinese Hindus joined a growing number of disenchanted Indonesian Buddhists in their conversion either "back" to Islam or to Christianity (see also Hefner 2004: 94, 99).

In the early 1990s, dissatisfaction with the official Hindu institutions was on the rise, too, among Balinese Hindus, especially among members of the growing middle class, for several reasons. First, these institutions failed to protect the Hindu community at large against denigrating behavior from members of the Abrahamic religions, particularly Islam. Second, their policies had resulted in a stifling bureaucratization of the Hindu religion, which had made people thirst for other sources of spirituality. This was aggravated by the fact that the official Hindu institutions were not investing enough in the religious education of the Hindu community. Many people felt stuck with their local traditions that proved less and less in synchrony with their increasingly well-to-do lifestyles. Last but not least, neither the PHDI nor the Office of Hindu Affairs took effective steps against the increasing commercialization of Hindu Balinese rituals prompted by the government's relentless promotion of tourism in Bali (Bagus 2004: 87–9; Ramstedt 2009: 333–42).

All these factors contributed to a renewed interest in things Indian among Balinese, which fortuitously met with a growing interest in Southeast Asian affairs on the part of the Indian government and diverse groups of Indian citizens. This interest on the part of the latter was prompted not the least by the dissolution of the Soviet Union in 1991, which had India lose its main trading partner (Ramstedt 2008: 1237). Pushing the Indian economy into the global market, the Indian government naturally found the booming Indonesian economy attractive, and until the Asia crisis of 1997, many Indian professionals found job opportunities in Indonesia (Ramstedt 2008: 1231).

Indian Hindu organizations took an enhanced interest in Indonesia in general and in Bali in particular, successfully relying on the different Indian-Indonesian networks throughout Indonesia to forge closer ties not only between Balinese and Indian Hindus but also between Balinese Hindus and diasporic Hindu communities around the world. In 1992, the World Hindu Federation convened in Bali, attended by Hindu scholars and spiritual leaders from Indonesia, Nepal, Bangladesh, Malaysia, Singapore, Fiji, Mauritius, the United Kingdom, and the United States (Ramstedt 2008: 1247). While the Hindu nationalist rhetoric of Rashtriya Swayamsevak Sangh (RSS) and Vishva Hindu Parishad (VHS) activists did not arouse much interest among Balinese Hindus or non-Balinese Indonesian Hindus, more and more Balinese were becoming interested in visiting India, and many were actually starting to do so.

Aside from this renewed enthusiasm for India, the 1990s in Bali were marked by a vocal public concern for the protection of local tradition against hostile "outsiders," above all foreign investors dominating Bali's tourism industry and Muslim migrants from neighboring islands allegedly taking advantage of Bali's thriving economy. In 1995, leading Balinese intellectuals, businessmen, and priests joined two Balinese lawyers in establishing the Forum of Those Concerned about Indonesian Hinduism (Forum Pemerhati Indonesia, FPHDI). One of the goals of the forum was to open a public debate on the possibility of turning Bali into an official Hindu territory. Support for this issue soon became widespread, boosted by frequent news of religious violence on the part of radical Muslims. In 1996, for example, riots erupted in which several Christian churches and a Buddhist temple were burned down. At the same time, vandalism against Hindu temples, particularly in Java and South Sulawesi, was on the rise (Purdey 2005: 56–66; Ramstedt 2012b: 325–7, 332).

The post–New Order period

When Soeharto was finally pressured to step down in May 1998, Indonesia began the first one-and-a-half years of its transition from dictatorship to a parliamentary democracy under the leadership of interim-President B. J. Habibie. With the support of the Breton Woods institutions, the IMF, and the World Bank, Habibie's legislature launched a legal scheme for a far-reaching decentralization, which was largely implemented under the presidency of Megawati Sukarnoputri between 2001 and 2004. Indonesia's transition from a strongly centralized and unitary form of governance to a highly decentralized one was, paradoxically perhaps, accompanied by an acceleration of normative and institutional recognition of Islam in the state legislation, as well as intense spells of violent inter-ethnic and inter-religious conflict in Kalimantan, Moluccas, Central Sulawesi, Lombok, West Irian/Papua, and, to a certain extent, Bali (Klinken 2007; Schulte Nordholt 2007: 403–7). Non-Muslim ethnic groups were starting to assert their local identities, frequently by lashing out against local Muslim migrant communities. While, after 2002, the violence largely subsided, efforts of reasserting local identities continued in the form of efforts to revitalize local customary law and to reaffirm, at least partially, traditional elites.

Hinduism in post–New Order Indonesia

The dissolution of Soeharto's New Order regime was marked by the abolition of tight state control over religious developments and organizations, thereby bestowing more freedom on local communities to determine their own affairs. Tamil-Indonesians, for instance, can now again celebrate their once prohibited rituals, Thaipussam and Dipavali (Basarsyah 2008: 26). For the Indonesian Hindu community as a whole this new freedom has paradoxically led to increasing fragmentation. Even though the tension between national and transnational orientation became much less pronounced in the course of the democratization of the country, a growing ethno-nationalism soon began to rival the newfound interest for universalistic Indian varieties of Hinduism (see also Picard 2011: 131).

Before focusing on the issue of the growing ethno-nationalism, let us first take a closer look at the interaction between Indonesian and Indian Hindus after the fall of Soeharto. During the New Order period, only a handful of Indonesian Hindus – most of them Balinese – had availed themselves of the scholarships provided by the Indian Council for Cultural Relations (ICCR) since 1955 to Indonesian students interested in studying at an Indian university. One of the few who did study in India was I Made Titib, who obtained his doctorate from the Gurukul Kangri University in Hardwar. Upon his return to Indonesia, Titib became a leading official in the PHDI and finally the director of the Hindu College in Denpasar. In 1990, he initiated regular pilgrimage tours by Indonesian Hindus to India. These pilgrimage tours, organized by specialized Balinese travel agencies, attracted more and more members of Bali's increasingly affluent middle class, as well as a few Hindu officials, intellectuals, and government officials from other ethnic groups. Between 1993 and 1999, some 6,000 Indonesian Hindus visited a variety of holy places on the Indian subcontinent. From 1999 onward, Air India offered special economy package tours from Bali to a couple of Indian destinations. Today, devotional images from India, as well as Indian devotional music, are ubiquitous in Hindu temples and settlements all over Indonesia (Ramstedt 2012b: 329) and an increasing number of Indonesian Hindus have taken the opportunity to deepen their understanding of Hindu Dharma at Indian universities.

Moreover, a number of prestigious Indian international schools in Jakarta and Denpasar, all of them espousing a universalist and integrationist Hindu ethos, have drawn the attention of affluent Indonesian parents, not only from a Hindu background. One of them is the well-reputed Bali Public School, an Ananda Marga neo-humanist school in Denpasar, offering playgroup, nursery schools, and elementary school education. The other three schools were established by the Taman Mahatma Gandhi Foundation on the basis of the principles of the Gandhi Education Movement, which in Indonesia reaches back to 1957. The oldest of the three schools is the Gandhi Memorial International School (GMIS) in Jakarta. It was officially recognized and registered by the Indonesian Ministry of Education and Culture in 1978. In 2007, a branch of GMIS opened in Denpasar. While both these schools have over the years downplayed their Hindu background in favor of a pronounced multi-religious and multi-ethnic admission policy, the third school managed by the Taman Mahatma Gandhi Foundation, the Taman Rama School, is more distinctly Hindu in the Gandhian sense. It was established in Denpasar in 1999.

The popularity among Indonesian Hindus of universalistic Indian Hinduism, as represented by Gandhism, Ananda Marga, Brahma Kumaris, ISKCON, or the Satya Sai Baba movement, is rooted in an absence of caste divisions, a rejection of ritualism, the cultivation of an egalitarian spirit, and an emphasis on spiritual self-development, largely with the help of meditation and yoga techniques. Such varieties of religiosity have meshed well with the spirit of the Indonesian democratization process.

In 2001, the national convention of the PHDI in Bali actually resulted in breaking the longstanding hegemony of Balinese Brahmins within the PHDI national board, and for the first time since its inception, it consisted of representatives from the whole range of currents within the Indonesian Hindu community. What was more, the newly elected head of the national board, I Nyoman Suwandha, was the first Balinese commoner in this post, and he was not even an ordained priest. Moreover, he shared the leadership of the national board, which formerly had been solely in the hands of Balinese Brahmin priests, with a Javanese, Adi Soeripto, who had been appointed as secretary-general and thus held the second highest rank within the board. A minority of Balinese conservatives was not willing to stomach such radical change. They openly rebelled against the election results, separating themselves from the PHDI Balinese board and in 2002 setting up a rival PHDI, the so-called PHDI Campuan; the rival board never received official recognition. In 2007, the PHDI Campuan officially changed its name to Parisada Dharma Hindu Bali. The conservatives thereby declared their return to the "true" Hindu Balinese religion, with its elaborate and costly ritual system and the unquestioned leadership of traditional Brahmin priests (Ramstedt 2009: 367–71; Picard 2011: 131–7).

Balinese traditionalists have strongly resented the spiritual competition by Indian gurus, who have posed a serious challenge to the spiritual authority of the Balinese Brahmin priests, particularly since varieties of Indian-style yoga became popular throughout Indonesia from the 1990s onward. One of the most influential proponents of Indian-style yoga living permanently in Bali today is Dr. Yadav Somvir, an Indian Sanskrit scholar and former member of a classical Indian reform-Hindu organization, the Arya Samaj, who had first come to Indonesia in 1993. In the late 1990s, he was a lecturer of Sanskrit at Udayana University in Denpasar and gave talks on Indian Hindu philosophy across Indonesia. At the beginning of the new millennium, he served as head of the Jawaharlal Nehru Cultural Centre (JNICC) branch office in Denpasar (see also Ramstedt 2008: 1230–1233). Thereafter, in 2006, he founded the Bali India Foundation, an organization with the mission to forge a friendship between Balinese and Indian Hindus, mainly through teaching Indian Hatha yoga and meditation to enrolled Balinese students and by providing ayurvedic treatments to interested Balinese clients. In 2009, he finally obtained Indonesian citizenship, not least in recognition of his cultural activities in Indonesia. One of his major projects was the construction of the Pasraman Gurukula Bangli (PKB), which started operating in 2006, after a planning and fundraising period of three years. Conceived as cultural translation of a traditional Arya Samaj gurukul into a Balinese setting, including an orphanage and a combined junior-senior high school, as well as a small herd of Indian cows providing the resident pupils with their daily milk Indian-style, the PKB offers a comprehensive Hindu education. The latter comprises daily yoga exercise, ayurvedic treatments, and the study of the Balinese language and sacred literature, as well as the arts.

Somvir had been able to raise funds not only from affluent members of the Indian–Indonesian community but also from the Indian tycoon, Lakshmi Mittal. While Somvir had originally planned to take residency in the Gurukula so as to oversee the management of the school himself, he finally decided to release the operation to a Balinese staff under the supervision of the district governor of Bangli, whose showcase project it had become.

In 2005, Somvir had already begun to design a similar project that resulted in the development of Markandeya Yoga City in the mountainous region of North Bali, in the District of Sukasada. Officially inaugurated by the incumbent governor of Bali, I Made Mangku Pastika, in March 2010, Markandeya Yoga City covers an area of ten hectares of land, dedicated to the practice and study of yoga and ayurveda. Within a short period of time, it has become a popular destination for domestic and international yoga lovers.

Already in the mid-1990s, the afore-mentioned dominance of foreign investors over Bali's tourist industries had prompted Balinese leaders to instigate a debate about the necessity to turn Bali into a Hindu realm. At the same time, they had started to align themselves with the indigenous rights movement that since the 1980s had gained currency among ethnic groups exposed to the detrimental effects of the relentless mining and logging activities of companies benefitting from cronyist Soeharto's license schemes. For conservative or traditionalist Balinese, Bali being Hindu was not enough. The island was to remain a Hindu Balinese realm, protected by traditional Hindu Balinese customary law. This idea rapidly gained currency in 2001, when the Alliance of Indonesia's Customary Law Communities (Aliansi Masyarakat Adat Nusantara, AMAN) opened a regional branch office in Bali. AMAN had been founded in 1999, when delegates of different ethnic groups involved in the Indonesian indigenous rights movement had gathered in Jakarta to replace the old Network for the Defense of the Rights of the Customary Law Communities (Jaringan Pembelaan Hak-Hak Masyarakat Adat, JAPHAMA), established in 1993, with a more up-to-date socio-political platform, untainted by roots in the Soeharto period. AMAN had soon developed close relations with the Asia Indigenous Peoples Pact (AIPP), the International Working Group of Indigenous Affairs (IWGIA), and the Indigenous Peoples Caucus, thus demonstrating it had become a force to be reckoned with. An AMAN representative in Bali fervently called for Hindu Balinese customary law courts to have the same status as the Islamic law courts. This call immediately resonated with the incumbent Balinese governor, I Dewa Beratha, and the Indonesian Democratic Party-Struggle (PDI-P), which at the time had the vast majority of seats in the Balinese Provincial Parliament. Several regional laws were drafted between 2001 and 2009 that juridified Balinese village customary law, without any further reference to AMAN (Ramstedt 2012b: 332–4, 2017: 57–9; Hauser-Schäublin 2013).

The juridification of Hindu Balinese customary law was facilitated by the contemporary decentralization process and entailed the zoning off of Bali from the secular jurisdiction of the Indonesian state, which was analogous to the effects of the special autonomy granted to the provinces of Aceh and Papua in 2001. While special autonomy was not granted to Bali, Bali Province Regulation No. 3/2001+2003 authorized the establishment of autonomous village jurisdictions on the basis of largely standardized and modernized versions of the old customary village institutions, rooted in a cosmology marked by ancestor worship and extensive ritualism. These village institutions were now endowed with a significant degree of legislative, administrative, adjudicative, punitive, and economic decision-making power that forced residents, irrespective of their individual convictions, into a tight neo-traditionalist regime. The regulation has nevertheless served as an effective bulwark against the alienation of village commons and the political emancipation of migrants in Bali, including Indian Hindus. The regulation was reconfirmed and supplemented by Bali Province Regulation No. 16/2009, stipulating that the sanctity of natural habitats, which have traditionally been revered as sites of important guardian spirits, including mountains and gorges, springs and lakes, coastlines and the sea, should be protected in the provincial spatial planning in years to come (Ramstedt 2009: 344–55, 2013: 117–24).

With the juridification of local village customary law, the Balinese have thus surreptitiously reversed the forced universalization of their rather heterogeneous local traditions, which had been going on under the heading of "Indonesian Hinduism" since the beginning of the 1950s (Ramstedt 2013: 112; see also Picard 2011). The renativization of religion in Bali has been echoed in the non-Balinese Hindu enclaves in Central and East Java, North Sumatra, South Sulawesi, and Central Kalimantan, thus exacerbating the fragmentation of the Indonesian Hindu community already suffering from a dwindling number of followers among the non-Balinese Hindus.

Buddhism in post–New Order Indonesia

The transition of the Indonesian Buddhist community from the Soeharto to the post–New Order period was first marked by the pogroms against Sino-Indonesians in Java, North Sumatra, and South Sulawesi, which were accompanied by an even fiercer vandalism of temples (Kimura 2003: 69; Purdey 2005: ix–xii, 66–8, 77–141). The pogroms prompted a wave of migration by Sino-Indonesians (particularly from Medan, Jakarta, and Surabaya), as well as Indian-Indonesians (also predominantly from Medan, Jakarta, and Surabaya), into Bali. Together with Javanese Muslims and Christian migrants from Timor and Flores, these groupings made up almost 15% of Bali's total population of 3.15 million people in 2000. The large majority of the new arrivals settled in the rapidly urbanizing area of Denpasar and Kuta, where Buddhists erected several large temples (see also Ramstedt 2012b: 327).

Apart from these external developments, there were also turbulent changes in the organization of Buddhism in Indonesia. In 1997, in the midst of the Asia Crisis, Bhante Giri passed away. In 1992, he had successfully lobbied so that a Sino-Indonesian businesswoman with close ties to both the military and the Soeharto family, Siti Hartati Murdaya, was appointed as chair of WALUBI. Without the backing of Bhante Giri, tensions over the leadership of Siti Hartati Murdaya, who had allegedly been trying to single-handedly control all WALUBI affairs, came to a head in 1998, eventually culminating in the unconstitutional dissolution of WALUBI. A month later, a new Buddhist organization was established under the same acronym, WALUBI, even though its constituent words had a slightly different meaning than before, namely "Representative Body" (instead of "Leadership") of Indonesian Buddhists (Perwakilan Umat Buddha Indonesia). Because Siti Hartati Murdaya was also at the helm of this new institution, it never received significant support (see also Steenbrink 2013: 10–11).

In mid-1999, some degree of communality among the different Buddhist currents was nevertheless regained, when the now four Buddhist orders (Sangha Buddhayana, Sangha Mahayana, Sangha Theravada, and Sangha Tridharma), together with the four councils of their respective lay-followers, formed the Conference of the Greater Indonesian Sangha (Konferensi Sangha Agung Indonesia, KASI) as their common representative body vis-à-vis MORA (Kimura 2003: 66).

In 1999, too, Bhante Ashin was internationally honored with the vice presidency of the World Buddhist Sangha Council. He passed away in 2002, having remained very active until the end of his life. His body was cremated in Bandar Lampung, South Sumatra. In the ashes, his followers found a number of crystal pearls that were immediately recognized as relics. These relics were then displayed to believers in ten towns in Sumatra and Java (Kimura 2003: 54, 67–8; Steenbrink 2013: 6). Subsequently, students and followers of Bhante Ashin established the Ashin Jinarakkhita Foundation. In 2007, it set about constructing an Indonesian Buddhist Education and Training Center (Prasadha Jinarakkhita) for monastics and lay Buddhist teachers and intellectuals in Jakarta, which became operational in 2012. The eight-story building houses a museum-cum-shrine hall that contains a small stupa with the relics of the late Bhante Ashin. The museum narrates the history of Buddhism in Indonesia in such a way that Bhante Ashin's work, that is, Indonesian Buddhayana, appears to directly descend from the Old Javanese Buddhist culture of the maritime empire Srivijaya in present-day Sumatra and the East Javanese empires of Singhasari and Majapahit.

In 2006, MORA finally granted Buddhism full independence from Hinduism with the establishment of the Directorate General for the Guidance of the Buddhist Community. Its inauguration came at a time when new state legislation, Law No. 12/2006 on Citizenship of the Republic of Indonesia, amended the precarious citizen status of Sino-Indonesians, thus following up on Abdurrahman Wahid's abolition of Soeharto's Presidential Instruction No. 14/1967, mandating the suppression of all Chinese cultural expressions in Indonesia, and Decision of the Indonesian Ministry of Home Affairs No. 477/805/Sj/1978, reversing the status of Confucianism as one of six recognized religions (Thung 2011: 197, 202ff.).

While Indonesian, especially Sino-Indonesian, Buddhists have appreciated these improvements, the community has mostly sought to remain inconspicuous. In 2013, a low-intensity bomb exploded outside the main Buddhayana temple-cum-monastery in West Jakarta, the Vihara Ekayana, injuring three people. The bomb had reportedly been placed there because of the ill treatment of Muslim Rohingyas in predominantly Buddhist Myanmar (see also Kimura 2003: 69). Indonesian Buddhists have tried to abate rising anti-Buddhist sentiments among their Muslim neighbors, by donating rice, clothes, and other goods to those in need and by playing down any aggressive acts recently committed against Indonesian Buddhists.

It is only in Bali that Buddhists have felt comparatively safe. Some Buddhist temples and meditation centers, like the afore-mentioned Brahmavihara Arama in North Bali or Merta Ada's Bali Usada Health Meditation Center in South Bali, have attracted a large following from all over Asia. They have thus contributed to Bali's growing spiritual tourism industry, simultaneously fueling Hindu Balinese fears of economic competition by outsiders.

References cited

Alexander, Robert J. 1991. *International Trotskyism 1929–1985: A Documented Analysis of the Movement* (Durham and London: Duke University Press).

Aritonang, Jan Sihar, and Karel Steenbrink. 2008. "The Spectacular Growth of the Third Stream: The Evangelicals and Pentecostals," in Jan Sihar Aritonang and Karel Steenbrink, eds., *A History of Christianity in Indonesia* (Leiden and Boston: Brill), pp. 867–902.

Ashiwa, Yoshiko and David L. Wank. 2005. "The Globalization of Chinese Buddhism: Clergy and Devotee Networks in the Twentieth Century," *International Journal of Asian Studies* 2(2): 217–37.

Bachtiar, W. Harja. 2006 (orig. 1993). "Indians in Indonesia: A Component of National Integration," in K. S. Sandhu and A. Mani, eds., *Indian Communities in Southeast Asia* (Singapore: ISEAS), pp. 131–50.

Bagus, I. Gusti Ngurah. 2004. "The Parisada Hindu Dharma Indonesia in a Society in Transformation: The Emergence of Conflicts Amidst Differences and Demands," in Martin Ramstedt, ed., *Hinduism in Modern Indonesia: A Minority Religion Between Local, National, and Global Interests* (London and New York: RoutledgeCurzon), pp. 84–92.

Baier, Martin. 1998. "Die Hindu Kaharingan-Religion als beispielloser Fall eines nachchristlichen Nativismus," *Tribus, Jahrbuch des Linden-Museums Stuttgart* 47: 49–54.

Basarsyah, Tuanku Luckman Sinar. 2008. *Orang India di Sumatera Utara/The Indians in North Sumatra* (Medan: FORKALA-SUMUT).

Benda, Harry J. and Ruth T. McVey. 2009 (1960). *The Communist Uprisings of 1926–1927 in Indonesia: Key Documents* (Singapore: Equinox Publishing).

Bourchier, David. 2010 (1984). *Dynamics of Dissent in Indonesia: Sawito and the Phantom Coup* (Singapore: Equinox Publishing).

Brown, Iem. 2004. "The Revival of Buddhism in Modern Indonesia," in Martin Ramstedt, ed., *Hinduism in Modern Indonesia: A Minority Religion Between Local, National, and Global Interests* (London and New York: RoutledgeCurzon), pp. 45–55.

Chen, Zhimin. 2005. "Nationalism, Internationalism and Chinese Foreign Policy," *Journal of Contemporary China* 14(42): 35–53.

Dharmawimala, Biksu. 2012. "Buddhayana dan Kontekstualisasi Agama Buddha di Indonesia," in Edij J. Heru Suherman Lim, ed., *Buddhayana Values* (Jakarta: Keluarga Buddhayana Indonesia), pp. 1–11.

Geertz, Clifford. 1972. "Religious Change and Social Order in Soeharto's Indonesia," *Asia* 27: 62–84.

Ginting, Juara R. 2004. "The Position of Hinduism in Karo Society (North Sumatra)," in Martin Ramstedt, ed., *Hinduism in Modern Indonesia: A Minority Religion between Local, National, and Global Interests* (London and New York: RoutledgeCurzon), pp. 226–41.

Hauser-Schäublin, Brigitta. 2013. "How Indigenous Are the Balinese? From National Marginalisation to Provincial Domination," in Brigitta Hauser-Schäublin, ed., *Adat and Indigeneity in Indonesia: Culture and Entitlements Between Heteronomy and Self-Ascription* (Göttingen: Universitätsverlag Göttingen), pp. 133–48.

Hefner, Robert W. 1985. *Hindu Javanese: Tengger Tradition and Islam* (Princeton: Princeton University Press).

———. 2004. "Hindu Reform in an Islamizing Java: Pluralism and Peril," in Martin Ramstedt, ed., *Hinduism in Modern Indonesia: A Minority Religion Between Local, National, and Global Interests*, pp. 93–108 (Leiden: KITLV Press).

Holleman, Johan F., ed. 1981. *Van Vollenhoven on Indonesian Adat Law: Selections from Het Adatrecht van Nederlandsch-Indië (Volume I, 1918; Volume II, 1931)* (Dordrecht: Springer Science+Business Media).

Hong Liu. 2011. *China and the Shaping of Indonesia, 1949–1965* (Singapore and Kyoto: NUS Press in Association with Kyoto University Press).

Howe, Leo. 2001. *Hinduism & Hierarchy in Bali* (Oxford and Santa Fe: James Currey and School of American Research Press).

Howell, Julia. 1977. *Vehicles for the Kalki Avatar: The Experiments of a Javanese Guru in Rationalized Ecstatic Religion* (Ann Arbor: University Microfilms International).

Juangari, Edij. 1995. *Menabur Benih Dharma di Nusantara: Riwayat Singkat Bhikkhu Ashin Jinarakkhita* (Bandung: Yayasan Penerbit Karaniya).

Kimura, Bunki. 2003. "Present Situation of Indonesian Buddhism: In Memory of Bhikkhu Ashin Jinarakkhita Mahasthavira," *Nagoya Studies in Indian Culture and Buddhism: Sambhasa* 23: 53–72.

Klinken, Gerry van. 2007. *Communal Violence and Democratization in Indonesia: Small Town Wars* (London and New York: Routledge).

Lev, Dan S. 2000. *Legal Evolution and Political Authority in Indonesia: Selected Essays* (Hague and Cambridge, MA: Kluwer Law International).

Ling, Haicheng. 2004. *Buddhism in China* (Beijing: China International Press).

Locher-Scholten, Elsbeth. 2000. *Women and the Colonial State: Essays on Gender and Modernity in the Netherlands Indies 1900–1942* (Amsterdam: Amsterdam University Press).

Loderichs, M. A. 1997. *Medan: Beeld van een stad* (Purmerend: Asia Maior).

Lyon, Margaret L. 1977. "Politics and Religious Identity: Genesis of a Javanese-Hindu Movement in Rural Central Java" (Ph.D. Thesis. Berkeley: Department of Anthropology, University of California).

MacDougall, John M. 2005. *Buddhist Buda or Buda Buddhists? Conversion, Religious Modernism, and Conflict in the Minority Buda Sasak Communities of New Order and Post-Suharto Lombok, Vol. I* (Ann Arbor: University Microfilms International).

Mani, A. 2006a (1993). "Indians in North Sumatra," in K. S. Sandhu and A. Mani, eds., *Indian Communities in Southeast Asia* (Singapore: ISEAS), pp. 46–97.

———. 2006b (1993). "Indians in Jakarta," in K. S. Sandhu and A. Mani, eds., *Indian Communities in Southeast Asia* (Singapore: ISEAS), pp. 98–129.

Mayor Polak, J. B. A. F. 1973. "De Herleving van het Hindoeïsme op Oost-Java" (MA Thesis. Amsterdam: South- and Southeast Asia Department, Anthropological-Sociological Centre).

———. 1977. "De Herleving van het Hindoeïsme op Oost-Java II," Working Paper No. 1 (Amsterdam: South- and Southeast Asia Department, Anthropological-Sociological Centre).

McGregor, Katharine E. 2009. "The Indonesian Killings of 1965–1966," in *Mass Violence and Resistance – Research Network*. www.sciencespo.fr/mass-violence-war-massacre-resistance/en/document/indonesian-killings-1965-1966 (Accessed 23 February 2017).

Mortimer, Rex. 2006 (1974). *Indonesian Communism Under Sukarno: Ideology and Politics, 1959–1965* (Singapore: Equinox Publishing).

Omveldt, Gail. 2003. *Buddhism in India: Challenging Brahmanism and Caste* (New Delhi, Thousand Oaks, and London: Sage Publications).

Pengurus Pusat Majelis Buddhayana Indonesia (PPIMBI). 2008. *Sarira 2008* (Jakarta: Majelis Buddhayana Indonesia – Sangha Agung Indonesia).

Picard, Michel. 2004. "What's in a Name? Agama Hindu Bali in the Making," in Martin Ramstedt, ed., *Hinduism in Modern Indonesia: A Minority Religion Between Local, National, and Global Interests* (London and New York: RoutledgeCurzon), pp. 56–75.

———. 2011. "From Agama Hindu Bali to Agama Hindu and Back: Toward a Relocalization of the Balinese Religion?" in Michel Picard and Rémy Madinier, eds., *The Politics of Religion in Indonesia: Syncretism, Orthodoxy, and Religious Contention in Java and Bali* (London and New York: Routledge), pp. 117–41.

Priastana, Jo. 2006. *Happy Vaisakh: Tiga Peristiwa Suci dan Maknanya Bagi Dunia Kehidupan* (Jakarta: Yasodhara Puteri).

Purdey, Jemma. 2005. *Anti-Chinese Violence in Indonesia, 1996–1999* (Leiden: KITLV).

Racheman, Harkiman. 2010. "Ekumenisme Buddhis di Indonesia: Sebuah Perspektif Buddhayan," in Edij J. Heru Suherman Lim, ed., *Buddayana Values* (Jakarta: Keluarga Buddhayana Indonesia), pp. 211–41.

Ramstedt, Martin. 2004a. "Introduction: Negotiating Identities – Indonesian 'Hindus' Between Local, National, and Global Interests," in Martin Ramstedt, (ed.), *Hinduism in Modern Indonesia: A Minority Religion Between Local, National, and Global Interests* (London and New York: RoutledgeCurzon), pp. 1–34.

———. 2004b. "Hinduization of Local Traditions in South Sulawesi," in Martin Ramstedt, (ed.), *Hinduism in Modern Indonesia: A Minority Religion Between Local, National, and Global Interests* (London and New York: RoutledgeCurzon), pp. 184–225.

———. 2008. "Hindu Bonds at Work: Spiritual and Commercial Ties Between India and Bali," *The Journal of Asian Studies* 67(4): 1227–1250.

———. 2009. "Regional Autonomy and Its Discontents: The Case of Post-New Order Bali," in Coen J. G. Holtzappel and Martin Ramstedt, eds., *Decentralization and Regional Autonomy in Indonesia: Implementation and Challenges* (Singapore: ISEAS), pp. 329–379.

———. 2011. "Colonial Encounters Between India and Indonesia," *South Asian History and Culture* 2(4): pp. 522–539.

———. 2012a. "Islamisation by Law and the Juridification of Religion in Anomic Indonesia," Max Planck Institute for Social Anthropology Working Papers, Working Paper No. 140 (Halle/Saale).

———. 2012b. "Processes of Disembedding and Displacement: Anomie and the Juridification of Religio-Ethnic Identity in Post-New Order Bali," *Asian Ethnicity* 13:(4):, pp. 323–339.

———. 2013. "Religion and Disputes in Bali's New Village Jurisdictions," in Franz von Benda-Beckmann, Keebet von Benda-Beckmann, Martin Ramstedt and Bert Turner, (eds.), *Religion in Disputes: Pervasiveness of Religious Normativity in Disputing Processes* (New York: Palgrave Macmillan), pp. 111–128.

———. 2017. "Cultural Translation, Traveling Law, and the Transposition of Indigenous Rights to Indonesian Contexts," *Translation and Translanguaging in Multilingual Contexts* 3(1), Special Issue: Valérie Dullion (ed.), *Between Specialised Texts and Institutional Contexts – Competence and Choice in Legal Translation* (Amsterdam: John Benjamins Publishing Company), pp. 47–63.

Schulte Nordholt, Henk. 2007. *Bali: An Open Fortress 1995–2005* (Singapore: NUS Press).

Seiwert, Hubert. 1997. "On the Religions of National Minorities in the Context of China's Religious History," in Thomas Heberer, ed., *Ethnic Minorities in China: Tradition and Transform* (Aachen: Rader Verlag), pp. 41–51.

Steenbrink, Karel. 2013. "Buddhism in Muslim Indonesia," *Studia Islamika* 20(1): 1–34.

Sudhamek, AWS. 2012. "Eksplorasi Nilai-Nilai Buddhayana (Sebuah Telaah dari Perspektif Transfomratif-Liberatif)," in Edij J. Heru Suherman Lim, ed., *Buddhayana Values* (Jakarta: Keluarga Buddhayana Indonesia), pp. 13–124.

Suwandi, Raharjo. 2000. *A Quest for Justice: The Millenary Aspirations of a Contemporary Javanese Wali* (Leiden: KITLV Press).

(*SvhKdN*) *Staatsblad van het Koninkrijk der Nederlanden 1883–1951* (Zwolle: Tjeenk Willink).

Thung Ju Lan. 2011. "Politik Identitas dan Proses Hukum: Kontestasi Pengertian Etnik Tionghua sebagai Subyek Hukum," in Martin Ramstedt and Fadjar I. Thufail, eds., *Kegalauan Identitas: Agama, Etnisitas, dan Kewarganegaraan pada Masa Pasca-Orde Baru* (Jakarta: Grasindo), pp. 195–217.

Vignato, Silvia. 2000. *Au nom de l'Hindouïsme: Reconfigurations ethniques chez les Tamouls et les Karo en Indonésie* (Paris and Montreal: L'Harmattan).

————. 2004. "Old Gods for the New World: The Ritual Struggle of the Tamil and the Karo Within Hinduism in North Sumatra," in Martin Ramstedt, ed., *Hinduism in Modern Indonesia: A Minority Religion Between Local, National, and Global Interests* (London and New York: RoutledgeCurzon), pp. 242–54.

Weinstock, Joseph A. 1984. *Kaharingan and the Luangan Dayaks: Religion and Identity in Central-East Borneo* (Ann Arbor: University Microfilms International).

Zuhdi, Muhammad. 2006. "Modernization of Indonesian Islamic Schools' Curricula, 1945–2003," *International Journal of Inclusive Education* 10(4–5): 415–27.

23

THE POLITICS AND LAW OF RELIGIOUS GOVERNANCE

Zainal Abidin Bagir

The most significant new development in religious governance in Indonesia since 1998 has undoubtedly been the strengthening of the constitutional and legal foundations of religious freedom. While religious freedom was already mentioned in the 1945 Constitution, it found firmer ground soon after the 1998 Reformasi in new laws on human rights and in the addition of a whole new chapter on human rights in the amended constitution. Yet, paradoxically, much of the politics and laws regulating religion inherited from the pre-1998 authoritarian era remains in existence. What seemed to be progress in commitment to religious freedom on the part of both the state and civil society has been held back by qualifications and limitations that stem from the old paradigm of religious governance as well as from the influence of new non-state forces, which have flourished in the free space of a democratized and decentralized Indonesia.

This chapter starts with a discussion of the historic change that started in 1998 and then looks at the tensions between it and three other elements influencing Indonesian religious governance. The three elements inherited from pre-1998 are in tension with efforts to strengthen religious freedom. *First*, recognition of Indonesian religious diversity remains limited, and this has been increasingly questioned recently because it becomes a basis of discrimination. *Second*, government action remains focused on attempts to maintain order or harmony, which can include advancement or even "protection" of religion. This basically means control over religious manifestations and expressions between religious groups, which, despite a general thread of peace among them, have sometimes been in tension. *Third*, a kind of Islamization in laws and regulations at both the national and local levels is ongoing in different degrees throughout the archipelago.

While much of the following discussion is critical of the present state of religious governance in Indonesia, we should not overlook important positive developments. Liddle and Mujani (2013) argue that the transition to democracy was completed by 2004, and Indonesia has been moving toward consolidated democracy since. Freedom House ranked Indonesia as "free" from 2006 until 2013, though in 2014, this designation was demoted to "partly free," and the status has not changed since.[1]

The arena where tensions inherent in the co-existence of the different paradigms of religious governance are played out is this new context of progressive developments toward consolidated democracy, which include the strengthening of societal forces and the weakening of the previously authoritarian state. These tensions are manifested concretely in such cases as discrimination against "non-orthodox" religious groups, the revitalization of the Defamation of Religion

Law, and conflicts over the construction of houses of worship. This chapter concludes with an assessment of the prospect of a fair and just management of religious diversity in the context of democracy in Indonesia.

Freedom of religion and belief

Only six months after the collapse of the New Order regime in May 1998, the People's Consultative Assembly issued a decree on human rights. The decree, the standing of which is right below the constitution in the hierarchy of laws, ordered the president and the parliament to ratify UN human rights instruments "insofar as they are not contrary to the Pancasila and the 1945 Constitution." Until now, eight international human rights documents, including the International Covenant on Civil and Political Rights, have become part of Indonesian law. Before May 1998, there were only two. The assembly's decree also included a text on what is called the Indonesian nation's view on human rights and a "Human Rights Charter," derived mainly from the Universal Declaration of Human Rights. Within just two years, the decree was followed by fundamental changes to Indonesian law, including the enactment of specific laws on human rights (No 39/1999). Most significant was the second amendment to the constitution (2000), which inserted a new chapter titled "Human Rights." Lindsey (2002) comments that the amendments constitute "the most radical change to the original philosophy of the Constitution . . . Chapter XA [on Human Rights] is a lengthy and impressive passage, granting a full range or protections extending well beyond those guaranteed in most developed states."

All this has provided an unprecedented foundation for religious freedom. The next move after the establishment of the rights was its mainstreaming. It was done partly by incorporating relevant clauses into a number of laws or lower-level regulations covering different issues. For example, the Management of Social Conflict Law (No.7/2012) encourages tolerance and respect for freedom of religion and belief in order to maintain peace, calling for a principle of non-discrimination (Art. 2n) in conflict resolution and setting a new norm of equality without discrimination based on religion and belief (Art. 7). Disaster Management Law (No. 24/2007, Art. 3 and its explanation) prohibits discrimination based on religion in the distribution of aid to disaster victims. The Indonesian Migrant Workers Abroad Law (No. 39/2004) names the freedom of religion and belief among the rights of overseas workers (Art. 8d). A regulation issued by the Head of Police (No. 8/2009) sets standards for the implementation of human rights in the execution of the duties of the Indonesian police.

Paradoxically, however, the complete picture, which was not fully noticeable in the first few years after 1998, now seems more ambiguous despite this progress. Some restrictive clauses in the constitution and other laws have turned out to have significant implications and, at the same time, the existing pre-1998 policies on religion remained in place without the changes that were called for. As a result, there continue to be tensions, if not contradictions, in the management of religious diversity and the resolution of conflict over religious issues. Some more recently enacted laws have also led to different kinds of restrictions on religious freedom. The restrictions concentrated on a few issues, such as how religion is defined and the significance of the phrase "religious values" in Article 28J of the constitution as part of legitimate restriction in exercise of rights, which will be discussed in the next section.

Recognition of religion and its limits

Indonesia is a pluralist state. Although it has a large Muslim majority, the state is not based on any religion. The state acknowledges the freedom of religion in its 1945 Constitution, but it has also been clear since the beginning that this recognition has limits set by a certain politics of religion and expressed, explicitly or implicitly, in the constitution, national and local laws, and lower-level regulations.

The first limit concerns how religion itself is defined (or constructed) by the state. The boundaries of the concept of religion have long been contested, in Indonesia like elsewhere (Picard 2011: 3). Furthermore, in practice, this definition is inevitably entangled with other types of identities that make up Indonesia's normative and legal pluralism, such as adat, or customary law, ethnicity, and region (Bowen 2005: 153–5). In addition, recent laws refer to other categories such as aliran kepercayaan (lit. streams of [local] beliefs; prevalent especially in Java, and usually syncretic) or even something called "local wisdom" that is entitled to a different set of rights. Even if their boundaries are not always clear, how an entity is named carries important legal consequences.[2] The complex entanglement of these identities would require extensive treatment not allowed in this chapter. Limiting the discussion here to religion, while keeping in mind that it may overlap with other elements of diversity, still requires starting from the central limit to the recognition of religious plurality, i.e., the problem of the way religion is defined. The problem is that there exists no explicit definition of religion anywhere in Indonesian laws or the constitution.

One example of the practical consequences of a restrictive definition of religion in the everyday lives of citizens is the religion column that has been part of the Indonesian national identity card since the 1970s. The main evidence of citizenship, this ID card is required for the enjoyment of public facilities and civil rights, such as education, health, and employment. Denial of ID cards for citizens with "unclear" religious affiliations has resulted in their children not being able to obtain birth certificates and in couples not being able to marry as well as the denial of employment and even problems with regard to burial. This policy of requiring one of the recognized religions to be named in that column was itself an expression of the Indonesian politics of religion, particularly the subject of tensions between some Muslim and aliran kepercayaan groups (Maarif 2017).

It is precisely because of problems like these that the law regulating these matters is currently being challenged in the Constitutional Court by representatives of groups experiencing that kind of discrimination (Elsam 2017 and Elsam 2016). The Civil Administration Law (2013, revised 2016) stipulates that the identity card must have a religion column but allows that it can be left blank in the cases of adherents to two categories of "religion": first, citizens whose "religion is not yet recognized as religion according to existing regulations," and, second, followers of aliran kepercayaan. The petition brought by the followers of aliran kepercayaan and indigenous/local religions asks the Constitutional Court to enable them to list their own religion/beliefs on their ID card, because, they feel, while leaving the religion column empty may be an improvement over being forced to fill it in with the name of a religion with which they do not identify, it is still a source of stigmatization and discrimination.

The wording of the law already indicates a fundamental confusion. It seems to regard aliran kepercayaan as a type of religion, as Art. 52 of the law mentions "agama/kepercayaan" as part of the information to be recorded in the official documentation database. Nevertheless, they are not of any of the "religions" that are already recognized (diakui) so citizens may not enter kepercayaan or the name of a kepercayaan in the religion column.

What religions then are recognized as religions (agama)? Where do the distinctions between religion and non-religion or between different categories of religions come from? While no explicit definition has yet been codified in Indonesian law, a general sense of definition may be traced to several sources. The first is the central position of the Pancasila in the constitution. In the early years after 1998, the Pancasila was not popular anymore because of its authoritarian misuse during the New Order, but more recently, many scholars and politicians have called for its revival in the face of threats, especially from Islamists calling for the establishment of an Islamic state (Raillon 2011). Yet, the first principle of Pancasila is belief in one God, which is inclusive of monotheistic religions but excludes both non-monotheistic religions and atheism.[3] The followers of religions such as Hinduism and Buddhism in Indonesia have been forced to reconstruct their faiths in the image of the monotheistic world religions, more specifically Islam and Christianity (Picard 2011, 3; Brown 1987). In some lower-level regulations and ministerial circulars in the 1950s up to the 1970s, the category of religion has the Islamic nuance of *din*, which assumes a tradition of prophecy, sacred scripture, and rituals (Mulder 1978; Atkinson 1983). Such circulars have a lower standing as sources of regulation and are often not even mentioned as part of the considerations of the civil administration law, but they reflect widespread cultural assumptions.

Another, more comprehensive source is Law No. 1/PNPS/1965 on Prevention of Misuse and/or Defamation of Religion. One function of this law is "religion-making" (Telle 2017). The Elucidation of the law recognizes several named religions and implicitly portrays a hierarchy of religions when explaining "the religions embraced by Indonesian people" that must be protected from deviant interpretations or practices. These are the six world religions (Islam, Christianity [Protestantism, Catholicism], Hinduism, Buddhism, and Confucianism) that have historically been embraced by significant populations of Indonesians; as such, they deserve to be protected and to receive government assistance. Next there are other (world) religions (the examples given are Judaism, Zoroastrianism, Shintoism, and Taoism), which are not outlawed and could be recognized by the state so long as they do not contradict the decree or other laws. So, more than just limiting what constitutes a "religion" to a certain narrow conception of world religions, the law further privileges mainstream expressions, defined as not deviant. These two aspects of state recognition of certain religious formations make up what Jeremy Menchik (2016) has called "Godly Nationalism."

Another category mentioned in the Elucidation are so-called "spiritual beliefs" (aliran kebatinan, an older name for aliran kepercayaan). They are implicitly not regarded as "religion" and the government's task in relation to them is to guide them to "sound beliefs in one God." What is also telling is what the Elucidation does not mention or suggest could be recognized as religion: what scholars of religion call indigenous or local religions as distinguished from transnational or world religions.

Based on the impacts of the existing regulation, it is possible to identify six categories of religious groups: the world religions, including the six recognized religions administered by the Ministry of Religious Affairs (MORA), as well as others defined as world religions, such as Baha'iism; non-mainstream groups within the world religions; the aliran kepercayaan; indigenous or local religions; and what contemporary literature calls "new religious movements." It is almost a truism to say that, using Hurd's (2015) terms, lived religion is much richer than governed religion which is recognized by the state (or other legitimizing institutions). But in a place where religion is heavily regulated, governed religion is consequential: the state determines not only whether a group is protected or even funded but also whether its members can enjoy equal access to health, education, and other civil rights. This kind of full recognition is now offered only to the first group in the previous list.

Freedom versus harmony

A central feature of religious governance in Indonesia is the idea of harmony (*kerukunan*). This term has deep roots in history. It is most commonly understood as the avoidance of conflict between religious groups through the imposition of, if needed, legal restrictions, but the term also connotes the provision of protection. Mukti Ali, a scholar of comparative religion who served as the Minister of Religious Affairs from 1971 to 1978, defined Indonesia as neither a secular nor a theocratic state but one based on the notion of one God; the state's responsibility is to "protect, assist, support and guide religious activities" (Sutanto 2011, 121–2). Djohan Effendi, a close aide of Mukti Ali, who has become known as a champion of inter-religious dialogue, has argued that harmony is achieved through dialogue. In contrast, Ali's successor, the former army officer Alamsyah Ratu Prawiranegara, sought harmony through increased regulation (Gaus 2009).

Taking into account differential power relations among religious groups, it is clear that "harmony" unavoidably privileges the majority, establishing the majority as the "mainstream" in contrast to minority "deviants" within one religion. The term does not always imply Islam is alone privileged, as efforts to enforce harmony may vary depending on the religious demography of different regions.

In the past decade, as the notion of religious freedom has gained more currency among civil society organizations, "harmony" is increasingly contrasted with freedom (Bagir 2014). One striking example of this tendency is the government's recent attempt to create a bill on "religious harmony," which was countered by human rights activists proposing an alternative bill on the "freedom of religion" (Crouch 2013). On two occasions since 1998 (in 2003 and 2011), different drafts have been circulated, but neither made it to the parliament because of sustained challenge, mostly by civil society organizations; a third draft (2016) is still being discussed by the MORA. Yet, Trisno Sutanto (2011) has argued that, regardless of these failures, the drafts were quite revealing of what he calls "harmonizing politics." The drafts have basically been compilations of existing lower-level regulations, particularly concerning restrictions on proselytization and houses of worship. Indeed, these two issues, in addition to the question of defamation of religion, have remained central to all regulations formulated in the name of maintaining harmony. Interestingly, however, the latest draft, which has been circulating since 2015, does not use "kerukunan" (harmony) in its title; instead it speaks of the "protection of religious communities." This change may not mean that kerukunan has lost its salience. Recently, the Research and Development Division of the MORA has attempted to formulate "harmony" more rigorously, as indicated by the creation of a "harmony index " conceived as an alternative measurement of the situation of religious life in contrast to the human rights-based measures of religious freedom released over the last ten years by civil society organizations (MORA 2017).

Revitalization of the Defamation of Religion Law

In its current form, the politics of harmony or maintenance of order is expressed in a number of regulations and laws, including some with penal sanctions. The most prominent of the laws concerns the defamation of religion. Two other central issues – proselytization and houses of worship – will be discussed later. Since 1998, the Defamation of Religion Law, discussed previously as an important source for the definition of the category of religion, has had another increasingly important function: justifying state strategies to maintain order or harmony through the use of Article 156A of the Penal Code, which is directly derived from it. Thus, paradoxically, despite the legal strengthening of religious freedom since 1998, the law has also been put to use in new and more dangerous ways. This tendency can be seen in four phenomena.

First, the number of court cases citing Article 156A has increased significantly since 2000. Where the law was used in courts in only ten cases between 1965 and 2000, since 2000, the number of prosecutions has grown to more than forty (Crouch 2012; Bagir 2015). It is also significant that the law has increasingly been used to target larger groups, such as the Ahmadiyah and Shi'a, a significant shift from its original target in 1965, aliran kebatinan, or suspected communists accused of demeaning religion, especially Islam. At that time, there were public debates concerning minority groups such as the Ahmadiyah and Shi'a, but it is only since 2000 that such disputes have been judicialized using this law.

Second, due to the increasing application of the law, it has been brought to the Constitutional Court twice, in 2009 and 2013, and, on both occasions, the court ruled that the law is constitutional despite the amendments from 2000 ensuring human rights and religious freedom. The Constitutional Court's ruling serves as one of the most vivid illustrations of the tension between freedom and harmony. The petitioners' main argument in 2009 was that the 1965 law contradicts the current constitution with its extensive bill of rights as well as the ICCPR, which Indonesia ratified in 2005. The court's ruling, however, upheld the law's constitutionality.

While petitioners in the 2009–2010 review invoked religious freedom arguments, the court's ruling underscored the necessity of the law to maintain order and harmony (Tømte 2012, Crouch 2012, and Bagir 2013). Since harmony is understood as involving restriction of freedom, a central debate in the Court was about the scope of permissible limitations on religious rights. In this regard, the limitation clause of "religious values" in the amended constitution (Art. 28J) played a crucial role in the court's decision to uphold the law. It functions as a basis for restrictions on religious freedom and disciplining non-conformist religious beliefs. The clause had indeed been a subject of debate during the ratification of the second amendment in 2000 and had been discussed again in relation to the fourth amendment (ratified in 2002), which states in Article 31 (5) on education that "The Government shall advance science and technology by respecting religious values and national unity" (Hosen 2005, 191ff; Salim 2008, 108–11). It is noteworthy too that the 2013 Social Organizations Law explicitly mentions an obligation to preserve "religious values," together with social norms, morality, and culture.

The review of the Defamation of Religion Law was also used by the court to affirm the nonsecular and non-liberal character of the Indonesian state, a characterization supported not only by conservative and hard-line religious organizations but also mainstream moderates, including NU and Muhammadiyah, as well as the religious councils of Hinduism, Buddhism, and Confucianism. Only the representatives of Protestantism and Catholicism dissented. The court decreed that the state has the obligation to protect religions, just as it is to protect cultures (which is less controversial), for the sake of maintaining Indonesian diversity. The court also signaled that religious values are central to state policy-making. While this standpoint may have been implicit, it had never before been stated so explicitly in an official document of such stature.

The *third* indicator of the revitalization of the law is the appearance of clauses on "defamation of religion" in several new national-level laws. These include laws pertaining to two institutions the function of which is to enforce the law, namely, the office of the state prosecutor (2004, Article 30) and police (2002, Article 15 (1.d)).[4] Three other recent laws – on societal organizations (No. 17/2013), Art. 5(c), Art. 21 (c) and Art. 59(2)), on electronic information and transactions (No. 11/2008, Arts. 28(2), 45(2), and on film (No. 33/2009, Art. 5, and Art. 30(6)) of governmental regulation No. 18/2004 establishing the film censorship board – explicitly forbid defamation of religion for the sake of protection of religious values and maintaining harmony; the law on electronic information allows for prison sentences of up to six years.

Fourth, the Defamation of Religion Law has become the basis for lower-level national and local regulations. In the past ten years, there have been two joint decrees issued by the minister of Religious Affairs, the attorney general, and the minister of Domestic Affairs to restrict the activities of groups regarded as deviant: in 2008, on the Jemaat Ahmadiyah Indonesia and in 2016, on the Gerakan Fajar Nusantara or Millah Abraham. The main considerations here are protection of religion (in this case, Islam) from deviancy and defamation – here regarded as an offense to mainstream religious groups, which in turn may take the law into their own hands. At the local level, there have been additional laws grounded on the Defamation of Religion Law. These include laws in the city of Tasikmalaya and the provinces of Aceh and East Java targeting an even wider spectrum of groups considered deviant, including some Sufi mystical groups (CRCS 2013, 15–17).

Proselytization

While there is no specific law against the range of activities labelled "proselytization," there are limits on proselytization activities, since they are seen as a possible source of disorder or conflicts among religious groups, especially if they result in conversion, which is not illegal but discouraged. The primary regulation prohibiting proselytization and foreign aid for religious groups is the 1979 Joint Decree of the Ministers of Religious and Domestic Affairs, which prohibits proselytization to people who have embraced a religion, leaving those whose faiths are not recognized as the only group open for proselytization. The decree specifically prohibits giving money, clothes, food, and medicine with the intention of converting the recipients as well as distributing publications or visiting houses for the purpose of proselytization. The 2007 Disaster Management Law (No. 24/2007) prohibits proselytization in distributing aid for victims of disasters.

The 2002 Child Protection Law contains detailed clauses designed to prevent the conversion of children. For example, children whose parents are not legally competent or whose whereabouts are unknown may be assigned a guardian by a court, but the guardian's religion or the religious affiliation of a custodial institution for the child must be the same as the child's. The same requirement applies to adoption, and "in the case where the child's background is unknown, the child's religion is to be adjusted with the religion of the majority in the area" (Art. 39 (5)). In 2005, a petition was submitted to the Constitutional Court concerning Article 86 of the law, which sets penal sanctions for violations of the law, after three Christian Sunday school teachers were sentenced to three years in prison on charges related to the article. The Constitutional Court rejected the petition, saying that as long as their actions did not show the criminal elements mentioned in Article 86 ("deliberately deceiving, lying to, or coaxing a child to choose a different religion to the child's own wishes"), religious adherents should not be prevented from doing missionary works as part of their freedom of religion (cf. Colbran 2010, Crouch 2014).

Another important regulation related to proselytization concerns the construction of houses of worship; one of the most common reasons for the denial of permits to build places of worship is suspicion, especially among Muslims, of Christian proselytization. The relevant regulation is the 2006 Joint Ministerial Decree of the Ministers of Religious and Domestic Affairs, which revised a 1969 regulation. The law states that houses of worship may be built based on the legitimate needs of religious communities, which is to be shown by the support of 90 "users," and, in addition, 60 residents from the adjacent neighborhood. The request then has to be approved by the Forum for Interreligious Harmony at the district/city level. If an application fulfills the 90-user requirement but does not gain the support from at least 60 neighbors, the application may be rejected, obliging the local government to work to find an alternate site for the petitioning congregation. In practice, this regulatory arrangement has yielded mixed results. There are examples of functional FKUBs and cases where religious groups are able to build their houses of worship but also many cases where the regulation has functioned instead as a justification to reject the public presence of minority religious communities (Ali-Fauzi, et.al. 2011). The majority of cases pertaining to the implementation of the 2006 Decree relate to difficulties in building churches by Christian communities, but there are also cases with regard to the building of mosques and other houses of worship in areas where Muslims or other religious communities are in the minority.

The broader impact of the regulations discussed in this section has been to maintain the dominance of the religious majority. In most areas, and at the national level in general, this means the dominance of Islam and Muslims, but a similar outcome occurs in non-Muslim majority areas. Placing limits on proselytization – thus, theoretically preventing conversion – is one way to maintain majority dominance.

"Islamization" of the law

"Islamization" here is understood as attempts to create laws based on Islamic teachings in order to change the character of society as a whole. Using the term *Islamization* to characterize this aspect of Indonesian religious governance does *not* mean that Islamic political interests – which can be represented by progressive, conservative, Islamist, and other kinds of Muslims – do not play roles in the other initiatives discussed previously, such as limitations on recognition of religions and politics of harmony. Quite the contrary, to a significant degree, these issues are actually also colored by contestations with and between different Muslim groups' interests and between them and other groups and the government. The main arenas for efforts at Islamization have been the constitution, national and local laws, and the Constitutional Court.

The failure of some Muslim groups to re-insert the clause about shariah originally proposed in the Jakarta Charter ("the obligation to perform the shari'a of Islam for its followers") into the constitution during the constitutional amendment process in 1999 does not mean that shari'a was removed from all public discussion. This perceived setback in 1999 was partially compensated by, as discussed earlier, the inclusion of the general term "religious values" in Article 28J as a limitation on human rights (Salim 2008, 110). The proponents of shari'a were also able to insert *iman* and *takwa*, two Islamic terms meaning "faith" and "piety," into the fourth amendment's article on national education. As with the "religious values" in Art. 28J, the term's use here could also be understood to be inclusive of all religions but became divisive along religious lines during the debates on the 2003 Education Law and the 2008 Anti-Pornography Law.

It is clear the largely unsuccessful attempt at "Islamization" during the amendment process was subsequently pursued through various national and local laws. We may distinguish different varieties of such laws. There are those that regulate only Muslims, such as laws on *zakat* and *halal* products, which in general are relatively non-controversial. There are national laws, such as the ones on education and pornography that have been advanced to accommodate the demands of certain Muslim groups. There are also a variety of local laws, such as those that regulate women's dress and conduct, prohibit prostitution, restrict the sale and distribution of liquor, and criminalize gambling. One lasting consequence of decentralization was the enactment of these laws, which now number more than 400 (Buehler 2016, 1; Butt 2010; Lindsey 2012). An important limitation within the Decentralization Law is the exclusion of matters of religion from regional lawmakers' jurisdiction. Even so, a number of local regulations do intervene in religious life, and there is practically no effective review mechanism in place. Such "shariah" legislation has been especially extensive in six regions: Aceh, West Sumatra, West Java, East Java, South Kalimantan, and South Sulawesi (Buehler 2016).

Another important legal battleground for Islamization is the Constitutional Court, which is the highest court for ruling on the constitutionality of laws. The court has issued several rulings on religious freedom. In addition to the judicial review of the Defamation of Religion Law discussed earlier, a number of other laws have been brought to the court, some by conservative Muslim groups (Butt 2016). For example, in 2007, a Muslim petitioner requested a review of the clauses that restrict polygamy in the 1974 Marriage Law, claiming that the clause restricted his religious rights (Constitutional Court Decision No.12/PUU-V/2007). In 2008, a petitioner argued that the 1989 (Islamic) Religious Court Law denied Muslims' religious freedom because this law limits the jurisdiction of Islamic Religious Courts only to civil matters, excluding criminal matters (Constitutional Court Decision No. 19/PUU-VI/2008). Both petitions were rejected by the court. One of the court's arguments is that Islamic law is one but not the only source of law in a multi-religious Indonesia. An ongoing judicial review has petitioned the court to change the definitions of adultery, rape, and sodomy in the penal code to prohibit all types of sexual relationship outside of marriage, with emphasis on same-sex relationships (Hermawan 2016).

In its rulings thus far, the Constitutional Court has made clear that the state can intervene in religious affairs, as in the cases of zakat and polygamy, and that it may use religion as a source of policy-making, as in matters related to Religious Defamation and Religious Courts. But the court has also signaled that it cannot accommodate Islamic law entirely (as shown in the cases of the Religious Court and Marriage Laws). In general, the Constitutional Court may be said to be striving to maintain a status-quo that reaches back to the New Order period. It is not as progressive as expected by the liberals but also not as religiously conservative as demanded by the conservatives.

Prospects

The tension within Indonesian religious governance, between post-1998 efforts to strengthen religious freedom and the politics and laws inherited from the earlier periods, may be seen as a failure of legal harmonization. Understood in this way, the key to advancing religious freedom is to remove objectionable laws and regulations, such as the old law on the defamation of religion. Efforts to carry out such reforms have thus far, however, not been successful, as shown most visibly by the two Constitutional Court rulings on the Defamation of Religion Law.

Rather than viewing the constitutional and legal supports for religious freedom strengthened after 1998 as a new normative benchmark, we can perhaps better understand Indonesian religious governance today as characterized by the co-existence of two or more elements, often in dynamic tension. The tension between these opposing forces was vividly captured in the 2010 review of the Defamation of Religion Law, when the Constitutional Court itself indicated it was trying to find a "middle path" (Constitutional Court Decision No.140/PUU-VII/2009, 270). It seems likely that tensions like these will continue to frame debates on freedom of religion for some time.

One of the most important institutions in these debates is the Constitutional Court with its role as the final interpreter of the constitution. Since its establishment in 2003, it has taken up nine cases that directly relate to religion.[5] The petitions were brought to the court by conservative as well as liberal groups and individuals. So far, the court has upheld the right of the government to intervene in the religious affairs of citizens and to restrict certain rights generally, but the court has also resisted demands to make certain laws more compatible with Islamic teachings as understood by certain petitioners. The court has made some improvements in practical issues but has shown itself unlikely to offer an interpretation of religious governance that departs radically from the existing paradigm, which struggles to accommodate both "freedom" and "harmony/control" elements.

Theoretical debates aiming to find a fair and just way of managing religious diversity are surely not unique to Indonesia, and the country may simply need time before a fair balance is achieved. In the meantime, however, a more unambiguous question is whether blatant discrimination against certain religious groups, such as non-world religions and non-mainstream groups within the world religions, can be eliminated even without altering the existing politics and law of religious regulation. A related concern is how the implementation of regulations on defamation of religion and houses of worship have become convenient legal instruments to create what one scholar terms "hate-spin" (George 2016), a technique employed by hard-line groups and often involving both state and non-state actors with the end result being the rise of intolerance (Lindsey and Pausacker 2016). An ethnographic study of a defamation of religion case shows how it has become an instrument of religious "lawfare" (Telle 2017). In this regard, initiatives such as strengthening the capability of the police to prevent and deal with potential conflicts are very important (Panggabean and Ali-Fauzi 2014). Another important avenue for improvement lies in the central government's capability to deal with the excesses of decentralization, especially in reviewing discriminatory local laws. An historic test will come when a new draft law on religion is written and debated in the parliament and in public. That moment will provide an opportunity to devise better religious governance for a multi-religious Indonesia. In the meantime, what may be more reasonably expected is, not comprehensive reform, but piecemeal progress with regard to particular problems in social life.

Notes

1 The demotion was due to the adoption of the Societal Organization Law in 2013. The law "restricts the activities of nongovernmental organizations, increases bureaucratic oversight of such groups, and requires them to support the national ideology of Pancasila – including its explicitly monotheist component." It should be noted, however, that the last requirement (support of Pancasila) is not a new feature of the regulation but actually a weakening of stronger wording in the earlier 1985 law, which stipulated that Pancasila be the only basis of such organizations, while the new law (2013) says that they may have bases other than Pancasila so long as they do not contradict it. See www.freedomhouse.org/report/freedom-world/2014/indonesia-0.

2 *Adat* has gained greater recognition recently in a number of laws; certain adat communities have recently been granted land custody of what are designated as adat forests (Parlina 2016). Some adat communities may also actually fit the definition of communities of indigenous or even recognized religion, but in general, they find they are better off when recognized as adat communities (cf. Maarif 2015).

3 Not surprisingly, the interpretation of this first principle of Pancasila is strongly debated. This is reflected in the many English translations of "Ketuhanan Yang Maha Esa." It is commonly translated as "Belief in One God" or "Belief in one and only God," an interpretation with a strongly Islamic flavor; for others "ketuhanan" does not necessarily refer to a monotheistic God but more like "Divinity" – a generous interpretation proposed by H. Agus Salim (1951), one of the founding fathers of Indonesia, that would make non-monotheistic and even atheistic beliefs the subject of state recognition. For further discussion, see Ropi (2017, 61–78).

4 The latter law includes police's monitoring of aliran that could threaten the unity of the state, and that, as explained in its elucidation, are deemed in opposition to the founding philosophy of the state. However a concern for human rights is also present in the 2009 regulation issued by the head of police on the implementation of the standards of human rights by police.

5 Butt (2016) discusses five of them, related to reviews on polygamy (2007), Religious Courts (2008), defamation of religion (2009), wedlock (2010), and divorce (2011); the four others include cases on defamation of religion (2013), zakat (2013), and two ongoing (2016–2017) judicial reviews on the religion column in the identity card as part of Civil Administration Law and adultery in the penal code.

References

Ali-Fauzi, Ihsan, Samsu Rizal Panggabean, Nathanael Gratias Sumaktoyo, Anick H. T., Husni Mubarak, Testriono, Siti Nurhayati. 2011. *Disputed Churches in Jakarta*. Trans. Rebecca Lunnon. Tim Lindsey and Melissa Crouch, eds. (The original Indonesian version was published in 2011 by the Center for Religious & Cross-cultural Studies, Universitas Gadjah Mada). Jakarta: Center for the Study of Religion and Democracy, Paramadina Foundation.

Atkinson, Jane. 1983. "Religions in Dialogue: The Construction of an Indonesian Minority Religion," *American Ethnologist*, 10(4): 684–96.

Bagir, Zainal Abidin. 2013. "Defamation of Religion Law in Post-Reformasi Indonesia: Is Revision Possible?" *Australian Journal of Asian Law* 13(2): 1–16.

———. 2014. "Advocacy for Religious Freedom in Indonesia," *The Review of Faith & International Affairs* 12 (4): 27–39.

———. 2015. "Indonesia," in Jaclyn Neo, ed., *Keeping the Faith: A Study of Religious Freedom in ASEAN Countries* (Jakarta: Human Rights Resource Center), pp. 138–94.

Bowen, John. 2005. "Normative Pluralism in Indonesia: Region, Religion, and Ethnicities," in Will Kymlicka and Baogang He, ed., *Multiculturalism in Asia* (Oxford: Oxford University Press), pp. 152–70.

Brown, Iem. 1987. "Contemporary Indonesian Buddhism and Monotheism," *Journal of Southeast Asian Studies* 18(1): 108–17.

Buehler, Michael. 2016. *The Politics of Shari'a Law: Islamist Activists and the State in Democratizing Indonesia* (Cambridge: Cambridge University Press).

Butt, Simon. 2010. "Regional Autonomy and Legal Disorder: The Proliferation of Local Laws in Indonesia," *Sydney Law Review* 32: 177–97.

———. 2016. "Between Control and Appeasement: Religion in Five Constitutional Court Decisions," in Tim Lindsey and Helen Pausacker, eds., *Religion, Law and Intolerance in Indonesia* (London and New York: Routledge), pp. 42–67.

Center for Religious and Cross-cultural Studies (CRCS). 2013. *Laporan Tahunan Kehidupan Beragama di Indonesia 2012* (Yogyakarta: Center for Religious and Cross-cultural Studies, Gadjah Mada University).

Colbran, Nicole. 2010. "Realities and Challenges in Realising Freedom of Religion or Belief in Indonesia," *The International Journal of Human Rights* 14(5): 678–704.

Crouch, Melissa. 2012. "Law and Religion in Indonesia: The Constitutional Court and the Blasphemy Law," *Asian Journal of Comparative Law* 7(1): 1–46.

———. 2013. "Shifting Conceptions of State Regulation of Religion: The Indonesian Draft Law on Inter-Religious Harmony," *Global Change, Peace & Security* 25(3): 1–18.

———. 2014. *Law and Religion in Indonesia Conflict and the Courts in West Java* (London: Routledge).

Elsam. 2016. "Pengosongan Kolom Agama bagi Penghayat Kepercayaan Inkonstitusional." http://elsam.or.id/2016/09/pengosongan-kolom-agama-bagi-penghayatpenganut-keprecayaan-inkonstitusional/ (Accessed 15 March 2017).

———. 2017. "Pengosongan Kolom Agama bagi Penghayat Kepercayaan Menutup Akses Pelayanan Publik Warga." http://elsam.or.id/2017/03/pengosongan-kolom-agama-bagi-penghayat-kepercayaan-ktp-menutup-akses-pelayanan-publik-warga/ (Accessed 15 March 2017).

Gaus, A. F. Ahmad. 2009. *Sang Pelintas Batas: Biografi Djohan Effendi* (Jakarta: ICRP and Kompas, 2009).

George, Cherian. 2016. *Hate-Spin: The Manufacture of Religious Offense and Its Threats to Democracy* (Cambridge, MA: MIT Press).

Hermawan, Ary. 2016. "Why AILA Is a Bigger Threat to Freedom Than the FPI?" *The Jakarta Post*, 30 August. www.thejakartapost.com/news/2016/08/30/commentary-why-aila-is-a-bigger-threat-to-freedom-than-the-fpi.html (Accessed 15 March 2017).

Hosen, Nadirsyah. 2005. "Religion and the Indonesian Constitution: A Recent Debate," *Journal of Southeast Asian Studies* 36(3): 419–40.

Hurd, Elizabeth Shakman. 2015. *Beyond Religious Freedom: The New Global Politics of Religion* (Princeton and Oxford: Princeton University Press).

Liddle, Bill and Saiful Mujani. 2013. "Indonesian Democracy: From Transition to Consolidation," in Mirjam Kunkler and Alfred Stepan, eds., *Democracy and Islam in Indonesia* (New York: Columbia University Press), pp. 24–50.

Lindsey, Tim. 2002. "Indonesian Constitutional Reform: Muddling Towards Democracy," *Singapore Journal of International and Comparative Law* 6: 244–301.

———. 2012. *Islam, Law and the State in Southeast Asia, Vol. I: Indonesia* (London: I.B. Tauris).

Lindsey, Tim and Helen Pausacker, eds. 2016. *Religion, Law and Intolerance in Indonesia* (London and New York: Routledge).

Maarif, Samsul. 2015. "Ammatoan Indigenous Religion and Forest Conservation," *Worldviews* 19(2): 144–60.

———. 2017. *Politik dan Hukum Agama Lokal Indonesia* (Yogyakarta: Program Studi Agama dan Lintas Budaya UGM).

Menchik, Jeremy. 2016. *Islam and Democracy in Indonesia: Tolerance Without Liberalism* (New York: Cambridge University Press).

Ministry of Religious Affairs (MORA). 2017. *Laporan Tahunan Kehidupan Keagamaan di Indonesia 2016* (Jakarta: Kementerian Agama).

Mulder, Niels. 1978. *Mysticism & Everyday Life in Contemporary Java: Cultural Persistence and Change* (Singapore: Singapore University Press).

Panggabean, Samsu Rizal, and Ihsan Ali-Fauzi. 2014. *Pemolisian Konflik Keagamaan di Indonesia* (Jakarta: Pusat Studi Agama dan Demokrasi, Yayasan Wakaf Paramadina and Magister Perdamaian dan Resolusi Konflik, Universitas Gadjah Mada).

Parlina, Ina. 2016. "Jokowi Grants Forest Rights to Indigenous Peoples," *The Jakarta Post*, 31 December. www.thejakartapost.com/news/2016/12/31/jokowi-grants-forest-rights-indigenous-peoples.html (Accessed 15 March 2017).

Picard, Michel, 2011. "Introduction: 'Agama', 'adat', and Pancasila," in Michel Picard and Rene Madinier, eds., *Politics of Religion in Indonesia: Syncretism, Orthodoxy, and Religious Contention in Java and Bali* (London and New York: Taylor & Francis), pp. 1–20.

Raillon, François. 2011. "The Return of Pancasila: Secular vs. Islamic Norms, Another Look at the Struggle for State Dominance in Indonesia," in Michel Picard and Rene Madinier, eds., *Politics of Religion in Indonesia: Syncretism, Orthodoxy, and Religious Contention in Java and Bali* (London and New York: Taylor & Francis), pp. 92–113.

Ropi, Ismatu. 2017. *Religion and Regulation in Indonesia* (Singapore: Palgrave Macmillan).

Salim, Arskal. 2008. *Challenging the Secular State: The Islamization of Law in Modern Indonesia* (Hawai'i: University of Hawai'i Press).

Salim, H. Agus. 1951. "Kementerian Agama Dalam Republik Indonesia," *Agenda Kementrian Agama, 1951/1952*. https://app.box.com/s/f1oo2bqtp08v1b08gdxb (Accessed 15 March 2017).

Sutanto, Trisno S. 2011. "Negara, Kekuasaan, dan 'Agama': Membedah Politik Perukunan Rezim Orde Baru," in Zainal Abidin Bagir, et al., *Pluralisme Kewargaan: Arah Baru Politik Keragaman di Indonesia* (Yogyakarta: Mizan and Program Studi Agama dan Lintas Budaya UGM), pp. 115–48.

Telle, Kari. 2017. "Faith on Trial: Blasphemy and 'Lawfare' in Indonesia," *Ethnos: Journal of Anthropology*. http://dx.doi.org/10.1080/00141844.2017.1282973.

Tømte, Aksel. 2012. "Constitutional Review of the Indonesian Blasphemy Law," *Nordic Journal of Human Rights* 30(2): 174–204.

24

ISLAMIC POPULISM IN INDONESIA

Emergence and limitations

Vedi R. Hadiz

Islamic populism is a variant of populism where the concept of the *ummah* (community of believers) substitutes for the concept of the "people." But like the "people" in more conventional populisms, the ummah is made up of internally diverse social interests that are notionally homogenized through juxtaposition against a set of purported oppressors, made up of economically exploitative or culturally remote elites or even foreign interests (Hadiz 2016). When successful, as seen most clearly in Turkey, an ummah-based politics has enabled cross-class alliances engaging effectively in competition over power and resources, in that case under the aegis of the ruling party since 2002, the AKP.

In Indonesia, however, Islamic populism has been less successful. Missing has been a pious big business component in extant alliances that have deployed Islamic identity in their engagement in contests over power and resources in the present democratic era. Furthermore, unlike in Egypt, where the Muslim Brotherhood was once successful in dominating civil society through middle-class-led charitable activities that helped to nurture a durable support base among the poor (Clarke 2004), the purveyors of Indonesian Islamic populism have achieved little of the sort. It is argued that, instead, Indonesia's Islamic organizational vehicles have been increasingly absorbed into the chaotic logic of its money-politics-fuelled democracy, either as direct or indirect players, thus contributing to the continued fragmentation of ummah-based politics in Indonesia and the incoherence of its Islamic populism.

But it is also shown that such a situation leaves room for fringe and often more "hard-line" groups, inherently unable to compete within an electoral democracy for lack of resources, to claim that they are themselves the truer representatives of the ummah. Typically, they can hardly assert to be "uncontaminated" by the profane nature of secular politics, often relying themselves on murky relationships with political elites and the state security apparatus (Wilson 2015). Such organizations suggest, nevertheless, that their rejection of democracy is reflective of adherence to pure Islamic teachings that demand matters of state be organized on the basis of Islamic law rather than secular tenets.

Islamic populism: tenuous and internally contradictory

In spite of their rejection of democracy, organizations like these do exercise an indirect influence on democratic political competition in Indonesia and on the shaping of its Islamic populism.

Most important, they are instrumental in "mainstreaming" compliance with conservative social positions as "proof" of genuine adherence to Islamic precepts and, therefore, of devotion to an implausibly undifferentiated ummah. Thus, recent developments in Indonesian Islamic populism have shown discernibly illiberal characteristics, such as in the much discussed proliferation, at one stage, of local government bylaws that placed restrictions on the behavior and dress of women (Bush 2008).

Most recently, this mainstreaming of Islamic conservatism was expressed in the mass mobilizations of lower- as well as middle-class Muslims directed against the ethnic-Chinese and Christian governor of Jakarta, Basuki Tjahaja Purnama, popularly known as "Ahok." Known for tough talk, the governor became susceptible to the charge of having committed blasphemy during an ad-libbed campaign speech – though his policies on administrative reform and urban redevelopment remained popular, if contentious. Reiterating the links between militant fringe Islamic groups and political elites, including at the national level, Fealy (2016) suggests that the mobilizations against Ahok "revealed how elite political forces have used religion to undermine the government and bolster their own prospects." He further suggests that these had "brought radical Islamists to the center of national attention and forced the state's most senior officials to appear beside them as if they represented the wider Islamic community."

Such developments seem to challenge the notion that Indonesia could serve as a ready-made model of democratization for other Muslim-majority societies. This notion has been favored by many Indonesian leaders, such as former president Susilo Bambang Yudhoyono (Alles 2016: 131). Ironically, however, it was the latter's own son who benefited from the aforementioned rallies coordinated by militant and conservative Islamic groups. This was Agus Harimurti Yudhoyono, a former rising star in the Indonesian military who was a contender in the Jakarta gubernatorial election of 2017 – which pitted him directly against Ahok. But it was the eventual victor, Muslim intellectual Anies Baswedan, who ultimately gained most from the anti-Ahok campaign.

But there is an even larger significance to the Jakarta case. What it demonstrates, in relation to the concerns of this chapter, is that Islamic populism does not necessarily take on characteristics of what Bayat has called "post-Islamism" – prompting change toward "a more rights-centered and inclusive outlook that favors a civil/secular state operating within a pious society" (Bayat 2013: 29). Bayat's concept is enlightening in many ways, having originated from analysis of Iran, where regularized institutions very similar to those found in secular states were established out of the necessities of operating a modern polity. However, post-Islamism tends to assume change that is too unidirectional in response to such necessities.

By contrast, the concept of Islamic populism, as utilized here, incorporates a greater element of historical contingency. As expressions of social alliances underpinned by internally contradictory coalitions of social interests, it allows for "conservative turns" (Van Bruinessen 2013), especially when the struggles of ummah through formal institutions have been only ambiguously successful, as in the Indonesian case. Furthermore, given the absence of organizational vehicles that can credibly claim monopoly on representing the interests of the faithful, anti-democratic and anti-market agendas could then permeate through Islamic populist discourse and practice even within a democracy and an economy with neoliberalizing tendencies.

A few more points are worth noting at this juncture. First, linking Islamic politics to the broader phenomenon of populism is not an entirely new intellectual endeavor (Colas 2004; Roy 2004). However, such a link had not been seriously explored until recently for the Indonesian case (Hadiz 2016). Second, there had been an attendant paucity in the Indonesian politics literature of attention to populism more generally, though this appears to be changing as well lately, especially since the Joko Widodo (Jokowi) versus Prabowo Subianto presidential contest of 2014, during which both presented themselves as rank outsiders to the political establishment

(Aspinall 2015; Mietzner 2015; Hadiz and Robison 2017). Finally, there is great diversity in the ways through which populism as a social and political phenomenon has been treated in the general theoretical literature. There have been approaches mainly concerned with addressing populism discursively (Laclau 2005), ideationally (Canovan 1981), and organizationally (Mouzelis 1985). More recently, some authors have presented populism as a form of political theater or as performance of politics (Moffitt 2016). They do so by latching on to populism's more demagogic proclivities.

In the remainder of this chapter, however, populism is understood in a somewhat different way. It is addressed with an emphasis on continually shifting or reconstituted social bases that bring together multi-class elements into what are – inevitably – internally contradictory social alliances. The major implication is that the Islamic variant of populism represents an attempt to forge these social alliances by recourse to available cultural and ideological resource pools, specifically the idioms and symbolisms associated with the Islamic religion. The resultant "Islamic" political lexicon thus enables a kind of "suspension of difference" within the ummah, which like the "people," can only be tenuously presented as a homogenous entity in the face of growing actual sociological diversity. Given that the purveyors of Islamic populism are inevitably entwined in modern forms of political competition, which are especially defined by contests over power and resources, the main objective of this suspension of difference is the facilitation of successful engagement in these contests.

While steeped in the assumptions of critical political economy (Hadiz and Robison 2012), the approach described owes a debt to Oxhorn's (1998) work on Latin America. Here, populism was viewed as being underpinned by "asymmetrical" class alliances, wherein those who are only relatively marginalized within a prevailing system of power – such as the middle class – take the lead in pushing forward agendas representing the interests of a notional uniformly oppressed "people." It also owes a debt to early, though rather inconsistent, endeavors to comparatively delineate the different social bases of various populist experiences (see especially Ionescu and Gellner 1969).

One of the effects of the approach deployed is to provide a "material base" for the way that theorists like Laclau (2005: 86) understand how the "plebs" come to be presented as the "populace," which entails that particularistic demands become generalized through a discursive mechanism known as "chains of equivalence." Or to put it another way, the approach provides the political economy underpinnings for processes of social inclusion and exclusion through which the identity of the "people" (or ummah, as in the case being analyzed here) becomes defined, albeit in ways always open to contestation. This is achieved mainly by linking them to social conflict, especially those over power and access to resources. In one sense, the approach harks back to Laclau's theoretical emphases before he tended to eschew historical analysis. These emphases were seen in Laclau and Mouffe (1985), where struggles for hegemony were placed in the context of prevailing, and shifting, material circumstances (Fenton 2016: 37) (also see Laclau 1977: 160–4, and the discussion of "class ideological practices").

This sort of analytical approach is useful because recent expressions of Islamic populism are related to the contradictions of capitalist development and the pressures of globalization (Hadiz 2016). In this way, Islamic populism is no different from populism in general, which is widely recognized as having experienced a resurgence in many parts of the world today (Müller 2016). Recognizing this means that the mutations within Islamic populism over time, whether in Indonesia or elsewhere, may be seen as part of broader developments that have produced an increasing variety of populisms, including in Europe, Latin America, and the United States in recent decades. Indeed – and as argued by Hadiz and Chryssogelos (2017) – it is increasingly difficult to understand the emergence and evolution of such populisms, whether in the developed

or developing parts of the world, as being unrelated to new social contradictions and disloca-
tions associated with neoliberal globalization, although always in their specific and contextual
manifestations.

Indonesian Islam populism: evolution and incoherence

Because of its emphasis on the shifting nature of social bases, the approach deployed here makes
possible concrete analysis of the sources of internal incoherence within Islamic populism. Given
that this demands attention to the dynamics of social change, Islamic populism's expression in
Indonesia in the democratic era can be usefully distinguished also from an older form that had
gained traction almost exactly one century ago. That was the kind of Islamic populism concerned
with safeguarding the position of petty propertied urban and rural interests in the late colonial
era even if its struggles became synonymous with the beginnings of a broader and notionally
more all-embracing nationalist movement. Its initial main vehicle was of course the storied
Sarekat Islam (SI), an organization that had emerged as a response to encroachment into the
traditional economic domains of such interests by a growing ethnic Chinese counterpart (Shiraishi 1990) that was seen to have benefited from the colonial era's arrangements of economic
power. In the present-day, there is far greater fragmentation within Indonesian Islamic populism,
however, with internal sociological diversity being accompanied by organizational incoherence,
thus leading to the inability to effectively bring together robust cross-class coalitions.

It was perhaps inevitable that organizations that had also emerged from the older tradition
of Islamic populism turned out to be the main representatives of the ummah in past interactions with the colonial as well as the early post-colonial state. It remains crucial, however, that
these organizations – most prominently, the Muhammadiyah and the Nahdlathul Ulama – as
well as the various Islamic political parties that have come, gone, or stayed in Indonesian political history, were never able to serve as a conduit for the production of a culturally Islamic big
bourgeoisie. The so-called Benteng program of the 1950s, which was intended to provide preferential treatment for "indigenous" and therefore largely Muslim-owned businesses didn't take
off (Robison 1986), with the licenses involved simply being pawned off to better positioned
ethnic-Chinese-owned enterprises. During the New Order, giant conglomerates did emerge
initially through state protection and support, but these were mainly ethnic Chinese-owned
again or linked to the Soeharto family and its assorted cronies. These business elements were
difficult to incorporate into a conception of a long-suppressed ummah. The establishment of
ICMI – the Association of Indonesian Muslim Intellectuals – in 1990 also was not geared to
produce a Muslim big bourgeoisie, having been established as a conduit to bureaucratic power
for Muslim intellectuals and activists (Hefner 1993). This took place in relation to a larger need
to outflank a military leadership that was becoming dismayed about its own declining position
within the New Order regime.

Nevertheless, any discussion of the way that the interests of the ummah are organized in
contemporary Indonesia will no doubt have to address the two venerable vehicles mentioned
earlier: the Muhammadiyah, a "reformist" entity historically associated with urban traders and
petty producers – as well the "traditionalist" Nahdlatul Ulama, customarily led by rural-based
landowning clerics and their families. These have long been recognized as the largest mass
organizations in the country, each claiming tens of millions of members. Established in the late
colonial period, both have survived the vicissitudes of Dutch rule, early post-colonialism, and the
authoritarian New Order and remain significant in the present era of decentralized democracy.

But the status of these organizations was never incontestable even before the social transformations linked especially to the New Order's economic development program had profoundly

altered and diversified the social composition of the ummah within Indonesia. Outside of these organizations, the Darul Islam (DI) movement had also made claims to being the genuine representative of Indonesian Muslims, which it did by waging an ultimately failed uprising against the nascent Republic of Indonesia from 1949 to1962 (Formichi 2012). Led by Kartosuwiryo, a former independence fighter who broke ranks with the leadership of the early Republic, it aimed to establish an Islamic State of Indonesia, after militia units that had fought the Dutch in West Java under his command were refused incorporation into the armed forces of the new nation-state.

In the present day, a number of vehicles compete in making the claim of articulating the interests of the ummah, though without ever approaching hegemonic status.This has been made possible in the first place because of the largely quietist nature of both the Muhammadiyah and NU, which had become integral parts of the vast system of patronage that characterized the New Order at the height of its powers.Though there were exceptional instances, neither was a vehicle for the strong expression of Islamic dissent against New Order repressive policies, including against Muslim activists, and an array of perceived social injustices. Moreover, the PPP (United Development Party), which was the "official" Islamic political party of the New Order – and whose leadership included large representations of Muhammadiyah and NU cadres – played a largely ornamental role in the highly state controlled system of electoral politics that the New Order established.

Hicks (2012) points out, therefore, that neither the Muhammadiyah nor NU could be said to have reliably provided blocs of support for Islamic or other political parties today, given that their memberships have become spread out across the entire political spectrum.There is good reason for this failing. Not only have they been unable to manufacture a big bourgeoisie, they have also been limited in their capacity to nurture and maintain the support of the poor masses when required by the imperatives of democratic political contests.This was a task that the Muslim Brotherhood in Egypt, for example, was able to achieve with outstanding success, including under the harsh authoritarian conditions of the Mubarak era (Clarke 2004), by delivering social services to the poor in the context of the inadequacy of their provision by the state.The New Order–created ICMI too had a similar problem. Declarations about the need to bring support to ICMI from workers (Hefner 2000: 149), for example, remained hyperbolic because mass mobilization went against the regime's obsession with political demobilization.

Among the most prominent of present-day vehicles that purport to represent the interests of a homogenous ummah within the Indonesian nation-state is the PKS (Justice and Development Party), a post–New Order political party that embodies the development of an urbanized and educated Muslim middle class. This is a political party that has been relatively successful in electoral competition, embracing democracy as well as the market, while relegating the aim of establishing an Islamic state to the background. Its origins, furthermore, lay in a broader *tarbiyah* (education) semi-clandestine movement that began in the 1980s, especially among middle-class university students.Though inspired by the AKP (and before that, the Egyptian Muslim Brotherhood), the PKS has never been able to develop real cross-class social alliances. Its business support is largely confined to small enterprises, for example, and it similarly lacks the resources to engage in large-scale delivery of social services that might cultivate enduring support from the poor. Thus, in spite of the pretense of representing the interests of the ummah as a whole, the party has had genuine difficulty transcending its middle-class origins.

Another notable vehicle is the Hizbut Tahrir Indonesia (HTI), which conversely eschews electoral politics in spite of identifying as a political party. Somewhat anachronistically, it also presents itself as a branch of much larger movement to establish a global caliphate, the Hizbut Tahrir founded in Palestine in 1953 (Munabari 2010). The HTI initially made its mark too through semi-clandestine organizing on university campuses during the authoritarian Soeharto era. It now plays a significant, albeit indirect, role in the dynamics of politics in the democratic era, such as through involvement in ad hoc alliances where mass mobilizations in the name of protecting the dignity of the ummah have taken place. Known for the use of anti-imperialist jargon – presented in conjunction with Islamic terminology and symbolism – its forays into mass mobilizations have not provided it with a solid cross-class basis of social support. Unlike other Hizbut Tahrir "branches," therefore, such as those in parts of Central Asia (Karagiannis 2010), it has not been able to take up the mantle of main opposition to a secular nation-state, which, in its narrative, continues to marginalize the virtuous masses.

There are other organizations, such as the notorious FPI (Islamic Defenders Front), that should be noted, as well as the multitude of militia groups that are active in Indonesia's teeming urban and peri-urban formations. In Solo, Central Java – for example – many operate under the umbrella of LUIS (Militia of the Ummah in Surakarta), frequently raiding entertainment venues where "immoral" acts reputedly occur (*Jakarta Post*, December 28, 2016). These appear to have developed limited bases of support among the precariously positioned urban poor of Indonesia (Mudhoffir 2017), to the extent of being able to instigate mass mobilizations, such as against the aforementioned Ahok. They claim to deliver an important service to society (Bakker 2016) by preventing the descent of alienated youths into vices involving drugs and alcohol, providing employment to members – for example as security guards or parking attendants – and training in various skills (including the martial arts). Some analysts have seen them as providing a sense of belonging to otherwise marginalized youths (Yasih 2016).

These organizations have tended to ban together on an ad hoc basis, such as within a front organization that coordinated the anti-Ahok rallies in Jakarta and whose name references the MUI (Indonesian Ulama Council) – the National Movement to Guard the MUI Fatwa (GNPF-MUI). Most organizations found here view democratic politics as anathema to the principle of an Islamic state led by the most pious. In reality, however, they are also not able to compete successfully in democratic competition, inherently constrained by their limited resources and confined social base. Unable to establish deeper roots in civil society by nurturing the enduring loyalty of a broader cross-section of the poor and precarious, many such organizations have cultivated ties with sections of the Indonesian security apparatus (Wilson 2015) instead. This is in spite of a professed hostility to the institutions of the secular nationalist state. The MUI itself is a parastatal organization established in the New Order as an instrument of control over Islamic religious life.

The picture we get from this discussion confirms the organizational incoherence of Indonesian Islamic populism. No vehicle can credibly claim a monopoly on articulating the interests of an increasingly socially diverse ummah. None has been able to emerge at the helm of a social alliance that would bring together multi-class interests under the banner of Islamic populism. Such a picture is quite different from that of Turkey, for instance, where under the leadership of the AKP, Islamic populism has embraced the Anatolian bourgeoisie and sections of the educated middle class as well as segments of the working class and broader urban poor. Evolving from previously existing Islamic vehicles and networks – the AKP has developed a political vernacular that, in its generous use of religious terminology, effectively binds together otherwise disparate groups in a brand of Islam that embraces globalization but claims to temper its social depredations. It does so not just through moral injunctions but also by provision of welfare services to the less materially fortunate. Önis (2012: 12) thus argues that the AKP's populism has been constructed out of "broad-based cross-class coalitions of political support" made possible by the social context out of which the party had emerged and evolved.

But just as the social bases of Islamic populism can shift or become reconstituted along with processes of social transformation, so too is the relationship between Islamic populism and democracy much less than pre-determined. Of course, the democratizing potential of Islam has long been an object of academic scrutiny (for the Indonesia case, see Hefner 2000). But that a strong element of contingency exists in that relationship is seen clearly in Turkey too, where the AKP embraced democracy to defend itself against entrenched foes within the Kemalist-dominated state apparatus, particularly the military. This is so in spite of recent authoritarian turns, where President Recep Tayyip Erdogan has clamped down on sources of opposition remaining within the state as well as in broader civil society (Tuğal 2016). In Indonesia, however, democracy has not brought the purveyors of Islamic populism anywhere as close to the main levers of power. As such, the legitimacy of opting for the democratic route has been always more open to question as an effective means of advancing the social, economic, and political interests of the ummah within the Indonesian nation-state.

While referring to the Turkish experience is important, it should be noted that the social agents of Islamic populism in Indonesia also gained inspiration from the Egyptian Muslim Brotherhood. The latter had forged links in the country, among others, through an organization called the DDII (Indonesian Islamic Propagation Council), founded by the late highly respected Masyumi party politician Mohamad Natsir and which had prioritized proselytizing activities after he was banned from politics in the early New Order period. This organization was also important for its role in disseminating financial assistance from the Middle East to Indonesia, including by funding study in various countries in the region by Indonesian students of the Islamic religion.

In turn, intersections between DDII and various continually reinvented DI groups (Alamsyah and Hadiz 2016), invariably claiming to be the political heirs of Kartosuwiryo, are noteworthy too. For example, Abdullah Sungkar and Abubakar Ba'asyir, founders of the Jemaah Islamiyah terrorist network, were DI activists as well as DDII functionaries. The Muslim Brotherhood connection in Indonesia is also significant for inspiring the so-called tarbiyah (education) movement on Indonesian university campuses in the 1980s, which as mentioned earlier, eventually gave rise to the PKS (Solahudin 2011). The movement was mainly founded by a group of Middle Eastern–educated activists who found promise in the Muslim Brotherhood's strategy of seeking state power through the back door of civil society.

The importance of these models lies in the fact that they provided impetus for the social agents of Islamic populism in Indonesia to think strategically about ways of gaining access to the levers of power, involving civil society organization, even in semi-clandestine fashion, and developed mechanisms for recruitment of cadres and possible alliance-building measures. Especially for the PKS, these lessons would serve them fairly well when they entered into formal electoral politics after the end of the New Order in 1998. This is so even if the party has yet to attain the sort of longstanding success of the AKP in Turkey or even the far more short-lived one of the Muslim Brotherhood in Egypt.

Islamic populism and economic power

The relationship between Islam and capitalism has been much debated. The classic Weberian claim that the two are inherently incompatible because of Islamic religious precepts and practices that obstruct capital accumulation has been criticized from different theoretical positions.

Half a century ago, the Marxist scholar, Rodinson (1966 [2007]), had already argued that there was nothing in Islamic doctrine that intrinsically blocked the emergence of capitalism, while explaining economic underdevelopment in Muslim societies by analysis of a host of historical and sociological factors. Gellner (1981) suggested that Weber missed elements in Islamic doctrine that might have provided the ideational basis for capitalism. From a more traditionally political liberal position, Nasr (2009) has argued that the obvious benefits of engaging in neo-liberal globalization for those who do so cannot be lost on Muslims. Rudnyckyj (2010), writing on Islam and capitalism in Indonesia, demonstrates the compatibility between Islam and capitalist development in a different way. He elaborates on managerial strategies at the firm level that build on references to religious values in order to instill the sort of work discipline among the labor force required for adaptation to the requirements of the market.

In spite of these highly insightful interventions, it is more likely that the relationship between Islam and capitalism is contingent on nature too. What seems especially critical is whether social alliances forged on the basis of Islamic populism are able to include major capitalists as a core element and whether these are well positioned to compete successfully in global markets. In other words, what matters is whether support for economically globalizing strategies is useful in the effort to advance themselves economically and therefore, notionally, the position of the ummah as a whole. In many ways, the Anatolian bourgeoisie in Turkey was able to grow precisely because it exploited the opportunities provided by the strategy adopted since the 1980s, along with broader economic restructuring under the technocratic Ozal government (Akça, Bekmen, and Ozden 2014), which expanded export markets in Europe, the Middle East, and Central Asia.

Thus it is common for the social agents of Islamic populism to approve of the principle of capital accumulation, although Islamic injunctions against extreme concentration of wealth are regularly cited as well (Tripp 2006: 103–24). So, rather than presenting a challenge to capitalism as such, Islamic populism aspires toward a capitalist state and society that would notionally assure a more just distribution of power and resources. Significantly, such a project would in itself assist those marginalized within the existing social order. This is of course attractive to those – such as in present-day Indonesia – who understand the ummah as consisting of people who have been historically and systematically marginalized, whether in the time of Western colonial domination or in the present age of secular nation-states and neoliberal globalization.

In fact, in Turkey, Islamic populism is closely associated with neoliberal economic policies, pursued by the AKP, which intensified the engagement of the Turkish economy with global capitalism (Tuğal 2009). In this case, such policies have benefited the Anatolian bourgeoisie. But the aim remains to confront the economic bulwarks of Kemalism by providing opportunities for social, economic, and political advancement for culturally Muslim sections of the bourgeoisie and middle class that had been peripheralized by those that had long dominated the state and the economy, as well as to provide the promise of a form of welfarism for the poor. Clearly, such aims do not necessitate an overtly Islamic state.

But this does not mean that calls for it disappear in all contexts. We see that in Indonesia, for example, the call is usually made by those least well positioned to make headway through the formal institutions of government and economy. This is the case particularly because the cross-class coalitions necessary to underpin Islamic populism's successful engagement in contests over economic resources remain largely wanting here.

Like all populisms, Islamic populism attempts to address the challenge of a number of socially explosive issues arising from the contradictions of development, thus affecting its own evolution. Across much of the Muslim world, these issues have been accentuated under conditions of neoliberal globalization. The most prominent of these in Indonesia, for instance, is of growing inequality, combined with chronic unemployment and underemployment (World Bank 2016), as well as persisting significant levels of poverty. Such matters are likely to be particularly combustible when they concern large numbers of youths, especially those whose aspirations have grown together with greater access to education and an increasingly consumerist culture.

Lying at the core of their social grievances is the broken promises of modernity itself, especially those pertaining to material advancement. Such grievances could be shared with the poor by sections of the population who are urban middle class in terms of education, occupation, and consumerist aspirations but for whom the future remains uncertain because of precarious material circumstances (Bayat 2013). In the Indonesian case, however, their coalescing into broader social alliances has not taken place in any robust sense, except in the way that lower- and middle-class members of society have been involved in ad hoc mass mobilizations.

Conclusion

The relationship among Islamic populism, democratization, and the growth of capitalism, including in its neoliberal manifestation, is complex and not pre-determined. Like all societies, Muslim-majority societies like Indonesia have experienced struggles over the organization of political and economic power. Islamic populism's evolution is intricately related to these struggles, having taken place within specific constellations of power and interest and historical contexts.

It has been suggested that Islamic populism is most powerful when it expresses robust multi-class alliances where differences within the ummah are suspended in favor of a political project that would notionally advance the social, economic, and political position of those who identify as its members. However, the development of such alliances is not inevitable. In Indonesia, for example, the absence of a big bourgeoisie component has been a major weakness, which contrasts sharply with the successful alliance brought together in Turkey by the AKP, incorporating a fast-rising, ambitious, and globalizing-oriented Anatolian bourgeoisie.

The consequence has been ambivalence in the ability of Islamic populism in Indonesia to navigate through – much less dominate – the democratic process. The organizational expression of Islamic populism remains fragmented and incoherent with no vehicle capable of claiming credible monopoly over the articulation of the interests of a notionally homogenous – but actually sociologically highly differentiated – ummah. This has opened the door for fringe groups to compete, bolstering their position by recourse to rigidly conservative social positions that can be tied to the values and teachings associated with the Islamic religion. These social positions are not infrequently asserted by way of aggressive actions that ostensibly underline their Islamic credentials, with the effect of mainstreaming conservative interpretations of Islam. This has impacted on the evolution of Islamic populism in Indonesia by significantly strengthening its politically illiberal tendencies.

References cited

Akça, Ismet, Ahmet Bekmen and Baris Ozden, eds. 2014. *Turkey Reframed: Constituting Neoliberal Hegemony* (New York: Palgrave Macmillan).

Alamsyah, Andi Rahman and Vedi R. Hadiz. 2016. "Three Islamist Generations, One Islamic State: The Darul Islam Movement and Indonesian Social Transformation," *Critical Asian Studies*. doi: 10.1080/14672715.2016.1260887

Alles, Delphine. 2016. *Transnational Islamic Actors and Indonesia's Foreign Policy: Transcending the State* (London: Routledge).

Aspinall, Edward. 2015. "Oligarchic Populism: Prabowo Subianto's Challenge to Indonesian Democracy," *Indonesia* 99: 1–28.

Bakker, Laurens. 2016. "Militias, Security and Citizenship in Indonesia," in Dale Eickelman, ed., *Social, Economic and Political Studies of the Middle East and Asia* (Leiden: Koninklijke Brill), pp. 125–54.

Bayat, Asef. 2013. "Post-Islamism at Large," in Asef Bayat, ed., *Post-Islamism: The Changing Faces of Political Islam* (Oxford: Oxford University Press), pp. 185–239.

Bush, Robin. 2008. "Regional Shariah Regulations in Indonesia: Anomaly in Symptom?" in Greg Fealy and Sally White (eds.), *Expressing Islam: Religious Life and Politics in Indonesia* (Singapore: ISEAS), pp. 174–91.

Canovan, Margaret. 1981. *Populism* (New York: Harcourt Brace Javonovich).

Clarke, Janine A. 2004. *Islam, Charity and Activism* (Bloomington and Indianapolis: Indiana University Press)

Colas, Alejandro. 2004. "The Reinvention of Populism: Islamicist Responses to Capitalist Development in the Contemporary Maghreb," *Historical Materialism* 12(4): 231–60.

Fealy, Greg. 2016. "Bigger Than Ahok: Explaining the 2 December Mass Rally," *Indonesia at Melbourne*, 7 December. http://indonesiaatmelbourne. unimelb.edu.au/bigger-than-ahok-explaining-jakartas-2-december-mass-rally/ (Accessed 1 January 2017).

Fenton, Natalie. 2016. *Digital, Political, Radical* (Oxford: Polity Press).

Formichi, Chiara. 2012. *Islam and the Making of the Nation: Kartosuwiryo and Political Islam in 20th Century Indonesia* (Leiden: KITLV Press).

Gellner, Ernest. 1981. *Muslim Society* (Cambridge: Cambridge University Press).

Hadiz, Vedi R. 2016. *Islamic Populism in Indonesia and the Middle East* (Cambridge: Cambridge University Press).

Hadiz, Vedi R. and Angelos Chryssogelos. 2017. "Populism in World Politics: A Comparative Cross-Regional Perspective," *International Political Science Review* 38 (4): 399–411.

Hadiz, Vedi R. and Richard Robison. 2012. "Political Economy and Islamic Politics: Insights from the Indonesian Case," *New Political Economy* 17(2): 137–55.

———— and Richard Robison. 2017. "Competing Populisms in Post-Authoritarian Indonesia," *International Political Science Review* 38 (4): 488–502.

Hefner, Robert W. 1993. "Islam, State and Civil Society: ICMI and the Struggle for Indonesian Middle Class," *Indonesia* 56: 1–35.

————. 2000. *Civil Islam: Muslims and Democratization in Indonesia* (Princeton: Princeton University Press).

Hicks, Jacqueline. 2012. "'The Missing Link': Explaining the Political Mobilisation of Islam in Indonesia," *Journal of Contemporary Asia* 42(1): 39–66.

Ionescu, Ghita and Ernest Gellner, eds. 1969. *Populism: Its Meaning and National Characteristics* (London: Weidenfeld and Nicolson).

Karagiannis, Emmanuel. 2010. *Political Islam in Central Asia: The Challenge of Hizb ut-Tahrir* (New York: Routledge).

Laclau, Ernesto. 1977. *Politics and Ideology in Marxist Theory* (London: Verso).

Laclau, Ernesto. 2005. *On Populist Reason* (London: Verso).

Laclau, Ernesto and Chantal Mouffe. 1985. *Hegemony and Socialist Strategy: Towards a Radical Democratic Politics* (London: Verso).

Mietzner, Marcus. 2015. *Reinventing Asian Populism: Jokowi's Rise, Democracy and Political Contestation in Indonesia.* Policy Studies No. 7 (Honolulu: East-West Centre).

Moffitt, Benjamin. 2016. *The Global Rise of Populism: Performance, Political Style, and Representation* (Stanford: Stanford University Press).

Mouzelis, Nicos. 1985. "On the Concept of Populism: Populist and Clientelist Modes of Incorporation in Semi-peripheral Polities," *Politics & Society* 14: 329–48.

Mudhoffir, Abdil Mughis. 2017. "Islamic Militias and Capitalist Development in Post-Authoritarian Indonesia," *Journal of Contemporary Asia* 47 (4): 495–514.

Müller, Jan-Werner. 2016. *What Is Populism?* (Philadelphia: Pennsylvania University Press).

Munabari, Fahlesa. 2010. "Hizbut Tahrir Indonesia: The Rhetorical Struggle for Survival," in Ota Atsushi, Okamoto Masaaki and Ahmad Sueady, eds., *Islam in Contention: Rethinking Islam and State in Indonesia* (Jakarta: Wahid Institute, CSEAS and CAPAS), pp. 169–213.

Nasr, Vali. 2009. *Forces of Fortune: The Rise of the New Muslim Middle Class and What It Will Mean for Our World* (New York: Free Press).

Önis, Ziya. 2012. "The Triumph of Conservative Globalism: The Political Economy of the AKP Era," *SSRN*, 10 February. https://papers.ssrn.com/sol3/papers. cfm?abstract_id=2003026 (Accessed 1 January 2017).

Oxhorn, Philip. 1998. "The Social Foundation of Latin America's Recurrent Populism: Problems of Popular Sector Class Formation and Collective Action," *Journal of Historical Sociology* 11(2): 212–46.

Robison, Richard. 1986. *The Rise of Capital* (Sydney: Allen and Unwin).

Rodinson, Maxime. 1966 (2007). *Islam and Capitalism* (London: Saqi).

Roy, Olivier. 2004. *Globalised Islam: The Search for a New Ummah* (London: Hurst).

Rudnyckyj, Daromir. 2010. *Spiritual Economies: Islam, Globalization, and the Afterlife of Development* (Ithaca and London: Cornell University Press).

Shiraishi, Takashi. 1990. *An Age in Motion: Popular Radicalism in Java 1912–1926* (Ithaca: Cornell University Press).

Solahudin. 2011. *NII sampai JI: Salafi Jihadisme di Indonesia* [NII to JI, Salafy Jihadism in Indonesia] (Jakarta: Komunitas Bambu).

Tripp, Charles. 2006. *Islam and the Moral Economy: The Challenge of Capitalism* (Cambridge: Cambridge University Press).

Tuğal, Cihan. 2009. *Passive Revolution: Absorbing the Islamic Challenge to Capitalism* (Stanford: Stanford University Press).

———. 2016. *The Fall of the Turkish Model: How the Arab Uprisings Brought Down Islamic Liberalism* (London: Verso).

Van Bruinessen, Martin, ed. 2013. *Contemporary Developments in Indonesian Islam: Explaining the "Conservative Turn"* (Singapore: ISEAS).

Wilson, Ian. 2015. *The Politics of Protection Rackets in Post-New Order Indonesia: Coercive Capital, Authority and Street Politics* (London: Routledge).

World Bank. 2016. "Indonesia's Rising Divide: Why Inequality Is Rising, Why It Matters and What Can Be Done." World Bank Report, March 2016. http://pubdocs.worldbank.org/en/16261460705088179/Indonesias-Rising-Divide-English.pdf.

Yasih, Diatyka W. P. 2016. "Jakarta's Precarious Workers: Are They a 'New Dangerous Class'?" *Journal of Contemporary Asia* 47(1): 27–45.

PART V

Gender and sexuality

25

GENDER CULTURE AND POLITICS IN POST–NEW ORDER INDONESIA

Kathryn Robinson

Noisy groups of women occupying the iconic roundabout outside Hotel Indonesia (Bundaran HI) in February 1998 were the first manifestation of the popular protest that eventually brought down the Soeharto regime. The women linked their concerns as mothers and housewives – the key definers of female citizenship under Soeharto – to the economic problems faced by Indonesian households as a consequence of Indonesia succumbing to the Asian Financial Crisis. Gender equity figured as a demand of the movement for democratic reform (Budianta 2006; Robinson 2009).

Occupation of the street has become a feature of the Indonesian political landscape, but in recent years, protestors are predominantly men and represent hard-line Islamist groups. A common theme has been an assertion of male prerogatives to define accepted forms of femininity – especially constraints on women's freedom of movement and (male) control of their bodies. While using Islamic rhetoric, their demands reflect a desire to shore up the masculine privilege challenged in Reformasi, through legislation or by protesting against visiting women figures (like Muslim feminist Irshad Manji or entertainer Lady Gaga), whom they accuse of transgressing Islamic norms of femininity (Robinson 2015).

These two faces of public performance encapsulate the main themes of claim and contestation that have emerged in regard to the politics of gender relations post-New Order. Indonesia is a majority-Muslim country, and there is a growing global discourse claiming that Islam is inherently antithetical to women's equal social participation. The democratic space of Reformasi encompassed greater freedom of religious expression, as well as enabling progress in the long-standing quest by Indonesian women for gender equity and women's greater involvement in "decision making" (*pengambilan keputusan*) from the household to the state. A gendered ideology of power was an important ideological underpinning of the militarized New Order, during which, the government emphasized wife and mother status as the basis of citizenship. While there have been many changes in the political system, the "gender order" (Robinson 2009) that was fundamental to the exercise of power in the New Order has been hard to shift. Demands for improved formal political representation and achievement of policy changes, such as outlawing domestic violence, but also public contestation over normative definitions of gender roles challenge this gender order.[1]

How do the (secular) ideologies of gender difference that were institutionalized during the New Order, as a well as gender ideologies presented in religious terms, play out in contemporary contestations over gendered power? How are they challenged by political claims for gender equity?

Women's political representation and women in leadership

Direct elections for both legislature and the executive were signature reforms of Reformasi, key to the move away from authoritarianism. Women's political representation is now firmly on the political agenda as an aspect of the democratic reshaping of Indonesia, unpacking the gender order of the New Order. There is a long tradition of Indonesian women being active in the economy and other aspects of public life (see Andaya this volume; Robinson 2009). Two significant examples are the women's groups that came together to demand changes to marriage laws in the colonial period and the Islamic women's mass organizations: NU and Fatayat NU, which are associated with Nahdlatul Ulama (NU) (present in 14,000 villages nationwide), and Aisyiyah, the women's wing of Muhammadiyah (with two million members nationwide). These Islamic mass movements have been very effective in delivering services in education and health, especially to women and girls, and providing opportunities for women to exercise secular and religious authority. However, during the New Order, the government drafted women into official corporatized women's organizations–Dharma Wanita for wives of civil servants and PKK (Family Welfare Movement) for women at the village level (Andaya this volume) that delivered health and well-being programs but as extensions of state power.

Women had held only a small number of seats in the national parliament in the Soeharto years, and at sub-national level, only two women had been appointed as district heads (*bupati*) (Dewi 2015:8). The New Order legacy is still strong in Indonesian public life. Women's exclusion from public life, far from being "traditional," is in many parts of the archipelago an innovation on traditional norms and practices (Andaya this volume, Robinson 2009). Activists argued for greater female political representation as a core pillar of democratic reform, but the first elections of the reform era in 1999 were a disappointment, resulting in only 9.6% of seats in the national parliament held by women, less than the proportion achieved under the New Order.

A conducive "social and structural context," which includes support for women's education, is considered a pre-condition for increased female political representation (Bessell 2010: 230). New Order programs to expand education benefited girls and women as much as men, and the economic policies that encouraged *inter alia* foreign investment in manufacturing and overseas labor migration propelled women into the formal economy. These changes undermined the effectiveness of New Order familist ideology in domesticating women. Female students accounted for 47.6% of students in higher education in 2010 (UNDP 2010: 21). Education has a positive effect on labor force participation, with rates for tertiary graduates at 80% (Manning and Pratono 2017). Around 50% of women participate in the workforce (as compared to around 75% of men) "higher than in India or Malaysia, very close to the Philippines but below Thailand, China and way below Vietnam," and they are moving more frequently into full-time jobs. These conditions would seem to provide a favorable climate for the entry of women into politics. In addition, Indonesia uses a system of proportional representation in its legislatures, an electoral system seen as favorable to the election of women candidates.

Activists argued for the need to "jump-start" women's parliamentary representation through implementing a quota, an affirmative action strategy supported by the UN but in 1995 implemented in only four countries (Hillman 2017: 38). Law 12/003 on political parties encouraged parties to "consider" that at least 30% of candidates on party lists for the multi-member electorates be women, at national, provincial, and district levels. The results for the 2004 elections were disappointing, however, with an increase to only 11.8% women's representation in the national parliament. The political climate was hostile to the quota, including active opposition from the then female president, Megawati Sukarnoputri (Bessell 2010: 228–9). The law provided no sanctions against parties that failed to comply, and many did not meet the quota. In addition, women were all too often ranked in unwinnable positions at the bottom of party lists (termed pejoratively the "shoe order" [*urutan sepatu*]). This policy failure led to further lobbying for a strengthened quota, and a coalition of NGOs drafted a clause that was included in the 2008 Law on Elections (Law No. 10/2008) that made it compulsory for parties to include a minimum of 30% women candidates on their lists and also required at least one out of the top three candidates to be a women (a limited "zipper" system). Although the political climate had shifted by the 2009 elections, and all major parties supported the idea of increasing numbers of women legislators (Bessell 2010: 231), six out of 38 parties failed to meet the quota, and only five placed women in one of the top three positions, as the law required. But overall, 34.7% of candidates for the national legislature were women, resulting in an increase in women members to 17.6%, close to the world average of 19% (Hillman 2017: 40).

A 2008 constitutional court challenge to the quota argued it was antithetical to the principle of equality. It was dismissed by the judges who found the state "had an obligation to foster substantive equality" (Bessell 2010: 233). But the court found in favor of the petitioner on another ground: the constitution required an open list system, so that parties no longer had the power to direct votes to ranked candidates on the party lists. The successful candidates were those who received the most votes. But this innovation in Indonesia's system of proportional representation halted the trend to greater women's representation.

The Constitutional Court decision had the result that candidates campaigned as individuals rather than as party blocs, so position on the party list became less relevant to success. This competition encouraged the rise in patronage and direct vote buying, considered by observers as barriers to capable and independent women candidates. It is possible that the pervasive stereotypes of women's lack of capacity (see below) may hinder the figures who bankroll candidates, and women's low levels of participation in parties and public bodies means that they have less opportunity to develop networks. On a positive note, during the 2014 election campaign, there seemed to be more commitment by the Electoral Commission (KPU) to enforce the quota, and several ministries implemented media campaigns encouraging voters to consider women candidates. While the proportion of women candidates increased to 37%, they won only 17.36% of seats, marginally *less* than in 2009.

Advocates of the need for policies to increase women's representation are looking for new strategies and suggestions include tighter regulation of campaign financing and a return to the closed list system (currently under discussion in the national parliament). But it cannot be assumed that women have greater moral rectitude and hence are reluctant to play "dirty politics." Some of the women who have been successful in politics have been as capable as male counterparts of nepotistic and self-advancing politics.

The Indonesian parliament is bicameral, with election to the upper house (Dewan Perwakilan Daerah or DPD) by proportional representation in single, non-transferable votes in multi-member electorates (provinces). Elections to the DPD do not have a gender quota, but nonetheless women have been more strongly represented than in the legislature – 26.5% in 2009 but falling to 25.8% in 2014. This relative success of female candidates is attributed to the lack of involvement of political parties in nomination of candidates and their campaigning. Candidates are judged on an individual basis, and success is based on their political and community work (Hillman 2017: 6).

In spite of a strong focus on women's election to the legislature as a significant step toward gender equity as a fundamental principle of democracy, the male-dominated institutions that serve as gatekeepers in the political system have resisted change. Nonetheless, there are a growing number of women with political aspirations who are knocking at the door.

Women representatives in provincial and regional parliaments

The Big Bang decentralization implemented from 2000 was intended to bring power holders, and hence accountability, closer to the people. The regional parliaments comprising directly elected representatives in multimember electorates were subject to the candidate quota in the 2008 law on elections. In 2009, women were elected to an average of 16% of seats in 33 provincial parliaments and 9% of seats at district and municipal levels, less than at the national level. In 2014, the proportion of women members in the provincial parliaments even declined to 14.6%, but there was a slight increase at district and municipal levels to 14.2%. These figures hide great diversity across the nation. Nine provincial parliaments have no female members, but 8 have more than 30% women members, and in West Kalimantan, for example, all 4 members are women. In elections, the pervasive stereotypes and gender politics of the New Order have been hard to shift.

The contestation at the local level in the period of democratization has seen the revival of "customary institutions" as one of the instruments of political competition, and in some cases, this has invoked (often putative) values on gender difference that shore up male privilege and attempt to exclude women. Patrilineal Hindu Bali has the lowest women's political participation at all levels. In spite of the 2008 quota, it is one of three provinces with no women elected to the national legislature, and in the revival of tradition that has accompanied decentralization, women are not eligible to vote in local political units (*banjar*) (Rhoads 2012).

Direct elections for district heads and provincial governors

Women have been far less successful in contestation for executive positions, which until 2004 were elected by the local legislatures. Only five female district heads (*bupati*) and one female vice governor had been successful. Law No 32/2004 on direct elections of governors and bupati has, however, been followed by a slow increase in women's success. Between 2005 and 2008, 11 women in Java and 15 outside Java were elected to the positions of bupati (district head), deputy bupati, governor, and deputy governor (Dewi 2015: 21–2). In 2015, there were 123 female candidates (7.44%) and 46 were elected (Bupati [24] and deputy Bupati [22]). Twenty-nine percent of female candidates were former members of the legislature, and 18.5% were incumbents. Overall, they were highly educated (85% university graduates) (Setyowati 2016).

Satriyo (2010) found that the factors leading to women candidates' success were the same as for men: party networks and the ability to raise the considerable funds needed for campaigning. In 2005, a successful constitutional court challenge to the party monopoly in nomination of candidates enabled independent candidates, avoiding the party gatekeepers. However, independents are required to provide a very large number of signatures of supporters, proportional to the population of their seat. This is a financial barrier for non-party-backed candidates.

A 2010 regulation restricting the incumbency of provincial and district heads to two terms has had a perhaps unexpected effect on female candidature. The Constitutional Court (in 2015) allowed the family of incumbents to stand for election, resulting in at least 16 candidates in 2015 having familial ties to the previous incumbent – as wife, daughter, and daughter-in-law (Setyowati 2016). This is a situation similar to the New Order period, where women in parliament most often held appointed seats, and incumbents were spouses or other relatives of powerful men. But in this current period of decentralized government, the dynamic of familial politics is creating local "dynasties."

Women in other public positions

Indonesia's remarkable strides in women's education and the historic involvement of women in the economy have not readily translated into women's participation in other areas of public life. A 2010 UNDP report found women's representation in a range of public institutions worse than their representation in national parliament. Women are poorly represented in the upper echelons of the civil service, for example. The situation has not changed greatly from the early reform era: women are still most heavily concentrated in the lower levels of the civil service and in the service areas of health and education, gender stereotyped positions for women (Oey-Gardiner 2002: 109). There have been very few women ministers in post–New Order cabinets and then mainly in the "soft" portfolios of women's affairs and social affairs. But in 2014, President Jokowi had eight women in his cabinet, including the foreign minister and some economic portfolios.

It is by no means certain that women legislators will see themselves as representing women's interests (the difference between "formal" and "substantive" representation). However, there is an increasing public discourse that women's voices need to be part of public decision making, as women's interests may differ from men's. Vice President Kalla put forward this argument, for example, before the 2014 elections. Women politicians and supporters have established support networks, such as the caucus of women politicians, both inside and outside parliament, to support and influence female (and male) members to adopt policies that advance women's interests.

Barriers to women's formal political participation

Indonesia has several of the characteristics shown to have a positive impact on women's parliamentary representation: the electoral system based on proportional representation, good levels of women's education and relatively high workforce participation, and legislated candidate quotas. The most significant barrier to women becoming candidates (and being elected) is the party machines, which control nomination and which are dominated by men. Parties claim they lack suitable women candidates. Experience as party functionaries is an important factor in nomination (Siregar 2010), and while the 2008 law required parties to adopt a 30% quota of women in executive positions, few have achieved this. Party leaders give the excuse that the people are not ready for women decision makers, but an Indo Barometer poll in March 2009 found that 75.8% of people surveyed supported women's right to run for president and 64.3% supported affirmative action for women candidates (Satriyo 2010: 253). A UNDP poll (2010: 28) found 55% of respondents were willing to see women in decision-making positions and 75% favored the legislative quota.

The terms used to justify support for male candidates over women reflect gender stereotypes: for example that a male candidate can provide "firm and solid leadership" and that a woman is more suited to be the running mate (Satriyo 2010: 249). Such views mirror the New Order ideological construct of the women standing behind the man or the legislated provision of the woman as the manager of the household under the husband's headship.

Another argument against female candidature was used in the case of Khofifah Indar Parawansa, a Muslimat NU leader who had been a cabinet minister under President Abdurrahman Wahid and who in 2013 stood for governor of East Java as candidate for the Islamic party PPP. This high-profile and capable politician was opposed by NU *kiyai* on the grounds that local leaders serve as prayer leaders in public ceremonies. As a woman, she could not be a prayer leader; hence, she was ineligible for office.[2] However, the Indo Barometer poll cited earlier found that 63% of people stated that they would ignore instructions of religious leaders who told them not to vote for women candidates (Satriyo 2010: 253).

It seems that while the party power brokers all fall back on ideological expressions of male prerogative, as formally instituted under the New Order, the people are ahead of them. This is not a surprise – male prerogative was so thoroughly shored up under the New Order, part of the "patriarchal dividend" that flowed to men in general from the capture of the state by a militarized male hegemonic elite, it is hardly surprising that they are reluctant to cede these advantages.

Attitudes regarding women's roles that reflect New Order ideology are impediments to change. A UNDP (2010: 24) survey of men and women found that 77.6% thought that men should be decision makers and leaders of the community; 95% thought men should be leaders of households; and 94% thought that women should not work outside the home without prior permission of their husbands.

A CSIS poll found that 86.3% agreed that "women's primary responsibility was to take care of the household"; 83.6% that women should not work at night; and that "politics was dirty and inappropriate for women." In this same poll, 2% agreed that women should obey their husbands, which Hillman (2017: 41) speculates extends to voting. These kinds of polling results are used to support "patriarchal attitudes," which see men as household heads and women as subordinating themselves to the male household head; both views mitigate against voters seeing women as legitimate candidates. However, such normative statements need to be contextualized with the realities of women's economic and other forms of public participation in Indonesia.

Dewi's (2015) study of three female politicians in Java gives a nuanced take on how these ideas play out. In their public performance of candidature, the women self-consciously present themselves as pious married women who defer to their husbands as family heads. But this is the basis of their claim to suitability to assume political power. It is now common to hear the view expressed by women, even those without a strong desire for changes in gender relations, that it is important to hear women's voices, accepting women's difference but desiring that it be heard in the political arena. These voices complement those that see women's representation as an essential prerequisite for gender equity.

Women's organizations

Indonesia has a long and rich tradition of women's organizations that have engaged in political advocacy for women's rights and also been significant in providing health and education services for women and children. These have included secular and religious groups and the groups associated with mass Islamic organizations (Aisyiyah Muhammadiyah and Fatayat and Muslimat NU), which have been especially important in delivering services, as well as providing Islamic education. Following Reformasi, membership of the state-sponsored organizations Dharma Wanita and PKK was no longer obligatory, and they are today regarded as "autonomous," but in many cases, they have continued to operate, as women see a benefit in their activities, which include provision of health and welfare services. Women's organizations provide important experience for prospective women candidates.

Several important feminist groups developed in the later New Order period and remain significant post New Order. For example, LBH Apik (The Women's Association for Justice) has continued its advocacy for legal reform, especially in relation to the 1974 Marriage Law, in addition to assisting individual women with legal redress. Kapal Perempuan (Alternative Education Circle) has been at the forefront of publicizing and challenging discriminatory legislation, especially in the districts. Solidaritas Perempuan (Women's Solidarity for Human Rights) has continued to advocate for women labor migrants. The effervescence of Reformasi and the expectations of change soon faded to disappointment at government inaction. Civil society organizations have taken advantage of the greater freedom of speech and action to take action on issues, rather than waiting for the government. Apart from groups of educated middle-class activists, there are emerging new forms of locality-based women's organizations, such as Suara Ibu Peduli, that draw on a rhetoric of motherhood and caring to act to support HIV and AIDS sufferers in Bandung urban *kampung*.

These new civil society organizations spring from a broad political spectrum and include Islamic groups advocating gender equity, like Rahima and Fahima. However, their message is challenged by women's groups associated with conservative Islamic groups, like the Hizbut Tahrir Indonesia (HTI) and the Prosperous Justice Party (PKS). These latter groups support the introduction of shariah and contest the feminist interpretations of Islamic doctrine discussed above. They reject feminism and gender equity as "Western" concepts.

The politics of the household

If elections have provided the stage for broad-based action challenging the masculinist gender order, the regulation of marriage has been the stage for the struggle over the gendered exercise of power in everyday life. While the constitution declares all citizens are equal, religious prescriptions impact on women's citizen rights – most notably in the area of marriage law and rights in the family. In contradistinction to the refusal of marriage as an institution that characterized second wave feminism in the West, Indonesian rights activists have focused on marriage reform through legislation and, more recently, court challenges. Gender rights activists see change as originating in legislation and court challenges but also in interpretations of fiqh (Islamic jurisprudence) (see below).

In the colonial period, family law was largely left to Islamic authorities, but Islamic law had accommodated the existing practices of the societies of the archipelago during its slow spread, particularly in regard to polygyny and property rights; the former was unpalatable in much of the archipelago, and "custom" commonly recognized women's inheritance (equal or near-equal, in contrast to the stipulations of Islamic fiqh) and other property rights. Women in the nationalist movement successfully pressed for pro-women government regulations in regard to Islamic marriage, especially limitations on polygyny, child marriage, and divorce by repudiation. Women's activism around marriage continued in the new nation state, and by 1974, they achieved some of their goals in the passage of a unified marriage law, which established a minimum age at marriage and provided greater protection in the case of divorce and polygyny. The Compilation of Islamic Law (KHI) in 1997 further strengthened customary rights, including women's common property rights on divorce (Robinson 2006).

The marriage law states that men are the household heads, a legal prescription that was strictly followed in the New Order period as it supported the regime's familist ideology – the *bapak* (father/president) at the head of the state mirrored the bapak at the head of the family. Men's prerogative in regard to wives and children formed part of the patriarchal dividend through which non-hegemonic males could benefit from the control of the state by a masculinist elite (Robinson 2009). Only married women could access contraceptives distributed through the state family planning program and only with consent of their husbands.

In the democratized political space of Reformasi, women's rights activists argued for a revision of the 1974 marriage law, to ban polygyny outright and further limit men's prerogatives in divorce. But at the same time some men (and women supporters) seized the moment to campaign for the restoration of rights to polygyny. In a constitutional court challenge in 2008, it was argued that the state restriction of polygyny was a violation of religious rights. The challenge was unsuccessful, however (see Lindsey chapter). The distaste of Indonesian women, including pious women, for polygyny was graphically illustrated in the fall from grace of television preacher AA Gym in 2006. His devoted and predominantly female audience deserted him, and his business empire collapsed, when it was revealed he had taken a second wife.

In 2016, the National Commission on Women (Komnas Perempuan) urged the government to speed up the process of amending the 1974 Marriage Law to strengthen monogamy. The Ministry of Women and Children has drafted a revision. But also in 2016, a group called the Sakinah Polygamous Family Forum (FKPS) announced their intention to request a further judicial review of the marriage law, in particular restrictions on polygyny, arguing it is in contradiction with clause 29 in the constitution "that promotes freedom" (Dipa 2016).

The 1974 Marriage Law was intended to disallow child marriage by setting a minimum marriage age of 16 for girls. However, this is now out of step with other regulations and changes, including the UN Convention on the Rights of the Child (to which Indonesia is a signatory) that sets a minimum marriage age of 18 years. As women enjoy the benefits of education and expectations change, this is now seen as a hot political issue. In 2014, a group of NGOs requested a judicial review of the marriage age by the court, but their case was not upheld. The court argued it would not enter into the religious domain of readiness for marriage and argued this was a legislative matter. Another challenge is being prepared with more argumentation about the Islamic provisions on marriage (I-CONnect 2015).

Middle-class households increasingly require two incomes, and this impacts male and female roles: a younger generation of Indonesian middle-class men are championing new and domesticated roles for husbands and fathers (http://lakilakibaru.or.id/). In less affluent circles, 60% of Indonesia's overseas labor migrants are women, mainly in domestic service. Men who are left behind are forced by circumstance to embrace such changes. Hence the political balance within households is challenged by economic changes, as well as improvements in education. As a result of the freedom of speech that has emerged in the reform period, people in all walks of life are exposed to mass media content and public debates about changing and emerging forms of masculinity and femininity.

Violence against women – today's key issue

Violence against women and children has been the subject of growing public debate and government action. The 1998 Jakarta riots that marked the violent end to Soeharto's New Order infamously involved orchestrated rapes of Chinese women, precipitating outrage and a practical response by new President B. J. Habibie to a request by women activists to establish Komnas Perempuan. This independent body has kept the issue of violence against women, including family violence, as a foregrounded political issue. It has sponsored legislative agendas concerned with family violence and the as-yet unsuccessful quest to reform the marriage law. These initiatives help keep gender issues at the forefront of government concerns. A recent survey on violence against women was conducted by the National Statistics Body, the Women's Ministry, and UNFPA: it found that one-third of women aged 15–64 experienced physical or sexual violence, almost 10% in the last year (BPS 2016).

A law outlawing domestic violence was passed in 2004 (Law 23/ 2004 on the Elimination of Violence in the Household). It provided stronger penalties for domestic violence than for common assault under the criminal code. However, as with all such law reform, the passage of the act is only a first step: judges and society in general have to be aware and accepting of the provision for it to be effectively implemented. In the era of decentralization, advocates have endeavored to have parallel provincial and even district legislation passed to ensure the legal changes are acknowledged and implemented. An important strategy in anti-violence has been the involvement of the police force in establishing crisis centers for victims of violence that ideally involve female police; thus far, however, the presence of women officers remains small (under 4%). The outlawing of a husband's right to exercise his leadership in the household through interpersonal violence is an important challenge to the assumption that men are kings of their own domains and that the household is an arena for the expression of the "patriarchal dividend" (see Robinson 2009; 2104) to men occupying non-hegemonic masculinities.

Female circumcision has also been a controversial issue, shrouded in secrecy for Indonesia's Muslim communities. Where in the past it had been practiced, it most often involved a symbolic drawing of blood. However, as an aspect of the middle-class piety movement, this practice began to spread in the 1990s and become standardized and more extensive (Feillard and Marcoes 1998). The government responded by regulating medical circumcision (Menkes regulation No. 1636/2010). Contested as official support for a practice that contravened human rights, this regulation was successfully repealed after negotiations between advocacy groups and the Ministries of Health and Women's Empowerment and Child Protection, supported by UN women. This case, like the policy on electoral quotas discussed above, exemplifies the ways in which women activists in Indonesia have been able to successfully leverage global links and the government ratification of international instruments like CEDAW, to effect change (see Robinson 1998).

Decentralization

The decentralization of government services to regions and districts led to concerns that previously centrally-funded programs that benefit women, such as contraceptive services or combatting maternal mortality (which remains high in Indonesia), would be under threat. District legislatures and executives would have to see the importance of women's issues to continue funding. Noerdin and Aripurnami (2007) invoke the idea of decentralization as a "narrative of opportunity" for women. Family planning, the name for the state delivery of contraception, had been a successful centralized program of the New Order that ran military-style programs but also used women's organizations and community networks to ensure continuity of supply in the villages. Between 1967 and 1997, the total fertility rate had dropped from 5.6 children per woman to 2.85.

In 2016, a report commissioned by Indonesia's Population and Family Planning Board (BKKBN, Badan Kependudukan dan Keluarga Berencana) found that decentralization had taken its toll on family planning and health programs, with a decreasing quality of public service (Dipa 2016). The report found that many local leaders have little understanding of how family planning links to development objectives and hence are reluctant to commit to policies and budgets. However, the authors also praised the family planning and public health programs in some provinces, which were creatively integrated in programs such as women's empowerment, public health, and activities for youth and far removed from the authoritarian top-down approaches of the New Order. Even when there was confusion of authority, men and women were still joining at the "grassroots" level, with health providers, civil society organizations, and faith-based groups keeping the program alive. This included the women's wings of the major Islamic organizations, NU Muslimat and Fatayat, and Muhammadiyah's Aisyiyah. In the era of decentralization, the retreat from the one-size-fits-all policies has made possible a more effective program that can embrace the diversity of Indonesia's constituent communities. Current prevalence seems relatively steady at just under 50% of married couples. Sexual and reproductive health services are critical cornerstones of gender equity and women's ability to make choices.

Challenges to gender equity using Islamic rhetoric

The opening up of democratic space post-Soeharto also emboldened and enabled anti-liberal Islamic groups (called Islam *keras*, "hard" Islam). Their view of Islam encompasses the expression of masculine prerogative. For example, in 2008, noisy street demonstrations by (usually) male supporters of groups like Islamic Defender's Front (FPI) were effective in pressuring the national legislature to pass a so-called anti-pornography law (Law No. 44, 2008). The Human Rights Commission (Komnas Ham) argued the law discriminated against and criminalized women who failed to meet dress standards or who engaged in proscribed actions in public. The legislation's proponents, by contrast, argued that restrictions on women's dress and behavior were expressions of morality and Islamic orthodoxy, while opponents argued it was an attempt to restrict women's freedom of movement justified in the name of Islam. While the law has led to few arrests, its rhetoric has influenced public discourse, for example framing official attempts to limit women's freedom through restrictive dress codes.

Following the 2001 implementation of decentralization, some newly empowered districts enacted local bylaws (purportedly) based on sharia law (perda syari'ah). These local regulations also mainly targeted women: restricting their movement in public, including curfews; imposing dress codes (e.g., requiring civil servants and schoolgirls to wear the jilbab, an especially encompassing Islamic headscarf); and even banning women's sitting astride motorcycles, as in one district in Aceh. In 2016, Komnas Perempuan identified some 422 regulations that directly or indirectly discriminated against women.

These regulations have been contested by men and women, including "Islamic feminist" activists – and they are also frequently ignored. But women appearing in public without head covering have been subject to "sweeping" by local police in some districts, and the regulations have licensed vigilante acts by men exercising a presumed masculine prerogative. In West Java, women returning home from work have been harassed and accused of immoral acts. Politicians (mostly from *non*-Islamic parties) deploy populist strategies to court male voters with promises to sustain masculine prerogatives through controlling women, utilizing an Islamic idiom (Robinson 2015).

Islamic feminism and female religious authority

Claims legitimating patriarchal authority in the name of Islam have not gone unchallenged, most notably by the proponents of feminist interpretations of Islam, which argue that equality before God is a fundamental Islamic value (Robinson 2007, 2008, 2009). The tertiary-level State Islamic Institutes (IAIN) have been important in developing the religious knowledge of women and men who have come through the pesantren (Islamic residential school) tradition. Grounded in the tolerant traditions of Indonesian Islam, these scholars provide a direct challenge to arguments for patriarchal authority legitimated by Islam. IAIN-educated scholars were at the forefront of a productive collaboration between religious scholars and secular feminists who provided the tools of "gender analysis" to develop "Islamic feminist" analysis. Many significant women Islamic scholars, including Musdah Muliah from the Research Institute of the Department of Religious Affairs, activists Lies Marcoes and Siti Ruhaini Dzuhayatin, and the late Lily Zakiyah Munir have been path blazers, not only in Indonesia, but globally. Male clerics have also been at the forefront of this movement, most notably Kiai Huscin Muhammad of Cirebon.

An interesting component of the growing piety movement in Indonesia has been the efflorescence of community level groups (*majlis taklim*) that provide religious instruction, especially for women. These groups serve as arenas for women leaders to hone their religious authority as well as a training ground in skills to enter other areas of public life, like local politics. In Indonesia, as in other parts of the Islamic world, women's religious groups are providing a platform for claims of religious authority by women preachers and scholars. These trends culminated in the Congress of Women Ulama held in Cirebon in April 2017, attended by 1,700 women and men. The Congress celebrated the history of women preachers and scholars, the tradition of gender equity in interpretation of Islamic texts, and the importance of Islamic Human Rights doctrine. Speakers were vociferous in their condemnation of polygyny, child marriage, rape in marriage, and all forms of violence against women. The congress was supported by the Religious Affairs Ministry and local government. Several of the international speakers commented this would be unthinkable in their own majority-Muslim countries.

An aspect of the piety movement that has attracted much comment, often negative, by foreign observers is the ever-growing trend for Indonesian Muslim women to adopt Islamic fashion, including headcovering, to a greater degree than in decades prior to the 1990s. For Western observers, the "veil" appears to be a symbol of women's oppression under Islam. But Indonesian Muslim activists and leaders embrace Islamic dress codes as expressions of their Muslim identities and also as a fashion statement. In Indonesia, the Islamic dress movement goes hand in hand with revitalization of Indonesian textile traditions by the middle class. Greater expression of piety and deepening Islamic knowledge are not challenging the tolerant traditions of Indonesian Islam and the Congress of Women Ulama was a living testimony to this.

Concluding remarks

Gender equity and an improvement in women's roles in decision making and in the family, civil society organizations, and the instruments of the state have been key demands of pro-democracy groups post Soeharto. A familist gender ideology that attempted to circumscribe women's social and political roles was a key element of the ideological apparatus of the New Order. In democratizing Indonesia, conservative forces have resisted increasing opportunities and power for women, falling back on arguments of the "traditional" nature of women's primary domestic role. In a practical way, this position has been challenged by the improvements in women's education, the significance of women's labor in sectors of the formal workforce, and also the regulation of fertility through contraception (see Robinson 2009). Male and female roles and responsibilities are continuously challenged by changes in all areas of social life and ideas in circulation in global and national mass media.

Global Islam and the piety movement have also provided a challenge to the ongoing fight for women to have "a seat at the table." Crude interpretations of Islamic texts have been deployed in ideological and power struggles, including in populist street politics and politicians' cynical attempts to shore up male privilege. But among Indonesia's educated Islamic population, with a long history of women-friendly accommodations in the practice of law and involvement of women in Islamic mass organizations, conservative anti-woman policies have not found firm purchase. For an important segment of educated middle-class Indonesians, Islam is accepted as supporting forms of gender equity or at least regarded as part of the terrain of struggle over ideologies and values. Women's rights and gender equity are not regarded as "Western values," existing outside the domain of Islam. For proponents of gender equity as a fundament of democracy, Islam is an ally.

Social change moves slowly, and the continuing advocacy for gender equity has brought the issue into the political mainstream. The government has embraced both gender mainstreaming and gender budgeting, and regular reporting to CEDAW (Convention on the Elimination of All Forms of Discrimination against Women) subjects progress toward gender equity to periodic scrutiny and provides a useful tool to focus political debate. Most recently (April 2017), Indonesia has been selected by the United Nations as one of 10 model nations for implementing gender equity, under the Sustainable Development Goals, a testimony to the progress achieved.

Nonetheless, there are entrenched secular institutional structures in the political domain that are mitigating against women gaining greater representation in formal politics. But formal politics is not the "only game in town," and civil society and religious organizations are also places for political action. Advocates for gender equity have been astute in using legal challenges and promoting changes in the law, but they operate on many fronts, including civil society groups that interface with the formal political system.

Notes

1 The change in the name of the women's ministry, to encompass the ideal of empowerment (*pemberdayaan*), a key political term in Reformasi, signaled the desire for change.
2 Similar arguments were developed in the debate about whether a woman could be president in 1997 (Robinson 2004).

References cited

Bessell, Sharon 2010. "Increasing the Proportion of Women in the National Parliament: Opportunities, Barriers and Challenges," in Edward Aspinall and Marcus Mietzner, eds., *Problems of Democratisation in Indonesia: Elections, Institutions and Society*, (Singapore: ISEAS), pp. 219–42.

BPS (Badan Pusat Statistik). 2016. "Satu dari Tiga Perempuan Usia 15–64 Tahun pernah mengalami Kekerasan Fisik dan/atau seksual selama hidupnya" [Report on Indonesian National Women's Life Experience Survey].www.bps.go.id/brs/view/id/1375 (Accessed 29 April).

Budianta, Melani, 2006. "Decentralizing Engagement: Women and the Democratization Process in Indonesia," *Signs* 31(4) pp. 915–23.

Dewi, Kurniawati Hastuti. 2015. *Indonesian Women and Local Politics* (Singapore: NUS Press).

Dipa, Arya. 2016. "Polygamists to File Judicial Review of Marriage Law," *The Jakarta Post*, 3 January. www.thejakartapost.com/news/2016/01/03/polygamists-file-judicial-review-marriage-law.html (Accessed 29 April 2017).

Feillard, Andree and Lies Marcoes. 1998. "Female Circumcision in Indonesia: To 'Islamize' in Ceremony or Secrecy," *Archipel* 56(1): 337–67.

Hillman, Ben. 2017. "Increasing Women's Parliamentary Representation in Asia and the Pacific: The Indonesian Experience," *Asia and the Pacific Policy Studies* 4(1): 38–49.

I-CONnect. 2015. "Developments in Indonesian Constitutional Law: The Year 2015 in Review." www.iconnectblog.com/2016/11/developments-in-indonesian-constitutional-law-the-year-2015-in-review/ (Accessed 27 April 2017).

Manning, Chris and Devanto Pratomo. 2017. "Labour Supply and Attachment to the Work Force," in Edimon Ginting, Chris Manning, and Kiyoshi Taniguchi, eds., *Improving Employment Outcomes in Indonesia* (Manilla: Asian Development Bank), pp. 47–69.

Noerdin, Edriana and Sita Aripurnami, eds. 2007. *Decentralization as a Narrative of Opportunity for Women in Indonesia* (Jakarta: Women Research Institute).

Oey-Gardiner, Mayling. 2002. "And the Winner Is … Indonesian Women in Public Life," in Kathryn Robinson and Sharon Bessell, eds., *Women in Indonesia: Gender Equity and Development* (Singapore: ISEAS), pp. 100–12.

Rhoads, Elizabeth. 2012. "Women's Political Participation in Indonesia: Decentralisation, Money Politics and Collective Memory in Bali," *Journal of Current Southeast Asian Affairs* 31(2): 35–56.

Robinson, Kathryn. 1998. "Indonesian Women's Rights, International Feminism and Democratic Change," *Communal/Plural* 6(2): 205–19.

———. 2004. "Islam, Gender and Politics in Indonesia," in Virginia Hooker and Amin Saikal, eds., *Islamic Perspectives on the new Millennium* (Singapore: ISEAS), pp. 183–96.

———. 2006. "Muslim Women's Political Struggle for Marriage Law Reform in Contemporary Indonesia," in Amanda Whiting and Carolyn Evans, eds., *Mixed Blessings: Laws, Religions, and Women's Rights in the Asia-Pacific Region* (Leiden, NL: Martinus Nijhoff Publishers), pp. 183–210.

———. 2007. "Islamic Influences on Indonesian Feminism," in Tony Day, ed., *Identifying With Freedom; Indonesia After Suharto* (New York and Oxford: Berghahn Books), pp. 39–48.

———. 2008. "Islamic Cosmopolitics, Human Rights and Anti-Violence Strategies in Indonesia," in P. Werbner, ed., *Anthropology and the New Cosmopolitanism: Feminist, Vernacular and Rooted Perspectives* (Oxford: Berg [ASA Monograph]).

———. 2009. *Gender, Islam and Democracy in Indonesia* (New York: Routledge).

———. 2015. "Masculinity, Sexuality and Islam: The Gender Politics of Regime Change in Indonesia," in Linda Rae Bennett and Sharyn Graham Davies, eds., *Sex and Sexualities in Contemporary Indonesia: Sexual Politics, Health, Diversity and Representations* (Abingdon and New York: Routledge), pp. 51–68.

Satriyo, Hana. 2010. "Pushing the boundaries: Women in Direct Local Elections and Local Government," in Edward Aspinall and Marcus Mietzner, eds., *Problems of Democratisation in Indonesia: Elections, Institutions and Society* (Singapore: ISEAS), pp. 243–66.

———. 2014. 'The 30%," *New Mandala*, 28 April AT www.newmandala.org/the-30/ (Accessed 12 April 2017).

Setyowati, Mg Retno. 2016. "Perempuan dalam Pilkada serentak," *Kompas*, 5 January. http://cdn.assets. print.kompas.com/baca/2016/01/05/Perempuan-dalam-Pilkada-Serentak (Accessed 29 April 2017).

Siregar, Wahidah Zein. 2010. *Gaining Representation in Parliament: A Study of the Struggle of Indonesian Women to Increase Their Numbers in Parliaments in the 2004 Elections* (Saarbruchen: Lambert Academic Publishing).

UNDP (United Nations Development Program) Jakarta. 2010. *Women's Participation in Politics and Government in Indonesia: A Policy Paper* (Jakarta: UNDP).

26

GENDER AND SEXUAL PLURALITY IN INDONESIA

Past and present

Sharyn Graham Davies

The early months of 2016 marked a watershed in the story of gender and sexual plurality in Indonesia. Unlike its closest neighbors, Indonesia had never criminalized homosexuality, and while prejudice and harassment were widespread, there had been no systematic political, legal, or religious persecution. The events of 2016 changed Indonesia's relationship to gender and sexual plurality, though. Beginning in January, politicians, lawyers, and Muslim clerics called for the confinement of lesbian, gay, bisexual, and transgender (LGBT) people, who were positioned as suffering mental illness, constituting a threat to national security, and violating Islamic norms. When President Joko Widodo finally weighed in on the debate in October of that year, his call for LGBT people to be protected from violence was qualified by the declaration that Indonesian beliefs do not support LGBT (Kine 2016). That the President and others ignored Indonesia's tradition of sexual and gender plurality is just one of the harms committed during 2016.

This chapter examines origin narratives, indigenous manuscripts, early traveler accounts, and colonial reports, in addition to material concerning independent Indonesia (1945–1998) to provide a view of gender and sexual plurality prior to democratic reform. The chapter then explores gender and sexual plurality in Reformation Indonesia (1998–2016), showing that despite hope of greater inclusion, events of 2016 precipitated unprecedented levels of discrimination against LGBT Indonesians. Drawing on Charles Lee's (2016) notion of ingenious citizenship, I argue that despite potential essentialist dangers, drawing on the past is one way LGBT Indonesians can push claims for contemporary legitimacy.

When Minister of Education Muhammad Nasir publicly stated in January 2016 that Indonesian universities should not support LGBT activities, a torrent of protest broke out. Protest heightened when media repeatedly misquoted Nasir as having stated that LGBT students should be banned from university. By the time Nasir qualified his statement, affirming that he was not against LGBT people per se but only against LGBT organizations, public debate had exploded, suggesting that an undercurrent of homophobia had been simmering just below the surface. Such was the fervor that even people who were not necessarily homophobic sensed an opportunity to win political and religious backing by espousing anti–LGBT rhetoric. While the fervor of vitriol took most people by surprise, a deeper analysis shows the antecedents to the crisis began with democratic reform in 1998. In fact, in an ironic twist, Indonesia's embrace of democracy, ushered into being by a call to protect the human rights of the most vulnerable and marginal segments of society, paved the way for both the decentralization and religious freedom that enabled the crisis to develop.

The "LGBT Crisis," as it became framed in the media, was unique not only in scale and vehemence but because it was the first time we have evidence in Indonesia of any sustained, systematic call for the persecution of people based on gender and sexuality. In such extraordinary times, extraordinary responses are needed. While activists and academics have often been reluctant to position Indonesia's gender and sexual past as a means of asserting contemporary legitimacy for LGBT subjects, we are now perhaps at a point where the risk is worth taking.

The chapter starts with an examination of the earliest evidence we have of gender and sexual plurality in Indonesia. Through origin narratives, indigenous manuscripts, the reports of early travelers, and colonial reports, as well as material from the reign of independent Indonesia's first two presidents, we can establish a picture of past gender and sexual plurality.

I focus primarily on Bugis South Sulawesi, as it is the area for which we have the best evidence. Some six million Bugis live in Sulawesi, Indonesia's third largest island. Most Bugis live in the southwestern province of South Sulawesi; however, because Bugis have long been travelers and entrepreneurs, their influence is felt across the island and indeed across the region. A central part of Bugis culture has been the subject position known as *bissu*, a term that can be roughly translated into English as "transgender shaman." Bissu played key roles in Bugis royal courts from at least the 1500s, and it was their combination of female and male elements that were considered to imbue bissu with particularly potent spiritual powers. In this chapter, I draw on accounts of bissu to show that what we now think of as transgenderism, and the mixing of feminine and masculine qualities, has a long history in South Sulawesi and indeed across the region in general.

I want to stress here that although the landscape of transgenderism in early Bugis society may have been among the more dramatically pluralized in the region, it was by no means unique. Elements of transgenderism, with its emphasis on the power that emerges from the combination in one human subject of masculine and feminine traits, has counterparts in other archipelagic sexualities. For instance, there are ritual traditions in Bali, Java, and elsewhere that emphasize the generative power of the interplay of masculine with feminine (B. Andaya 1994; Blackwood 2005a; Hefner 1990; Oetomo 1996).[1] It is therefore not possible to dismiss the Bugis case as exceptional or irrelevant to a broader understanding of sexual and gender plurality in Indonesia.

After an examination of aspects of the past, the chapter moves to analyze gender and sexual plurality from the end of authoritarian rule in 1998 through democratic transition until the "LGBT crisis" of 2016. The chapter concludes by noting that while there are dangers in drawing upon the past to make current claims of legitimacy, in such times of repression and harassment, Indonesia's queer past should be exploited for contemporary political and social advantage.

Gender and sexual plurality before reformation

A key source of information we have on past Bugis gender and sexual plurality comes in the form of origin narratives, which began to be composed in formulaic oral form between the ninth and fourteenth centuries (Caldwell 1988; Cummings 2002, 2003; Davies 2015a; Enre 1983: 31; Nyompa 1992; Pelras 1996: 56). Origin narratives are told as everyday forms of entertainment and education. During my early fieldwork in the late 1990s, when cell phones and Internet were scarce and electricity unreliable, elder members of my Bugis host family shared stories of how the world was created, telling of gods descending from the heavens and ascending from the oceans to populate earth. In these narratives, transgender bissu shamans accompanied the main protagonists, advising on such things as whom to form alliances with, reciting lineages, and officiating at royal weddings. It was told that bissu were invested with the ability to communicate between the gods and humans on account of combining female and male qualities. Origin narratives are in constant flux, however, with particular nuance developed to resonate with events occurring at the time of their telling. What the contemporary recitation of origin narratives suggests is that there is an ideal vision of bissu playing instrumental roles in past Bugis social life. To help verify the actual historical role of bissu, we can turn to indigenous documents.

Writing was in use in South Sulawesi by at least the fifteenth century (Noorduyn 1965), although some evidence suggests that the Bugis script had been developed as early as the tenth century (Hunter 1998). The oldest known surviving Bugis manuscript was obtained in 1784 and is written on lontar palm leaf (Koolhof 1999). Many thousand subsequent manuscripts exist, a large segment of which form part of the La Galigo cycle. The La Galigo cycle is the collective name given to a selection of scattered manuscripts written at various times, by various people, for various political purposes. If collected together, the La Galigo cycle, named after the main protagonist in the adventures recounted, I La Galigo, would comprise over 300,000 lines of text (Pelras 1996: 34). The cycle forms a kind of cultural encyclopedia telling about the origins of humanity and how to live an ethical and enjoyable life (Macknight 1993: 25–37; Pelras 1996: 32). For instance, the cycle gives advice on sustaining fulfilling marital sexual relations, encouraging husbands to focus on foreplay (Hadrawi 2016), and offering suggestions on how wives can maintain a dry vagina, considered to increase sexual pleasure for both partners (Idrus 2003: 181–223). The La Galigo cycle became especially well-known after American avant-garde director Robert Wilson developed the 2003 *I La Galigo* stage play, performing it in New York, London, Milan, Singapore, Jakarta, and Makassar (Davies 2015a).

The manuscripts of the La Galigo cycle recount bissu playing key roles in state affairs. Manuscripts analyzed by Leondard Andaya (2004: 54) recount battles occurring between the sixteenth and twentieth centuries where bissu helped Bugis secure key victories against the Dutch. Other manuscripts record battles where one hundred bissu marched toward the invading army, impervious to the onslaught of bullets (L. Andaya 2000). Combining female and male energies enabled bissu to communicate with the gods and thus seek protection during battle. La Galigo manuscripts consistently recount bissu occupying significant roles across generations of Bugis royal courts, advising rulers about whom they should marry, when to go to war, and with whom to trade.

Early Bugis documents are silent, however, on the position of other gendered categories, such as calabai' (transgender women) and calalai' (transgender men). This silence leaves open the possibility that calalai' and calabai' are more recent subject positions than bissu or that the positions of calalai' and calabai' were never documented. Hamonic (1977a) posits that in social life there was little difference between bissu, calabai', and calalai' (cited in L. Andaya 2000: 42), but we have no evidence to affirm this claim. As historical narratives focus on aspects of concern to the higher classes, it is not surprising that bissu, and not calalai' or calabai,' are mentioned, as bissu were so closely associated with royal courts. As La Galigo manuscripts are political texts, we can surmise that the elites who commissioned the manuscripts wanted to present bissu as playing strategic political and spiritual roles and that bissu were positioned as able to undertake such roles because they combined male and female elements in a way that differentiated them from women and men.

A further source of material we have on gender and sexual plurality in Indonesia's past comes from the reports of travelers and colonialists. Indeed, the earliest account we have of gender and sexual plurality among Bugis comes from the writings of Portuguese merchant and missionary Antonio de Paiva, who visited the region in the 1540s (see Jacobs 1966; cf. Pelras 1996: 35). In a letter written from South Sulawesi in 1544, de Paiva clearly expressed his repugnance for bissu, a repugnance based not only on his orthodox Christian background but also, as the second quote reveals, the influence bissu had over the king:

> Your Lordship will know that the priests of these kings are generally called bissus. They grow no hair on their beards, dress in a womanly fashion, and grow their hair long and braided; they imitate [women's] speech because they adopt all of the female gestures and inclinations. They marry and are received, according to the custom of the land, with other common men, and they live indoors, uniting carnally in their secret places with the men whom they have for husbands. This is public [knowledge], and not just around here, but on account of the same mouths which Our Lord has given to proclaim his praise. These priests, if they touch a woman in thought or deed, are boiled in tar because they hold that all their religion would be lost if they did it; and they have their teeth covered in gold. And as I say to Your Lordship, I went with this very sober thought, amazed [that] Our Lord would destroy those three cities of Sodom for the same sin and considering how a destruction had not come over such a wanton people as these in such a long time and what was there to do, for the whole land was encircled by evil.
>
> *(cited in Baker 2005: 69)*

De Paiva tried relentlessly to convert Bugis rulers to Christianity and expressed exasperation at his failure, blaming bissu for being key impediments:

> I was thus awaiting a reply from the king [about whether he would convert to Christianity], which was already late one day beyond the nine which he took and the reason was because of the tremendous debating over Christianity by this race of abominable priests [bissu] which I already mentioned, because of whom it took the greatest possible labour, and all the delay was for the reconciliation he [the king] wanted to have with them [bissu].
>
> *(cited in Baker 2005: 70–1)*

While de Paiva makes clear his draconian views, he also notes that bissu held significant power within Bugis royal courts. Indeed, such was the power of bissu that they helped sway Bugis rulers to adopt Islam rather than Christianity. When de Paiva first visited Sulawesi, the city of Makassar, on the southwest tip of the island, was fast becoming an economic powerhouse because of its strategic location and acceptance of diverse peoples, including Muslims from Mecca, Christians from Portugal, and Confucians from China (Aritonang and Steenbrink 2008). De Paiva was warmly welcomed by Bugis royalty both because Bugis wanted Portuguese goods, such as weapons, and because Bugis were actively courting conversion. Recognizing the tactical importance of being linked into a global religion, rulers in Makassar and elsewhere were weighing up the relative advantages of conversion to either Christianity or Islam. Given that pork was the only meat eaten by people in Makassar, as de Paiva pointed out, Christianity had a great deal of appeal. However, the lack of Portuguese follow-through led bissu and others to successfully advise conversion to Islam. We might then say that Islam owes its acceptance in South Sulawesi to people currently being persecuted by the very religion they welcomed.

While de Paiva's reports are the earliest evidence we have recounting the position of bissu, subsequent travelers to the region commented on gender and sexual plurality. For instance, three hundred years after de Paiva, Englishman James Brooke (1848: 82–3) alluded to bissu, calalai' (etymologically "false men"), and calabai' (etymologically "false women"):

> The strangest custom I have observed is, that some men dress like women, and some women like men; not occasionally, but all their lives, devoting themselves to the occupations and pursuits of their adopted sex. In the case of the males, it seems that the parents of a boy, upon perceiving in him certain effeminacies of habit and appearance, are induced thereby to present him to one of the rajahs, by whom he is received. These youths often acquire much influence over their masters.

Subsequent Western travelers, such as B. F. Matthes (1872) and H. T. Chabot (1950), also commented on the role and position of bissu. For instance, Chabot refers to the examination of bissu conducted by J. A. Slot (1935):

> [Slot] examined a number of these bissu for their physical characteristics and reported that their sexual organs were completely normal; there was no question of hermaphroditism. A number of secondary sex characteristics can be called feminine. Among these he [Slot] reports a hyper-extendibility of the elbow, little muscular development, and broad hips.
>
> *(cited in Chabot 1950: 192)*

Clearly a product of his time, Chabot included Slot's discussion of bissu in a section entitled "Phenomena of Maladjustment: Homosexuality" (Chabot 1950: 187–94).

What we learn from sources such as those cited here is that bissu have been included in Bugis society since at least the 1500s, and probably earlier, and that bissu are positioned in these texts as being held in high esteem by Bugis, who see bissu occupying an intermediate position between women and men. When President Joko Widodo claims that homosexuality and transgenderism are not part of Indonesia's tradition or that LGBT are not compatible with Islam, he is clearly ignoring this rich past.

The proclamation of Indonesia's independence in 1945 had little direct impact on gender and sexual pluralism in the archipelago. Unlike former British colonies, such as Singapore and Malaysia, Dutch and Japanese occupation left homosexuality and transgenderism untouched by law. There is little evidence then of what life was like for Indonesians who publicly deviated from heteronormativity during Indonesia's early independence. The little evidence we have speaks largely of instances of intolerance and the declining position of subjects such as bissu. For instance, in interviews I conducted with bissu in the late 1990s and 2000s, bissu often reminisced about a time prior to 1957 when bissu were still formally attached to Bugis royal courts and granted patronage and social legitimacy. Prior to 1957, bissu noted that they were allocated land by the royal courts that they could farm, keeping the produce. But as the power of the royal courts declined, so too did the position of bissu. Bissu Mariani also told me that during the 1950s and 1960s, s/he and other bissu went into hiding at various points because of a number of events, including the communist purges of the 1950s, militant Islamic violence, and the Sulawesi Rebellion (see also Boellstorff 2005; Davies 2011; Peletz 2006: 669).

By the late 1970s and early 1980s, gender and sexual plurality in Indonesia were increasingly influenced by the lesbian and gay rights movement in the West. In addition, the HIV/AIDS epidemic meant that increasing funding was being funneled into sexual health in Indonesia, and LGBT Indonesians accessed this funding to advocate for both health and identity politics. While lesbian and transgender rights were still rather mute, gay liberation was becoming more prominent through organizations such as Lambda Indonesia and later GAYa NUSANTARA, both spearheaded by prominent gay rights activist Dede Oetomo (b. 1953).

Despite President Sukarno's and subsequently President Soeharto's authoritarian rule, gender and sexual pluralism were not specific targets of either regime. While discrimination and harassment haunted the lives of LGBT Indonesians between 1945 and 1998, there was no sustained systematic state or religious persecution. Soeharto's forced resignation, due in part to his appalling human rights record, created hope that LGBT Indonesians would go from a largely overlooked segment of society to one accorded full human rights.

Reformation and the LGBT crisis

President Soeharto's downfall, due to widespread disaffection with corruption, collusion, and nepotism, created hope that gender and sexual pluralism would be acknowledged and LGBT Indonesians would be welcomed as legitimate citizens. Indeed, in 1999, I listened to the mayor of Sengkang give a speech recognizing *waria* (transgender women) as a vital part of Bugis society. The mayor ended his speech stating "Long Live Waria." There is a wealth of ethnographic and media studies on gender and sexual plurality from this period, with much of it tracing a historical dimension (Blackwood 2010; Boellstorff 2005; Davies 2011; Murtagh 2013; Wieringa 1999).

A host of democratic reforms took place in the early years of Indonesia's reformation. Key among these reforms was decentralization, which gave increasing power to local governments to enact laws. While it was hoped that decentralization would enable local governments to operate in ways sensitive to local communities, in reality, many local governments ratified homophobic and transphobic laws. In 2002, South Sumatra implemented the Eradication of Immoral Behavior Act, classifying anal sex between men as immoral and illegal. In 2004, Palembang issued the City Ordinance on the Eradication of Prostitution; it conflated homosexuality with prostitution (Allen 2007). In 2015, Aceh implemented the Qanun Jinayat, an Islamic Criminal Code Bylaw used to penalize homosexuality (Simanjuntak 2016). Austere laws were also implemented at a national level. In 2008, ratification of the Anti-Pornography Law prohibited depiction, production, and distribution of pornography. While the law did not criminalize LGBT Indonesians, there was the possibility that same-sex sexuality would be considered pornographic.

Another significant reform that took place during Indonesia's reformation was the loosening of state repression over religion. While President Soeharto had sought to initially repress and then develop an Islam that acquiesced to his authoritarian rule (Hefner 2000), post-1998 reform provided space for Islamist politics to flourish (Robinson 2015). While religious freedom was welcomed, unrestrained Islamist discourse grew, preaching hatred of Indonesia's LGBT community. Militant religious groups, such as the Islamic Defenders Front (Front Pembela Islam, FPI), openly attacked LGBT activities (Davies 2015b) and pressured the government to regulate non-normative genders and sexualities (Marching 2010).

Homophobia is not new to Indonesia. In 2013, the Pew Research Center reported that 93% of Indonesians thought homosexuality should not be accepted – a higher percentage than any other Asia-Pacific country surveyed and worryingly close to Nigeria's score of 98% (Pew Research Center 2013). While we should not take this figure as reliable – only 1000 people were surveyed and the framing of the question was loaded toward getting a homophobic response – it certainly suggested that Indonesia was not an LGBT paradise. Nevertheless, while there was increasing persecution from segments of society against LGBT, namely from religious extremists (Liang 2010), for almost the first two decades of Indonesia's Reformation, anti-LGBT violence remained limited to isolated events.

Gender and sexual plurality in Indonesia were dramatically challenged, however, in the first months of 2016. Religious leaders, politicians, psychiatrists, and the general public weighed in on the debate, condemning LGBT Indonesians as spreading disease, threatening state security, and having no place in Indonesia. A characteristic feature of the vitriol was that it was not aimed at individual LGBT people but rather at LGBT as a visible collective group framed as attempting to stake a claim as national subjects (Boellstorff 2016). Indeed, after Minister Nasir's call to ban support for LGBT organizations at university, he clarified that "We are not against LGBTs but the activity . . . [T]he problem is when they are showing romance, kissing, and making love (in public)" (Rappler 2016b). Speaker of the People's Consultative Assembly Zulkifli Hasan similarly commented, "As a movement, the existence of LGBT must be opposed. We must limit its room to move. However, as individual people, they must be protected like any other citizen" (Nurbianto 2016). Gender and sexual plurality would only continue to be tolerated, it seemed, as long as LGBT remained collectively invisible (Davies 2016a).

While there are examples of LGBT Indonesians being visible and politically active – transwoman Dorce Gamalama has appeared alongside President Joko Widodo at public events (Karibo 2015) – tolerance and at times acceptance have been accorded to LGBT Indonesians largely through the community keeping a low profile by marrying heterosexually, ostensibly reinforcing heteronormativity and undertaking strategic political engagement (Yulius 2016). The events of 2016 thus marked a turning point where gender and sexual pluralism became seen as a threat because society might have to tolerate LGBT collectively as recognized citizens.

In the months following Nasir's statement, various incendiary statements and actions came to light. The conservative Islamic newspaper, *Republika*, ran the headline "LGBT poses serious threat to nation" (Mariani and Sampeliling 2016). The largest Muslim organization, Nahdlatul Ulama, declared non-heterosexual orientation incompatible with human nature and stated that LGBT activities must be criminalized (Yosephine 2016). The secretary general of the People's Conscience Party claimed, "Being LGBT is an infectious and dangerous disease. LGBT must be banned, like we banned communism and drug trafficking" (Curve 2016). Former Communications Minister Tifatul Sembiring exhorted his one million Twitter followers to kill any gay people they met (Rappler 2016a).

LGBT Indonesians were positioned as a threat to state sovereignty. Mahfudz Siddiq, the person in charge of defense, foreign affairs, communications, information, and intelligence, claimed that "LGBT issues can damage national security, identity, culture and the faith of Indonesians" (Goodenough 2016). Defense Minister Ryamizard Ryacudu described LGBT rights as an effort by Western nations to undermine Indonesia's sovereignty. He went further to declare the LGBT movement a "proxy war" brainwashing Indonesians (Tempo 2016). Indonesia's Vice President Jusuf Kalla rejected UN funding earmarked to support ending stigma, discrimination, and violence toward LGBT people.

The Indonesian Psychiatric Association declared, "We need to promote, prevent, cure and rehabilitate LGBT people" (BBC 2016). Psychiatrist Suzy Yusna Dewi noted, "We really do care about them. What we are worried about is, if left untreated, such sexual tendencies could become a commonly accepted condition in society" (Yosephine 2016). Following the World Health Organization's 1990 lead, Indonesia declassified homosexuality as a psychiatric disorder in 1993, although gender identity disorder remained. The association's move to now classify homosexuality as a treatable disorder drew on Indonesia's Law No. 18/2014 on Mental Health and the Mental Disorder Diagnostic Guidelines. While neither the law nor the guidelines mention LGBT, such omission did not stop the association from using it as support for framing homosexuals and bisexuals as "people with psychiatric problems" and transgender people as having "mental disorders" (Davies 2016b).

Radio and television stations were barred in February 2016 from airing programs portraying LGBT behavior as "normal" (Sundaryani 2016a). Lawmakers claimed a ban would protect children and teenagers "susceptible to duplicating deviant LGBT behaviors" (Tang 2016). Politicians wanted to mandate "rehabilitation for every person who has LGBT characteristics" (Sundaryani 2016b) and prohibit online content viewed as promoting homosexuality (Goodenough 2016). The Social Affairs Minister was (mis)reported as advocating bathing LGBT in boiling water infused with spices to cure homosexuality – she actually stated this would only work for drug addicts. The Minister rather promoted spiritual training as a cure for homosexuality (Coconuts Jakarta 2016). The world's first Islamic school for transwomen was forced to close (Muryanto 2016b). While the school covertly continued advocacy work, pressure from large Muslim organizations and other groups made this work exceedingly difficult (pers. comm. Dédé Oetomo and Bob Hefner, November 2, 2016). Anti-LGBT protests took place unhindered (BBC 2016), while police suppressed pro-LGBT demonstrations (Muryanto 2016a).

The fear and anxiety caused by the aforementioned events, which mostly occurred between January and March 2016, forced the LGBT community into hiding. LGBT Indonesians changed their mobile phone numbers, moved out of their boardinghouses to undisclosed safe houses (Tang 2016), deleted social media postings, and un-friended people for fear of being identified and blackmailed. Police checked identity cards at LGBT haunts, detaining those without proper ID. Dédé Oetomo, who founded GAYa NUSANTARA almost two decades previously, told employees to stay away from the office for fear of harassment. Forced reclusion meant people needing sexual health care and HIV treatment were afraid to access services.

The events of 2016 severely compromised gender and sexual plurality in Indonesia. Extending from fear that LGBT would stake a collective claim on Indonesia, the LGBT community was framed as a subversive movement (*gerakan*) to draw on negative connotations with the outlawed communist movement (Paramaditha 2016). Strangely, though, the crisis was not precipitated by actual LGBT demands for the right to marry or to adopt children or for discrimination to be banned. Indeed, the timing of the crisis led one commentator to note that the furor came about just as revisions were made to anti-corruption law (Croft-Cusworth 2016).

In analyzing further the causes of the LGBT crisis, the tensions surrounding perceptions of moral decay stand out. Reformation was synonymous for some with sexual promiscuity (Pausacker 2008; Smith-Hefner 2009), and in response, people wanted gender and sexual pluralism replaced with heteronormativity. An increasingly conservative religiosity in much of Indonesia provided ammunition and support for anti-LGBT rhetoric. While religious freedom is a democratic good, left unchecked, it can be used to justify violence and persecution. Antagonistic relations between Indonesia and the West fueled further anti-LGBT sentiment with LGBT being framed as a Western import threatening Indonesia's sovereignty, security, and traditional culture. Indonesia's embrace of social media fostered swift and widespread public engagement with the debate and Twitter hashtags, such as #TolakLGBT (reject LGBT), and the banning of LGBT emojis (The *Guardian* 2016) provoked extraordinary fervor. All of this torment grew on the back of the enduring repercussions of the 1997 financial crisis, which caused severe lasting economic depression in Indonesia (Bunnell and Miller 2011).

While 2016 gave rise to concern about the future of gender and sexual plurality in Indonesia, responses to the crisis also gave hope. Survey data on Indonesian Muslims indicate that the great majority of people reject sexual pluralism; however, it appears only a minority of people want such diversity criminalized. Islam can accept and accommodate sexual and gender plurality (cf. Sheridan 2016). Ministers who railed against the LGBT community also exhorted people to condemn violence and accept LGBT as part of Indonesia (Jong, Dipa, and Salim 2016). Moreover, the crisis made visible LGBT in a way not previously possible. What emerged was a community of LGBT and their advocates, both in Indonesia and across the world, committed to supporting LGBT Indonesians (Widianto 2016).

Conclusion

It is unsettling that Indonesia's "LGBT crisis" came at a time when slow but steady progress was taking place in much of the world in respect to LGBT inclusion. By 2016, 24 countries permitted same-sex marriage and 34, including Thailand, had introduced anti-discrimination laws. Even conservative nations, such as Singapore, were officially tolerating LGBT talent in the name of economic progress (Chua 2014).

Indonesia's "LGBT crisis" was the culmination of various converging factors, including the lasting effects of the 1997 financial collapse, increasing religious conservativism, decentralization, the perception of growing moral laxity, and emerging LGBT rights internationally. Anti-LGBT rhetoric espoused by politicians, religious figures, and members of the general public repeatedly asserted that LGBT were not part of Indonesian culture or tradition and that Islam (indeed religion in general) does not accept LGBT.

One way to counter these claims is drawing on what Lee (2016) calls ingenious agency to acknowledge and assert Indonesia's diverse gender and sexual past. Ingenious agency requires that we move from a fight of purity to a fight of contamination, such that LGBT rights are pushed forward by exploiting neoliberal discourse, religious conservatism, heteronormativity, and history. By drawing on the past, despite the risks of doing so, we can promote the idea that people in South Sulawesi might have converted to Christianity, rather than Islam, had it not been for the efforts of bissu – a subject position Islamists see as having no place in Islam or Indonesia. It would seem that Indonesia and Islam are indeed indebted to the country's LGBT subjects.

Paying attention to the past enables understanding of gender and sexual legacies, showing how "attendant identities and practices produce new kinds of subjects in the present moment" (Grewal and Kaplan 2001: 667). It is thus important to heed calls made by Towle and Morgan (2002) and Peletz (2006) to give attention to historical contexts in which subjects are produced and modified. As Blackwood (2005a: 871) shows, while state and Islamic discourses provide a dominant frame of reference and worldview for gender and sexual plurality in today's Indonesia, "faint echoes of older gender mythologies are also perceptible." We can push the LGBT movement forward by making these echoes reverberate. Indeed, prominent Indonesian gay rights activist, Dédé Oetomo (2006: 330), recollects how he used the work of van der Kroef (1956) to frame his own legitimate arguments for homosexuality.

There are at least four key dangers, however, in asserting contemporary legitimacy for LGBT subjects based on historical precedent. First, deploying the past for current purposes encourages romanticization of the past. We see such romanticization in accounts comparing the supposed current near extinction of transgender bissu shamans with a past where bissu commanded great power (Grauer 2004; Holt 1939; Lathief 2003). However, a closer look at the sources provides a more complex picture with bissu indeed formerly commanding great power but also being harshly punished for transgressions. Moreover, while bissu numbers may be decreasing at present, bissu are reinventing ways to actively participate in a globalized world.

A second risk in deploying the past is that claiming contemporary space for gender and sexual plurality through recourse to history may suggest that LGBT subjects are unaffected by neoliberal modernity. We must continually affirm then that no gender or sexual subject transcends time and place (Blackwood 2005b). Indeed bissu participation in an international stage play reveals that their current subjectivity is keenly reconfigured in a contemporary world.

A third risk in deploying the past to serve current concerns is that we necessarily view the past with contemporary eyes. While we know from early Bugis documents that bissu were considered to occupy an intermediate position between women and men, we do not know whether the authors of these documents considered bissu as constituting an alternative gender. Moreover, we do not know what bissu themselves or the general population thought about bissu gender. Indeed, it is only in the last few decades that academic language has developed to even disarticulate identity, gender, and sexuality.

A fourth risk in using the past to legitimize contemporary claims is that subject positions that cannot claim a historical legacy may be disenfranchised. As Boellstorff (2005: 36) poignantly notes, "[I]t can appear that without an unbroken historical timeline one must view gay and lesbian [Indonesians] as derivative, converging on a single global conception of homosexuality." Using historical precedent to justify contemporary legitimacy thus potentially marginalizes LGBT Indonesians.

While recognizing potential hazards of using the past, the events of 2016 brought persecution of LGBT Indonesians to such heights that more weapons are needed and today are being constructed to fight for gender justice. LGBT Indonesians use forms of ingenious agency, and in this chapter, I hope to have developed an account of past gender and sexual plurality that strengthens the argument that LGBT are indeed part of Indonesian culture. Drawing on Indonesia's historical past means that when President Joko Widodo and others claim that LGBT individuals and organizations have no place in Indonesia, LGBT can respectfully retort, but we do Pak President, we do.

Note

1 Peletz and the academics who replied to his article give a good overview of gender and sexual pluralism in Southeast Asia since early modern times (Blackwood 2006; Boellstorff 2006a, 2006b; Geertz 2006; Johnson 2006; Loos 2006; Manalansan 2006; Oetomo 2006; Peletz 2006, 2009; Sinnott 2006; Thompson 2006).

References cited

Allen, Pam. 2007. "Challenging Diversity?: Indonesian's Anti-Pornography Bill," *Asian Studies Review*, 31 (June): 101–15.

Andaya, Barbara Watson. 1994. "The Changing Religious Role of Women in Pre-Modern South East Asia," *South East Asia Research* 2(2): 99–116.

Andaya, Leonard. 2000. "The Bissu: Study of a Third Gender in Indonesia," in Barbara Watson Andaya, ed., *Other Pasts: Women, Gender, and History in Early Modern Southeast Asia* (Honolulu: Center for Southeast Asian Studies, University of Hawai'i), pp. 27–46.

———. 2004. "Nature of War and Peace Among the Bugis-Makassar People," *South East Asia Research* 12(1): 53–80.

Aritonang, Jan Sihar, and Karel Adriaan Steenbrink, eds. 2008. *A History of Christianity in Indonesia* (London: Brill).

Baker, Brett. 2005. "South Sulawesi in 1544: A Portuguese Letter," *Review of Indonesian and Malaysian Affairs* 39(1): 61–85.

BBC. 2016. "The Sudden Intensity of Indonesia's Anti-Gay Onslaught," *BBC News*, 10 August. www.bbc.com/news/world-asia-35657114

Blackwood, Evelyn. 2005a. "Gender Transgression in Colonial and Postcolonial Indonesia," *The Journal of Asian Studies* 64(4): 849–79.

———. 2005b. "Transnational Sexualities in One Place: Indonesian Readings," *Gender and Society* 19(2): 221–42.

———. 2006. "Comments to Peletz's Article 'Transgenderism and Gender Pluralism in Southeast Asia Since Early Modern Times'," *Current Anthropology* 47(2): 325–6.

———. 2010. *Falling into the Lesbi World: Desire and Difference in Indonesia* (Honolulu: University of Hawai'i Press).

Boellstorff, Tom. 2005. *The Gay Archipelago: Sexuality and Nation in Indonesia* (Princeton: Princeton University Press).

———. 2006a. "Comments to Peletz's Article 'Transgenderism and Gender Pluralism in Southeast Asia Since Early Modern Times'," *Current Anthropology* 47(2): 326–7.

———. 2006b. "Domesticating Islam: Sexuality, Gender, and the Limits of Pluralism," *Law & Social Inquiry* 31(4): 1035–53.

———. 2016. "Against State Straightism: Five Principles for Including LGBT Indonesians," *E-International Relations*, www.e-ir.info/2016/03/21/against-state-straightism-five-principles-for-including-lgbt-indonesians/

Brooke, James. 1848. *Narratives of Events in Borneo and Celebes Down to the Occupation of Labuan, From the Journals of James Brooke, Esq* (Vol. 1). London: John Murray.

Bunnell, T., and Michelle Ann Miller. 2011. "Jakarta in Post-Suharto Indonesia: Decentralisation, Neoliberalism and Global City Aspiration," *Space and Polity* 15(1): 35–48.

Caldwell, Ian. 1988. "South Sulawesi AD 1300–1600: Ten Bugis Texts." (Ph.D. Canberra: Australian National University).

Chabot, Hendrik Theodorus. 1950. *Kinship, Status, and Gender in South Celebes*. Vol. 1996 (Leiden, Netherlands: Koninklijk Instituut voor de Taal-, Land- en Volkenkunde (KITLV) Press).

Chua, Lynette J. 2014. *Mobilizing Gay Singapore: Rights and Resistance in an Authoritarian State* (Singapore: National University of Singapore Press).

Coconuts Jakarta. 2016. "Social Affairs Minister: We Wouldn't Treat LGBT With 'boiling' Water and Spices, Just Drug Users." http://jakarta.coconuts.co/2016/03/14/social-affairs-minister-we-wouldnt-treat-lgbt-boiling-water-and-spices-just-drug-users (Accessed 3 July 2016).

Croft-Cusworth, Catriona. 2016. "This Week in Jakarta: Terror, Corruption and Moral Panic." *Lowy Institute for International Policy* [Online]. www.realclearworld.com/articles/2016/02/26/terror_corruption_and_moral_panic_in_jakarta_111726.html (Accessed 20 March 2016).

Cummings, William. 2002. *Making Blood White: Historical Transformations in Early Modern Makassar* (Honolulu: The University of Hawai'i Press).

———. 2003. "Rethinking the Imbrication of Orality and Literacy: Historical Discourse in Early Modern Makassar," *The Journal of Asian Studies* 62(2): 531–51.

Curve. 2016. "Indonesia Sees Rising Discrimination Against LGBT Community." www.curvemag.com/News/Indonesia-Sees-Rising-Discrimination-Against-LGBT-Community-1008/.

Davies, Sharyn Graham. 2011. *Gender Diversity in Indonesia: Sexuality, Islam, and Queer Selves* (London: RoutledgeCurzon).

———. 2015a. "Performing Selves: The Trope of Authenticity and Robert Wilson's Stage Production of *I La Galigo*," *Journal of Southeast Asian Studies* 46(3): 417–43.

———. 2015b. "Sexual Surveillance," in Linda Rae Bennett and Sharyn Graham Davies, eds., *Sex and Sexualities in Contemporary Indonesia: Sexual Politics, Health, Diversity and Representations* (London: Routledge), pp. 10–31.

———. 2016a. "Indonesia's Anti-LGBT Panic," *East Asia Forum* 8(2): 8–11.

———. 2016b. "Indonesian 'Tolerance' Under Strain as Anti-LGBT Furore Grows." *Asian Currents*, March. http://asaa.asn.au/indonesian-tolerance-under-strain-as-anti-lgbt-furore-grows/.

Enre, Fachruddin Ambo. 1983. *Ritumpanna Wélenrénngé: Telaah Filologis Sebuah Episoda Sastra Bugis Klasik Galigo (Ritumpanna Wélenrénngé: Philological Study of an episode of Classical Bugis Literature of Galigo)*. Jakarta: Universitas Indonesia.

Geertz, Clifford. 2006. "Comments to Peletz's Article 'Transgenderism and Gender Pluralism in Southeast Asia Since Early Modern Times'," *Current Anthropology* 47(2): 327–8.

Goodenough, Patrick. 2016. "World's Biggest Islamic Country Pushes Back Against LGBT Promotion." *CNSNews* [Online]. www.cnsnews.com/news/article/patrick-goodenough/worlds-biggest-islamic-country-pushes-back-against-lgbt-promotion (Accessed 10 May 2016).

Grauer, Rhoda. 2004. *The Last Bissu: Sacred Transvestites of Sureq Galigo*. Indonesia

Grewal, Inderpal and Caren Kaplan. 2001. "Global Identities: Theorizing Transnational Studies of Sexuality," *GLQ: A Journal of Gay and Lesbian Studies* 7(4): 663–79.

The Guardian. 2016. "Indonesia Bans Gay Emoji and Stickers From Messaging Apps," *The Guardian*, 12 February. www.theguardian.com/world/2016/feb/12/indonesia-bans-gay-emoji-and-stickers-from-messaging-apps

Hadrawi, Muhlis. 2016. "Narratives of Sexuality in Bugis and Makassar Manuscripts," *International Journal of Asia Pacific Studies* 12(1): 187–206.

Hamonic, Gilbert. 1977a. "Les 'fausses-femmes' du pays Bugis (Celebes-sud)," *Objects et Mondes* 17: 39–46.

Hefner, Robert. 1990. *Hindu Javanese: Tengger Tradition and Islam* (Princeton: Princeton University Press).

———. 2000. *Civil Islam: Muslims and Democratization in Indonesia* (Princeton: Princeton University Press).

Holt, Claire. 1939. *Dance Quest in Celebes* (Paris: Les Archives Internationales de la Dance).

Hunter, T. H. 1998. "Inscriptions," in John H. McGlynn, ed., *Language and Literature: Indonesian Heritage* (Vol. 10) (Jakarta: Editions Didier Miller), pp. 12–13.

Idrus, Nurul Ilmi. 2003. "'To Take Each Other': Bugis Practices of Gender, Sexuality and Marriage (Ph.D. Canberra: Australian National University).

Jacobs, Hubert. 1966. "The First (Locally) Demonstrable Christianity in Celebes, 1544," *Studia, Rome* 17 (April): 251–305.

Johnson, Mark. 2006. "Comments to Peletz's Article 'Transgenderism and Gender Pluralism in Southeast Asia Since Early Modern Times,'" *Current Anthropology* 47(2): 328.

Jong, Hans Nicholas, Arya Dipa, and Tama Salim. 2016. "Luhut Defends LGBT Groups," *The Jakarta Post*, 13 February. www.thejakartapost.com/news/2016/02/13/luhut-defends-lgbt-groups.html.

Karibo, Anto. 2015. "Dorce Gamalama Bangga Makan Malam Bersama Presiden Jokowi." *Vidio* [Online]. www.bintang.com/celeb/read/2392531/dorce-gamalama-bangga-makan-malam-bersama-presiden-jokowi (Accessed 10 July 2016).

Kine, Phelim. 2016. "Indonesia President Jokowi Defends LGBT Rights." *Dispatches* [Online]. www.hrw.org/news/2016/10/20/indonesia-president-jokowi-defends-lgbt-rights.

Koolhof, Sirtjo. 1999. "The 'La Galigo': A Bugis Encyclopaedia and Its Growth," *Bijdragen, Tot de Taal-, Land- en Volkenkunde* 155(3): 362–87.

Lathief, Halilintar. 2003. "Bissu: Para Imam yang Menhibur (Bissu: The Entertaining Priests)," in Nurhayati Rahman, Anil Hukma, and Idwar Anwar (eds.), *La Galigo: Menelusuri Jejak Warisan Sastra Dunia (La Galigo: Following the Footprint of a World Literature Legacy)* (Makassar, Indonesia: Cetakan Pertama), pp. 517–33.

Lee, Charles T. 2016. *Ingenious Citizenship: Recrafting Democracy for Social Change* (Durham: Duke University Press).

Liang, Jamison. 2010. "Homophobia on the Rise." *Inside Indonesia* [Online]. www.insideindonesia.org/homophobia-on-the-rise.

Loos, Tamara. 2006. "Comments to Peletz's Article "Transgenderism and Gender Pluralism in Southeast Asia Since Early Modern Times'," *Current Anthropology* 47(2): 329.

Macknight, Charles Campbell. 1993. *The Early History of South Sulawesi: Some Recent Advances* (Melbourne: Monash University).

Manalansan, Martin F. 2006. "Comments to Peletz's Article "Transgenderism and Gender Pluralism in Southeast Asia Since Early Modern Times'," *Current Anthropology* 47(2): 329–30.

Marching, Soe Tjen. 2010. "ILGA dan Anak Itik (ILGA and Duck)," *Bhinneka Magazine*, 6.

Mariani, Evi, and Aldrin Rocky Sampeliling. 2016. "LGBT Group Faces State Persecution," *The Jakarta Post*, 5 January. www.thejakartapost.com/news/2016/01/25/lgbt-group-faces-state-persecution.html

Matthes, B. F. 1872. "Over de Bissoe's of Heidensche Priesters en Priesteressen der Boeginezen," *Verhandelingen der Koninklijke Akademie can Wetenschappen, Afdeeling Letterkunde* 17: 1–50.

Murtagh, Ben. 2013. *Genders and Sexualities in Indonesian Cinema: Constructing Gay, Lesbi and Waria Identities on Screen* (London: Routledge).

Muryanto, Bambang. 2016a. "Police Ban Rally Held by LGBT Supporters," *The Jakarta Post*, 24 February. www.thejakartapost.com/news/2016/02/24/police-ban-rally-held-lgbt-supporters.html

———. 2016b. "Yogyakarta Transgender Islamic Boarding School Shut Down," *The Jakarta Post*, 26 February. www.thejakartapost.com/news/2016/02/26/yogyakarta-transgender-islamic-boarding-school-shut-down.html

Noorduyn, J. 1965. "Origins of South Celebes Historical Writing," in Soedjatmoko, ed., *An Introduction to Indonesian Historiography* (Ithaca: Cornell University Press), pp. 137–55.

Nurbianto, Bambang. 2016. "More Political Leaders Speak Out Against LGBT," *The Jakarta Post*, 21 March. www.thejakartapost.com/news/2016/03/04/more-political-leaders-speak-out-against-lgbt.html

Nyompa, Johan. 1992. *Mula Tau: Satu Studi Tentang Mitologi Orang Bugis (Beginning of Knowledge/Humanity: A Study of Bugis Mythology)*. Ujung Pandang: Fakultas Ilmu Sosial dan Ilmu Politik, Universitas Hasanuddin.

Oetomo, Dede. 1996. "Gender and Sexual Orientation in Indonesia," in Laurie Sears, ed., *Fantasizing the Feminine in Indonesia* (Durham: Duke University Press), pp. 259–69.

———. 2006. "Comments to Peletz's Article Transgenderism and Gender Pluralism in Southeast Asia Since Early Modern Times," *Current Anthropology* 47(2): 330–1.

Paramaditha, Intan. 2016. "The LGBT Debate and the Fear of 'gerakan'," *The Jakarta Post*, 27 February. www.thejakartapost.com/news/2016/02/27/the-lgbt-debate-and-fear-gerakan.html

Pausacker, Helen. 2008. "Hot Debates." *Inside Indonesia* [Online]. www.insideindonesia.org/hot-debates.

Peletz, Michael G. 2006. "Transgenderism and Gender Pluralism in Southeast Asia Since Early Modern Times," *Current Anthropology* 47(2): 309–40.

———. 2009. *Gender Pluralism: Southeast Asia Since Early Modern Times* (New York: Routledge).

Pelras, Christian. 1996. *The Bugis* (Oxford: Blackwell Publishers).

Pew Research Centre. 2013. "The Global Divide on Homosexuality." www.pewglobal.org/2013/06/04/the-global-divide-on-homosexuality/ (Accessed 20 August 2016).

Rappler. 2016a. "Indonesian Officials on LGBT: 'Kill them', Contagious." *Rappler* [Online]. www.rappler.com/world/regions/asia-pacific/indonesia/123865-lgbt-government-comments-officials (Accessed 20 July 2016).

———. 2016b. "Minister: I'm Not Against LGBT, Just Their Public Displays of Affection." *Rappler* [Online]. www.rappler.com/world/regions/asia-pacific/indonesia/bahasa/englishedition/120353-lgbt-ban-campus-minister-nasir (Accessed 20 October 2016).

Robinson, Kathryn. 2015. "Masculinity, Sexuality, and Islam: The Gender Politics of Regime Change in Indonesia," in L. R. Bennett and S. G. Davies (eds.), *Sex and Sexualities in Contemporary Indonesia* (London: Routledge), pp. 51–68.

Sheridan, Greg. 2016. "Indonesian Islam Is a Good-News Story for Peace," *The Australian* 10 March. www.theaustralian.com.au/opinion/columnists/greg-sheridan/indonesian-islam-is-a-goodnews-story-for-peace/news-story/b9a6f8da391868f6b89e254e9752041c

Simanjuntak, Hotli. 2016. "'Qanun Jinayat' Becomes Official for All People in Aceh." *The Jakarta Post*, 23 October. www.thejakartapost.com/news/2015/10/23/qanun-jinayat-becomes-official-all-people-aceh.html

Sinnott, Megan. 2006. "Comments to Peletz's Article 'Transgenderism and Gender Pluralism in Southeast Asia Since Early Modern Times'," *Cultural Anthropology* 47(2): 331–2.

Slot, J. A. 1935. "Koro in Zuid-Celebes," *Geneeskundig Tijdschrift voor Nederlandsch Indie* 75: 811–20.

Smith-Hefner, Nancy J. 2009. "'Hypersexed' Youth and the New Muslim Sexology in Java, Indonesia," *RIMA: Review of Indonesian and Malaysian Affairs* 43(1): 209–44.

Sundaryani, Fedina S. 2016a. "Commission Wants TV, Radio Free of LGBT," *The Jakarta Post*, 14 February. www.thejakartapost.com/news/2016/02/14/commission-wants-tv-radio-free-lgbt.html

———. 2016b. "NU Joins Anti-LGBT Bandwagon With Edict," *The Jakarta Post*. www.thejakartapost.com/news/2016/02/27/nu-joins-anti-lgbt-bandwagon-with-edict.html

Tang, Alisa. 2016. "Under Attack, Indonesian LGBT Groups Set Up Safehouses, Live in Fear." *Yahoo! News* [Online]. http://news.yahoo.com/under-attack-indonesian-lgbt-groups-set-safehouses-live-010538655.html (Accessed 24 June 2016).

Tempo. 2016. "Minister: LGBT Movement More Dangerous Than Nuclear Warfare," *Tempo.Co*, 23 February. http://en.tempo.co/read/news/2016/02/23/055747534/Minister-LGBT-Movement-More-Dangerous-than-Nuclear-Warfare.

Thompson, Eric C. 2006. "Comments to Peletz's Article 'Transgenderism and Gender Pluralism in Southeast Asia Since Early Modern Times'," *Current Anthropology* 47(2): 332–3.

Towle, Evan B. and Lynn M. Morgan. 2002. "Romancing the Transgender Native: Rethinking the Use of the 'Third Gender' Concept," *GLQ: A Journal of Lesbian and Gay Studies* 8(4): 469–97.

van der Kroef, J. 1956. "Transvestism and the Religious Hermaphrodite," in J. van der Kroef, ed., *Indonesia in the Modern World* (Vol. 2) (Bandung: Masa Baru), pp. 182–95.

Widianto, Stanley. 2016. "Bound by Culture and Religion, Indonesia Is Paranoid About LGBT Rights, But We Won't Be Silenced," *The Guardian*, 26 February. www.theguardian.com/commentisfree/2016/feb/26/bound-by-culture-and-religion-indonesia-is-paranoid-about-lgbt-rights-but-we-wont-be-silenced

Wieringa, Saskia. 1999. "Desiring Bodies or Defiant Cultures: Butch-Femme Lesbians in Jakarta and Lima," in Evelyn Blackwood and Saskia Wieringa, eds., *Female Desires: Same-Sex Relations and the Transgender Practices Across Cultures* (New York: Columbia University Press), pp. 206–31.

Yosephine, Liza. 2016. "Indonesian Psychiatrists Label LGBT as Mental Disorders," *The Jakarta Post*, 24 February. www.thejakartapost.com/news/2016/02/24/indonesian-psychiatrists-label-lgbt-mental-disorders.html#sthash.kzahehOM.dpuf

Yulius, Hendri. 2016. "What Does the Indonesian LGBT Movement Want? *The Jakarta Post*," 19 February. www.thejakartapost.com/news/2016/02/19/what-does-indonesian-lgbt-movement-want.html.

27

COURTSHIP AND MARRIAGE IN INDONESIA'S NEW MUSLIM MIDDLE CLASS

Nancy J. Smith-Hefner

The social demographer Gavin W. Jones has described shifts in Indonesian marriage patterns since the 1960s as nothing short of a "revolution." Jones was referring in particular to the rapid increase in the age of first marriage for young women. Up until the 1960s, one-third of Indonesian women were married by age sixteen. By the late 1970s, only 10% of women were marrying by that age (Jones 1994: 76). Urban areas saw more rapid rises than rural areas, but by 1985, the mean age at marriage among Indonesian women had reached 20.7 (Jones 1994: 83). During this same period, marriage age rose for men as well, although not quite as dramatically. Much of this shift was the result of socio-economic programs put into place during the New Order (1966–1998). These programs offered new educational and economic opportunities for young people – opportunities that were especially attractive to women. Revised marriage regulations also played a role in the changes. The 1974 Marriage Law set the minimum age of marriage as 16 for girls and 18 for boys and "enshrined the principle that the consent of both parties must be obtained prior to marriage" (Robinson and Utomo 2003: 6). It also tightened restrictions on divorce and on polygyny.

Changes in the situation of Indonesian youth have only accelerated since the fall of Soeharto in the spring of 1998, a period which has seen the rapid rise of Indonesia's middle class and the renewed interest among young people in more normative forms of Islam. By 2010, the mean age at first marriage for Indonesian women had climbed to 22.2 years and to 25.6 for men (Jones and Yeung 2014: 1570). In urban areas like Jakarta and Yogyakarta, women's age at first marriage rose even higher, and increasing numbers of educated women began to express anxiety about the dearth of suitable marriage partners. These and related developments have had significant repercussions for contemporary patterns of youth sociability, courtship, and marriage.

Unmarried singlehood

An important concomitant of the delay in marriage age has been the lengthening of the period of unmarried singlehood. Whereas in previous generations, a young woman's parents would begin to entertain marriage inquires as their daughter approached the end of high school (or even earlier), parents now encourage their daughters as well as their sons to finish high school and if possible to pursue a tertiary degree in the hope of gaining a foothold in the new middle class. In 2014, almost 83% of Indonesian young people were attending secondary school. In that same year, 29.4% of men and 32.8% of women were enrolled in tertiary institutions (http://data.uis.unesco.org/?queryid=142).

For many young people, the pursuit of education and new economic opportunities have involved moving to the city and living away from home for an extended period of time, leaving young people on their own and away from the watchful eyes of family and neighbors. It is a situation that has raised parental fears and has resulted in repeated public moral panics concerning the possibility of sexual improprieties among unmarried youth (Parker and Nilan 2013; Smith-Hefner 2006). Parental fears focus on the possibility that sons or daughters might fall in love and ask to stop studying in order to marry, thereby jeopardizing their economic futures. An out-of-wedlock pregnancy would lead to a similar outcome: the rapid arrangement of a marriage to "cover up the shame" (*menutupi aib*) and one if not both of the young couple dropping out of school.

Muslim conservatives have stepped to the fore in these public debates and vigorously promoted polygyny (*poligami*), early marriage (*nikah dini*), and unofficial marriage (*nikah sirih* or *nikah dibawah tangan*) as solutions to what they view as a moral crisis among today's Muslim youth (Smith-Hefner 2009). Puspo Wardoyo, a popular and vocal supporter of polygyny (and the owner of a well-known chain of fried chicken restaurants), has appeared frequently in public forums to argue that the taking of multiple wives by Muslim men would radically reduce extramarital affairs and prostitution by addressing men's greater libidinal requirements (Brenner 2006; Nurmila 2009; van Wichelen 2013). Wardoyo holds up his own life as an example of how polygyny can be successful. He is often shown in newspaper and magazine articles surrounded by his four smiling, veiled wives, each of whom manages one of his fried chicken restaurants located in various cities throughout Java. Wardoyo and other proponents of polygyny voice support for the loosening of marriage laws to allow earlier marriage without parental permission. They argue that young people should be allowed, even encouraged, to marry before finishing their degrees, because it would facilitate the taking of multiple wives and would prevent immoral pre-marital relationships from occurring during long engagements.

Pacar

Despite public and parental panics surrounding pre-marital relationships, many young people admit to having boyfriends or girlfriends (*pacar*) beginning in late grade school or early middle school (Smith-Hefner 2005: 451). Typically, boys and girls meet at school or in school-related activities or through friends. Indonesian schools, with the exception of explicitly religious schools, are co-ed and young people socialize in their classes and after school. These early relationships are usually regarded with a measure of amusement and are not seen as significant. They are often described as "puppy love" (*cinta monyet*; lit. "monkey love") and as "not (yet) serious" (*belum serius*). In many cases, these exploratory relationships are limited to simply the passing of notes or a whispered rumor. In conversations with me on the topic, young people laughed, wondering aloud whether these interactions even "counted" as pacaran ("having a boyfriend or girlfriend") or not; they were, after all, still "young/immature" (*masih kecil/belum dewasa*) at the time and were "just having fun" (*having fun saja, main-main saja*). For their part, parents reported that if they knew about their daughter's or son's early interests, they ignored the situation, assuming it was nothing to be concerned about and that the fascination would soon fade.

Young people who attend Muslim boarding schools (pesantren) are of course prohibited from having boyfriends or girlfriends. Male and female students (*santri*) live in separate residences and receive instruction in same-sex classrooms. In their religion classes, students are taught that unchaperoned interactions between members of the opposite sex inevitably lead to *zina* "promiscuity," even "adultery." An expression of a gendered double standard, however, the punishment for male santri who break the rule is less severe than is the case for female santri. Whereas a male santri might have his head shaved or be forced to clean the pesantren yard or toilets if caught, a female santri is typically expelled.

Regardless of their religious background and orientation, parents become more vigilant once their daughters approach adolescence (Smith-Hefner 2005: 452). Innocent flirtations and friendships aside, beginning at this stage, most parents do what they can to limit their adolescent daughters' relationships with boys. Adolescent girls are described as *masih labil* "still changeable" and easily caught up in their emotions. They may suffer emotional trauma (*traoma*) from break-ups or from early crushes that are unreciprocated. Parents say they have fewer concerns about their sons engaging in pacaran. Although they may well worry that a son's involvement with a member of the opposite sex might interfere with his studies or lead to sexual impropriety, young men are regarded as being better able to take care of themselves. Of course, young men too may experience emotional trauma and depression (*depresi*) from failed romances. But parents say they have less ability to directly control the behavior of sons than is the case with daughters. "All I can tell him is to be careful," is a common refrain from parents.

It is significant that the first translation given for *pacar* in Echols and Shadily's (1998: 401) Indonesian-English dictionary is actually "fiancé/fiancée." In an earlier era, when marriages were parentally arranged, the time between engagement and wedding was often very short and there was little time for the couple to get to know each other prior to marriage in an unchaperoned setting. Pacaran on the Western model of "having a boyfriend/girlfriend, dating" as a method of premarital familiarization is a relatively modern development and in fact is sometimes referred to as "modern pacaran" (*pacaran modéren*; cf. Bennett 2005: 69). Modern pacaran is understood to involve a young couple going out alone together for the express purpose of getting to know one another more intimately. In the 1980s, modern dating sites that facilitate such encounters had begun to spring up in most major Indonesian cities and towns. These sites include Western-style restaurants and coffee shops, movie theaters, and malls but also bars and nightclubs. Other favorite destinations that offer a degree of anonymity and the possibility for romance to young couples are popular tourist spots, such as temple grounds, parks, and beaches. The relative novelty of pacaran modéren and its Western connotations are reflected in the number of words and phrases that have been borrowed into Indonesian from English to talk about such relationships. These include such revealingly ambivalent terms as "having fun," "trauma," "serious," "concern," "enjoy," "commitment," "care," and "playboy" (*having fun, traoma, serius, konsern, enjoi, komitmen, ker,* and *playboy*) among others, terms which have only gained widespread currency within the past twenty years or so.

"To come courting"

Although pacaran on the Western model is relatively new, a pattern of premarital familiarization called *ngapel* (Jav. "to visit to the house of one's girlfriend, to come courting")[1] has long been common in many areas of Java and is evidenced in similar forms in many other areas of Indonesia (Smith-Hefner 2005; cf. Bennett 2005). These visits allow young people to get to know each other in a more carefully supervised setting prior to making a long-term commitment. More specifically, *ngapel* involves a young man calling on a young woman at her home in the late afternoon or evening, most commonly on Saturday night. After introducing himself to the girl's parents, the young man will sit in the front room (*ruang tamu*) chatting with the young woman over tea and snacks. Although a family member is not necessarily present in the same room, elders are always aware of the interaction, and a parent or older sibling may step in on occasion to monitor the situation. It is not uncommon for young people, both males and females, to entertain several of these types of relationships at any one time. It is also not uncommon for a young man to bring along a friend or two for moral support or in cases where the couple is trying to hide their mutual interest from the girl's parents. If her parents press their daughter to indicate which one among the group of male visitors is her boyfriend (pacar), the young woman will often deny any element of seriousness, insisting that she doesn't care for any one visitor in particular; they are all simply "friends" (*teman*).

In fact the line between "courting" (ngapel) and just "dropping by to visit" (*main-main ke rumah*) is not always clear, not only to parents but to the young people as well. A young man may not be "courageous" (*berani*) enough to openly declare his interest in a young woman. Even if he does, the young woman out of shyness or embarrassment may not make clear the interest is shared. Notwithstanding this uncertainty, ngapel gives young couples a space for exploring a possible mutual attraction, while also allowing parents a measure of control and oversight of their children's social interactions. The delicately choreographed interaction also affords the parents of a young woman the opportunity to assess a young man's manners and intelligence, his degree of religiosity, his education and career prospects, and his compatibility with their daughter and with their family more generally.

If parents decide they approve of the young male visitor, he might eventually be allowed to join the family in the back areas of the house for meals or invited into the family room to join in activities, such as watching television together. Conversely, parents can attempt to intercede if they are unhappy with their daughter's choice. If the parents disapprove of a relationship, they may restrict the couple's interactions to the front room and refuse to leave the couple alone by posting a family member as a constant chaperone (cf. Bennett 2005). Alternately, they may take sterner measures in an attempt to force the young couple apart or to keep them from meeting.

Some young women whose parents forbid them from pacaran resort to *pacaran bekstrit* (lit. "backstreet pacaran"); that is, meeting with their boyfriends without their parents' knowledge. Backstreet meetings often take place in the mall or at a coffee shop or restaurant. If a young woman lives at home, she might leave the house accompanied by a girlfriend and then meet up with her boyfriend at an agreed-upon spot, returning home later with the same girlfriend. Some women resort to pacaran bekstrit, fearing that if their parents knew about their relationship, they might insist that the couple stop seeing one another or (more rarely) would push them into marriage (Smith-Hefner 2005: 452). Others simply aren't yet ready to reveal their romantic interest to their parents. Sometimes backstreet relationships involve a young man of whom the girl's parents disapprove because of his family background, personal characteristics, or religion. The couple might cling to the hope that eventually the girl's parents would come to accept their relationship or that one or the other would decide to convert. Because backstreet meetings can occur in more private spaces with limited or no social surveillance, they offer the possibility of greater freedom for the expression of physical affection than is available in other modes of courtship (cf. Bennett 2002: 110). Some young couples eagerly take advantage of the opportunity to hug and kiss or even have sex in a secluded tourist spot or a boyfriend's unsupervised boardinghouse room. Nonetheless, young people insist that backstreet relationships are not *necessarily* any more serious – sexually or otherwise – than those that are aboveboard.

Courtship practices like ngapel are still engaged in by many young people, especially those who continue to live at home with parents. Some of these early relationships eventually develop into serious commitments and result in lengthy engagements, as one or both partners finish school and work to put aside money for a future home of their own. By the time they have graduated high school and are entering college, however, many young people report breaking off earlier relationships that have no possibility of becoming "serious" and especially those that face strong parental objection.

Not only parents, but young people themselves, emphasize the distinction between "serious" and "not serious" relationships. Non-serious relationships do not quite matter; they are "just having fun," and they may involve individuals who are not in the long view candidates for marriage. By the time they are in their twenties, however, most young women – and the majority of young men – insist they are only interested in a serious relationship that could possibly "lead to matrimony" (*yang menuju ke jenjang perkawinan*). Those young women who find themselves approaching twenty-five without a serious partner evince particular anxiety. By that age, a woman is considered an "old maid" (*prawan tua*), and anxious concern is expressed over her "marketability" and, in particular, her declining fertility. Young men also express anxiety about marrying but are generally accorded somewhat more leeway. By their late twenties, however, many young men begin to feel the pressure (and desire) to marry as well.

An example of how these various concerns come into play in modern courtship is that of Wati, now in her late thirties and a lecturer at a leading Islamic university. When she was in her mid-twenties, she posted a letter along with her picture in a regional magazine, requesting a pen pal. She received multiple responses, most of them from young men. After several months of exchanging letters, she said she became bored with the process and told the writers to contact her only when they had something new to report. Four of the young men nonetheless persisted in writing to her and eventually asked to be allowed to come courting. Wati's mother was thrilled that her daughter – who had never had a boyfriend – now had four suitors.

The first three candidates, Wati said, turned out to be unacceptable; for a variety of reasons, they were just "not a good fit" (*tidak cocok*). Only the fourth, Fadjar, was a possibility. Wati explained,

> By this time, my mom was really impatient. Because you know, if a daughter is approaching 25, her parents are really worried. My mom told Mas Fadjar right away, "If you're interested in her, then go ahead and propose!" She wasn't picky. She said to me, "If you like him, I'll go along with it."

But Wati said she wasn't certain that she wanted to marry Fadjar. The couple continued to exchange letters for over a year while Wati engaged in serious prayer, asking for guidance (*solat istikharah*) in making her decision. During that time, Fadjar happened to get sick and didn't write for a week. Wati suddenly realized that she missed his letters. "And then I began to think, wow, I must really like him!"

Once Wati finally accepted Fadjar's proposal, it took the couple three months to make the necessary arrangements. This afforded Wati the time to finish her final semester of her degree while Fadjar looked for more secure employment. Their marriage has been a happy one, and the couple now has a daughter in middle school. The important thing, Wati said, and what convinced her that Fadjar was right for her, was that they shared a similar religious understanding. "We were sekufu, you know, on the same level" with regard to religion. Both of us were pretty religious and had strong religious educations. And that's what really matters."

The perfect match

Young women describe the ideal marriage candidate as someone who has finished his education, with secure employment or the promise of secure employment. He should ideally have some form of transportation and possibly a place for the newlyweds to live – although many young couples in fact live with one or the other set of parents until they are ready to establish a household of their own. It almost goes without saying that any potential candidate must be Muslim. Although two generations ago, mixed marriages between Christian and Muslims were tolerated in some Indonesian families, in recent years, attitudes in most Muslim circles have changed. Young women echo what is taught in schools and religion classes and supported by the 1974 marriage legislation: that marriage outside of one's religion inevitably results in discord and a "broken home" (cf. Lindsey 2012: 75; Parker, Hoon, and Raihani 2014). Young men reiterated this spousal religious requirement (although there are some who mentioned the possibility of converting a non-Muslim fiancée). Males, however, place relatively more emphasis than do females on attractiveness in describing an ideal spouse, often remarking that they find women who wear the headscarf particularly alluring. Most indicate that they would prefer a wife who is educated, although a college degree is not a prerequisite, and if she wants to work after marriage, most agree she should be allowed to, so long as she is able to take care of the children and household. After *kesalehan* (piety) the spousal characteristic most commonly cited by men, however, is *keibuan* or "motherliness."

Marriage goes hand in hand with childbearing, and the normative expectations that surround childbearing also show a surprising measure of overlap or ethical consensus between those who regard themselves as casual in their religious observance and those who regard themselves as observant Muslims. Children are referred to as "gifts" (*anugrah*) and "blessings" (*berkat*) from God who bring good fortune (*rejeki*) to their parents. Young people from all backgrounds regularly volunteer, "If I'm ready to get married, I'm ready to have a child." Newlyweds anticipate producing a "fruit of their love" (*buah hati*) as quickly as possible. If, after several months of marriage, they have not yet made a happy announcement, people begin to ask if something is the matter.

Although Indonesian parents warn their daughters to avoid relationships that could interfere with their studies and possibly keep them from obtaining their degrees, the fear of never marrying is a source of considerable tension for both young women and their parents. As their daughters approach their twenties and are close to attaining their educational goals, many parents are willing – even delighted – to accept a relationship with a young man from a good background and with good future prospects who is "serious" in his intentions. In fact, across religious backgrounds, if a young woman does not have a serious boyfriend at graduation or soon after, family members begin pressing her to find someone.

Marital anxieties

Although increasing numbers of Indonesian young people are postponing marriage in order to pursue an education or employment, they have hardly abandoned it. Within Indonesian Islam and as is the case in other Muslim-majority countries, there is a powerfully felt "marital imperative" (cf. Adely 2012: 125; Singerman 2007: 5). Marriage is strongly enjoined by Islam, but for ordinary Muslims, it is also an important marker of social maturity; any who opt not to marry face social stigmatization (Parker 2008: 23). There is a widespread assumption that those who do not marry are in fact defective or incomplete (*tidak sempurna*). Even homosexuals in Indonesia feel strong social pressures to enter into heterosexual unions and produce an offspring so as to take up an identifiable position within Indonesian society and graduate from the category of "unmarried youth" (Blackwood 2010; Boellstorff 1999, 2005).

New opportunities for Indonesian women have led, however, to what is widely perceived as a "marriage crisis" or what some have referred to as a "marriage squeeze" (Jones 1994: 122–5, Jones and Yeung 2014: 1579–1580; Utomo 2014). This widely observed and, for many young women, deeply unsettling phenomenon refers to the difficulties many educated young women face in finding partners because of an imbalance in the number of available men or to young women putting off marriage for "too long" and aging out of the marital market. Most Indonesian men still prefer to marry "down," that is, wed a woman who has less education and experience than themselves. This leaves a dearth of available men "at the top."[2] Facing a narrowing pool of marriageable men, educated women scramble to identify an appropriate partner, one who has a similar level of education and who is also willing to negotiate work and family roles within the context of a "modern," companionate marriage. Women's life histories indicate that many have had to adjust both their strategies and their expectations in their search for a suitable spouse.

Despite the difficulties educated women face in finding a partner, very few say they would consider asking their parents to arrange a marriage for them. For their part, parents say they do not dare to make arrangements for their daughters, fearing they would be blamed later if the marriage didn't work out. They often add, "I gave her an education so that she can make her own decisions." And yet, although young women are insistent about finding a partner on their own, a surprising number report they have never had a boyfriend. Many say they put off having a relationship in order to pursue their education or to work – a pattern many parents endorse. They describe feeling awkward (*canggung, kaku*) and nervous (*grogi, gugup*) around eligible, unmarried men. This is especially true of women who have absorbed the message of their religion teachers who warn that interactions with unrelated members of the opposite sex can easily lead to sinful thoughts and interactions (*zina, dosa besar*) and should be avoided. They accept the commonly heard religious admonition that "there is no dating in Islam only *ta'aruf*" (meeting for the purpose of deciding whether or not to marry).

Contemporary trends in courtship and marriage among educated youth are a response to these shifting realities. In addition to the trend of increasingly – and in some estimations, alarmingly – long courtship and engagement periods of young people who postpone marriage, there are today social models that radically limit or even completely reject premarital familiarization and surrender individual choice of martial partner to a recognized religious authority (Smith-Hefner 2005). These latter models include shorter or non-existent engagements and more modest wedding celebrations that emphasize conservative Muslim norms over traditional societal values.

The new Muslim romance

For women who are anxious to marry but have no available prospects, religious organizations are often willing to identify a candidate for them (cf. Widiarti 2010). On campuses like Gadjah Mada University in Yogyakarta, student groups like the Indonesian Muslim University Student Action Union (KAMMI) and Hizbut Tahrir have committees that facilitate the process of finding a marriage candidate for their members. These organizations promote a conservative view of Islam as systematic, comprehensive, and all-encompassing (*kaffah*) and believe that if shariah (Islamic law) were implemented, Indonesia would become a more just and peaceful nation. Conventional understandings of shariah severely limit interactions between unrelated men and women and restrict premarital familiarization (*pacaran*). When a member of one of these organizations is ready to marry, he or she simply submits his or her "biodata" to the committee. Biodata typically include a candidate's age, height and weight, educational level, employment, home address, and telephone number as well as a brief statement of one's personal aspirations and preferences with regard to a marital partner; the information is usually accompanied by a passport-style photo. The committee then uses the data to identify someone who is a good match. The group will also supply chaperones so that the couple can meet and come to a decision without ever being alone with one another.

By 2010, there were multiple groups and organizations that had sprung up in Yogyakarta offering free matchmaking services. These groups do not necessarily embrace the conservative Islamic views of KAMMI or Hizbut Tahrir but nonetheless encourage young people who are serious about marrying to marry quickly with a minimum of pre-marital familiarization. The services they offer include monthly "mass matchmaking events" (*perjodohan masal, ta'aruf masal*) advertised in local newspapers. Some of these events are sponsored by religious organizations, others by concerned parties – local religious leaders or private individuals who had successfully gone through the matchmaking process themselves and had decided to help others achieve the same pious and happy outcome.[3] Although it is not necessarily their primary motivation, these services also address the concerns of many young women who have put off marriage to pursue their educations and, as a result, find their marital options rapidly narrowing. These mass meetings attract a much larger and more diverse group than the university-based *dakwah* organizations and are less tightly controlled; nonetheless, their operational principle is similar. The ads for the services, which appear in local newspapers, emphasize the importance of seriousness of intent and the sincere desire to marry quickly on the part of participants. Some organizations offer chaperones to allow the couple to meet for the purposes of negotiating marriage; others offer a safe, public place to meet. There are even organizations that enlist pious and affluent donors willing to cover the wedding costs for couples who decide to marry quickly. A few of these sponsors go so far as to offer all-expenses-paid honeymoon trips to Singapore.

Nindy used this process to find her husband, Hermawan. Nindy is tall and attractive and did not seem to be the type of young woman who would have any problem attracting a marriage partner. She had a college degree in child psychology and was working as a teacher's aide in a school for children with disabilities. She had taken the civil servant test in the hope of becoming a full-time teacher. Nindy was 35, however, when she turned to matchmaking services, an age considered to be "well past the standard for marriage." In addition, she was, by her own admission, almost painfully shy and lacking in self-confidence (*kurang pede*). In fact, she said, she hadn't planned on attending the mass matchmaking event at all and had only gone along because her cousin had signed her up and had even filled out the form for her.

The event was held in the south of the city of Yogyakarta in the sub-district of Sewon in the regency of Bantul and was sponsored by the Bureau of Religious Affairs (Kantor Urusan Agama, KUA). Nindy said that when she and her cousin arrived, there were already hundreds of people gathered in the courtyard. They were met by a welcoming committee whose members greeted each of the guests individually and helped those who had not yet filled out the biodata form to do so. The information sheets were then collected into two books, one for men and one for women. At the end of the meeting, all of the participants would be given access to the biodata of the other participants.

After a short speech by the organizer, reminding everyone that the event was only for those who were serious about marriage, there was a brief Muslim prayer. Then the participants were each invited to stand up one by one, to give their name and a description of what they were looking for in a spouse. Most of the women said more or less the same thing. They wanted a man with at least the same level of education as themselves, a steady job, around their age or maybe a little older, and of the same faith. The participants were then divided into smaller groups and urged to use the opportunity to get to know one another. Nindy said she was too shy to say much of anything, and she and her cousin left soon afterward.

In the days and weeks following the meeting, however, Nindy began to receive phone calls and text messages from interested men who had made note of her telephone number from the book of collected biodata. One of those men was Hermawan. After some initial reluctance on Nindy's part and repeated difficulties identifying a date and time when they were both available, they arranged to meet at a nearby mall. Nindy said she immediately felt some sympathy or compassion for Hermawan – even though he was younger than she was (he was 33) and had only a grade school education. Hermawan had quit school when he was twelve because his father had died and the family did not have the money for him to continue. He had postponed his own marriage because he wanted to see his younger siblings marry first and had helped to pay for their wedding expenses. Now he was free of his obligations and could marry; his siblings were all married and had families. He had a steady, though modestly paying job in the office supply store. Their wedding took place just two weeks after the couple's first meeting at the mall. Their daughter was born ten months later.

Young women like Nindy have turned to Muslim matchmaking services as a strategy for marriage in a marital market straining under the weight of new social and ethical pressures. The pressure has multiple sources. It comes from the proponents of the new Islamic normativity, who seek to bring courtship and marriage into conformity with far stricter notions of pre-marital contact and sociability. It also comes from families anxious about their children's futures, especially about daughters at risk of sexual impropriety or surpassing the socially acceptable age for marriage. Finally, the pressure arises from young people themselves who are trying desperately to balance new educational and economic opportunities with the desire to marry and establish families of their own. The latter pressure is greater for young women than it is for young men. Young women see themselves as having less control over their choices than do men. They realize that it is still young men who are typically the ones to signal their interest and initiate relationships and are more likely to play a decisive role in the final choice of partner. But women also feel under pressure because those who have delayed marriage to pursue an education are painfully aware of their narrowing window of fertility. Given these pressures, some young women are willing to make certain compromises, hoping that commitment to a shared set of ethical principles will ensure marital stability.

Courtship and marriage in the new Muslim middle class

At a time when social and educational developments have led to the prolongation of the period of premarital singlehood and when social mobility has created new opportunities for unsupervised encounters between members of the opposite sex, some young people have found a solution to the marital problem in a course of action that they regard as submitting to an ethical imperative greater than themselves. These young people eschew pre-marital familiarization as sinful and urge a radically shortened period of courtship or even no courtship at all. And while the majority of Indonesians now accept the "modern" right of individual choice of marital partner, many youth are turning to a variety of matchmaking services that narrow the field by screening candidates to ensure their religious credentials and suitability.

This shift in Indonesia's marital economy represents a radical departure from trends apparent in the Indonesian middle classes beginning in the 1980s. At that time, researchers reported that they saw that long courtship and extended engagement periods were giving rise to a new sense of individualized sexual autonomy. The trend was most apparent in the growing incidence of "Western-style" dating and, according to some sources, heightened rates of premarital sex. It is clear that this latter trend has not come entirely to a halt. However, what is also clear is that in the intervening years, the marital economy has undergone a small if still unfinished normative revolution. One of the revolution's most distinctive features has been the arrival on the public scene of a small army of Islamic sex counselors, pamphleteers, and anti-promiscuity activists. They have struggled tirelessly to promote "more Muslim" patterns of courtship and wedding celebrations, which exclude elements identified as non-Islamic. These and related developments distinguish

Indonesia from many other countries in East and Southeast Asia that have experienced soaring rates of premarital cohabitation and non-marriage over the past 25 years (Jones and Yeung 2014). It is difficult to forecast how long it might be before Indonesia's youth will follow suit. Depending on the course of current religious and ethical trends, the answer may be never.

Notes

1 There are very close parallels between Javanese ngapel and the practice known as *midang* among Muslim Sasak in Lombok described by Linda Rae Bennett (2002, 2005).
2 Uneducated and working class men may face a similar problem; however, men still have the advantage of playing the more active role in courtship. They are the ones who are expected to *menembak dulu* or "shoot first."
3 Helping others to marry is an act of piety (Bouhdiba 2004: 90).

References cited

Adely, Fida. 2012. *Gendered Paradoxes: Educating Jordanian Women in Nation, Faith, and Progress* (Chicago: University of Chicago Press).

Bennett, Linda Rae. 2002. "Modernity, Desire, and Courtship: The Evolution of Premarital Relationships in Mataram, Eastern Indonesia," in Lenore Manderson and Pranee Liamputtong, eds., *Coming of Age in South and Southeast Asia* (Richmond, Surry: Curzon), pp. 96–112.

———. 2005. *Women, Islam and Modernity: Single Women, Sexuality and Reproductive Health in Contemporary Indonesia* (London and New York: Routledge).

Blackwood, Evelyn. 2010. *Falling into the Lesbi World* (Honolulu: University of Hawaii Press).

Boellstorff, Tom. 1999. "The Perfect Path: Gay Men, Marriage, Indonesia," *GLQ: A Journal of Lesbian and Gay Studies* 5(4): 475–509.

———. 2005. *The Gay Archipelago: Sexuality and Nation in Indonesia* (Princeton: Princeton University Press).

Bouhdiba, Abdelwahab. 2004. *Sexuality in Islam* (London: Saqi Books).

Brenner, Suzanne A. 2006. "Democracy, Polygamy, and Women in Post-'Reformasi' Indonesia," *Social Analysis* 50(1): 164–7.

Echols, John M., and Hassan Shadily (revised by John U. Wolff and James T. Collins). 1989. *Kamus Indonesia Inggris* (Indonesian English Dictionary) (Ithaca: Cornell University Press).

Jones, Gavin W. 1994. *Marriage and Divorce in Islamic South-East Asia* (Oxford: Oxford University Press).

Jones, Gavin W. and Wei-Jun Jean Yeung. 2014. "Marriage in Asia," *Journal of Family Issues* 35(12): 1567–83.

Lindsey, Timothy. 2012. *Islam, Law, and the State in Southeast Asia Volume 1: Indonesia* (New York: I.B. Tauris).

Nurmila, Nina. 2009. *Women, Islam and Everyday Life: Renegotiating Polygamy in Indonesia* (London: Routledge).

Parker, Lyn. 2008. "Theorising Adolescent Sexualities in Indonesia – Where 'Something Different Happens.'" *Intersections: Gender and Sexuality in Asia and the Pacific*, 18 October. http://intersections.anu.edu.au/issue18/parker.htm (Accessed 16 January 2014).

Parker, Lyn and Pam Nilan. 2013. *Adolescents in Contemporary Indonesia* (London and New York: Routledge).

Parker, Lyn, Chang-Yau Hoon, and Raihani. 2014. "Young People's Attitudes Towards Inter-Ethnic and Inter-Religious Socializing, Courtship and Marriage in Indonesia," *South East Asia Research* 22(4): 467–86.

Robinson, Kathryn and Iwu Dwisetyani Utomo. 2003. "Introduction," in Kathryn Robinson, Iwu Dwisetyani Utomo, and Christine Campbell, eds., volume on "Youth, Sexuality and Personal Life in Indonesia," *Review of Indonesian and Malaysian Affairs* 37(1): 5–16.

Singerman, Diane. 2007. "The Economic Imperatives of Marriage: Emerging Practices and Identities Among Youth in the Middle East," The Middle East Youth Initiative Working Paper, 6 September. www.meyi.org/uploads/3/2/0/1/32012989/singerman_-_the_economic_imperatives_of_marriage-_emerging_practices_and_identities_among_youth_in_the_middle_east.pdf (Accessed 30 March 2015).

Smith-Hefner, Nancy J. 2005. "The New Muslim Romance: Changing Patterns of Courtship and Marriage Among Educated Javanese Youth," *Journal of Southeast Asian Studies* 36(3): 441–59.

———. 2006. "Reproducing Respectability: Sex and Sexuality Among Muslim Javanese Youth," *Review of Indonesian and Malay Affairs* 40(1): 143–72.

————. 2009. "'Hypersexed' Youth and the New Muslim Sexology in Contemporary Java," *Review of Indonesian and Malay Affairs* 43(1): 209–44.

Utomo, Ariane J. 2014. "Marrying Up? Trends in Age and Education Gaps Among Married Couples in Indonesia," *Journal of Family Issues* 35(12): 1683–1706.

van Wichelen, Sonja. 2013. "Polygamy Talk and the Politics of Feminism: Contestations Over Masculinity in a New Muslim Indonesia," *Journal of International Women's Studies* 11(1): 173–88.

Widiarti, Asri. 2010. *Tak Kenal maka Ta'aruf: Panduan Lengkap Proses Ta'aruf Hingga Pernikahan Aktivis Dakwah* (Unacquainted and yet Engaged: The Complete Guide to the Marriage Process for Religious Activists) (Solo: Era Adicitra Intermedia).

28

WOMEN'S RESPONSES TO THE IMPLEMENTATION OF ISLAMIC LAW IN ACEH

Dina Afrianty

The Islamic Criminal Code was introduced in the Islamic Province of Aceh in 2015. Its implementation is seen by many observers as discriminatory against women and other minority groups. It contravenes national legislation, among others, Law No. 39/1999 on Human Rights; it also contradicts the principles of the Convention on the Elimination of all Forms of Discrimination Against Women or CEDAW that the Indonesian government ratified in 1984. Despite this, the Indonesian Supreme Court rejected a lawsuit submitted by local and national civil society groupings seeking to overturn this legal regime (Serambi Indonesia 2016).

Since the introduction of the code, the international and national media regularly circulate video clips showing Acehnese men and women lashed by sharia police with a rattan cane for violating the law. Most women were lashed for allegedly committing *khalwat* activities or illicit proximity with the opposite sex, while men were lashed for committing illicit relations, gambling, or consumption of alcohol. The punishment usually takes place in the front yard of the district mosque. Typically dozens of onlookers, including men, women, and children, look on during the event. Wearing a white robe and with their heads covered by headscarves, female convicts attempt to stand still with their heads down unable to face the crowd who jeer at them every time the rattan cane strikes their back. Behind the stage and sitting under a big tent, officials from the sharia office and the prosecutor's office and religious leaders sit quietly observing the event. A medical team is also present to provide assistance to those who collapse or become ill during or after execution of the sentence.

The punishment regime clearly demonstrates the local government's determination to "fully implement" Islamic law or "pelaksanaan syariat Islam secara kaffah." In the early years following its introduction in 2000, many Acehnese as well as other Indonesian nationals had in fact expressed doubt if Islamic law would really be fully implemented (Salim 2009). Apart from divided opinions on whether or not formalizing sharia into legislation will rectify the social, political, and moral problems facing Aceh, the overlapping duties and mandates of institutions that oversee the implementation of sharia law such as the Sharia Court, the Sharia Office, the prosecutor's office, and the Sharia police contributed to skepticism about a full implementation of Islamic law.

What does the implementation of the Islamic criminal code mean for Indonesia's democracy, the future of its moderate Islam, and, particularly, the status of women in the world's most populous Muslim nation? Why has the national government allowed the implementation of local regulations that contradict higher laws in Indonesia's legal hierarchy? This chapter examines these questions while paying particular attention to how Acehnese women have been targeted by and responded to the implementation of Sharia law. Stories of women being caned for being in close proximity with the opposite sex or committing sex outside marriage (*zina*) or being publicly abused for having their hair uncovered and for wearing jeans have become reference points for how "Islam" treats women. These events reinforce the stereotype of Islam as a religion that oppresses and discriminates against women and that does not respect human rights.

The experience of Acehnese women is important because the treatment of women under Aceh's Islamic law contradicts what people outside this region have long believed to be among the region's special characteristics – including its early history of female sultanas and the prominent role of women as leaders in the war against the Dutch colonial occupation (Siapno 2002).

I open this chapter with a brief discussion of sharia law and what Muslim feminists say about the place of women in sharia law. Then I focus on the experiences of Acehnese women under the implementation of sharia law and how they have responded to it. This chapter demonstrates that, despite the restrictions imposed on women's rights and mobility, as believers of Islam, Acehnese women, including women activists, academics, and female religious leaders, have challenged the way sources of sharia have been interpreted and then implemented in Aceh – but they have done so in a highly limited way. It could be argued that the way Acehnese women activists, women scholars, and the female religious leaders challenge and demand reform to the introduction of sharia falls within the framework of Islamic feminism. As believers of Islam, they do not want to engage in the debate over whether or not Aceh should be based on Islam. What matters for Acehnese women is that Islamic law must be gender sensitive, as they believe the true teaching of Islam guarantees equality and respect of women's rights. Thus, Acehnese women use the available means, such as public participation, which has been allowed under Indonesia's democracy, to demand equality.

Sharia and Muslim women

Sharia is central in Islam and fundamental to every Muslim's life. Sharia derives from the Quran, the Holy Book consisting of God's revelation to the prophet Muhammad, and Hadith, the canonical compilation of the prophet's words and deeds. Muslims believe sharia is a comprehensive guide that serves as the basis for their personal and public lives, both in relation to God and to other human beings.

How sharia should be understood and manifested in worldly affairs has long been a matter of debate and tension among Muslims. Some Muslims believe that sharia must be institutionalized in the form of legal rulings, but others believe it is intended more as religious guidance, which serves as inspiration for spiritual well-being but not as a blueprint for a socio-political order (Mir-Hosseini 2000; An-Na'im 2009).

According to Muslim feminist Ziba Mir-Hosseini (2000: 1), this tension with regard to how sharia should be understood and implemented has its origins in that fact that sharia is manifest in two dimensions, one "sacred," as divine revelation, and the other "temporal," a product of centuries of juristic interpretations. The Moroccan Muslim feminist Fatima Mernissi (1991) argues that what many Muslims refer to as "sharia" in modern times, particularly those who define and limit women's roles and status, is based on the works of male authorities since the seventh century who attempted to maintain their "male privileges." As she boldly argues, "If women's rights are a problem for some modern Muslim men, it is neither because of the Koran nor the Prophet, nor the Islamic tradition, but simply because those rights conflict with the interests of a male elite" (Mernissi 1991: ix).

Muslim women's scholars and male reformists believe that the interpretation of sharia that limits women's mobility or freedom is unjust and discriminatory, deriving not from revelation but from the legal methodologies used during the early period of Islam when patriarchal culture colored the thought of male religious authorities (Mir-Hosseini 2006: Mernissi 1991). This is the reason Muslim feminists insist that in modern times, the sources of sharia must be reread and reinterpreted before they are transformed into legal regulations.

In recent times, the attempt to Islamize the social and legal order in Muslim societies, including in Indonesia, often begins with attempts to regulate women's religiosity. The Malaysian Muslim feminist Zainah Anwar (2005: 237) notes that women's roles often become the first target in Islamizing society, defining what women can and cannot do both in private and public; these efforts unfold because changing women's behavior is considered essential for rectifying social problems. Aceh is no exception in this regard. Among the first statutory laws (Qanun) enacted was Qanun No. 11/2002 on the Implementation of Islamic Law. While it regulates both men and women's clothing, its primary focus had to do with covering women's hair and regulating the tightness of their clothing. This was the beginning of an era when women's dress and mobility became primary foci of governmental and public scrutiny.

There are several major offenses of sharia regulated under the Islamic Criminal Code that directly and seriously affect women. These include the regulation on khalwat or illicit relations (Article 23) and zina or sexual relations of people who are not legally married (Article 26). Other offenses include homosexuality, sexual harassment, and rape. Unlike the previous Qanun, the Qanun regulating khalwat stipulates that the violator is subject to ten lashes (Article 23); zina is punishable with one hundred lashes (Article 33).

Women activists and female religious leaders in Aceh strongly criticized this legislation on the grounds that it is discriminatory. As will be discussed in the following section, women activists in urban areas as well as female religious authorities are today working to challenge the Qanun, by examining the way the sources of sharia have been interpreted; they are also demanding that the government of the special district of Aceh consult women during the process of crafting Qanun (Afrianty 2015; Kloos 2016; Srimulyani 2016).

Women living under the Islamic law

Data from the Mahkamah Syari'at or the Provincial Shariah Court in Aceh demonstrate a steady increase in the number of criminal cases that involve the Islamic Criminal Code. In 2015, around four hundred criminal cases were handled by the Mahkamah Syari'at Court. Throughout 2016, there were 339 Acehnese men and women who had been whipped by the rattan cane after being charged for violating the code. While most men were charged for *maisir* (gambling) and consumption of alcohol, 37 cases involved women charged with khalwat offenses. Between January and February 2017 alone, there were twenty-six men and women prosecuted and caned.

The most pressing concern of Acehnese women is how the implementation of Islamic law has targeted their religiosity and bodies. Women's religiosity is being evaluated in terms of how they cover their hair and bodies and how they move about. Article 13 (1) of Qanun No. 11/2002 on the Implementation of Islamic Law states that "all Muslims are obliged to wear Islamic dress." It defines Muslim clothing for women as dress that covers her "intimate parts" or *aurat* and that is not transparent and does not show the shape of the body. Women's mobility has also become the target of sharia implementation in which women are restricted from being in close proximity with male friends as they could be targeted under khalwat. Recently authorities have banned women from straddling motorbikes and performing in traditional dances.

Covering their hair is not new for most Acehnese women, and they are used to wearing proper Muslim clothing or *baju muslim*. But the new Qanun is based on a new definition of "head covering." The traditional practice for Acehnese women is to simply drape a shawl to cover their hair; the new Qanun stipulates that a proper covering must be in the form of jilbab, a more encompassing head covering. As a result, even when women considered themselves to have followed sharia law by covering their hair, they may be targeted by sharia police in "jilbab raids."

In addition, many Acehnese women activists and religious leaders have also resented the way men lacking adequate mastery of Islamic sources assumed that they have the authority to scrutinize whether or not women follow Islamic law (Afrianty 2015: 74–5, 78; Otto 2016; Srimulyani 2016). Kloos (2014: 61) argues that the implementation of Islamic law represents a new type of social control in which certain individuals think they possess a monopoly of moral authority to define and interpret sources of sharia. The continuing public humiliation and harassment many Acehnese women have experienced have inspired resistance to the implementation of sharia law and to the institution that oversees it, the sharia police or the Wilayatul Hisbah (WH). Many young Acehnese women particularly resent the way WH check their jilbab and measure how loose their clothing is. Dilla, a young Acehnese female teenager, told BBC Indonesia that when WH apprehended her and questioned her for not wearing what they consider "proper Muslim clothing," her answer was that she never wears the headscarf because her parent never asked her to do that (Lestari 2012). When she was told by WH that it is sinful for women not to wear a headscarf, she said to WH, "They have no authority to define whether or not she commits sinful act, it is God's authority to define it." Dilla told BBC Indonesia that in her opinion the government has no right to regulate people's private religious life including determining what women must wear. She said, "The choice of clothing cannot be forced, wearing a headscarf is not my choice . . . and I wear short skirt when I hang out with friends or families." Although no women have been convicted, prosecuted, and lashed by sharia police for not wearing "proper Muslim clothes," this has been a source of resentment and anger for Acehnese women.

Restriction on women's mobility can also be seen in the regulating of khalwat and zina in the Islamic criminal code. Khalwat is most generally understood as illicit relations outside marriage, but in practice, it is interpreted to mean anything from sexual activities outside marriage to a situation where a man and a woman who are not legally married are in close proximity, whether in public or private. Many women have been caught, prosecuted, and convicted for allegedly being in close proximity with the opposite sex. Some of them were accused of committing sexual relations or zina while caught being in close proximity with men who are not their legal husbands (Kloos 2014).

The loose definition of khalwat and how it has been practiced has – sadly – taken a toll. In 2012, a young girl in the district of Bireun decided to hang herself after she was caught at night by WH and was accused of being a prostitute. Understanding that she might be taken to the sharia court to be prosecuted and accused of prostitution, she decided to end her life. She could not bear the embarrassment and how the accusation would humiliate her parents and family. In a letter she left her parents, she explained that she was out at night with friends only to enjoy live music and had never engaged in prostitution as alleged by the sharia police (Baiquni 2012).

The Islamic Criminal Code imposes a penalty of up to one hundred lashes for those who are convicted of zina (Article 33). The first to receive the full one hundred lashes was a couple who were caught committing zina in the district of Takengon. Both were caught and handed by the villagers to the sharia police before being detained at the prosecutor's office. The Mahkamah Syari'ah verdicts were that the couple was committing zina and subject to one hundred lashes. The punishment was carried out on May 26, 2016 (*Tribun News* 2016).

Discriminatory practice can also be seen in the way minority groups are targeted. A sixty-year-old female Chinese non-Muslim was subject to twenty lashes by the Sharia Court in Takengon District on April 2016, following a conviction for selling alcoholic beverages. This news made headlines as sharia law is supposed to apply only to Muslims. The head of the Sharia Office in Banda Aceh issued a statement acknowledging that the punishment could have been imposed because of a "misinterpretation" of the Qanun resulting in a non-Muslim being prosecuted under the Islamic Criminal Code (Hidayat 2016). Article 5 of the Islamic Criminal Code states that the regulation applies only to Muslims and to a) those who are not Muslim but commit *jarimah, any action or behavior that is considered an offense to sharia,* along with b) Muslims who are given the option to voluntarily follow the Islamic Criminal Code. Activists protested that the victim was not given this latter option.

Responses of Acehnese women

These stories show how ordinary Acehnese women living their everyday lives under Aceh's version of Islamic law deal with and respond to the way it is implemented. Previous research has demonstrated that varied actors, including female ulama, women scholars, and women gender activists have responded to the implementation of Islamic law by not only criticizing the way sources of Islamic law have been interpreted and implemented but by also demanding legal reform (Afrianty 2015; Srimulyani 2016; Kloos 2014; Grosmann 2016). As Muslim believers, their demand for legal reform has focused on the importance of working through an Islamic framework and carefully evaluating which modern discourses of gender justice, equality, and rights can be effectively incorporated into their struggles (Afrianty 2015; Grossman 2016).

In the context of Aceh, the struggle for legal reform by Acehnese women activists, scholars, and religious leaders faces an especially serious challenge in that it has to deal with a very conservative religious community that has a dearth of women in possession of public influence. The lack of female leaders and religious leaders with enough access and resources to engage with male orthodox religious leaders is a serious impediment to the struggle for legal reform and equality.

During the early period of the introduction of Islamic law, a number of women activists from local women's organizations played a central role in promoting the need for a just and equitable legal framework in formulating Qanun. It was these local women activists who mobilized scholars, female religious ulama, and women leaders to work together for gender-sensitive Islamic law (Afrianty 2015). Among the local women's activists were Soraya Kamaruzzaman from Flower Aceh, Syarifah Rahmatillah from MISPI or Mitra Sejati Perempuan Indonesia (True Partner of Indonesian Women), Khairani Arifin from RPUK or Relawan Perempuan Untuk Kemanusiaan (Women's Volunteer for Humanity), and Fatimah Syam from Women's Legal Aid. Participation by qualified female religious scholars, however, was far more limited with only Professor Nurjannah Ismail and academics from the Gender Studies Centre at the State Institute of Islamic Studies (IAIN) Ar-Raniry actively engaged in public fora.

Given the conservative character of the larger Acehnese population, women activists were regularly reminded of how they need to frame their struggle for gender equality in Islamic legal terms. Activists like Soraya Kamaruzzaman and Syarifah Rahmatillah chose to engage and emphasize local Acehnese culture and tradition in explaining the issue of equality (Afrianty 2015). Other than engaging in the debate of whether Aceh should have Islamic law, they thought they had to work closely with the male religious leaders and the authorities to make sure that Islamic law would not discriminate against women.

Similarly, Srimulyani's work demonstrates how female religious leaders are also at work in challenging the way sharia is interpreted and formalized as Qanun. While most women scholars and activists agree with the introduction of Islamic law, they are critical of the way it has been implemented especially with regard to women. During meetings of women's Quranic reading groups regularly organized in villages or in *dayah* (traditional Islamic schools), female religious leaders often brought up the issue of the status of women in the implementation of sharia. They criticized the way Qanun restrict women's movement by banning women from wearing trousers or traveling alone. One female religious leader argued that Acehnese women have always been active in public by going to paddy fields and selling their harvest to the market and they have always worn trousers (Srimulyani 2016: 158–9).

Most Indonesians view Acehnese as pious Muslims and understand that Islam is strongly entrenched in Acehnese identity. As Muslim believers, activists and female religious leaders who are critical of sharia implementation argue that advocating gender equality must be based on Islamic teachings. This is consistent with what the Malaysian Muslim feminist Zainah Anwar has argued (2005: 235), namely, that as believers, Muslim women "find liberation, truth, and justice within their own faith." Therefore, in presenting their arguments, Acehnese women advocate the importance of re-reading and re-interpreting the sources of Islamic law (Afrianty 2015; Grosmann 2016).

During the post-tsunami reconstruction period (i.e., post December 2004), Acehnese women activists learned from the experience of national Muslim women's organizations, such as the Fahmina Institute based in Cirebon, about the need for a substantive re-interpretation of sharia before it is institutionalized and enforced in formal legislation. Foreign donors such as UNIFEM (United Nations Development Fund for Women) organized a number of seminars and workshops designed to facilitate Acehnese women's learning from the experience of women in other countries living under sharia law. Speakers from other Muslim countries came to Aceh to talk about the necessity to re-read and re-interpret the sources of Islamic law and to ensure that Acehnese women are involved in the legislative process (Afrianty 2015).

Women in Aceh were also introduced to international women's rights instruments, such as CEDAW, and were encouraged to explore how such legal mechanisms can be incorporated into Aceh's regional regulations (Afrianty 2015: Grosmann 2016). However, local women activists are careful in their referring to international norms of women's rights, as they find some of the ideas are "Western" and therefore problematic with regard to Islamic teachings and local cultural values (Afrianty 2015: 151–2). Women's organizations, like MISPI (Mitra Sejati Perempuan Indonesia), for example, were of the opinion that most Acehnese accept the right of the Acehnese to implement Islamic law based on the fact that there was an overwhelming response of the Acehnese when Aceh was granted the right to implement sharia law (Afrianty 2015: 163). Therefore, for MISPI, what is important is how the implementation of sharia law would not discriminate against women.

Acehnese women's participation in public life is formally guaranteed under the Helsinki Peace Agreement signed in 2005. The Helsinki Peace Agreement, which ended almost three decades of military conflict, marked an opening for women's wider political participation, as the accord stipulated that Aceh would have its own local political parties. The agreement also stipulated that women's gender interests and justice must be included in the formulation of future Qanun. These provisions would seem to have provided a solid foundation for women's organizations and activists to participate in the drafting of Qanun.

There were some instances in which women activists, scholars, and religious leaders did manage to influence the formulation of Qanun. In 2004, a group of women's activists mobilized through the Jaringan Perempuan Untuk Kebijakan (JPUK) or the Women's Policy Network (Afrianty 2015: 125–6). This network consisted, not only of women activists, but also female religious leaders, academics, and other civil society activists from across the province. They met and discussed the draft Law on the Governance of Aceh (LOGA). Representatives from the

JPUK became involved in drafting the LOGA by advocating 26 themes related to gender interests. Through their advocacy, some of the themes they proposed were accepted and included in the LOGA (Afrianty 2011). These included provisions for local political parties to have 30% women's membership, gender mainstreaming in all government policies, women's representation at the Aceh Provincial Ulama Council (Majelis Pemusyawaratan Ulama, MPU), women's access to government credit for women-owned businesses, the empowering of women through education, and urging the government to play a consistent role in the protection of women's rights.

Another milestone for women's activists was their role in influencing the formulation of Qanun No. 7/2006 on Local Elections (Afrianty 2011). An earlier draft excluded women's participation as candidates in elections, because it stipulated that all who wished to run as candidates had also to already qualify for serving as a leader (*imam*) or a preacher (*khatib*) in a mosque – roles limited to men in Aceh. Qanun No. 7/2006 on Local Elections finally removed the clause and stipulated instead that political parties must be made up of at least 30% of women and that the leadership of political parties should consist at least of 30% women.

Women were also involved in the process of drafting Qanun Jinayah or the Islamic Criminal Code, which was launched in 2007 (Grosmann 2016). Among the demands put forward by RPUK's leading women's rights activist, Khairani Arifin, was the inclusion of passages establishing the law's conformity to international conventions concerning human and women's rights, as well as provisions dealing with sexual harassment and rape (Grosmann 2016: 99). These provisions were incorporated into the first draft bill – but were subsequently dropped from the final bill passed by the local parliament in 2009 (Grosmann 2016: 87).

Conclusion

Injustices and discriminatory practices against women in the implementation of Islamic regional regulations have given Acehnese women a new reason to mobilize. Challenged by the introduction of a particular version of Islamic law, women activists have sought to ensure that local regulations take account of principles of gender justice and women's rights.

The early phases of the formulation and introduction of sharia Qanun demonstrate that under appropriate circumstances, Muslim women can make a difference and adjust and revise Islamically inspired laws. However, since these early phases, the body of sharia law in Aceh has only continued to expand, and much of it can be and has been criticized from an Islamic feminist perspective. That is, the content and intention of the Qanun have been aimed at controlling women and confining their public appearance and activity. What is now needed is additional and deeper research on the ways in which Acehnese women can mobilize to influence law and law reform or, equally, analyze the barriers to effective legal reform.

Women have called for the sources of sharia, the Quran and Hadith, to be re-read, re-interpreted, and contextualized within the Acehnese setting; they have also demanded that women be represented equally in Aceh's law- and policy-making. This last point has been made formally possible in as much as the Law of Local Government of Aceh (LOGA) grants Acehnese women the rights to participate equally in the political, religious, and socioeconomic development of Aceh. The response of Acehnese women in challenging the interpretation of sharia is similar to that of Muslim women's movements in other part of the Muslim world. The injustices and discrimination against women as a result of neo-conservative interpretations of sharia have paved the way to the resurgence of Islamic feminism (Sharify-Funk 2005).

The prospects for additional gender-sensitive reform of Islamic law in Aceh today are not entirely clear. It may be that the particular conditions at play in Aceh following the peace agreement and period of post-tsunami assistance were more conducive to facilitating female engagement. If so, this means that the contemporary political and social conditions are hostile to a broadly feminist, gender-sensitive suite of religiously inspired laws. The presence of international and national organizations at work in Aceh was a significant factor in facilitating women's engagement with the formulation of local law, which at the time was in the early stages of development. The disruption to life caused by the tragedy opened public space in a way that was not previously possible and in a way that is not possible today. Women are now largely constrained by the status quo – social and economic roles and a legal framework that, together, constrict their public policy engagement. With a considerable body of law now in place, the focus will need to be on monitoring implementation and constructing a comprehensive and constructive reform platform.

References cited

Afrianty, Dina. 2011. "Local Women's Movements in Aceh and the Struggle for Equality and Justice: the Women's Network for Policy," *Review of Indonesia and Malaysia Affairs* 45(1 and 2): 37–68.

Afrianty, Dina. 2015. *Women and Sharia Law in Northern Indonesia: Local Women's NGOs and the reform of Islamic Law in Aceh* (London and New York: Routledge).

An-Na'im, Abdullahi. 2009. *Islam and the Secular State Negotiating the Future of Shari'a* (Cambridge: Harvard University Press).

Anwar, Zainah. 2005. "Sisters in Islam and the Struggle for Women's Rights," in Nouraie-Simone, Fereshteh, ed., *On Shifting Ground: Muslim Women in the Global Era* (New York: the Feminist Press), pp. 233–79.

Baiquni. 2012. "Cerita remaja putri Aceh gantung diri karena dituduh melacur," *Merdeka*, 13 September. www.merdeka.com/peristiwa/cerita-remaja-putri-aceh-gantung-diri-karena-dituduh-melacur.html (Accessed 28 February 2017).

Grosmann, Kristina. 2016. "Women's Rights Activists and the Drafting Process of the Islamic Criminal Law Code (Qanun Jinayat)," in Michael Feener, David Kloos, Annemari Samuels, eds., *Islam and the Limits of the State: Reconfiguration of Practice, Community and Authority in Contemporary Aceh* (The Netherlands: Brill), pp. 87–117.

Hidayat, Rafki. 2016. "Cambuk perempuan non-muslim, pusat diminta tegur Aceh," *BBC Indonesia*, 15 April. www.bbc.com/indonesia/berita_indonesia/2016/04/160414_indonesia_aceh_qanun_hakim (Accessed 20 February 2017).

Kloos, David. 2014. "In the Name of Syariah? Vigilante Violence, Territoriality, and Moral Authority in Aceh, Indonesia," *Indonesia* 98: 59–90.

———. 2016. "The Salience of Gender: Female Islamic Authority in Aceh, Indonesia," *Asian Studies Review* 40(4): 527–44.

Lestari, Sri. 2012. "Isu Syariat Islam di Pilkada Aceh," 9 April. www.bbc.com/indonesia/berita_indonesia/2012/04/120409_acehsyariat.shtml (Accessed 20 February 2017).

Mernissi, Fatima. 1991. *The Veil and the Male Elite: a Feminist Interpretation of Women's Rights in Islam* (Cambridge, MA: Perseus Publishing).

Mir-Hosseini, Ziba. 2000. *Marriage on Trial: A Study of Islamic Family Law* (London and New York: IB Tauris).

———. 2006. "Muslim Women's Quest for Equality: Between Islamic Law and Feminism," *Critical Inquiry* 32: 629–45.

Otto, Jan Michiel, ed. 2016. *Sharia Incorporated: A Comparative Overview of the Legal Systems of Twelve Muslim Countries in Past and Present* (Leiden: Leiden University Press).

Salim, Arskal. 2009. "Islam and Modernity: Syariah, Terrorism and Governance in Southeast Asia," *ARC Federation Fellowship* (Melbourne: Melbourne Law School).

Serambi Indonesia. 2016. "MA Tolak Guggatan terhadap hokum Jinayat," 18 July. http://aceh.tribunnews.com/2016/07/18/ma-tolak-gugatan-terhadap-hukum-jinayat (Accessed 22 February 2017).

Sharify-Funk, Meena. 2005. "Women and the Dynamics of Transnational Networks," in Nouraie-Simone, Fereshteh, ed., *On Shifting Ground: Muslim Women in the Global Era* (New York: The Feminist Press), pp. 250–68.

Siapno, Jacqueline. 2002. *Gender, Islam, Nationalism and the State in Aceh* (New York: Routledge Curzon).

Srimulyani, Eka. 2016. "Teungku Inong Dayah: Female Religious Leaders in Contemporary Aceh," in Michael Feener, David Kloos, Annemari Samuels, eds., *Islam and the Limits of the State: Reconfiguration of Practice, Community and Authority in Contemporary Aceh* (The Netherlands: Brill), pp. 141–65.

Tribunnews. 2016. "Hukuman cambuk 100 kali untuk pasangan zina di Takengon," 27 May. www.tribunnews.com/regional/2016/05/27/hukuman-cambuk-100-kali-untuk-pasangan-zina-di-takengon (Accessed 23 February 2017).

PART VI

Indonesia in an age of multiple globalizations

29

POPULAR CULTURE AND IDENTITY POLITICS

Ariel Heryanto

For too long, the study of Indonesia has been narrowly focused on its political and economic institutions and elite, at the expense of other issues of concern experienced on a daily basis by the majority of its many millions of citizens. Even when culture is taken seriously, academic studies of Indonesia tend to concentrate their inquiry around three types: the so-called "traditional," "ethnic," or "folk" cultures (which are often exoticized and presented as the "authentic" culture of the people), the state-sanctioned official version of national culture (as often propagated in schools and ceremonies), or the avant-garde or "high" cultures of the nation's intelligentsia (celebrated in the academy, theaters, and prestigious galleries). The everyday life, where popular culture permeates, is significantly understudied.

This continued neglect is even less forgivable in the early twenty-first century, as major political and economic institutions in Indonesia (along with many other countries around the world) suffer from a serious legitimation deficit. At the same time, increased access to mobile technologies and the proliferation of social media platforms have enabled the billions of the globe's "ordinary" population to make a strong presence in the world. In the public life of contemporary Indonesia, such trends have assumed an outward expression with Islamic features, as the scope of Islamization continues to expand at an unprecedented scale.

The above observation is not intended to suggest that political institutions or their elite can be considered as separate from, or less important than, popular culture. The rise of Joko Widodo's (best known as Jokowi) political career to presidency in 2014 served as a big wake-up call from millions of ordinary citizens. To a lesser extent, so did the case of the preceding president, Susilo Bambang Yudhoyono (better known locally as SBY), who became the first directly elected president of the republic a decade earlier. Prior to his ascent, Jokowi was a furniture trader and a long-term dedicated fan of heavy metal music. Yudhoyono was a retired military officer before being elected president for two terms from 2004 to 2014. During his presidency, he composed pop songs and released four albums.

The electoral success story of both presidents reads like a David and Goliath contest, demonstrating the seemingly miraculous power of passionate volunteers and non-party groups against the old political establishments, and against all odds. Right up to the eleventh hour, the rapidly turned politician Jokowi was reluctant to run for the presidency and challenge an extremely well-connected Prabowo, who already enjoyed the benefits of a well-established political network and the strong support of nearly all of the mainstream media outlets in the country.

Unlike Prabowo, Jokowi had not built a career or network in political parties. In sharp contrast to Prabowo, Jokowi had limited resources and interest in mobilizing the masses to support him. In contrast to the flow of the familiar "money politics," a large number of individual citizens proudly published their bank slips on social media, showing off their laughably small donations to Jokowi's election campaign.

Jokowi's success in the 2014 presidential election can be attributed to many things, not least of all the spontaneous popular support of largely unorganized groups of ordinary Indonesians during the last few weeks before the election day. They converged in various forms, exhibiting a high degree of fluidity, and estimated to be as many as 1,000-odd groups of varying sizes. Most important among them were the Jakarta-based pro-Jokowi artists who were behind the July 5 music concert, which attracted over 100,000 people. Unpaid volunteers with no political party affiliation designed and ran the entire event. The term "people power" is inadequate for describing Jokowi's supporter base. Such a term is strongly associated with street mobilization, depicting masculine forces and creating martyrs of violence in the downtowns of cities like Manila, Bangkok, or Cairo. In contrast, Jokowi's supporters were inclined toward soft power, such as puns, visual arts, and music on YouTube, Facebook, and Twitter. It is significant that in this group women and the underprivileged were overrepresented, while others in this group could be characterized by the absence of politics in their daily lives, proudly belonging to none of the contesting political parties.

Like Jokowi, his predecessor SBY was never seriously considered a political leader, let alone a presidential candidate, prior to formally running for the elections in 2004. His Democratic Party was a fledgling underdog when it contested the elections and was in no way a rival to the other major party candidates. While its achievement impressed many, it won only a minority position in the parliamentary election. However, SBY won Indonesia's first direct presidential election. To explain SBY's sudden rise to power, and his reelection for a second term in 2009, it would be remiss if one completely overlooked the success of his campaign team in mobilizing the power of the mass media and popular culture.[1]

SBY's main rival was Megawati Sukarnoputri, chair of the Indonesian Democratic Party, one of the few big parties with a long history dating back to the struggle for Indonesia's independence. Her party already enjoyed the largest number of parliamentary votes. The major difference between the two presidential hopefuls was in their public presentations. Megawati often evaded media coverage; when confronted by journalists, she always said very little, if anything at all. In contrast, SBY paid generous attention to the demands of the media. He even went as far as singing at public functions, releasing three albums of his own songs, and attending the finals of the Indonesian Idol competition.

To highlight the importance of the populous and the popular in selected events of political significance, however, is not the main aim of this chapter. Merely emphasizing how popular culture can serve or subvert the interests of the political elite, or exert influence over national politics, misses the point. It would risk a common error in reducing the significance of the former by subordinating it to the latter and in the process reproducing the elitist perspectives that require a serious critique. In contrast, this chapter aims to show how elite national politics and everyday cultural practices and contestations are mutually constitutive in complex and indirect ways, with a focus on identity politics in contemporary Indonesia as manifest in popular cultures. In a later section, I will present selected cases from Indonesian cinema and music performance to illustrate this point. Before we set out an empirical analysis of the dynamics of identity politics in contemporary Indonesia, it is worth examining the broader context, and consider why such an important topic has remained understudied for much of the history of Indonesian studies, as well as detailing why an in-depth investigation into identity politics in popular culture is a critical component to studying the social life of the world's fourth most populated nation.

Framework and history

There are many reasons why a privileged focus on elitism within the political and economic institutions prevails in most studies of Indonesia. Here it will be sufficient to note some of the more obvious contributing factors. As Ruth McVey (1995) has observed, for a very long time, the intellectual framework in Southeast Asian studies, including Indonesian studies, has centered too much on nation-state building and modernization (see also Bonura and Sears 2007; Heryanto 2005). Alternatively, the study of Indonesia has been dominated by a set of commonly perceived problems as essentially impediments to nation-state building and modernization: militarism, human rights abuses, rampant corruption, violent ethno-religious conflicts, and, lately, Islamist militants.

Pop culture's close and unashamed association with profit-making in the entertainment industry has made it difficult for it to gain respectable status among educators, moralists, religious leaders, or serious scholars and researchers. For this reason, the pejorative term "mass culture" has occasionally been used to describe it (Macdonald 1998: 22; Strinati 1995: 10). The latter term "represents a debased, trivialized, superficial, artificial and standardized culture" (Strinati 1995: 21). As acknowledged by many,[2]

> the consumption of popular culture by the general population has always been a problem for "other people," be they intellectuals, political leaders or moral and social reformers. These "other people" have often held the view that this population should ideally be occupied with something more enlightening or worthwhile than popular culture.
>
> *(Strinati 1995: 41)*

Another reason for the preoccupation with Indonesia's elite and its political and economic institutions is the presence of a strong masculine bias (Stivens 1991). As is the case globally (see O'Connor and Klaus 2000: 379–82), issues concerning modernization, nation-state building, the economy, religion, war, and corruption are primarily stories about men and masculinity. It is taken for granted that these issues are of public importance, while other less valued genders are relegated to the secondary "private" or "domestic" sphere – a place where mass-mediated entertainment and pop culture are commonly consumed. Thus, we have the familiar and deeply problematic division between the masculine world news and the feminine soap operas or between serious news magazines and so-called women's magazines.

To be fair, popular culture is a product of an industrialized society. Its production and distribution requires technologies of mass production, distribution, and duplication. Since Indonesia's independence, sustained industrial expansion of significance only took place in the 1980s, at the height of the militarist rule of the New Order government (1966–1998). During the same period, the urban middle classes underwent phenomenal growth. Understandably then, a serious and sympathetic study of popular culture has arrived fairly late. Even as late as the 1970s, when popular culture began to make its presence difficult to ignore, the nation's intelligentsia tended to discuss the phenomena with disgust or contempt (see Henschkel 1994). More often than not, popular culture was perceived primarily as the unintended and undesirable excess of modernization and industrialization, comparable to air pollution or traffic jams.[3] Of course, such a negative perspective is not uniquely Indonesian.[4] It is only from the 1980s that we witness a growing interest and sympathetic, albeit critical, analysis of the issues, in Indonesia and overseas, with Heider (1991), Kitley (2000), Lockhard (1998), and Sen and Hill (2000) among the pioneering authors of books in English on Indonesian media and popular culture (for more, see those cited in Heryanto 2008: 6; Heryanto 2014).

Notwithstanding recent booms in the media and entertainment industry, another less obvious problem is the fact that the majority of Indonesians today are unaware of the rich and complex history of popular culture prior to independence. Indonesian studies that have developed outside the country have not done enough to help Indonesians see this past either. A strong nativist vision of the Indonesian self since the 1950s has been responsible for driving a contemporary ethno-nationalism and rampant amnesia. Building the new nation-state in Indonesia meant denying or forgetting that history immediately prior to independence, a time when many non-natives took on pioneering and critical roles, including liberal or progressive Europeans, Chinese Indonesians, and the Left of various ethnic backgrounds. Independent Indonesia wants not only to "reject" its colonial cultural heritage but to deny and forget it, while it ambitiously attempts to "invent" a new culture (Reid 2016: 6). As Foulcher succinctly describes it, Indonesia "never looked back to ask questions that produce post-colonialist answers. . . . Rather, it looked forward" (Foulcher 1995: 161). When it looks back, it does so in a self-orientalizing fashion, indulging in the delusion of the past glory of the ostensibly authentic traditions of the various ethnic groups. The works of Barendregt (2013, 2014) Cohen (2006, 2009, 2016), Cohen and Noszlopy (2010), Strassler (2008, 2010), and Winet (2010) are just a few of a longer list of literature that redress this lacuna in the field of popular culture.

Methodologically, studying popular culture poses another challenge. The fast-changing life cycle of what comes to be considered a "popular" product or popular consumption often occurs on a massive scale in a relatively short period of time. As Chua comments in a slightly different context: "Film, television programmes, popular music and musicians . . . are often already off the screen [or the stage, or shops] way before any analysis is completed" (Chua 2004: 204). However, it is not the specific products of popular culture that should form our main object of analysis. Rather, popular cultures can be fascinating and highly instructive when considered from a wider perspective: as materials and sites for the performative contestation of various ideologies, class dispositions, moral inclinations, and identity politics. The rest of this chapter will be devoted to highlighting some of the most important identity politics in contemporary Indonesia. Before that, it will be useful to delineate the concept of popular culture adopted for this study.

For the purpose of this study, the term *popular culture* refers broadly to a variety of genres of circulated communicative practices, which figure prominently for a large number of "ordinary" people or by such people or a combination of both. Some products of popular culture are commercially produced (including music, films, and television) for mass consumption by the largest possible segment of people. Others are non-industrialized, relatively independent, communicative practices that circulate through various means (public events, parades, festivals), often, but not always, in opposition or as an alternative to the mass-produced commodities of entertainment and lifestyle. Of course, these categories are in practice not entirely separated. History shows a continuous and considerable borrowing or mutation of particular elements across one category and another. What they all share in common are the communicative practices ("culture") of, to, or by people of diverse backgrounds, who are "neither [exclusively or distinctly] members of the philosophical, aesthetic, or political elites, nor . . . of the new proletariat or underclasses" (Kahn 2001:19).[5]

Identity politics

It has been often repeated that Indonesia is a nation of extremely diverse cultures, languages, religious beliefs, and traditions. That is an understatement. Pisani (2014) more aptly describes Indonesia as an "improbable" nation. Diversity is a common feature of most metropolitan cities around the globe, and such diversity has often been celebrated by locals. However, it is limited by the fact that these local residents visit the same or similar chain of grocery stores, exchange the same monetary currency, and share many television news and other programs with power from the same major suppliers of electricity. For the same reasons, the middle class population of Indonesia's capital city Jakarta shares a lot in common with its counterparts in San Francisco, Shanghai, or Melbourne in lifestyle, education, and aspiration.

What distinguishes most of Indonesia from these metropoles are the remarkable gaps and disconnections among the hundreds of distinct and scattered ethnic communities that inhabit the thousands of islands across this world's largest archipelagic nation. For students of Indonesian culture, an in-depth discussion of any select part of the nation's culture or history would necessarily require some sort of reduction and generalization. But for many citizens of Indonesia, "national identity" has always been a soul-searching question, a central and highly emotional topic of heated public debate and communal conflict, sometimes fatally so. Indonesia's vast territory and cultural diversity are a constant source of national pride, as well as a source of apprehension – about its fragile unity and potential breakup, its lack of security in the face of real or perceived foreign threats, and the unjustified domination of selected groups of fellow nationals over the rest.

What should never get lost in the necessarily generalized or reductive analysis of Indonesia's identity politics, are the fascinating, as well as dangerous, tensions among the four major forces that make the foundation or backbone of Indonesia. One of these four forces can generally be understood as the many vernacular "traditions" in the archipelago, of which what has been conveniently called Javanese (itself diverse and complex) has been salient. The other three competing forces are commonly identified as exogenous and distinctively "modern": Islamic, liberal, and for want of a better term, "socialist."[6] A few words on each of these four major social forces will be useful.

For many decades, students of Indonesian culture have deconstructed the notion of local culture as something pristine, authentic, essential, or indigenous. Many of these local traditions have a long history of change and interaction with one another. They have also interacted with and adopted elements from other traditions that have traveled across the globe. In several parts of Indonesia's archipelago, Hinduism and Buddhism have been embraced with varying modification in form and scale, giving new life to the traditions of the local ancestors (see Chalmers 2006: Chapters 2, 4). What has come to be known variably as "Javanese" culture, Javanism, or Javanist mysticism are products of a long history of such traditions blending from local and distant places. In any case, "Javaneseness" is never one and the same thing for the long-term residents of the island of Java, including those who have been identified or self-identify as ethnically Javanese and members of the sub-ethnic groups. To varying degrees and complexity, the same can be said about other ethnic groups of Indonesia.

Of the three major modernizing forces that have shaped Indonesia, Islam was the earliest to arrive on the archipelago and has become the most prominent in the early decades of the millennium. The other two sources of modernity are a little more difficult to label with accuracy. For want of a better term, they will be referred to here as the various streams of thought inspired by liberalism and socialism respectively. Liberalism is regarded as a dirty word by some in independent Indonesia; the term "developmentalism" has been preferred among those who subscribe to some of the basic tenets of liberalism in the past and present. Problematic as they may be, terms like "leftist" or "populist" are often used conveniently to refer to those people who show a marked orientation toward, or affinity with, Marxist or socialist thoughts and ideological orientation.

Certainly, there are more than a few derivatives, variants of, and names for each of these four moral, intellectual, and ideological orientations that have shaped Indonesia past and present. For the purpose of analysis, they are portrayed here as ideal types and conceptualized in the simplest terms; they do not provide an empirical description of Indonesia's overwhelmingly complex history. It is also worth noting that in reality there are no clear-cut boundaries that would separate out these four identified forces, although in some major conflicts their distinctions can be overdrawn and their occasional overlaps denied.

The challenge of keeping the "improbable" nation intact is managing these four major forces. In the 1960s President Sukarno tried to strike a balance with three major ideologies in his concept of NASAKOM, an acronym of Nasionalisme, Agama, and Komunisme (nationalism, religion, and communism). The impetus for this slogan was the looming crisis of a country clearly teetering on the brink of civil war, and also partly the unresolved questions since independence about the nation's identity and subsequently the heat of the global Cold War. The army (backed by liberal democracies in the West) in alliance with the intelligentsia from both "developmentalist" quarters and "Muslim" quarters confronted the Indonesian Communist Party (the world's largest outside the Soviet Union and the People's Republic of China). From the end of 1965 and for the next several years, the socialist/Marxist/Communist oriented segments of the population and their cultural works were physically annihilated. Survivors and their relatives were systematically stigmatized for decades. President Sukarno was marginalized before being put under house arrest where he remained until his death in 1970.

For the next three decades, a version of Javanese political culture (called the *priyayi*) took center stage in national politics under the military dictatorship of General Soeharto's New Order government (1966–1998). During this period, Indonesia witnessed an illiberal "developmentalism," which sponsored an expansion of industrialization. The history of the Indonesian left, including its brutal demise in the 1960s, was completely erased from the history textbooks. Any contemporary public discussion regarding its fate or legacy risked official censure, legal prosecution, or threats of retaliations from non-government groups.

Throughout much of the 1970s and 1980s, Islam became the next target of suppression by the military dictatorship. Many Islamic political leaders were jailed under the draconian anti-subversion law. The suppression of political Islam lasted for about 20 years, ironically marking a period of strongly anti-Muslim politics over an extended period in the world's largest Muslim nation (see TAPOL 1987). However, serious division within the top political elite of the New Order led President Soeharto in 1990 to make a radical change to his political strategy by actively courting Islamic groups of various ideological orientations. This shift heralded the beginning of an unprecedented wave of Islamization, continuing into the early decades of the twenty-first century. Since then, the question of Islam versus non-Islam, as well as the more intricate question of what is (not) Islamic, has dominated Indonesia's social life from the top of national politics right down to the banality of everyday life. As will be shown in the next section, these issues are clearly visible and resonate loudly in social media and the popular culture of everyday life.[7]

In the opening section of this chapter, I referred to Jokowi's remarkable political career and his rapid ascent to the presidency. It is worth noting that the single most serious challenge that he confronted during his presidential nomination was the smear campaign launched by his opponent, which questioned his religious faith, as well as the accusation of his having a past association with the communist movement. Furthermore, in late 2016, Jokowi's key political confidant, Basuki Tjahaja Purnama (a.k.a. Ahok), Jakarta's governor, became the target of two large street protests – the largest since the 1998 mobilizations that brought the military dictatorship of Soeharto to its knees. These rallies were presented as an Islamic protest against Ahok, a Chinese Indonesian and a Christian. The official pretext for the protest was an allegation that Ahok had made a blasphemous statement against Islam. But not all Muslim leaders in Jakarta were in agreement about this accusation. Most observers saw the protest as a blatant campaign to undermine Ahok's nomination for the upcoming governorship election, in competition with two other candidates, both of whom had capitalized on their Muslim credentials in an attempt to woo Muslim voters.

Politics of identity in popular culture

Certainly, popular cultures are often designed, produced, and distributed with no intention of ever becoming a conduit for political messages. The majority of mass-produced products are intended to provide entertainment for the potential consumer as a source of profit. Likewise, most consumers patronize these commodities with no interest in politics. So, it is important not to politically over-read such cultural products. However, Indonesia has many examples of culture (popular or otherwise), which have been overtly designed to make political statements and are celebrated for exhibiting political values. Some are banned for being politically subversive. The music of Rhoma Irama in the 1970s and 1980s (Frederick 1982), the music of Iwan Fals in the 1980s and 1990s (Murray 1991), the literary works of Pramoedya Ananta Toer, and the theatrical productions of Rendra's Bengkel Teater and Nano Riantiarno's Teater Koma (Zurbuchen 1990) are some of the best known examples of politically engaged artworks that bore the brunt of the New Order censorship.

My main concern in this chapter, however, is not the kind of cultural works with overtly political content or intent. Rather, more fascinating and instructive are cases where what is crafted and performed with the pure intention to entertain unintentionally acquires political value when circulated in public or is received as such by the audience, beyond the control of the producer or performers. This section is devoted precisely to such cases, including one in 2003, when popular singer-dancer Inul Daratista found herself at the center of a national controversy.

Needless to say, the relationship between national politics and popular culture at any given time is never simple, straightforward, one-directional, or homologous. While popular culture is not entirely autonomous from its immediate political environment, it is not its mirror either. As briefly mentioned above, Soeharto's New Order government (1966–1998) delegitimized leftist politics and culture. It suppressed political Islam, before making a complete about-face in 1990, marking the beginning of a huge wave of Islamization. For most of the period of the New Order rule, a gentrified version of Javanese culture and political etiquette enjoyed a dominant position. With considerable support from Western investment – minus the Western liberal thinking – Indonesia's capitalist industrialization expanded stridently while labor unions were controlled as tightly as the press, the parliament, the justice institution, and the universities. In brief, it was a political environment where the production and consumption of pop culture was caught in the polarity between those for and those against the status quo, centered as the official ideology of the regime, which was a combination of Javanism, secularism, militarism, developmentalism, and indigenism.

Keith Foulcher's (1990) analysis of *Selamat Tinggal Jeanette* (Goodbye Jeanette) (1987 Sandy), a commercially successful film released at the height of the New Order rule, is highly instructive. Undoubtedly, the melodramatic film was intended mainly as entertainment.[8] But Foulcher's critical and considered analysis demonstrates persuasively how the film can be read as a case where a non-state agent voluntarily and unconsciously created a fictional narrative that reproduced the hegemonic ideologies of the time and where a contemporary version of a priyayi perspective was central. Here priyayi implies

> an eclectic combination of aspects of a *kebatinan* [Javanese mysticism] world view and the Dutch colonial mix of public morality and private self-interest, all elaborated against a backdrop of the arts, customs and etiquette of the courts of Central Java.
>
> *(Foulcher 1990: 303)*

The film tells the love story of Suryono, a male Javanese artist from a priyayi family and two very different women: Jeanette (his French wife) and Trima, a peasant woman who works as a housemaid in the house of Suryono's mother in the city of Solo (the home of Javanese court culture). For most of the story, Suryono and his wife live in his mother's house. Jeanette and Trima are polar opposites. Jeanette is highly animated, independent-minded, confident, and thoroughly if not excessively "modern." Following the stereotype of the "liberal" West commonly portrayed in Asia, Jeanette is presented as a woman from a rich family, who having fallen victim to drugs in the past, travels to Indonesia to seek spiritual and emotional tranquility. Trima, in contrast, is a peasant girl, with no school education. She is timid, especially in showing her secret love for the married son of her employer-cum-patron. When their marriage breaks down, Jeanette leaves Suryono and returns to Europe. After some time, Suryono rapes Trima, and she becomes pregnant. To cover the shame, Trima is forced to resign from work and return to her village with a false story about a thief having raped her.

Suryono's mother plays a third important woman in the story. Her deceased husband was unfaithful to her, leaving her with painful memories of their marriage. Having Suryono as her only child, and her only next of kin, she is strongly attached to him. Until near the end of the film, Suryono's mother does not approve of his marrying a Westerner, or worse still, a housemaid. She sees Trima's pregnancy out of wedlock not so much as her son's shortcomings. Rather, her priyayi perspective confirms her conviction of the low character of low-class Javanese peasant folk.

Foulcher suggests that the relations between Suryono and these three women resemble the New Order state-sponsored notions of three significant others: the enchanting but also flawed and intimidating West (Jeanette), the vernacular traditions whose qualities of innocence and backwardness seem exploitable and disposable (Trima), and the modern-day priyayi Java (Suryono's mother) as the foundation and antecedent to the Indonesian nation-state (Suryono's self). The film, presumably unconsciously, also asserts a local version of a hyper-masculinist self (in Suryono) by distinguishing itself from the "others" as female. It reaffirms its entitlement and desire to dominate all three females.

The intention to unite these others under one dominating self is never a total success in the film, just as in New Order Indonesia. Near the end of the story, Suryono marries Trima. Jeanette returns to Solo with a baby (Suryono's son) to learn the truth about Suryono's new status. She decides not to reunite with her husband but manages to reconcile with her mother-in-law thanks to the newborn baby. These two women are disappointed by their respective husbands. This potentially subversive ending must have not been intended by the producer. Neither was it taken as such by many of its viewers, if the reception and published reviews of the films are any indicator.

Significantly, two major forces are absent from *Selamat Tinggal Jeanette*, and their absence goes without comment in Foulcher's otherwise excellent analysis. There are no elements with an identifiable orientation toward Islam or with socialist aspirations. As indicated earlier, these two major forces were unwanted during much of the New Order rule. Off screen, they were either dead, in prison, or "released" with no civil rights and under regular surveillance. From 1990, Soeharto began to court Islamic politicians in an attempt to reaffirm his grip on state power. Immediately after the official end of Soeharto's New Order rule in 1998, Islamization began in earnest. How Islamization altered the production, circulation, and reception of popular culture in Indonesia (and Malaysia) has been addressed in Weintraub's edited volume (2011). Following Foulcher's steps, and reading specific cinematic text as an allegory, I found the hugely successful feature film *Ayat-ayat Cinta* (2008, Bramantyo) remarkable for the ways in which it threw light on the ideological changes occurring in post–New Order Indonesia.

No film – and certainly no "Islamic" film – has attracted the amount of public attention and celebration in contemporary Indonesia as the film *Ayat-ayat Cinta* at the time of its release. Not all Muslims agreed that it contains Islamic values or serves the interests of the Muslims (Yumiyanti 2008); some even alleged it is anti-Islam. Notwithstanding the controversy, the film broke new records as soon as it was commercially released. Viewed by more than three million Indonesians in the first few weeks of its release, the film surpassed all other titles previously screened in the country, regardless of country of origin, language, or genre. The film was based on a best-selling novel of the same title by Habiburrahman El Shirazy, an Islamic intellectual and proselytizer.

To put it in a broader perspective, the downfall of the New Order left in its wake a vast political, cultural, and ideological vacuum and led the various surviving social forces (indigenous mysticism, Islam, and liberalism were among the strong contenders) to compete for dominance. The success of such a story as *Ayat-ayat Cinta* marked a high point of Islamic cultural strength in this ideological battle, not least in cinema. Significantly, prior to the production of *Ayat-ayat Cinta*, the two most commercially successful films shown in Indonesia were *Jelangkung* (2001) and *Ada Apa Dengan Cinta?* (2002). The first is a horror film, but not in the tradition of the genre from previous decades or the longer history of mystical practices among the more devoted followers of Javanese tradition. Rather, *Jelangkung* represented a new generation of horror films that are distinctly based in the urban middle classes. The film tells the story of a group of very critical and competent university students who, with much earnest curiosity, endeavor to find out about the possible existence of ghosts. The second film, *Ada Apa Dengan Cinta?* is a shamelessly Americanized melodramatic love story between two middle-class Jakartan youths. Both titles attracted slightly over one million viewers, outdoing the major Hollywood blockbusters that had dominated the nation's cinema for nearly half a century. The arrival and success of *Ayat-ayat Cinta* not only brought contemporary Islam on par with the more Western-oriented and indigenized-oriented popular cultures on the nation's cinematic screen in terms of box office sale figures but well surpassed them.

Perhaps it is not purely accidental that both priyayi-centric *Selamat Tinggal Jeanette* and (supposedly) Islamic *Ayat-ayat Cinta* tell a love story with a male protagonist who is surrounded by several women who are in love with him. However, when read as political allegory, their contrast is striking and instructive. *Ayat-ayat Cinta*'s male protagonist, Fahri, appears to resemble post-1998 Indonesia during a period of a post-economic crisis. Fahri has a very modest family background. As a quasi-superhuman, he is a capable and conscientious student, with heart-throb charm and a certain naïveté. Such attributes are in line with the official propaganda, spouting a self-delusion about Indonesia's magnificent potential and natural resources, which have attracted the world's superpowers over many centuries.

In a post-9/11 environment, Indonesia's Islamization has also been a cautious one. Indonesia is proud to be seen as the world's largest Muslim country, striving to be a respectable player in contemporary world politics but preferring to maintain its own "authentic" identity rather than ape the West or become Arabized. It is committed to retaining its status as a secular state. The male protagonist in *Ayat-ayat Cinta* is a pious Muslim who welcomes pluralism and globalism with a moderate stance and a Western lifestyle. He speaks Arabic, English, and a little German in addition to Indonesian. He is neither a militant jihadi nor a syncretic-cum-traditionalist mystic follower; neither is he Arabized in his appearance or cultural orientation. He duly remembers his origins, respectfully stays true to his Indonesian identity, and remains in contact with his mother in the motherland.

We have seen how the film *Selamat Tinggal Jeanette* can be read as an unconscious testament to a late-1980s ideological perspective, dominant during the New Order rule, where Javanese priyayi represented the state-sponsored image of the nation's self. Both Islam and the Left are significantly missing. We also considered how two decades later, the film *Ayat-ayat Cinta* articulated the significant alteration Indonesia had undergone with Islamization becoming the single most dominant feature of public life. I wish to conclude this discussion with a brief mention of the case of Inul Daratista, a non-priyayi Javanese popular culture performer who came to prominence for a short while in the early 2000s, provoking a major backlash from all directions, especially from the Islamic-oriented elite.

In 2003, the sensual singer-dancer Inul Daratista stirred up a nationwide controversy. Her performance represented a resurgence of an old tradition of non-priyayi Javanese cultural practice, this time from the lower classes of East Java, which celebrates bodily pleasure and sexuality. Being the single largest ethnic and cultural group, the Javanese, with their resilient mysticism, have for centuries been the main buffer preventing Indonesia from becoming an Islamic state. Although Inul's critics are drawn from a wide variety of backgrounds, the staunchest and loudest critics have been those with an Islamic institutional basis or background. She was banned from performing in several cities (and in Malaysia), while being much lauded in others.

Partly triggered by Inulmania, but also in response to a broader expansion of other related erotic-focused elements in the entertainment industry, a proposal for a new anti-pornography law was tabled before parliament in 2006 and ratified on October 30, 2008, with a significant number of lawmakers walking out of the session in protest.[9] The controversy about both Inul and the anti-pornography law has a lot more to do with Indonesia's identity politics than with issues of decency in general or with an individual artist. By many traditional standards among many ethnic groups in Indonesia, Inul's eroticism was mild, but the ideological war brewing among the major political forces in contemporary Indonesia was definitely not.

The controversy over Inul and the anti-pornography law can be considered as another iteration of a series of ideological contests among the four major forces outlined earlier, that have shaped Indonesia. Elsewhere, I have elaborated how this contest has taken shape in the case of Inul (Heryanto 2011). Suffice to note here that the Inul controversy encompasses a multidimensional ideological battle in at least four overlapping areas. The first is the teetering tension between local sentiment (East Java) and the national authority (Jakarta); the second is between syncretic Javanism and the new, rising Islamic piety; the third is the tension between a feminist consciousness, which is gaining momentum, and the old established patriarchy; and finally the fourth involves class conflict between Inul's lower-class fans and the middle- and upper-middle-class citizens who have long dominated the nation's cultural scene.

Concluding note

It is a miracle that the unity of an "improbable nation" as large and diverse as Indonesia has survived imminent divisions. I have identified four major social and cultural forces that have dominated the nation and have been competing with each other over the past seven decades since independence. Indonesian history is to some extent a history of the dynamic relations among these four forces, fraught with occasional fatal conflicts among the segments of two or more of these major forces. While analyses of political and economic elites and institutions abound in Indonesian studies, their power relations in everyday life among the millions of Indonesians, mediated by the new power of digital technology, remain understudied.

From an enlarged perspective in the twenty-first century, there are additional reasons for a more serious study of Indonesia's identity politics. Violent conflicts, which have raged in many parts of the globe after the end of the Cold War, have been more concerned with identity politics than having any legitimate control over a population, natural resources, or a territory. Kaldor

(1999) and McDonald (2013) call them the "new wars." But identity politics has not always been about conflicts and wars. For millions of Indonesians and non-Indonesians alike, everyday forms of identity politics also mean an articulation of their visions, aspirations, and commitments to solidarity or simply the apprehensions or pleasures pertaining to their personal life or immediate social circles. Popular cultures abundantly demonstrate these sentiments on a massive scale in quotidian fashion.

Notes

1 I am grateful to Mark Hobart, who helped me see this point through an informal communication exchange.
2 For similar elitist perspectives in contemporary Indonesia, see Hobart (2006).
3 Indonesia's most prestigious social sciences journal, *Prisma*, dedicated its June 1977 issue specifically to discussing the general theme "pop culture." With very few exceptions, the dominant tone throughout the issue in articles, commentaries, and interviews is one of condemnation, scorn, and pillory. Such a view was commonly shared by scholars, critics, and artists.
4 Macdonald (1998) is a classic example of the elitist American view in the 1950s of popular culture as "mass culture."
5 For other equally familiar concepts of "popular culture," see equally valid concepts of "popular cultures" (Strinati 1995; Storey 2006).
6 For a different take on the matter, to which my analysis here is partly indebted, see Cribb (1999). Elsewhere, I have made similar attempts in Heryanto (2005: 63–5, and 2008: 9–11).
7 I attempted a more nuanced account of these changes in Heryanto (2014).
8 The film was based on a novel of the same title, authored by Titie Said (1986). Foulcher's analysis, which I sum up here, is based on the film, which departs slightly from the novel.
9 The bill may have a longer history of antecedents. It had already been the subject of much serious discussion in parliament in 1997 but was not formally drafted and submitted for ratification in parliament until February 14, 2006. Since then, it has continued to provoke an unabated nationwide controversy.

References cited

Barendregt, Bart, ed. 2014. *Sonic Modernities: Popular Music in the Malay World* (Leiden: Brill).
Barendregt, Bart and Els Bogaert, eds. 2013. *Recollecting Resonances: Indonesian Dutch Musical Encounters* (Leiden: Brill).
Bonura, Carlo and Laurie Sears. 2007. "Knowledges That Travel in Southeast Asian Studies," in Laurie Sears, ed., *Knowing Southeast Asia* (Seattle: University of Washington), pp. 3–32.
Chalmers, Ian. 2006. *Indonesia: An Introduction to Contemporary Traditions* (Melbourne: Oxford University Press).
Chua Beng-Huat. 2004. "Conceptualizing an East Asian Popular Culture," *Inter-Asia Cultural Studies*, 5(2): 200–21.
Cohen, Matthew. 2006. *The Komedie Stamboel: Popular Theater in Colonial Indonesia, 1891–1903* (Leiden: KITLV Press).
———. 2009. "Hybridity in *Komedi Stambul*," in D. Jedamski, ed., *Chewing Over the West: Occidental Narratives in Non-Western Readings* (Amsterdam and New York), pp. 275–301.
———. 2016. *Inventing the Performing Arts: Modernity and Tradition in Colonial Indonesia* (Honolulu: University of Hawaii Press).
Cohen, Matthew and Laura Noszlopy, eds. 2010. *Contemporary Southeast Asian Performance: Transnational Perspectives* (Cambridge: Cambridge Scholars Publishing).
Cribb, Robert. 1999. "Nation: Making Indonesia," in D. K. Emmerson, ed., *Indonesia Beyond Suharto* (Armonk, NY: Asia Society), pp. 3–38.
Foulcher, Keith. 1990. "The Construction of an Indonesian National Culture: Patterns of Hegemony and Resistance," in A. Budiman, ed., *State and Civil Society in Indonesia* (Clayton: Centre of Southeast Asian Studies), pp. 301–20.
———. 1995. "In Search of the Postcolonial in Indonesian Literature," *Sojourn* 10(2): 147–71.
Frederick, William. 1982. "Rhoma Irama and the Dangdut Style," *Indonesia*, 34 (Oct): 103–30.

Heider, Karl. 1991. *Indonesian Cinema; National Culture on Screen* (Honolulu: University of Hawaii Press).

Henschkel, Marina 1994. "Perception of Popular Culture in Contemporary Indonesia," *Review of Indonesian and Malayan Affairs* 28(2): 53–70.

Heryanto, Ariel. 2005. "Ideological Baggage and Orientations of the Social Sciences in Indonesia," in V. R. Hadiz and D. Dhakidae, eds., *Social Science And Power In Indonesia* (Jakarta and Singapore: Equinox and ISEAS), pp. 69–101.

———, ed. 2008. *Popular Culture in Indonesia: Fluid Identities in Post-Authoritarian Politics* (London and New York: Routledge).

———. 2011. "Upgraded Piety and Pleasure: the New Middle Class and Islam in Indonesian Popular Culture," in A. Weintraub, ed., *Islam and Popular Culture in Indonesia and Malaysia* (London: Routledge), pp. 60–82.

———. 2014. *Identity and Pleasure: The Politics of Indonesian Screen Culture* (Singapore and Kyoto: NUS Press and Kyoto CSEAS Series on Asian Studies).

Hobart, Mark. 2006. "Entertaining Illusions: How Indonesian Elites Imagine Reality TV Affects the Masses," *Asian Journal of Communication* 16(4): 393–410.

Kahn, Joel. 2001. *Modernity and Exclusion* (London: Sage).

Kaldor, Mary. 1999. *New and Old Wars: Organized Violence in a Global Era* (Cambridge: Polity Press).

Kitley, Philip. 2000. *Television, Nation, and Culture in Indonesia* (Athens: Center for International Studies).

Lockhard, Craig. 1998. *Dance of Life: Popular Music and Politics in Southeast Asia* (Honolulu: University of Hawaii Press).

Macdonald, Dwight. 1998. "A Theory of Mass Culture," in John Storey, ed., *Cultural Theory and Popular Culture*, 2nd Edition (Athens: The University of Georgia Press), pp. 22–36.

McDonald, Kevin. 2013. "Grammars of Violence, Modes of Embodiment and Frontiers of the Subject," in Kevin McSorley, ed., *War and the Body: Militarisation, Practice and Experience War Politics and Experience* (London: Routledge), pp. 138–51.

McVey, Ruth. 1995. "Change and Continuity in Southeast Asian Studies," *Journal of Southeast Asian Studies* 26(1).

Murray, Alison. 1991. "Kampung Culture and Radical Chic in Jakarta," *Review of Indonesian and Malayan Affairs*, 25 (Winter): 1–16.

O'Connor, Barbara and Elisabeth Klaus. 2000. "Pleasure and Meaningful Discourse: An Overview of Research Issues," *International Journal of Cultural Studies* 3(3): 369–87.

Pisani, Elizabeth. 2014. *Indonesia Etc.: Exploring the Improbable Nation* (New York and London: W. W. Norton & Company).

Reid, Anthony. 2016. "Humanities in Indonesia for a Global Age," *Humaniora: Journal of Culture, Literature and Linguistics* 28(1): 3–11.

Said, Titie. 1986. *Selamat Tinggal Jeanette* (Jakarta: Alam Budaya).

Sen, Krishna and David Hill. 2000. *Media, Culture and Politics in Indonesia* (Melbourne: Oxford University Press).

Stivens, Maila, ed. 1991. *Why Gender Matters in Southeast Asia Politics* (Clayton, Victoria: Centre for Southeast Asian Studies, Monash University).

Storey, John. 2006. *Cultural Theory and Popular Culture: An Introduction* (New York: Pearson Prentice Hall).

Strassler, Karen. 2008. "Cosmopolitan Visions: Ethnic Chinese and the Photographic Imagining of Indonesia in the Late Colonial and Early Postcolonial Periods," *Journal of Asian Studies*, 67(2/May): 395–432.

———. 2010. *Refracted Visions: Popular Photography and National Modernity in Java* (Durham and London: Duke University Press).

Strinati, Dominic. 1995. *An Introduction to Theories of Popular Culture* (London: Routledge).

TAPOL. 1987. *Indonesia: Muslims on Trial* (London: TAPOL).

Weintraub, Andrew, ed. 2011. *Islam and Popular Culture in Indonesia and Malaysia* (London: Routledge).

Winet, Evan. 2010. *Indonesian Postcolonial Theatre* (London: Palgrave Macmillan).

Yumiyanti, Iin. 2008. "Kontroversi Dongeng Cinta Fahri," *detikNews*, 18 March.

Zurbuchen, Mary S. 1990. "Images of Culture and National Development in Indonesia: The Cockroach Opera," *Asian Theatre Journal* 7(2): 127–49.

Filmography/Videography

Ada Apa Dengan Cinta? (Indonesia 2002, Rudi Soedjarwo)

Ayat-Ayat Cinta (Indonesia 2008, Hanung Bramantyo)

Jelangkung (Indonesia 2001, Rizal Mantovani and Jose Poernomo)

30

NATION, ISLAM, AND GENDER IN DANGDUT, INDONESIA'S MOST POPULAR MUSIC

Andrew N. Weintraub

In this chapter, I wish to sketch out competing notions of musical cosmopolitanism in Indonesia by drawing from some of my research on popular music, politics, identity, and performance (Weintraub 2011; 2010; 2006). I will focus on *dangdut* (pronounced "dahng-doot"), a massively popular genre of music in Indonesia, especially among the country's majority middle- and underclass population. "Musical cosmopolitanism" signifies "the located ambitions, desires and dreams that situate the music we make and listen to in a 'world'" (Stokes 2007: 6). This approach to cosmopolitanism "invites us to think about how people in specific places and at specific times have embraced the music of others and how, in doing so, they have enabled music styles and musical ideas, musicians, and musical instruments to circulate (globally) in particular ways" (ibid.). "Worldmaking" through music and sound takes on many forms, and we must be careful to specify the social actors, ideas, histories, and practices, as well as their different bases of power and influence.

One would be hard-pressed to find a more pervasive type of music than dangdut in contemporary Indonesia. Dangdut's upbeat rhythms and plaintive melodies shape the soundscape of homes and alleyways, as well as buses and taxis, roadside food stalls, nightclubs, karaoke bars, and outdoor concerts. Performance contexts include election campaign rallies, village celebrations, and eroticized dancing in nightclubs. Its broad appeal and wide circulation via electronic media (radio, audio and video recordings, television, the Internet, and cellular/ring back tones) and the fact that its audience comprises the majority of Indonesia's population have earned dangdut the moniker "Indonesia's most popular music."

On one hand, dangdut's ubiquitous presence, hybrid repertoire, and adaptability to diverse performance contexts point to a kind of social inclusiveness associated with cosmopolitanism. In recent years, it has even attracted attention in other parts of Asia, namely Malaysia and Japan, and since the 1990s has been promoted as a form with the potential to "go international." On the other hand, dangdut has become a site for national debates about a particular kind of Islamic morality and the regulation of women's bodies in public, which suggest a kind of social exclusiveness or "counter-cosmopolitanism" (Appiah 2006). From this perspective, its *Melayu* (read: Muslim) roots, predominantly Muslim fan base, and promotion of certain kinds of Muslim values might seem to neutralize its potential to "go international." These competing and sometimes colliding worlds are the subject of this chapter.

How is the world imagined in the history, discourse, and practice of dangdut? How does dangdut's identity as a form of national music relate to its cosmopolitan heritage and its potential

to "go international"? How does the association of dangdut with Islam promote and simultaneously constrain its cosmopolitanism? I will explore particular modes of Indonesian cosmopolitanism through dangdut, whose history of celebrating and integrating foreign ideas and material
practices articulate well with cosmopolitanism. However, this analysis also attempts to theorize
a politics of cosmopolitanism, that is, the conditions of possibility that have allowed different
forms of cosmopolitanism to take place, from above and below, and the uneven and power-laden
nature of dangdut's "roots and routes" (Gilroy 1993).

A historical overview of the genre will show how the symbolic and material practices of
dangdut both reflect and activate different ways of imagining the world.[1] These mainly come
into view through dangdut as a form of national music, which is part and parcel of its cosmopolitanism. I then focus on the place of Islam and women in dangdut, which are often in tension
in contemporary Indonesia. Musical examples from fifteen years of fieldwork will illuminate the
possibility of dangdut as a form of alternative or vernacular cosmopolitanism.

Dangdut and the nation

As a geographical and commercial crossroads, the archipelago that makes up what we now call
Indonesia has long been a "traveling culture" (Clifford 1992) constituted by rich and diverse
flows of musical ideas, values, and meanings from many different places. Music is a particularly
potent site for imagining different worlds across these spatial borders because sound travels easily
and can be incorporated and transformed readily. As musicians encountered diverse people, languages, and sounds, they interacted with and internalized those different worlds as part of their
habitus. They created hybrid forms that would have meaning for diverse listeners, in accordance
with localized circumstances and social needs.

Dangdut's multicultural musical mélange of Malay, Indian, Arab, Euro-American, and Latin
musical elements suggest a cosmopolitan view of culture. Indeed, dangdut has its routes in the
movement of people, languages, and religions shaped by contact, commerce, and conquest, or
"cosmopolitanism from below" (Gilroy 2005: 67). Dangdut's progenitors include the commercial *stambul* and *bangsawan* theatrical troupes of the late nineteenth and early twentieth centuries
and the Melayu bands (*orkes Melayu*) of the 1930s, which played a mixed repertoire of music
for diverse audiences in the urban supercultures of colonial Indonesia (Tan 1993; Cohen 2006).
After independence in 1945, musicians brought a new modern sensibility to orkes Melayu,
especially in the urban centers of Medan, Jakarta, and Surabaya, by appropriating and transme-
diating Indian film melodies that dominated the Indonesian cinemascape of the 1950s. It would
take developments in the 1970s, particularly the influx of rock music elements from the United
States and Great Britain, as well as the spread of cheap cassettes and dangdut films that played
across the archipelago, to secure dangdut's place as a dominant commercial force in Indonesian
popular music.

Dangdut crystallized in urban areas in the early 1970s during a period of industrial expansion, Western-style capitalism, intensified commodification, and a culture of consumerism. The
neoliberal Soeharto regime opened the door to Western music and enabled the development of
entertainment media, outdoor parks, and nightclubs where dangdut was played. The construction of dangdut as the "music of the people" (*musik rakyat*) developed under these conditions,
and it has been a common theme ever since. Dangdut was popular in economically and socially
marginalized urban neighborhoods including Bangunrejo (Surabaya), Sunan Kuning (Semarang), and Planet Senen (Jakarta). The music appealed to *becak* (pedicab) and *bajaj* (motorized
cab) drivers, soup and cigarette peddlers, and market sellers and traders who lived in the streets,
alleys, and slums of Jakarta and other urban areas. Urban industrial workers – those who worked

in the most dangerous, dirty, and difficult working environments (Heryanto 1999) – did not inhabit the soft, dreamy music of sentimental pop. Dangdut's raw percussion-driven sound, lyrics about everyday life, and brazen performance style accommodated the gritty urban soundscape that surrounded its listeners.

While the Malay band music saturated the soundscape of streets and poor urban neighborhoods (*kampung*), the name "dangdut" was actually an insulting term used by "the haves" toward the music of the "have-nots." Social elites coined the term *dangdut* after the genre's signature drum sounds "dang" (dahng) and "dut" (doot). Musicians took the negative slang term used to demean the underclass and turned it into a marker of positive self-definition. The song "Dangdut," composed by Rhoma Irama in 1973, celebrated people singing and dancing to "a song from India" accompanied by a flute and a drum.

Rhoma Irama, the central figure associated with dangdut from the mid-1970s to the present, was not one of the subalterns associated with the socially marginalized underclass. His father was a captain in the army, and like other socially mobile male teenagers of the early 1960s, he played American rock 'n' roll and pop at parties in the well-heeled neighborhoods of Jakarta. He began his professional career imitating the vocal styles of pop singers like Tom Jones and Elvis Presley, but around 1970, he began to realize the great financial and creative possibilities in orkes Melayu. Rhoma Irama and his band Soneta (named after the English "sonnet") modernized orkes Melayu by adding American and English rock guitar, new electronic technologies, and a wide variety of percussion. He drew visual elements from rock shows, including flashy costumes, bright lights, stage props, and dry ice. The lyrics of his songs expressed social criticism and Islamic messages (see below). His political affiliation with the Islamic opposition party, the United Development Party (PPP), challenged the dominance of Soeharto's Golkar regime, and he was banned from performing on state-run television and radio from 1977 to 1988. In the late 1980s, as Islam began to liberalize and state restrictions against Islam loosened, politicians began endorsing dangdut and building alliances with dangdut performers to gather popular support. Rhoma Irama switched his allegiance to Golkar, thus gaining access to state-run media. In the 1990s, a period when Islam was publicly embraced by Soeharto, Rhoma Irama moved even closer to the New Order.

The sound world of dangdut expanded in the mid- to late 1970s, following the commercial success of Rhoma Irama's music recordings, live concerts, and films, and a cultural industry around dangdut began to take shape. A genre of "dangdut films" created a visual culture around dangdut and made stars out of singers Rhoma Irama, Elvy Sukaesih, and A. Rafiq. Production teams created spinoff genres, including "sweet dangdut," "pop dangdut," "rock dangdut," and "Mandarin dangdut," among others. By branching out musically and visually, dangdut grabbed a large market share of music sales in relation to other popular genres (including pop Indonesia, *langgam, kroncong,* and Western popular music).

As its sound world expanded, dangdut spread across spaces of dance and pleasure in nightclubs, bars, and discos. The combination of emotionally powerful lyrics, upbeat dancing, and a camp performance style captivated diverse audiences. Performers used a heightened sense of theatricality, costumes, and movements to express a range of emotions. Song lyrics in this era of production centered on male-female relationships and everyday social issues and portrayed emotional pain and suffering, economic hardship, and social injustice. Instead of offering advice about how to fix one's problems or countering difficulties with a higher moral power (as in songs by Rhoma Irama), the lyrics reflected fatalism, acceptance, and idealism.

Dangdut's hybrid border-crossing led critics and commentators to ask whether dangdut could be considered "Indonesian" music at all. Its tuning is Western (diatonic), and its instruments comprise a core ensemble of two electric guitars (rhythm and lead), electric bass, keyboard, bamboo flute, drums, and additional percussion. Its main rhythm, called *chalte* (or *calte*) and played on a set of two drums similar to the Indian *tabla*, indexes its Indian associations. Many of its melodies were copied from Indian film songs and given Indonesian lyrics. The song "Viva Dangdut" (1996) sums up its origin story: "Melayu music, originally from Deli [north Sumatra], influenced by the West and India" ("musik Melayu berasal dari Deli, Lalu kena pengaruh, Dari Barat dan Hindi").

However, scholars of Indonesian music have argued that it is precisely dangdut's hodgepodge hybrid character that established its identity as Indonesia's national music in the 1980s (Hatch 1985; Yampolsky 1991; Sutton 2003). First, dangdut's lyrics are sung in the national language, not regional languages, making it understandable to people across the archipelago. Second, its musical elements (instruments, tuning, timbres, and melodic, rhythmic, and formal organization) are not tied to one ethnic group or another, thus appealing to all. Third, in its early stages of development, recordings were produced in the capital city of Jakarta by a centralized group of producers and disseminated via national media (radio and television) for a national market of consumers.[2]

How does dangdut's identity as a form of national music relate to its cosmopolitan heritage and its potential to "go international"? Despite dangdut's huge success in Indonesia's cultural industry, critics of the 1980s denigrated songs that memorialized people's emotional and material suffering within the contexts of dance and pleasure. Government cultural officials labeled dangdut texts of this period "pornographic" (*porno*) and "weepy" (*cengeng*). Members of the "middle class and up" referred to dangdut as hickish (*kampungan*), excessive (*lebay*), and vulgar (*seronok*). Vulgar lyrics allegedly led to sexual excess, while weepy lyrics led to indolence.

These top-down positions, however, did not allow space for everyday audiences to create the multiplicity of meanings that gave dangdut its pleasure and meaning. By its very nature, dangdut's attractive and sometimes outrageous style of performance tested the sonic, visual, and linguistic boundaries of what could be expressed in the public sphere. As commercial music, dangdut adapted to changing markets, media, and technologies. Songs were created for particular audiences in particular places, and addressed themes avoided by other genres, including drunkenness and gambling ("Mabuk dan Judi"); poverty ("Termiskin di Dunia"/The Poorest in the World); unemployment ("Gelandangan"); and infertility ("Mandul"), among others.

Overdressing or wearing ostentatious jewelry was part of dangdut's spectacle of excess. Excess (expressed in the slang term, *lebay*) referred to the pleasure of speaking what is conventionally unspoken. In performance, it was the uncontainable or "excessive" quality of dangdut that resonated with listeners, dancers, and spectators. It was the surplus of erotic elements that popular audiences found so exciting and compelling. It was what made people shake their heads in comic disbelief while they exclaimed, "It's too much!" (*Keterlaluan!*). It was an imagined world that seemingly knew no bounds.

As dangdut's popularity and influence grew, the state attempted to incorporate dangdut into its program of national development. Dangdut's place in Indonesia's national political culture was cemented in the 1990s when Secretary of State Moerdiono declared that "Dangdut is our music, the music of our people" ("Moerdiono Bergoyang Dangdut" *Suara Pembaruan* 1994). In this period, the New Order, which was ousted from power a few years later in 1998, was losing touch with its citizenry and began looking to dangdut for support. Using the New Order language of "development," Moerdiono called dangdut a "commodity with potential for unlimited development . . . [and] a chance to go international" in the 1990s (quoted in Piper 1995: 44).

However, dangdut's "cosmopolitanism from below" did not resonate with the goals of the cultural state apparatus. The emotionally excessive, overblown, and extreme nature of dangdut would have to be tempered in order for dangdut to be fully integrated as part of the Indonesian national character. In order for dangdut to "go international," according to official government channels, it would have to be transformed and repackaged. Social criticism, Islam, and the erotic spectacle of dangdut were all out of place in the national version of the New Order state. In this "cosmopolitanism from above," reformers created stories about how dangdut was for everyone, not just the "middle classes on down." Pictures and stories about the glamorous lives of dangdut celebrities flooded the tabloid market. As media regulations were lifted to give airtime to private television stations, dangdut shows on TV proliferated. Female singers began appearing on television in glamorous evening gowns on brightly lit stages and red carpets. In the 1990s, the genre continued to branch out as new styles of dangdut embraced house music, remix, reggae, and others. There was even a TV show about how to shake one's hips in the proper way (*goyang*). In its reconstructed international commodity form, dangdut was "going international," symbolically representing Indonesia among the nations of the world.

Dangdut and Islam

Dangdut has wide public appeal among Indonesian Muslims of different classes, ethnicities, genders, and generations. It is arguably the most widely circulated music of the majority-Muslim nation of Indonesia and generally has little appeal for non-Muslims in the country. Although some dangdut songs have Islamic inspiration, characteristics, or content, dangdut is not a genre of Islamic music (*musik islami*). However, many prominent dangdut singers in the 1970s grew up learning vocal techniques of Quranic recitation (*tilawa*), including phrasing, diction, breathing, and pronunciation, as well as the ability to memorize and repeat sections of the Quran. Songs reflecting Islamic themes and Arabic words include "Takdir" (Divine Decree), "Keagungan Tuhan" (The Majesty of God), "Munafiq" (Hypocrite), and "Qais dan Laila" (names of lovers from a love story that took place in seventh-century Arabia), among others.

As a form of Melayu music, dangdut bears strong connections to a "core culture" of Islamic ideas, beliefs, values, and symbols (Reid 2001:297) that make it important in discourses about Islam and music in Indonesia. But in a country with so many varieties of Islamic ideology and practice, which variants are sanctioned and institutionalized and which ones are marginalized and even prohibited? By clarifying dangdut's often-controversial relationship with Islamic ideas, values, and discourse, I aim to shed light on the role of popular music in revealing and framing the boundaries of morality in contemporary Indonesian Islam.

After taking the hajj in 1975, Rhoma Irama began shaping dangdut into an instrument to spread messages about Islam (dakwah). He transformed the urbanized, mass-mediated, and commodified dangdut into a form of popular Islam. He localized Islam by addressing specific social and political concerns in his music. As a professional religious orator (*mubaligh* or *juru dakwah*), he blended the world of Islam with the world of dangdut lyrics, stage shows, and films.

However, despite its discursive and material connection with Islam, dangdut unveils and exposes deep ideological conflicts about morality in contemporary Indonesian Islam, which contest the notion of cosmopolitanism as a set of universally shared moral principles (Appiah 2006). No other form of popular music in this majority-Muslim nation has been so clearly defined by sex, eroticism, and women's bodies as dangdut. These associations would appear to make the music more worldly and cosmopolitan, enabling it to "go international." But this has not necessarily been the case.

Dangdut and women

Eroticized styles of female dance have long been a part of rural performances commissioned by hosts in conjunction with important life-cycle events on Java (Suharto 1980; Hefner 1987; Foley

1989; Hughes-Freeland 1990). At these events, women dance and sing, and money is passed from audience members (both men and women) to performers. This practice of tipping, called *sawéran* (in Javanese), is a cultural practice traditionally associated with weddings and circumcisions on the island of Java.

It is *nyawer* in the verb form – giving money to the (female) performers – that is performed at musical performances in conjunction with communal celebrations (*hajatan*) (Simatupang 1996: 20; Browne 2000, 21; Bader 2013). In these contexts, it is common (and arguably expected) that a female performer will sing sexually suggestive songs and move her body in eroticized ways on a raised stage in front of an audience. Spectators include men and women of all ages, as well as children. Males nyawér for all sorts of reasons: to bring good luck to the family, couple, or child being celebrated; to exchange money for status (either individual or as part of a larger family or village unit); to show their enjoyment of the music and dance as artistic expression; and to show their appreciation for the performing group, among others. Giving money can be a way of showing off one's masculine status to other males (Spiller 2010). In most cases, the singer/dancers are not prostitutes and touching onstage between the female singers and the male patrons is discouraged (Bader 2013).

In the early 2000s, dangdut on national television merged with local performance practices in which eroticized dance took place. The most famous example is Inul Daratista, a female singer from a village in East Java who came to national attention in 2003 for her "drilling dance" (*goyang ngebor*). Inul gained a large national following in early 2003 among dangdut fans, especially women, who admired her energetic, expressive, and erotic style of dance. They interpreted the "drilling dance" as a symbol of female agency and desire. A small but powerful segment of Muslim religious authorities interpreted her drilling dance as overly sexualized and too "aggressive" as a symbolic representation of women. They argued that the drilling dance would have a negative moral influence on Indonesian citizens, and they called for censorship of her televised and live performances. The drilling dance challenged conservative or hard-line Islamic views about gender. Inul's rise to fame coincided with transformative political events, including the fall of Soeharto in 1998, the subsequent calls for political reform in the name of democracy, and the simultaneous ascension of an Islamicist discourse in the public sphere. In the politically charged atmosphere of Reformasi Indonesia, feminists, artists, intellectuals, and highly placed political leaders rallied behind her. The contest over Inul's body became a struggle over religious authority, freedom of expression, women's rights, and the future of Indonesia's political leadership.

As dangdut was "going international," it was also "going local." Local varieties of dangdut (*dangdut daerah*) strengthened dangdut's status as national music, although not in the way that the state intended. These regional expressions often featured eroticized female dancing in public performances, as part of local practices that had become part of dangdut's reach. This is not to say that all dangdut singers tried to outdo one another with more sexually explicit moves, but it became a mark of distinction in an increasingly competitive and lucrative market.

It is important to view the music, performance, and song texts of regional dangdut in context rather than separating out women's bodies for examination and censure according to the top-down national standards of political Islam. In an offshoot of dangdut called *koplo*, songs from the early 2000s included such shocking titles as "Goyang Heboh" (Outrageous Movements), "Selingkuh" (Having an Affair), "Belah Duren" (Splitting the Durian Fruit), "Cinta Satu Malam" (Love for One Night), "Hamil Duluan" (Pregnant before [Marriage]), and "Wanita Lubang Buaya" (a syntactically ambiguous but unmistakably lewd title). Eroticized female singers/dancers delighted audiences with these songs as well as their trademark dance moves while hard-line Muslim leaders and organizations continued to denounce this trend as lowering the moral standards of Indonesia's majority-Muslim society.

In the 2010s, the regional genre of *dangdut pantura* across the northern coast of Java highlighted these creative eroticized forms of dangdut on public stages and in YouTube videos. As prohibitions on women's dancing bodies increased, their movements became more eroticized and their outfits more revealing. In post-Inul Indonesia, almost every dangdut band had a group of "sexy" dancers for weddings and circumcisions. So, it seems that the "porno wars" stimulated rather than curbed the public appetite for eroticized female bodies in both regional performances and national media. These struggles over defining morally acceptable behavior reflected the ideological tensions and contradictions that characterize life in early-twenty-first-century Indonesia. Inspired by the co-opted dangdut on television in the 1990s and 2000s, the TV station Indosiar created a nationally televised contest of dangdut pantura in 2015. The very singers censored for their allegedly unruly behavior in the early 2000s, including Inul Daratista, comprised the jury. One could hardly make the connection between the scantily clad dancers moving in sexually provocative ways and singing risqué lyrics and the fully covered bodies whose movements were restricted by tight-fitting evening gowns. In the case of singers showing too much skin, TV stations began blurring parts of the body in 2015.

This brief historical view of dangdut through the lens of cosmopolitanism demonstrates several points about dangdut's past, present, and future. Dangdut has always been a place to create "sound worlds," as "bodily ways of knowing and being in the world" (Feld 2000: 173). Belonging to a history of cosmopolitanism from below, the mixture of different rhythms, instruments, and languages enabled people to speak a common "musical language." They created a musical world by building musical alliances and crafting musical selves with whomever they came into contact with. For the "middle classes on up," which was not its main audience, dangdut needed to be repackaged for the sake of New Order "development." As the ideas, images, and meanings related to dangdut became even further removed from most people's everyday lives, the form took on new meanings in regional forms far from the centers of media. As Indonesian national music, dangdut is often metaphorized as a barometer for the future of Indonesia. Will dangdut continue to celebrate and absorb foreign influences? Will it restrict its messages to Islamic ideas, values, and behavior? If so, what kind of Islam will it be? Will women's bodies continue to be subject to monitoring and censure, despite being the dominant attraction for dangdut?

The Jakarta gubernatorial election in April 2017 demonstrates the tensions of these different worlds that I have been outlining in dangdut. In a hotly contested run-off, voters chose the candidate Anies Baswedan, whose platform was clearly aligned with Islam, rather than the incumbent candidate Basuki Tjahaja Purnama (popularly known as "Ahok"). Although many voters felt that Ahok was more experienced and, in many cases, a better choice, Ahok is not only non-Muslim, but he is also Chinese. Clearly the people were choosing political Islam as opposed to democratic pluralism. Although Anies is not a hard-line Muslim politician, he has publicly sided with and received support from hard-line groups including the Islamist militia and the Islamic Defenders Front (FPI), as well as military strongman Subianto Prabowo, who has an eye on the presidency in 2019. On the day before the election, I watched Anies address a large crowd at a dangdut concert sponsored by Rhoma Irama. He spoke about the need to have a Muslim leader in a Muslim-majority nation, raising the specter of discrimination against Chinese Indonesians embodied in the acronym of SARA ("ethnicity, religion, race, and group relations"). As people imagine their world in terms defined by democratic pluralism, or as one moving closer to political Islam, dangdut is taking center stage.

Notes

1 Stokes argues against the concept of "musical globalization," which tends to view cultural flows as a by-product of rapid technological change in late capitalism. Musical cosmopolitanism "restores human agencies and creativities to the scene of analysis, and allows us to think of music 'worlds,' rather than a passive reaction to global 'systems'" (Stokes 2007: 6).

2 In the 1970s, local (also called regional or ethnic) popular musics, on the other hand, were sung in local languages and had indigenous musical ingredients. Local tended to be coterminous with small communities, linguistically and culturally specific.

References cited

Appiah, Kwame Anthony. 2006. *Cosmopolitanism: Ethics in a World of Strangers* (New York: W.W. Norton & Company).

Bader, Sandra. 2013. "Intersubjective Realities: Women Dangdut Performers and Their Lived Experience in Indramayu and Jakarta, Indonesia" (Ph.D. Thesis. Clayton, Victoria, Australia: Department of Anthropology, Monash University).

Browne, Susan. 2000. "The Gender Implications of Dangdut Kampungan: Indonesian 'Low-Class' Popular Music," Working Paper No. 109 (Clayton, Victoria, Australia: Centre of Southeast Asian Studies, Monash University).

Clifford, James. 1992. "Traveling Cultures," in Lawrence Grossberg et al. (eds.), *Cultural Studies* (New York: Routledge), pp. 96–116.

Cohen, Matthew. 2006. *The Komedie Stamboel: Popular Theater in Colonial Indonesia, 1891–1903* (Athens: Ohio University Press).

Feld, Steven. 2000. "Sound Worlds," in P. Kruth and H. Stobart (eds.), *Sound* (Cambridge University Press), pp. 173–98.

Foley, Kathy. 1989. "Of Gender and Dance in Southeast Asia: From Goddess to Go-Go Girl," in *Proceedings of the 20th Anniversary CORD Conference* (New York: Congress on Research in Dance).

Gilroy, Paul. 1993. *The Black Atlantic: Modernity and Double Consciousness* (London and New York: Verso).

———. 2005. *Postcolonial Melancholia* (New York: Columbia University Press).

Hatch, Martin. 1985. "Popular Music in Indonesia," in D. Horn, ed., *Popular Music Perspectives 2: Papers from the Second International Conference on Popular Music Studies, Reggio Emilia, September 19–24, 1983* (Goteborg, Exeter: IASPM).

Hefner, Robert. 1987. "The Politics of Popular Art: Tayuban Dance and Culture Change in East Java," *Indonesia* 43: 75–94.

Heryanto, Ariel. 1999. "The Years of Living Luxoriously: Identity Politics of Indonesia's New Rich," in M. Pinches, *Culture and Privilege in Capitalist Asia* (London: Routledge).

Hughes-Freeland, Felicia. 1990. "Tayuban: Culture on the Edge." *Indonesia Circle* 52: 36–44.

"Moerdiono Bergoyang Dangdut Bersama Camelia Malik." 1994. *Suara Pembaruan*, 4 September.

Piper, Suzan. 1995. "Performances for Fifty Years of Indonesian Independence: Articles from the Indonesian Press, translated by Tony Day and Suzan Piper," *Review of Indonesian and Malaysian Affairs* 1 and 2: 37–58.

Reid, Anthony. 2001. "Understanding *Melayu* (Malay) as a Source of Diverse Modern Identities." *Journal of Southeast Asian Studies* 32(3): 295–313.

Simatupang, G. R. L. L. 1996. "The Development of Dangdut and Its Meanings: A Study of Popular Music in Indonesia" (Ph.D. Thesis. Clayton, Victoria, Australia: Department of Anthropology and Sociology, Monash University).

Spiller, Henry. 2010. *Erotic Triangles: Sundanese Dance and Masculinity in West Java, Indonesia* (Chicago: University of Chicago Press).

Stokes, Martin. 2007. "On Musical Cosmopolitanism," The Macalester International Roundtable 2007. Paper 3. http://digitalcommons.macalester.edu/cgi/viewcontent.cgi?article=1002&context=intlrdtable (Accessed 21 April 2017).

Suharto, Ben. 1980. *Tayub: Pengamatan dari Segi Tari Pergaulan serta Kaitannya dengan Unsur Upacara Keseuburan* (Tayub: A Study of a Social Dance and Its Relationship to Fertility Rites). Yogyakarta: Proyek Pengembangan Institut Kesenian Inodnesia, Departemen Pendidikan dan Kebudayaan.

Sutton, R. Anderson. 2003. "Local, Global, or National? Popular Music on Indonesian Television," in S. Kumar and L. Parks (eds.), *Planet TV: A World Television Reader*, New York: New York University Press.

Tan, Sooi Beng. 1993. *Bangsawan: A Social and Stylistic History of Popular Malay Opera* (Singapore: Oxford University Press).

Weintraub, Andrew. 2006. "Dangdut Soul: Who Are 'The People' in Indonesian Popular Music?," *Asian Journal of Communication* 16(4): 411–31.

———. 2010. *Dangdut Stories: A Social and Musical History of Indonesia's Most Popular Music* (New York: Oxford University Press).

———. 2011. "Morality and Its Dis(contents): Dangdut and Islam in Indonesia," in David Harnish and Anne Rasmussen, eds., *Music and Islam in Indonesia* (Oxford University Press), pp. 318–36.

Yampolsky, Philip. 1991. "Indonesian Popular Music: Kroncong, Dangdut, and Langgam Jawa." Liner Notes to Smithsonian/Folkways SF 40056, v. 2, Music of Indonesia series, edited by P. Yampolsky (Washington, DC: Smithsonian Folkways).

31

LANGUAGE DIVERSITY AND LANGUAGE CHANGE IN INDONESIA[1]

Zane Goebel

This chapter provides a sociolinguistic perspective on language diversity and language change in Indonesia. I do this by first sketching out how five terms – *language, diversity, change, value,* and *imitation* – are conceptualized within contemporary sociolinguistics, before then viewing the case of Indonesia through these concepts. I draw upon a wide range of empirical data that range from everyday conversations to representations of them on television and from texts in newspapers to texts on political billboards. In looking at these data, I argue that nation-building infrastructures, such as educational institutions, the bureaucracy, and the mass media, helped to regiment ideas about language, ethnicity, diversity, and citizenship until the early 1990s. This process helped to create a hierarchy of languages in Indonesia where pure unitary forms were at the top and mixed everyday vernacular language practices were at the bottom.

I go on to point out that from the early 1990s onward new value projects – including the search for profit by television broadcasters and uptake of decentralization ideas – and the unintended consequences of these projects helped reconfigure this hierarchy. In short, everyday vernacular varieties of ethnic languages and mixed language gained social value in many social domains. For many Indonesians, an unintended consequence of this was an increased familiarity with fragments of ethnic languages not their own. This enabled some Indonesians to relate to other Indonesians in new ways. For example, in inter-ethnic settings where the national narrative had prescribed Indonesian, it was increasingly common to find fragments of ethnic languages.

Ideas about language, diversity, and language change

Within sociolinguistics, especially linguistic ethnography and one of the four fields of American anthropology, linguistic anthropology, the concepts of language, diversity, and change have undergone some rethinking in recent years.[2] This chapter works with these three concepts as well as two other concepts, value and imitation. Here I will briefly introduce these five concepts.

Since the mid-1990s, sociolinguists have been exploring the processes of how the idea of what constitutes a named language comes about (e.g. Errington 2001; Inoue 2006; Kroskrity 2000; Schieffelin, Woolard, and Kroskrity 1998). Much of this work points to how ideas about territory, group, personhood, and linguistic form have been combined to become what we commonly refer to as a named language. Often these formulas of language also ideologized language as unitary, pure, and unmixed with other languages.

In tandem with work on the construction of ideas about language at the nation-state scale, there has been an increased skepticism about the usefulness of using a named language from the nation-state scale when trying to understand everyday communicative practices at another scale (e.g. Agha 2007; Blommaert 2010; Blommaert and Rampton 2011). At the scale of face-to-face everyday communication, especially in settings increasingly characterized by contact between those from different backgrounds, people cobble together just enough linguistic and other semiotic resources to get a communicative job done. While such encounters cannot be characterized as an encounter in Language X or Language Y, we can talk about how fragments used enable people engaged in interaction to align with each other and with ideas about language that are reproduced by institutions of the nation-state (e.g. Agha 2007). For example, in inter-ethnic interaction in urban Java, non-Javanese can use fragments of Javanese to align with ideas of community (Goebel 2010). In other contexts, such as rural Java or the island of Sumba, fragments of Indonesian can be used in a co-ethnic interaction to align with ideas of expertise and authority (e.g. Errington 1998b; Kuipers 1998; Wolff and Poedjosoedarmo 1982).

Like the concept of language, the concept of *diversity* and its relationship with other concepts such as *multi-culturalism* have been changing since the late 1990s. One stream of work within the social sciences has increasingly used the notion of *superdiversity* (Vertovec 2007). This concept contrasts with common ideas around multilingualism and multiculturalism by seeking to reflect the outcomes of an increasingly mobile world where, in Europe at least, migration was no longer a pattern of waves from another country but rather from multiple countries for multiple reasons (e.g. voluntary and involuntary displacement). These new migrants often settled in areas already considered diverse because of earlier waves of migration and required assistance (linguistic and otherwise) for which the receiving bureaucratic infrastructures simply were not prepared. In short, superdiversity meant the diversification of diversity.

The term *superdiversity* was further developed in sociolinguistics by a group of scholars who looked at some of the sociolinguistic manifestations and outcomes of mobility and contact (e.g. Blommaert 2010; Blommaert and Rampton 2011; Goebel 2010). As work on superdiversity continued, it became increasingly obvious for the need to encompass a wider range of communicative activities in the study of diversity. These activities included multimodal aspects of communication (e.g., gesture, posture, the use of space, how texts are represented on signage, and so on), historical antecedents (e.g., what brought particular people together), the relationship of classroom practices to students' everyday communicative practices, and how superdiversity could also be a condition created from within a nation through nation-building and market forces (Arnaut, Blommaert, Rampton, and Spotti 2015; Arnaut, Karrebæk, Spotti, and Blommaert 2016; Blommaert 2013; Goebel 2015, 2016).

Another emerging theme in sociolinguistics builds upon a long-term concern with change by linking it with one set of ideas relating to value, markets, and nationhood (Bourdieu 1991; Hobsbawm 1992; Wallerstein 2004), and another relating to continuity and governmentality (Bakhtin 1981; Foucault 1977, 1978). In a nutshell, the first set of ideas sees social change as linked with the idea that market saturation and the search for new niche markets has increasingly become tied to languages (e.g. Heller, Bell, Daveluy, McLaughlin, and Noel 2015; Heller and Duchêne 2012; Pietikäinen and Kelly-Holmes 2013). In cases where there is more than one language competing for status as the language of the nation, typically those that lose out have less social value than the national language and soon find themselves in a hierarchical relationship with the national language (Blommaert 2010). In other cases, especially settings that have experienced major economic change, formerly undervalued languages (e.g., minority or ethnic) have gained value as part of efforts to sell goods.

The second set of ideas sees all change – whether political, communal, linguistic, or economic – as constant and constantly surveilled (Agha 2007; Errington 1986; Goebel 2017a; Lempert 2014; Wortham 2006). This view of change, or *semiosis*, sees change as occurring from one interaction to the next, always consisting of something from the past and something new: something old makes an utterance, policy, politician, and so on recognizable, while something new makes this new configuration noticeable. Being noticeable also turns these common aspects of social life into an event worthy of evaluative commentaries, which are a form of everyday governmentality. Ultimately, such commentaries create emergent configurations of normativity that are susceptible to new rounds of *imitation* (i.e., replication not as precise copy) via the process described here. Where such configurations appear long-lived, longevity is typically facilitated through forms of imitation that are part of nation-building infrastructures, such as schools, bureaucracies, and the mass media. Such *infrastructures for imitation* have the capacity to facilitate imitation on a larger scale than that found in face-to-face encounters.

In what follows, I look at changing conceptualizations of language in Indonesia with reference to the ideas discussed here. I start by looking at how unitary and pure perspectives of language are increasingly being replaced by ones where the mixing of linguistic and other semiotic resources from multiple languages is common. I follow this by looking at how social change has reconfigured the value of Indonesian vis-à-vis ethnic languages. Before doing so, however, I provide a brief historical backdrop.

Nation-building via infrastructures of imitation

Large-scale investment in nation building started to occur in Indonesia in the late 1960s (Dick 2002). Nation building and building a sense of pride in Indonesia were achieved through investment in schooling, communication, transportation infrastructures, and language planning activities. These activities helped regiment ideas that languages were unitary and pure and that using Indonesian language properly, especially with those who did not speak your regional language, was part of what it meant to be a citizen (e.g., Bjork 2005; Dardjowidjojo 1998; Errington 1998b, 1998a, 2000; Goebel 2015; Kitley 2000; Sneddon 2003). Language planning activities had their basis in a long history of Dutch thought and colonial administrative practices (e.g., Errington 2001; Maier 1993; Moriyama 2005; Sneddon 2003). The massive diversity that the Dutch encountered was simplified by a series of governors, administrators, educators, and settlers. Ultimately, this process constructed language as a named entity, conceptualized it as pure, and constituted it through the equation of territory + linguistic forms + group.

As with the period from the 1900s onward, the period from the late 1960s until the early 1990s became one where this equation was imitated and where diversity management continued on a massive scale, most commonly within ever-expanding education, media, and bureaucratic infrastructures (Goebel 2015). In Java, and many of Indonesia's islands, a pure standard version of Indonesian (*bahasa baku*) was constructed and offered as the language of the nation in schools, universities, the mass media, and the bureaucracy. In doing so, it was linked to interethnic communication, the nation, knowledge, power, and appropriate behavior (Errington 2000; Goebel 2015). In Java, and much less so in the other Indonesian islands, regional languages (*bahasa daerah*) were standardized and taught from primary school onward, often with very patchy success because of poor resourcing (Bjork 2005; Kurniasih 2007; Sudarkam 2014).

By the early 1990s, these nation-building activities, especially as they related to language, had created a hierarchy of languages within Indonesia. This hierarchy can be brutally summarized as one where standard pure Indonesian (typically as written and spoken on national television and radio) was at the top, and standardized pure versions of ethnic languages with large numbers of speakers (such as Javanese, Balinese, and Sundanese) sat below. In the case of Javanese, the label "Javanese" often referred to more prestigious *kromo* varieties of Javanese, even though these were actually increasingly uncommon in many communicative contexts (Errington 1985, 1998b, 1998a, 2000; Goebel 2007; Smith-Hefner 1983, 1988b, 1988a).

At the nation-state level, these standardized versions of ethnic languages sat above much less valued colloquial forms of ethnic languages, as well as above varieties of Malay and everyday colloquial Indonesian, both of which vary significantly from region to region. Everyday communicative contexts were typically characterized by the use of fragments of Malay, Indonesian, and ethnic languages in co-ethnic interaction (Errington 1998b, 2000; Kuipers 1998) and inter-ethnic interaction (Goebel 2002; Jacob and Grimes 2006). Finally, at the base of this language hierarchy, there were the endangered and dying ethnic languages from the island peripheries. These were valued neither by the nation-state nor often by their own speakers because of the social value of Indonesian, which was seen as a means of social and economic mobility (e.g. Jukes 2010; Kuipers 1998).

While statistics from the 1990s onward may indicate that the majority of Indonesia's population could use standard Indonesian, most of the population actually fit into the third category of speakers in the hierarchy noted above. These Indonesians would have competence to comprehend but often not to use standard forms of Indonesian. In general, in everyday interaction, Indonesians would use a mixture of languages, as in example 1. This example was recorded in 1996 and is taken from a monthly women's meeting in an ethnically diverse middle-class city neighborhood in Semarang, Central Java. At this meeting, six of the 13 participants were not Javanese. *Ngoko* Javanese is in bold, and Indonesian is in plain font.

Example 1: A public address in an inter-ethnic meeting

bu tobing **kui lho**, ditarik **wong** kan ngga pernah ketemu **yo, ndeweké karepé kih**, lepas **ngono lho, soko** tanggung jawab rt, **iki ndeweké kih emoh**.	**That** Mrs. Tobing, [if] asked [for contributions] by **someone**, right? [She] can never be found, **yeah her wish is** to let go **you know,** of neighborhood responsibilities, [she] doesn't want to.

As can be seen, this public address by the ward head, Mrs. Naryono, contains much Javanese. Part of the reason for this was the need to pursue and maintain convivial social relations with neighbors. Using Indonesian often worked against the building and maintenance of positive social relations in this and other neighborhoods in Semarang. Some neighbors, especially those who were not perceived as Javanese or those of Chinese ancestry, were socially ostracized and in some cases verbally threatened with violence, for not adopting local ways of interacting, including speaking fragments of Javanese in inter-ethnic encounters (Goebel 2009, 2010, 2014b).

In addition to differing from actual everyday communicative practices, national ideologies of language as pure, unitary, and anchored to a territory and particular group also started to be challenged in the early 1990s through a deregulated television industry's search for profit. To summarize this period, market forces in the area of television production and consumption helped usher in a period where the representation of ethnic-ness became highly profitable because of its ability to attract wider and niche audiences (Goebel 2008; Kitley 2000; Loven 2008; Sen and

Hill 2000). Most of these television representations used just enough emblems of ethnicity and fragments stereotypical of a particular ethnic language to engender a sense of ethnic-ness. The upshot of these practices was that everyday conversations, both in co-ethnic and inter-ethnic encounter, were increasingly represented as being conducted in a mix of languages. This practice also started to undermine another ideology that the language of doing "unity in diversity" was solely Indonesian (Goebel 2010, 2013a, 2013b, 2015).

Imitating mixed language practices on contemporary television

By 2009, practices of representing fragments of ethnic languages could be found in almost all television genres, including children's shows, quiz shows, celebrity gossip shows, soaps, and local language news services (Goebel 2015). Example 2 is taken from the comedy, *Office Boy Shift 2*, broadcast on RCTI in August 2009. This example is of representations of talk between those of different ethnolinguistic backgrounds in an urban Jakartan office (Sundanese is in bold caps and Betawi is in small caps). Note that in this comedy, characters are represented as understanding one another, despite their use of ethnic languages instead of Indonesian (plain font).

Example 2: Representations of inter-ethnic talk on television

Susi:	a ha ha (slaps Ipul on the arm) kebetulan LU datang ha, gantiin GUÉ ya	A [here is someone to take my place] as it happens YOU have come by, replace ME yeah!
Ipul:	Eh, gantiin **NAON TEH**	Eh replace **WHAT OLDER SISTER?**
Susi:	ndak jangan kebanyakan nanya (while grabbing shirt and moving around Ipul and pushing him in front of toilet door) nah LU diam aja di sini, berdiri di sini, ya, ntar kalau misalnya ada cewek yang mau masuk, jangan dikasih, ngerti KAGAK, ya itu pun kalau LU KAGAK mau dimarahin, ngerti nggak	Stop, don't ask too many questions. Now, YOU just stay here, stand here, OK? Later, if for example a woman comes to use the toilet, don't let them in. Understand or NOT? That is if YOU DON'T want to get in trouble. [Do you] understand or not?
Ipul:	**ENYA ENYA ATUH ENYA**	YES, YES, OK, YES.

Example 3 is taken from the quiz show *Siapa Lebih Berani* (Who Is Braver?), which was aired on RCTI to a national audience. During the two episodes that I have footage of, the two hosts (Helmy and Alya) moved between using fragments from a number of languages. These included Betawi/Jakartan forms of reference (*gué* "I/me and *lu* "you"), Sundanese terms of references (*neng* "younger unmarried woman," *teteh* "older sister"), invitation (*mangga* "please go ahead"), and descriptions of cultural practices (*munjungan* "description of a greeting practice"), and as in example 3, a Javanese interrogative (*sopo* "who"). In example 3, one contestant, Agus, presses the buzzer and the following interaction ensues. Indonesian is in plain font and Javanese is in bold caps.

Example 3: I also know and can speak some Javanese

Agus:	mel lisen	Mel Lisen
Helmy:	mel salah	Mel is wrong.
Alya:	**SOPO** sih agus, melan **SOPO**	**WHO** do [you] think it is Agus? Melan **WHO**?
Helmy:	mel **SOPO**, ngerti bukan mel shandy chintami sini aja sayang	Mel **WHO**? [I] understand, It's not Mel Shandy. Chintami come here please.

Source: Siapa Lebih Berani broadcast on RCTI, Tuesday August 12, 2009, 7:00–8:00 a.m.

What examples 2 and 3 show is that fragments of ethnic languages continue to be widely used, rather than whole sentences being spoken in ethnic languages. The hosts' talk suggests that they imagine their audience as having some familiarity with Betawi, Sundanese, and Javanese. This representation of addressing both a local audience (the contestants and studio audience) and a national one in Indonesian and fragments from a number of regional languages presents a model for the doing of unity in diversity that does not exclusively involve Indonesian. Ultimately, these representations challenge the long-running narrative about pure Indonesian being used in the media and inter-ethnically.

In sum, whereas pure forms of language were socially valued up to the early 1990s, in the years since, the commodification of language on television helped to change the value of ethnic languages, by making them more visible and valuable as a means of reaching niche markets. Making these languages more visible via the large participation framework of television also helped to increase many Indonesians' familiarity with languages that were not their own. For example, some of my research shows that Indonesians who report no experience living or interacting with Sundanese speakers, nevertheless will use and evaluate fragments of Sundanese in some settings to achieve certain interactional ends (Goebel 2012, 2013a, 2015). One unintentional outcome of the commodification of ethnic languages on television is that it has engendered new ways to relate to other Indonesians from different backgrounds.

Revaluing regional languages in other domains

In addition to the media industries' challenges to the conceptualization of language as pure, unitary, and immobile, the value of Indonesian vis-à-vis regional languages became increasingly challenged through practices that emerged from 2001 onward as part of ongoing political and fiscal decentralization. Since 1998, there has been significant social, economic, political, and cultural change in Indonesia (e.g. Aspinall and Mietzner 2010; Holtzappel and Ramstedt 2009). Decentralization contributed to increases in the social value of ethnicity and ethnic languages in Indonesia (Davidson and Henley 2007). For example, fragmentation and the remaking of internal political boundaries have often been justified through claims about linguistic and cultural authenticity (e.g. Aspinall 2011; Davidson and Henley 2007).

As sociolinguistic research on contemporary language practices in Indonesia emerges, it seems that local institutions now have the resources and the political and constitutional support to further promote ethnic languages. This change in the social value of ethnic languages vis-à-vis Indonesian can be seen in increased discourses about entitlement and authenticity (Arps 2010; Kurniasih 2016; Zentz 2014) and increases in the use of ethnic languages for political purposes (Donzelli 2016; Goebel, Jukes and Morin 2017; Harr 2016; Kurniasih 2016; Morin 2016). Example 4, extracted from Harr (2016:73–4), demonstrates how fragments of a regional language are used at the beginning of a campaign speech by a candidate for the post of district head in Ende district in Flores, in 2008. This interaction occurs after the candidate, who is currently the vice regent, arrives late in a village in Ende. Indonesian is in plain font, and the local language, Lio, is in bold font.

Example 4: Mixing languages to get votes in Ende, Flores

Vice regent:	Sore ini saya sudah di tiga tempat. **Neabuga aku mena Demulaka**.	This afternoon, I've been to three places. **This morning, I was mena**[3] Demulaka.
Audience:	**Ghale**.	**Ghale**[4].
Vice regent:	**Ghale?**	**Ghale?**
	Saya melantik duapuluh-delapan orang Badan Permuyawaratan Desa. Jam satu **neanea**. **Ghale** juga?	I installed 28 members of the Village Assembly. At one o'clock **this afternoon**. **Ghale**, too?
Audience:	**Lau!**	**Downriver!**

While the vice regent's efforts were ultimately unsuccessful, this example and the rest of his speech provide many examples of the use of what the vice regent thought were just enough Lio fragments to get the communicative job done. We also get to see how his audience reacted to these attempts, which in part might even provide some predictive power in relation to how he would ultimately fare in the political contest.

While many of the language policy changes that occurred and were implemented at provincial and district levels, typically following the old unitary formula of territory + linguistic form + group (Goebel 2016), there were increasing numbers of exceptions. Example 5 is from a copy of text found on signage sponsored by the city of Jayapura in Papua in mid-2015 (Morin 2016). This sign is meant to encourage youth to get an electronic identity card. This is done by implying that the soccer celebrities pictured on the sign have one and through the use of Papuan Malay (PM) mixed with Indonesian. Example 5 reproduces the text in this sign. PM is in bold and Indonesian is in plain font. Morin's (2016) work shows that this use of PM is not an isolated case but one that has emerged in a number of social domains since the early part of the new millennium, including films, television broadcasts, and the Internet.

Example 5: Mixed language at the city scale in Jayapura, Papua

Kalau **ko** Punya KTP-Elektronik **Ko tra kosong** Ayo. . .! **Urus tempo**	If **you** own an electronic ID card **You are somebody** Come [and] **get one as quick as you can**

We find similar examples of mixed language on political signage in Tomohon city, located in Minahasa, North Sulawesi (Goebel, Jukes, and Morin 2017). The text in one political campaign poster for Johny Runtuwene ("Jonru"), a candidate running for the position of mayor of Tomohon, is *Jonru adalah torang* "Jonru is us." It is a mix of two varieties, including the Indonesian copula *adalah* and the Manado Malay (MM) first person inclusive pronoun, *torang*. This mixing helps address two audiences, those who can read Manado Malay and those who can read Indonesian.

If we move to other social domains, we find many other contexts where mixed language practices are increasingly part of ideologies and everyday language practices. This includes teen literature (Djenar 2016), the Internet (Goebel 2015; Manns and Musgrave 2016), regional newspapers (Goebel 2017a), consumer goods (Cole 2016), everyday conversations among university students (Errington 2014; Ewing 2016; Zentz 2014), the teaching of ways of performing in public (Cole 2010), and within the Indonesian bureaucracy (Goebel 2007, 2014a). At the ideological level, which can be accessed via attention to political rhetoric, opinion, and prescriptive pieces found in newspapers, blogs, and so on, regional languages have also increased in social value (Goebel 2017b; Kurniasih 2016; Moriyama 2012; Quinn 2003, 2012). Even so, ideology can differ significantly from interactional practice. For example, Smith-Hefner (2009) has found a continued emphasis on the importance of learning Indonesian over an ethnic language among parents of children in early childhood centers. In another context, in rural Java, Zentz (2014) found that some elements of ethnic languages, such as speaking *kromo* Javanese, while desired, are rarely practiced among youth studying at university.

Conclusion: Indonesian(-ness), ethnic-ness, and sociability

In this chapter, I have examined how language, diversity, change, and value are thought about and analyzed in the broad field of sociolinguistics. In applying these ideas to Indonesia, I have pointed out that change is constant and can be found in every situation that involves any type of communication. In such situations, change is a produce of discursive noticing and evaluation. In the case at hand, ideas about Indonesian, Indonesian-ness, and ethnicity have continued to be reconfigured through this process and through other value projects, such as the Indonesian television industry's search for profit or politicians' search for votes. At the same time, these processes have contributed to the further diversification of Indonesia through the positive revaluing of varieties of regional languages that were previously ignored.

In comparison to the New Order period (1966–1998), language is increasingly conceptualized as a commodity to be bought and sold and one that can contain fragments from other languages. This reconfiguring of the language hierarchy from the New Order period has meant that ethnic languages now have co-equal status with Indonesian in some public settings. At the same time, the circulation of fragments of ethnic languages within the mass media has also helped engender new forms of sociability, where familiarity with fragments of ethnic languages enables Indonesians to recognize and use fragments of ethnic languages for specific interactional projects.

Notes

1 This chapter builds upon some ideas presented in a working paper: Goebel, Zane, 2016, *A sociolinguistic critique of ACARA*.
2 For recent surveys about what sociolinguistics is and what it studies, see Duranti 2009; Rampton 2008.
3 *Mena* is a locational/directional term. For an explanation of how this works, see Harr 2016.
4 *Ghale* is a locational/directional term. For an explanation of how this works, see Harr 2016.

Zane Goebel

References cited

Agha, Asif. 2007. *Language and Social Relations* (Cambridge: Cambridge University Press).

Arnaut, Karel, Jan Blommaert, Ben Rampton, and Massimiliano Spotti, eds. 2015. *Language and Superdiversity* (New York: Routledge).

Arnaut, Karel, Martha Karrebæk, Max Spotti and Jan Blommaert, eds. 2016. *Engaging Superdiversity: Recombining Spaces, Times and Language Practices* (Bristol: Multilingual Matters).

Arps, Ben. 2010. "Terwujudnya bahasa using di Banyuwangi dan peranan media elektronik di dalamnya (selayang padang, 1970–2009)," in Mikihiro Moriyama and Manneke Budiman, eds., *Geliat Bahasa Selaras Zaman: Perubahan Bahasa-bahasa di Indonesia Pasca-orde Baru* (Tokyo: Tokyo University of Foreign Studies), pp. 225–48.

Aspinall, Edward. 2011. "Democratization and Ethnic Politics in Indonesia: Nine Theses," *Journal of East Asian Studies* 11: 289–319.

Aspinall, Edward and Marcus Mietzner, eds. 2010. *Problems of Democratisation in Indonesia: Elections, Institutions and Society* (Singapore: ISEAS).

Bakhtin, Mikhail. 1981. *The Dialogic Imagination: Four Essays*, Caryl Emerson and Michael Holquist, trans. Michael Holquist, ed. (Austin: University of Texas Press).

Bjork, Christopher. 2005. *Indonesian Education: Teachers, Schools, and Central Bureaucracy* (New York: Routledge).

Blommaert, Jan. 2010. *The Sociolinguistics of Globalization* (Cambridge: Cambridge University Press).

———. 2013. *Ethnography, Superdiversity and Linguistic Landscapes: Chronicles of Complexity* (Bristol: Multilingual Matters).

Blommaert, Jan and Ben Rampton. 2011. "Language and Superdiversity," *Diversities* 13(2): 1–21.

Bourdieu, Pierre. 1991. *Language and Symbolic Power* (Cambridge: Polity Press in Association with Basil Blackwell).

Cole, Deborah. 2010. "Enregistering Diversity: Adequation in Indonesian Poetry Performance," *Journal of Linguistic Anthropology* 20(1): 1–21.

———. 2016. "The Material Force of Signs and the Reconfiguration of Superdiverse Identities," in Zane Goebel, Deborah Cole and Howard Manns, eds., *Margins, Hubs, and Peripheries in a Decentralizing Indonesia* (Tilburg Papers in Culture Studies, special issue number 162), pp. 112–25.

Dardjowidjojo, Soenjono. 1998. "Strategies for a Successful National Language Policy: The Indonesian Case," *International Journal of the Sociology of Language* 130: 35–47.

Davidson, Jamie and David Henley, eds. 2007. *The Revival of Tradition in Indonesian Politics: The Deployment of Adat from Colonialism to Indigenism* (London: Routledge).

Dick, Howard, ed. 2002. *The Emergence of a National Economy: An Economic History of Indonesia, 1800–2000* (Crows Nest, NSW: Allen & Unwin).

Djenar, Dwi Noverini. 2016. "Adolescent Interaction in Fiction and Peripheralisation of Languages," in Zane Goebel, Deborah Cole and Howard Manns, eds., *Margins, Hubs, and Peripheries in a Decentralizing Indonesia* (Tilburg Papers in Culture Studies, special issue number 162), pp. 42–50.

Donzelli, Aurora. 2016. "Transnational Neoliberal Democracy and the Vintage Aesthetics Of the Margins in Post-Suharto Political Oratory," in Zane Goebel, Deborah Cole and Howard Manns, eds., *Margins, Hubs, and Peripheries in a Decentralizing Indonesia* (Tilburg Papers in Culture Studies, special issue number 162), pp. 77–100.

Duranti, Alessandro. 2009. "Linguistic Anthropology: History, Ideas and Issues," in Alessandro Duranti, ed., *Linguistic Anthropology: A Reader* (London: Blackwell), pp. 1–60.

Errington, Joseph. 1985. *Language and Social Change in Java: Linguistic Reflexes of Modernization in a Traditional Royal Polity* (Athens: Ohio University Press).

———. 1986. "Continuity and Change in Indonesian Language Development," *Journal of Asian Studies* 45(2): 329–53.

———. 1998a. "Indonesian('s) Development: On the State of a Language of State," in Bambi B. Schieffelin, Kathryn A. Woolard and Paul V. Kroskrity, eds., *Language Ideologies: Practice and Theory* (New York: Oxford University Press), pp. 271–84.

———. 1998b. *Shifting Languages: Interaction and Identity in Javanese Indonesia* (Cambridge: Cambridge University Press).

———. 2000. "Indonesian('s) Authority," in Paul V. Kroskrity, ed., *Regimes of Language: Ideologies, Polities, and Identities (Advanced Seminar Series)* (Santa Fe, NM: School of American Research), pp. 205–27.

———. 2001. "Colonial Linguistics," *Annual Review of Anthropology* 30: 19–39.

386

———. 2014. "In Search of Modern Indonesian: Linguistic Dynamics in an Urban Periphery," in Gerry Van Klinken and Ward Berenschot, eds., *In Search of Middle Indonesia: Middle Classes in Provincial Towns* (Leiden: Brill), pp. 199–219.

Ewing, Michael. 2016. "Localising Person Reference Among Indonesian Youth," in Zane Goebel, Deborah Cole and Howard Manns, eds., *Margins, Hubs, and Peripheries in a Decentralizing Indonesia* (Tilburg Papers in Culture Studies, special issue number 162), pp. 26–41.

Foucault, Michel. 1977. *Discipline and Punish: The Birth of The Prison* (New York: Vintage books).

———. 1978. *The History of Sexuality (Volume 1: An Introduction)*, Robert Hurley, trans. (New York: Pantheon books).

Goebel, Zane. 2002. "Code Choice in Inter-Ethnic Interactions in Two Urban Neighbourhoods of Indonesia," *International Journal of the Sociology of Language* 158: 69–87.

———. 2007. "Enregisterment and Appropriation in Javanese-Indonesian Bilingual Talk," *Language in Society* 36(4): 511–31.

———. 2008. "Enregistering, Authorizing and Denaturalizing Identity in Indonesia," *Journal of Linguistic Anthropology* 18(1): 46–61.

———. 2009. "Semiosis, Interaction and Ethnicity in Urban Java," *Journal of Sociolinguistics* 13(4): 499–523.

———. 2010. *Language, Migration and Identity: Neighborhood Talk in Indonesia* (Cambridge: Cambridge University Press).

———. 2012. "Enregisterment, Communities, and Authenticity: Watching Indonesian Teledramas," *Journal of Linguistic Anthropology* 22(2): 1–20.

———. 2013a. "Competence to Comprehend and Knowledging," *Language & Communication* 33(4): 366–75.

———. 2013b. "Representations of Doing Unity in Diversity on Indonesian TV," *Review of Indonesian and Malaysian Affairs* 47(1): 89–114.

———. 2014a. "Doing Leadership Through Signswitching in the Indonesian Bureaucracy," *Journal of Linguistic Anthropology* 24(2): 193–215.

———. 2014b. "Stigmatising Others Through Neighbourhood Talk in Indonesia," *PORTAL Journal of Multidisciplinary International Studies* 11(1): 1–20.

———. 2015. *Language and Superdiversity: Indonesians Knowledging at Home and Abroad* (New York: Oxford University Press).

———. 2016. "Superdiversity from Within: The Case of Ethnicity in Indonesia," in Karel Arnaut, Martha Karrebæk, Max Spotti and Jan Blommaert, eds., *Engaging Superdiversity: Recombining Spaces, Times and Language Practices* (Bristol: Multilingual Matters), pp. 251–76.

———. 2017a. "Imitation, Interdiscursive Hubs, and Chronotopic Configuration," *Language & Communication* 53: 1–10.

———. 2017b. "Infrastructures for Ethnicity: Understanding the Diversification of Contemporary Indonesia," *Asian Ethnicity* 18(3): 263–76.

Goebel, Zane, Anthony Jukes, and Izak Morin. 2017. "Linguistic Enfranchisement," *Bijdragen tot de Taal, Land- en Volkenkunde* 173: 273–295.

Harr, Adam. 2016. "Recentering the Margins? The Politics of Local Language in a Decentralizing Indonesia," in Zane Goebel, Deborah Cole and Howard Manns, eds., *Margins, Hubs, and Peripheries in a Decentralizing Indonesia* (Tilburg Papers in Culture Studies, special issue number 162), pp. 70–6.

Heller, Monica, Lindsay Bell, Michelle Daveluy, Mireille McLaughlin, and Hubert Noel. 2015. *Sustaining the Nation: The Making and Moving of Language and Nation* (New York: Oxford University Press).

Heller, Monica and Alexandre. Duchêne, eds. 2012. *Language in Late Capitalism: Pride and Profit* (Hoboken: Routledge).

Hobsbawm, Eric. 1992. *Nations and Nationalism Since 1780: Programme, Myth, Reality* (Cambridge: Cambridge University Press).

Holtzappel, Coen and Martin Ramstedt, eds. 2009. *Decentralization and Regional Autonomy in Indonesia: Implementation and Challenges* (Singapore: ISEAS).

Inoue, Miyako. 2006. *Vicarious Language: Gender and Linguistic Modernity in Japan* (Berkeley: University of California Press).

Jacob, June and Barbara Grimes. 2006. "Developing a Role for Kupang Malay: The Contemporary Politics of an Eastern Indonesian Creole." Paper read at Tenth international conference on Austronesian Linguistics, Puerto Princesa City, Palawan, Philippines, 19–20 January.

Jukes, Anthony. 2010. "Someone Else's Job: Externalizing Responsibility for Language Maintenance." Paper read at *Fourteenth Foundation for Endangered Language Conference: Reversing Language Shift: How to Re-Awaken a Language Tradition*, 13–15 September at Carmathan, Wales.

Kitley, Philip. 2000. *Television, Nation, and Culture in Indonesia* (Athens: Ohio University Press).

Kroskrity, Paul V., ed. 2000. *Regimes of Language: Ideologies, Polities, and Identities* (Santa Fe: School of American Research).

Kuipers, Joel. 1998. *Language, Identity and Marginality in Indonesia: The Changing Nature of Ritual Speech on the Island of Sumba* (Cambridge: Cambridge University Press).

Kurniasih, Yacinta. 2007. "Local Content Curriculum 1994: The Teaching of Javanese in Yogyakarta Schools." Paper read at the *First International Symposium on the Languages of Java (ISLOJ)*, 15–16 August at Graha Santika Hotel, Semarang, Indonesia.

———. 2016. "Local Activism Versus Recentralization: The Case of Javanese in Municipal Offices in Central Java," in Zane Goebel, Deborah Cole and Howard Manns, eds. *Margins, Hubs, and Peripheries in a Decentralizing Indonesia* (Tilburg Papers in Culture Studies, special issue number 162), pp. 137–47.

Lempert, Michael. 2014. "Imitation," *Annual Review of Anthropology* 43(1): 379–95.

Loven, Klarijn. 2008. *Watching Si Doel: Television, Language, and Cultural Identity in Contemporary Indonesia* (Leiden: KITLV Press).

Maier, Hendrik. 1993. "From Heteroglossia to Polyglossia: The Creation of Malay and Dutch in the Indies," *Indonesia* 56 (October): 37–65.

Manns, Howard and Simon Musgrave. 2016. "On the Internet, No-One Knows You're From Suroboyo: Ethnic Identity From the Digital Margins to the Mainstream Core," in Zane Goebel, Deborah Cole and Howard Manns, eds. *Margins, Hubs, and Peripheries in a Decentralizing Indonesia* (Tilburg Papers in Culture Studies, special issue number 162), pp. 126–36.

Morin, Izak. 2016. "Marginalizing and Revaluing Papuan Malay: The Impact of Politics, Policy and Technology in Indonesia," in Zane Goebel, Deborah Cole and Howard Manns, eds. *Margins, Hubs, and Peripheries in a Decentralizing Indonesia* (Tilburg Papers in Culture Studies, special issue number 162), pp. 101–11.

Moriyama, Mikihiro. 2005. *Sundanese Print Culture and Modernity in Nineteenth-Century West Java* (Singapore: NUS Press).

———. 2012. "Regional Languages and Decentralization in Post-New Order Indonesia: The Case of Sundanese," in Keith Foulcher, Mikihiro Moriyama and Manneke Budiman, eds., *Words in Motion: Language and Discourse in Post-New Order Indonesia* (Tokyo: Research Institute for Languages and Cultures of Asia and Africa, Tokyo University of Foreign Studies), pp. 82–100.

Pietikäinen, Sari and Helen Kelly-Holmes. 2013. "Multilingualism and the Periphery," in Sari Pietikäinen and Helen Kelly-Holmes, eds., *Multilingualism and the Periphery* (New York: Oxford University Press), pp. 1–16.

Quinn, George. 2003. "Coming Apart and Staying Together at the Centre: Debates over Provincial Status in Java and Madura," in Edward Aspinall and Greg Fealy (eds.), *Local Power and Politics in Indonesia: Decentralisation and Democratisation.* (Singapore: ISEAS), pp. 164–178.

Quinn, George. 2012. "Emerging From Dire Straits: Post-New Order Developments in Javanese Language and Literature," in Keith Foulcher, Mikihiro Moriyama and Manneke Budiman, eds., *Words in Motion: Language and Discourse in Post-New Order Indonesia* (Tokyo: Research Institute for Languages and Cultures of Asia and Africa, Tokyo University of Foreign Studies), pp. 65–81.

Rampton, Ben. 2008. "Disciplinary Mixing: Types and Cases," *Journal of Sociolinguistics* 12(4): 525–31.

Schieffelin, Bambi, Kathryn Woolard, and Paul Kroskrity, eds. 1998. *Language Ideologies: Practice and Theory* (New York: Oxford University Press).

Sen, Krishna and David T. Hill. 2000. *Media, Culture and Politics in Indonesia* (Oxford: Oxford University Press).

Smith-Hefner, Nancy. 1983. "Language and Social Identity: Speaking Javanese in Tengger." (Ph.D. Thesis. Michigan: University of Michigan).

———. 1988a. "The Linguistic Socialization of Javanese Children in Two Communities," *Anthropological Linguistics* 30(2): 166–98.

———. 1988b. "Women and Politeness: The Javanese Example," *Language in Society* 17: 535–54.

———. 2009. "Language Shift, Gender, and Ideologies of Modernity in Central Java, Indonesia," *Journal of Linguistic Anthropology* 19(1): 57–77.

Sneddon, James. 2003. *The Indonesian Language: Its History and Role in Modern Society* (Sydney: University of New South Wales Press).

Sudarkam, Mertono. 2014. "The Decentralization of Schooling in Palu, Central Sulawesi, Indonesia." (Ph.D. Thesis. Melbourne: Department of Asian Studies, La Trobe University).

Vertovec, Steven. 2007. "Super-diversity and its Implications," *Ethnic and Racial Studies* 30(6): 1024–53.

Wallerstein, Immanuel. 2004. *World-Systems Analysis: An Introduction* (Durham: Duke University Press).

Wolff, John and Soepomo Poedjosoedarmo. 1982. *Communicative Codes in Central Java* (New York: Cornell University).

Wortham, Stanton. 2006. *Learning Identity: The Joint Emergence of Social Identification and Academic Learning* (Cambridge: Cambridge University Press).

Zentz, Lauren. 2014. "'Love' the Local, 'Use' the National, 'Study' the Foreign: Shifting Javanese Language Ecologies in (Post-)Modernity, Postcoloniality, and Globalization," *Journal of Linguistic Anthropology* 24(3): 339–59.

32

A "TOLERANT" INDONESIA? INDONESIAN MUSLIMS IN COMPARATIVE PERSPECTIVE

Jeremy Menchik and Katrina Trost

At the 2015 meeting of the world's largest Islamic organization, Nahdlatul Ulama, Indonesian president Joko Widodo stated, "NU has used religion as a source of tolerance, peace and progressiveness" and said that he hoped NU would continue to promote peace in a time of religious radicalism. Likewise, longtime NU observer, academic Martin van Bruinessen said that Islam in Indonesia was relatively more tolerant toward minorities within Islam, such as the Shi'ites and Ahmadis, than elsewhere in the Muslim world (Junaidi 2015). That same week, members of Indonesia's second largest Islamic organization, Muhammadiyah, saw Jokowi make a similar appeal to uphold and promote religious tolerance: "We should also become an example of a nation that can live in peace and harmony" (Jakarta Post 2015). At a time of sectarian violence in the Middle East and Islamist extremism elsewhere, Indonesian Muslims are widely seen as a stronghold of tolerance and moderation, by some accounts "immune" to radicalization (Defense One 2016).

Poorly understood, however, is whether this view is consistent with more systematic measures of tolerance. Are Indonesian Muslims exceptionally tolerant? How do Indonesian Muslims compare to other countries in levels of tolerance toward non-Muslims? How do they compare to populations in other developing countries? Other Muslim-majority countries? Other newly democratic countries? Within Indonesia, what are the best predictors of tolerance and intolerance? Despite the frequent assertion of tolerance, scholars have not thoroughly compared the views of Indonesian Muslims with those of other Muslims on the issue of interfaith tolerance.

Drawing on three data sets on tolerance, as well as indicators from five other related data sets, this chapter argues that contrary to the conventional wisdom, Indonesian Muslims are neither exceptionally tolerant nor intolerant. Instead, Indonesian Muslims are about as tolerant as one would expect for a developing, newly democratic country with low levels of higher education. Within Indonesia, individuals with greater education and income are more tolerant than those with less. The Indonesian state is also different from many other Muslim-majority states in that it is relatively less involved in religion, while it remains non-secular. Indonesia is distinct, however, in being home to mass Islamic organizations whose leaders are more tolerant than one would expect, are highly socially and politically engaged, and have been active in promoting the rights of religious minorities. Future research should investigate what tolerance means to members of these organizations and whether their influence is fading in order to explain the implications for democratic governance.

Literature review

Perhaps the most influential scholar of Indonesian Islam, Clifford Geertz, directly contrasted religious culture in Java with that of the Middle East. "Compared to North Africa, the Middle East, and even to Muslim India, whose brand of faith it most closely resembles, Indonesian Islam has been, at least until recently, remarkable malleable, tentative, syncretistic, and most significantly of all, multivocal" (Geertz 1968: 12). While Moroccan Muslims followed medieval texts, religio-political leaders, and orthodox interpretations of Islam, Javanese Muslims combined Islamic practices with Buddhism and Hinduism, followed ethnic or tribal leaders, and practiced syncretic or mystical interpretations of Islam. Geertz's belief that Indonesian Muslims were syncretic, culture-oriented rather than religion-oriented, and open to multiple faiths is a major reason why subsequent scholars and the public believe Islam in Indonesia to be more tolerant than in other Muslim societies. This reputation was bolstered by the Islamic renewal (*pembaharuan pimikiran*) movement of the 1970s and 1980s, when prominent Muslim leaders appeared to support liberal, secular, and pluralist ideas. Abdurrahman Wahid, leader of the massive Islamic organization Nahdlatul Ulama, declared his opposition to an Islamic state and helped found liberal NGOs to promote a strong civil society. Nurcholish Madjid argued against Muslims supporting Islamic political parties. And Syaafi Maarif made strong arguments for supporting religious pluralism and cooperation with Indonesia's non-Muslim population as head of the country's second-largest Islamic organization, Muhammadiyah. These prominent leaders further cemented Indonesia's reputation for tolerance, moderation, and even liberalism in contrast to Middle-East Muslims.

The Geertzian view has, however, been repeatedly challenged over the past four decades. Geertz's work has been criticized for overstating the influence of Hinduism on Java and the strength of the abangan (Hodgson 1974; Woodward 1989). Indeed, there is no evidence that the abangan existed before the mid-nineteenth century (Ricklefs 2006, 2007). Instead, scholars have pointed to the importance of Islamic leaders in Cairo and the hijaz in shaping Indonesian Islam. Michael Laffan's 2003 book *Islamic Nationhood and Colonial Indonesia*, which maps the writings of Muslims from Southeast Asia who studied in the Hijaz and Cairo during the late nineteenth century, suggests that Islamic reform played a key role in Indonesian nationalism. Chiara Formichi shows how pan-Islamic and then Indonesian Islamic nationalist ideals endured long beyond the late colonial period in the writings of the influential leader of *Darul Islam*, Kartosuwiryo (Formichi 2012). Kevin Fogg reveals how pious Muslims experienced the 1945 revolution as an explicitly Islamist struggle (Fogg 2012). Jeremy Menchik suggests that rather than being grounded in either secular or Islamic nationalism, Indonesian nationalism occupies a middle ground where belief in God is mandatory but also plural. "Godly nationalism" is based on a common, orthodox theism and helps to explain the state's demand that Indonesians adhere to a world religion and renounce support for heterodox, syncretic, or animist views, including those of the abangan (Menchik 2014). Most recently, Martin van Bruinessen argues that the liberal or progressive turn of Indonesian Islam has been confounded by a "conservative turn" marked by increased intolerance toward minority Muslims like the Ahmadiyah (Bruinessen 2013).

Absent from this debate between the Geertzian view of Indonesian Islam as syncretic, plural, and tolerant and the revisionist view of Indonesian Islam as also orthodox and intolerant are more empirical comparisons across Muslim societies. This is surprising given the fact that scholars now have access to cross-national indicators of public opinion in Indonesia, the Middle East, and elsewhere in the Muslim world. By assembling this data from the fifth wave of the World Values Survey (WVS), the fourth wave of the Indonesian Family Life Survey (IFLS), Jeremy Menchik's and Robin Bush's surveys of the leaders of the mass Islamic organizations

Muhammadiyah and Nahdlatul Ulama (NU), Saiful Mujani's survey of Indonesian Muslims, economic development indicators from the World Bank, and political development indicators from Freedom House, this chapter seeks to provide a more systemic and comprehensive answer to the question: are Indonesian Muslims exceptionally tolerant?

To do so, it may be helpful to introduce readers to the survey research literature on tolerance. The first major social science survey on tolerance was a 1955 study by Samuel Stouffer on American's tolerance toward groups that were known to be disliked: communists, socialists, atheists, and accused communists. The Stouffer questions asked whether the disliked groups should be permitted by the state to give a speech, teach in a high school, teach in a college or university, work in a defense plant, and be a radio singer. In 1972, the Stouffer questions were adopted by the General Social Survey and appeared on nearly every national survey since. Stouffer's impact on the questions developed by Sullivan, Pierson, and Marcus (1982) has shaped the prevailing conceptualization of tolerance in survey research. Sullivan, Pierson, and Marcus developed a "content-controlled" strategy, where respondents picked their "least-liked" group from a list including communists, Black Panthers, and other disliked groups. The respondents' attitudes were then assessed using questions about the least-liked group's right to teach in the public schools, make a speech in the city, hold public rallies in their city, and become president of the United States. The least-liked strategy was an improvement on Stouffer in that it included a broader range of targets, and respondents who "liked" communists no longer distorted the sample; Stouffer under-estimated the degree to which non-communists disliked communists because he included communist sympathizers in his sample. The downside of this strategy, however, was its vagueness. Rather than assessing tolerance toward multiple targets, only one target was assessed. And rather than assessing tolerance toward rights in difference contexts, only a single site was assessed. Similarly, the content of the speech, course taught at school, and public rally were left unspecified.

The Sullivan et al. questions proved highly influential for subsequent researchers. Caspi and Seligson (1983) used the questions in Israel and Costa Rica. Shamir and Sullivan (1985) used the questions in Israel. Barnum and Sullivan (1989) used the questions in Britain. Gibson and Duch (1993) used the questions in the Soviet Union. Sullivan, Walsh, Shamir, Barnum, and Gibson used the questions in Israel, Britain, and New Zealand (Sullivan et al. 1993). Single country studies outside the United States have also adopted the Sullivan et al. questions. Wang and Chang (2006) asked whether Taiwanese supporters and opponents of unification with China should be permitted to hold rallies and express their opinions, teach in schools, and run for government positions. Mujani combined the Stouffer and Sullivan items to ask whether respondents in Indonesia would tolerate a Christian as a teacher in a public school and if they objected to a church in a predominantly Muslim community, to Christian religious services in a predominantly Muslim community, and to a Christian becoming president of the country (Mujani 2003, 174).

In 1990, the WVS picked up the Sullivan et al. "least-liked group" strategy for a question on social tolerance, asking, "On this list are various groups of people. Could you please sort out any that you would not like to have as neighbors?" This question was used again in 1995, 2000, and 2005. In the 1995 wave, the WVS expanded their questions to include political tolerance. After choosing their least-liked group from a list, respondents were asked whether the group should be allowed to hold public office, teach in schools, or hold public demonstrations. The 1995 wave of the WVS was done in 180 countries, and researchers have since published papers using its data to measure tolerance in 18 countries (Peffley and Rohrschneider 2003), Turkey (Tessler and Altinoglu 2004), 16 countries (Weldon 2006), 33 countries (Hutchison 2007), 33 countries (Hutchison and Gibler 2007), 14 countries (Marquart-Pyatt and Paxton 2007), and 35 countries (Anderson and Fetner 2008).

The two most recent waves of the WVS asked respondents who they would not like to have as neighbors and included nine groups: people of a different race, heavy drinkers, immigrants/ foreign workers, people who have AIDS, drug addicts, homosexuals, people of a different religion, unmarried couples living together, and people who speak a different language. These questions make it impossible to know the specific religion or ethnicity of whoever the respondent is thinking about, but they do allow for cross-national comparisons of levels of tolerance toward groups that are perceived as different. These are the questions utilized in the following.

As with any cross-national survey data, more nuanced questions and concepts are forsaken for the benefit of comparison and replicability. This tradeoff is most apparent in the questions on tolerance toward a neighbor of a different religion; other research has demonstrated that levels of tolerance are specific to the religion of the neighbor rather than being a general value (Stouffer 1955; Gibson 2006). In the Indonesian context, Muslims are significantly more tolerant of Christians and Hindus than Ahmadi, Muslims, Shi'ite Muslims, or communists (Menchik 2016). Likewise, as we will discuss, Menchik's research demonstrates that leaders of Indonesia's mass organizations think about tolerance in ways that are ignored by the WVS questions.

Yet this oversight does not mean that cross-national indicators are useless. They help us understand how Indonesian Muslims answer these questions in comparison to their co-religionists abroad. And this is an important concern in Indonesia's democratic age. Tolerance is a cornerstone of a stable democracy. In a political system based upon the mutual respect of citizen and government, intolerance can threaten stability, especially when anti-system movements like Hizb ut-Tahrir Indonesia (Indonesian Party of Liberation) and Front Pembela Islam (the Islamic Defenders Front) are quick to mobilize against any perceived threat to the majority. By comparing Indonesians to other populations, this chapter elucidates the levels of tolerance in Muslim-majority democracies, suggests ways to strengthen pluralism in other developing and Muslim-majority states, and suggests future avenues of research for scholars of Indonesia.

Indonesian Muslims compared

The World Value Survey (WVS) is a cross-national, longitudinal survey of trends in people's values and beliefs. Over the last three decades, the WVS has grown to include over 100 countries and provides the most comprehensive cross-national database of public opinion. The most recent wave that includes Indonesia and questions on tolerance was undertaken in 2006 and asks respondents one question relevant to our inquiry: "On this list are various groups of people: Mention any that you would not like to have as neighbors." People of another race, another religion, and who speak another language are possible answers with the answers moving in tandem. For that reason, we choose to focus primarily on the number pertaining to religious intolerance. Figure 32.1 compares levels of intolerance by Indonesian Muslims with Muslims in the other Muslim-majority countries of Jordan, Iran, Morocco, Turkey, Iraq, and Mali. Jordanian Muslims have the highest levels of intolerance, followed by Iranians and Moroccans. Mali's Muslims have the lowest levels of intolerance toward a neighbor of a different religion. Indonesian Muslims sit in the middle of sampled countries. Figure 32.1 suggests that statements lauding Indonesian Muslims as exceptionally tolerant are not warranted.

Modernization theory predicts that levels of intolerance should decrease with increases in economic development, since post-industrial societies will emphasize "post-material values" (Norris and Inglehart 2011). By incorporating indicators of economic development from the World Bank with the WVS indicators of intolerance, we can assess whether Indonesians are exceptionally tolerant for a low-income country. Figure 32.2 shows countries with WVS data on religious intolerance compared to their gross national income per capita with a 95%

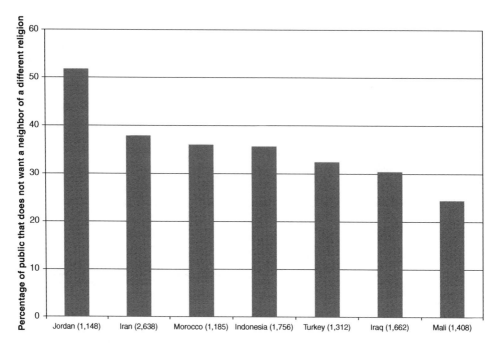

Figure 32.1 Religious intolerance in Muslim-majority countries

Note: Indicator of religious intolerance from 2005–2009 WVS, using only Muslim respondents.

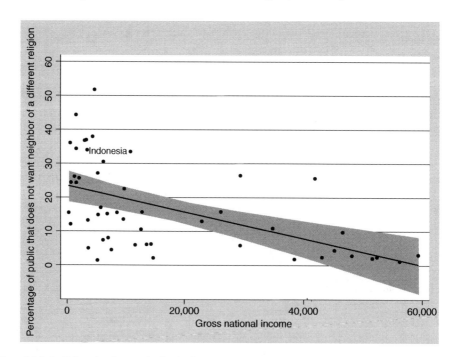

Figure 32.2 Religious intolerance by level of economic development

Note: Indicator of religious intolerance from 2005–2009 WVS; GNI per capita from the World Bank's Global Development Indicators for 2012 (World Bank 2017).

confidence interval. Richer countries have lower levels of intolerance than poorer countries, but there is a great deal of variation, suggesting that other variables are necessary to explain levels of religious intolerance. More important for this chapter, Indonesians are not exceptionally tolerant for a poor country.

Modernization theory further predicts that levels of religious intolerance should decrease as societies undergo political development. By incorporating indicators of democratic freedom from Freedom House with the WVS indicators of religious intolerance, we can assess whether Indonesians are exceptionally tolerant for a newly democratic country. Freedom House uses a simple 1–7 score, with the lower number indicating more political and social rights for citizens. Figure 32.3 shows countries with WVS data on religious intolerance compared to their level of democratic development with a 95% confidence interval. More democratic countries have lower levels of intolerance than more authoritarian countries, but there is a great deal of variation suggesting, again, that other variables are necessary to explain levels of religious intolerance. More important for our purposes, Indonesians are not exceptionally tolerant for a newly democratic country.

Combining the focus on levels of economic development and democratic consolidation together suggests that Indonesians are likely to be substantially less tolerant than populations in rich Western countries with consolidated democracies. Figure 32.4 uses WVS indicators for intolerance to having a neighbor of a different religion, having a neighbor who speaks a different language, and having a neighbor of a different ethnic group. We find that Indonesians are

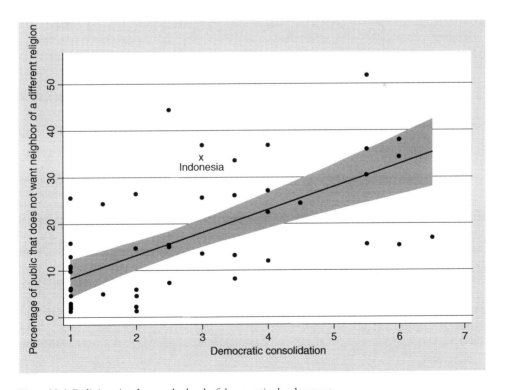

Figure 32.3 Religious intolerance by level of democratic development

Note: Indicator of religious intolerance from 2005–2009 WVS; Democracy indicators from Freedom House 2012.

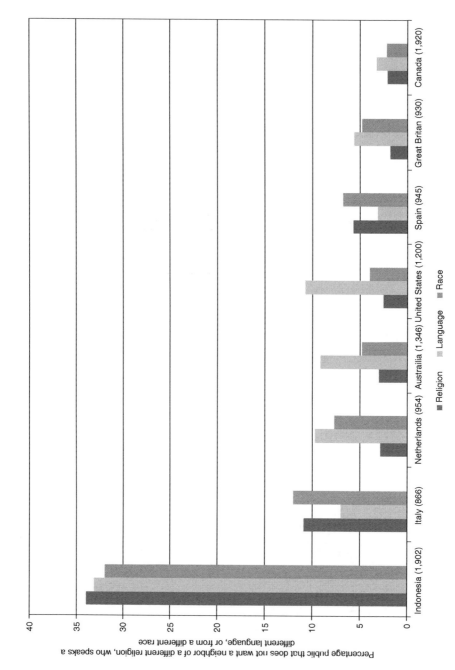

Figure 32.4 Intolerance in Indonesia and Western democracies

Note: Indicators of religious, language, and racial intolerance from 2005–2009 WVS.

substantially more intolerant than publics in rich, consolidated democracies on all indicators. While Western respondents never rise over 15% intolerance, Indonesians never fall below 30%.

Our findings suggest that Indonesia is not exceptionally tolerant for a developing Muslim-majority country. Now that Indonesia has proven itself to be unexceptional in terms of Muslim-majority democracies, low-middle income countries, and new democracies, it is worth investigating the determinants of tolerance within Indonesia. Geertz divides Javanese society into three groups: priyayi, abangan, and santri (Geertz 1976: 5–6). The priyayi are the administrative upper classes who practice a form of "Javanese religion" that combines Islam with mystical and Hindu practices. Their class status differentiates them from the abangan. The abangan are then contrasted with the santri, who are outwardly orthodox Muslims in their dress, living arrangements, and religious rituals. Owing to the abangan's syncretic beliefs, a Geertzian explanation stresses the relative intolerance of the santri compared to abangan Muslims. The Geertzian view, then, would predict significantly higher levels of intolerance among orthodox, observant Muslims compared to syncretistic, nominal Muslims.

The WVS data do not support this view. The WVS contains two questions that can be used as a proxy for the santri and abangan distinction. The first asks, "Apart from weddings and funerals, about how often do you attend religious services these days?" We coded as "observant Muslims" respondents who attend religious services once per week or more and coded as "nominal Muslims" those who report attending once per month, only on holy days, once per year, less often, and never. Some 30% of santri Muslims object to a neighbor of a different race, while 33% of abangan Muslims object. Thirty-four percent of santri Muslims object to a neighbor of a different religion, while 33% of abangan Muslims object. And 32% of santri Muslims object to a neighbor who speaks a different language, while 35% of abangan Muslims object. So the WVS finds that the santri/abangan Muslim distinction is unhelpful for explaining attitudes of tolerance.

The second question asks, "Do you consider yourself a religious person, not a religious person, atheist, etc.?" Here we find evidence against the Geertzian view: self-proclaimed religious people are *more* tolerant of neighbors of a different race (30% intolerant to 38% intolerant), neighbors of a different religion (33% intolerant to 37% intolerant), and neighbors who speak a different language (32% intolerant to 44% intolerant). While neither question is an ideal proxy for the santri–abangan distinction, the WVS data suggest that the distinction between syncretic and orthodox Muslims is a poor predictor of levels of tolerance. The WVS data also upends the Geertzian (and more broadly held) notion that more orthodox, observant Muslims are more intolerant than their syncretistic, nominal Muslim neighbors.

In addition to religious observance, education is another factor that shapes attitudes toward other religious groups. More educated individuals are thought to be better at understanding and embracing religious pluralism. Separating respondents by the highest education level produces some of the more powerful, if unsurprising, results. In general, more education leads to less intolerance so that university and college students have the lowest levels of intolerance. Figure 32.5 presents the average levels of intolerance based on forms of education using the question, "How do you feel if someone with a different religion lives near your home?" Figure 32.5 demonstrates that education is a powerful explanation for levels of tolerance.

In addition to education, some scholars argue that ethnicity is a good predictor of levels of tolerance. They argue that individuals from ethnic groups that are homogenously Muslim may have less contact with individuals from other religious backgrounds and less incentive to work with individuals from other religious backgrounds and be less trusting of individuals from other religious backgrounds. Conversely, when the ethnic composition stretches across multiple religions, tolerance is more likely. Menchik (2016) makes this argument by using Lipset and

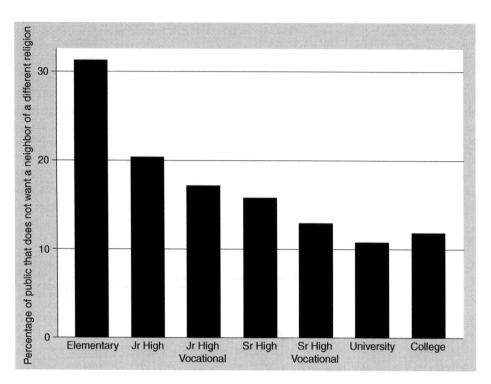

Figure 32.5 Education level and intolerance

Note: Indicators of tolerance and education from the fourth wave IFLS (Strauss et al. 2009)

Rokkan's contention that cross-cutting cleavages are important for understanding conflict and coexistence and applies it to the behavior of religious organizations (Lipset and Rokkan 1967). Figure 32.6 uses the IFLS data to suggest that ethnicity is indeed a good predictor of tolerance. Using the aggregate indicator of tolerance and respondent's self-identified ethnic group, those Muslims from more heterogeneous ethnicities, such as the Torajans (12% Muslim), Nias (19% Muslim), Balinese (3.6% Muslim), and Chinese (16.7% Muslim), tend to be more tolerant than those from homogenous ethnic backgrounds, like the Sasak, Banjarese, Bima-Dompu, Acehnese, Gorontalo (100% Muslim), and largely homogenous backgrounds like Sundanese (99.6%), Madurese (99.3%), Minangkabau (99.6%), Makassarese (99.5%), Sumbawans (99%), Malay (99.7%), and Cirebonese (99.8%).

Separately but related, whether an Indonesian is a member of the Muslim majority or non-Muslim minority is a good predictor of tolerance. According to the IFLS data, Indonesian Muslims are less tolerant than non-Muslim Indonesians. Some 23.7% of Muslim respondents object to having a neighbor of a different faith. Hindus are the next least tolerant, with 8.32% respondents stating they would object to someone of a different faith. Protestants follow with 4.67%, and Catholic respondents have the lowest levels of intolerance, with only 2.67% responding they would object to having a neighbor of a different faith. Gaduh likewise notes that Muslims in Indonesia are slightly more intolerant than their non-Muslim compatriots (2012).

Another way in which Indonesia is not exceptional but noteworthy is in exercising a relatively small amount of regulation of religion for a Muslim-majority country and especially in not heavily privileging Islam over other recognized religions. Using Jonathan Fox's data set

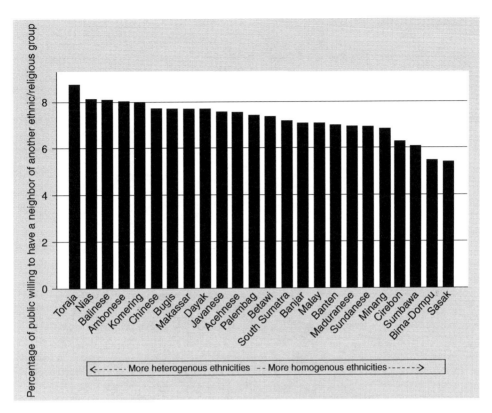

Figure 32.6 Tolerance and ethnicity

Note: Indicators of tolerance and education from the fourth wave IFLS.

on state involvement in religion in 2008, we created a figure that aggregates four indicators of government regulation of religion and the privileging of Islam: whether there is a favored religious branch, whether the government funds some things related to religion, proportion of laws based on religious law, and whether conversion is limited or restricted (Fox 2008). The aggregate scale ranges from 0–12 with higher numbers indicating more regulating and privileging of Islam. While these indicators are theoretically crude and normatively biased toward secularism and Protestant faiths, they provide a useful snapshot of the degree to which these states regulate religion and privilege Islam. As Figure 32.7 indicates, Indonesia is on the lower end of government regulation of religion and privileging of Islam but is still not a secular state.

A final determinant of attitudes toward other religions is membership in one of Indonesia's mass Islamic organizations, like Muhammadiyah or Nahdlatul Ulama. These organizations are believed to be the backbone of Indonesian civil society and have proved crucial in tamping down intergroup conflict during the country's democratic transition (Hefner 2000; Mujani and Liddle 2004). Do the members and leaders of these organizations share the attitudes of other Indonesians?

The compiled data suggests that membership in Islamic civil society organizations predicts higher levels of tolerance and lower levels of intolerance, for both the members and the leaders. The 2007 IFLS data reports that 23.7% of Indonesian Muslim respondents object to having a neighbor of a different religion, and the 2006 WVS reports that 33.9% of Indonesians objects to

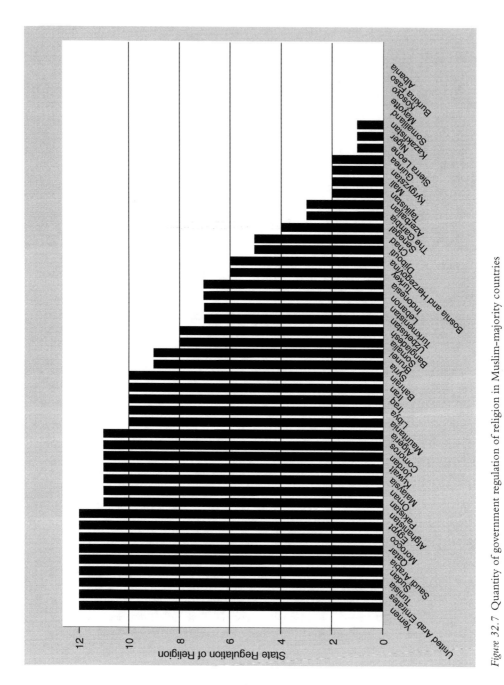

Figure 32.7 Quantity of government regulation of religion in Muslim-majority countries

Note: Indicators of regulation from the 2008 US Department of State's International Religious Freedom Reports and downloaded from the Association of Religion Data Archives.

having someone of a different religion in their neighborhood. Bush's survey of the membership of NU shows slightly less intolerance than the WVS data: Bush finds that 30% of members of Muhammadiyah and 29% of NU members object to a non-Muslim living in their community (Bush 2014). Menchik, however, finds a bigger difference between the leadership and the members: only 14.2% of NU and 18.3% of Muhammadiyah leaders object, suggesting lower levels of intolerance than the members and than the broader Muslim population. Additionally, IFLS reports that 83% of Muslims object to a group of another religion building a house of worship in their community. Bush and Menchik find slightly lower levels of intolerance: Bush finds that 76% of Muhammadiyah's mass members object and 63% of NU members object, while Menchik finds that 78% of Muhammadiyah leaders and 71% of NU leaders do not think a Christian church should be allowed to be built in their community. So on the second question, too, leaders of Islamic civil society organizations are more tolerant than the general public, and members of Islamic civil society are slightly more tolerant. On both questions, NU members and leaders are considerably more tolerant than the general public.

These differences become even more pronounced if we use more theoretically sophisticated indicators of tolerance and intolerance. Menchik's 2016 book suggests that the leadership of NU and Muhammadiyah think *differently* about the rights of Muslims and non-Muslims than classical liberal political theory would suggest. For that reason, it is important to describe some of those differences between showing the implications quantitatively.

The term "brotherhood" (*persaudaraan*) is often used by Muhammadiyah to describe the virtue of fostering warm, supportive relationships between Christians and Muslims (*persaudaraan sesama mahluk*). Abdul Mu'ti, a longtime leader and currently the secretary general of Muhammadiyah for 2015–2020, published a book titled *KrisMuha* (a shortening of the words for "Christian" and "Muhammadiyah") that laid out the institutional manifestation of this vision (Mu'ti and Riza ul Haq 2009). Muhammadiyah schools operate in Flores, West Kalimantan, and North Sumatra, where the students are majority Christian or Buddhists. Teachers of any faith provide instruction in math, history, English, and other secular subjects to students of any religion. Doctrine is taught according to religious identity. These schools and curricula date back to the 1970s, before the central government required that religious education be given in accordance with the religion of the students and by a teacher of the same religion. Like non-religious education, in regards to other aspects of social relations like health, economic development, and neighborhood relations, Muhammadiyah places a high emphasis on inter-religious brotherhood and tolerance.

Similarly, in an influential book written in 1979, *Goals of the Members of Nahdlatul Ulama*, Achmad Siddiq, the head of the Islamic law board (*Syuriyah*) of NU from 1983–1989, explained NU's values as based on moderation (*al-tawāssut*), justice (*al-i'tidāl*), and balance (*al-tawāzun*; Siddiq 2006 [1979]). Highly broad and somewhat vague, NU's principles provide the organization a great degree of fluidity and support for social harmony. In addition to moderation, justice, and balance, a similar NU value is *al-amr bi al-ma'rūf wa nahy 'an al-munkar* (enjoining right and forbidding wrong). One manifestation of these values is NU's strong emphasis on respecting the highly heterogeneous practices of Sunni traditionalism in Java, including support for the already diverse Sunni mazhabs, local religious beliefs like the veneration of the nine saints of Java (*wali songo*), and Islamic mystical sects (*tarekat*). Similarly, in applying the principle of moderation to Islamic law, NU recognizes the uncertainty that accompanies the interpretation of Islamic law and urges its members to withhold condemnation of Muslims following different theologies.

At the same time, however, both NU and Muhammadiyah place clear limits on tolerance. While Mu'ti has called for respect and tolerance of Ahmadi Muslims, other leaders and the central board seem to disagree. Former Muhammadiyah chair Syafi'i Maarif touted Mu'ti's research as an example of Muhammadiyah's tolerance, while also making clear that there would never be a book on *AhMuha* (a shortening of the words for "Ahmadiyah" and "Muhammadiyah" (Syafi'i Maarif 2009, interview with Jeremy Menchik and Alfred Stepan, September 30). Muhammadiyah, like NU, draws the boundary of tolerance at interactions that corrupt or undermine Muslims' faith. Brotherhood does not extend to matters that might confuse respect for other religious people with admiration for beliefs that are inferior to Islam. Their distinction between permissive interactions in social matters and curtailed interaction in matters of faith stems from their commitment to the primacy of religious belief over other values like political or religious freedom. Any interactions that might lead Muslims to devalue their own faith, confuse the tenets of their faith with those of another faith, or convert to the other faith should be avoided. In interviews, Menchik's informants would frequently joke that different religions should not be combined like "gado-gado," a mixed vegetable salad with peanut sauce. The point is not that Muhammadiyah or NU are opposed to cooperation with non-Muslims. The point is that by privileging faith over brotherhood, these organizations are cautious about sanctioning activity that might corrupt the beliefs of their members.

These views are manifest in survey data. NU and Muhammadiyah leaders are likely to be tolerant of Christians as elected leaders in a predominantly Christian area like Manado and somewhat tolerant in the heterogeneous area of Jakarta. But they are less likely to tolerate Christian mayors in a predominantly Muslim area like Banda Aceh. Similarly, the presidency of a country that is almost 90% Muslim, a highly symbolic seat, is likely to be seen as only appropriate for a Muslim. Similarly, NU and Muhammadiyah leaders are unwilling to tolerate political behavior by the minority that interferes in religious affairs. On the question of demonstrating about a topic of broad social interest – gas prices – Islamic elites are highly willing to tolerate demonstrations. Demonstrations in favor of inter-faith marriage or against Islamic law in the region of Aceh are not tolerated. They are unwilling to put up with demonstrations by Christians that interfere in matters of Islamic marriage or Islamic community governance.

Finally, Menchik finds that NU and Muhammadiyah do not hold individual freedom as their most important value. Even after decades of political inclusion and moderation, they are not liberals, nor are they likely to become liberals. NU and Muhammadiyah leaders are willing to live next door to Christians at high rates of 82%. This is a high level of tolerance similar to wealthy, industrialized, consolidated democracies. Yet, there is a marked decrease in tolerance as soon as the subject is religious. Islamic leaders are unwilling to allow Christians to teach an unspecified subject in a private Islamic boarding school, nor to build a church in an Islamic neighborhood. These data suggest that NU and Muhammadiyah leaders are tolerant but not in the secular-liberal sense.

Conclusion

This chapter has argued that contrary to the conventional wisdom, Indonesian Muslims are not exceptionally tolerant. Instead, they are about as tolerant as we should expect given their relatively low levels of higher education and economic development and the recent introduction of democracy. What does make Indonesian Muslims exceptional, however, is that members of the mass civil society organizations Nahdlatul Ulama and Muhammadiyah are more tolerant than their co-religionists within Indonesia and abroad. Insofar as public attitudes have enabled Indonesia's successful democratic transition and relatively low levels of ethnic conflict compared to the Middle East, the country should credit NU and Muhammadiyah for being one important contributor to the country's relative stability and continued resilience against more anti-democratic forces.

These findings raise the question of why scholars and the public mistakenly think that Indonesian Muslims are exceptional. The most obvious answer is Geertz's legacy and Indonesia's association with Hinduism, which in the public imagination is thought of as more tolerant than Islam in the Middle East. Less obvious, but perhaps more important, are Indonesia's neighbors. In the United States, Jordan and Egypt are frequently invoked as home to moderate Muslim populations in contrast to the extremists in Iran or Saudi Arabia. But on most all measures of women's equality – political leadership, access to education, justification for the use of reproductive health tools such as abortion in cases of rape, incest, or genetic diseases for the child – the public in Egypt and Jordan is equally or more extreme than in Iran and Saudi Arabia (2005–2009 WVS). Attitudes in Jordan are the most extreme anywhere in the Muslim world about women's right to have abortion in case of incest, rape, or congenital defects. And attitudes about female political leadership are the most extreme in Egypt, with 93% of the public believing that men make better political leaders than women (compare to 74% in Saudi Arabia). The reason that Jordan and Egypt are considered moderate is political: both regimes have foreign policies that are considered moderate in terms of the US alliance with Israel. We say this not to critique US foreign policy but rather to demonstrate that the category of "moderate Muslim" may reveal more about the speaker than the population to which it is applied.

Regardless of the origins of the misunderstanding, future scholars should go beyond the relatively blunt instruments of the World Values Survey and Indonesian Family Life Survey to better understand the meaning of tolerance to Indonesian Muslims and especially to the members and leaders of Islamic civil society. Understanding determinants of tolerance among this group is likely to hold the most potential for increasing interfaith understanding and cooperation and minimizing the religious intolerance that too often accompanies political change.

References cited

Anderson, Robert and Tina Fetner. 2008. "Economic Inequality and Intolerance: Attitudes Toward Homosexuality in 35 Democracies," *American Journal of Political Science* 52(4): 942–58.

Barnum, David G., and John L. Sullivan. 1989. "Attitudinal Tolerance and Political Freedom in Britain." *British Journal of Political Science* 19(1): 136–146.

Bruinessen, Martin van. 2013. "Introduction: Contemporary Developments in Indonesian Islam and the 'Conservative Turn' of the Early Twenty-First Century," in Martin van Bruinessen, ed., *Contemporary Development in Indonesian Islam: Explaining the "Conservative Turn"* (Singapore: ISEAS), pp. 1–20.

Bush, Robin. 2014. *Nahdlatul Ulama and the Struggle for Power within Islam and Politics in Indonesia* (Singapore: Institute of Southeast Asian Studies).

Caspi, Dan and Mitchell A Seligson. 1983. "Toward an Empirical Theory of Tolerance: Radical Groups in Israel and Costa Rica," *Comparative Political Studies* 15(4): 385–404.

Defense One, 2016. "Why Indonesia is Immune to ISIS," 16 January. www.defenseone.com/ideas/2016/01/why-indonesia-immune-isis/124821/ (Accessed 27 February 2017).

Fogg, Kevin. 2012. "The Fate of Muslim Nationalism in Independent Indonesia." (Ph.D. Thesis. New Haven, CT: History, Yale University).

Formichi, Chiara. 2012. *Islam and the Making of the Nation: Kartosuwiryo and Political Islam in 20th Century Indonesia* (Leiden: KITLV; Manoa: University of Hawaii Press).

Fox, Jonathan. 2008. *A World Survey of Religion and the State* (New York: Cambridge University Press).

———. 2011. "Building Composite Measures of Religion and State," *Interdisciplinary Journal of Research on Religion* 7(8): 1–39.

Freedom House. 2012. "Freedom in the World 2012." https://freedomhouse.org/report/freedom-world/freedom-world-2012 (Accessed 5 July 2017).

Gaduh, Arya. 2012. "Uniter or Divider? Religion and Social Cooperation: Evidence from Indonesia." Unpublished Working paper. from http://comp.uark.edu/~gaduh/papers/relsocap_latest.pdf (Accessed 20 November 2017).

Geertz, Clifford. 1968. *Islam Observed: Religious Development in Morocco and Indonesia* (Chicago: University of Chicago Press).

————. 1976. *The Religion of Java* (Chicago and London: University of Chicago Press).

Gibson, James L. 2006. "Enigmas of Intolerance: Fifty Years After Stouffer's Communism, Conformity, and Civil Liberties," *Perspectives on Politics* 4(1): 21–34.

Gibson, James L., and Raymond M. Duch. 1993. "Political Intolerance in the USSR: The Distribution and Etiology of Mass Opinion," *Comparative Political Studies* 26(3), 286–329.

Hefner, Robert W. 2000. *Civil Islam: Muslims and Democratization in Indonesia* (Princeton: Princeton University Press).

Hodgson, Marshall. 1974. *The Venture of Islam: Conscience and History in a World Civilization* (Chicago: University of Chicago Press).

Hutchison, Marc Lawrence. 2007. "The Contextual Elements of Political Tolerance: A Multilevel Analysis of the Effects of Threat Environment and Domestic Institutions on Political Tolerance Levels." (Ph.D. diss. University of Kentucky).

Hutchison, Marc Lawrence and Douglas M. Gibler. 2007. "Political Tolerance and Territorial Threat: A Cross-National Study," *The Journal of Politics* 69(1): 128–42.

The Jakarta Post. 2015. "Muhammadiyah Should Become 'Engine of Reform': Jokowi," *The Jakarta Post,* 8 August. www.thejakartapost.com/news/2015/08/03/muhammadiyah-should-become-engine-reform-jokowi.html (Accessed 3 August 2015).

Junaidi, Ahmad. 2015. "NU Vows to Maintain Tolerant, Peaceful Islam," *The Jakarta Post,* 3 August. www.thejakartapost.com/news/2015/08/03/nu-vows-maintain-tolerant-peaceful-islam.html (Accessed 3 August 2015).

Lipset, Seymour and Stein Rokkan. 1967. "Cleavage Structures, Party Systems, and Voter Alignments: An Introduction," in Seymour Lipset and Stein Rokkan, eds., *Party Systems and Voter Alignments* (New York: Free Press), pp. 1–64.

Marquart-Pyatt, Sandra and Pamela Paxton. 2007. "In Principle and in Practice: Learning Political Tolerance in Eastern and Western Europe," *Political Behavior* 29(1): 89–113.

Menchik, Jeremy. 2014. "Productive Intolerance: Godly Nationalism in Indonesia," *Comparative Studies in Society and History* 56(3): 591–621.

————. 2016. *Islam and Democracy in Indonesia: Tolerance Without Liberalism* (New York: Cambridge University Press).

Mujani, Saiful. 2003. "Religious Democrats: Democratic Culture and Muslim Political Participation in Post-Suharto Indonesia." (Ph.D. Thesis. Columbus, OH: Political Science, The Ohio State University).

Mujani, Saiful and R. William Liddle. 2004. "Politics, Islam, and Public Opinion," *Journal of Democracy* 15(1): 109–23.

Mu'ti, Abdul and Fajar Riza ul Haq. 2009. *Kristen Muhammadiyah: Konvergensi Muslim dan Kristen Dalam Pendidikan* (Jakarta: Al-Wasat).

Norris, Pippa and Ronald Inglehart. 2011. *Sacred and Secular: Religion and Politics Worldwide* (New York: Cambridge University Press).

Peffley, Mark and Robert Rohrschneider. 2003. "Democratization and Political Tolerance in Seventeen Countries: A Multi-Level Model of Democratic Learning," *Political Research Quarterly* 56(3): 243–57.

Ricklefs, Merle C. 2006. *Mystic Synthesis in Java: A History of Islamization From the Fourteenth to the Early Nineteenth Centuries* (Norwalk: Eastbridge).

————. 2007. *Polarizing Javanese Society: Islamic and Other Visions (c. 1983–1930)* (Singapore: NUS Press).

Shamir, Michal, and John L. Sullivan. 1985. "Jews and Arabs in Israel: Everybody Hates Somebody, Sometime." *The Journal of Conflict Resolution* 29(2): pp. 283–305.

Sullivan, John L., James Pierson, and George E. Marcus. 1982. *Political Tolerance and American Democracy* (Chicago: University of Chicago Press).

Sullivan, John L., Pat Walsh, Michel Shamir, and David G. Barnum. 1993. "Why Politicians Are More Tolerant: Selective Recruitment and Socialization Among Political Elites in Britain, Israel, New Zealand and the United States," *British Journal of Political Science* 23(1): 51–76.

Stouffer, Samuel Andrew. 1955. *Communism, Conformity and Civil Liberties: A New Cross-Section of the Nation Speaks Its Mind* (New York: Doubleday & Co., Inc.).

Strauss, John., F. Witoelar, B. Sikoki and A. M. Wattie. 2009. "The Fourth Wave of the Indonesian Family Life Survey (IFLS4): Overview and Field Report." WR-675/1-NIA/NICHD.

Tessler, Mark and Ebru Altinoglu. 2004. "Political Culture in Turkey: Connections Among Attitudes Toward Democracy, the Military and Islam," *Democratization* 11(1): 21–50.

Wang, T.Y. and G. Andy Chang. 2006. "External Threats and Political Tolerance in Taiwan," *Political Research Quarterly* 59(3): 377–88.

Weldon, Steven A. 2006. "The Institutional Context of Tolerance for Ethnic Minorities: A Comparative, Multilevel Analysis of Western Europe," *American Journal of Political Science* 50(2): 331–49.

Woodward, Mark. 1989. *Islam in Java: Normative Piety and Mysticism in the Sultanate of Yogyakarta* (Tucson: The University of Arizona Press).

World Bank. 2017. *World Development Indicators 2017* (Washington, DC: World Bank). http://data.world bank.org/data-catalog/world-development-indicators (Accessed 5 July 2017).

World Values Survey Association. 2014. *World Values Survey Wave 5, 2005–2008 Official Aggregate v. 20140429*. Aggregate File Producer: Asep/JDS, Madrid Spain. www.worldvaluessurvey.org (Accessed 5 July 2017).

33

PUBLIC DIPLOMACY AND THE GLOBAL DISSEMINATION OF "MODERATE ISLAM"

James Bourk Hoesterey

For much of Indonesia's history, Islam did not play a particularly prominent role in the styles and strategies of the country's foreign policy (Azra 2015; Sukma 2003; Anwar 2008). President Sukarno's anti-imperialist rhetoric played well with former colonies around the world, culminating in the historic Asia-Africa Conference in Bandung. Yet, it was Sukarno's bold non-alignment posturing and willingness to stand up to the imperial West – not his role as president of the largest Muslim-majority country in the world – that earned great admiration among formerly colonized peoples around the globe. During the New Order (1965–1998), President Soeharto's foreign policy was decidedly non-confessional. In fact, Soeharto wanted to consciously marginalize political Islam in both domestic affairs and foreign policy.

After the fall of Soeharto in 1998, Islam played an increasingly important and public role. There was a proliferation of Islamic media, new Islamic political parties emerged, and in the process, Islam acquired a particular symbolic power and political currency. Indonesians, it appeared, were also beginning to take pride in what they perceived as a distinctly Indonesian style of Islam. In the wake of the terrorist attacks of September 11, 2001, and in response to the 2002 bomb blasts in Bali, Indonesia's Ministry of Foreign Affairs announced a new Directorate of Information and Public Diplomacy, whose task was to showcase Indonesia as the home of "moderate Islam" and provide proof for the compatibility between Islam and democracy.

The directorate of information and public diplomacy, in cooperation with the Ministry of Religious Affairs and various civil society organizations, launched a broad range of person-to-person public diplomacy programs, including inter-faith dialogues, religion advisory boards, and youth and scholar exchange programs. Over the course of a decade, Indonesia worked to revamp its global image from one of political instability on the brink of Balkanization to one of Asia's leading promoters of democracy and religious pluralism. Indonesian politicians and diplomats were now eager to share what they viewed as their success story: consolidating democracy, resolving ethno-religious conflict, and cultivating a distinct form of "moderate Islam."

This chapter traces the development and impact of the "Islamic turn" in Indonesia's foreign policy, paying particular attention to how religious diplomacy connected a diverse range of people (diplomats and religious leaders), government institutions (ministries and initiatives), and civil society and religious organizations (Nahdlatul Ulama, Muhammadiyah, and beyond). This chapter bridges anthropological analyses of the politics of piety with conversations in political science and international relations about diplomacy and foreign policy. Only recently have scholars of foreign policy acknowledged some of the false assumptions of the secularization thesis (namely, that secularism would eventually eclipse the public role of religion) and begun to research the connections between religion, diplomacy, and soft power (Haynes 2011). As Petito and Thomas have observed, "the merging of 'modern' political values and practices with traditional local references and ways of living, often rooted in religious traditions, will in all like-lihood be the rule rather than the exception in the 21st century" (2015: 43). At the same time, there has been a burgeoning interest to exert "soft power" – a non-coercive approach to foreign policy that seeks influence through cultural exchange and shared political values (Nye 1990). Central to this discussion is the shift away from formal government-to-government programs, in favor of person-to-person diplomacy that reaches civil society and religious organizations.

The foundation of Indonesia's soft power diplomacy during the 2000s was the soft power strategy of promoting Indonesia's "moderate Islam." Whereas countless diplomats herald Indo-nesia as an exceptional home of "moderate Islam," such an abstract, decontextualized concept – whether it originates in the language of America's "War on Terror" or the foreign ministry of the world's largest Muslim-majority nation – runs the risk of perpetuating the perceived dichotomy between "good Muslims" and "bad Muslims" (Mamdani 2004). In this chapter, I consider how a network of diplomats, politicians, and religious elite *manufacture and market* the category of "moderate Islam." I am more interested in exploring the production, possibilities, and pitfalls of this soft-power strategy than declaring whether or not Indonesia is truly a model for "moderate Islam" (cf. Harsono 2012).

What counts as "moderate Islam," even among its proponents in Indonesia, does not easily adhere to Western liberal-secular ideas about citizenship and belonging. "Moderate Islam" has lives of its own and cannot be simply reduced to a Western hegemonic discourse projected outward as part of the War on Terror (of course, that is certainly part of the story). Of equal importance are the ways Muslims themselves craft and contest the concept, inflecting it with new meanings and local nuance. As we will see, the narrative of Indonesia's "moderate Islam" was eagerly adopted by countries in the West but did not really resonate with co-religionist countries in the Middle East. Thus, "moderate Islam" is perhaps best understood not in singular terms of what Islam is but as competing visions and projects about what Islam could be.

The (minimal?) role of religion in Indonesia's foreign policy (1945–2002)

Although space considerations preclude an exhaustive history of the role (or lack thereof) of religion in Indonesia's foreign policy, a brief recap of Indonesia's foreign policy trends will help us appreciate the novelty of recent public diplomacy programs designed to engage religious actors and promote Indonesian Islam. As noted above, Sukarno's global popularity was due to his anti-imperialist swagger, not any allegiance to Islam as a political ideology or the umma as a political community. Subsequently, Soeharto was famously adept at co-opting cultural forms of Islam, while also preventing expressions of political Islam. Political scientist-turned-ambassador Dr. Rizal Sukma puts it succinctly (2012: 85):

> Before 1998 Islam was never a determining factor in Indonesia's foreign policy, because neither Sukarno nor Suharto would allow foreign policy to be dictated by Islamic considerations. Islam became part of the national identity only after reformasi, when the rise of several Islamic-based political parties placed political Islam at the centre of national politics. The effect on foreign policy has been most evident in the attempts to shape Indonesia's image as a moderate Muslim country.

Some scholars have begun to challenge this prevailing scholarly narrative that Islam played an inconsequential role throughout most of Indonesia's history. Kevin Fogg (2015) rightly observes that non-state Muslim actors, working in partial conjunction with formal state officials, absolutely drew from the religio-political repertoire of Islam when trying to solicit support from Arab countries for Indonesia's claim to independence. Islam also structured much of the bilateral relationship between Indonesia and Pakistan during the early 1960s. These exceptions are important not only because they emphasize that Islam did indeed play a role in particular contexts but also in the sense that their approach to diplomacy and foreign policy is not limited to state actors and institutions (Umar 2016; Schlehe and Nisa 2016). Regardless of disputes about the exact role of Islam during the twentieth century, few scholars would dispute that Indonesian foreign policy took a dramatic shift following the fall of Soeharto's New Order regime (1966–1998), especially with the appointment of Dr. Wirajuda as foreign minister in 2001 and the eventual consolidation of democracy marked by the election of Susilo Bambang Yudhoyono (SBY) in 2004.

The advent of public diplomacy and the making of moderate Islam

In the immediate wake of authoritarian rule, parts of Indonesia experienced a range of inter-ethnic and inter-religious conflicts, leading some international observers to fret whether these were early signs of an imminent "Balkanization." Many of these conflicts simmered or ceased, though, and East Timor (with a quite different colonial history and only annexed by Indonesia in 1975) was the only province that became independent. Then, in 2002, terrorist bomb blasts killed over 200 people on the tourist island of Bali, causing Western governments to worry about the state of Indonesian Islam and the government's ability to combat violent extremism. While Western media offered a rather gloomy view and outlook, Indonesia's politicians and diplomats wanted to tell a different story about Indonesian exceptionalism – with its unique form of "moderate Islam," rooted in the spread of Islam through culture and arts, not conquest and invasion. These diplomatic strategies also revealed a growing confidence in Indonesian Islam, which, unsurprisingly, had different meanings for different people.

In contemporary configurations of religious authority, Indonesians typically study the exegetical commentaries of Middle-Eastern scholars, not the other way around. They can easily purchase translated books by Yusuf al-Qaradawi and televangelist Amr Khaled, yet very few, if any, Egyptians have ever read books by Indonesian scholars Syafii Maarif, Nurcholish Madjid, Quraish Shihab, or Abdurrahman Wahid. As Martin van Bruinessen has observed, "Indonesian Muslims have developed a wide range of unique expressions of Islam, but they have shown no great zeal in propagating them to other parts of the Muslim world" (2012: 122). However, as Indonesia began to successfully consolidate its democracy and manage several conflict zones, its leaders increasingly felt a sense of optimism and confidence. With "great power aspirations" (Fealy and White 2016), Indonesian politicians and diplomats wanted to assert Indonesia's new profile on the global stage.

One of the key architects of this foreign policy shift was Dr. Hasan Wirajuda. With degrees from Harvard, University of Virginia, and Tufts Fletcher School of Law and Diplomacy, Wirajuda was a career diplomat who held several important posts and, between 2001 and 2009, served as minister of Foreign Affairs. In 2002, Wirajuda created the Directorate of Information and Public Diplomacy in order to craft and implement a new soft-power strategy – an approach he referred to as "total diplomacy." In a 2009 speech at the Carnegie Endowment for International Peace in Washington, DC, Wirajuda outlined his soft power vision:

A few days ago in Cairo, President Obama invited the Muslim world to a partnership to address an array of critical issues: violent extremism, the Middle East situation, nuclear disarmament, democracy, religious freedom, women's rights, and economic development and opportunity. I am here to tell you that Indonesia, the country with the world's largest Muslim population, has long prepared itself to answer President Obama's call for partnership.

Wirajuda keenly understood Indonesia's strategic position as the world's largest Muslim-majority democracy. With the newly established Directorate of Public Diplomacy, he launched an ambitious plan for person-to-person diplomacy that would connect a broad range of religious and civil society organizations across a diverse group of countries and multilateral organizations. At that time, however, the ministry of foreign affairs was a relatively secular institution, and Wirajuda himself was not well-connected with the religious and civil society leaders he needed to help launch his public diplomacy vision. With this in mind, he began to host foreign policy breakfasts in order to forge relationships with a range of journalists, religious leaders, and civil society actors.

Wirajuda knew that public diplomacy programs could only succeed with the support, authority, and legitimacy of Indonesia's largest Islamic organizations, Nahdlatul Ulama (NU) and Muhammadiyah. In turn, leaders of these organizations also saw an opportunity to promote their own religious visions (and political aspirations). Despite some early stumbles, these state, civic, and religious leaders were able to find common ground around the idea of Indonesia as a model for "moderate Islam." During the mid-2000s, the directorate sponsored an ambitious range of public diplomacy programs. The following list is only a partial account of the more prominent and recurring programs that reflect Indonesia's new positioning as peacemaker, problem-solver, and champion of "moderate Islam":

The first APEC Inter-Cultural and Faith Symposium (October 2004)
The first Asia-Pacific Regional Interfaith Dialogue (Yogyakarta, 2004)
International Conference of Islamic Scholars (ICIS; 2004, 2006, 2009, 2014); in cooperation
    with NU
Sponsored the first Inter-faith dialogue for the Asia Europe Meeting (ASEM; 2005)
Key religious leaders and intellectuals of various faiths visit London's Chatham House
    (July 2006)
Interfaith fora held in New Zealand, Slovakia (November 2006)
Interfaith fora held in Czech Republic, Hungary, United States, Poland (2007)
Bilateral interfaith dialogues with Netherlands, Canada, Vatican, United Kingdom
World Peace Forum (WPF) in coordination with Muhammadiyah
Sent peacekeeping troops to Lebanon (2006)
Hosted the Sunni-Shi'ite Conference in Bogor to bring together Iraqi factions (April 2007)
Offered venue for diplomatic talks between Fatah and Hamas

The International Conference of Islamic Scholars (ICIS) included scholars from around the world but was really intended to showcase Indonesian Islam. ICIS was among the first and highest-profile public diplomacy programs. Beyond the Ministry of Foreign Affairs' own interests, ICIS became an important public diplomacy vehicle for NU leaders to increase NU's domestic and global profile. The late KH Hasyim Muzadi, who was the leader of NU from 1999–2010, served as secretary-general of ICIS and participated in a range of inter-faith public diplomacy programs. In each setting, Muzadi promoted NU's version of "moderate Islam" in terms of the Quranic description of Islam as *rahmatan lil alamin* ("a blessing for humankind and the universe"). To provide a sense of the cross-over and conceptual borrowing between state ministries and civil society at this time, the phrase *rahmatan lil alamin* was also chosen as the title for a Ministry of Religion's program, launched in 2015, to train 200,000 public school religion teachers how to teach moderate Islam.

International public diplomacy, and its slick slogans about moderate Islam, reflect dynamics between domestic politics and religious authority. For example, the first ICIS gathering was held amid Muzadi's 2004 vice-presidential campaign, leading some scholars to question the domestic political motives involved in global public diplomacy (van Bruinessen 2012). In 2010, KH Said Aqil Siradj replaced Muzadi as the chair of NU. Whereas Muzadi has remained strongly committed to branding moderate Islam in the Quranic terms of "rahmatan lil alamin," Siradj wanted to take NU's version of "moderate Islam" in a different direction, and a rift began to form. Thus, understanding NU's multiple articulations of "moderate Islam" sheds light on internal power dynamics and the struggle for religious authority and authenticity.

Siradj promoted NU's version of "moderate Islam" in terms of *Islam Nusantara*, or "Islam of the archipelago" (Sahal and Aziz 2015). According to Siradj, who earned both his undergraduate and doctoral degrees in Saudi Arabia, many Indonesians were too preoccupied with mimicking Arab culture as if it represented authentic Islam. Siradj argued that the nine saints (*wali songo*) spread Islam throughout the Indonesian archipelago by respecting and encouraging the expression of local customs, as long as they did not transgress Islamic teachings. Siradj and the NU's central board chose Islam Nusantara as the theme for NU's 2015 Muktamar gathering to choose new leadership. In a volume launched for that event, Muhadjir describes Islam Nusantara as "an effect of the dialectics between written Islamic law and local realities and cultures" (2015: 67). Even Indonesian president Joko "Jokowi" Widodo began to adopt the language of Islam Nusantara, contrasting it with Arab Islam: "Our Islam is Islam Nusantara, a friendly, anti-radical, inclusive, tolerant Islam full of politeness" (Affan 2015). NU central leadership has been keen to leverage the concept of Islam Nusantara as a way to increase its influence on the Jokowi administration, brandish its moderate image on the global stage, and provide an alternative theology to counter the so-called Islamic State at home and abroad.

In May 2016, NU sponsored the International Summit of Moderate Islamic Leaders (ISOMIL), which brought together over fifty ulama from over thirty countries worldwide (reportedly with financial assistance from several sponsors, including Indonesia's National Agency for Combatting Terrorism, BNPT). The grandiose theme for the gathering was "Islam Nusantara: Inspiration for World Civilization." In his opening speech delivered in fluent Arabic, Siradj recounted the spread of Islam in Indonesia through culture, not coercion. As he has written elsewhere,

> this kind of approach is suited to our nation, as it was employed by the Wali Songo when they prevailed against the Pajajaran, Majapahit, and Sriwijaya kingdoms within only 50 years, without a single war. These kingdoms were not conquered by war, but by a cultural approach.
>
> *(2015:65)*

Siradj defended Islam Nusantara as well within the theological contours of Islamic doctrine and argued for the permissibility within Islam to allow, indeed to celebrate, local cultural expressions. Toward the end of his speech, he playfully chided ulama visiting from the Middle East. He acknowledged that Indonesia is currently experiencing intolerance and instances of terrorism, yet characterized such violence in terms of extremist discourse exported from the Middle East to Southeast Asia (see also Staquf 2015).

For Siradj and many NU elite, Indonesia is uniquely positioned to address the problems experienced by the global umma, and Islam Nusantara represents Indonesia's antidote to what many perceive as the violence and intolerance of "Arab Islam." As Gus Yahya Cholil Staquf proclaimed,

> Because we are the world's largest Muslim nation, we cannot consider violence in this world to be distant from Indonesia. It is high time that Indonesia assumes the role and takes the initiative to gather the world's Muslim leaders to discuss this problem. Indonesia's strength lies in the fact that we do not have an invested interest, unlike Iraq, Iran, Syria, and even Saudi Arabia.
>
> *(Kompas, March 24, 2016)*

In the formal 16-point ISOMIL Declaration, NU leadership was careful to note that they did not intend to export this concept to the Middle East, rather to make the case for why culture and context (and thus, Indonesia) matter, especially in the contemporary moment when religious scholars around the world try to formulate a version of fiqh (jurisprudence) that could counter violent extremism in the name of Islam.

Members of NU's central board even produced a documentary film, *The Divine Grace of Islam Nusantara*, characterized in a *New York Times* headline as a "Muslim challenge to the ideology of the Islamic State" (Cochrane 2015). In the film, shots of religious scholars explaining the history of the nine saints and the spread of Islam in Indonesia are cut with clips of Islamic State fighters killing people deemed as infidels. Other parts of the film describe practices of the veneration of saintly tombs. It should be noted, however, that such grave visitation practices (*ziarah*) are not only proscribed by the Saudis or Islamic State but also by members of Indonesia's modernist Muslim organization, Muhammadiyah.

The concept of Islam Nusantara played well with Western audiences. At home, however, the concept met significant resistance. Critics referred pejoratively to advocates of Islam Nusantara as the "Islam Nusantara Network" (Jaringan Islam Nusantara), whose acronym JIN refers to other-worldly beings (jinn) described in the Quran (the acronym also evokes the oft-derided JIL, "Liberal Islam Network"). Popular female televangelist Mama Dedeh proclaimed that there was no theological basis for Islam Nusantara in either the Quran or the tradition of Prophet Muhammad. Further, the celebrity preacher from Cirebon, Buya Yahya, characterized Islam Nusantara as "[haram] pig meat wrapped in halal goat meat" (daging babi dikemas kambing). Even the former NU leader, KH Hasyim Muzadi publicly and consistently derided the concept of Islam Nusantara, insisting instead that Indonesians promote his own formulation of Islam Rahmatan lil alamin. The struggle over Islam Nusantara within NU became even more pronounced with the emergence of NU Garis Lurus, the self-described "straight path" wing of NU, who waged a social media campaign to belittle the concept and its proponents.

Beyond NU, Muhammadiyah promoted its own notion of "Progressive Islam" (Islam Berkemajuan), the theme for its own 2015 muktamar. Although one could consider "Progressive Islam" as Muhammadiyah's alternative to Islam Nusantara, Muhammadiyah has not yet shown the same zeal in promoting the concept at home or abroad. This is not to say that Muhammadiyah has not played an important role in global public diplomacy. On the contrary, Muhammadiyah has a special committee devoted to international relations, and its leaders also travel the world building cultural and religious bridges between Indonesia and other countries. Muhammadiyah co-sponsors the World Peace Forum (WPF). WPF was co-sponsored by the Center for Dialogue and Cooperation among Civilizations (CDCC), founded by Din Syamsuddin, former chair of Muhammadiyah (2005–2015) and vice chair for the Council of Indonesian Ulama (MUI, 2000–2005). For the sixth WPF gathering in 2016, President Jokowi delivered the opening address to over 180 participants. Also in attendance was Yayah Khisbiyah, one of Muhammadiyah's prominent inter-faith activists who participates in similar religious diplomacy events around the world. With respect to both NU and Muhammadiyah, Indonesia's public diplomacy has relied on developing state-society partnerships with leading Islamic organizations with their own incentives and initiatives for engaging in global religious diplomacy.

The Bali Democracy Forum and Institute for Peace and Democracy

During his tenure as foreign minister, Wirajuda asserted Indonesia's emerging confidence in its new role as champion of democracy, human rights, and religious harmony. In 2008, Indonesia launched the Bali Democracy Forum (BDF) in order to promote democracy and showcase Indonesia's success story. Wirajuda, SBY, and other patrons founded the Institute for Peace and Democracy (IPD) as the implementing agency for the BDF. What began as a small regional forum with a handful of countries from the Asia-Pacific region has turned into a gathering of high-ranking diplomats from over 100 countries as well as official observers from Europe and North America. Nonetheless, BDF has been criticized for being simply a space of dialogue but without any concrete achievements as a result (articulated by some critics with the acronym "NATO" – No Action, Talk Only). Other observers have lamented the fact that the BDF, which consciously does not bar countries with questionable records of governance and human rights (itself part of SBY's broader "Million Friends, Zero Enemies" policy) can actually lend legitimacy to dictators (Emmerson 2012: 70).

Civil society activists protested the BDF for being yet another elite-level diplomatic gathering that fails to connect with actual citizens and civil society. Others pointed to what they perceived as the discrepancy between SBY's self-presentation as model statesmen who champion the rights of religious minorities and their own experiences of a state apparatus that systematically refuses to safeguard the rights of Shi'a and Ahmaddiyah communities. In an ironic twist in 2014, protests at the Bali Democracy Forum were banned. The possibilities of soft power can thus occasionally collide with the realities of *real politik*. To address some of these concerns, the BDF now sponsors side sessions (prior to the formal BDF) that invite participants from media and civil society.

In 2009, when Marty Natalegawa became Indonesia's foreign minister, Wirajuda devoted his energies to expanding the visibility and role of the Institute for Peace and Democracy. In addition to serving as the implementing agency for the Bali Democracy Forum, IPD has sponsored an array of governance training and public diplomacy programs throughout Southeast Asia. In 2010, as the Arab Uprising was transforming the political and religious fault lines in the Middle East, Wirajuda conceived a plan to invite diverse stakeholders in Egypt and Tunisia to gather in Indonesia, where Wirajuda and other political and religious leaders would share Indonesia's lessons of democratization and religious conflict.

Over the next eighteen months, IPD sponsored four additional workshops: "Building Electoral Democracy in Egypt: Lessons Learned from the Indonesian Experience" (July 25, 2011, in Cairo); "Empowering the Electoral Management Body" (October 20–2, 2011, in Semarang); "Islam, the State, and Politics" (April 11–12, 2012, in Jakarta); and "Constitutional Reform and Constitution Building" (November 5–7, 2012, in Bali). Similar to the *modus operandi* of the BDF, Wirajuda explicitly stated that Indonesia's role was not to point fingers or provide some cookie-cutter approach to democracy but simply to share lessons.

In his opening speech to convene the Egypt-Indonesia dialogue, Wirajuda was careful not to alienate his guests. In subsequent written reflections on the gathering, Wirajuda noted that he was aware of the sensitivity of unsolicited advice during a political crisis: "I believe that democracy is a universal value. But as universal as it is, we cannot impose it on others, because when we impose values on others they tend to reject those values. So our aim is to share" (2011: 150). Wirajuda told his Egyptian colleagues that, despite Indonesia's consistent 7 to 8% economic growth during Soeharto's authoritarian rule, "there was corruption, a lack of checks and balances, violations of human rights by the military, a monopoly on power, and a monopoly on the truth" (2011: 150). Perhaps more important than the substance of Wirajuda's remarks was the style and tone with which he spoke: "We made our presentations with humility. At the same time, we made the workshop a closed session because we didn't want to give them the impression that it was a publicity event for us" (2011: 152). Wirajuda's comments reflect Indonesian diplomats' renewed confidence in both what Indonesia has accomplished and what the Indonesian model offers.

Public diplomacy under Jokowi

When Joko Widodo (Jokowi) began his presidency in 2014, he maintained an insular domestic focus, proclaiming that Indonesia's foreign diplomacy must serve its national interests. This marked a dramatic shift from SBY's policy of a "Million friends, zero enemies." The early months of Jokowi's presidency were marked by media spectacles of blowing up foreign vessels that were illegally fishing in Indonesia's waters. Compared with his predecessor, Jokowi also did not appear as invested in the BDF, which he reportedly perceived as a diplomatic relic from SBY's era. However, in the wake of an ISIS-affiliated terror attack in Jakarta in January 2016, Jokowi appeared more interested in leveraging Indonesia's model of Islam into his own foreign policy. At a breaking of the Ramadan fast with NU ulama, Jokowi publicly embraced Islam Nusantara, which he characterized as "friendly, anti-radical, inclusive, tolerant Islam full of politeness" (Affan 2015).

After an initial year of a relatively insular foreign policy focused on national interests, Indonesian Islam became more central to Jokowi's foreign policy posturing. During his speech before the UK parliament in April 2016, Jokowi touted Indonesia as the example of moderate Islam. Several months later, Jokowi spoke about the Indonesian model in his opening address at the BDF (whose theme was "Religion, Democracy, and Pluralism"). On the second day of the BDF, and in keeping with what had become a staple of Indonesian religious diplomacy, the Indonesian foreign minister, Retno Marsudi, personally escorted delegates on a visit to experience the religious tolerance and harmony at the Bina Insani Islamic boarding school, located on the Hindu-majority island of Bali. In stark contrast to the diplomatic glitter of Indonesia's "moderate Islam," participants at the BDF civil society and media side events struck a less optimistic tone, bemoaning Indonesia's rising religious intolerance, exemplified by the high-profile blasphemy trial of Jakarta's Chinese-Christian governor (among other examples).

Jokowi appears to have taken to heart critiques of being too inwardly focused. His administration began to recalibrate its foreign policy and public diplomacy to more consciously leverage Indonesia's image as the home of "moderate Islam." In April 2017, Jokowi joined an interfaith delegation of intellectuals and religious leaders to promote Indonesia's version of "moderate Islam" throughout the Middle East, Europe, and the United States. Judging from the past, however, the idea of Indonesia's exemplary form of "moderate Islam" will be received quite differently in the West versus the Middle East.

To what end? Concluding thoughts on the efficacy of soft Islam

Total diplomacy and the image of Indonesia's "moderate Islam" played especially well in Western diplomatic circles. Consider the public praise by senior American diplomats like Secretary Albright and Secretary Clinton, who each lauded Indonesia as proof of the compatibility of Islam, democracy, modernity, and women's rights. During President Barack Obama's 2010 visit to Indonesia, he nostalgically recollected the religious harmony of his childhood years in Jakarta:

> And while my stepfather, like most Indonesians, was raised a Muslim, he firmly believed that all religions were worthy of respect. And in this way, he reflected the spirit of religious tolerance that is enshrined in Indonesia's Constitution, and that remains one of this country's defining and inspiring characteristics ... *Bhinneka Tunggal Ika* – unity in diversity. This is the foundation of Indonesia's example to the world, and this is why Indonesia will play such an important part in the 21st century.

The homecoming of Indonesia's adopted son seemed to solidify around Indonesia's international image as a consolidated Muslim-majority democracy. A cottage industry developed around both the role of soft power and the place of Southeast Asia – specifically, Indonesia – in the "War on Terror." As Bond and Simons (2009) note,

> The fact that Islam in Southeast Asia, although under rising fundamentalist pressure, is not yet in crisis, should be all the encouragement the United States needs to step up to the challenge by putting what foreign policy experts know as 'smart power' to work in the region.

Western government officials, especially from Australia, the United States, and the United Kingdom, were eager to support and engage Indonesia's soft power diplomacy (while also pursuing hard power approaches of weapons sales and military training).

Indonesia's revamped image of "moderate Islam" plays much better with Western governments anxious about terror than with the anxious monarchies of the Middle East. As Saudi Arabian King Salman's recent visit to Indonesia suggests, the ruling class of Middle East monarchies are more interested in Balinese beaches than Indonesia's Sufi-inflected Islam. As Rizal Sukma cautions, "It is not immediately clear how attractive Indonesia's brand of Islam is to its co-religionist partners in the Arab Muslim world" (2012: 87). Martin van Bruinessen puts it more forcefully, "The Arab world has shown a remarkable lack of interest in Asia in general, let alone in the social and cultural forms of Islam in Southeast Asia" (2012: 117). To be sure, it seems unfathomable that the king of Saudi Arabia would embrace Islam Nusantara.

Given this lack of authority in the Middle East, Indonesia has struggled to assume any significant role as peace broker. Azyumardi Azra laments, "Despite renewed Indonesian activism in Middle Eastern affairs, the hopes that Indonesia can be a bridging and mediating force among the conflicting parties in the Middle East seem to be very difficult to realize" (2015: 151). This is certainly not due to any lack of effort. In March 2016, Indonesia hosted the Organization of Islamic Cooperation's (OIC) extraordinary summit for Palestine, yet the much-heralded "Jakarta Declaration" has certainly not brought about any real political change. Despite the grandest of aspirations, Indonesia has yet to project any serious power or influence that might mitigate conflict in the Middle East.

Soft power is also expensive. If recent budget cuts are any indication, Indonesia has not seriously invested in the institutions, training, and expertise necessary to become an effective diplomatic player (Sukma 2011). Noting that the Ministry of Foreign Affairs has only a handful of China specialists and not a single diplomat who speaks Hindi, Fealy and White conclude that Indonesia's "Foreign Affairs shows little signs of being able to rise to the challenges posed by Indonesia's growing diplomatic prominence" (2016: 97–8). Without a significant budget and adequate human resources, public diplomacy and soft power can go only so far.

In the long run, Indonesia's ability to promote itself as a home of "moderate Islam" – at least in the West – will not depend on its slick slogans or diplomatic stunts. It will largely depend on Indonesia's own record. When it comes to safeguarding the rights of Shi'a, Ahmadiyyah, and LGBTQ citizens, many of Indonesia's politicians and religious leaders nowadays do not exactly embody the sort of "moderate Islam" applauded by the West (Harsono 2012). As Dewi Fortuna Anwar has astutely observed:

> Indonesia's efforts to promote a new face for Indonesia which is moderate, democratic and progressive will be meaningless and futile if the international news on Indonesia is dominated by stories about the burning of churches, attacks against groups accused of deviating from Islam, such as Ahmadiyyah, women being forced to wear the jilbab [headscarf] and other non-democratic and non-progressive acts . . . Indonesia's public diplomacy would be received with a degree of cynicism by the international community.
>
> *(2008: 11; cited in Sukma 2012: 87)*

This is *not* to mandate some liberal-secular litmus test of who can legitimately claim to be a "moderate." It is to underscore, however, that the future success of Indonesia's soft power strategies (at least in the West) will rest on the veracity of the claim that Indonesia is indeed the home of "moderate Islam." With respect to the Middle East, Indonesia's great challenge will be to convince co-religionists of the authenticity of Indonesian Islam and the authority of its religious scholars. This difficult, but not impossible, undertaking will demand greater financial investment and human resources capacity. Given the bleak prospect of a long Arab Winter ahead, compounded by setbacks in Turkey's democracy, uncertainty about Tunisia's future, and rising religious intolerance in America and Europe, Indonesia's promotion of civic religious pluralism and "moderate Islam" – notwithstanding the political and theological challenges at home and abroad – continues to be an important endeavor and will undoubtedly shape Indonesia's image on the global stage.

References cited

Affan, Hayder, 2015. "Polemik di Balik Istilah Islam Nusantara [The Polemics Behind the Concept of Islam Nusantara]," *BBC Indonesia*, 15 June. www.bbc.com/indonesia/berita_indonesia/2015/06/150614_indonesia_islam_nusantara (Accessed 12 March 2017).

Anwar, Dewi Fortuna. 2008. "Peran Diplomasi Publik dalam Kebijakan Luar Negeri Republik Indonesia [The Role of Public Diplomacy in Indonesia's Foreign Policy]." Paper presented at the Syarif Hidayatullah State Islamic University, Jakarta, December 5.

Azra, Azyumardi. 2015. "Indonesia's Middle Power Public Diplomacy: Asia and Beyond," in Jan Melissen and Yul Sohn, eds., *Understanding Public Diplomacy in East Asia: Middle Powers in a Troubled Region* (New York: Palgrave Macmillan), pp. 131–54.

Bond, Christopher S. and Lewis M. Simons. 2009. *The Next Front: Southeast Asia and the Road to Global Peace with Islam* (Hoboken, NJ: John Wiley & Sons).

Cochrane, Joe. 2015. "For Indonesia, a Muslim Challenge to the Ideology of the Islamic State." *The New York Times*, 26 November 2015. www.nytimes.com/2015/11/27/world/asia/indonesia-islam-nahdlatul-ulama.html?_r=0 (Accessed 28 February 2017).

Emmerson, Donald K. 2012. "Is Indonesia Rising? It Depends," in Anthony Reid, ed., *Indonesia Rising: The Repositioning of Asia's Third Giant* (Singapore: ISEAS), pp. 49–76.

Fealy, Greg and Hugh White. 2016. "Indonesia's 'Great Power' Aspirations: A Critical View," *Asia and the Pacific Policy Studies* 3(1): 92–100.

Fogg, Kevin. 2015. "Islam in Indonesia's Foreign Policy: 1945–1949," *Al-Jami'ah: Journal of Islamic Studies* 53(2): 303–35.

Harsono, Andreas. 2012. "No Model for Muslim Democracy." *The New York Times*, 21 May 2012. www.nytimes.com/2012/05/22/opinion/no-model-for-muslim-democracy.html (Accessed 12 March 2017).

Haynes, Jeffrey, ed. 2011. *Religion, Politics, and International Relations: Selected Essays* (New York: Routledge).

Mamdani, Mahmood. 2004. *Good Muslim, Bad Muslim: America, the Cold War, and the Roots of Terror* (New York: Three Leaves Press).

Muhadjir, Afifuddin. 2015. "Islam Nusantara untuk Peradaban Indonesia dan Dunia," in Akhmad Sahal and Munawir Aziz, eds., *Islam Nusantara: Dari Ushul Fiqh Hingga Paham Kebangsaan* (Bandung: Mizan), pp. 61–8.

Nye, Joseph S. Jr. 1990. "Soft Power," *Foreign Policy* 80 (Autumn): 153–71.

Obama, Barack. 2010. Speech given at University of Indonesia. November 10. https://obamawhitehouse. archives.gov/the-press-office/2010/11/10/remarks-president-university-indonesia-jakarta-indonesia (Accessed 10 December 2017).

Petito, Fabio and Scott M. Thomas. 2015. "Encounter, Dialogue, and Knowledge: Italy as a Special Case of Religious Engagement in Foreign Policy," *The Review of Faith and International Affairs* 13(2): 40–51.

Sahal, Akhmad and Munawir Aziz, eds. 2015. *Islam Nusantara: Dari Ushul Fiqh Hingga Paham Kebangsaan* (Bandung: Mizan).

Schlehe, Judith and Eva F. Nisa. 2016. "The Meanings of Moderate Islam in Indonesia: Alignments and Dealignments of Azharites." *Occasional Paper Series, Southeast Asian Studies at the University of Freiburg (Germany)* 31: 1–10.

Siradj, K. H. Said Aqil. 2015. "Indonesia's 'Peaceful, Gracious, Polite' Islam," *Strategic Review* 5(4): 62–5.

Staquf, Yahya Cholil. 2015. "How Islam Learned to Adapt in 'Nusantara'," *Strategic Review* 5(2): 18–28.

Sukma, Rizal. 2003. *Islam in Indonesian Foreign Policy* (New York: Routledge Curzon).

———. 2011. "Soft Power and Public Diplomacy: The Case of Indonesia," in Sook Jong Lee and Jam Melissen, eds., *Public Diplomacy and Soft Power in East Asia* (New York: Palgrave Macmillan), pp. 91–116.

———. 2012. "Domestic Politics and International Posture: Constraints and Possibilities," in Anthony Reid, ed., *Indonesia Rising: The Repositioning of Asia's Third Giant*. Singapore: ISEAS), pp. 77–92.

Umar, Ahmad Rizky Mardhatillah. 2016. "A Genealogy of Moderate Islam: Governmentality and Discourses of Islam in Indonesia's Foreign Policy," *Studia Islamika* 23(3): 399–434.

Van Bruinessen, Martin. 2012. "Indonesian Muslims and Their Place in the Larger World of Islam," in Anthony Reid, ed., *Indonesia Rising: The Repositioning of Asia's Third Giant* (Singapore: ISEAS), pp. 117–40.

Wirajuda, Hassan J. 2009. "Speech at the Carnegie Endowment for International Peace." 8 June. http://carnegieendowment.org/2009/06/08/indonesian-foreign-minister-wirajuda-on-u.s.-indonesian-comprehensive-partnership/mds (Accessed 19 June 2012).

———. 2011. "Seeds of Democracy in Egypt: Sharing Is Caring," *Strategic Review* 1(1): 147–58.

GLOSSARY

Routledge Handbook of Contemporary Indonesia

abangan: Javanese term for a Muslim of non-observant or syncretic persuasion

adat: customary practices, ethics, or law

agama: religion

Ahlus Sunnah wal Jamaah: term used to refer to orthodox Sunni Muslims self-identifying as upholders of the *Sunna* and the community of Prophet Muhammad

Ahmadiyah, Ahmadi: a movement self-identifying as Islamic and established by Mirza Ghulam Ahmad in late nineteenth century India and today regarded as heretical by many Sunni Muslims

Aisyiyah: the women's association linked to the Muhammadiyah

aliran: lit., "current," a term for a social grouping or religious sect in society

aliran kebatinan: a mystical sect or spiritual tradition

aliran kepercayaan: a spiritualist sect or tradition

Banser: *Barisan Ansor Serbaguna Ansor:* civilian security units sponsored by Nahdlatul Ulama

Bhineka Tunggal Ika: "unity in diversity," Indonesia's official national motto

bid'a, bidah: religiously unjustifiable "innovation" with regard to Islamic practice and creed

bissu: a traditional transgender medium or shaman among ethnic Buginese

bupati: district (*kabupaten*) head, regent

CEDAW: Convention on the Elimination of All Forms of Discrimination Against Women

dakwah   (Ar. da'wa): Islamic "appeal" or "calling," i.e. outreach with the intention of inviting Muslim believers to a more observant profession of Islam

dangdut: a bawdy genre of contemporary Indonesian pop music

Darul Islam: lit., "abode" or "territory" of Islam; a radical Muslim insurgent movement established in Indonesia in the late 1940s

dayah: traditionalist Islamic schools, typically in the special district of Aceh

Dewan Dakwah Islamiyah Indonesia: Indonesian Council for Islamic Predication, an Islamic organization founded in 1967 by Mohammad Natsir with ties to the Saudi-sponsored Muslim World League

dhimmi: a social category in classical Islamic jurisprudence for "protected" (non-Muslim) minorities abiding in Muslim lands and subject to taxes and public restrictions different from Muslims

DPD, Dewan Perwakilan Daerah: Regional Representative Council

fatwa: legal opinion of a Muslim jurist or scholar

fiqh: Islamic jurisprudence

FKAWJ, Forum Komunikasi Ahlus Sunnah wal Jamaah: Community Forum for Followers of the Sunnah and the Community of the Prophet

FKUB, Forum Kerukunan Umat Beragama: government-established Forum for Harmony between Religious Communities operative at all levels of state administration since 2006

GAM: Gerakan Aceh Merdeka: Free Aceh Movement

Golkar, Golongan Karya: political party established by New Order regime and still active today

hadith, hadis (Ind.): canonical words and deeds of Prophet Muhammad and the second major source of religious guidance for Muslims after the Quran

halal: religiously permissible or allowed

HAM, Hak Asasi Manusia: human rights

haram: religiously forbidden

hijab: term for a headscarf or "cover" worn by women that typically envelops the hair, neck, and chest

Hizbut Tahrir Indonesia/HTI: Indonesian Party of Liberation: the Indonesian branch of an international Islamist organization founded in Jerusalem in 1953 and established in Indonesia in the 1980s

IAIN/UIN: Institute Agama Islam Negeri/Universitas Islam Negeri: Indonesia's state-sponsored network of colleges and universities for Islamic higher education

ICMI, Ikatan Cendekiawan Muslim Indonesia: Indonesian Association of Muslim Intellectuals, a government-established association of Muslim intellectuals and leaders influential in social and political affairs in the 1990s

Jemaah Islamiyah: a secretive Islamist organization with branches in several Southeast Asian countries, established in 1993 and linked to a series of terrorist attacks on non-Muslims and Indonesian state officials from 1999 on

jihad: struggle in the cause of Allah, holy war

jilbab: a woman's headscarf

jinayah: criminal law according to Islamic jurisprudence

kabupaten: administrative district below the level of province

kaffah: comprehensive or complete, as in the performance of Islam or the implementation of Islamic ethics and laws

KAMMI, Kesatuan Aksi Mahasiswa Muslim Indonesia: Muslim (university) student action committee

kampung: neighborhood, residential quarters in or adjacent to a town

Kantor Urusan Agama (KUA): Indonesia's national Bureau of Religious Affairs

Katolik: Catholic

kebatinan: spiritual "esotericism" or mysticism once widely practiced in Indonesia, especially on the island of Java

kepercayaan: "spirituality," a category of religious tradition accorded less extensive protections in Indonesia than state-recognized religions (agama)

ketuhanan: belief in an Almighty God

***kewarganegaraan*:**   citizenship

***khalwat*:**   "illicit proximity" between a man and a woman not related by kinship

***Khonghucu*:**   Confucianism

***kitab*:**   holy book, scripture

***kitab kuning*:**   lit., "yellow scriptures," classical Islamic jurisprudential and religious texts typically studied in Islamic boarding schools

***kodrat*:**   (gendered) code of ethical behavior assumed to be based in both nature and religion

***Komisi Pemberantasan Korupsi*:**   Commission for the Eradication of Corruption

***KOMNAS HAM*:**   *Komisi Nasional Tentang Hak Asasi Manusia*: Indonesia's National Commission on Human Rights

***Komnas Perempuan*:**   the National Commission on Women

Kompilasi Hukum Islam: the Compilation of Islamic law introduced in 1991 and used in Indonesia's Religious Courts for matters of inheritance, marriage, pious endowments, and Islamic finance

Konstituante: national assembly elected in 1955 and holding meetings from 1956–1958 to draw up a permanent constitution for Indonesia; dissolved by President Sukarno in July 1959

KPK, Komisi Pemberantasan Korupsi: the Commission for the Eradication of Corruption

Kristen: Indonesian term for a Christian of Protestant persuasion

Laskar Jihad: Holy war militia; Salafist paramilitary established in 1999 with the aim of battling non-Muslim belligerents in eastern Indonesia; disbanded in October 2002

***madhhab*:**   a school of Islamic law

***madrasa(h)*:**   an Islamic school; in the medieval Middle East, an Islamic boarding school for intermediate and advanced study in the Islamic sciences; in contemporary Indonesia, an Islamic school that combines general education with Islamic studies

***Mahkamah Agung*:**   Indonesia's Supreme Court

***Mahkamah Konstitutsi*:**   Indonesia's Constitutional Court

***Mahkamah Syari'ah*:**   shariah court, in particular in the special district of Aceh

***majlis taklim*:**   community based council or association, dedicated to the informal study of Islam

***maksiat*:**   vice, immorality

***MOEC*:**   Indonesian Ministry of Education and Culture

***MORA*:**   Indonesian Ministry of Religious Affairs

***MPR*:**   *Majelis Permusyawaratan Rakyat*, People's Consultative Assembly, Indonesia's supreme consultative assembly

***Muhammadiyah*:**   Indonesia's second largest Muslim social and educational welfare association, established in 1912 and today the largest reformist Muslim association in the world

***MUI*,**   *Majelis Ulama Indonesia*: Indonesian Council of Ulama

***mut'a(h)*:**   temporary marriage, long recognized in Shi'a Islam but not in Sunni Islam

***Nahdlatul Ulama*:**   a federation of traditionalist Islamic scholars, schools, and associations established in 1926 and today recognized as the largest Islamic educational and social welfare organization in the world

***NASAKOM: Nationalisme, Agama, Komunisme*:**   a coalitional formula introduced by President Sukarno in the late 1950s to unite nationalist, religious, and communist organizations

***New Order*:**   military-dominated government that came to power in 1965–1966 and ended with President Soeharto's resignation in May 1998

***nikah*:**   marriage

OKB, orang kaya baru: "new rich person," a term for the new, Reformasi-era middle- and upper-middle class

OPM: Organisasi Papua Merdeka: Free Papua Organization

ormas: organisasi masa, social organization

pacar: "boyfriend," "girlfriend," i.e., a person with whom one is having a still casual romantic interaction

Pancasila: the "Five Principles" on which the Indonesian nation is officially based, including belief in Almighty God, just humanitarianism, national unity, democratic consultation, and social justice

Parisada Hindu Dharma: state-recognized association for Hindu religious and educational life

pemekaran: the legal process by which administrative districts are divided into smaller units

pengadilan agama: religious court

peranakan: Indonesians of Chinese descent resident for many generations in Indonesia and regarded as culturally assimilated to local language and culture

perda, alt.: *peraturan daerah*: regional bylaws implemented by provinces, districts, and municipalities, especially in the aftermath of Indonesia's administrative decentralization in 1999–2000

pesantren, alt.: *pondok pesantren*: an Islamic boarding school, typically for intermediate and advanced study of the Islamic sciences including jurisprudence

poligami: lit., "polygamy," the Indonesian term for polygyny, the practice of a husband having more than one wife

pribumi: lit., "of the soil," indigenous, as opposed to a person of foreign descent

priyayi: an individual of aristocratic background, especially in Java; more generally, a high-ranking government official

propinsi: province, the highest level of state administration below the national government

PRRI, *Pemerintah Revolusi Republik Indonesia*: the Revolutionary Government of the Republic of Indonesia; a revolutionary government established in Sumatra in 1958 in opposition to the government in Jakarta

Reformasi: lit., "Reformation": term for the period of democratic reform initiated in the aftermath of President Soeharto's resignation in May 1998

Repelita: official Indonesian five-year development plan

Qanun: Islamic laws implemented in the special district of Aceh

Salafism: a current within the global Muslim community that seeks to reform the practice of Islam by grounding it on the words and practices of the first three generations of Muslim believers, thereby marginalizing the religious and jurisprudential commentaries of the medieval and early-modern periods

santri: lit., a student of an Islamic boarding school (pesantren), often used to refer to any Muslim who is religiously observant

sesat: "deviant," especially with regard to recognized principles and practices of Islam

Shi'a (also Ind., Syiah): the second of Islam's two major sects after Sunni Islam

Sumpah Pemuda: national youth pledge first pronounced in 1929

Sunna: the traditions of Prophet Muhammad as derived from his words and actions as recorded in the Hadith

Sunna(h): the way or tradition of the Prophet, as based on his words and deeds as expressed in the Hadith

syariah: Indonesian and Malaysian spelling for shariah, Islamic "law"

takfir: the act of declaring a Muslim a non-Muslim

tarbiyah: education, especially of a religious and ethical nature

***tasawwuf*:**   Islamic traditions of esotericism or spirituality

***tauhid*:**   the Islamic principle of God's unicity or oneness

***TNI, Tentara Nasional Indonesia*:**   Indonesian Armed Forces

***totok*:**   Chinese Indonesians of a recently arrived immigrant background and typically regarded as less assimilated to Indonesian language and culture

***Tuhan yang Maha Esa*:**   the first of the principles affirmed in the Pancasila and expressing belief in God as Almighty and One

***ulama* (Ar. singular, *alim*):**   Islamic religious scholar or scholars

***uleebalang*:**   traditional aristocrat in Aceh

***VOC, Vereenigde Oost–Indische Compagnie*:**   the East Indies Company, a mercantile alliance that first established Dutch sovereignty in parts of the early modern Indonesian archipelago

***waqf*/Ind. *wakaf*:**   "pious endowments," trusts set aside in perpetuity for some religious or public benefit and recognized in Islamic law

***zakat*:**   religious alms, one of Islam's five "pillars," required of all adult Muslims of sufficient means

***zina*:**   sexual relations outside of marriage

INDEX